A TEXTBOOK OF
TRACTOR AT A GLANCE
(A UNIQUE BOOK OF FARM POWER)

Er. Sanjay Kumar, M.Tech.

Deptt. of Farm Power & Renewable Energy,
College of Agriculture Engineering,
Dr. Rajendra Prasad Central Agricultural University,
Pusa, Distt. Samastipur - 848 125, Bihar

CBS

CBS Publishers & Distributors Pvt. Ltd.

New Delhi • Bengaluru • Chennai • Kochi • Kolkata • Mumbai
Hyderabad • Nagpur • Patna • Pune • Vijayawada

A Textbook of Tractor at a Glance

ISBN: 978-93-86310-90-3

First CBS Reprint: 2017

Published by **Satish Kumar Jain** and produced by **Varun Jain** for
CBS Publishers & Distributors Pvt. Ltd.,
4819/XI Prahlad Street, 24 Ansari Road, Daryaganj, New Delhi - 110002
delhi@cbspd.com, cbspubs@airtelmail.in • www.cbspd.com
Ph.: 23289259, 23266861, 23266867 • Fax: 011-23243014

Corporate Office: 204 FIE, Industrial Area, Patparganj, Delhi - 110 092
Ph: 49344934 • Fax: 011-49344935
E-mail: publishing@cbspd.com • publicity@cbspd.com

Branches:
- *Bengaluru:* 2975, 17th Cross, K.R. Road, Bansankari 2nd Stage,
  Bengaluru - 70 • Ph: +91-80-26771678/79 • Fax: +91-80-26771680
  E-mail: cbsbng@gmail.com, bangalore@cbspd.com
- *Chennai:* No. 7, Subbaraya Street, Shenoy Nagar, Chennai - 600030
  Ph: +91-44-26681266, 26680620 • Fax: +91-44-42032115
  E-mail: chennai@cbspd.com
- *Kochi:* Ashana House, 39/1904, A.M. Thomas Road, Valanjambalam,
  Ernakulam, Kochi • Ph: +91-484-4059061-65
  Fax: +91-484-4059065 • E-mail: cochin@cbspd.com
- *Kolkata:* 6-B, Ground Floor, Rameshwar Shaw Road, Kolkata - 700014
  Ph: +91-33-22891126/7/8 • E-mail: kolkata@cbspd.com
- *Mumbai:* 83-C, Dr. E. Moses Road, Worli, Mumbai - 400018
  Ph: +91-9833017933, 022-24902340/41 • E-mail: mumbai@cbspd.com

Representatives:
- Hyderabad: 0-9885175004
- Patna: 0-9334159340
- Vijayawada: 0-9000660880
- Nagpur: 0-9021734563
- Pune: 0-9623451994

Printed at:
Neekunj Print Process, Delhi

Dedicated to
My Respected Father-in-law & Mother-in-law
Late Bal Krishan Singh
&
Smt. Shanti Singh

Dr. A.P. Mishra
Vice-Chancellor

Rajendra Agricultural University, Bihar
Pusa (Samastipur) 848 125
Phone : Off. 06274-240226
E-mail : raupusa@sancharnet.in

Foreword

It is a great privilege for me to write foreword for the book entitled "Tractor at a Glance" written by Er. Sanjay Kumar. This book will provide as a reference material as well as a text book for the students of Agricultural Sciences, in general and Agricultural Engineering, in particular, in the country and abroad. This book will also provide as a key book for the students of GATE, ARS and IFS.

The author has tried his best to add some more information than available at present and much emphasis has been given in understanding of fundamental concept of I.C. Engine and Hydraulic System and Traction Theory.

This book has main thrust on improving the numerical solving ability of students.

The salient features of this book are:

1. The subject matter is abide with the new syllabus of various Agricultural Engineering Colleges.
2. The language used in this book is pertaining to the students.
3. S.I unit has been used in this book.
4. Each Chapter of this book contains numerical example, multiple choice and fill in the blanks.

I wish to compliment Er. Sanjay Kumar for putting his effort in bringing out such a book in a nice manner.

(A.P. Mishra)

Dr. J.P. Gupta
M.Tech. FMP (IIT), Ph.D. (IIT)
Dean
Faculty of Agricultural Engineering

Bidhan Chandra Krishi Viswavidyalaya
P.O. Krishi Viswavidyalaya, Distt. Nadia
Telefax : 03473-222657,
Tel 03473-223257/58/59
E-mail: jpgupta_bckv@yahoo.co.in

Foreword

I feel extremely happy in conveying my heartiest congratulation on the occasion of writing a new book entitled "*TRACTOR AT A GLANCE*" by Er. Sanjay Kumar. The book appears to be of very good quality and will be certainly of a good use by the students of Agricultural Engineering. The book has been written in accordance with the new syllabus of different Agricultural Engineering Colleges, ARS and GATE examination. A large number of multiple choice questions, fill in the blanks and other numerical problems have been appended at the end of each chapters for practice of the students. S.1. units have been used in the book to enrich the knowledge of the students as per latest trend. Apart from the above, this book also contains questions of GATE and ARS with their solutions which will be a great boon to the students. Once again I wish all success to Er. Sanjay Kumar for publishing the book.

11/01/07

(J.P. Gupta)

Preface

Encouraged and enthused by the popularity of our books among the candidates appearing in various Competitive Examination and continuous demand from them for bringing out a text book on "Tractor Power", prompted in to take up this project. The subject matter in this book is comprehensive, rigorous & yet very simple. Even an average student will find no difficulty in understanding the various concepts.

The salient features of this book are:

1.   The subject matter is abide with the new syllabus of different Agril. Engg. College.
2.   The language used in this book is pertaining to the students.
3.   S.I unit has been used in this book

The requirement of the candidates has been a major factor kept in mind during the compilation of this book. We are sure that the book will serve the purpose of leading the readers to success.

I am very grateful to Dr. A. P. Mishra, Vice-Chancellor, RAU, Pusa and Dr. J.P. Gupta, Dean. Faculty of Agricultural Engineering, BCKV, Mohanpur Nadia, West Bengal.

For taking all pains and interest in the publication of this book, Author expresses his deep sense of appreciation to many of the professors and staff members of CAE, RAU, Pusa specially Er. Kranti Kumar, HOD, Farm Power and Renewable Energy, Er. Subhash Chandra, Er. Reyaz Ahamd, Er. Sunil Kumar, Er. Sanjay Kumar Choudhary Er. Manoranjan Kumar, Er. Shailesh Kumar and my parents. I am also thankful to my friends specially Manoj Kumar Rai (SMS), Virmani Prasad, Dr. Shatruhan Kumar Raushan and Anil Kumar. In addition to this I am thankful to all of the students of CAE specially Pramod, Tausif, Gunjan, Chandan and others.

I also convey my sincere thanks to my Wife Neetu Singh for encouraged appreciation at each & every tenure writing of this book.

I am thankful to Dharmendra Kumar, Avinash Kumar and Mr. K.M. Prasad, Assistant, RAU, Pusa for sincere help during preparation of manuscript. I am very thankful to M/s International Book Distributing Co., Lucknow for helping in publication of this book.

The author would fortunate that any criticism and suggestion for improvement of subject matter has appreciated.

Place : Pusa

Date: 10.3.07

SANJAY KUMAR

CONTENTS

Chapter 1
Farm Power in India and Tractor Development

1.1 INTRODUCTION:

Power is the basic requirement for agriculture. In agriculture power is required for : (1) Tillage (2) Sowing (3) Weeding and Mulching (4) Harvesting (5) Transportation (6) Irrigation (7) Threshing (8) winnowing (9) Feed grinding (10) Cane crushing (11) Chaff cutting and (12) Cotton ginning in addition to numerous other jobs of similar nature. The nature of these works is classified into two main groups:

(1) Tractive works (2) Stationary works

Tractive works are those which require pulling force. The first five of the above examples come under tractive works. The remaining exampls are of stationary works.

1.2 Sources of Power:

The sources of power, for different farm operations in India, are as follows:

1. Human power   2. Animal Power

3. Stationary internal Combustion engines. 4. Tractor power 5. Electrical Power

1.3 Nature of the Power:

The nature of these powers is classified into two main groups.

(1) Animate power (2) Inanimate power

The first two of above examples under Animate power. The remaining examples are of inamimate power.

1.3.1 Animate Power: The following are the main sources of animate power

(A) Human Power: Human energy is predominantly used in agriculture for all operations from seedbed preparation to threshing and transport. The 1991 census report estimated the population of agricultural workers at 187 million. The number of agricultural workers at 187 million. The number of agricultural workers in 1997 in estimated to be about 205 milion as shown in Table 3. Assuming each agricultural worker being capable of supplying an average 0.1 hp for a period of 8 to 10 hours per day the total human horse power amounts to

1

Annual workforce available is given in Table = 15.293 GW.

The following are the advantages and disadvantages of human power in Indian agriculture.

Advantages of human power. The following are the main advantages of human power.

(i)   Easily available

(ii)   Adaptable to practically all farm operations.

(iii)   Source of reserve power for emergency and temporary over loads

(iv)   Produced on the farm.

(v)   Falling sick of one man does not stop the work.

(vi)   Used for varying power requirements.

(vii)   Survives mostly on farm produce.

Disadvantages of human power: The following are the main disadvanages of human power:

(i)   Cost power compared to all other forms of power

(ii)   Very low efficiency.

(iii)   Requires full maintenace when not in use.

(iv)   Cannot be continuously used for longer duration.

(v)   Mangement is very difficult.

(vi)   Affected by weather condition and seasons.

(B) Animal Power: Draught animals in India continue to be a major power sources for field operations, In the sloppy hill regions and on small farms the draught animals will remain the main power source, besides human power. The number of draught animals, as result of adoption of mechanical power in agriculture, is however, decling. A recently published Live stock. Census report indicated that the population of draft animals has decreased from 80.9 millions to 1961 to about 70.7 million in 1992, although the total borin population increased from 22.7 to 28.5 million in the same period as shown in Table 1. The population of draft animals is estimated to 61.5 millions in 1997. Assuming a bullock is capable of supplying on average of 0.5 hp for a period of 8 to 10 hours per day, the total animal horsepower amounts to

$$61.5 \times 0.5 = 30.725 \text{ million hp}$$
$$= 22.92 \text{ GW}$$

The following are the advantages and disadvantages and disadvantages of animal power in Indian agriculture.

Advantages of Animal Power: The following are the main advantages of animals power.

(i)   Easily available.

(ii)   Most suitable for tractive farm works

(iii)   Low initial investment.

(iv)   Lives on farm products.

(v)   Source of reserve power for emergency and temporary over loads.

(vi)   May be produced on farm.

(vii)   Lay up of one animal does not stop the work.

(viii) Can be used in wet or loose soils.

(ix)   Cheaper than human power.

Disadvantages of Animal Power: The following are the main disadvantages of animals power

(i)   It is not very efficient

(ii)   Requires full maintenance when not in use

(iii)   Creats dirty and unhealthy atmosphere near the residue

(iv)   Affected by wheather and season condition

(v)   Low efficiency

1.3.2 In Animate Power:

(A) Tractor Power:

Tractor is the chief source of mechanical power for tractive farm works. The tractors in India were introduced in the late forties by importing was surplus tractors from Europe. The number of tractors in use estimated by Jain (1971) was 8,500 in 1951 and 37,000 in 1960, all of these were imported. The tractor manufacturing stored in 1961 with 881 units. This rose to 20,000 units in 1970, 71,000 units in 1980 and 1,40,000 units in 1990. The production of tractors during 1997 was 2,55,000 units (Singh, 1999). The number of tractors in use in India at the end of 1997 was estimated to be over two million units shown in Table 1.1 Based on 142 Mha cultivated land, the gross cropped area per tractor in India, has reduced from 14,800 ha in 1951 to 71 ha in 1997.

The power tiller although introduced in the 1960s has not become popular as shown in Table 3. The yearly production is about 10,000 with as total population of 66,000 units only (Singh, 1999). These are mainly used in the states of West Bengal, tamil Nadu, Andhra Pradesh , Kerela, Karnataka and Assam where rice is major crop.

Advantages of Tractor Power:

(i)   Higher efficiency as compared to human and animal power.

(ii)   Require lesser space for storage.

(iii)   No maintentance is required when not in use.

(iv)   Cheaper form of power.

(v)   Can run for longer duration.

(vi)   Adaptable to stationary works.

(vii)   Not affected by weather.

(viii)   Speed of operation varies considerably.

(ix)   Timeliness of operation.

Disadvantages of Tractor Power

(i)   High initial cost.

(ii)   Requires skill of operation.

(iii)   Repairs and maintenance needs technical knowledge.

(iv)   Creats problem of fuel storage.

(v)   Lay up of the tractor will stop the work.

(vi)   Limited overload capacity.

(B)   Electric Power:

One of the major inputs adopted by the Indian farmers for modernization of agriculture in irrigation pumps. The irrigated area has increased from 21 million hectare during 1950 to 1955 million hectares in 1997 as shown in Table. The population of electric motor-operated pumps has incrased from 1.6 millions in 1970 to 12 million in 1997 and the diesel engine pumps from 1.7 to 5.5 million as shown in Table 1.1.

Advantages of Electric Power:

(i)   Cheapest cost of operation per unit energy.

(ii)   Highest efficiency.

(iii)   Can work at stretch.

(iv)   Maintenance and operating cost is very low.

(v)   Requires lesser space for installation.

(vi)   No maitentance is required when not in use.

(vii)   Not affected by seasons.

(viii)   Adaptable to varying speeds.

Disadvantages of Electric Power:

(i)   Higher initial cost.

(ii)   Limited over load capacity.

(iii)   Requires costly transmission system.

(iv)   Risky if not handled carefully.

(v)   Requires good amount of technical knowldege.

1.4.   Other sources of power: Besides, animate (human and animal) and inanimate (mechnical and electric), Renewable energy is also used as power source in agriculture. It includes (i) wind energy (ii) Solar energy (iii) Biogass (iv) Geothermal energy.

Biogass energy, wind energy and solar energy are used in agriculture and domestic purposes with suitable devices. It can be used for processing, water pumping, diesel engine operation and electric generation. This type of energy is inehaustible in nature. Renewable energy has bee discussed in details in fuel chapter.

Thouh farm power' refers various sources of non-conventional energy, but tractor remain the single power system which can be harnessed for both tractive as well as stationary forming activities in addition in this a tractor can also be used for transportation and haulage of farm products. These facts prompt the author to go through details of tractor.

1.5. Development of Tractor

1.5.1 Introduction of Development of Tractor: In the later part of the eighteenth century when the German scientist Nichlos Auto developed an in internal combustion enengine, thereafter the engine was used to pull the agricultural implements in the field.

The journey of the modern tractor started in 1855 with the introduction of steam engine for the purpose of operating agricultural therefore in U.S.A. Later, on these engines were made self-propelled steam traction engines. During 1870-80, a system for rear wheels was provided, which used to get drive through a chain or belt from the steam engine fly wheel. During last decade of nineteenth century (1890), these self-propelled steam engines with clutch, gear, etc were in the market under the name of 'steam plows'. The steam plows remained in use till starting of 20th century during which lot of improvement took place.

Real tractors were introduced in the beginning of ninteenth century when a three wheeler tractor was developed. America and other countries started making tractors run by both steam and internal combustion engines. These tractors had iron wheels and were heavy in weight. one such tractor 'IVEL' made in the year 1902 is shown in Fig. 1.1. The tractor has iron wheels and w as very heavy. Tractors run by steam were slowly replaced by tractors run with internal combustion engine. Iron wheels were replaced with rubber types.

In the year 1856, all such machines used for traction purposes were known as traction motors. In year 1906, these were redesignated as tractor by tailing half the word from, traction i.e., trac and other half from motor. i.e., tor. The tractor is a machine which is used to pull or push agricultural implements in fields.

Early ploughing tractors well able to exert considerable draft, but were of slow speed and therefore had rather low horse power ratings.

1.5.2 International Tractor Development:

The present tractor is the result of gradually development of machine in different stages. History of tractor development is given below in chronological order.

1890: The word tractor appeared first on record in a patent issued on a tractor or traction engine invented by George H. Harris of Chicago.

1906: Successful gasoline tractor was introduced by Charles W. Hart and Charles H. Parr of Charles City, Iowa.

1961-70 : (a) Power of tractors continued to increase.

(b)   Ergonomy was considered and emphasis was placed on operator (driver) comfort and safety.

(c)   Full Power-shift transmission became available.

(d)   Radial-pig tractor types becomes available.

1970-78 : (a) Turbacharger and intercoolers were added to diesel engines.

(b)   Most large tractors were equipped with cabs.

(c)   Nebraska tractor tests included sound level measurments.

(d)   Four wheel drive became popular.

1979-85 (a) Tractors eqipped with electronic sensing and control system popular.

(b)   Tractor size and power have appeared to upper limits.

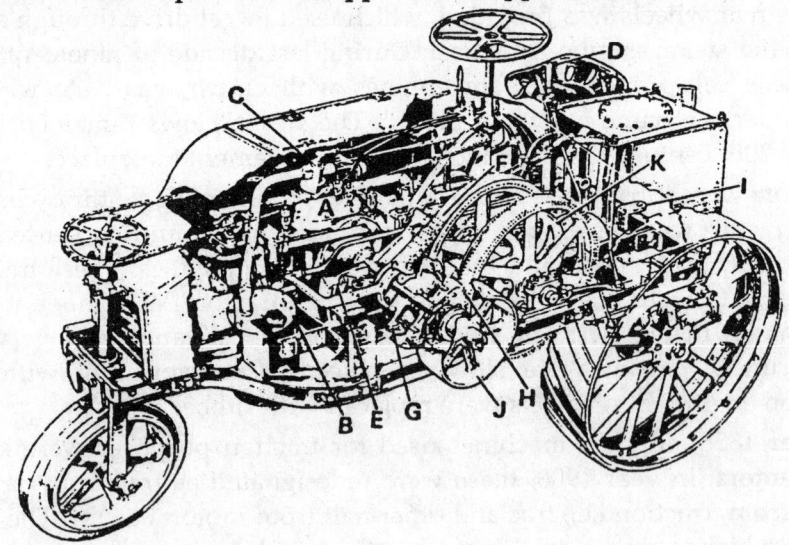

A-Horizontally opposed twin cylinder engine, B- Fuel system, C- Air fuel mixture control chamber, D- Forward and reverse drive lever, E- Inner cone clutch, F- Chain, G- Outer cone clutch, H- Reverse drive gear, I- Hetch point, J- Crankshaft pulley, K- Counter pulley.

Fig. 1.1 IVEL Tractor made in the Year 1902

1.5.3 Trctor Development in India: The tractors in India were introduced in the late forties by importing war surplus tractors from Europe. The number of tractors in use, as estimated by Jain (1971) was 8,500 in 1951 and 37,000 in 1960 all of these were imported. The manufacturing of the tractor started in 1961 with 880 units. This increased to 20,000 units in 1970, 71000 units in1980 and 1,40,000 units in 1990. The production of tractors during 1997 was over 2,55,000 units (Singh (1999). The number of tractor in use in India at the end of 1997 was estimated to over two million units as shows in Table 1.2. Based on 142 Mha cultivated land, the grass croped area per tractor in India was reduced from 1,48,00 in 1951 to 71 ha in 1997. The highest concentration of tractor is in northern India, especially Punjab, Haryana and Western Utter Pradesh, where Wheat is a major crop. Tractors are increasing rapidly in Madhya Pradesh, Rajashtan, Gujrat and Maharastra as shown in Table 1.3.

History of tractor development in India is given below in chronological order.

1960-61 Manufacturing of tractor started in India by first manufactures M/S Eicher Good Earth.

1962-70: Manufactures like Tractor and farm Equipment Madras, Hindustan Tractors at Baroda, Escorts Tractors at Faridabad and International Harvester in Bomaby started their work during this period.

1971: Escorts Tractor Ltd. started producing Ford-Tractor.

1973: Manufacturing of HMT Tractor was launched.

1974: Pitti and Kirlosker Tractors were launched.

1975 : Harsha Tractors were established.

1981: Auto Tractor were started.

1982: Universal Tractors were started.

1997: Manufacturing of Sonalica International Tractor was launched.

1998: Manufacturing of Standrard Tractor was launched.

2000: Manafacturing of L and T Joh n Deere Tractor was launched.

Besides above these are Mitsubishi, Ford New Holland Tractors, Greaves, Davi Brown made tractors also.

Table 1.1 Major Sources of Farm Power, 1950-97

Year	Worker (million)	Animal (million)	Tractor (100)	Avg. size (hp)	Power tiller (hp)	Avg. size (hp)	S.P. Combine (000)	Diesel engine (million)	Electric motor (million)	Total power available (Mhp)
1950	95.6	65.0	8	34.1	0.0	-	0.0	0.07	0.02	42.8
1955	112.4	72.0	20	34.1	0.0	-.	0.0	0.12	0.05	48.8
1960	11.0	80.4	37	34.1	0.0	-	0.0	0.23	0.20	55.2
1965	120.0	81.4	63	34.1	1.5	6.5	0.1	0.50	0.50	59.9
1970	124.2	82.6	168	34.1	9.6	9.0	0.2	1.70	1.60	76.1
1975	136.2	83.4	292	34.1	17.9	9.1	0.3	2.32	2.28	88.4
1980	149.3	73.4	531	34.1	16.2	9.1	0.3	2.88	3.35	101.0
1985	165.9	72.6	810	34.2	19.6	9.4	1.5	5.40	4.33	129.5
1990	183.5	70.9	1,192	33.9	31.2	9.7	3.2	4.80	8.07	159.2
1995	199.0	65.2	1,707	35.3	55.2	9.7	4.1	5.20	11.13	195.3
1997	305.0	62.6	2,032	35.5	65.9	9.7	4.4	5.55	41.99	212.6

Source: AMA Vol 32 No. 2 SPRING 2001

Note: Assumed average power of agricltural worker: 0.1 hp draft animal: 0.5 hp, seft propelled combine harvester: 85 hp, electric motor and diesel engine for irrigations pump: 5 hp.

Table 1.2. Availability of Tractors and power-tller in various years

Year	1950	1955	1960	1965	1970	1975	1980	1985	1990	1995	1997
Tractor (000)	8	20	37	63	168	292	530	810	1,192	1,707	2,032
Power-tiller (000)	0.0	0.0	0.0	1.5	9.6	17.9	16.2	19.6	31.2	55.2	65.9

Source: AMA Vol 32 No. 2 SPRING 2001

Table 1.3 Availability of Tractors and Power Tillers in various States, (1997)

States	Agriculture land (1000 ha)	Tractor		Power tiller	
		Population	units/000 ha	Population	units/000 ha
Jammu and Kashmir	1,104	3,700	3.7	20	0.0
Himanchal Pradesh	1,010	2,200	2.0	10	0.0
Punjab	4,033	332,700	82,5	20	0.0
Uttar Pradesh	17,986	434,400	24.2	260	0.0
Harayana	3,711	233,400	62.9	20	0.0
Rajashan	20,971	175,300	8.4	30	0.0
Assam	3,205	6,400	2.0	6.130	1.7
Bihar	10.743	74,100	6.9	740	0.1
West Bengal	5,656	16,100	2.9	17,400	2.8
Madhya Pradesh	22,111	195,100	8.9	410	0.0

Gujarat	10,292	146,500	14.2	1,710	0.2
Orissa	5,296	13,000	2.5	1,550	0.3
Maharashtra	20,925	110,800	5.3	3,150	0.1
Andhra Pradesh	14,460	100,100	6.9	3,560	0.2
Karataka	12,321	73,900	6.0	9,230	0.7
Tamil Nadu	7,474	85,100	11.4	12,400	1.5
Kerala	1,796	7,700	4.3	5,120	2.6
Others	2,505	5,200	2.1	4,180	1.7
Total	165,509	2015,600	12,2	65,930	0.4

Source: AMA Vol 32 No. 2 SPRING 2001

1.6 Classification of Tractors: Generally tractors are classified on the basis of construction, type of drive and purpose for which it is used.

1.6.1 Classification on the basis of construction: They are classified as follows:

(a)   Riding type: Tractor in which driver can sit & drive.

(b)   Walking type: Tractor with which the operator walks along.

16.2. On the basis of type of drive: They are classified as follows:

Track type (i) Full track type

(ii)   Half track type

(b)   Wheel type

(i)   Two wheels

(ii)   Three wheels

(iii)   Four Wheels

(i)   **Full Track Type Tractoer:** In this type of tractors instead of wheels one track is provided on either side as shown in Fig. 1.2. This track gets drive from the sprnket run by rear axle shaft. Steer the tractor no stearing gears are provided. The tractor is steered by applying brakes to one side of the track with the other track moving.

(ii)   **Half Track Type:** In this type of tractor tractor a small track chain is provided at the rear end only while at front axle types are mounted. types are fitted. Track type of tractors are mostly used for reclaiming barron bands and are seldom used for general agricultural purpose. As these are provided the tracks which has more contact area to the ground as such the traction power of the tractor increases considerably. Track type of tractors play any important role on dams for earth moving work. At one time crowles tractors were larger than wheel tractors, and thus they were used on some large farm.

9

Fig. 1.2 Track types Tractor or Crawler Tractor

(b)   Wheel Type of Tractors: Wheel types of tractors are most commonly used for agricultural pupuses. As they can run fast and tyre fitted in it can absorb a certain amount of fields shocks also.

(i) Two wheel types of tractors are used for small farms, hilly area and for gardening purposes.

(ii)   Three Wheel or Tricle Type: Three wheeles tractors were very popular 45 years' back but now it has been replaced by four wheelers. These tractors had single or dual wheel fitted at the front end in th centre and were considered good for negotiated shorter turns.

(iii)   Four-wheel Drive Tractor With Smaller Front Wheel: A four-wheel drive tractor with smaller front wheels is simply a standard or a row-crop tractor with the front wheels also being driven with regard to prices and traction, this type of tractor comes between the standard and the four-wheel drive tractor with equal-sized wheels as shown in Fig. 1.3. The particular tractor has become popular in Japan because of its excellent steering and tractin characteristics in soft, wet rice fields.

Fig. 1.3 Four Wheel Drive Tractor with Smaller
Steering Wheels in Front.
(Courtesy Long Mfg. N.C. Inc.)

Fig. 1.4 Four Wheel Drive Tractor

iv) Four-wheel-drive or simple 4WD: Four-wheel-drive tractors have been developed so as to be in able to produce more drawbar power. The size of 4WD tractor varies in United States and Canada from 100 kW to more than 300 kW. In Europe, 4WD tractors may be small as 15 kW and are used especially in vineyards. Four-wheel-drive tractors can be steered by pivaiting the tractor in the centre (frame steer) or steering the wheels as shown in Fig. 1.4.

1.6.3 Classification on the Basis of Purpose of Use: They are classified as follows:

(I) Utility tractor	(II) Orchard tractor
(III) Lawn and garden tractor	(IV) Multipurpose tractor
(V) Power tiller	(VI) Row crop tractor
(VII) Standard tractor	(VIII) Earth moving tractor

(I) Utility Tractor: It is as shown in Fig. 1.5. They have generally less clearance than standard a row-crop tractors. They are used for many on the farm and are often equipped with a front loades. A special use for that tractor is cleaning a feedlot.

(II) Orchard Tractor: An orchard tractor slightly differs from an utility tractor except that it is a few centrimeters lower. It is only used in orchards. No part of the tractor is produced outside, therefore, tractor can easily go in between trees safely.

Fig. 1.5 A small 28 hp utility Tractor (Courtesy Long Mfg. N.C. Inc.)

(III) Lawn and Garde Tractor: It is as shown in Fig. 1.6. these tractors are in the ranges of 1.5 to 15 kW and are primarily designed for the care of large lawns. They can carry a lawn moves, a sweeper, a snowblower and many other attachments. The wheels, provided to such tractors are of scooter size but thicker in width.

Fig. 1.6 Lawn and Garden tractor.

(IV) Multipupose Tracter: It is shown in Fig. 1.7. These tractors are designed to operate in either direction. it not only carries the implement but also supplies the power. A large general purpose tractor is shown in Fig. 1.8.

Fig. 1.7 Multipurpose or All Tractor (Courtesy Tractor Operations)

(V) Power Tiller: It is as shown in Fig. 1.8. A power tiller is a two-wheeled tractors operated by the operator walking behind it. It also knwon as hand tractor or walking type tractor. It is used commonly in the rice-growing areas of Japan and Southern Asia. Power tillers and are in the range of 5 to 12 kW and powered by a horizontal single cylinder engine.

Fig. 1.8 (a) Power Tiller

1.8 (b) A medium-size garden tractor. (Courtesy of Bolens Products Division.)

(VI) Row crop Tractor: It is all purpose tractor as shown in Fig. 1. They are designed for the care of all agricultural purposes like ploughing, horrowing, levelling, pulling seed drills, planters, streep and drills or for weed control or for running other machines like water pumps, threshers etc through its belt pulley. They have followig characteristics:

(i) It should have provisions for adjustment of row spacing.

(ii) It should have more ground clearance.

(iii) It should be easy to steer and can take shorter turns.

(iv) It should be easy and convenient to operate.

(v) It should attach and deattach agricultural machines quickly and conveniently.

(vi) It should have provisions for P.T.O. drive.

(vii) It should have power lift for lowering or lifting agricultural machines.

(VII) Standard Tractors: They are designed primarily for traction as shown in Fig. 1.9. They are characterized by a drive through the two rear wheels, with centre of gravity located at approximately two-third the wheelbase behind the front axles.

Fig. 1.9 Standard or Row Crop Tractor.
(Courtesy John Deere, Molinef)

(VIII) Earth Moving Tractor: They are available in track and type types both. They are heavy in weight and strongly built. These are mainly used for earth moving work on dawns, quaries and other constructional works.

(IX) Implement Carries: It is a special type of tractor as shown in Fig. These tractors have and extended charis frame between the front and rear types where all the implements, like seed drills, duster, sprayer, loader, platform can be mounted only easily.

(XX) Tree Skidder; These tractors are a four-wheel-drive. They are deisgned especially for moving tree trunks out of the forest to an area where they can be loaded on trucks.

Fig. 1.10. Industrial Tractor

1.7 Variations in Tractor in various Countries:

1. Tractors designed and used in Japan are usually provided with cagewheel tyres.

2. The power to mass ratio is more for Japanese tractors than others.

3. European tractors mostly used radia-ply tyres for traction.

4. Tractors manufactures outside Northern America may have as many as four different speeds on the power take off.

5. In northern America, 4-wheel drive (4WD), is mostly on, tractors above 100 kW, in Japan, however, tractors as small as 10 kW may have 4-wheel drive.

6. In United Kingdam, Europe, and Japan 4-WD with frontwheels smaller than rear is popular, whereas almost all 4-WD tractors in Northern America have equal-sized wheels.

7. Crawler tractors are more popular in United Kingdom and Europe.

8. Power tillers are quite popular in Japan and Southern Asia, primarily because of the smaller rice farms and soft, wet land conditions are found there.

1.8 System of Tractor: The tractor is divided into two main system namely the engine system and tractor system.

(i) Engine System: It provides the source of power to drive the tractor. It includes following systems:

(a)   Fuel system

(b)   Ignition system

(c)   Cooling system

(d)   Lubrication system

(e)   Governor system

(ii) Tractor System: Power generated from engine system is available on flywheel. Then it goes to transmission system. The tractor system starts beyond the flywheel. It includes following system.

(a)   Tranmission system

(b)   Hydraulic and Hitching system

(c)   Traction Mechanism

(d)   Chasis

(e)   Steering system

(iii) Tractor Accerrories: Main accessories of the tractor are shwon in Fig. Although we will discuss them in detail in the respective chapters but here we would like you to get familiar with the accerrories which are as under:

1.   **Engine:** A tractor can have powerine, petrol or desiel engine. But now-a-days all the tractors have diesel engine. Engine provides the source of power to drive the tractor.

2.   **Clutch:** Clutch is fitted between engine and gearbox and is used to connect and disconnect the tractor engine from the transmission gears and drive wheels. Clutch transmits power by means of friction between driving members and driven members.

3. **Transmission:** Gearbox is assembled in the tractor to increase the driving torque so as to enable the tractor to pull more load. In the gear box housing differential and reduction gears are also mounted. The differential helps the tractor to take turn without its inner wheel spinning while the reduction gear mounted further to increases the driving torque of the wheel.

4.   **Wheels.** Two wheels are mounted to the front axle and two rear wheels to the reduction gear shaft, drive is transmitted through the gear wheels.

5.   **Front Axle:** Front axle is mounted at the front of the tractor and two stub axles are provided at either end through which the steering linkage is connected and wheels are steered.

6.   **Steering System:** Operator steers the tractor through a steering system either left or right as desired.

7.   **Brake System:** Operator stops the moving tractor through brake system as desired.

8. Electrical System: Electrical system is provided in the tractor which makes it to work in the right through the electricity produced by the dynamo. Moreover engine is also started through starter which draws its electric current from battery.

9. Hydraulic Lift: Implements are lifted or lowered through hydraulic lift, Moreover, draft and depth are controlled through it.

10. Power Take Off: Provisioin is made in the tractor to drive stationary or moving implements like thresher, water pump, sprayes dusters and etc.

1.9. Technical Terms: Certain techhnical terms are used in this book. These are as under and shwon in Fig. 1.10 (a) to (c).

1. Track: It is the distance between centres of front two tyres.

2. Ground Clearance: It is the height of the lowest point of the tractor from a level supporting surface, the tractor being loaded to its maximum permissible weight.

3. Wheel base: It is the horizontal distance btween front and rear wheels measured at ground contact.

4. Height of Fame: It is the distance from the upper edge of the frame from the ground level.

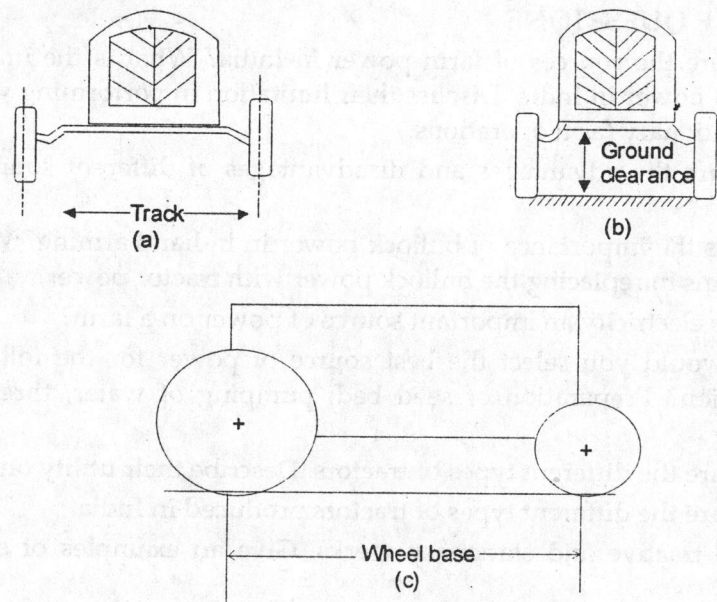

Fig. 1.11 Showing Technical Terms

1.10. Functions of Farm Tractor: Now-a-days agricultural tractor is a versatile vehicle is used to propel and power agricultural implements for agricultural production. Impliment applications, therefore have considerable effect on tractor

17

designs, and the tractor engineer must be aware of implements to weigh properly such design consideration like crop clearance, ground clearance, tracks, wheel base, power to mass ratio and mass distribution as well as to provide placement of controls to satisfy the number of operation. Every design will necessarily include some compromises.

Implements may be attached to and operated by tractors in one of four ways.

1. Trailed, single-point-hitch
2. Mounted, three-pont-hitch
3. Semi mounted, three-point-hitch
4. Frame mounted

Power may be transmitted to the implement by a power take-off shaft or by oil-hydraulic boxes. Each new tractor creates many engineering problems related proper hitch point, and implement clearance.

The wide spread adoption of hitch-mounted and frame mounted implement is probably the result of one or both of two primary factor decreased and increased versatility. A part from it the extra weight transfer of mounted implements adds significantly to the tractive ability of the tractor.

SUBJECTIVE QUESTIONS

1. What are the sources of farm power in India? What is the importance of human power in India. Discuss their limitation in performing various field and stationary farm operations.
2. What are the advantages and disadvantages of different sources of farm power?
3. What is the importance of bullock power in Indian Farming? What are the problems in replacing the bullock power with tractor power?
4. How is electricity an important source of power on a farm?
5. How would you select the best source of power for the following farm operation? Preparation of seed bed, pumping of water, threshing, chaff cutting.
6. What are the different types of tractors. Describe their utility on farm.
7. What are the different types of tractors produced in India.
8. Define tractive and stationary works. Give an examples of each type of work.
9. Write short note on:
    (a) System of tractor
    (b) Transmission in the tractor
    (c) Ground clearance

(d) Track

(e) Wheel base

4. Differentiate between:

(a) Conventional and of non-convention sources of energy.

(b) Biomass and biogas.

(c) Solar Energy and Nuclear energy

MULTIPLE TYPE QUESTIONS

1. The journey of the modern tractor started in
   (a) 1855   (b) 1955
   (c) 1755   (d) 1655

2. Successful gasoline tractor was introduced by
   (a) Charlas W. Hart   (b) Charles H. Parr
   (c) both   (d) none

3. All purpose tractor was developed in
   (a) 1910-14   (b) 1915-1919
   (c) 1920-24   (d) 1936-37

4. The power take was introduced in
   (a) 1910-14   (b) 1915-1917
   (c) 1920-24   (d) 1936-37

5. Automatic hydraulic draft control was introduced in
   (a) 1936-37   (b) 1937-41
   (c) 1941-49   (d) 1950-60

6. Turbo charger and intecooler was introduced in
   (a) 1941-49   (b) 1950-60
   (c) 1961-70   (d) 1970-1978

7. Manufactuing of tractor was started in India in
   (a) 1960-61   (b) 1970-71
   (c) 1980-81   (d) 1990-91

8. First tractor manufacture of India was
   (a) M/S Eicher Good Earth   (b) Harsa Tractor
   (c) Universal Tractor   (d) Escorts Tractor

9. Manufacturing of HMT-Tractor was started in
   (a) 1970   (b) 1971
   (c) 1973   (d) 1974

10. Power of Lawn and garden tractors varies in between
    (a) 1.5 to 15 kW   (b) 15-20 kW
    (c) 20-25 kW   (d) 25-30 kW

11. The word tractor first appear in
    (a) 1890   (b) 1906
    (c) 1908   (d) None of thea bove

12. Successful gasoline tractor was introduced by
    (a) Charles H. Hart and H. Parr (b) James Watt
    (c) both   (d) none of the bove

13. Successful gasoline tractor was introduced in
    (a) 1890   (b) 1906
    (c) 1908   (d) 1910

14. The power take-off was introduced in between
    (a) 1915-1919   (b) 1906-1908
    (c) 1910-1914   (d) 1937-1941

15. Automatic hydraulic draft control was introduced in between
    (a) 1906-1908   (b) 1915-1919
    (c) 1910-1914   (d) 1937-1941

16. Tractor manufacturing was started in India in
    (a) 1960   (b) 1971
    (c) 1973   (d) 1974

17. Tractor manufacturing was started in India by first manufacturer
    (a) M/S Eicher Good Eearth   (b) M/S Escorts tractor
    (c) M/S Harsha tractor   (d) M/S HMT tractor

18. Which of the following is a renewable source of energy
    (a) Coal   (b) Petroleum
    (c) Natural gas   (d) Solar energy

19 Which of the following is a tractor system
    (a) Fuel system   (b) Ergonomics
    (c) Governor system   (d) None of the above

20. Which of the following is non-renewable source of energy
    (a) Coal   (b) Petroleum
    (c) Natural gas   (d) All of the above

21. The S.I. unit of energy is
    (a) J   (b) W
    (c) kgm   (d) None of the above

22. The distance between centres of the front tyres in known as
    (a) Track   (b) Ground clearance
    (c) Wheel base   (d) None of the above

23. The distance between centres of hubs of front and rear wheel is known as
    (a) Track   (b) Wheel base
    (c) Ground clearance   (d) height of frame
24. Clutch is fitted between
    (a) engine and gear box   (b) Front axle and rear axle
    (c) both   (d) none of the above
25. Gear box is fitted inthe tractor to increase
    (a) driving torque   (b) momentum
    (c) force   (d)   all of the above

FILL INTHE BLANKS

1. Biogas is a mixture of .... and ....
2. Solar constant is approximately .... J/m²s.
3. .... is the distance between centre of hubs of front and rear wheels.
4. .... is used to connect and disconnect the engine drive to the gear box.
5. Power tiller are quite popular in .... and South East Asia.
6. The tractor manufactuing started in India in ....
7. The word tractor appeared first in ....
8. Diesel engine was used in tractor in between.
9. Biogas contains about .... carbondioxide.
10. Directly or indirectly all forms of energy originate from .... energy.

Ans. 1. methane and carbondioxde 2. 1.4 3. wheel base 4. Clutch 5. Japan 6. 1961
    7. 1890 8. 1936-37 9. 30-40% 10. solar.

FILL UP THE BLANKS

1. The first tractor demonstration was held in United States at ...., Nebraska in.............................
2. Diesel engine was used in tractor in ....
3. Tractor 'IVEL' made in year.
4. Power tillers in the range of .... to .... kW.
5. Successful gasoline tractor was introduced in ....
6. Clutch connect and disconnect the tractor engine from ....
7. .... is the distance between centres of front two types.

8.   .... is the height of the lowest point of the tractor from a level supporting surface, the tractor being loaded to its .... permissible weight.

9.   The tractor is divided into .... and .... systems.

10. Power is provided in tractor through .... system.

Ans. Omaha, 1911, 2. 1936-37. 3. 1902 4. 5 to 12 5. 1906 6. transmission system 7. Track 8. Ground clearance 9. engine tractor 10. Engine.

ANSWER OF MULTIPLE CHOICE QUESTIONS

1(a) 2 (c) 3 (b) 4 (b) 5 (b) 6 (d) 7 (a) 8 (a) 9 (a) 10 (a) 11 (a) 12 (a) 13 (b) 14 (a) 15 (d) 16 (a) 17 (a) 18 (d) 19 (b) 2 0(d) 21 (a) 22 (a) 23 (b) 24 (a) 25 (a)

Chapter 2
Basic Mechanics

2.1. Displacement (S):

2.1.1 If the body is moved from initial position A to final position B, then a straight line distance AB is knwon as the displacement, So it is the movement of the particle from initial point to final point measured along a straight line.

2.1.2. Fig. 2.1 Shows that the body may follow various path to move from A to B but the shortest possible path or distance between A and B in the displacement. It is shown in Fig. 1.1.

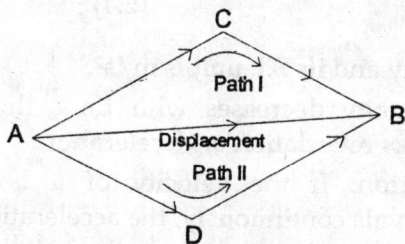

Fig. 2.1 Various path from A to B

2.1.3. Displacement in a vector quantity having magnitude and direction. It S.I. unit is metre (m).

2.2. Velocity (v).

2.2.1. Definition: Velocity is defined as the rate change of displacement (ds) with time (dt). It is given as

$$v = \frac{ds}{dt} \qquad (2.1)$$

It is also defined as the disatance (S) convered per unit time (t) in the direction. It is given as

$$v = \frac{s}{t} \qquad (2.2)$$

2.2.2. Velocity is a vector quantity having magnitutde and direction.

2.2.3 Its S.I. unit is metre per second (m/s)

2.2.4. Instantaneous velocity: It is the velocity of a particle at any instant of time.

23

2.2.5. Average velocity: It is defined as the ratio of the resultant displacement to the total time required to cover it. If the instantaneous velocity is changing from time to time, taken.

$$V_{av} = \frac{\text{Resultant displacement}}{\text{Total time required}} = \frac{S_R}{t} \qquad (2.3)$$

2.2.6 **Unifrom velocity:** If the velocity of a particle is constant in magnitutde and direction with respect to time, then it is known as uniform velocity.

2.3. Speed

2.3.1 Definition: Speed is defined as the rate of covering the distance w.r.t. time irrespctive of its direction.

2.3.2 Speed is a scalar quantity and its S.I. unit is m/s.

2.4. Acceleration (a):

2.4.1. **Definition:** Acceleration is defined as the rate of change of velocity with respect to time. It is given as

$$a = \frac{dv}{dt} \qquad (2.4)$$

2.4.2 It is a vector quantity and its S.I. unit is m/s².

2.4.3 **Retardation:** If velocity decreases with time, the acceleration becomes negative which is known as retardation or deceleration.

2.4.4 **Uniform Acceleration:** If the velocity of a body changes by equal magnitudes in equal intervals continuously, the acceleration is known as uniform acceleration or constant acceleration.

2.4.5 **Variable Acceleration:** If the change in velocity per unit time is not constant in a continuous motion, then the corresponding acceleration is called as variable acceleration.

2.5 Equations of motion with uniform acceleration.

2.5.4	$v = u + at$	(2.5)
2.5.2	$s = ut + \dfrac{1}{2} at^2$	(2.6)
2.5.3	$v^2 = u^2 + 2as$	(2.7)
2.5.4	$S_n = u + a (n - 0.5)$	(2.8)

where,

s = Displacement, m

u = Initial velocity, m/s

v = Final velocity, m/s

Sn = Distance travelled during nth seconds.

2.6   Motion under gravity:

  2.6.1 $v = u \pm gt$ (2.9)

  2.6.2 $s = ut \pm \dfrac{1}{2}\, gt^2$ (2.10)

  2.6.3 $v^2 = u^2 \pm 2as$ (2.11)

Note: Negative sign is taken when motion is vertically upward.

2.7   Force

2.7.1 A concept of force is concerned with the action of one body on another. This force may be exerted by actual contact or at a distance as in case of gravitational force and magnetic force.

2.7.2 The force is specified by its point of application, magnitude and direction just like vector.

2.7.3 Definition: The external agency, which tends to change the state of a body is known as a force.

2.7.3 Representation: It is a vector quantity. Force (F) is represented graphically by a straight line as 'ab' where length is proportional to the magnitude of froce and the arrow drawn shows the direction of force 'F' as indicated in Fig.1.2.

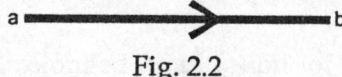

Fig. 2.2

2.7.4 Unit of force: S.I. unit of force is Newton (N).

2.7.5 Resultant: If any number of forces acting upon a body are replaced by a single force which has the same effect as the force together, then this single force is called the resultant force.

A resultant force may be found out analytically, graphically or by following three laws:

(a)   Parallelogram law of forces: It states, "If two forces acting simultaneously on a particle be represented in magnitude and direction by the two adjacent sides of a paralleogram taken in order, there resultant may be represented in magnitude and direction by the diagonal of the parallelogram passing through the point."

(b)   Triangle law of force: It states, "If two forces acting simultaneously on a particle be represented in magnitude and direction by the sides of a triangle taken in order, their resultant may be represented in magnitude and direction by a third side of the triangle taken in opposite order".

(c)   Polygon law of forces: It states, "If a number of forces acting simultaneously on a particle be represented in magnitude and direction by the sides of a polygon taken in order, their resultant may be represented in magnitude and direction by the closing side of the polygon taken in opposite order".

Centripetal and centrifugal force:

Consider a particle of mass m moving with a linear velocity v in a circular path of radius r.

We know that centripital acceleration,

$$a_c = \frac{v^2}{r} = \omega^2 . r \qquad (2.12)$$

∴ Centripetal force = Mass x centripetal acceleration

$$F_C = \frac{mv^2}{r} = m\omega^2 r \qquad (2.13)$$

This force acts radially inwards and is essential for circular motion.

We have discussed above that the centripetal force acts radially inwards. According to Newton's Third Law of motion, action and reaction are equal and opposite. Therefore, the particle must excert a force radially outwards of equal magnitude. This force is known as centrifugal force whose magnitude is given by

$$F_C = \frac{mv^2}{r} = m w^2 r \qquad (2.14)$$

2.9 Moment:

2.9.1 Moment of force about a point: It is turning effect that would be produced by the force about the point.

2.9.2 It is a vector quantity and its S.I. unit is Nm.

2.9.3. Moment is given by the Cross product or vector product of two vectors, the force ($\bar{F}$) and its distance (position vectors $\bar{r}$) from the given point, out side the line of action of the force, about which the moment in taken. It is mathematically expressed as

$$\bar{M} = \bar{r} \times \bar{F} \qquad (2.15)$$

2.9.4 The magnitude of the moment is given by

$$M = r F \sin\theta \qquad (2.16)$$

2.10 Momentum (M): The momentum of a moving body is the total motion in possesion of the body. The momemtum of a body is measured by the product of its mass and velocity. Mathematically, it is expressed as

$$M = mv \qquad (2.17)$$

where,

m = mass of the body, m

v = velocity of the body, m/s

2.11 Torque (T):

2.11.1 Definition: Application of force at any point to develop turning effect is called torque. Mathematically, it is expressed as

$$T = F \times r \qquad (2.18)$$

Where, r is the distance of applied force (F) from the centre of shaft.

2.11.2 Unit : Its S.I unit is Nm.

2.12 Work (W):

2.12.1 Definition: Work is defined as the effect or transformation or expenditure of energy.

2.12.2 Mechanical work: It is defined as the product of force and the displacement in the direction of force for linear motion.

$$W = F.S \text{ or } W_{12} = \int_{1}^{2} Fds \qquad (2.19)$$

2.12.3 Gravitational work (WG): It is given as

$$W_G = \text{Gravitational Force} \times \text{height} = mgh \qquad (2.20)$$

2.12.4 Electrical work (WE): it is given as

$$W_E = V. Q, J \qquad (2.21)$$

where,

V = Potential difference, volt

Q = Charge, columb

2.11.5 Unit: S.I. unit of work is Newton-meter or Joule (Nm or J)

2.11.6 Joule: One joule is defined as the work when a force of 1-newton moves a body through a distance of 1-metre in the direction of force.

2.11.7 Work done during Rotation (Wr): The work done by a couple is given by

$$W_r = T \theta \text{ or } W_{12} = \int_{\theta_1}^{\theta_2} T.d\theta, J \qquad (2.22)$$

where,

T = Moment of couple or Torque, Nm

θ = Angular displacement, rad./s

2.12 Power (P):

2.12.1 Definition: Power is defined as the rate of doing the work.

2.12.2 It is given by following relationship for linear motion.

$$P = \frac{W}{t}, \text{watt} \qquad (2.23)$$

$$P = F. \ v, \ watt \qquad\qquad (2.24)$$

where,

W = work done, J

v = Velocity, m/s

2.12.2 It is given by following relationship for rotational motion.

$$P = \frac{dw}{dt} = T\omega = F. \ v \qquad\qquad (2.25)$$

we know that

$$\omega = 2 \pi N$$

Substituting the value of w in equation, we have

$$P = \frac{2\pi NT}{60}, \ watt \qquad\qquad (2.26)$$

where,

ω = Angular velocity, rad/s

N = Speed, rpm

T = Torque, Nm

2.13 Energy (E):

2.13.1. Definition : Energy is defined as a capacity to do work. Thus the energy something which appears in various forms and gets converted from one form into another. During such conversion certain work is done by it and its SI unit is Joule (J)

2.13.2 Foms of Energy : Various forms of energy are as follows :

(a) Mechanical Energy : It exists in two forms

(i) Potential Energy (P.E) : It is defined as the energy possessed by the body due to its position w.r.t. certain reference level.

Case I: **Potential energy due to gravity :** If a body is raised to a height above a certain reference level, then its P.E. w.r.t to that level is given by

$$P.E. = m.g.h \ , \ J \qquad\qquad (2.27)$$

where,

m = Mass of body, kg

g = Gravitational acceleration, m/s^2

h = Height above reference level, m

Case II : Strain Energy : If the length of the spring is changed due tension or compression, its P.E. w.r.t. to normal position is given by

$$P.E. = \frac{1}{2} K\delta^2 = \frac{1}{2} \frac{F^2}{K}, J \qquad (2.28)$$

Where,

K = stiffness of the spring, N/m

δ = change in length, m

F = Force exerted, N

unstretched, PE = 0

$$\therefore PE = \frac{1}{2} k\delta^2$$

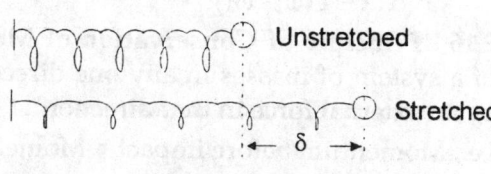

Unstretched

Stretched

Fig. 2.3 Strain

(b)   Kinetic Energy (K.E): It is defined as the energy possessed by the body due to its motion or velocity. Kinetic energy for linear motion is given by following relationship

$$K.E. = \frac{1}{2} mv^2, J \qquad (2.29)$$

where,

m = mass of body, kg.

v = velocity, m/s

2.14   Principle of Conservation of energy: It states "The energy can niether be created nor destroyed, through it can be transformed from one form into any of the forms, in which the energy can exist". i.e.; The loss of energy is any one form is always accompanied by an equivalent increase in another form.

2.15 Impulse and Impulsive Force: Impulse may be defined as product of force and time. Mathematically, it is expressed as,

Impulse = F x t

where, F = Force

t = time

If m is the mass of body Let a force F changes its velocity from an intial velocity v1 to a final velocity v_2.

We know that the force is equal to the rate of change of linear momentum, therefore,

$$F = \frac{m(v_2 - v_1)}{t}$$

or, F x t = m (v₂-v₁)

i.e., Impulse = change of linear momentum.

Note: 1. If a force acts for a very short, it is then called as impulsive force or blow.

2. When the two rotating gears with angular velocities w_1 and w_2 mesh each other, then an impulsive torque acts on the two gears, until they are both rotating at speeds corresponding to their velocity ratio. The impulsive torque

$$T. t = I (\omega_2 - \omega_1)$$

2.16 Principle of Conservation of Momentum: It states "The total momentum of a system of masses in any one direction remains constant, unless acted upon by an external force in that direction".

i.e., Momentum before impact = Momentum of per impact

$$m_1v_1 \pm m_2v_2 = (m_1+m_2) v$$

Note: Consider two rotating bodies of mass moment of Inertia I_1 and I_2 and intially apart from each other and are made to engage as in the case of a clutch. If they reach a common angular velocity w, after slipping has ceased, then

$$I_1\omega_1+I_2\omega_2 = (I_1+I_2) \omega$$

The $\pm$ sign depends upon the direction of rotation

Prob. 2.1.   A particle is moving along a circular track of radius r. What is the distance traveled by particle in half revolution? What distance is displacement?

Sol. Refening Fig.

Given: radius AC = CB = 4 r

Distance $\overset{\frown}{AB}$ = πr

Displacement AB = AC + CB

= r + r = 2r

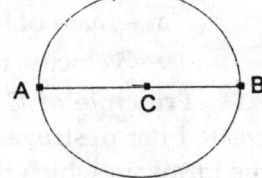

Fig. 2.4

Prob. 2.2 A particle thrown vertically upward reaches a height ո and then returns to intial position. What are displacement and distance travelled by particle.

Sol.   Refering Fig.

Distance = AB + BA

h + h = 2h

Displacement = $\overrightarrow{AB} + \overrightarrow{BA}$

= h + (-h) = 0

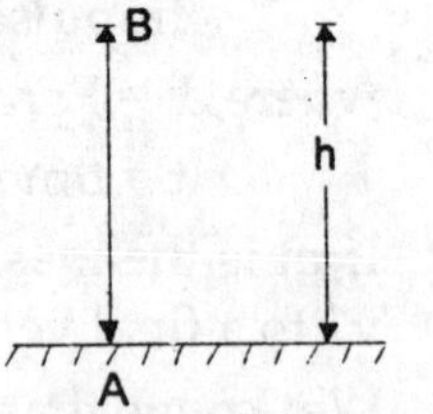

Prob. 2.3. A train travels from one station to another at a speed of 40 km/h and returns to the first station at a speed of 60 km/h. Calculate the average speed and average velocity of the train.

Sol. Given : v_1 = 40 km/h ; v_2 = 60 km/h

Let S Km be the distances between two stations.

Time taken by train from one station to another.

Fig. 2.5

$$t_1 = \frac{\text{Distance}}{\text{Velocity}} = \frac{S}{40} \, h$$

Time taken by train for return journey

$$t_2 = \frac{S}{60} \, h$$

Therefore, Average speed = $\dfrac{\text{Total distance}}{\text{Total time}}$

$$= \frac{S + S}{\dfrac{S}{40} + \dfrac{S}{60}} = \frac{2 \times 40 \times 60}{40 + 60}$$

$$= 48 \text{ km/h}$$

The displacement of the train for the whole journey is zero; therefore;

average velocity = $\dfrac{\text{Total displacement}}{\text{Total time}}$

$$= \frac{0}{t_1 + t_2} = 0$$

Prob. 2.4 A tenis ball is dropped on to the floor from a height of 4.000 m. It rebounds to a height of 3.0m. If the ball was is contact with the floor for 0.010 s, What was its average acceleration during contact?

Sol. Given : $h_2 = 3m$; $h_1 = 4.0m$; $\Delta t = 0.015 \text{ S}$

Average accelaration $(\vec{a}) = \dfrac{\vec{v}_2 - \vec{v}_1}{\Delta t}$

$$= \frac{\sqrt{2gh_2} - \sqrt{2gh}}{\Delta t}$$

$$= \frac{\sqrt{2 \times 9.8 \times 3} + \sqrt{2 \times 9.8 \times 4}}{0.010}$$

$$= 165.2 \text{m/s}^2.$$

Prob. 2.5 The motion of a particle along a straight line described by the function.

$$x = 6 + 4t^2 - t^4$$

where x is in meter (m) and t is positive time in second(s).

(a) Find the position, velocity and acelearation at t = 2s

(b) During what time interval is the velocity positive.

(c) During what time interval is x-positive.

(d) What is the maximum possible velocity attained by the particle

Sol. Given $x = 6 + \Delta t^2 - t^4$

where x is in meter and $\bar{t}$ in second.

(a)   At $= 2s$, position, $x = 6 + 4 \times 2^2 - (2)^4$

$$= 6 + 16 - 16 = 6m$$

velocity $(v) = \dfrac{dx}{dt} = 8t - 4t^3$

At $t = 2s$.

$v = 8 \times 2 - 4 \times 2^3$

$= 16 - 32 = -16 m/s$

Acceleration $a = \dfrac{dv}{dt} = 8 - 12\, t^2$

$\Delta t = 2s$

$a = 1 - 12 \times (2)^2 = -40\ m/s^2$

(b)   The velocity (v) is positive if $v = 8t - 4t^3 \geq 0$

or $\Delta t (2 - t^2) = 0$

i.e., $t = 0$ or $2 - t^2 > 0$ i.e., $t < \sqrt{2}$ s

Thus velocity is positive for time t such that

$0 < t < \sqrt{2}$ or < 1.41

(c)   The position x is positive if $x = 6 + 4t^2 - t^4 \geq 0$

Solving for

t^2, we get $t^2 \leq 2 \pm \sqrt{10}$ or $t^2 \leq 2 \pm 3.16$

As t is positive, t ties between 0 and $\sqrt{5.16} = 2.27$ s

Thus position x is positive for time t given by $0 \leq \theta \leq 2.27$

(d)   The velocity is maximum for time t given by

$$\dfrac{dv}{dt} = 0 \text{ or } 8 - 12\ t^2 = 0$$

or $t = \sqrt{\dfrac{2}{3}} = 0.816$ s

Maximum velocity $(V_{max}) = (8t - 4t^3)$

$t = 0.816$

$= 8 \times 0.816k - 4 \times (0.816)^3$

$= 6.528 - 2.173$

$= 4.355\ m/s$

Prob. 2.6 Find the power used in pumping 2500 kg of water per minute from a well 1500 m deep to the surface. Supposing 40% of the power of the engine during pumping is wasted, what is the power of the engine.

Sol. Given: m = 2500 kg; h = 15.00 m

work done per minute (w) = mgh

$$= 2500 \times 9.8 \times 15$$

$\therefore$ Power of engine (P) $= \dfrac{W}{t} = \dfrac{2500 \times 9.8 \times 15}{60}$

$$= 6125 \text{ w}$$

Pactual $= \dfrac{P}{0.6} = \dfrac{6125}{0.6} = 120208.33 \text{ W}$

$$= 10.208 \text{ KW}$$

Prob. 2.7 A truck can move up a road having a a grade of 1.0 m rise every 50 m with a speed of 24 km/h, the resisting force is equal to one-twenty-fifth the weight of the truck. How fast will the same truck move down the hill with the same power?

Sol. Given : v = 24 km/h; $\sin \theta = \dfrac{1}{50}$

If W_t is the weight of truck, then the total force required for constant speed up the incline

$F = W_t \sin\theta + \dfrac{Wt}{25}$

$\therefore F = \dfrac{Wt}{50} + \dfrac{Wt}{25}$

$= \dfrac{3Wt}{50}$

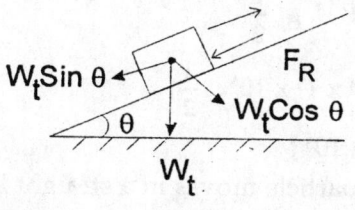

If V is the speed to truck up the incline, then

$\therefore$ Power of the engine (P) = F. v.

$$= \left(\dfrac{3W}{50}\right) \times v$$

If truck moves down the incline, the resisting force is up the incline parallel to plane.

$F' = \dfrac{Wt}{25} - w \sin\theta$

$= \dfrac{Wt}{25} - \dfrac{Wt}{50} = \dfrac{Wt}{50}$

Therefore, v is the constant speed of truck down the incline, then

Power of engine $P' = F'v' = \dfrac{Wt}{50} v'$

But given $P = p'$

$$\dfrac{Wt}{50} v' = \dfrac{3Wt}{50} v$$

$$\therefore v' = 3 v = 3 \times 24 = 72 \text{ km/h.}$$

Prob. 2.8 What is the gravitational potential energy of water completely, filled in a cubical tank of edge 1m, taking bottom as reference level?

Sol. Take a differential (or elementry) strip of mass dm at a height 'h'. The gravitational potential energy is

$$du = (dm) gh$$

where $dm = l^2 dh . \rho$

$$\therefore du = l^2 dh \, \rho \, gh$$

$$U = \int du = \rho l^2 g \int_0^l h \, dh$$

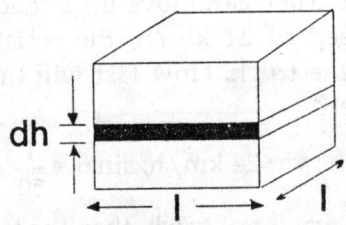

Fig. 2.5

$$= \left[\rho l^2 g \dfrac{h^2}{2} \right]_0^l$$

$$U = P \, l^3 . \, g. \dfrac{1}{2}$$

$$= 10^3 \times 1^3 \times 10 \times \dfrac{1}{2}$$

$$= 5 \times 10^3 \text{ J}$$

Prob. 2.9 A particle moves in a straight line with constant acceleration. If it covers 10 m in first second and 20 m in next second, find its intial velocity.

Sol. Let the initial speed be V_0 and the acceleration be 'a'

Applying, $s = v \mu_0 t + \dfrac{1}{2} at^2$

$$10 = v_0 \times 1 + \dfrac{1}{2} a \times (1)^2$$

or $10 = v_0 + \dfrac{a}{2}$ .... (i)

and from 2nd coordinate

$$30 = v_0 \times 2 + \dfrac{1}{2} a \times (2)^2$$

or $30 = 2v_0 + 2a$ .... (ii)

From equation (i) and (ii) we have

$v_0 = 5$ m/s Ans.

PROBLEMS

1. A man goes on drive, using tractor on a hill slope of in 20 with the velocity of 10 kmph. If mass of tractor is 3000 kg. Calculate the power of tractor. (Ans. 4.083 kW)

2. A railway wagon 200 kN weight moving at 8 kmph strikes the buffer springs and comes to a stop after compressing it by 18.5 cm Friction is 5% by weight. Calculate the average resistance offered by the buffers. Use the work and energy principle only. (Ans. 262.103 kN)

3. Find the kp used for pumping 2000 kg of water per minute from a 12 m deep well. Assume 40% energy loss during operation. (Ans. 7.35)

4. A pump is installed at the ground floor of building to fill the water tank of 30 m3 capacity in 15 minutes. The height of tank from the ground is 40 m. Calculate the power required by the pump, if efficiency of pump is 40%. (Ans. 25.925 kW)

5. A kpump is required to lift 1000 kg water per minute from a well 20 m deep and eject it at a speed of 20 m/s. Calculate.
   (a) How much work is done per minute in lifting the water> 1
   (b) How much is giving K.E.?
   (c) What up of engine is needed?
   (Ans. 1.95×19^5 J, 2×10^5J, 8.85)

SUBJECTIVE QUESTIONS

1. What do you understand by displacement? Explain clearly.
2. What is energy? Explain the various forms of mechanical energies.
3. What are power and work? Explain the various types of work.
4. Distinguish clearly between speed and velocity. Give examples.
5. What do you understand by the term 'accceleration'? Define positive and negative acceleration.

MULTIPLE CHOICE

1. The unit of linear acceleration is
   (a) kg.m   (b) m/s
   (c) m/s^2 (d) rad/s^2

2. The linear velocity of a body rotating at w rad/s along a circular path of radius r is given by
   (a) w.r   (b) w/r
   (c) w^2.r   (d) w^2/r

3. Joule is a unit of
   (a) force   (b) work
   (c) power   (d) none of the above

4. Which of the following is a scalar quantity.
   (a) electric current   (b) force
   (c) velocity   (d) linear momentum

5. The resultant of two forces -5 N and 10 N can never be
   (a) 12 N   (b) 5 N
   (c) 10 N   (d) 4 N

6. The magnitude of resultant of two forces F and F acting at a point is also F, then the angle between the two forces is
   (a) 0°   (b) 60°
   (c) 120°   (d) 90°

7. A particle is moving at a speed of a 5m/s along east, after 10 s its velocity changes and becomes 5m/s along north what is the average acceleration during this interval
   (a) 0   (b) $\frac{1}{\sqrt{2}}$ m/s² north west
   (c) $\frac{1}{\sqrt{2}}$ m/s² north east   (d) $\frac{1}{\sqrt{2}}$ m/s² north west

8. Two masses 1g and 4 g are moving with equal equal K.E. The ratio of magnitudes of their momentum is
   (a) 4:1   (b) $\sqrt{2:1}$
   (c) 1:2   (d) 1:6

9. A body falls freely under gravity. If its speeds is v when it has lost an amount v of gravitational potential energy, then its mass is
   (a) $v\,g/v^2$ (b) v^2/g
   (c) $2\,v/v^2$ (d) $2\,v/gv^2$

10. Which of the following is a form of energy.
    (a) pressure   (b) momentum
    (c) light   (d) power

11. A pumping machine pumps a liquid at a rate of 60 cc per minute at a pressure of 1.5 atmosphere. The power of the machine is
    (a) 9W   (b) 6W
    (c) 9 kW   (d) none of these

12. When a mass walks on a horizontal surface with constant velocity work done by
    (a) friction is zero   (b) contact force is zoro
    (c) gravity is zero   (d) mass is zero

13. A machine delivers power to a body which is proportional to velocity of the body. If the body starts with a velocity which is almost negligible, then distance curved by the body is proportional to

(a) $\sqrt{v}$

(b) $\sqrt[3]{\dfrac{v}{2}}$

(c) $v^{5/3}$

(d) v^2

13. An elevator is moving upward with an acceleration is 'a' and velocity 'v' when a man inside the elevator little a body of mass m through a height h in time 't'. The average power developed by the mass is

(a) m (g+a)h/t

(b) mgh/t

(c) mg(v+½ at)

(d) none of these

FILL UP THE BLANKS

1. Displacement is a .... quantity.
2. S.I. unit of force is.................. .
3. S.I. unit of angular velocity is...................... .
4. S.I. unit of moment is W.................. .

Ans. 1. vector. 2. Newton 3. rad/s 4. Nm

ANSWER OF MULTIPLE CHOICE QUESTIONS

1(c) 2(a) 3 (b) 4 (a) 5 (d) 6 (c) 7 () 8 (c) 9 () 10. (c) 11 (a) 12 (d) 13 (a)

Chapter **3**

Basic Thermodynamic Principles of Cycles of Internal Combustion Engine

3.1 Gas Laws:

3.1.1 Boyle's Law: It states that "At constant temperature, the volume of a given mass of gas is inversely proportional to pressure.

For a given mass of a gas at constant temperature, Let V be its volume when pressure is P, then

$$V \alpha \frac{1}{P}$$

or PV = K (constant)   (3.1)

Thus, $P_1V_1 = P_2V_2 = PnVn$ (3.2)

This means that the product of the volume and its corresponding pressure at a given temperature is always constant.

The relationship between pressure and volume can be represented by a rectangular hyperbola as shown in Fig 3.1.

3.1.2 Boyle's Law in Terms of Densities

Let mass of a given gas is M gram. Also at pressure P_1 and P_2 their densities be D_1 and D_2

$$V_1 = \frac{M}{D_1} \text{ and } V_2 = \frac{M}{D_2}$$

From Boyle's Law

$P_1V_1 = P_2V_2$ ......

Substituting the value of V_1 and V_2 in equation, we have

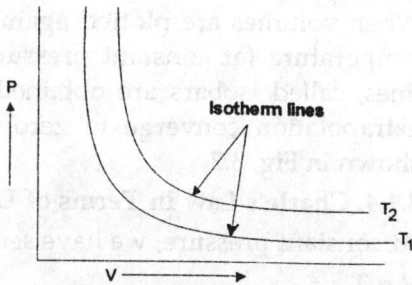

Fig 3.1 Relationship between Pressure and Volume at Constant Temperature

$$\frac{P_1 M}{D_1} = \frac{P_2 M}{D_2}$$

or $\dfrac{P_1}{D_1} = \dfrac{P_2}{D_2}$ (3.3)

or $\dfrac{P}{D} = \text{Constant}$ (3.4)

or $P \propto D$ .....

Therefore, at constant temperature, the pressure of a given mass of gas is directly proportional to its density.

3.1.3. Gay-Lussac or Charle's Law: It states that "At constant pressure, the volume of given mass of gas is directly proportional to the absolute temperatures".

For a given mass of gas at constant pressure, Let V be its volume when absolute temperature, T, then

$V \propto T$

or $\dfrac{V}{T} = \text{Constant}$ (3.5)

Thus, $\dfrac{V_1}{T_1} = \dfrac{V_2}{T_2} = \dfrac{V_n}{T_n}$ (3.6)

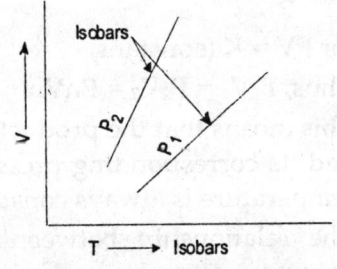

When volumes are plotted against absolute temperature (at constant pressure) straight lines, called isobars are obtained which an extrapolation converge to zero volume as shown in Fig. 3.2

3.1.4. Charle's Law in Terms of Densities

At constant pressure, we have seen that
$V \propto T$

Fig. 3.2 Relationship between volume and Tempreature at constant Pressure

But also, $V \propto \dfrac{1}{D}$ ...., where 'D' is the density of gas

Combining equations and , we have

$T \propto \dfrac{1}{D}$

or $DT = \text{Constant}$ (3.7)

3.1.5. Avagadro's Law: It states that, "Equal volume of all gases under similar conditions of temperature and pressure contain equal number of molecules or mole. Mathematically, it is expressed as

40

V α n

Where,

V = volume of gas

n = number of moles of gas

The quantity, 'n', usually expressed in gram moles so that if W g of gas of molecular wt (Mm) be taken, the

$$n = \frac{W}{Mm} \qquad (3.8)$$

3.1.6 Derivation of Ideal gas Equation or Gas Equation: This equation can be derived with the help Boyle's law, Charle's law and Avogadro's law:

(i) According to Boyle's :

$V \alpha \dfrac{1}{P}$, when and T are constant

(ii) According to Charle's Law: V α T, when n and P are constant

(iii) According to Avagadro's law: V α n, when P and T are constant

Combining all the three laws, we have

$V \alpha n \dfrac{T}{P}$

or PV = nRT   (3.9)

Where, R is constant and is known as universal gas constant.

Thus, $D_1T_1 = D_2T_2$ = ... = DnTn ; at constant Pressure   (3.10)

3.2. Relationship between Absolute Temperature and Celsius Temperature

T = 273 + t   (3.11)

Where,

T = absolute temperature, K

t = Celsius temperature, °C

3.3. Standard Condition (STP or NTP): Standard Temperature and Pressure (STP) or Normal Temperature and Pressure (NTP) refers a temperature of 0°C (273.15 K, round off for most problems in this book to 273 K) and normal atmospheric pressure (1 atm= 760 mm =760 torr of Hg) of any gas.

3.4. Numerical Values of Gas Constant (R) in different units.

The numerical value of R depends on the units in which P, V and work measured.

(a) Value in Absolute Units: Consider the gas equation PV, nRT

or $R = \dfrac{P \times V}{n \times T}$

When, P = 1 atmosphere, V = 22.4 L; n = 1 mole

T = 273 K

then

$$R = \frac{1 \times 22.4}{1 \times 273} = 0.0821 \text{ atm L. mole}^{-1} \text{ K}^{-1}$$

= 0.0821 atm L mole^{-1} K^{-1}

= 82.1 ml atm K^{-1} mole^{-1}, (D in at, V is cm^3)

= 62.3 L mm K^{-1} mole^{-1}, (P in mm, V in litre)

(b) Value in S.I. Units:

For one mole of gas at STP

Pressure = 1 atm = 1.013 x 10^5 Pa

Volume = 22.4 L = 22.4 x 10^{-3} m^3

T = 273 K

$$\therefore R = \frac{Dv}{nT} = \frac{1.013 \times 10^5 \times 22.4 \times 10^{-3}}{1.0 \times 273}$$

= 8.314 J mole^{-1}K^{-1}

= 8.314 Pa dm^3 mole^{-1}K^{-1}

= 8.314 x 10^7 erg mole^{-1}K^{-1}

(P in dynes cm^{-2}, V in mm^3)

$$= \frac{8.314 \times 10^7}{4.184 \times 10^7} \quad [\because 4.184 \times 10^7 \text{kg} = 1 \text{ cal}]$$

= 1.987 cal K^{-1} mole^{-1}

3.5. Thermodynamic Process: The operation by which the changes from one state to other are made, are known as thermodynamic process. The operation are made in either of the way:

(1) Isothermal Process (a) It is a slow process in which temperature remains constant through out the process.

(b) $\Delta T = 0$ and also $\Delta E = 0$

(c) Achieved by thermostatic bath.

(d) A gas under isothermal process obey's Boyle's Law

PV = constant for constant mass & temperature

(e) Slope on PV diagram for isothermal process of a gas

$$\left(\frac{dP}{dv}\right)_{\text{isothermal}} = -\frac{P}{V} \quad (3.12)$$

(2) Adiabatic Process: (a) This is the rapid process in which heat of system remains constant. In other words a process during which no exchange of heat takes place in between system and surrounding.

(b) q = 0

(c) Achieved by insulating the system boundries.

(d) For an adiabatic change of a perfect gas, the Poisson's equation holds which is given by

$Pv^\gamma = k$ (3.13)

$TV^{\gamma-1} = k$ (3.14)

$T^\gamma p^{1-\gamma} = k$ (3.15)

(3) Isobaric Process (a) A process in which pressure of the system remains constant throughout the investigation.

(b) $\Delta P = 0$

(4) Isochoric Process : (a) A process in which volume of the system remains constant throughout the investigations.

(b) $\Delta V = 0$

Graphical representation of four basic thermodynamic process:

It is shown as in Fig. 3.3 (a) Fig. 3.3. (b), Fig. 3.4 and Fig. 3.5

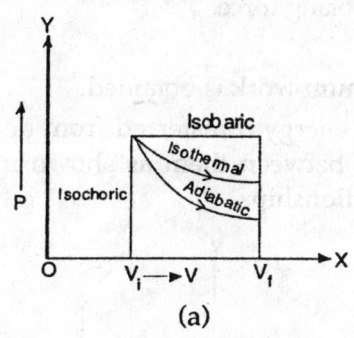

(a)

Fig. 3.3. Showing Four Basic Thermodynamic Process

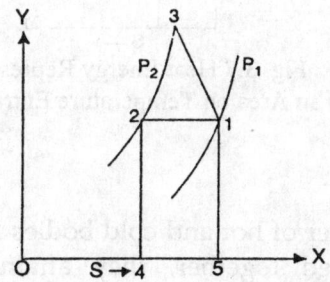

Fig. 3.4 Isothermal and Adibatic Compression Lines on Temperature - Entropy

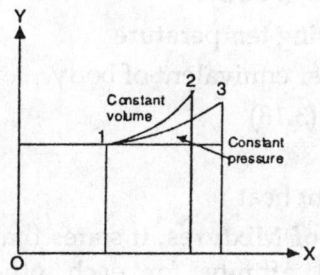

Fig. 3.5. Isothermal and Adiabatic Compression Lines on Pressure-Volume

43

5. Reversisble Process: A reversible or quasi-static process is one in which all changes occuring at any part of the process can be exactly reversed. When it is carried out in opposite direction as shown in Fig. 3.6.

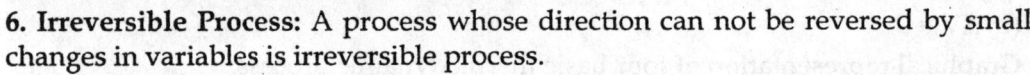

A reversible process involves

(a) A slow change during investigation.

(b) Driving force is infinitesimally greater than the opposing force and vice versa.

(c) The process may take place in either direction.

(d) Maximum possible work is obtained.

Fig. 3.6 Reversible Process

6. Irreversible Process: A process whose direction can not be reversed by small changes in variables is irreversible process.

(a) A fast change during investigation.

(b) Driving force is much different from opposing force.

(c) It is unidirectional process.

(d) Net work is somewhat lesser than maximum work is obtained.

3.6. Heat (Q): It is a measure of quantity of energy transferred from one body to other as a result of temperature difference between them as shown in Fig. 3.7. Mathematically, it is given by following relationships,

$$Q = S\,m\,\Delta t \qquad (3.16)$$

$$= W\,\Delta t \qquad (3.17)$$

Where,

S = sp. heat

m = Mass of body

Δt = Raising temperature

W = water equivalent of body

$$Q = m\,L \qquad (3.18)$$

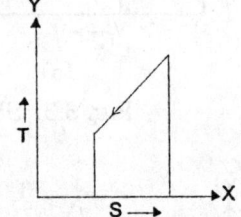

Fig. 3.7 Heat Energy Represented as an Area on Temperature Entropy Plane

Where,

L = Latent heat

3.7 Law of Mixtures: It states that "If a number of hot and cold bodies having as chemical affinity for each other are mixed together, they attain thermal equilibrium and the total heat gained by cold bodies is equal to heat lost by the hot bodies i.e.;

$$\text{Heat gained} = \text{Heat lost} \qquad (3.19)$$

3.8. Specific Heat: Specific heat of a substance is defined as the amount of heat required to raise the temperature of 1 g of the substance through 1°C. It is generally expressed in calories.

A calories is defined as the amount of heat required to raise the temperature of 1 g of water through 1°C (from 15.5 to 16.5°C)

3.9. Molar Heat: Molar heat of a substance is defined as the quantity of heat required to raise the temperature of one mole of the substance through 1°C, i.e.,

Molar Heat: sp. heat & molecular wt. of substance. In SI units, molar heat is expressed in terms of J/mole K.

Since, with rise of temperature, there may be increase in pressure, as well as volume, it is necessary to measure sp. heat either at constant pressure or at constant volume. The two values differ appreciably from each other in gases but not in solids and liquids whose coefficient, of expansion are very small.

(a) Molar Heat of a Gas at Constant Volume: In case the volume of gas is kept constant, there is no external work done by the gas when it is heated. Thus if the temperature of one mole of a gas is raised through (say, from T to (T +1), the increase in its kinetic energy itself is equal to the molar heat at constant volume (C_v).

We know that,

Kinetic energy per mole at temperature (T) $= \dfrac{3}{2} RT$

Similarly Kinetic energy per mole at temperature $(T +1) = \dfrac{3}{2} R (T+1)$

Therefore, increase in K.E. per mole for one degree rise of temperature is expressed as

$$\Delta E = C_v = \dfrac{3}{2} R (T+1) - \dfrac{3}{2} RT$$

$$\dfrac{3}{2}R \approx \dfrac{3}{2} \times 2 \approx 3 \text{ cal} \approx 12.55 \text{ J} \qquad (3.20)$$

Thus, the molar heat of every gas at constant volume should be nearly equal to 3 calories (12.55J). This is true only for monatomic gases such as helium, neon, argon, etc.

(b) Molar Heat at Constant Pressure (C_p) When a gas is heated at constant pressure, there will be increase in its volume, i.e., the gas will expand and do some external work. Hence, extra heat must be supplied to the gas to enable it to perform this external work. i.e., $C_p > C_v$.

The work done by the gas in expansion may be calculated as below:

Suppose, one mole of a gas is contained in a cylinder of cross-section (A) provided with an air-tight piston AB, as shown in Fig. 3.8 Let the pressure on the piston be P.

Suppose, the piston is raised to the new portion C through a height (l). The work done (W) against pressure (P) is given by

dW = Force x displacement

= (PA) x dl

= P (Adl)

W = Pdv   (3.25)

on integrating equation we have

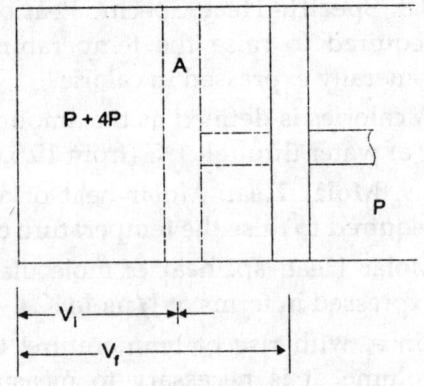

Fig. 3.8 Displacement Work

p [v_f -v_i] = PΔV

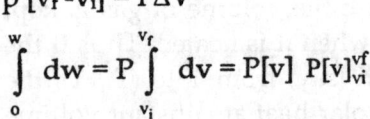

where,

ΔV = increase in volume (ΔV) of the gas as resultant of expansion.

Again, for one mole of a gas

PV = RT   (3.22)

When the temperature is raised by 1° from T to (T+1), so that the volume is (V+ΔV), then

P (V+ΔV) = R (T+1)   (3.23)

Substrating equation from equation we have

PΔV = R

Thus, the work done by the gas in expanding when heated through 1°C is equal to R,

∴ C_p -C_v = R   (3.24)

3.10 Poisson's Ratio (γ): It is the ratio of molar heat at constant pressure to molar heat at constant volume. It is given as

$$\gamma = \frac{Cp}{Cv} \qquad (3.25)$$

Molar heats of a few common gases at constant pressure and those at constant volume, along with their ratios are given in Table 3.1.

Table 3.1 Molar Heat of Gases (in calories)

S.No.	Gas	C_p	C_v	$C_p - C_v$	$C_p / C_v = \gamma$	Atomicity
1.	Helium	5.00	3.09	1.91	1.66	1
2.	Argon	4.98	2.99	1.99	1.67	1
3.	Nitrogen	6.90	4.92	1.98	1.40	2
4.	Oxygen	6.92	4.84	2.08	1.42	2
5.	Hydrogen	6.33	4.32	2.01	1.46	2
6.	Hydrogen chloride	7.07	5.01	2.06	1.41	2
7.	Carbon Dioxide	8.75	6.71	2.04	1.30	3
8.	Nitrogen oxide	8.81	6.76	2.05	1.30	3
9.	Sulphur dioxide	9.70	7.52	2.18	1.29	3
10.	-	-	-	-	-	-

3.11. Internal Energy: Each substance is associated with definte amount of energy. Energy envoloved upon the chemical nature of substance and the conditions of P, V, T. It includes many types of energies such as translational, vibrational, rotational, coulombic, potential energy, etc. Therefore, exact or absolute magnitude of internal energy cannot be determined. Furthermore, it is a state function and denoted by E and is independent of path. In thermodynamics, we deal with the change in internal energy of two states,

$\Delta E = E_2 - E_1$ (3.26)

It is also given by following relationship

$\Delta E = n \, C_v \, \Delta T$ (3.27)

3.12. Heat Enthalpy or Heat Content: It is defined as the sum of internal energy (E) and product of pressure (P) and volume (V) of system. It is also a state function and independent of path. It is denoted by 'H' and is expressed as

$H = E + PV$ (3.28)

Like E, in thermodynamics, we deal with changes in heat enthalpy (ΔH),

$\Delta H = H_2 - H_1$

3.13. Relationship in between ΔH and ΔE: The two are related by

$\Delta H = \Delta E + P \Delta V$ (3.29)

at constant volume

$(\Delta H)_v = \Delta E + P \times O$

$\therefore (\Delta H)_v = \Delta E$ (3.30)

3.14. First Law of Thermodynamics: It states that "Mass and energy of an isolated system remains constant. Mathematically, the law is expressed as dq = dE - dW; for an infinitesimal change (3.31)

where,

dE = Changes in internal energy

dq = Heat supplied to system

-dW = Work done by the system

Also, from first law of thermodynamics

q = ΔE - W   (3.32)

or ΔE = q +W, for finite change   (3.33)

3.15. Some Useful Formulae Based upon 1st law of thermodynamics are: The following are the useful formulaes.

(a) Isothermal Process: $\because \Delta T = 0$

$\therefore \Delta E = 0$

Therefore, by equation (3.32) we have

q = -W (3.34)

i.e.; Heat given to a system is used in work done by the system

(b) Adiabatic process: q = 0

Therefore, by equation (3.32), we have

+ ΔE = W

or - ΔE = -W   (3.35) i.e; work is done by the system on the cost of its internal energy

(c) Cyclic Process: $\because \Delta E = 0$

Therefore, by equation (3.32) , we have

 q = -W   (3.36)

(d) Isochoric process: $\because \Delta V = 0$

Therefore, by equation (3.32), we have

 q_v = ΔE (3.37)

i.e; Heat given to a system under constant volume is used in increasing interval energy.

(e) Isobaric Process: $\because \Delta P = 0$

Consider a system showing increase in volume from V_1 to V_2 at constant pressure p, during absorption of heat q. The expansion work or work done by system is

W = - PΔV

Therefore, by equation (3.32), we have

q_P = ΔE- (-PΔV)

= E_2 - E_1 - (-P (V_2-V_1)

= (E_2 + PV_2) - [E_1 + PV_1]

$= H_2 - H_1$

$[\because H = E + PV]$

or $q_P = \Delta H$ (3.38)

i.e., Heat given to a system under constant pressure (P) is used up in increasing heat enthalpy of system.

(f) Work done in irreversible isothermal process: Suppose an ideal gas expands against external pressure (P) and its volume changes by an amount dv then work done (W) can be given by

$W = - P\, dv$

For a finite change V_1 to V_2

Total workdone on the system W is derived by

$W = - P\, (V_2 - V_1)$

$W_{irr} = - P\, (V_2 - V_1)$ (3.39)

Case I: if $V_2 > V_1$ then W_{irr} is - ve; expansion work or work done by system.

Case II: If $V_2 < V_1$ then W_{irr} is +ve, i.e; compression work or work done on the system.

Case III : If $V_2 = V_1$

$W_{irr} = 0$

(g) Workdone in Isothermal Reversible Process: Consider a system under isothermal condition, showing reversible expansion of an ideal gas by a volume dv, then

$\Delta E = 0$

$\therefore q = -dW = - pdV$ (3.39)

The total workdone during expansion of gas from V_1 to V_2

$$\int_0^W dw = \int_{V_1}^{V_2} Pdv$$

$$= \int_{V_1}^{V_2} -\frac{nRT}{v} dv \quad [\because pv = nRT]$$

$$= - nRT\, [lnv]_{V_1}^{V_2}$$

$$W_{rev} = - nRT\, l_n \frac{V_2}{V_1} \quad\quad (3.40)$$

$$W_{rev} = 2.303\, nRT \log \frac{V_1}{V_2} \quad\quad (3.41)$$

$$\therefore\ P\, \alpha\, \frac{1}{v}$$

$\therefore$ Wrev = - 2.303 nRT log $\dfrac{P_1}{P_2}$ (3.42)

(h) Workdone in Adiabatic Reversible Process: Consider a system, under adiabatic conditions, showing reversible expansion of an ideal gas by volume dv, then from I-law of thermodynamics,

$\because$ dq = 0

$\therefore$ + dE = dw   (3.43)

$\because$ dE = nCvdT

Substituting the value of dE in equation ( ), we have

dW = n Cv dT   (3.44)

on integrating eqn. ( ) within temperature limits of T_1 and T_2 we have

$$\int_0^W dw = \int_{T_1}^{T_2} nCvdT$$

or $\displaystyle\int_0^W dw\, n\,\dfrac{R}{\gamma-1} \int_{T_1}^{T_2} dt \left[\because Cv = \dfrac{R}{\gamma-1}\right]$

$[W]_0^W = \dfrac{nR}{\gamma-1}\,[T]_{T_1}^{T_2}$

or W = $\dfrac{nR}{\gamma-1}$[T2-T1]

or Wrev = $\dfrac{nR}{\gamma-1}[T_2 - T_1]$ (3.45)

Case I : If $T_2 > T_1$ then Wrev = + ve, i;e; workdone on the system.

Case II : If $T_2 < T_1$ then Wrev = -ve, i.e; workdone by the system.

Case III : If $T_2 = T_1$

$\qquad\qquad$ Wrev = 0

3.16. General or Polytropic Changes: The general law for the expression and compression of gasses is given by

PV^n = Constant

Where,

n = polyptropic index, 0 to ∞

The various equations for polytropic process may be expressed by changing the index n for γ in the adiabatic process, i.e;

$\dfrac{T_1}{T_2} = \left(\dfrac{V_2}{V_1}\right)^{n-1}$ (3.46) and $\dfrac{T_1}{T_2} = \left(\dfrac{P_1}{P_2}\right)^{\frac{n-1}{n}}$ \hspace{1cm} (3.47)

(A) Work done during polytropic Process:

$Wpol = \dfrac{m\,R\,(T_1 - T_2)}{n-1}$ \hspace{1cm} (3.48)

$= \dfrac{P_2 V_2 - P_1 V_1}{1-n}$ \hspace{1cm} (3.49)

(B) Heat absorbed or rejected during polytropic Process,

$Q = \dfrac{\gamma - n}{\gamma\,1-n} \times$ work done \hspace{1cm} (3.50)

3.17. Introduction of Thermodynamic Cycles: A thermodynamic cycles or a cyclic process consists of thermodynamic processes, which take place in certain order such that the initial condition are restored at the end of the process.

Air cycles: Cycles using a ideal gas as medium is said to be air cycles. i.e; a certain uses of air operates in a complete thermodynamics cycle. The following assumptions are made for the analysis of cycles.

(i) The working fluid (air) : Air is taken as working fluid.

(ii) The properties of the working substances can be computed by the application of ideal gas equation.

PV = n RT \hspace{1cm} (3.51)

= mRT \hspace{1cm} (3.52)

Where,

n = Mole of air

m = Mass of air

P = Pressure of air or gas

R = Universal gas constant

(iii) The specific heat (C_p and C_v) of the working substance remains constant during the process in the cycle.

(iv) Cycles are reversible in nature.

(v) The gas does not undergo any chemical changes during cycles.

(vi) The piston has zero friction in the cylinder.

(vii) No heat transfer takes place through the engine walls.

With these assumption in mind, we may proceed to the consideration of air cycles. The following air cycles are given below:

3.17.1 Otto Cycle (1876): One very common type of internal combustion engines is the spark ignition (S.I.) engine generally used in automobiles. The otto cycle is

51

the air standard cycle of such an engine. It comprises two isochoric processes and two reversible adiabatic process. On the P-V co-ordinates and T-S co-ordinates, it is shown in Fig. 3.9 (a) and Fig. 3.9 (b). If we consists all the processes to take place in a cylinder all these will be treated as non-flow processes. The heat transfer and pressure-volume work quantities are shown in Table 3.2

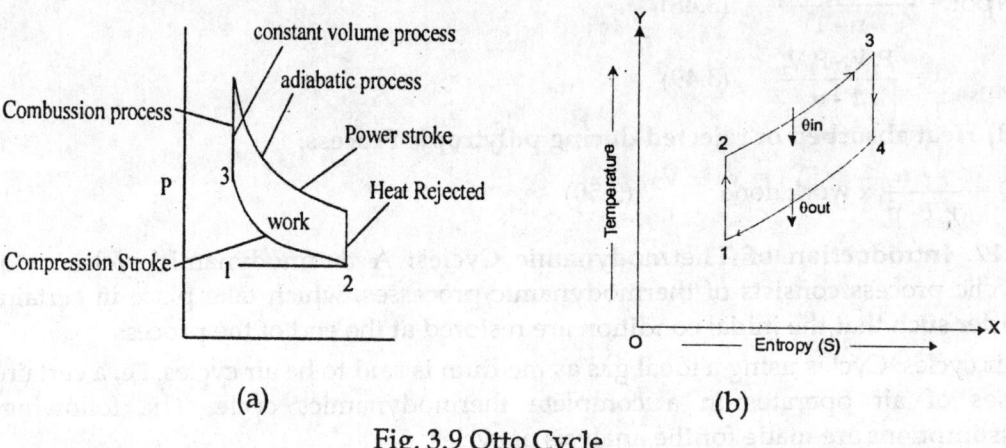

(a)   (b)

Fig. 3.9 Otto Cycle

Table 3.2

S.No.	Process	Nature of Process	Heat transfer	Pressure volume work
1.	1-2	Reversible adiabatic compression	0	$-(E_2-E_1) = -C_v (T_2-T_1)$
2.	2-3	Isochroic process (Heat addition)	$Q_{in} = C_v (T_3-T_2)$	0
3.	3-4	Reversible adiabatic expansion	-	$E3-E4 = (T3-T4)$
4.	4-1	Isochroic Process (Heat rejection)	$Q_{out} = C_v (T_4-T_1)$	0

Heat added during the cycle per kg of working substance

Q_{in} $Q_{2-3} = C_v (T_3-T_2)$

Net work done per kg of working substance (W) = $W_1 + W_2$

$= C_v [(T_3 - T_4) - (T_2 - T_1)]$

$= C_v [(T_3 - T_2) - (T_4 - T_1)]$

Thermal efficiency (notto) = $\dfrac{\text{Net work done per cycle}}{\text{Heat added per cycle}}$

$= \dfrac{C_v\left[(T_3 - T_2) - (T_4 - T_1)\right]}{C_v (T_3 - T_2)}$

$$= 1 - \frac{(T_4 - T_1)}{(T_3 - T_2)}$$

Also we have

$$\frac{T_2}{T_1} = \left(\frac{V_1}{V_2}\right)^{\gamma-1}$$

and $\frac{T_3}{T_4} = \left(\frac{V_4}{V_3}\right)^{\gamma-1}$

But $\frac{V_1}{V_2} = \frac{V_4}{V_3}$ [$\because V_1 = V_4 \,\&\, V_2 = V_3$]

Therefore, $\frac{T_4}{T_3} = \frac{T_1}{T_2} = \frac{T_4 - T_1}{T_3 - T_2}$

Therefore,

$$\eta_{otto} \; 1 - \frac{T_1}{T_2}$$

$$= 1 - \left(\frac{V_2}{V_1}\right)^{\gamma-1}$$

or $\eta_{otto} \; 1 - \dfrac{1}{\left(\dfrac{V_1}{V_2}\right)^{\gamma-1}}$ \qquad (3.53)

$$\eta_{otto} = 1 - \frac{1}{r.^{\gamma-1}} \qquad (3.54)$$

Where, r = Volume ratio, popularly known as Compression ratio.

The net work done per kg in otto cycle can be expressed in term of PV and may be computed as

$$W = \frac{P_3 V_3 - P_4 V_4}{\gamma - 1} + \frac{P_2 V_2 - P_1 V_1}{\gamma - 1}$$

or From conversion of energy

$$W = Q_{in} + Q_{out}$$

$$= Cv\,(T_3 - T_2) - Cv\,(T_4 - T_1) \qquad (3.55)$$

Mean effective pressure is given by

$$P_m = \left[\frac{P_3 V_3 - P_4 V_4}{\gamma - 1} - \frac{P_2 V_2 - P_1 V_1}{\gamma - 1}\right](V_1 - V_2) \qquad (3.56)$$

3.17.2. Characteristics of otto cycles: From equation (3.53), we see that the thermal efficiency of otto engine depends upon compression ratio (r) and poisson ratio (γ).

The poisson ratio of 1.4 is selected on the assumption that the working fluid is standard cold air with constant specific heats.

The pressure ratio has absolutely no influence on the theoretical otto cycle thermal efficiency. This is turn signifies that theoretical otto cycle thermal efficiency is independent of the amount of heat added.

The mean effective pressure which is an indication of the internal work output, increases with pressure ratio at a fixed value of compression ratio and poisson ratio or adiabatic index (γ).

The following Fig. 3.10 shows the relationship of mean effective pressures and thermal efficiency vs compression ratio.

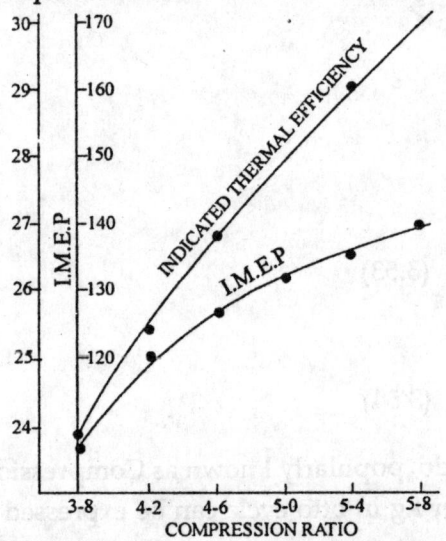

Fig. 3.10 Showing Relationship of Mean effectve Pressue and Thermal Efficiency Vs Compression Ratio

3.17.4 Diesel Cycle or Constant Pressure Heat Addition Cycle (1892): The limitation on compression ratio in the S.I. engine can be overcome by compression air alone, instead of the fuel-air mixture, and then enjecting the fuel into the cylinder in spray form when combustion is desired. The cycle differes from the otto cycle is one respect. The heat is added at constant pressure instead of at constant volume. Thus it comprises two isentropic process, one constant pressure heat

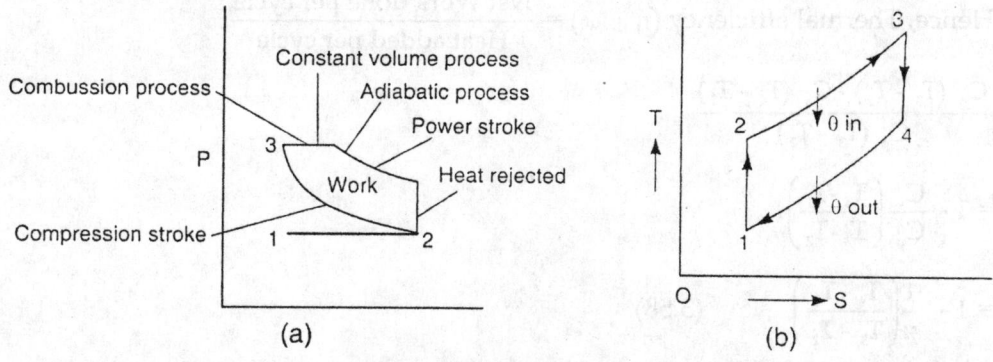

Fig. 3.11 Diesel Cycle

addition process and one constant volume heat rejection process. The cycle analysis is given in table. The cycle is shown on the P.V. and T-S diagram in Fig. 3.11 (a) and Fig. 3.11 (b). The heat and work analysis is done in tabular form per kg of working substance is shown in Table 3.3.

Table 3.3

Process	Classification	Heat transfer per kg	Pdv work per kg
1-2	Reversible adiabatic compression	0	$-C_v (T_2-T_1)$
2-3	Constant Pressure (Isobaric) Heat addition	$Q_{in} = C_p (T_3-T_2)$	$R (T_3-T_2)$
3-4	Reversible adiabatic expansion	0	$C_v (T_3-T_4)$
4-5	Constant volume heat rejection	$Q_{out} = -C_v (T_4-T_1)$	0

Thus heat added during the cycle $(Q_{in}) = Q_{2-3} = C_p (T_3-T_2)$

Net work done per kg of working substance during cycle

$W = C_v (T_3-T_4) + R (T_3-T_2) -C_v (T_2-T_1)$

$= C_v (T_3-T_4) + (C_p-C_v) (T_3-T_2) - C_v (T_2-T_1)$

$= C_vT_3-C_vT_4 + C_p T_3 - C_p T_2 - C_vT_3 + C_vT_2 - C_vT_2 + C_vT_1$

$= C_p (T_3 - T_2) - C_v (T_4-T_1)$

Alternate method

$W = Q_{in} + Q_{out}$

$= C_p (T_3-T_2) + (-) C_v (T_4-T_1)$

$= C_p (T_3-T_2) - C_v (T_4-T_1)$ \hfill (3.57)

Hence, Thermal efficiency $(\eta_{\text{diesel}}) = \dfrac{\text{Net Work done per cycle}}{\text{Heat added per cycle}}$

$$\dfrac{C_p\,(T_3 - T_2) - C_v\,(T_4 - T_1)}{C_p\,(T_3 - T_2)}$$

$$= 1 - \dfrac{C_v}{C_p}\left(\dfrac{T_4 - T_1}{T_3 - T_2}\right)$$

$$= 1 - \dfrac{1}{\gamma}\left(\dfrac{T_4 - T_1}{T_3 - T_2}\right) \qquad (3.58)$$

Let,

$$\dfrac{V_1}{V_2} = \text{Compression ratio (r)}$$

$$\dfrac{V_3}{V_2} = \text{Fuel cut off ratio } (r_e)$$

Isenthropic process 1-2

$$T_2 = T_1\left(\dfrac{V_1}{V_2}\right)^{\gamma-1} \qquad (i)$$

along the constant pressure 2-3

$$\dfrac{T_3}{T_2} = \dfrac{V_3}{V_2} = r_c \qquad (ii)$$

Therefore, from (i) and (ii), we have

$$T_3 = T_2\, r_c$$

$$= T_1 r^{\gamma-1}\, r_c \qquad (iii)$$

Similarly,

$$T_4 = T_3\left(\dfrac{V_3}{V_4}\right)^{\gamma-1} = T_1\, r^{\gamma-1}\, r_c \qquad (iv)$$

Therefore,

$$\eta_{\text{diesel}} = 1 - \dfrac{T_1 r_c^{\gamma} - T_1}{\gamma\left(T_1 r^{\gamma-1} rc - Tr^{\gamma-1}\right)}$$

$$\eta_{\text{diesel}} = 1 - \dfrac{1}{r^{\gamma-1}}\left[\dfrac{r_c^{\gamma}-1}{\gamma(r_c - 1)}\right] = \dfrac{1}{r^{\gamma-1}}\left[\dfrac{r_c^{\gamma}-1}{\gamma(r_c - 1)}\right]$$

$$= 1- \left(\frac{1}{r}\right)^{\gamma-1} \left[\frac{r_c^{\gamma}-1}{\gamma(r_c-1)}\right]$$

It may be observed that equation ( ) for efficiency of the diesel cycle is different from that of the otto cycle only in the bracket factor. This factor is always greater than unity, because $r_c>1$. Therefore, a given compression ratio, the otto cycle is more efficient.

The net work for diesel cycle can be expressed in terms of PV

$$W = \quad P_2 (V_3 - V_2) + \frac{P_3V_3-P_4V_4}{\gamma-1} - \frac{P_2V_2-P_1V_1}{\gamma-1} \qquad (3.60)$$

$$= P_2V_2 (r_c-1) + \frac{P_3 r_c V_2 - P_4 r V_2}{\gamma-1} - \frac{P_2 V_2 - P_1 r V_2}{\gamma-1}$$

$$= \frac{V_2 \left[P_2 (r_c -1)(\gamma-1)+P_2 r_c - P_4 r - (P_2 - P_1 r)\right]}{\gamma-1} \quad [\because P3 = P2]$$

$$= \frac{V_2 \left[P_2 (r_c-1)(\gamma-1) + P_2 \left(r_c - \frac{P_4}{P_2}\right) - P_2 \left(1-\frac{P_1 r}{P_2 r}\right)\right]}{\gamma-1}$$

$$= \frac{P_1 V_1 r^{\gamma-1} \left[(r_c-1)(\gamma-1) + r_c - r_c^{\gamma} r^{1-\gamma} - (1-r^{1-\gamma})\right]}{(\gamma-1)}$$

$$\frac{P_1 V_1 r^{\gamma-1} \left[\gamma(r_c-1) - r^{1-\gamma}(r_c \gamma^{-1})\right]}{(\gamma-1)} \qquad (3.62)$$

And mean effective pressure is given by

$$P_m = \frac{P_1 V_1 r_{\gamma-1} \left[\gamma (r_c-1) - r^{1-\gamma}(r_c^{\gamma}-1)\right]}{V_1(\gamma-1)\frac{(r-1)}{r}}$$

$$= \frac{P_1 r^{\gamma} \left[\gamma(r_c-1) - r^{1-\gamma}(r_c^{\gamma}-1)\right]}{(\gamma-1)(r-1)} \qquad (3.63)$$

3.17.4 Characteristics of Diesel Cycle or Constant Pressure:

From equation ( ), it is clear that increase in compression ratio (r) results in higher thermal efficinecy. But the increase of cut-off ratio decreases thermal efficiency. Also the variation of mean effective pressure with cut-off ratio shows that with increase of mean effective pressure.

The following Fig. 3.12 shows the relationship of mean effective pressure and compression ratio and thermal efficiency and compression ratio.

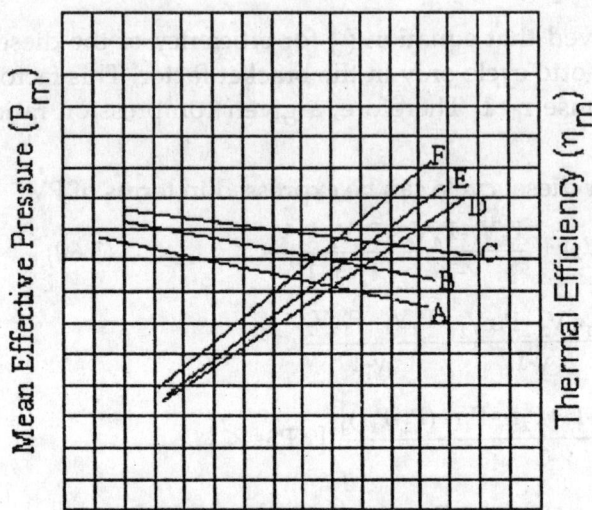

Fig. 3.12 Showing Mean Effective Pressure & Compression Ratio and Thermal Efficiency and Compression Ratio

P = 1 atm

For A, η_{th} at γ = 1.4 & r = 15

For B, η_{th} at γ = 1.4 & r = 17

For C, η_{th} at γ = 1.4 & r = 20

For D, η_{th} at γ = 1.4 & r = 15

For E, η_{th} at γ = 1.4 & r = 17

For F, η_{th} at γ = 1.4 & r = 20

3.17.6 Dual Cycle or Mixed Cycle: The Air Standard Diesel cycle does not stimulate exactly the pressure volume variation in an actual compression ignition engines, where the fuel injection is started before the end of compression stroke. Duel cycle consists of heat to addition process at constant volume and partially at constant pressure. The cycle is represented on the P-V diagram and T-S diagram in Fig. 3.13 (a) and Fig. 3.13 (b).

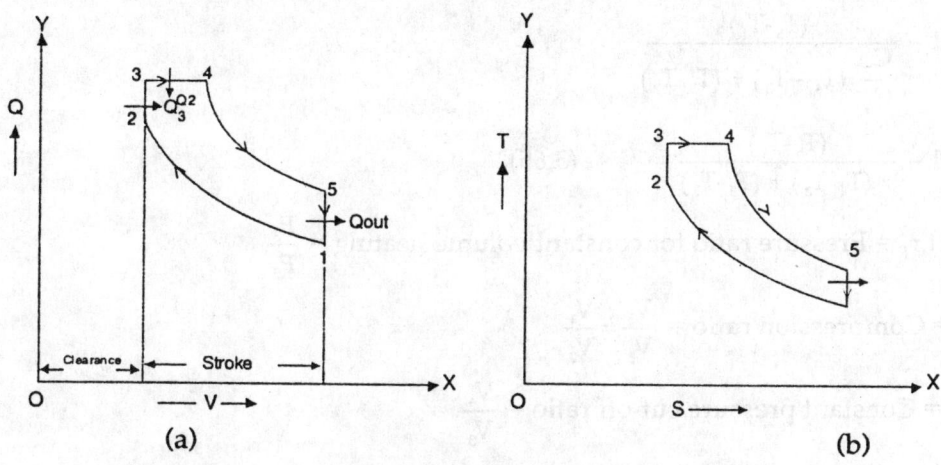

Fig. 3.13 Dual Cycle

The heat transfer and Pdv work quantities are shown in Table 3.4.

Table 3.4

Process	Classification	Heat transfer per kg	Pdv work per kg
1-2	Reversible adiabatic compression (Isentropic)	0	$C_v (T_1-T_2) = -C_v (T_2 - T_1)$
2-3	Constant volume heating (Heat added)	$Q_1 = C_v (T_3-T_2)$	0
3-4	Constant pressure heating (Heat added)	$Q_1 = C_p (T_4-T_3)$	$R (T_4-T_3)$
4-5	Reversible adiabatic expansion (Isentropic)	0	$Cv (T_4-T_5)$
5-1	Constant volume Cooling (Heat rejected)	$-C_v (T_5-T_1)$	0

Heat added during the cycle = $C_v (T_3-T_2) + C_p (T_4-T_3)$

Net Pdv work output = $R (T_4-T_3) +C_v (T_4-T_5) - C_v (T_2-T_1)$

$= (C_p -C_v) (T_4- T_3) + C_v (T_4 - T_5) - C_v (T_2-T_1)$

$= C_pT_4 - C_pT_3 - C_vT_4 + C_vT_4 + C_vT_3 + C_vT_4 - C_vT_5 - C_v T_2 + C_v T_1$

$= C_p (T_4 - T_3) + C_v (T_3 - T_2) - C_v (T_5 - T_1)$ (3.64)

Thermal efficiency (η_{dual}) = $\dfrac{\text{Net work out put per cycle}}{\text{Heat added per cycle}}$

$= \dfrac{C_p (T_4-T_3) + C_v (T_3-T_2) - Cv (T_3-T_1)}{Cp (T_4-T_3) + C_v (T_3-T_2)}$

$= 1 - \dfrac{C_v (T_5-T_1)}{C_p (T_4-T_3) + C_v(T_3-T_2)}$

$$= 1 - \frac{(T_5 - T_1)}{\dfrac{C_p}{C_v}(T_4 - T_3) + (T_3 - T_2)}$$

$$= 1 - \frac{(T_5 - T_1)}{\gamma(T_4 - T_3) + (T_3 - T_2)} \qquad (3.65)$$

Let r_p = Pressure ratio for constant volume heating = $\dfrac{P_3}{P_2}$

r = Compression ratio = $\dfrac{V_5}{V_3} = \dfrac{V_1}{V_2}$

r_c = Constant pressure cut-off ratio = $\dfrac{V_4}{V_3}$

From the reversible adiabatic compression process 4-5

$$\frac{T_4}{T_5} = \left(\frac{V_5}{V_4}\right)^\gamma = \left(\frac{V_5}{V_3} \times \frac{V_3}{V_4}\right)^{\gamma-1}$$

$$= \left(\frac{r}{r_c}\right)^{\gamma-1} \qquad (i)$$

Similarly from the reversible adiabatic process 1-2.

$$\frac{T_2}{T_1} = r^{\gamma-1} \qquad (ii)$$

$$\frac{T_3}{T_2} = \frac{P_3}{P_2} = r_p$$

$$\therefore T_2 = \frac{T_3}{R_p} \qquad (iii)$$

From the constant pressure process 3-4.

$$\frac{T_4}{T_3} = \frac{V_4}{V_3} = r_c$$

$$T_4 = r_c T_3 \qquad (iv)$$

Substituting equation (iv) in equation (i), we have

$$T_5 = T_4 \left(\frac{r_c}{r}\right)^{\gamma-1} = T_3 \cdot r_c \left(\frac{r_c}{r}\right)^{\gamma-1} \qquad (v)$$

Substituting equation (iii) in equation (ii), we have

$$T_1 = \frac{T_2}{r^{\gamma-1}} = \frac{T_3}{r_p \; r^{\gamma-1}} \qquad \text{(vi)}$$

Therefore,

$$\eta_{dual} = 1 - \frac{\left[T_3 \cdot r_c \left(\dfrac{r_c}{r}\right)^{\gamma-1} - \dfrac{T_3}{r_p - r^{\gamma-1}} \right]}{\left(T_3 - \dfrac{T_3}{r_p} \right) + \gamma \; (r_c \; T_3 - T_3)}$$

$$= 1 - \frac{1}{r^{\gamma-1}} \left[\frac{r_c^{\; r} - \dfrac{1}{r_\rho}}{\left(1 - \dfrac{1}{r_p}\right) + \gamma(r_{c-1})} \right]$$

$$= 1 - \frac{1}{r^{\gamma-1}} \left[\frac{r_p r_c^{\; r} - 1}{(r_p - 1) + r_p \gamma (r_c - 1)} \right] \qquad (3:66)$$

The net work of dual cycle can be expressed in term of PV

$$W = P_3 \left(v_4 - v_3 \right) + \frac{P_4 V_4 - P_5 V_5}{\gamma - 1} - \frac{P_2 V_2 - P_1 V_1}{\gamma - 1}$$

$$= P_3 V_3 \left(r_c - 1 \right) + \frac{(P_4 r_c V_3 - P_5 r V_3) - P_2 V_3 - P_1 r V_3}{\gamma - 1}$$

$$= \frac{P_3 V_3 \left(r_c - 1 \right) (\gamma - 1) + P_4 V_3 \left(r_c - \dfrac{P_5}{P_4} r \right) - P_2 V_2 \left(1 - \dfrac{P_1}{P_2} r \right)}{\gamma - 1}$$

Also $\dfrac{P_5}{P_4} = \left(\dfrac{V_4}{V_5}\right)^{\gamma} = \left(\dfrac{r_c}{r}\right)^{\gamma}$

And $\dfrac{P_2}{P_1} = \left(\dfrac{V_1}{V_2}\right)^{\gamma} = r^{\gamma}$

Also, $P_3 = P_4$, $V_2 = V_3$ and $V_5 = V_1$

Therefore,

$$W = \frac{V_3 \left[P_3 (r_c - 1)(\gamma - 1) + P_3(r_c - r_c^{\gamma} r^{1-r}) - P_4(1 - r^{1-\gamma}) \right]}{\gamma - 1}$$

$$= \frac{P_2 V_2 \left[r_p (r_c - 1)(\gamma - 1) + r_p(r_c - r_c^{1-\gamma}) - (1 - r^{1-\gamma}) \right]}{\gamma - 1}$$

$$= \frac{P_1 r^{\gamma} \dfrac{V_1}{r} \left[r_p^{\gamma} (r_c - 1) + (r_p - 1) - r_c^{1-\gamma}(r_p - 1) - r^{\gamma-1}(r_p - r_c^{\gamma-1}) \right]}{\gamma - 1}$$

$$= \frac{P_1 v_1 r^{\gamma-1} \left[r_p \gamma (r_c - 1) + (r_p - 1) - r^{\gamma-1}(r_p r_c^{\gamma-1}) \right]}{\gamma - 1} \qquad (3.67)$$

Mean effective Pressure (Pm)

$$P_m = \frac{W}{v_1 - v_2}$$

$$= \frac{W}{v_1 \left(\dfrac{r-1}{r} \right)}$$

$$= \frac{P_1 V_1 \left(r^{1-\gamma} r_p^{\gamma} (r_c - 1) + (r_p - 1) - r^{1-\gamma}(r_p r_c^{\gamma-1}) \right)}{(\gamma - 1) \left(\dfrac{r-1}{r} \right)}$$

$$= \frac{P_1 r^{\gamma} \left[r_p (r_c - 1) + (r_p - 1) - r^{1-\gamma}(r_p r_c^{\gamma} - 1) \right]}{(\gamma - 1)(r - 1)} \qquad (3.68)$$

3.17.7 Characteristics of Dual Cycles:

The thermal efficiency of a cycle with heat addition at constant pressure and also at constant volume depends on adiabatic index (γ), compression ratio (r), the pressure ratio (r_p) and cut off ratio (r_c) for heat and addition at constant presure.

If amount of heat received reduces due to reduction in constant pressure cut-off ratio with pressure ratio for constant volume heatinmg remains constant the thermal efficiency of the cycle increases.

For a fixed value of a heat supplied, mean effective will be greater with greater value of pressure ratio and smaller value of cut-off ratio.

Prob. 3.1: What will be the volume of gas at 27°C and 700 mm pressure , if it occupies a volume of 22.4 litre at NTP.

Soln

Given P_1 = 700 mm   P2 = 760 mm

V_1 = ? V_2 = 22.4 L

T_1 = 273 + 27 = 300 K T_2 = 273 K

we know that,

$$= \frac{P_1 V_1}{T_1} = \frac{P_2 V_2}{T_2} \quad \therefore V_1 = \frac{P_2 V_2 T_1}{P_1 T_2} = = \frac{760 \times 22.4 \times 300}{273 \times 700}$$

= 26.725 L Ans.

Prob. 3.2. Calculate the temperature of 4.0 moles of a gas occupying 5 L at 3.22 bar. (R = 0.9085 bar L K^{-1} mole^{-1})

Soln. Given P = 3.22 bar, n = 4

v = 5 L, R = 0.083 bar L K^{-1} mole^{-1}

we know that

PV = nRT

$$T = \frac{PV}{nR} = \frac{3.32 \times 5}{4 \times 0.083} = 50, K$$

Prob. 3.3. A balloon of diameter 20 m weight 100 kg. Calculate its pay-load, if it is filled with helium (He) at 1.0 atm. and 27°C. Density of air is 1.2 kg m^{-3}.(R = 0.082 atm L K^{-1} mole^{-1})

Soln.

Given: Diameter of ballon (d_b) = 20 m

Radius of ballon (r_b) = $\frac{20}{2}$ = 10 m

Pressure (P) = 1 atm.

Temperature (T) = 273 + 27 = 300 K

Molecular wt. of He (μm) = 4

Air density (P_a) = 1.2 kg m^{-3}

we know that

volume of sphere = $\frac{4}{3} \pi r^3$

i.e; volume of ballon = = $\frac{4}{3} \pi r_b^3$

= 4190.47 10^3 L

= 41.90.47 m^3

Mass of displaced air = volume of sphere x density of air

= 4190.47 x 1.2

= 5028.57 kg

Again, we know that

$$PV = n\,RT = RT = \frac{m}{M_m}RT$$

or $m_{He} = \dfrac{PVMm}{RT} = \dfrac{1 \times 4190.47 \times 10^3 \times 4}{0.082 \times 300}$

= 681.377 x 10³ g

= 681.377 kg

Therefore, total weight of gas and ballon

= 681.377 + 100

= 781.377 kg

Pay load = weight of air displaced - weight of gas and ballon

= 5028.57 - 781.377

= 4247.193 kg Ans.

Prob 3.4 : A spherical balloon of 21 cm diameter is to the filled up with hydrogen at NTP from a cylinder containing the gas at 20 atmospheres at 27°C, of the cylinder can hold 2.80 litres of water, calculate the number of balloons that can be filled up.

Soln.

Given r_b = 10.5 cm

P_1 = 1 atm, P_2 = 20 atm.

T_1 = 273 K, T_2 = 273 + 27 = 300 K

V_1 = ?, V_2 = 2.82 L

we know that,

$$\frac{P_1 V_1}{T_1} = \frac{P_2 V_2}{T_2}$$

$$V_1 = \frac{P_2 V_2 T_2}{T_2 P_1} = \frac{20 \times 2.82 \times 273}{300 \times 1}$$

= 51.324 L

= 51324 ml

Volume of H_2 left in the cylinder = 2820 ml

Actual volume transferred to balloon = 51324 - 2820

= 48504 ml

64

Volume of each ballon $= \dfrac{4}{3} \pi r_b{}^3$

$= \dfrac{4}{3} \times 3.142\ 0 \times (10.5)^3$

$= 4849.69$

$= 4850$ ml

Number of ballon which can be filled up $= \dfrac{48504}{4850} = 10$ (approx)

Prob. 3.5. What is difference in pressure between the top and bottom of a vessel 76 cm deep at 27°C, when filled with (i) water (ii) mercury ? Density of water at 27°C is 0.99 g/cm³

Soln.

Given : $\int w = 0.990$ g cm^{-3}

$\int m = 13.50$ g cm^{-3}

$g = 981$ cm S^{-2}

we know that,

$P = \int gh$

Case (i), Pressure $(P_w) = 76 \times 0.990 \times 981$

$= 7.38 \times 10^4$ dynes cm$^{-2} = \dfrac{7.38 \times 10^4}{1.013 \times 10^6}$

$= 0.073$ atm Ans.

($\because$ 1 atm = 1.013 × 10⁶ dynes cm^{-2})

Case (ii) Pressure $(P_m) = 76 \times 13.6 \times 981$

$= 1.013 \times 10^6 = 1$ atm Ans.

Prob. 3.6 A chemist while studying the properties of dichlodiflurs ethene a chlorifluro carbon refrigerant, cooled a 1.25 g sample at constant atmospheric pressure of 1.0 atm from 320 K to 293 K. During the process sample volume decreased 274 to 248 ml. Calculate ΔH, ΔU for chlorofluro carbon for this process for $C_2Cl_2F_2$, $C_p = 80.7$ J/mole/K.

Soln. Given : W = 1.25 g, Mm of $C_2Cl_2F_2 = 2 \times 12 + 2 \times 35.5 + 19 \times 2 = 133$

$P = 1$ atm $= 1 \times 10^5$ N/m², $=$

$C_p = 80.7$ J/mole/K, $V_i = 274$ ml

$T_i = 320$ K, $T_f = 293$ K, $V_f = 248$ ml

$\therefore \Delta V = V_f - V_f = 274 - 248$

$= -26$ ml

$= -27 \times 10^{-6} \text{ m}^3$

we know that,

$\Delta H = nC_p \Delta t$

$= \dfrac{W}{M_m} C_p (293 - 320)$

$= \dfrac{1.25}{133} \times 80.7 \times (-27)$

$= 20.47 \text{ J}$

$W = P.\Delta V = 10^5 \times (-26 \times 10^{-6})$

$= -2.6 \text{ J}$

Again, applying equation

$\Delta H = \Delta E + W$

$\therefore \Delta E = \Delta H - W$

$= -20.47 - (-2.6)$

$= -17.8 \text{ J Ans.}$

Prob. 3.7: A gas expands from 5L to 3L against a constant pressure of 3 atm. The work done during expansion is used to heat 10 mole of water at 290 K. Calculate the fixed temperature of water. (Specific heat = 4.2 J/g/K)

Soln. Give: $\Delta V = (5-3) = 2L = 2 \times 10^{-3} \text{ m}^3$, S = 4.2 J g⁻¹ K⁻¹

$n = 10$, $P = 3 \text{ atm} = 3 \times 10^5 \text{ N/m}^2$, $M_m = 18$

We know that

$W = P\Delta V$

$= 3 \times 10^5 \times 10^{-3} \times 2$

$= 6 \times 10^2 = 600 \text{ J}$

weight of water (m) = n x Mm

$= 10 \times 18 = 180 \text{ g}$

Applying equation,

$W = m\,s\,\Delta t$

$= 180 \times 4.2 (t - 290)$

$t - 290 = 0.793 = 0.8 \text{ K}$

$\therefore t = 0.8 + 290 = 290.8 \text{ K Ans.}$

Prob. 3.8: 2 moles of oxygen (C_v = 4.95 cal/mol/degree) are compressed adiabatically and reversibly from a volume of 75 L at 1atm to 100 atm. Calculate work done to compress the gas.

Soln.

Given: $P_f = 100$ atm, $P_i = 1$ atm $= 10^5$ N/m^2

$V_f = ?$, $V_i = 75$ L $= 75 \times 10^{-3}$ m^3

$C_v = 4.95$ cal/mol/degree, $\gamma = 1.4$

we know that

$Pv^\gamma = K$

or $P_i v_i^\gamma = P_f V_f^\gamma$

or $\dfrac{V_f}{V_i} = \left(\dfrac{P_i}{P_f}\right)^{\frac{1}{\gamma}}$

or $\dfrac{V_f}{V_i} = \left(\dfrac{1}{100}\right)^{\frac{1}{1.4}}$

$V_f = 0.037 \times v_i$

$= 0.037 \times 75 = 2.775$ L $= 2.775$ m^3

Applying

$W = \dfrac{P_i v_i - P_f V_f}{\gamma - 1}$

$= \dfrac{1 \times 10^5 \times 75 \times 10^{-3} - 100 \times 10^5 \times 2.775}{1.4 - 1}$

$= \dfrac{10^2 \, [75 - 2.775 \times 100]}{0.4}$

$= \dfrac{100 \, [75 - 277.5]}{0.4}$

$= \dfrac{100 \times [-202.5]}{0.4}$ $= -50625$ J $= 50.625$ kj

Prob. 3.9: In an air standard diesel cycle, the compression ratio is 16, and at the beginning of isoentropic compression the temperature, at the end of constant pressure is temperature 1480°C. Calculate (a) the cut off ratio (b) the heat supplied per kg of air (c) the cycle efficinecy (d) mean effective pressure. ($C_p = 1.005$ kJ/kg K, $C_v = 0.718$ kJ/kg K)

Soln.

Referring Fig. 3.8

Given $T_1 = 273 + 15 = 288$ K, $P_1 = 0.1$ MPa $= 100$ kPa

$r = 16$, $T_3 = 1480 + 273 = 1753$ K

$C_v = 0.718$ KJ

$$\frac{T_2}{T_1} = \left(\frac{V_1}{V_2}\right)^{\gamma-1} = (16)^{0.4}$$

or $\dfrac{T_2}{T_1} = 3.03$

$\therefore T_2 = 288 \times 3.03 = 873$ K

$$\frac{P_2 V_2}{T_2} = \frac{P_3 V_3}{T_3} \quad [P_2 = P_3]$$

$$\frac{V_3}{V_2} = \frac{V_3}{T_2}$$

(a) cut-off ratio (ρ) = $\dfrac{V_3}{V_2} = \dfrac{1753}{873} = 2.01$

(b) Heat supplied (Q_{in}) = $C_P (T_3 - T_2)$

= 1.005 (1753- 873)

= 884.4 kJ/kg.

$$\frac{T_3}{T_4} = \left(\frac{V_4}{V_3}\right)^{\gamma-1} \quad \text{or} \quad \frac{T_3}{T_4} = \left(\frac{V_1}{V_2} \times \frac{V_2}{V_3}\right)^{1.4-1}$$

$$= \left(\frac{16}{2.01}\right)^{0.4} = 2.29$$

$\therefore T_4 = 766$ K

Heat rejected (Q_{out}) = $C_v (T_4 - T_1)$

= 0.718 (766 - 288)

= 343.2 KJ/kg.

(e) $\eta_{cycle} = 1 - \dfrac{Q_{out}}{Q_{in}}$

$= 1 - \dfrac{343.2}{884.2}$

= 0.612 or 61.2%

(d) m.e.P. (P_m) = $\dfrac{W}{V_1 - V_2}$

68

$$= \frac{541.3}{0.775} = 698.45 \text{ kKPa}$$

$$= 698.45 \text{ kPa}$$

Prob. 3.10: An air standard dual cycle has a compression ratio of 16, and compression begins at 1 bar, 50°C. The maximum pressure is 70 bar. Th heat transfered to air at constant pressure is equal to that of at constant volume. Detemine (a) Cycle efficiency and temperature at the cardinal points of the cycle (b) the cycle efficiency and (c) the m.e.p. [C_v = 0.718 kJ/kg K, C_p = 1.005 kJ/kg K]

Soln. Refering, Fig. 3.

Given: T_4 = 273 + 50 = 323 K, r = 16

$$\frac{T_2}{T_1} = \left(\frac{V_1}{V_2}\right)^{\gamma-1}$$

or $\dfrac{T_2}{T_1} = (16)^{1.4-1} = 16^{0.4}$

or $T_2 = T_1 \times (16)^{0.4} = 323 \times (16)^{0.4}$

$\therefore T_2 = 979$ K

$$P_2 = P_1 \left(\frac{V_1}{V_2}\right)^{\gamma} = 1.0 \times (16)^{1.4} = 48.5 \text{ bar}$$

$$T_3 = T_2 \cdot \frac{P_3}{P_2} = 979 \times \frac{70}{4.5} = 1413 \text{K}$$

$Q_{2\text{-}3} = C_v (T_3 - T_2) = .718 (1413 - 979)$

= 312 kJ/kg

Now, $Q_{2\text{-}3} = Q_{3\text{-}4} = C_p (T_4 - T_3)$

$$T_4 = \frac{312}{1.005} + 1413 = 1723 \text{ K}$$

$$\frac{V_4}{V_3} = \frac{V_4}{T_3} = \frac{1723}{1413} = 1.22$$

$$\frac{V_4}{V_3} = \frac{V_1}{V_2} \times \frac{V_3}{V_4} = \frac{16}{1.22} = 13.1$$

$$T_5 = T_4 \left(\frac{V_4}{V_5}\right)^{\gamma-1}$$

$$= 1723 \times \frac{1}{(13.1)^{0.4}}$$

$$= 615 \, K$$

$$P_5 = P_1\left(\frac{T_5}{T_1}\right) = 1.0 \times \frac{615}{323} = 1.9 \, bar$$

$$\eta_{cycle} = 1 - \frac{Q_{out}}{Q_{in}} = 1 - \frac{C_v(T_5 - T_1)}{C_v(T_3 - T_2) + C_p(T_4 - T_3)}$$

$$= 1 - \frac{0.718\,(615 - 323)}{312 + 312}$$

$$1 - \frac{0.718 \times 292}{624}$$

$$= 0665 = 66.5\%$$

$$v_1 = \frac{RT_1}{P_1} = \frac{0.287 \times 323}{10^2} = 0.927 \, m^3/kg$$

$$V_1 - V_2 = V_1 - \frac{V_1}{16} = \frac{15V_1}{16}$$

$$W = Q_{in} \times \eta_{cycle} = 0.665 \times 624$$

$$\therefore \, m.e.p. = \frac{W}{V_1 - V_2} = \frac{0.665 \times 624}{\frac{15}{16} \times 0.927} = 476 \, kN/m^2$$

$$= 4.76 \, bar \, Ans.$$

Prob. 3.11: A diesel engine has a compression ratio of a 14 and cut-off ratio takes place at 6% of the stroke. Findthe air standard efficinecy.

Soln. Refering Fig.

Given : $r = \dfrac{V_1}{V_2} = 14, \; \rho = \dfrac{V_3}{V_2}$

$\gamma = 1.4$ (taken)

According to question,

$$V_3 - V_2 = 0.06\,(V_1 - V_2)$$

$$= 0.06\,(14V_2 - V_2)$$

$$= 0.06\,(13\,V_2)$$

$$= 0.78\,V_2$$

$\therefore V_3 = 1.78\ V_2$

Therefore,

$$\rho = \frac{V_3}{V_2} = \frac{1.78\ V_2}{V_2} = 1.78$$

$$\eta_{\text{diesel}} = 1 - \left(\frac{1}{r}\right)^{\gamma-1} \cdot \left(\frac{r_c^{\gamma}-1}{\gamma\ (r_c-1)}\right)$$

$$= 1 - \left(\frac{1}{14}\right)^{1.4-1} \cdot \left(1.78^{1.4}-1\right) / 1.4\ (1.78-1)$$

$= 0.605 = 60.\ \%$ Ans.

Prob. 3.12: An engine working on the otto engine is supplied with air at 0.1 MPa, 35°C. The compression ratio is 8. Heat supplied is 2100 kJ/kg. Calculate the maximum pressure and temperature of the cycle, the cycle efficiency and the m.e.p. (C_p = 1.005, C_v = 0.718, R = 0.287 kJ/kg K)

Soln. Refering Fig.

Given : P_1 = 0.1 MPa = 100 kPa, T_1 = 273 + 35 = 308 K

$r = 8$, Q_{in} = 2100 KJ/kg, $\gamma = \dfrac{C_p}{C_v} = \dfrac{1.005}{0.718} = 1.4$

$C_p = 0.718$, $C_p = 1.005$

$$\eta_{\text{otto}} = 1 - \left(\frac{1}{r}\right)^{\gamma-1}$$

$$= 1 - \left(\frac{1}{8}\right)^{0.4}$$

$$= 1 - \frac{1}{2.3}$$

$= 0.565 = 56.5\%$

Applying gas equation,

$$V_1 = \frac{RT_1}{P_1} = \frac{0.287 \times 308}{100} = 0.884\ m^3/kg$$

$$\because r = \frac{V_1}{V_2}$$

or $8 = \dfrac{0.884}{V_2}$

$\therefore V_2 = \dfrac{0.884}{8} = 0.11 \text{ m}^3/\text{kg}$

$\dfrac{T_2}{T_1} = \left(\dfrac{V_1}{V_2}\right)^{\gamma-1} = 8^{0.4}$

or $\dfrac{T_2}{T_1} = 2.3$

$\therefore T_2 = 2.3 \times T_1 = 2.3 \times 308 = 708.4 \text{ K}$

$Q_{in} = C_v (T_3 - T_2)$

or $2100 = 0.718 (T_3 - 708.4)$

or $T_3 = \dfrac{2100}{0.718} + 708.4$

$= 3633 \text{ K}$

$\dfrac{P_2}{P_1} = \left(\dfrac{V_1}{V_2}\right)^{\gamma} = 8^{1.4}$

or $P_2 = (8)^{1.4} \times P_1 = 18.37 \times 10^5$

$= 18.37 \times 10^5 \text{ Pa} = 1.837 \text{ MPa}$

Again,

$\dfrac{P_3 V_3}{T_3} = \dfrac{P_2 V_2}{T_2}$

or $P_3 = P_{max} = \dfrac{P_2 V_2}{T_2} \times \dfrac{T_3}{V_3}$ $[\therefore V_2 = V_3]$

$= \dfrac{1.837 \times 363}{708} = 9.426 \text{ MPa}$

$W = Q_{in} \times \eta_{cycle}$

$= 2100 \times 0.565$

$= 1186.5 \text{ kJ/kg}$

Now

$P_m (V_1-V_2) = W$

or $P_m = \dfrac{W}{V_1 - V_2} = \dfrac{1186.5}{0.774} = 1553 \text{ kPa}$

$= 1.533 \text{ MPa}$

Prob. 3.13: Prove that for otto-cycle, the optimum compression ratio for maximum work done is given by $r = \left(\dfrac{T_2}{T_1}\right)^{1.25}$ where T_2 is the maximum cycle temperature, T_1 is the minimum cycle temperature and is the compression ratio.

Soln.

We know that, work for per kg working substance,

$W = C_v (T_3 - T_2) - C_v (T_4 - T_1)$

$= C_v (T_3 - T_1 r^{\gamma-1}) - C_v \left(\dfrac{T_3}{r^{\gamma-1}} - T_3\right)$ \hspace{1cm} (i)

Differentiating equation (i) w.r.t. r, we have

$\dfrac{dw}{dr} = C_v (\gamma - 1) . T_1 r^{\gamma-2} + (\gamma - 1) C_v T_3 r^{-(\gamma-1)-1}$

For maximum work done, $\dfrac{dw}{dr} = 0$

$0 = C_v (\gamma-1). T_1 r^{\gamma-2} + (\gamma-1) C_v T_3 r^\gamma$

$\dfrac{T_3}{T_1} = r^{2\gamma-2} = r^{0.8}$

or $T_3 r -g = T_1 r \, g - w$

or $r = \left(\dfrac{T_3}{T_1}\right)^{\frac{1}{0.8}}$

or $r = \left(\dfrac{T_3}{T_1}\right)^{1.25}$

Prob. 3.14. The enthalpy change during the oxidation of glucose is -2880 kJ/mole. 25% of this energy is available for muscular work. If 100 kJ of muscular work is needed to walk 1km. What is the maximum distance that a person will be able to walk after eating 120 g.

Soln. Energy envolved from 120 g of glucose $= \dfrac{2880}{180} \times 120$

$= 1920 \text{ kJ}$

Energy utilization for walking = $\dfrac{25}{100} \times 1920$

= 480 kJ

$\because$ 100 KJ = 1 km.

$\therefore 480 = \dfrac{1}{100} \times 480$

= 4.8 km Ans.

Prob. 3.15. An oil engine works on the ideal diesal cycle with a comparission ratio of 18:1. The constant pressure energy addition ceases at 10% of the stroke. The intake pressure & temperature are 100 kP & 300 k respectively. The hourly air comsumption is 100m3. If the ratio of specific ehats is 1.4. The maximum temperature in the cycle is

(a) 953.3k   (b) 1334.6 k   (c) 2154.5 k   (d) 2573.9 k   (GATE 2007)

Soln. Refering Fig. 3.14

Since pressure energy addition ceases at 10% of the stroke. And it will cease at point 3, 50, To find T_3 (max)

Given, T_1 = 300k

P_1 = 100 kPa

$\therefore r = \dfrac{V_1}{V_2} = 18$

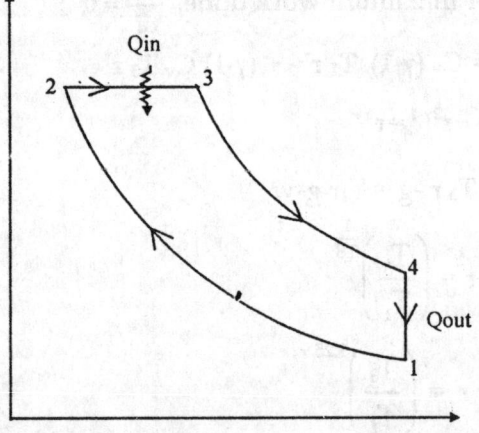

$V_3 - V_2 = 0.1\,(V_1 - V_2)$

$\dfrac{V_3}{V_2} - 1 = 0.1\left(\dfrac{V_1}{V_2} - 1\right)l$

$= 0.1\,(18-1)$

$\dfrac{V_3}{V_2} - 1 = 0.1 \times 17$

$\dfrac{V_3}{V_2} = 1.7 + 1 = 2.7$

Fig. 3.14

$V_3 = 2.7\,V_2$

for the process 1-2

$P_1 V_1 \gamma = P_2 V_2 \gamma$

$100 \times v_1{}^\gamma = P_2 \times V_2{}^\gamma$

$P2 = 100 \times \left(\dfrac{V_1}{V_2}\right)^\gamma = 100 \times 18^{1.4} = 5719.8$ kPa

Again for 1-2

$P_1{}^{1-\gamma}. T_1{}^\gamma = P_2{}^{1-v}. T_2{}^\gamma$

$\left(\dfrac{P_2}{P_1}\right)^{\gamma-1} = \left(\dfrac{T_2}{T_1}\right)^\gamma$

$\left(\dfrac{5719.8}{100}\right)^{1.4-1} = \left(\dfrac{T_2}{300}\right)^{1.4}$

$5.05 = \left(\dfrac{T_2}{300}\right)^{1.4}$

$T_2{}^{1.4} = 300^{1.4} \times 5.05$

$T_2 = 300 \times (5.05)1/1.4$

$T_2 = 953.29$ k

for process 2→3

$\dfrac{T_2}{V_2} = \dfrac{T_3}{V_3}$

$\dfrac{T_2}{V_3} = \dfrac{V_2}{V_3} = \dfrac{1}{2.7}$

$T_3 = 2.7 \times T2$

$T_3 = 2.7 \times 953.29$

$T_3 = 2573.9$ k

It is the required maximum temperature

Prob. 3.16. The mechanical efficiency of the power tiller engine developing 7.5 kw is 80%. The calorific value of diesel is 45 Mj/kg if the indicated thermal effecient is 35% the brake specific fuel comsumption of engine.   (GATE 2007)

Soln. Given

B.P. = 7.5 kw

ηmech = 0.80

C.V. = 45 × 10³ kJ/kg

ηin = 0.35

ηmech = $\dfrac{n_b}{n_{in}} = \dfrac{n_b}{0.55}$

nb = 0.35 x 0.80 = 0.28

$$B.S.f.c = \frac{3600}{c.v \times n_b}$$

$$\frac{3600}{45 \times 10^3 \times 0.28} = 0.286 \text{ kg/b. kwh}$$

PROBLEMS

1.   10 g of oxygen is introduced in a vessel of 5 litre capacity at 27°C. Calculate the pressure of the gas in bar in the container. (Ans. 155.887 kPa)

2.   Density of a gas is found to be 5.46 g/dm^3 at 27°C at 2 bar pressure. What will be its density at STP. (Ans. 3.04 g/dm^2)

3.   Calculate the volume occupied by 5.0 g of acetylene gas at 50°C and 740 mm pressure (Ans. 5.23L)

4.   A open vessel at 27°C is heated until three fifth of the air in it has been expelled. Assuming the volume of the vessel remains the same, find the temperature to which the vessel has its be heated. (Ans. 477°C)

5.   What will be the volume at 450 K of a gas which occupies 200 cm^3, at 300 K, the pressure remaining constant throughout. (Ans. 300 cm^3).

6.   Calculate the temperature of 4.0 moles of gas occuping 5 x 10^{-3} m^3 at 3.22 bar. (R = 0.083 bar L K^{-1} mol^{-1}) (Ans. 50 K)

7.   A person exhales 0.75 kg of CO_2 per day. Suppose the person is in a sealed room with the dimensions of 3.0 m by 3.0 m by 2.5 m at a temperature of 290 K. Calculate the pressure of CO_2 in the room after one day.   (Ans. 1.9 kPa)

8.   Determine the work done by a gas system following an expansion pressure as shown in Fig. 3.14. (Ans. 292 kPa)

9.   Calculate the work done when 1.0 mole of water at 100°C vaporizes against on atmospheric pressure of 1 atm. Assume ideal behaviour and volume of liquid water to be negligible.   (Ans. -3.1 KJ)

10. . 500 cm^3 of a sample of ideal gas is compressed by an average pressure of 0.5 atm to 250 cm^3. During this process 10 J of heat flows out to the surroundings. Calculate the change in internal energy of the system.   (Ans. 2.67 J)

11.   A sample of Argon gas at 1.0 atm and 27°C expands reversibly and adiabatically from 1.25 dm^3 to 2.5 dm^3. Calculate the enthalpy change in this process. C$_v$ for Argon is 12.48 JK^{-1} mole.   (Ans. -115 4 J)

12. An athlete is given 100 g of glucose ($C_6H_{12}O_6$) of energy equivalent to 1560 kJ. He utilizes 50 percent to this gained energy in the event. In order to avoid storage of energy in body, calculate the weight of water he would need to perspire. The enthalpy of water is 44 kJ/mole. (Ans. 4.8 km)

13. An engine equipped with a cylinder having a bore of 150 mm and stroke of 450 mm operates on an otto cycle. If the clearance volume is 2000 cm³, compute the air standard efficiency. (Ans. 47.4%)

14. In an air standard diesel cycle, the compression ratio is 15. Compression begins at 0.1 MPa, 40°C. The heat added is 1.6575 MJ/kg. Compute,

(a) The maximum temperature of cycle (b) The work done per kg of air (c) The cycle efficiency (d) the temperature at the end of the inetropic expansion (e) the cut-off ratio (f) the maximum pressure of the cycle and (g) the mean effective pressure of the cycle.

15. A air standard limited pressure cycle has a compression ratio of 15 and compression begins at 0.1 MPa, 40°C. The maximum pressure is limited to 6 MPa and the heat added is 1.6575 MJ/kg. Calculate, (a) the heat supplied at constant volume per kg of air, (b) the heat supplied at constant pressure per kg of air (c) work done per kg of air, (d) the cycle efficiency (e) the temperature at the end of the constant volume heating process, (f) the cut-off ratio and (g) m.e.p. of the cycle. (Ans. (a) 235 kJ/kg (b) 1440 kj/kg (c) 1014 kJ/kg (d) 60.5% (e) 1252 K (f) 2.144 (g) 1.21 MPa

16. At what temperature will be the Celsius and Fahrenheit scales show the same readings? (Ans. -40°C)

17. The peak pressure in an otto cycle is 2.1 MPa and the minimum pressure is 0.1 MPa with thermal efficiency of 47.5%. Determine a compression ratio. (b) mean effective pressure. The working substance has $C_p = 0.25$ and $C_v = 0.18$. (Ans. 5, 340. 5 kPa)

18. Any engine working on semi-diesel cycle has cylinder bore of 20 cm and stroke of 40 cm. The compression ratio is 14.5 and the pressure ratio for constant volume in that addition process is 1.5. If the ideal air standard efficiency is 56.3, determine the point of cut-off for the constant pressure heat addition process as a percentage of the stroke. Assume necessary data. (Ans. 0.91% of stroke)

SUBJECTIVE QUESTION

1. Why gas balloons burst at high altitudes?
2. What is the universal gas constant? What are its units

3.   State Boyle's Law, Charles' Law. Derive the equation of state with the help of these law. Discuss the significance of gas constant R and give its value in JK^{-1} mol^{-1} and in atmosphere litre K^{-1} mol^{-1}.

4.   Show that the heat absorbed at constant volume is equal to the increase in the internal energy of the system, whereas that at constant pressure, is equal to the increase in the enthalpy of the system.

5.   What are the macroscopic properties? Explain extensive and intensive properties with at least two examples.

6.   Explain isothermal, adiabatic, isochoric, and isobaric process with at least one example in each case.

7.   Derive the expression for work done for isothermal and adiabatic process?

8.   With the help of p-v diagram and T-S diagram explain otto cycle and diesel cycle. Clearly showing the process during which heat is supplied and rejected.

9.   Derive an expression for the air standard efficiency of otto cycle and diesel cycle in terms of compression ratio and shows the efficiency of disel cycle is always lower than efficency of otto cycle for the same compression ratio.

9.   Derive an expression for mean effective pressure of diesel cycle.

10.   Compare the otto, diesel and dual cycles for same compression and same heat inputs.

MULTIPLE CHOICE QUESTIONS

1.   20% N_2O_4 molecules are dissociated in a sample of a gas at 27°C and 760 torr pressure. Density of N_2O_4 is
      (a) 3.1 g L^{-1} (b) 6.2 g L^{-1}
      (c) 12.4 gL^{-1} (d) 18.6 g L^{-1}

2.   20 ml of gas was collected at STP. The pressure was then doubled and the temperature was gradually changed until the volume becomes 20 ml again. The temperature at which this happened was
      (a) 173 K   (b)   576 K
      (c) 473 K   (d)   373 K
      (e) 273 K

3.   If 10 g of a gas at 1 atm pressure is cooled from 273°C to 0°C keeping the volume constant, its pressure would become
      (a) $\frac{1}{2}$ atm   (b) $\frac{1}{273}$ atm
      (c) 2 atm   (d)   273 atm

4. Equal weights of methane and hydrogen are mixed in an empty container at 25°C. The fraction of total pressure exerted by hydrogen is
    (a) 1/2 (b) 8/9
    (c) 1/9 (d) 16/17

5. At 100°C and 1 atm if the density of liquid water is 1.0 g/cm³ and that of water vapour is 0.006 g/cm³, then the volume occupied by water molecules in 1 litre of steam at that temperature is
    (a) 6 cm³ (b) 60 cm³
    (c) 0.6 cm³ (d) 0.06 m³

6. 4.4 g of a gas at STP occupies a volume of 2.24 L, the gas can be
    (a) O_2 (b) CO
    (c) NO_2 (d) CO_2

7. The volume of 2.8 g of CO at 27°C and 0.821 atm pressure is R (0.082 L atm⁻¹ K⁻¹ mole⁻¹)
    (a) 3.0 L (b) 0.3 L
    (c) 1.5 L (d) 30 L

8. Vibrational energy is
    (a) Partially potential and partially kinetic
    (b) only potential
    (c) only kinetic
    (d) none of the above.

9. Which of the following expression expresses the first law of the themodynamics
    (a) $q = \Delta E - W$ (b) $\Delta U = q - W$
    (c) $\Delta H = q + W$ (d) $\Delta U = P\Delta v + \Delta H$

10. In an adiabatic process which of the following is true
    (a) $q = + W$ (b) $q = 0$
    (c) $\Delta E = q$ (d) $P\Delta V = 0$

11. The relationship between enthalpy change and internal energy change is
    (a) $\Delta H = \Delta E + P\Delta V$ (b) $\Delta H = - (\Delta E + P\Delta V)$
    (c) $\Delta H = \Delta E - P\Delta V$ (d) $\Delta H = \Delta PV - \Delta E$

12. Heat of combustion of carbon is 96 kcal, when some quantity of carbon is burst in oxygen, 48 Kcal of heat is liberated. What is the volume (in lit) of oxygen at STP created with this carbon?
    (a) 48 (b) 22.4
    (c) 1 (d) 11.2

13. Which one of the following statements is false?
    (a) work is state function

(b) Temperature is a state function

(c) work appears at the boundary of the systems

(d) None of the above

14. One mole of a non-ideal gas undergoes a change of state (2.0 atm, 3.01L, 95 K) → (4.0 atm, 5L, 245 K) with a change in internal energy, $\Delta E = 30.0$ L atm. The change in enthalpy (ΔH) of the process in L. atm is.

15. Specific heat at constant pressure (C_p) of a real gas

(a) increases with increase in temperature

(b) decrease with increase in temperature

(c) remains constant with increase in temperature.

(d) None of the above

16. Specific heat at constant volume (C_v) of a real gas

(a) increase with increase in temperature

(b) decrease with increase in temperature

(c) remains constant with increase in temperature

(d) first increases with increase in temperature and then decrease with further increase in temperature.

17. Specific heat at constant pressure (C_p)

(a) increases with increase in moisture content in air

(b) decrease with increase in moisture content in air

(c) remains same irrespective of the moisture content of air

(d) none of the above

18. The ratio of sp. heats $\left(\dfrac{C_p}{C_v} = \gamma \right)$ for air

(a) increases with increases in moisture content in air

(b) decrease with increase in moisture content in air

(c) remains constant irrespective of the increase in moisture content in air.

(d) none of the above

19. The concept of air standard cycle predicts the performance characteristics of actual engines.

(a) for compression ratio variations

(b) for heat addition with actual full combustion

(c) both (a) and (b) (d) none of the above

20. The air standard efficiency of otto cycle is

(a) $\eta_{otto} = 1 - \left(\dfrac{1}{r} \right)^{\frac{\gamma-1}{\gamma}}$ (b) $\eta_{otto} = 1 - \left(\dfrac{1}{r} \right)^{\gamma-1}$

(c) $\eta_{otto} = 1 - r\left(\dfrac{\gamma-1}{\gamma}\right)$ (d) None of the above

21. The mean effective pressure (P_m) for the otto cycle is given by (P_1 = lowest pressure in the cycle)

    (a) $P_m = \dfrac{P_1 r(r^{\gamma-1}-1)\,(r_p-1)}{(\gamma-1)\,(r-1)}$

    (b) $P_m = \dfrac{P_1(r^{\gamma-1}-1)\,(r_p-1)}{(\gamma-1)\,(r-1)}$

    (c) $P_m = \dfrac{P_1 r\,(r^{\gamma-1}-1)\,(r-1)}{(\gamma-1)\,(r_p-1)}$

    (d) none of the above

22. The thermal efficiency of theoretical otto cycle:
    (a) Increase with increase in compression ratio.
    (b) increases with increase in in-sentropic index γ.
    (c) is independent of the pressure ratio
    (d) all of the above

23. The work output of theoretical otto cycle
    (a) increases with increase in compression ratio (r)
    (b) increases with increases in pressure ratio
    (c) increases with increases in adiabatic index (γ)
    (d) all of the above

24. The thermal efficiency of theoretical otto cycle with fixed compression ratio operates on Air, Nitrogen, and Carbon di oxide.
    (a) η_{otto} (Air) > η_{otto} (Nitrogen) > η_{otto} (Carbondioxide)
    (b) η_{otto} (Air) = η_{otto} (Nitrogen) = η_{otto} (carbondioxide)
    (c) η_{otto} (Air) < η_{otto} (Nitrogen) < η_{otto} (Carbondioxide)
    (d) none of the above

25. The graph shown in Fig. Shows variation of work output versus pressure ratio for otto cycle with fixed compression ratio and fixed value of adiabatic index (γ).

    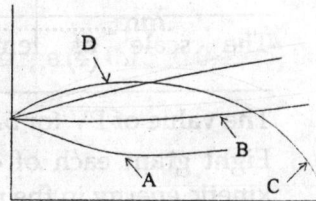

    (a) A   (b) B
    (c) C   (d) D

27. The graph shown in Fig. shows variation of thermal efficiency versus compression ratio for otto cycle for fixed value of pressure ratio and adiabatic index (γ).

(a) A

(b) B

(c) C

(d) D

27. For same compression ratio

(a) $\eta_{th\ otto} > \eta_{th\ diesel}$

(b) $\eta_{th\ otto} > \eta_{th\ diesel}$

(c) $\eta_{th\ otto} = \eta_{th\ diesel}$

(d) none of the above

28. In air standard diesel cycle, at fixed compression ratio and fixed value of adabatic index (γ).

(a) Thermal efficiency increases with increases in heat cut-off ratio addition of

(b) Thermal efficiency decreases with increases in heat addition cut-off ratio

(c) Thermal efficiency remains same with increase in heat addition cut-off ratio

(d) None of the above

29. In a dual cycle at fixed compression ratio, the heat added at constant volume is x and at constant pressure is y. Also x + y = constant

(a) If x is increased, the thermal efficiency increased

(b) If y is increased, the thermal efficiency increased

(c) If x = y is thermal efficiency is the maximum

(d) none of the above

FILL IN THE BLANKS

1. The law which describes the relationship between the volume and temperature of a gas at constant pressure is called Charle's law average kinetic energy of a molecule of a gas at temperature TK is _____

2. The scale of temperature with -273°C as zero is called - _____

3. The value of PV for 5.6 litres of an ideal gas is _____ at STP.

4. Eight gram each of oxygen and hydrogen at 27°C with have the total kinetic energy in the ratio of _____.

5. Law of conservation of energy is also known as _____.

6. As per the reaction

$N_2 (g) + 2O_2 (g) \rightarrow 2 NO_2 (g)$; 4 H = 66 kJ

The heat of formation of nitrogen dioxide is 33. kJ.

7. H_2O (l) $\rightarrow$ H_2O (s) ; ΔH = - 6.01 kJ

   ΔH is heat of _____ of water.

8. At STP one gram of hydrogen occupies a volume of _____ lites 24.0
   g of methane at STP occupies a volume of _____ litres.

ANSWER OF FILL IN THE BLANKS

1. $\frac{3}{2}$ KT   2. Kelvin temperature scale   3. 0.25 RT   4. 1:16

5. 1st law of thermodynamics   6. 33 kJ   7. Fusion   8. 11.2, 33.6

ANSWER OF MULTIPLE CHOICE QUESTIONS

1 (a) 2 (b) 3 (c) 4 (b) 5 (c) 6 (d) 7 (a) 8 (a) 9 (b) 10 (b) 11 (a) 12 (d) 13 (a) 14 ( ) 15 (a) 16 (a) 17 (a) 18 (b) 19 (a) 20 (b) 21 (a) 22 (d) 23 (d) 24 (a) 25 (d) 26 (c) 27 (a) 28 (b) 29 (a)

9.2 Necessity of Cooling System

(i)   Melting point of different metals is lower than heat generated in the engine.

(ii)   ...burning or the lubrication oil ...deposition of carbon on the sliding and ...components results in rough running.

(iii) ...stress may arise in different components.

(iv)   ...wear on parts is increased, when engine is operated at over cooling ...higher cooling ...

(v)   ...vaporization of the fuel takes which results in fall of combustion ...rate of flame occurring when engine is operated ...over cooling.

(vi)   Temperature differences between atmosphere and heated surface.

9.4 ...law of Cooling (Newton's Law of Cooling).

It states that, the rate of heat radiated or lost by a body is directly proportional to the excess temperature ...provided that the excess temperature is less as compared

Chapter 4
Power Unit and Mutli Cylinder Engine

4.1 Power Unit: All the tractors are fitted with internal combustion engine, which is the power unit of the tractor. Both petrol engine and compression-ignition engines operate on the four-stroke cycle or the two-stroke cycles and are used for the construction of tractor.

4.2 Internal Combustion Engines: It is a type of engine which converts sotred energy of gaseous or liquid fuels into useful work, within the engine cylinder.

In other words, in internal combustion engine fuel in burnt within the engine cylinder.

4.3 Classification of Internal Combustion Engine: Internal combustion engines may be classified in many different ways as follows:

4.3.1. On the Basis of Working Cycle Employed:

(a) Two stroke engine (b) Four stroke engine

4.3.2. On the Basis of Fuel Used:

(a) Petrol engine (b) Diesel engine

(c) Gas engine and (d) Bi-fuel engine.

4.3.3. On the Basis of Themodynamic Cycle Used:

(a) Otto cycle (b) Diesel cycle and (c) Duel cycle

4.3.4. On the Basis of Ignition

(a) Spark ignition engine (b) Compression ignition engine

4.3.5. On the Basis of Arrangement of Engine Cylinders:

(a) Horizontal engine (b) Vertical engine

(c) V. engine (d) In-line engine (e) opposed piston engine

(f) Opposed cylinder engine (g) Radial engine

4.4. Two Stroke Engine:

4.4.1 Introduction:

In two stroke engine, cycle is completed in two storke of the piston or one revolution of the crank-shaft and is shown in Table 4.1

Table 4.1.

Stroke	During the stroke	At the end of stroke
First	Compression	Suction
Second	Power	Exhaust

4.4.2 Working Principle of the Two Stroke Engine: Two stroke of engines are namely upward stroke and downward stroke. It works as follows:

1. Upward Stroke or Ist Stroke [Suction and Compression]: During upward movement of piston, it covers two of the ports, exhaust port and transfer port which are normally almost opposite to each other. Allowing the mixture to come in during the compression stroke of the piston. Further upward movement of the piston compresses this charge and further movement of the piston also uncovers a third port in cylinder called Suction port. More fresh mixture is drawn throught this port into the crankcase just before the end of this stroke, the mixture in the cylinder ignited.

From above discussion we have observed that there are three stages of compression stroke as shown in Fig. (a) (b) and (c). These are starting of first stroke, piston at BDC exhaust port opens changes enters the cylinder from crank case, drying compression of charge both ports closed, compression is complete, inlet ports open and charge enters in the crank case.

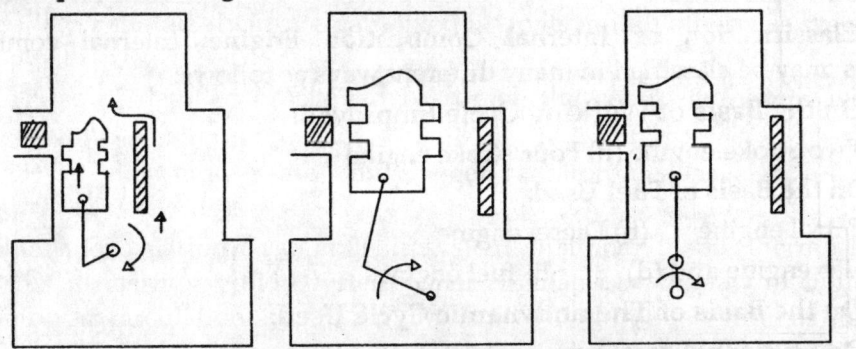

(a) Pistonat BDC (b) Piston in between BDC and TDC (c) Piston at TCC

Fig. 4.1 Three Stages of Compression Strokes

2: Second Sroke: The explosion of the mixture pushes the piston to move down in the cylinder. When the piston goes down, it covers and closes the suction port, trapping the mixtures drawn into the crankcase during the previous stroke then compressing it. Further downward movement of the piston uncovers first the exhaust port and then transfer port. This allows the burnt gases to flow out through exhaust port. Also the fresh mixture under pressure in the crankcase is transfered into the cylinder through transfer port during this stroke.

From above discussion we have observed that there are three stages of power stroke. These are beginning stoke which are shown in Fig. 4.2 (a), (b) and (c).

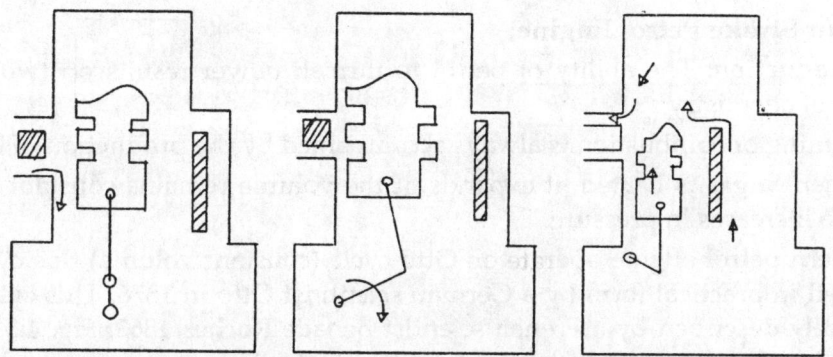

(a) Piston TDC (b) Piston in between BDC and TDC (c) Exhaust port open

Fig. 4.2. Three Stages of Power Stroke

4.5 Four Stroke Engine

4.5.1 Introduction: In four Stroke engine, cycle is completed in four stroke of the piston or two revolution of the crank shaft in shown as Table 4.2. Fig. 4.3 shows contructional details of 4-stroke spark ignition engine.

Table 4.2. Cycle of 4-Stroke Engine

Strokes	Events
First	Suction
Second	Compression
Third	Power
Fourth	Exhaust

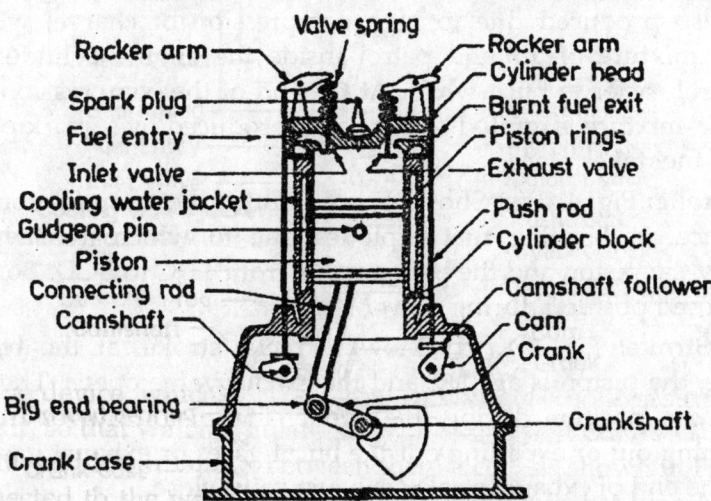

Fig. 4.3. Constructional Details of a 4-Stroke Spark Ignition (petrol) Engine

4.6   Four Stroke Petrol Engine:

4.6.1 Introduction: The ability of petrol to furnish power results on two basics principle of chemistry:

(i)   Burning or combustion is always accompanied by the production of heat.

(ii)   When a gas is heated, it expands, if the volume remains constant results into increases in pressure.

The modern petrol engine operate on Otto cycle (constant volume) this cyle was introduced in practical form by a German scientitist Otto in 1876. This cylce was theoretically described by a French scientist Benade Roches 1862. Fig. 4.3 shows Construction details of a 4-stroke spart ignition (petrol) engine.

4.6.2. Working principles: In a 4-stroke spark ignition engine, the four strokes are as follows:

(i)   Suction Stroke: Fig 4.4. (a) shows suction stroke of a constant volume cycle engine. During suction stroke, the piston is moved downward by the crank shaft which is revolved either by the mometum of fly-wheel or power generated by the electric starting motor. The intake valve (11) is open and due to higher pressure of ambient air, a fuel-air mixture in the cylinder from the carburettor through the open inlet valve. Here, the charge (mixture of air-petrol), broken up into a mixed form and paritally vapourised in the carburettor. At the end of suction strokes, the inlet valve closes.

(ii) Compression Stroke: Fig. 4.4. (b) Shows compression stroke. During compression stroke both the valves remain in closed postion. The piston travels from BDC to TDC. This upward movement of the piston compresses the charge. The heat is also produced due to high compression of charge, which makes homogeneous mixture of air and petrol inside the engine cylinder. The heat makes the petrol easier to burn while. At the end of the compression stroke, the compressed air mixture is ignited by the spark produced by a spark plug and the combustion of fuel takes place.

(iii) Power Stroke: Fig. 4.4. (c) Shows Power stroke due to spark combustion of fuel takes place an burning fuel explodes due to which a heavy thrust is experienced by the piston and the piston move from TDC to BCD. Both the valve remains in claosed position during power stroke.

(iv) Exhaust Stroke: Fig. 4.4. (d) Shows exhaust stroke, at the begnining of exhaust stroke, the piston is at BDC and the exhaut valve opens. The inlet valve remains in closed position during this stroke. The piston moves from BDC to TDC and pushing out or expelling out the burnt gases or exhaust gases from the cylinder. At the end of exhaust stroke, exhaust valve close.

After the exhaust storke, the cycle is again repeated till the engine starts or is running.

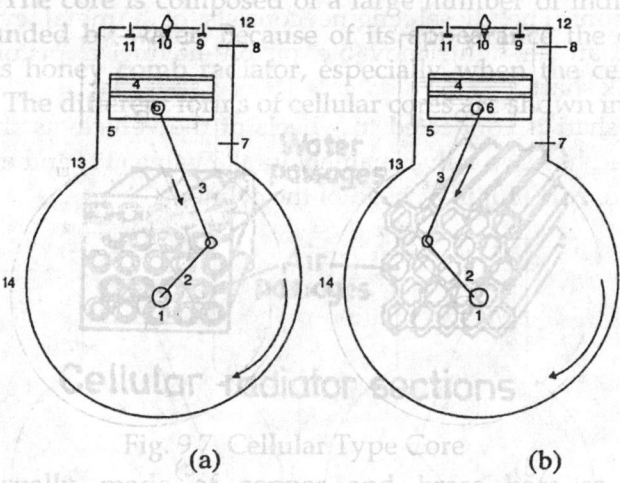

(a)   (b)

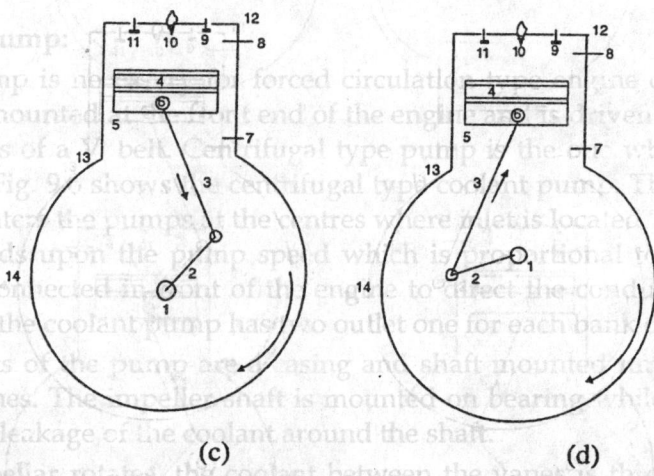

(c)   (d)

Fig. 4.4 Details of 4-stroke Petrol engine

1. Crank shaft, 2. Crank arm, 3. Connecting rod, 4. Piston ring, 5. Piston, 6. Piston pin, 7. BDC, 8. TDC, 9. Exhaust valve, 10. Spark plug, 11. Inlet valve, 12. Head, 13. Cylinder.14. Crank case.

4.7 Four Stroke Diesel Engines

4.7.1 Introduction:

It was invented by a scientist Rudolph diesel in 1807. In a 4-stroke diesel engine diesel is used as a fuel. In this engine, the enjected fuel is ignited by the heat of the air which is compressed by the piston within the cylinder head. It is also called compression ignition engine.

4.7.2 Construction: The diesel engine consists of a metal cylinder which is connected with an air-tight, movable piston having a piston rod which is conected to crank shaft.

And this crank shaft is connected to wheels of the vehicle as shown in Fig. 4.5. The cylinder head has two valves namely intake valve (11) and exhaust valve (9). There is also a nozzole (10) in th head of the cylinder.

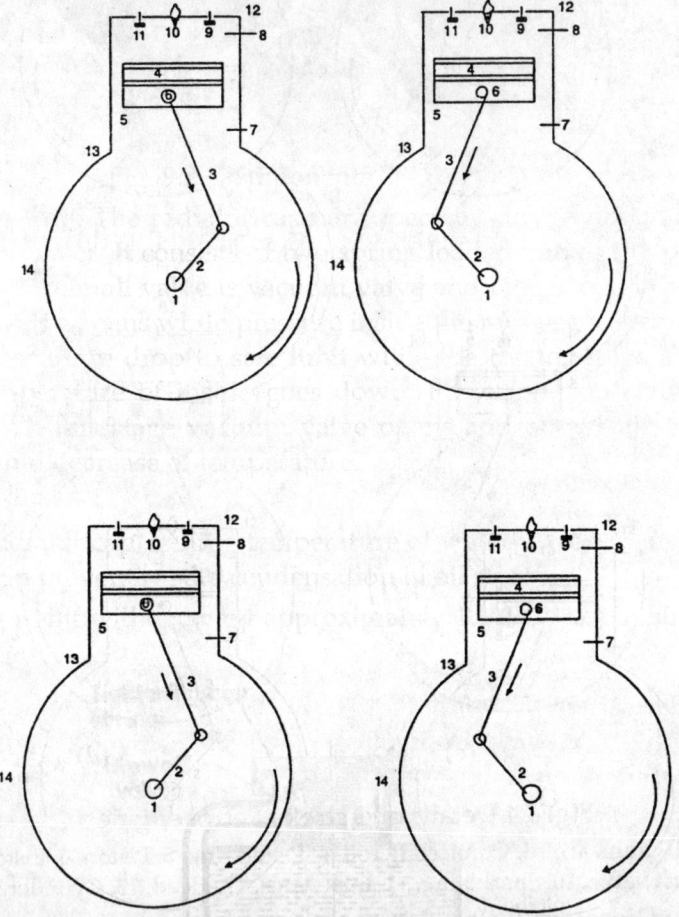

1. Crank shaft, 2. Crank arm, 3. Connecting rod, 4. Piston ring, 5. Piston, 6. Piston pin, 7. BDC, 8. TDC, 9. Exhaust valve, 10. Spark plug, 11. Inlet valve, 12. Head, 13. Cylinder.14. Crank case.

Fig. 4.5 Details of 4-Stroke of Diesel Engine

4.7.3. Working Principle: The working of a diesel engine is divided into '4-step', called "4-stroke" of the engine. These 4-strokes are as follows:

(i) Intake Stroke: When piston moves downwards then intake valve 11 opens up and air is sucked into the cylinder of diesel engine.

(ii) Compression storke: the intake valve (11) closes when sufficient air has entered into the cylinder. Now, the piston moves upward and compresses the air in the cylinder to about $\frac{1}{16}$ th parts of its original volume. This high compression of air produces a lot of heat due to which air in the cylinder becomes very hot and it temperature rises up to 1273 K.

(iii) Power Stroke: When the air has been fully compressed, then a fine spray of diese oil is injected into the cylinder through the atomizer (nozzle). Due to high temperature of air in the cylinder, the diesel oil burns rapidly and produces an extremely large volume of hot gases. The gases, now at high temperature and pressure expand against the piston and push the piston downward with a great force. The piston rod then pushes the crank shaft which in turn rotates the wheels of the vehicle.

(iv) Exhaust Stroke: When the piston has been pushed down then the exhaust valve (9) opens. Now due to momentum gained by wheels, the piston pushed upwards. This upward movement of piston expels the burnt gasxes into exhaust pipe and from there to the atmosphore through the exhaust valve (9). The exhaust valve then gets closed, again the intake valve opens up and the abvoe 4-siroke of the diesel engine are repeated again and again.

4.8 Difference between 2-Stroke and 4-Stroke Single Cylinder Engine: It is given in Table 4.3

Table 4.3 Difference between 2-Stroke and 4-Stroke Single Cylinder Engine

S.No.	Item	2-Stroke Engine	4-Stroke Engine
1.	Working stroke	obtained each revolution of crankshaft	obtained two revolution of crank shaft
2.	Turning moment of crank shaft	Even	Uneven
3.	Weight of engine per unit power	Light	Heavy
4.	Mechanical efficiency	Low	High
5.	Power out put	More	Less
6.	Running temperature	High	Low
7.	Fuel consumption	High	Low
8.	Space requirement	Less	large
9.	Lubricating system	Simple	Complex
10.	Noise	High	Less
11.	Use	Generally in moped scooters, motocycle	Generally in car, tractor, truck, buses etc.
12.	Comsumption of Lubricating oil	More	Less
13.	Mechanism of valve	Absent because it has ports.	Present

14.	Speed	High speed engine only	All types, low, medium and high
15.	Direction of operation	Both, clock and anti clock wise	One
16.	Size of flywheel	Small	Big
17.	Effectiveness of piston	Both side	One side
18.	Cank case	Fully closed and air tight	x
19.	Cost	Low	High
20.	Scavenging	Poor	Good

4.9. Advantages of 2-Stroke. Engine over 4-stroke Engine.

There are followings advantages of 2-stroke engine over 4- stroke engine

1. For same speed (rpm), number of power stroke is double in case of 2-stroke engine than 4-stroke.

2. Power developed at same speed (rpm) by two stroke engine should be doubled the 4-stroke engine. But in actual practice, the above increase in power is only 50 to 60 percent only due to poor scavenging.

3. 2-stroke engine requires smaller cylinder volume as compared to 4-stroke engine for same power, Therefore, weigth and size is smaller than 4-stroke engine.

4. 2-stroke engine requires smaller flywheel due to availability of power stroke in each revolution.

5. Friction loss in less due to absence of suction, exhaust valve, rocker arm, camshaft and timing gears.

6. Direction of rotation can be reverssed in two-stroke engine.

4.10. Disadvantage of 2-Stroke Engine Over 4-Stroke Engine.

There are followings disadvantages of 2-stroke engine over 4-stroke engine

1. Poor scavenging, results in low thermal efficiency.

2. Due to lack of separate lubricating system, wear and tear of parts are more.

3. Fuel consumption per unit power is more than 4-stroke due to flow of some of the fule from the exhaust.

4. At heavy loads engine gets heated and at lighter load it does not give smooth running.

5. It consumes more lubricating oil due to greater amount of heat generation.

6. Compression ratio for the same diameter is lower incase of 2-stroke due to constant opening of the ports.

7. Efficiency is lower in case of 2-stroke because it is directly proportional to compression ratio.

4.11. Difference Between Petrol and Diesel Engine. It is given in Table 4.4.

Table. 4.4 Difference Between Petrol and Diesel Engine

S.No.	Item	Diesel Engine	Spark Petrol or Ignition engine
1.	Components	It has got no carburretor ignition coil and spark plug	It has got carburetor, ignition coil, and spark plug.
2.	Fuel	Diesel are used	Vapouring fuels like petrol, powering or kerosene is used.
3.	Compression ratio	14:1 to 22:1	5:1 to 8:1
4.	Ignition of fuel	By the heat of air which is compressed by piston within the cylinder head.	By the spark which is produced by spark plug.
5.	Thermal efficiancy	32 to 38%	25 to 32%
6.	Engine weight	High per horse-power	Low per horse-power
7.	Temperature	It runs at a lower temperature on part load and less fuel consumption.	It runs at higher temperatures comparatively.
8.	Specific fuel consumption	tons (0.26 kg/kW/h)	0.396 kg/kW/h
9.	Noise during working	More	Less
10.	Wormfing up time	Less	More
11.	Initial cost	High	Low
12.	Compression pressures inside the cylinder	1.2 Mpa or 1200 kPa to 2.5 Mpa or 2500 kPa	0.6 Mpa or 600 k Pa to 1.0 Mpa or 1000 Kpa
13.	Temperature attained	500°C	260°C
14.	Luging ability	More	Less
15.	Transmission	Heavy	Lighter
20.	Air amount used	Constant	Variable
21.	Running cost	Less	More
22.	Starting the engine	Harder	easier
23.	Speed (rpm)	600-2500	400-6000
24.	Sound	More	Less

4.12 Multi Cylinder Engine

4.12.1 Introduction

Most of the problems in engine opearation may be solved by the use of more than one cylider. Although the use of a single cylinder engine is still in tractors, these days trend is towards multi cylinder engine. Farm tractors are built-with engine having 3 to 8 cylinders. The use of a multicylider engine brings a problems of proper firing orer which is ultimately related to the problems of balancing and vibration.

4.12.2. Classfication of Engine on the basis of Cylinder Arrangements:

They are classified as follows:

(i)   In line Engine: Most of the tractors present in India are equipped with one, two, three or four cylinders in line engines as showsn in Fig. 4.5 (a). These cyliders are vertically fittled to a common crankshaft below them. The cylinders are numbers from the radiator side to the flywheelside. But some manufactures, however, specify the cylinder from the flywheel side to the radiator side like Deuts, Excort 3036.

(ii)   V-Type Engines: A few tractors are available with V-shape engines. The cylinders are fitted in V-shape in two banks consisting of half the numbers of cylinders in each banks shown in Fig. 4.5 (b). The banks usually from 90o angle, however, other angular spacings are also used. This engines gives a smaller and more rigid engine. It shows less tendency towards torsional vibration.

(iii)   Horizontally oppsed Cylinders: Although it is not popular, a few of these engines are also available, which has two banks, opposite to each other and connected to a common crank shaft as shown in fig. 4.6 (c). Since, cylinders are arranged horizontally oppsite to each other , thus arrangment is called horizontally opposed, such as the starling engine D-4 crawler is of this type.

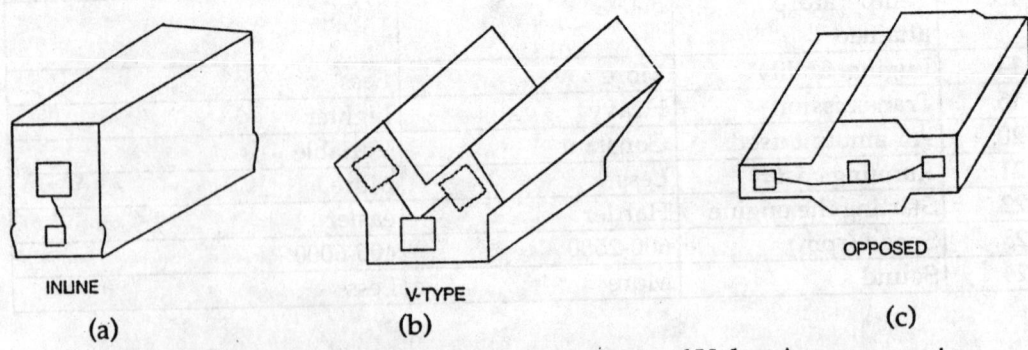

INLINE	V-TYPE	OPPOSED
(a)	(b)	(c)

Fig. 4.6. Classification of Engine on the Basis of Valve Arrangement

4.13. Classification of Engine On The Basis of the Valve Arrangement: They are classfiied as follows,

(i) L-Head: In the L-head design, both the inlet and enhaust valves are provided in the cylinder block of the engine and are one side of block. Both the valves are operated by a single camshaft with the helps of push rod rocker arm as shown in Fig. 4.7 (a).

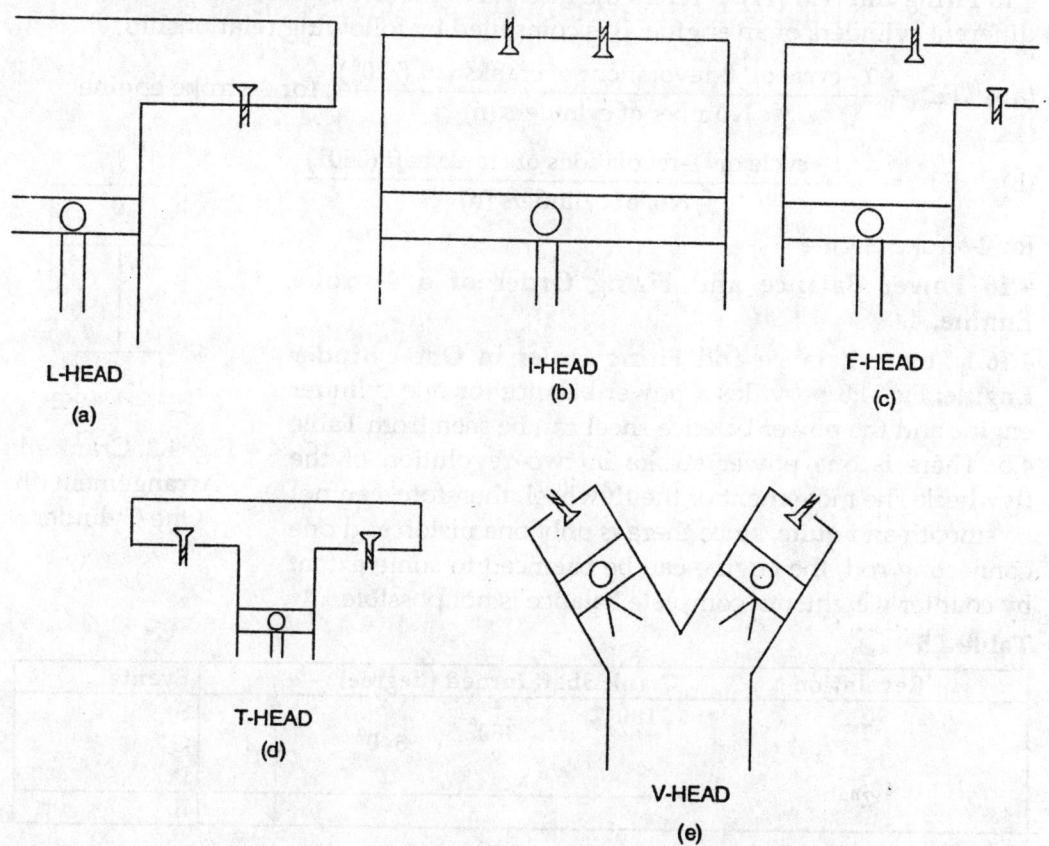

Fig. 4.7. Different Types of Valve Arrangement

(ii) I-Head Engine: It is also known as overhead valve engine. In this type of engine both the valves are provided in the cylinder head as shown in Fig. 4.7 (b). A single camshaft operates both the inlet and outlet valves with the help of push rod and rocker arm.

(iii) F-Head Engine: In this type of engine, one valve in the block whereas the other is in the head as in the case of Willey's Jeep, which is shown in Fig. 4.7 (c).

95

(iv) T-Head Engine: T-head design, both valves are provided in cylinder block and are operated by separate cam shafts one on each side of block, which in shown in Fig. 4.7 (d).

(v) V-Head Engine: It is similar to I-head, valves on each arm of the V is operated by reparate camshaft, as shown as Fig. 4.7 (e).

4.14. Firing Order (F.O) It refers to the sequence of power stroke in each cylinder of an engine. The arrangement of the crankpin on the crankshaft and design of the camshaft both determine the firing order.

4.15 Firing Interval (FI): It refers the interval between successive power strokes in different cylinders of an engine. It is computed by following relationship.

(a) $\quad$ F.I. $= \dfrac{1 - \text{cycle or 2-revolations of crankshaft } (720°)}{\text{Number of cylinders (n)}}$; for 4-stroke engine

(b) $\quad$ F.I. $= \dfrac{1 - \text{cycle or 1-revolations of crankshaft } (360°)}{\text{No. of cylinders (n)}}$;

for 2-stroke engine

4.16 Power Balance and Firing Order of a 4-stroke Engine:

4.16.1 Power Balance and Firing Order in One cylinder Engine: Fig. 4.8 provides a power balance for one cylinder engine and the power balance sheet can be seen from Table 4.5. There is one power stroke in two revolution of the flywheel. The movement of the flywheel, therefore, can not be smooth and quite, since there is only one piston and one connecting rod, the engine can be balanced to some extent by counter weightsbut complete balance is not possible.

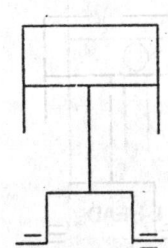

Fig. 4.8. Crank-pin Arrangement on One Cylinder

Table 4.5

Revolution	Crank Shaft turned (degree)				Events
1st	180° ↕	360°	540°	720° ↑	S
		↓	↓		C
					P
2nd					E

4.16.2. Power Balance and F.0 in Two Cylinder Engine: Fig. 4.9 provides a power balance for two-cylinder engine with 180° out of hase crank shaft i.e., one piston is going down the other goes up. Power balance sheet can be seenfrom Table 4.6.

In both cases, mechanical balance with reference to primary force in ggood but power power impulses occur with an interval of 180° and 540° instead of 360° which results into irregular production of power which comes vibrations in the engine and can it to turn unevenly. But in Fig. 4.9 (b) gives an equal firing interval 360° and power balance sheet can be seen from Table 4.6 (b). Due to difficulty in securing mechanical balance, it is not prefered.

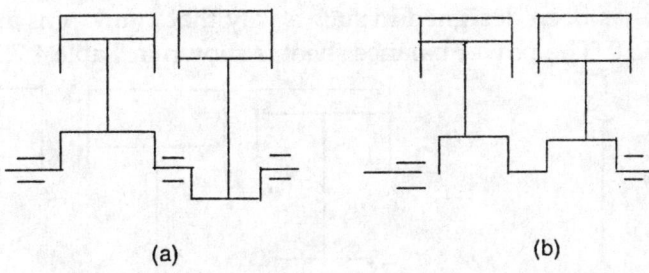

Fig. 4.9. Crank pin Arrangement of a Two Cylinder Engine

Table 4.6 Power Balance Sheet of a Two-cylinder Engine

Revolution	Crank shaft turn (degree)	Cylinder No.1	Cylinder No.2
1st	180 360 540 720	P	C
		E	P
2nd		S	E
		C	S

(a)

Revolution	Crank shaft turn (degree)	Cylinder No.1	Cylinder No.2
1st	180 360 540 720	P	S
		E	C
2nd		S	P
		C	E

(b)

4.16.3 Firing Balance and Firing Order in Three-Cylinder Engine: The firing interval in three cylinder engines,

$$FI = \frac{720}{3} = 240°C$$

The crankshaft has been designed in such a way that crank pins are 120° apart, as shown in Fig. 4.10. The power balance sheet is shown in Table 4.7.

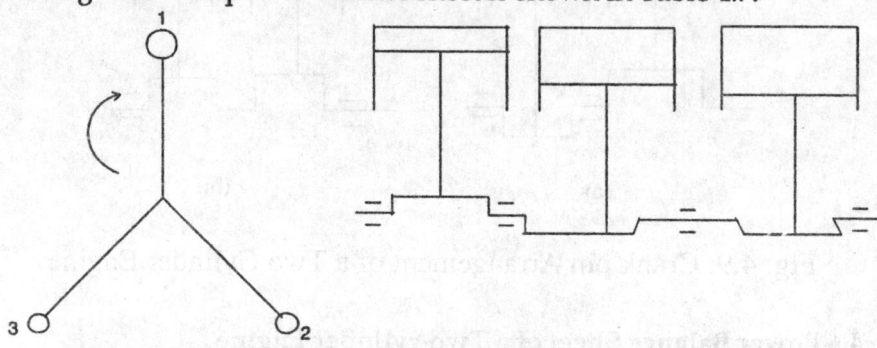

Fig. 4.10. Crank pin Arrangement in Three Cylinder Engine

Table 4.7 Power Balance Sheet of a Three-cylinder Engine

Firing order	One complete cycle, i.e., 720° of crank shaft rotation											
	180°			180°			180°			180°		
Cylinder 1	P	P	P	E	E	E	S	S	S	C	C	C
Cylider 2	S	C	C	C	P	P	P	E	E	E	S	S
Cylinder 3	E	E	S	S	S	C	C	C	P	P	P	E

4.16.4 Firing Balance and Firing Order in Four Cylinder Engine: The firing interval for 4-cylinder engine is 180°. The carnk-shaft is designed in such a way that crankpin 1and 4 lie in one direction and 2 and 3, 180° apart. As the position of 1 and is always moving opposite to that of a and 3-as shown in Fig. 4.11. They tend to neutralise the effect of primary inertia forces if the pistons are equal weight and a good mechnaical balance is obtainbale. By arrangement of cams, two popular firing orders, can be achieved as shown in Table. 4.7 (a) and 4.7 (b).

But the most popular firing order is 1-3-4-2 It is apperent that every time the power impulse is available, in one of the cylinders depending upon the firing order. Hence, the crank depending upon the firing order. Hence, the crank revolution is more smooth. Flow diagram of a four cylinder-engine is shown in Table 4.8.

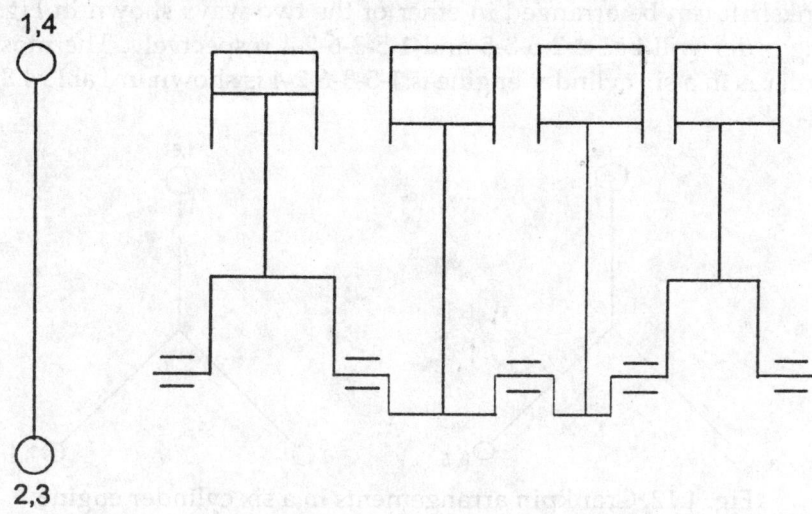

Fig. 4.11. Crank pin arrangement in a four-cylinder engine

Table 4.7 Power Balance Sheet for a Four-Cylinder Engine.

Cylinder	1	2	3	4
	P	E	C	S
Ist rev.	E	S	P	C
2nd rev.	S	C	E	P
	C	P	S	E

(a)

Cylinder	1	2	3	4
	P	C	E	S
Ist rev.	E	P	S	C
2nd rev.	S	E	C	P
	C	S	P	E

(b)

4.16.5. Firing Balance and Firing Order in Six-Cylinder Engine: The firing interval is $\dfrac{720}{6}$ =120°. The crankshaft is arranged in such a way that the 2 and 5, 3 and 4 are in the same radial plane 120° apart. Six strokes will be available with a firing interval of 120° in two revolution of the crank shaft. In other words, after every 120° there will be a power overlap for 60° as shown in Table 4.8.

99

The crankshaft can be arranged in ether of the two ways shown in Fig. 4.12 and the firing order will be1-4-2-6-3-5 and 1-5-3-6-2-4 respectvely. The most popular firing order is in a six cylinder engine is 1-5-3-6-2-4 is shown in Table 4.8.

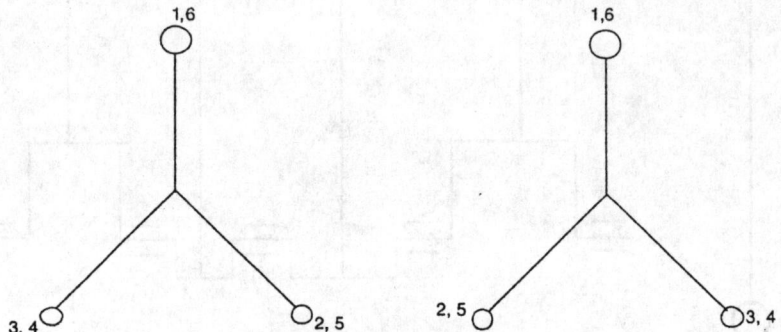

Fig. 4.12. Crankpin arrangements in a six cylinder engine.

Note: Engines with 5-cylinders or more having overlapping power strokes. In such instance the flywheel function of providing power between engine power stroke is unncessary but the flywheel in steel used to store energy which is given up in the event of sudden overloads.

Table 4.8 Power Flow Diagram of Six-Cylinder Engine

Firing order	2 revolutions or 720°											
	360° or one revolution						360° or one revolution					
	180°			180°			180°			180°		
	60°	60°	60°	60°	60°	60°	60°	60°	60°	60°	60°	60°
1	P	P	P	E	E	E	S	S	S	C	C	C
5	C	C	P	P	P	E	E	E	S	S	S	C
3	S	C	C	C	P	P	P	E	E	E	S	S
6	S	S	S	C	C	C	P	P	P	E	E	E
2	E	E	S	S	S	C	C	C	P	P	P	E
4	P	E	E	E	S	S	S	C	C	C	P	P

4.17. Difference Between, 4-stroke Large Single-Cylinder Engine and Multicylinder Engine. It is given in Table 4.9.

Table 4.9. Difference between 4-Stroke Large Single Cylinder Engine and Multi Cylinder Engine

S. No.	Items	Large single - cylinder engine	Multi-cylinder engine
1.	No. of powre stroke per cycle	Only one	Two or more than two.
2.	Nature of torque	Jerky	Smooth
3.	Requirement of flywheel	Heavy	Lighter
4.	Size of piston and valves	Large, giving considerable cooling diffculties	Small, giving cooling easier.
5.	Size of the engine	Tall	Small
6.	Nature of exhaust pulsations	Larger	Smaller

SUBJECTIVE QUESTIONS

1. What is internal combustion engine? How does it work?
2. Explain the working of two strokes cycle engine with neat sketches.
3. Explain the working of four strokes cycle engine.
4. Compare the advantages and disadvantages of four stroke cycle engine and two strokes engine.
5. What are the advantages of multicylider engine?
6. What are differences between diesel engine and petrol engine?
7. Write short notes on
(a) In line engine (b) V-type engines.
(c) Firing interval (d) Power balance sheet of 3, 4 and 6 cylinders engine.
8. What are the different arrangements of valve in an engine?

MULTIPLE CHOICE QUESTIONS

1. Choose the best alternative for four stroke cycle petrol engines
   (a) inlet valve open $10°$ before top dead centre and closes $45°$ after top botton dead centre.
   (b) inlet valve open $45°$ before top dead centre and closes $10°$ after TDC.
   (c) inlet valve open TDC and closes at BDC.
   (d) none of the above

2. Which of the operation in four stroke cycle petrol engines continues from $50°$ before bottom dead centre to $10°$ after top deal centre.
   (a) Suction (b) Compression
   (c) Expansion (d) Exhaust

3. The therml efficiency of petrol engines as compared to diesel engine in
    (a) higher
    (b) lower
    (c) same for same power output
    (d) same for same speed

4. The specific fuel consumptions of diesel engine as compared to that for petrol engine is
    (a) higher
    (b) lower
    (c) same for same output
    (d) same for same speed

5. The thermal efficiency of a good internal combustion engine at rated load in the range of
    (a) 10 to 20%
    (b) 30 to 35%
    (c) 60 to 70%
    (d) 80 to 90%

6. For best thermal efficiency of spark ignition engine, the fuel air mixture ratio should be
    (a) chemically correct
    (b) rich
    (c) lean
    (d) may be rich or lean

7. For maximum power of spark ignition engine the fuel-air mixture ratio should be
    (a) chemically correct
    (b) rich
    (c) lean
    (d) may be rich or lean

8. Relative fuel air ratio (FR) for maximum power in spark ignition engine is:
    (a) 0.8
    (b) 0.6
    (c) 1.2
    (d) 1.5

9. Relative fuel-air ratio (FR) for maximum thermal efficiency of spark ignition engine may be
    (a) 0.8
    (b) 0.6
    (c) 1.2
    (d) 1.5

10. I-head engine is also known as
    (a) overhead valve engine
    (b) T-head engine
    (c) L-head engine
    (d) none of the above

11. In I-Head engine, both valves are operated by
    (a) single camshaft
    (b) separate camshaft
    (c) both
    (d) none of the above

12. In V-head engine, both valves are operated by
    (a) single camshaft
    (b) separate camshaft
    (c) both
    (d) none of the above

13. F-head engine has both valve in
    (a) one valve in block and one in head
    (b) both valve in block
    (c) both valve in head
    (d) none of the above

102

14. The first I.C. engine was invented by
    (a) Nicolaus Otto   (b) Watersman
    (c) James Watt   (d) none of the above
15. The first I.C. engine was invented in
    (a) 1876   (b) 1800
    (c) 1775   (d) 1910
16. During compression stroke of 4-stroke diesel engine, the volume of air in the cylinder, becomes about
    (a) 20% of its original volume   (b) 10% of its original volume
    (c) 15% of its original volume   (d) 6.28% of its original volume
17. Firing interval in 4-stroke three cylinder engine in
    (a) $120°$ (b) $240°$
    (c) $360°$ (d) $480°$
18. In internal combustion engine, fuel is burnt:
    (a) Within the engine cylinder   (b) Out of the engine cylinder
    (c) both   (d) none of the above
19. Power unit of tractor is
    (a) internal combustion engine   (b) external combustion engine
    (c) both   (d) none of the above
20. In two stroke engine, cycle is completed in
    (a) two stroke of the pistons   (b) one revolution of crankshaft
    (c) both   (d) none of the above
21. In two stroke engine, first stroke includes
    (a) suction and power   (b) suction and compression
    (c) power and exhaust   (d) compression and power
22. Both valve are closed during
    (a) compression stroke   (b) power stroke
    (c) both   (d) none of the above
23. Number of power stroke in case of 2-stroke engine than 4-strone engine is
    (a) same   (b) double
    (c) triple   (d) none of the above
24. Direction of rotation can be reversed in
    (a) 4-stroke engine   (b) 2-stroke engine
    (c) both   (d) none of the above
25. Thermal efficiency of diesel engine varies from
    (a) 25 to 32%   (b) 32 to 38%
    (c) 40 to 45%   (d) 45 to 50%

26. Thermal efficiency of petrol engine varies from
    (a) 25 to 32%   (b) 32 to 38%
    (c) 40 to 45%   (d) 45 to 50%
27. Compression ratio of diesel engine varies from
    (a) 14 : 1 to 22 : 1   (b) 5 : 1 to 8 : 1
    (c) 4 : 1 to 6 : 1   (d) none of the above
28. Compression ratio of petrol engine varies from
    (a) 14:1 to 22:1   (b) 5:1 to 8:1
    (c) 20:1 to 25:1   (d) 30:1 to 35:1
29. Firing order depends on
    (a) arrangement of the crank   (b) camshaft design
        pin on the crank shaft
    (b) both   (d) none of the above

FILL UP THE BLANKS

1. Petrol engine is also known as................... engine.
2. In the L-head design, both valves are provided in and .... of the block.
3. In T-head design, both valves are operated by................... cam shaft.
4. I-head engine is also called................... valve engine.
5. In I-head design, both valves are operated by .... cam shaft.
6. .... refers to the sequence of power stroke in each cylinder of an engine.
7. .... refers the interval between successive power stroke in different cylinders.
8. The firing interval in three cylinder 4-stroke engine is...................
9. The most popular firing order is................... in the 4-stroke four cylinder engine.
10. There will be a power overlap of 60° after every 120° in 4-stroke...............cylinder engine.
11. In F-head engine one valve in .... where as other in.
12. Specific fuel consumption of diesel engine is................... than petrol engine.

Ans. 1.S.I. 2. cylinder block, one 3. separate 4. over head 5. single 6. firing order 7. firing interval 8. 120° 9. 1-3-4-2 10. 6 11. block, head, 12. less

ANSWER OF MULTIPLE CHOICE QUESTION

1 (a) 2. (d) 3 (b) 4 (b) 5 (b) 6 (c) 7 (b) 8 (c) 9 (a) 10 (a) 11 (a) 12 (b) 13 (a) 14 (a) 15 (a) 16 (d) 17 (b) 18 (a) 19 (a) 20 (c) 21 (b) 22 (c) 23 (b) 24 (a) 25 (b) 26 (a) 27 (a) 28 (b) 29 (c)

Chapter 5

Engine Parts and their Kinematics

5.1 Introduction: Engine consists of many parts, some of them are stationary during operating that are known as stationary parts. The parts which are in motion during operation are known as Moving Parts. All parts of a tractor are shown in Fig. 5.1 (a) and (b).

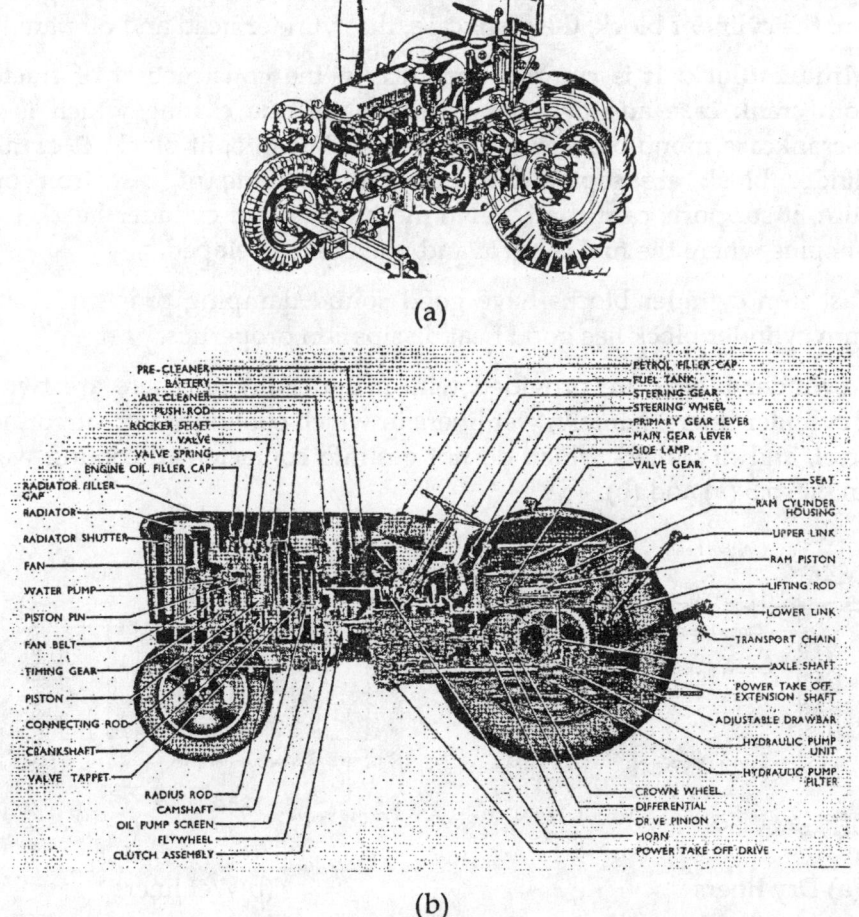

(a)

(b)

Fig. 5.1. Section view of 4-Wheel Drive Tractor

(Source : Farm Machinery by Clude Culpin, Crosby Lockwood & Son. Ltd. London)

5.2 Stationary Parts or Components: Its includes following parts:

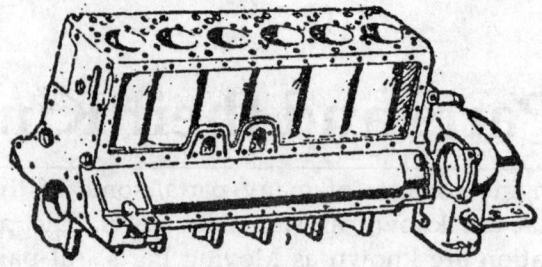

Fig. 5.2. Monoblock Cylinder

5.2.1 Engine Block: It is the heaviest single part of the engine. The engine block consists of the cylinder block, the crankcase, the cylinder head and oil pan.

5.2.2 Cylinder Block: It is common practice in the construction of tractors to make both crank case and cylinder block out of one casting which is called cylinder-crankcase mono block show in Fig. 5.2 But in split block, & crank case and cylinder block are separately casted. It is made of cast iron or cast aluminium. It supports cam shaft, valve mechanism and cylinder head. It is the heart of engine where the fuel is burnt and power is developed.

Note: Cast iron cylinder blocks have good sound damping properties whereas aluminium cylinder block has good heat dissipation properties.

Usually cylinder blocks are provided with cylinder liners. There are two main types of cylinder liners, namely, wet liners in which cooling water surrounds the liner barrel, and dry liners which do not get into contact with cooling water as shown in Fig. 5.3 (a) and (b).

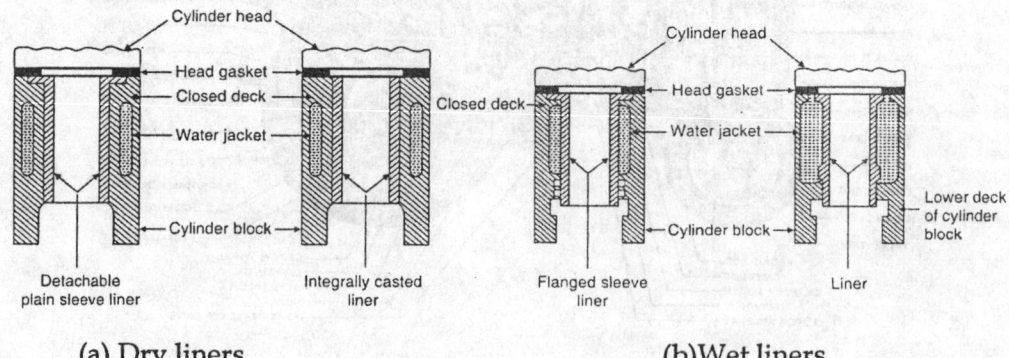

(a) Dry liners   (b)Wet liners

Fig. 5.3. Cylinder liners

1. Engine block; 2. Cylinder liners; 3. Cooling water; 4. Packing rings

A nickel chromium alloy steel of the following composition is much useful for liners of heavy, duty engines is given in Table 5.1

Table 5.1 Composition of lines

Name of constituents	Percentage
Iron	93.92 to 92.22
Carbon	3 to 3.5
Silicon	1.8 to 2.4
Maganese	0.5 to 0.8
Phosphorous	04. to 0.7
Sulphur	0.08
Chromium	0.3

Because it has following characteristics

(i)   It has capability to withstand working temperature and pressure.

(ii)   It has resistance to corrosion and wear

(iii)   It has very hardness with maximum flexibility

(iv)   It has high durability

(v)   It is cheaper.

5.2.2.2 Crank Case: The crankcase houses the revolving parts. These include, above all, the crankshaft and the camshaft. In the case of four-stroke engines, the oil filler pipe and the oil dipstick are arranged at the crank case in such a way that they are accessible from the outside. The crankcase of tractors a built in the unitired construction must be very sturdy, a requirement which is not raised in motor-car construction.

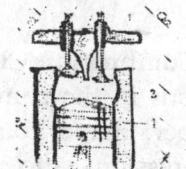

Fig. 5.4. Cooling water duets in the cylinder 1. Cooling water duct 2. Valves 3. Combustion chamber

5.2.2.3 Cylinder Head: The cylinder head is the top cover of the cylinder block. The combustion chambers, bore-holes for the above valve and enable threads holding the sparking plugs or and injection-nozzle holders are provided in the cylinder head.

The cylinder head is exposed to the high temperature produced in combustion to a particularly high degree. That is why cooling water passes through it as shown in Fig. 5.4.

Cylinder head is made of cast irion or aluminium alloy. The Ford motors composition of cylinder heaps and block is given in Table 5.2

Table 5.2 Composition of Cylinder Head & Block

Name of constituents	Percentage
Total carbon (C)	1.20 to 3.40
Silicon (Si)	1.80 to 2.10
Maganese (Mn)	0.60 to 0.80
Copper (Cu)	0.50 to 0.75
Phosphorus (P)	0.25 to 0.32
Sulphur (S)	0.10 (Maximum)

A heat-resisting gasket is inserted between cylinder head and cylinder block to produce a gas-tight seal between the two coolings. This gasket consists of heat-proof material which is exposed both the great head and high pressure. Further, the gasket prevents the penetration of cooling water into the combustion chambers and seals off the individual cylinder from each other as shown in Fig. 5.5

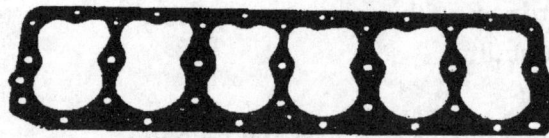

Fig. 5.5. Cylinder Head Gasket

5.2.3 Combustion Chamber: A combustion chamber is a space inside combustion reactions in the combustion chamber differ according to fuel type, combustion chamber. Shape, cooling system efficiency. Locations of spark plugs and valves. Compression ratio and the quality of the intake. Changes one of the most important of these factors is the combustion chambers shape. The combustion chambers shape primarily depends on the shape of the top of the piston and the shape of the pocket formed in the cylinder head. These shapes have a great affect on the control of combustion smoothness.

Classification of Combustion Chamber: They are classified as follows:

(i)   Direct in injection chamber

(ii)   Indirect injection chamber

(i)   **Direct Injection chamber:** Fuel is injected directly in the compressed air of the cylinder. The entire fuel does not burn quickly. Only a part of the fuel comes in contact with the heated air of the engine which gets ignited immediately. Starting the engine is easy in this case. The combustion of the wheel fuel takes place very slowly which result in low efficiency of high speed engines and high efficiency of low speed engines. It is shown in Fig. 5.6 (a)

(ii)   **Indirect Injection Chamber:** It may be of following types:

(a)   **Per Combustion Chamber:** There is small chamber above the cylinder of engine. The shape of chamber may be spherical or cylindrical. Fuel is injected directly in this chamber. At the time of the fuel injection the air of the chamber is distributed by the upward movement of the piston. As the combustion takes place, very high pressure is produced inside the small chamber which forces the unburnt fuel with high velocity into the main chamber. Starting the engine is not very easy due to relatively low temperatures of the cylinder due to the cooling effect of the surrounding wall which is shown in Fig. 5.6. (b).

(b)   Air cell chamber: It is a space provided in the piston or cylinder to trap air during the compression stroke. Later air blows out into the Combustion chamber. There is spherical cavity in the cylinder head, piston head, or the cylinder wall. Fuel is injected in the main chamber and combustion of th fuel takes place inside the cylinder. When the piston moves downward, the air cell discharges air in the forms of spray inside the cylinder which results in rapid burning of the fuel. It is shown in Fig. 5.6 (c).

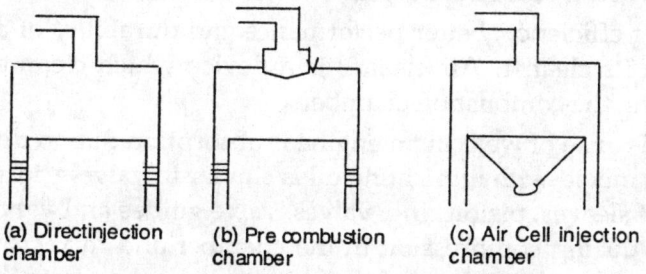

(a) Directinjection chamber   (b) Pre combustion chamber   (c) Air Cell injection chamber

Fig. 5.6 Combustion Chambers

Difference between Open and Divided Combustion Chamber

Open Combustion Chamber	Divided Combustion Chamber
1. Sensitive to spray characteristics	Insensitive to spray characteristics.
2. Can consume fuel of good ignition quality	Ability to use single hole injection nozzle and moderate pressure
3. Requires multiple hole injection nozzles and high injection pressure	Ability to use single-hole injection nozzle and moderate pressure.
4. Mixing of fuel and air is not so efficient and thus high fuel-air ratios are not feasible without smoke	Ability to use higher fuel-air ratios without smoke, due to proper mixing and consequent higher air utilization factor.
5. Cylinder construction is simple	More expressive cylinder construction.
6. Easy cold starting	Difficult cold starting
7. Open combustion chambers are thermally more efficient	It is thermally less efficient than open combustion chamber

5.2.4 Intake and Exhaust Ports: The intake and exhaust ports are the passages east in the cylinder head leading from the manifolds to the respective valves. In line engines have both intake and exhaust ports made on the same side of the engine. Often two of cylinder share the some port because of restricted spaced available.

5.2.5 Intake Manifold: The inlet manifold is required to deliver in to the cylinder either a mixture of fuel and air from the carburetor or only air from air cleaners.

The manifolds are made in one or two pieces either from cast iron or aluminium alloy. They are also blotted from separate castings into a single unit. The manifold flanges are connected to the cylinder block or cylinder head by means of asbestos-copper gasket studs and nuts.

5.2.6 Air Cleaner: An internal combustion engine uses large quantities of the air from atmosphere for combustion, the ratio is 15-17 kg of air for every kg of fuel burns. Unfilterd air may contain. Millions of particles of abrasive dust and other matter which could cause rapid wear of the combustion chamber.

The operating efficiency, better performance and durability of an engine depend mainly upon its cleaner. Air cleaner is a device which clean and filters the air before entering the combustion chamber.

The principal cause of wear in an engine is absorption due to dust formation. The effect of dust mixed with lubricating oil is similar to valve-griding paste. It causes rapid wear of sleeves, piston ring, valves, valve guides and valve seats whenever, the air leaks during compression in the chamber and mixes with the oil causes rapid wear of crank and crankshaft bearing and results into early engine overhauling becomes essential. Therefore, the air cleaner must be high efficient at any time especially when working in dusting condition like threshing and preparation dry lands.

Classification of Air Cleaner: There are many types of air cleaners depending upon the environment of use. The types commonly used in tractors are (i) oil wetted mesh type (ii) dry air type

(i) Oil Wetted Mesh Air Cleaner: It consists of a copper mesh or nylon wire, wetted with oil trap the dust particles from the air which are made to pass through it. This type, through very efficient, however, gets eloged with dust quickly, thus seriously affecting the air flow through it and reducing its efficiently in removing the fine particles of dust from the air.

(ii) Dry Air Cleaner: This type of air cleaner are two stage cleaners that contain three main parts (i) pre cleaner, main housing and cleaning element. These are sealed into one unit. The intake air is conducted through appropriate filtering materials of the dry filter like multi-wire netting, finest fabric or felt. They trap dust particles having or diameter in the order of 0.005 mm.

Dry air cleaners are mounted (i) vertically infront of tractor radiator and (ii) horizontally on the overhead engine. This type of air cleaner, are mounted in John Dears 2020 and Richard continental Crawler tractors.

110

Advantages of Dry Air Cleaner: The following are the main advantages of the dry air cleaner.

(i) Easy service (ii) More efficient at high speeds (iii) Good performance in gradient and in rough field (iv) Straw and chaff cause less restriction to air passage.

Disadvantage of Dry Air Cleaner:

(i) Contrail to maintain than or both type are because the filter elements require replacements very often.

(ii)   Some times, dust particles outer the cylinder.

5.2.7 Exhasut Manifold: The exhaust manifold collects exhaust gases from the exhaust parts of various cylinders and conducts thun from each end to a central exhust passage. It is usually made of cast iron. The exhaust manifolds are designed to avoid the overlapping of exhaust as much as possible, thus keeping the back pressure to a mimimum. This is often done by dividing the exhaust manifolds into or more braches so that no two cylinders will exhaust into the same branch at the same time.

5.2.8 Muffler: The muffler reduce the noise of the exhaust gases by reducing the pressure of the used gases by slow expansion and cooling. On the other hand, the muffler must not cause any appreciable restriction to the flow of oil that could raise the back pressure excessively. The muffler contains a number of chamber through which the gas flow. The gas is allowed to expand from the first passage into a much larger second one and then to a still larger third one and so on, to the final and the largest passage which is connected to the tail (outlet) pipe of the muffler.

5.3 Engine Moving Parts:

Power from the burnt gases in the combustion chamber is delivered to the crankshaft through the pistoin, piston pin, and connecting rod. The crank shaft changes the reciprocating motion of the piston in the cylinder to the rotary motion of the fly-wheel. i.e., carnk shaft, cam shaft, piston piston pin, connecting rod and flywheel etc that are the engine moving parts.

5.3.1 Crank Shaft: The crank shatt runs under the action of pistion through the connecting rod and crank pin located between carank webs or cheeks, and transmits the works from the piston to the driven shaft. The parts of crank shafts supported by and rotating inthe main bearing are called the jounals. Generall,y I-shaped cross-section of forged or cast steel is used which in shown in Fig. 5.7. The distance between crank pin axis and crank shaft axis is known as carnk throw as shown in Fig. 5.7.

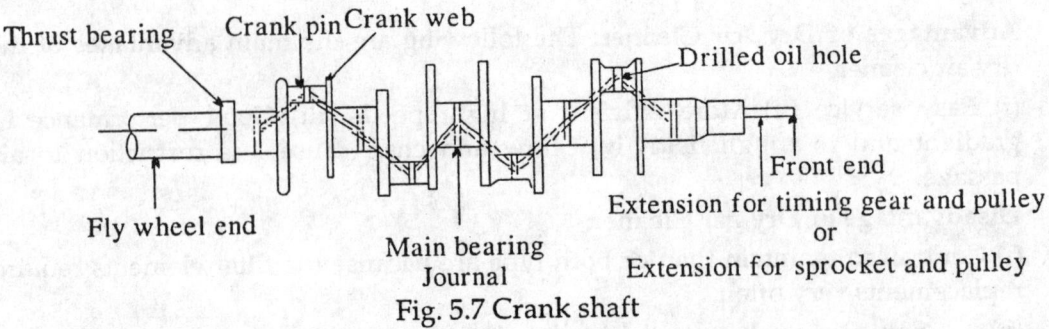

Fig. 5.7 Crank shaft

5.3.2 Piston

(A) Introduction:

It is a component, of the engine, which is cylinderical in shape, closed at the tip and open at the bottom. It transmits power of expanding gases to the connecting rod. Just below the piston head, there are grooves fro compression and oil, cast iron piston rings which press outword against the cylinder wall and forms seal between piston and cylinder, which is shown in Fig. 5.8.

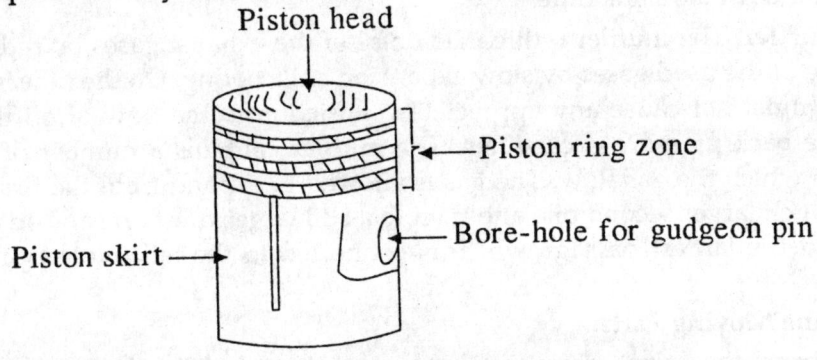

Fig. 5.8 Piston

(B) Function of Piston: The following are the main functions of the piston

(i)   To transmit the force of expansion to the crankshaft.

(ii)   To form a seal, so that the high pressure gases in the combustion chamber do not escape into the crank case.

(iii)   To serve as a guide and a bearing for samll end of the connecting rod.

(C) Material for Piston: A number of different alloys (alluminum alloy) are used for piston, but practically all contain small amount magmonial which improvestheir bearing propertiess. Generally piston, is made of cast iron or alluminium alloy.

Aluminium and its alloys are preferred mainly due to piston to the high heat conductivity of cast iron and no part of alluminium alloy piston gets as hot in service as the corresponding part of the cast iron.

(D) Piston carnk Kinematics: (i) Velocity of piston: Referring Fig. 5.9 let OC bethe crank PC the connectingrod. Consider crank rotates with angular velocity ω rad/s and crank turns through an angle θ_c from the dead centre (DC). Let x be the piston displacement from TDC after time t seconds.

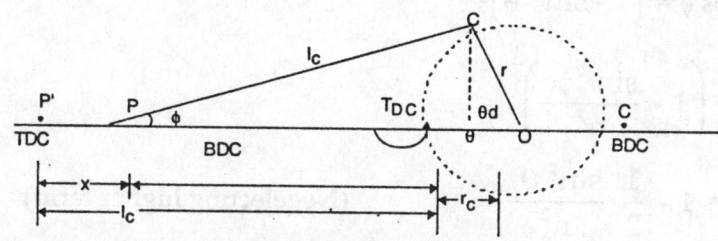

Fig. 5.9 Kinematic of Piston

Let l_c = Length of connecting rod

r_c = Radius of crank

ϕ = Inclinition of connecting rod to line of stroke PO

n = Ratio of length of connecting rod to the radius of crank $\left(\dfrac{l_c}{r_c}\right)$

velocity of piston

From Fig. 5.7

x = p'p = OP'-OP

(P'C' + C'O) - (PQ + QO)

= $(l_c + r_c) - (l_c \cos \phi + r \cos \theta_c)$

$\left[\because PQ = l_c \cos\phi \text{ and } QO = r_c \cos\theta_c\right]$

= $r_c (1 - \cos \theta_c) + l_c (1 - \cos \phi)$

= $r_c \left[(1 - \cos \theta c) + \dfrac{l_c}{r_c}(1-\cos\phi)\right]$

= $r_c [(1 - \cos \theta_c) + n (1 - \cos\phi)]$ (5.1)

From triangles CPQ and CQO

CQ = $l_c \sin \phi = r_c \sin \theta c$

or $\dfrac{l_c}{r_c} = \dfrac{\sin \theta_c}{\sin \phi}$

or $n = \dfrac{\sin \theta_c}{\sin\phi}$

$$\therefore \sin \phi = \frac{\sin \theta_c}{n} \qquad (5.2)$$

We know that,

$$\cos \phi = \left(1 - \sin^2 \phi\right)^{\frac{1}{2}}$$

$$= \left(1 - \frac{\sin^2 \phi c}{n^2}\right)^{\frac{1}{2}}$$

$$= 1 - \frac{1}{2} \frac{\sin^2 \theta_c}{n^2} \qquad \text{(Negelecting higher term)}$$

$$\text{or } 1 - \cos \phi = \frac{\sin^2 \theta_c}{2n^2} \qquad (5.3)$$

Substituting the value of $(1 - \cos \phi)$ in equation (5.1) we have

$$x = r_c \left[(1 - \cos \theta_c) + n \times \frac{\sin^2 \theta c}{2n^2}\right]$$

$$= r_c \left[(1 - \cos \theta_c) + \frac{\sin^2 \theta c}{2n}\right] \qquad (5.4)$$

Differeating equation (5.4) w.r.t. θ, we have

$$\frac{dx}{d\theta} = r_c \left[\sin \theta_c + \frac{1}{2n} \times 2 \sin \theta_c . \cos \theta_c\right]$$

$$= r \left[\sin \theta_c + \frac{\sin 2\theta_c}{2n}\right] \qquad (5.5)$$

$$\because (2 \sin \theta . \cos \theta = \sin 2\theta)$$

$$\therefore \text{Velocity of Piston P } (Vp) = \frac{dx}{dt} = \frac{dx}{d\theta} \times \frac{d\theta}{dt}$$

$$\text{or } V_p = \frac{dx}{d\theta} \times \omega$$

Substitating the value of $\frac{dx}{d\theta}$ from equation (5.5) we have

$$V_p = w r_c \left(\sin \theta c + \frac{\sin 2\theta_c}{2n}\right) \qquad (5.6)$$

It is noted that the values of θ_c at which the piston velocities are maximum or minim,um depand upon the connecting-rod-to-crank ratio. Usually the

114

pistionattains its maximum velocity at 75° to 80° from top dead centre (TDC) at which the angle between the crank arm and connecting rod is close to being perpendicular.

(ii) Aceleration of the Piston: Since the acceleration is the rate of change of velocity therefore acceleration of the piston P,

$$a_p = \frac{dV_p}{dt} = \frac{dV_p}{d\theta_c} \times \frac{d\theta_c}{dt}$$

$$= \frac{dV_p}{d\theta_c} \times \omega$$

Differentiating equation (5.6) with respect to θ, we have

$$\frac{dv_p}{d\theta_c} = \omega\, r_c \left[\cos\theta_c + \frac{\cos 2\theta_c \times 2}{2n} \right]$$

$$= \omega_c\, r_c \left[\cos\theta_c + \frac{\cos 2\theta_c}{n} \right]$$

Substituting the value of $\dfrac{dV_p}{d\theta}$ in the equation, we have

$$a_p = w.\, r_c \left[\cos\theta + \frac{\cos 2\theta_c}{n} \right] \times \omega$$

$$= \omega^2.\, r_c \left[\cos\theta_c + \frac{\cos 2\theta_c\, 2}{n} \right] \qquad (5.7)$$

Case I: When the carnk is at the TDC then $\theta_c = 0$

$$\therefore\ a_p = \omega^2.r_c \left[\cos\theta + \frac{\cos\theta}{n} \right]$$

$$= \omega^2.\, r_c \left[1 + \frac{1}{n} \right] \qquad (5.8)$$

Case II: When the crank is BDC then $\theta = 180$

$$\therefore\ a_p = \omega^2.r_c \left[\cos 180° + \frac{\cos 2 \times 180°}{n} \right]$$

$$= \omega^2\,.r_c \left[-1 - \frac{1}{n} \right] \qquad (5.9)$$

115

As the direction of motion is reversed at the BDC, therefore changing the sign of the above expression,

$$a_p = \omega^2 . r_c \left[1 + \frac{1}{n} \right] \qquad (5.10)$$

5.3.3 Piston Pins: It is hollow case hardened steel with precision finishing. It is used to join the connecting rod to the piston. It provides a flexiable or hinge like connection between the piston and the connecting rod. Normal piston pin clearance range from 0.0127 to 0.017^8 mm.

Piston pin holes located in the pistion are not centred but have on effect of approximately 1.57 mm from the piston slap centre line. Pin offset is designed to reduce the piston and noise which results from crossover action as the large end of the connecting rod swings part both upper and lower dead canters. piston pin is also known as gudgeon or wrist pin.

5.3.4. Piston Rings

(A) Introduction: Rings located in the groves of the piston usually near the top of the piston said to the be compression ring below the compression ring is said to be oil ring.

The functions of the rings are as follows:

(i)   It forces a gas tight combustion chamber for all positions of piston.

(ii)   It controls the flow of oil over the cylinder walls.

(iii)   It dissipates heat through cylinders wall.

(iv)   It reduces contact between cylinder wall and pistionwallfor preventing friction losses and excessive wera.

(B) Classification of pistion rings: The following are types of piston-ring

(a) Compression ring and (b) Oil control ring

(a) Compression Ring: Six or more compression rings at the top-depending upon the size and type of piston. The compression rings help to obtain maximum power from the combustion, chamber pressure by maintaining a seal with the cylinder wall while keeping the friction at maximaum. It is done with mechanical pressure.

Mechnical pressure of th ring results from the ring shape, material characteristics and expanders. It is usually plain, single piece. Chromium- faced and molybdenum faced piston rings are generally used. But under abrasive wear conditious, chromium faced rings have a better service life.

(b) Oil Rings: The oil ring uses steel rails with chromium. These rings are grooved eitehr in lowest groove above the piston pin or in a groove above the pistion scrit. It controls the distribution of lubrication oil in the cylinder and the piston. They prevent excessvie oil consumption also. Oil ring is provided with small holes through which excess oil returns back to the crank case chamber. Ring clearance is leansion the gap at the joint of thr ring, measured when the ring is inside the cylinder. The gap is ually .1 mm pe 200 mm diameter of the piston.

5.3.5 Connecting Rod

(A) Introduction: As the same implies, connects the piston through Gudgean pin at one end and crankshaftpin at the other end. The end connecting the piston is called small end and the other end is called big end. As the connecting rod is experinced to heavy force during power stroke, it is made of froged steel and the section is of the I-beam.

(B) Kinematic drop forged of Connecting Rod:

(i) Angular velocity: Consider the motion of a connecting rod and a crank as shown in Fig. From the geometry of the figure, we have,

$$C\theta = l_c \sin\phi = r_c \sin\theta c$$

or $\sin\phi = \dfrac{r_c}{l_c} \times \sin\theta c$

or $\sin\phi = \dfrac{\sin\theta_c}{n}$ \qquad\qquad (5.11) ,

Differentiating both sides with respect to time t,

$$\cos\phi \times \frac{d\phi}{dt} = \frac{\cos\theta_c}{n} \times \frac{d\theta_c}{dt}$$

$$= \frac{\cos\theta_c}{n} \times \omega$$

Since, the angular velocity of the connecting and PC is same as the angular velocity of point D with repeat to C and is equal to $\dfrac{d\phi}{dt}$, therefore angular velocity of the connecting rod

$$\omega_{PC} = \frac{d\phi}{dt} = \frac{\cos\theta_c}{n} \times \frac{\omega}{\cos\phi}$$

we know that,

$$\cos\phi = (1 - \sin^2\phi) = \left(1 - \frac{\sin^2\theta c}{n^2}\right)^{\frac{1}{2}}$$

$$\therefore \omega_{PC} = \frac{\omega}{n} \times \frac{\cos\theta_c}{(1 - \frac{\sin^2\theta_c}{n^2})^{\frac{1}{2}}}$$

117

$$= \frac{\omega}{n} \times \frac{\cos\theta_c}{\frac{1}{n}(n^2 - \sin^2\theta_c)^{\frac{1}{2}}}$$

$$w_{PC} = \frac{\omega\cos\theta c}{(n^2 - \sin^2\theta_c)^{\frac{1}{2}}} \qquad (5.12)$$

(ii) Angular Acceleration of the connecting rod PC,

α_{PC} = Angular acceleration of P with respect to C

$$= \frac{d(\omega_{PC})}{dt}$$

we know that

$$\frac{d\omega_{pc}}{dt} = \frac{d(\omega_{pc})}{d\nu_c} \times \frac{d\theta_c}{dt}$$

$$= \frac{d(\omega_{pc})}{d\theta} \times \omega \qquad (5.13)$$

Differentiating equation (i) we have

$$\frac{d(\omega_{pc})}{d\theta_c} = \frac{d\theta_c}{dt}\left[\frac{\omega\cos\theta c}{(n^2 - \sin^2\theta_c)^{1/2}}\right]$$

$$= \omega\left[\frac{(n^2 - \sin^2\theta_c)^{1/2}(-\sin\theta_c) + (n^2 - \sin^2\theta_c)^{1/2}\sin\theta c\cos^2\theta_c}{(n^2 - \sin^2\theta_c)}\right]$$

$$= -\omega\sin\theta_c\left[\frac{(n^2 - \sin^2\theta c) - \cos^2\theta c}{(n^2 - \sin^2\theta)^{3/2}}\right] \quad \text{(Dividing \& multiplying by } (n^2 -$$

$\sin^2{}_c)\ \frac{1}{2}$

$$= \left(\frac{-\omega\sin\theta_c}{(n^2 - \sin^2\theta_c)^{3/2}}\right)(n^2 - (\sin^2\theta + \cos^2\theta)$$

$$= \left(\frac{-\omega\sin\theta_c(n^2 - 1)}{(n^2 - \sin^2\theta_c)^{3/2}}\right)$$

$$\therefore \alpha_{pc} = \frac{d(\omega_{PC})}{d\theta} \times \omega$$

$$= \left(\frac{-\omega^2 \sin \theta_c \ (n^2 - 1)}{(n^2 - \sin^2 \theta_c)^{\frac{3}{2}}} \right) \qquad (5.14)$$

Notes: 1. Since, $\sin^2\theta_c$ is small a compared to n^2, therefore it may neglected. Thus, equations (5.12) and (5.13) are reduced to

$$w_{PC} = \frac{\omega \cos \theta_c}{n}$$

and $\alpha_{PC} = \dfrac{-\omega^2 \sin \theta_c (n^2 - 1)}{n^3}$ $\qquad (5.15)$

Note 2: Also in equation (iii) unity is small as compared to n^2, hence the term unity may be neglected.

$$\alpha_{pc} = \frac{-\omega^2 \sin \theta_c}{n} \qquad (5.16)$$

Prob 5.1 If the crank and connecting rod are 300 mm and 1 m long respectivty and the crank rotates at a constant speed of 250 rpm,; determine. The crank angle at which maximum velocity obtainable and maximum velocity of the piston.

Soln. Given $r_c = 300$ mm = 0.3 m; N = 250 rpm

$l_c = 1$m $\omega = 2\pi N$

$= 2 \times \pi \times 250$

$= 26.2$ rad/s

Let θc = crank angle fromthe top dead centre to BDC at which the maximum velocity obtained.

$$n = \frac{l_c}{r_c} = \frac{1}{0.3} = 3.33$$

we know that

$$V_p = \omega. r \left(\sin \theta_c + \frac{\sin 2\theta_c}{2n} \right) \qquad (i)$$

For maximum velocity of the piston,

$$\frac{dv_p}{d\theta} = 0$$

i.e., $\omega. r \left(\cos\theta + \dfrac{2\cos 2\theta}{2n} \right) = 0$

$n \cos \theta + 2 \cos\theta - 1 = 0$

119

∵ (cos 2θ = 2cos 2 θ - 1)

or 2 cos 2 θ + 3.33 - 1 = 0

$$\because \cos\theta = \frac{3.33 \pm \sqrt{(3.33)^2 + 4 \times 2 \times 1}}{2 \times 2} = 0.26$$

θ = 75°

Maximum velocity of the piston

Substituting the value of θ = 75° in equation (i), maximum velocity of the piston,\

$$V_p(max) = \omega.r_c \left[\sin 75° + \frac{\sin 150}{2 \times n} \right]$$

$$= 26.2 \times 0.3 \left[0.966 + \frac{0.5}{3.33} \right] m/s$$

=8.12 m/s

Prob 5.2. The crank and connecting rod of a diesel engine are 0.2 m and 1.0 m in lenght. The crank rotates at 180 rpm clockwise. Determine the velocity and acceleration of the piston when the crank is at 40 degrees from the inner dead centre piston. Also determine the piston of the crank for zero acceleration of the piston.

Soln. Given r_c = 0.2 m; l_c = 1.0 m; N = 180 rpm

θc = 40° ω = 2π N = 2 π × 180 = 18.85

Velocity of the piston

We know that

$$n = \frac{l_c}{r_c} = \frac{1}{0.2} = 5$$

∴ Velocity of the pistion $(V_p) = \omega. r \left[\sin\theta + \frac{\sin 2\theta}{2n} \right]$

$$= 18.85 \times 0.2 \left[\sin 40° + \frac{\sin 80°}{2 \times 5} \right]$$

Acceleration of the piston

$$a_p = \omega^2. r_c \left[\cos\theta_c + \frac{\cos 2\theta_c}{n} \right]$$

$$= (18.85)^2 \times 0.3 \left[\cos 40° + \frac{\cos 80}{5} \right]$$

Piston of the crank for zero acceleration of the piston

Let θ_1 = Piston of the crank from the inner dead centre for zero acceleration we know that,

$$a_P = \frac{\omega^2 r_c}{n} \ [n \cos \theta_1 + \cos 2\theta_1] = 0$$

$\therefore \ n \cos \theta_1 + 2 \cos 2\theta_1 = 0$

or $2 \cos^2 \theta_1 + 5 \cos \theta_1 - 1 = 0$

$$\therefore \ \cos \theta_1 = \frac{-5 \pm \sqrt{5^2 + 4 \times 1 \times 2}}{2 \times 2} = 0.1862 \ \text{(taking)}$$

$\theta_1 = 79.27°$ or $280.73°$ Ans.

(C) Force on the Reciprocating parts of the Engine: Neglecting the weight of the connecting rod.

The many forces acting on the reciprocating parts of a horizontal are shown in Fig. 5.10.

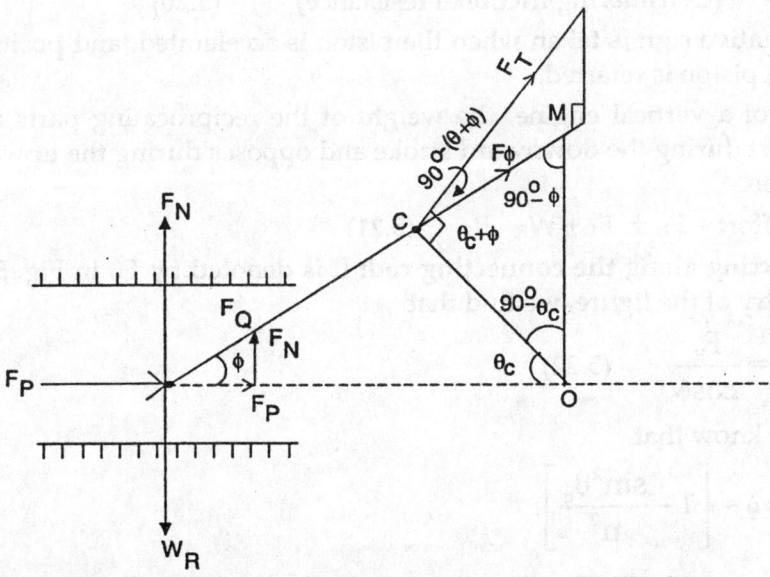

Fig. 5.10. Forces on the Reciprocating parts of an Engine

(i) Piston Effort:

Let

M_R = Mass of the reciprocating parts

W_R = weight of reciprocating parts = $m_R.g$

we know that acceleration of the piston

$$a_R = a_P = \omega^2 . \ r_c \left[\cos\theta_c + \frac{\cos 2\theta_c}{n} \right] \qquad (5.17)$$

Therefore, Accelerating force of Inertia of the reciprocating parts

$$F_1 = m_R . a_R$$

$$= m_R \omega^2 . r_c \left[\cos\theta_c + \frac{\cos 2\theta_c}{n} \right] \qquad (5.18)$$

It has been observed that in a horizontal engine, the reciprocating parts (piston) are accelerated from BDC to TDC and vice versa.

The inertial force due to acceleration of the reciprocating parts, opposes the force on the piston due to the difference of pressure in the cylinder on the two sides of the piston. On the other hand, the inertia force due retardation of the reciprocating parts, helps the force on the piston.

Therefore,

F_P = Net load on the piston = Inertia force

$= F_L \pm F_1$ (Neglecting frictional resistance) $\qquad$ (5.19)

$= F_L \pm F_1 - F_R$ (Considering frictional resistance) $\qquad$ (5.20)

Note: Negative sign is taken when the piston is accelerated, and positive sign is used when piston is retarted.

2. Incase of a vertical engine, the weight of the reciprocating parts assists the piston effort during the downward stroke and opposes during the upward stroke of the piston.

∴ Piston effort $= F_L \pm F_1 + W_R - R_F \qquad$ (5.21)

II. Force acting along the connecting rod: It is denoted by Fθ in Fig. 5.10. From the geometry of the figure, we find that

$$F_Q = \frac{F_P}{\cos\phi} \qquad (5.22)$$

we know that,

$$\cos\phi = \left[1 - \frac{\sin^2\theta_c}{n^2} \right]$$

$$\therefore F_Q = \frac{F_P}{\sqrt{1 - \dfrac{\sin^2\theta_c}{n^2}}} \qquad (5.23)$$

III: Thrust on the sides of the cylinder walls or normal reaction on the guide bars: It is denoted by F_N in Fig. 5.10. From the figures, we find that

$$F_N = F\theta \sin\phi = \frac{F_P}{\cos\phi} \times \sin\phi \qquad (5.24)$$

$$= Fp. \tan \phi \qquad (5.25)$$

$$\left[F_Q = \frac{F_P}{\cos\phi} \right]$$

(iv) Crank-pin effort and thrust on crank shaft bearings: The force acting on the connecting rad F_Q may be resolved in to the components, one perpenducular to the crank and the other along the crank. The component of F_Q perpendicular to the crank is known as crank-pin effort and it is denoted F_T in Fig. 5.10 The component of F_Q along the crank produces a thrust on the crank shaft bearings and is denoted by F_B in Fig. 5.10

Resolving F_Q perpendicular to crank,

$$F_T = F_Q \sin(\theta_c + \phi) = \frac{F_P}{\cos\phi} . \sin(Q_c + \phi) \qquad (5.26)$$

and resolving F_Q along the crank

$$F_B = F_Q. \cos(\theta_c+\phi) = \frac{F_P}{\cos\phi} . \cos(\theta_c + \phi) \qquad (5.27)$$

(v) Crank effort or turning moment or torque on the crank shaft: It is defined as the product of the crank pin effort (F_T) and the crank pin radius (r_c) Mathematically, it is given by following relationship,

$$\text{Crank Effort (T)} = F_T \times r = \frac{F_P \sin(\theta_c+\phi)}{\cos\phi} \times r$$

$$= \frac{F_P (\sin\theta_c. \cos\phi + \cos\theta_c. \sin\phi)}{\cos\phi} \times r$$

$$= F_P \left[\sin\theta_c + \cos\theta_c \times \frac{\sin\phi}{\cos\phi} \right] \times r$$

$$= F_P (\sin\theta_c + \cos\theta_c. \tan\phi) \times r \qquad (5.28)$$

we know that, $1 \sin\phi = r \sin\theta_c$

$$\sin\phi = \frac{r}{l} \sin\theta_c = \frac{\sin\theta_c}{n}$$

and $\cos\phi = \sqrt{1 - \sin^2\phi}$

$$= \sqrt{1 - \frac{\sin^2\theta_c}{n^2}}$$

$$= \frac{1}{n}\sqrt{n^2 - \sin^2\theta_c}$$

$$\therefore \tan\phi = \frac{\sin\phi}{\cos\phi} = \frac{\sin\theta_c}{n} \times \frac{n}{\sqrt{n^2 - \sin^2\theta_c}}$$

$$= \frac{\sin\theta}{\sqrt{n^2 - \sin^2\theta_c}} \qquad (5.29)$$

Substituting the value of tanϕ in equation (5.27) we have

$$T = F_P\left[\sin\theta_c + \frac{\cos\theta_c \cdot \sin\theta_c}{\sqrt{n^2 - \sin^2\theta_c}}\right] \times r$$

$$= F_P \times r\left[\sin\theta_c + \frac{\sin 2\theta_c}{2\sqrt{n^2 - \sin^2\theta_c}}\right] \qquad (5.30)$$

Note: Since $\sin^2\theta$ is very small as compared to n^2 therefore neglecting $\sin^2\theta$, we have,

$$T = F_P \times OM$$

From figures we have

$$OM = r\left[\sin\theta_c + \frac{\sin 2\theta_c}{2n}\right] \qquad (5.31)$$

Therefore, it is convenient to find OM instead of solving the large expression.

(A) Co-efficient of Fluctuation of speed: The difference between the maximum and minimum speeds during a cycle is called the maximum fluctuation of speed. The ratio of the maximum fluctuation of speed to the mean speed is called the co-efficient of fluctuation of speed. It is denoted by C_S and expressed as

$$C_s = \frac{\Delta N}{\overline{N}} \qquad (5.32)$$

Where, ΔN = Difference in maximum and minimum speeds,rpm

$$\Delta N = N_1 - N_2$$

$$\overline{N} = \frac{N_1 + N_2}{2}$$

Where,

N_1 and N_2 = Maximum and minimum speeds during the cycle, rpm

(i) Co-efficient of fluctuation of speed in terms of angular speeds:

$$C_s = \frac{\omega_1 - \omega_2}{\omega} = \frac{2(\omega_1 - \omega_2)}{\omega_1 + \omega_2} \qquad (5.33)$$

(ii) Co-efficient of flucutation of speed in terms of linear speed

$$C_s = \frac{v_1 - v_2}{v} = \frac{2(v_1 - v_2)}{v_1 + v_2} \qquad (5.34)$$

The co-efficient of fluctuation of speed is a limiting factor in the design of flywheel. It varies depending upon the nature of service to which the flywheel is employed.

Note: The reciprocal of the co-efficient of fluctuation of speed is known as co-efficient of steadiness and is denoted by m and expressed as

$$m = \frac{1}{C_s} = \frac{N}{N_1 - N_2} \qquad (5.35)$$

5.26 Flywheel: A flywheel used in machine serves as energy reservoir, which stores energy during the period when supply of energy is more than requirement and releases it during the period when the requirement of energy is more than supply flywheel is made of cast-iron and its main functions are as follows:

(i) It stores energy during power stroke and returns back the same energy during the idle strokes, providing an uniform rotary motion by virtue of the inertia.

(ii) It also carries ring gear that meshes with the piston of starting motor.

(iii) The rear surface of the flywheel serves as one of the pressure surfaces for the clutch plate.

(iv) Engine timing marks are usually stamped on the fly wheel, which helps in adjusting the timing of the engine.

(v) Sometime the flywheel serves the purpsoe of a pulley for transmitting power.

Note: A flywheel controls the speed variation caused by the fluctuation of engine turning moment during each cycle of operation.

5.2.7. Kinematics of Flywheel Energy Stored in a Flywheel: A flywheel is shown in Fig. It has been observed that when a flywheel absorbs energy, its speed increases and when it gives up energy, its speeds decreases.

Let

m_f = Mass of flywheel, kg

K = Radius of gyration of the flywheel, m

I = Mass Moment of inertia of the flywheel about its axis of rotation, kg m².

N_1 and N_2 = Maximum and minimum speeds differing the cycle, rpm

ω_2 and ω_2 = Maximum and minimum angular speeds during cycles, rad/s

$\overline{N}$ = Mean speed during the cycle rpm, $= \dfrac{N_1 + N_2}{2}$

$\overline{\omega}$ = Mean angular speed during the cycle, rad/s, $= \dfrac{\omega_1 + \omega_2}{2}$

C_s = Co-efficient of fluctuation of speed, $= \dfrac{\Delta N}{\overline{N}} = \dfrac{\Delta \omega}{\overline{\omega}}$

we know that the mean kinetic energy of the flywheel,

$$E = \frac{1}{2} I\omega^2 = \frac{1}{2} m_f k^2 \omega^2 \qquad (5.36)$$

As the speed of the flywheel changes from ω_1 and ω_2, the maximum fluctuation of energy,

ΔE = Maximum K.E. - Minimum K.E.

$$= \frac{1}{2} I. \omega_1^2 \frac{1}{2} \times I \omega_2^2$$

$$= \frac{1}{2} I. [\omega_1^2 - \omega_2^2]$$

$$= \frac{1}{2} (I. (\omega_1 + \omega_2) . (\omega_1 - \omega_2) \qquad (5.37)$$

$$= I. \overline{\omega} . (\omega_1 - \omega_2) \qquad (5.38)$$

$$= I \overline{\omega}^2 \left(\frac{\omega_1 - \omega_2}{\overline{\omega}} \right)$$

$$= I. \overline{\omega}^2 . Cs = m. K^2 \overline{\omega}^2 . C_s \qquad (5.39)$$

$$= 2 ECs \qquad (5.40)$$

The radius of gy ration (K) may be taken equal to the mean radius of the Rim (R), because the thickness of rim is very small as compared to the diameter of rim. Therefore, substituting K = R in equation (5.37), we have

$$\Delta E = m. R^2. \omega^2. C_s = mv^2. C_s \qquad (5.41)$$

where, v = mean linear velocity, m/s, ωR

Notes: 1. Since $\omega = 2\pi N/60$, therefore equation (5.36) may be written as

$$\Delta E = I \times \frac{2\pi N}{60} \left(\frac{2\pi N_1}{60} - \frac{2\pi N_2}{60} \right)$$

$$= \frac{4\pi^2}{3600} \times I \times N \, (N_1 - N_2) \qquad\qquad (5.42)$$

$$= \frac{\pi^2}{900} \, m \, K^2 \, N \, (\Delta N) \qquad\qquad (5.43)$$

$$= \frac{\pi^2}{900} \cdot m \, k^2 \, N^2 \cdot C_s \qquad\qquad (5.44)$$

In the above expression, only the mass moment of inertia of the flywheel rim (I) is considered and the mass moment of inertia of the hub and arms is neglected because the major portion of the mass of the flywheel is in rim and small portion is in the hub and arms. Also hub and arms are nearer to the axis of rotation therefore mass moment of inertia of the hub and arms is small

(C) Dimension of the Flywheel Rim:

Consider a rim of the flywheel as shown in Fig. 5.111

Let

D = Mean diameter of rim, m

R = Mean radius of rim, m

A = Cross-sectional area of rim, m²

ρ = Density of rim material, kg/m³

N_f = speed fo the flywheel, rpm

ω = Angular velocity of the flywheel rad/s

v = Linear velocity at the mean radius, m/s

$= \omega R = \pi \Delta N / 60$

σ = Tensile stress or hoop stress in N/m² due to centrifugal force.

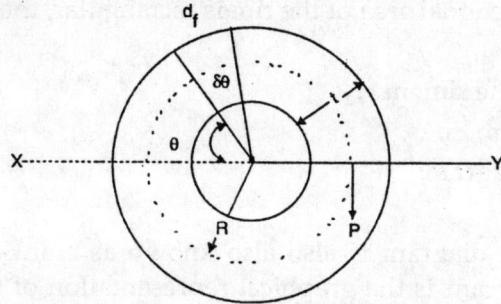

Fig. 5.11. Small Element of the Rim

Consider a small element of the rim as shwon in Fig. 5.11.

Let it subtends as angle $\delta\theta$ at the centre of the flywheel.

Volume of the small element = $A \times \delta\theta$

$\therefore$ Mass of the small element = $dm = \rho . A . R. \delta\theta$

and centrifugal forc on the element acting radially out wards,

$dF = dm, \omega^2. R = \rho .A. R^2. \omega^2 \delta\theta$

Vertical component of dF

= $dF \sin\theta = q . A . R^2. \omega^2 \delta\theta. \sin\theta$

$\therefore$ Total vertical upward force tending to burst the rim across the diameter XY.

$$= r. A.R^2.\omega^2. \int_0^\pi \sin\theta \, d\theta = \rho A R^2 \omega^2 (-\cos\theta)_0^\pi$$

$$= 2 \rho A R^2 \omega^2 \qquad (5.45)$$

This vertical upward force will produce tensile stress or hoop stress (also called centrifugal stress), and it is resisted by 2P, such that

$2P = 2\sigma A \qquad (5.46)$

Equating equations (5.43) and (5.44)

$2 \rho A R^2 \omega^2 = 2\sigma A$

$\sigma = \rho R^2 w^2 = \rho v^2$

$$\therefore v = \sqrt{\sigma/\rho} \qquad (5.47)$$

we know that mass of the rim,

m = Volume x density = $\pi DA\rho$

$$A = \frac{m}{\pi. D .\rho} \qquad (5.48)$$

From euation (5.47) and (5.48), we may find the value of the mean radius and cross-sectional area of the rim.

Consider the cross-sectional area of the rim is rectangular, then

A = b xt

Where b = Width of the rim, m

t = Thickness of the rim, m

Turning Moment Diagram:

Introduction:

The turning moment diagram is also also known as crank-effort diagram. The turning moment diagram is the graphical representation of the turning moment or crank-effort for various positions of the crank. It is plotted on cartesion coordinates, in which the turning moment is taken as the ordinate and crank angle as abscissa.

(i) Turning Moment Diagram for a Four Stroke Cycle Internal Combustion Engine: It is shown in Fig. 5.12. The vertical ordinate represents the turning moment and the horizontal ordinate represents the crank angle.

From equation (5.28), we have that the turning moment on the crankshaft.

$$T = Fp \times r \left[\sin \theta_c + \frac{\sin^2 \theta_c}{2\sqrt{n^2 - \sin^2 \theta_c}} \right] \qquad (5.49)$$

From the above the expression, we see that the turning moment (T)

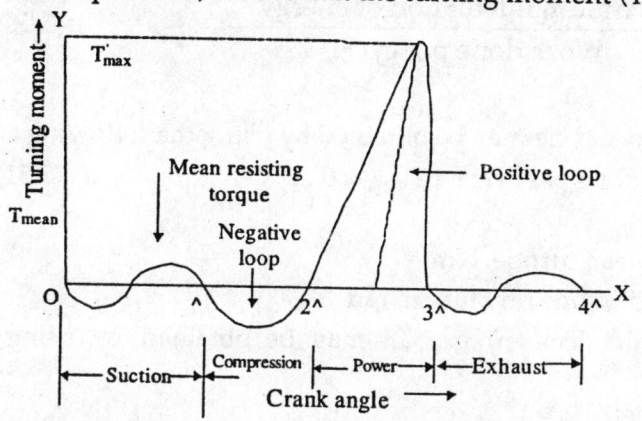

Fig. 5.12. Turning Moment Diagram

is zero, when the crank angle is zero. It is maximum when the crank angle is 90° and it is again zero when crank angle is 180°. Since the work done is the product of the turning moment and the angle turned, therefore, the area of the turning moment diagram represents the work done per revolution. In actual practice,the engine is around to work against the mean resisting torque.

Notes: 1. Accelerating torque on the rotating parts of the engine is expressed as T - T_{mean}

2. If (T-T_{mean}) is positive then flywheel accelerates and if (T-Tmean) is negative then the flywheel retards. We know that in four stroke cycle internal combustion engine, there is one power stroke after the crank has turned through two revolutions. i.e. 720°.

Since the pressure inside the engine cylinder is less than the atmostpheric pressure during the suction stroke, therefore a negative loop is formed as shown in Fig. During the compression stroke, the work is done on the gases, therefore a higher negative loop is obtained. During expansion or power stroke, the fuel burns and the gases expand, therefore a large positive loop is obtained. In the stroke, the work is done by the gases. During exhaust, the work is done on the gases, therefore a negative loop is formed.

(E) Fluctuation of Energy: The variation of energy above and below the mean resisting torque line are called fluctuations of energy and the differences between the maximum and the minimum energies is known as maximum fluctuation of energy.

(F) Co-efficient of fluctuation of Energy: It may be defined as the ratio of the maximum fluctuation of energy to the work done per cycle. Mathematically, co-efficient of fluctuation of energy. It is denoted by C_e and expressed as

$$C_e = \frac{\text{Maximum fluctuation of energy}}{\text{Work done per cycle}} \qquad (5.50)$$

The work done per cycle may be obtained by using the following two relations:

1. Work done per cycle = $T_{mean} \times \theta$, J $\qquad$ (5.51)

Where,

T_{mean} = mean toruqe, Nm

q = Angle turned in one revolution, rad

The Mean torque (T_{mean}) in Nm may be obtained by using the following relation:

$$T = \frac{P \times 60}{2 \pi N} = \frac{P}{\omega} \qquad (5.52)$$

where,

P = Power transmitted, W

N = Speed, rpm

ω = Angular velocity, rad/s

2. The work done per cycle may also be obtained by using the following relation:

$$\text{Work done per cycle} = \frac{P \times 60}{n} \qquad (5.53)$$

n = number of working strokes per minute

i.e.; n = N for steam engine and two stroke I.C. engines

$$n = \frac{N}{2} \text{ for four stroke I.C. engine}$$

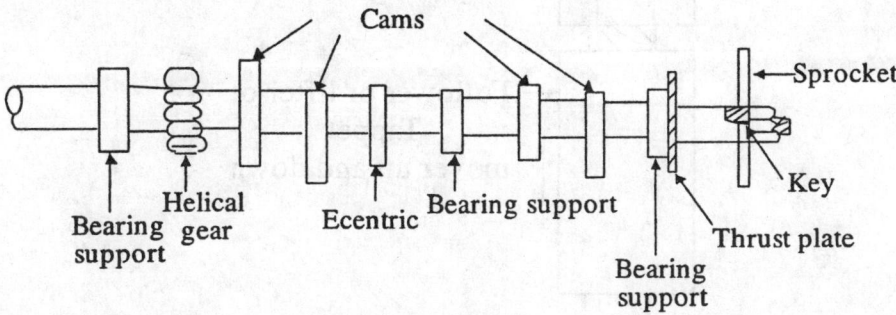

Fig. 5.13

Cam Shaft: The cam shaft provides a means of actuating the opening and controlling the period before closing, both from the inlet as well as the exhaust vales. It also provides a drive for the ignition distributor, oil pump and mechanical fuel pump. The cam shaft consists of a number of cams of suitable angular position for operating the valves at approximate timings relative to the piston movement and in a sequence according to the firing order as shown in Fig. 5.13. There are two lobes on the cam shaft of each cylinder of the engine, one to operate the intake valve and to other to operate the exhaust valve. The number of integral bearing journals support the shaft in bearing. Cam shaft bearing journals are always larger than the cam lobes so that the cam shaft may be installed in the engine through the cam bearings. Usually, there is integral spiral toothed gear on the camshaft to drive the distributor and other oil pump as shown in Fig. 5.14. The fuel pump is operated from an integral eccentric. Endwise movement of the camshaft is limited by a thrust plate between the front bearing journal and the drive gear or the sprocket.

The camshaft is forged from alloy steel or cast from hardenable cast iron. A typical cast iron alloy for a camshaft would consist of 3.3% carbon, 2% silicon, 0.65% mangnese, 0.65% chromium, 0.25% molybodenum (Mo) and the remaining iron.

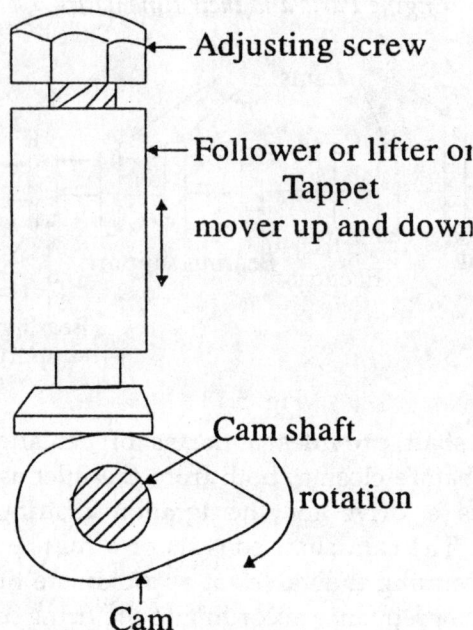

Adjusting screw

Follower or lifter oɪ
Tappet
mover up and down

Cam shaft

rotation

Cam

Fig. 5.14

Cam Shaft Drive: The camshaft rotates at half the crank shaft speed so as to open and close one in every two revolution of the crankshaft. The drive from crankshaft to the camshaft may be either chain or sprocket drive. Fig. 5.15 (a) or Fig. 5.15 (b) where camshaft gear or sproket wheel is twice as large as camshaft gear or gears of the cam shaft and the crankshaft to ensure correct valve twing. In a chain-drive a separate idles gear may be provided. A long chaindrive tends to whip in order to avoid it a tensioning device (chain tensioner) is implemented which may be automatic type. Gears drive, on the other hand, need no tensioner, but are noisy and are suitable only for camshaft mounted close to the crankshat. Gear type is not suitable for overhead camshaft. The latest type of drive is by means of a toothed rubber belt, which is made of rubber moulded on to a non stretching chord. Such belts operating relatively silently, do not need any lubrication.

Cam: A cam is a rotating machine systemwhich gives reciprocating motion or another component or element known as follows (knife edge follower, roller follower, plate faced flower, spherical faced follower) as shown in Fig. The cam and the follower have a line contact and constitute a higher pair. Cams are rotated by a shaft with uniform speed whereas the follower speed is predetermined and will be according to the shape of the cam. Inlet and exhasut valves of internal combustion engines are operated by cam. Generally raidal same are used in internal combustion engine.

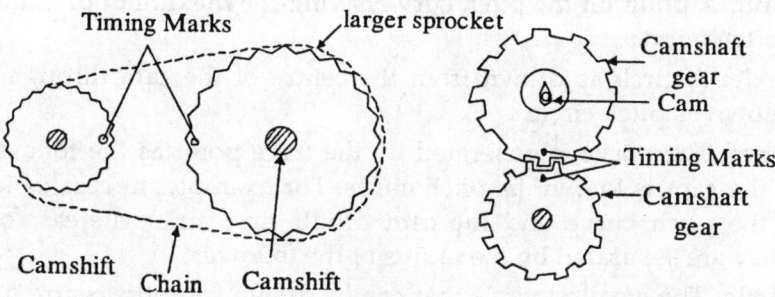

Fig. 5.15

Radial or Disc Cam: In radial cam, the follower oscillates in a direction perpendicular to the cam axis. The cams shown in Fig. 15.16 all radial cams.

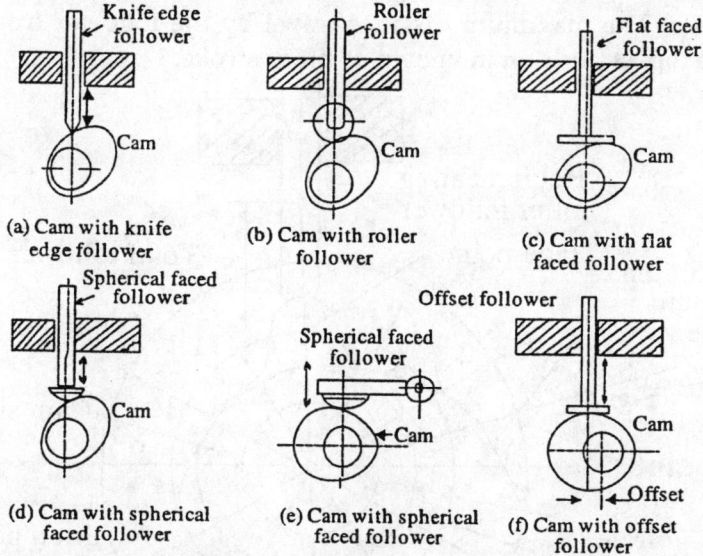

Fig. 5.16. Classification of Followers

Fig. 15.17 shows related to redial cam.

Terminology Related to Radial Cam:

1. Base Circle: Smallest circle that that can be drawn to the cam profile is called base circle.

2. Trace Point: It is the contact point between cams and follower and considered as reference point on the follower into predict the pitch curve depending upon the shape of cam. Such as, in case of knife, edge follower, the knife edge is representd as trace point.

3. Pressure Angle: The angle between the direction of follower motion and normal to pitch curve is known as pressure angle.

Note: If the pressure angle is too large, a reciprocating follower will jam in its bearings.

4. Pitch point: A point on the pitch curve having the maximum pressure angle is known as pitch point.

5. Pitch circle: A circle is drawn from the centre of the cam through the pitch points is known as pitch circle.

6. Pitch curve: The curve is generated by the trace point as the follower moves relative to the cam is known as pitch curve. For example, in case of knife edge follower, the pitch curve and the cam profile are same whereas for a roller follower, they are separated by the radius of the follower.

7. Prime circle: The smallest circle that can be drawn from the centre of the cam and tangent to the pitch curve. For example, in case of knife edge follower and flat edge folower, the prime circle and the base circle are same but for a roller follower, the prime circle is larger than the base circle by the radius of roller.

8. Lift or stroke: The maximum distance travel by the follower from its lowest position to the topest position in known as lift or stroke.

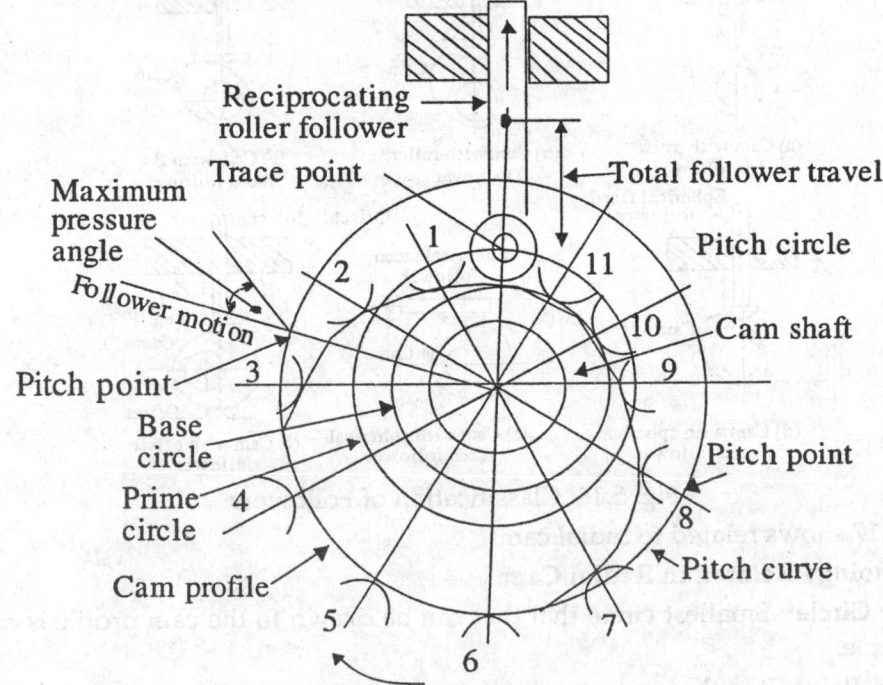

Fig. 15.17 Redial cam

Tangent Cam with Reciprocating Roller of Follower: When the flanks of the cam are straight and tangential to the base circle and nose circle, then the cam is called tangential cam as shown in Fig. They are symmetrical about the centre line of the cam shaft. Inlet and exhaust valves of internal combustion engines are operated by such type of cam.

Kinetmatics of Tangent Cam with Reciprocating Roller Follwer:

Case I: When the roller has contact with the straight flanks:

Let,

r_B = Radius of the base circle

r_R = Radius of the roller

r_N = Radius of the nose

α = Angle of contact

θ = Angle truned by the cam from the begining of the roller displacement.

ϕ = Angle turned by cam for contact roller with the straight flank.

ω = Angular velocity of cam

Fig. 15.18. shows a roller having contact with straight flanks. The point O and point K are the centre of cam shaft and nose respectively. EG and PQ are striaght flanks of cam. When the roller is in lowest position, the centre of roller lies at B on the pitch curve. Consider the cam has turned through an angle θ (less than tanθ, since the cam is assumed to stationary, the angle θ is turned by roller), for the roller, to have contact at any point (say F) between the straight flanks EG. The centre of roller at this stage lies at C. Therefore displacement (or lift or stroke) of the roller from its lowest position in given by

$$x = OC - OB = \frac{OB}{\cos\theta} - OB$$

$$= OB \left(\frac{1 - \cos\theta}{\cos\theta}\right)$$

$$= (r_B + r_R) \left(\frac{1 - \cos\theta}{\cos\theta}\right)$$

$$[\because OB = OE + EB = r_B + r_R] \qquad (5.54)$$

Differenting eqquation: with respect to t, we have velocity of the follower,

$$v = \frac{dx}{dt} = \frac{dx}{d\theta} \times \frac{dv}{dt} = (r_B + r_R) \left(\frac{\sin\theta}{\cos^2\theta}\right) \frac{d\theta}{dt} \qquad (5.55)$$

$$= \omega (r_B + r_R) \left(\frac{\sin\theta}{\cos^2\theta}\right) \left(\because \frac{d\theta}{dt} = \omega\right) \qquad (5.56)$$

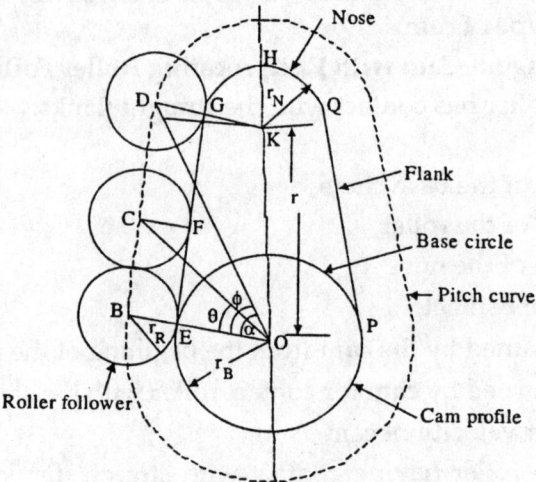

Fig. 15.18 Tangent cam with reciprocating roller having
contact with straight flanks

From equation (ii) we see that when Q increases, $\sin\theta$ increases and $\cos\theta$ decreases i.e., $\dfrac{\sin\theta}{\cos^2\theta}$ increases. Thus the velocity is maximum where θ is maximum. This happens when $\theta = \phi$

$\therefore$ Maximum velocity of the folower,

$$V_{max} = w\,(r_B + r_R)\left(\frac{\sin\phi}{\cos^2\phi}\right) \qquad (5.57)$$

Acceleration of folower: Now differentiating equation (5.54) with respect to t, we have acceleration of the follower,

$$\alpha = \frac{dv}{dt} = \frac{dv}{d\theta} \times \frac{d\theta}{dt}$$

$$= \omega\,(r_B + r_R)\left(\frac{\cos^2\theta.\cos\theta - \sin\theta\,.\,2\cos\theta\,(-)\sin\theta}{\cos^4\theta}\right)\left(\frac{d\theta}{dt}\right)$$

$$= \omega 2\,(r_R + r_R)\left(\frac{\cos^2\theta. + 2\sin^2\theta}{\cos^3\theta}\right)$$

$$= \omega^2\,(r_B + r_R)\left(\frac{\cos^2\theta. + 2(1 - \sin^2\theta)}{\cos^3\theta}\right)$$

$$= w^2\,(r_B - r_R)\left(\frac{2 - \cos^2\theta}{\cos^2\theta}\right) \qquad (5.58)$$

Minimum and maximum accleration of follower are

$$a_{min} = \omega^2 (r_B + r_R) \qquad (5.59)$$

$$a_{max} = \omega^2 (r_B + r_R) \frac{2-\cos^2\phi}{\cos^3\phi} \qquad (5.60)$$

Case II: When the roller contact with Nose: Fig. 5.19 shows a roller having contact with circular nose at G. The centre of roller lies at D on the pitch curve. The displacement in computed from the top position of the roller i.e., centre of roller lies at J on the pitch curve.

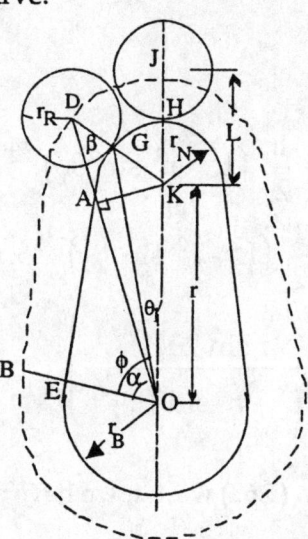

Fig. 5.19. Tangent Cam with Reciprocating Roller Follower Having Contact with the Nose.

The displacement of roller is given by

$$x = OJ - OD = OJ - (OA + AD)$$
$$= (OK + KJ) - (OA + AD)$$

Substituting OK = r and KJ = KH + HJ = r_N + r_R, we have,

$$x = (r + L) - (OK \times \cos \theta_1 + DK \cos \beta)$$
$$= (r + L) - (r \cos\theta_1 + L \cos \beta)$$
$$= L + r - r \cos\theta_1 - L \cos \beta$$
$$[DK = KJ = r_N + r_R = L]$$

Now from right angled triangled OAK and DAK

$$AK = DK \sin \beta = OK \sin \theta_1$$
$$\text{or } L \sin \beta = r \sin \theta_1 \qquad (5.61)$$

Squaring equation (5.59) both sides, we have

$$L^2 \sin^2 \beta = r^2 \sin^2 \theta_1$$

or $L^2 (1 - \cos^2 \beta) = r^2 \sin^2 \theta_1$,

or $L^2 - L^2 \cos^2 \beta = r^2 \sin^2 \theta_1$

or $L^2 \cos^2 \theta = L^2 - r^2 \sin^2 \theta_1$

$\therefore L \cos \beta = (L^2 - r^2 \sin^2 \theta_1)^{\frac{1}{2}}$

Substituting the values of $L \cos \beta$ in equation (i), we have

$$x = L + r - r \cos \theta_1 - (L^2 - r^2 \sin^2\theta_1)^{\frac{1}{2}} \qquad (5.62)$$

Differntiating equatin (5.62) with respect to K, we have

velocity of follower,

$$v = \frac{dx}{dt} = \frac{dx}{d\theta} \times \frac{d\theta}{dt}$$

$$= r \times -\sin\theta_1 \times \frac{d\theta_1}{dt} - \frac{1}{2} \left(L^2 - r^2 \sin^2\theta_1\right)^{-\frac{1}{2}} (-r^2 \times 2 \sin\theta_1 \cos\theta_1) \frac{d\theta_1}{dt}$$

$$= r \times \sin\theta_1 \times \frac{d\theta_1}{dt} + \frac{1}{2} \left(L^2 - r^2 \sin^2\theta_1\right)^{-\frac{1}{2}} \times r^2 \times \sin 2\theta_1 \times \frac{1}{2}$$

$$= \omega \times r \left(\sin\theta_1 + \frac{r \sin 2\theta_1}{2\left(L^2 - r^2 \sin^2\theta_1\right)^{\frac{1}{2}}} \right) \left(\because \frac{d\theta_1}{dt} = \omega \right)$$

(5.63)

Now differentiating equation (5.63) w.r.t. t, we have acceleration of follower,

$$a = \frac{dv}{dt} = \frac{dv}{d\theta_1} \times \frac{d\theta}{dt}$$

$$= \left(\cos\theta_1 + \frac{(L^2 - r^2 \sin\theta_1)^{\frac{1}{2}} (r \times 2\cos\theta_1 + r\sin 2\theta_1 \times \frac{1}{2}(L^2 - r^2 \sin^2\theta_1)^{-\frac{1}{2}} (r^2 \times 2\sin\theta_1\cos\theta_1))}{2\left(L^2 - r^2 \sin^2\theta_1\right)} \right) \frac{d\theta}{dt}$$

$\frac{d\theta_1}{dt}$

Substituting $\frac{d\theta_1}{dt} = \omega$ and multiplying the numerator and denominator of second term by $(L^2 - r^2 \sin^2\theta)$, we have

$$a = w^2.r \left[\cos\theta_1 + \frac{L^2 - r^2 \sin^2\theta_1 . \cos^2\theta + \frac{1}{2} \times r^3 \left(2\sin\theta_1 . \cos\theta_1\right)^2}{2 \left(L^2 - r^2 \sin^2\theta_1\right)^{\frac{3}{2}}} \right]$$

$$= w2.r \left[\cos\theta_1 + \frac{\cos\theta.r\cos\theta_1((1-2\sin^2\theta_1)+2r^3\sin^2\theta_1(1-\sin^2\theta_1)}{2(L^2-r^2\sin^2\theta_1)^{3/2}} \right]$$

$$= w^2.r \left[\cos\theta_1 + \frac{L^2.r.\cos2\theta_1+r^3\sin^4\theta_1}{(L^2-r^2\sin^2\theta_1)^{3/2}} \right] \quad (5.62)$$

Notes:

1. Since θ_1 is measured from the top position of the roller, therefore the roller to have contact at the apex of the nose (i.e. at point H), then $\theta_1 = 0$, and for the roller to have contact where straight flank merges into a nose (i.e., at point (G), then $\theta_1 = \alpha - \phi$

2. The velocity is zero at H and maximum at G.

3. The acceleration is maximum at H and maximum at G.

Valve: Valve is a device which is used to open and close the passage.

The engine valves admit the air fuel mixture in the engine cylinder and forces out the exhaust gases at correct timing, following are the three types of engine valve

(i) Poppet valve or Mushroom valve

(ii) Sleve valve and (iii) Rotary valve

Poppet Valve: Its motion is popping up and down

This is also called mushroom valve because of its shape like mushroom. It consits of a head and stem as shown in Fig. 5.20. The following are the main advantages of poppet valve

(i)   Simplicity of construction

(ii)   These are self contering

(iii) These are free to rotate about the stem in new position.

Generally the inlet valves are larger than the exhaust valve because speed of incoming charge is less than the velocity of exhaust gases, exhaust gases leave at high pressure as well as have high density. Generally inlet valve and exhaust valves are 45% and 38% of the cylinder bore respectively.

Valve Tappet Clearance: A slight clearance is kept between the valve tappet and the valve stem tip in the case of side valve mechanism and between the rocker arm end and valve stem in the case of over head mechanism, and is known as valve tappet clearance or simply tappet clearance or valve lash. This clearance allows for expansions o the valve stem as the engine heated. If sufficient clearance is not given,the vlave will not sit properly. The engine becomes heated which will cause power and lifting of the value. The exhaust valve has more clearance than the inlet valve & valves of tappet clearnce depends upon length of the valve stem, material of the valve and temperature at which valves work.

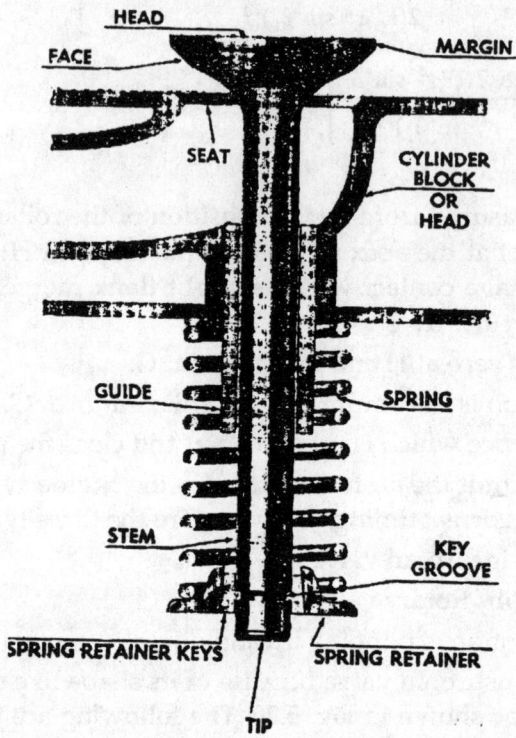

Fig. 5.20. Poppet valve or Mushroom Headed valve

Note: The clearance between the valve guide and stem is from 0.378 mm to 0.882 mm in the intake valves and 0.063 mm to 0.1008 mm in the exhaust valve.

Valve operating Mechanism

The following are main types of valve operating mechanism:

(i) Over head valve mechanism

(ii) Side valve mechanism

Over Head Valve mechanism: Fig. 5.21 shows the valve mechanism to opearate the valve when it is in the cylinder head (i.e., I and F-head design). The components of over head mechanism is shown in Fig. 5.21 As the cam rotates, it lifts the valve tappet of the lifter which actuates the push rod. The push rod rotates the rocker arm about a shaft which is called rocker arm shaft. This motion of rocker arm causes one need of it to push down on the valve stem to open the valve, thus connecting the valve part with combustion chamber.

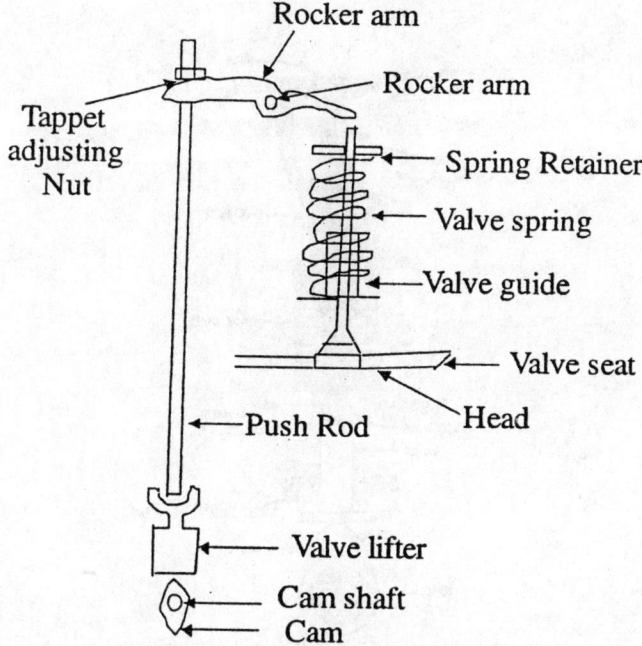

Fig. 5.21. Showing Head Mechanism

In this mechanism the valve tappet clearance is between the rocker arm end and the valve stem tip. It is adjusted by means of an adjusting hut on the rocker arm end that connect the push rod.

Side Valve Mechanism: Fig. 5.22 shows the valve mechanism to operate the valve, when it is in engine block (i.e., L, F and T design). The valve stems slides up and down in the valve stem guide, which acts as as slipper bearing. It also prevents the gases from passing through the valve part to the chamber of the engine blocks.

Valve spring is fitted between the engine block and spring retainer,which keeps the valve closed tightly on the valve seal, untill lifted by the valve tappet by the rotation of the cam. The tappet or lifter is held betwen guids which is generally a part of engine block, adjusting screw is provided on the tappet to adjust the clearance between the upper end of the tappet and the bottom of the valve stem As the cam rotates, it lifts the tappets which lifts the valve to open position, thus connecting the valve part to the combustion chamber valve-seat-inserts are fitted on the valve seat. These inserts are in the form of ring tapered grounded to suit the valve fous and made of special alloy steel. They reduce wear and can be replaced when worn out.

Note: Most of today's tractors use an overhead valve placed design.

141

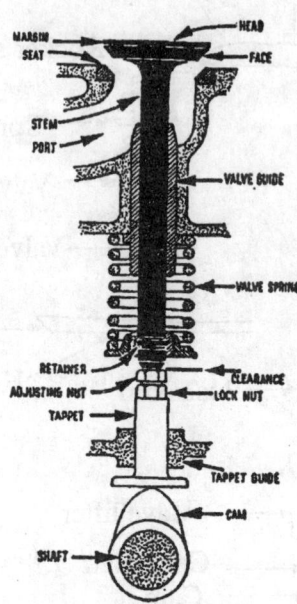

Fig. 5.22. Showing Side Valve Mechanism

Face Angle: The valve face angle is generally kept 30° or 45°. A smaller face angle provides greater valve operating for a given left but poor sealing because of the reduced sealing pressure for a given valve spring loaded. Exhaust valve operaters under relatively more reverse conditions on account of higher temperature involves.

Requirement of Exhaust Valve Material: The following the main requirements of exhaust valve material,

(i)   High strength and hardness to resist loads.

(ii)   High heat strength and hardness to face wearing.

(iii) High fatigue resitance

(iv)   High corrosion resistant

(v)   Less co-efficient of thermal expansion.

(vi)   High thermal conductivity for better heat dissipation.

Valve Cooling: The exhaust valve temperature in modern engines reach very high values of the order of 750°C. In heavy duty engines, it may still be higher, therefore cooling of exhaust valves becomes very important, to arrange this cooling water jackets as near the valve possible. In many cases, nozzles are directed towards the hot spot caused by the exhaust valve.

In heavy duty engines, sodium cooled valve are used. Sodium is a high conductiviting metal which melts at 105°C. Thus sodium is in liquid state at the operating temperature. Sodium is filled up to about 40% volume of the hollow stem of the valve. When the valve is operating, the liquid sodium moves up and down in the hollow stem. When it goves up it absorbs heat from the hot valve head and on coming back down it gives the same hat to the stem, to the cylinder block and from there to the cooling water circulating in water jackets. This arrangement cools the valve by about 100°C.

Valve Timing: The opening and closing times vary, depending on the type of the engine and are stated in the operating instruction by the manufacturer. These times are given in degrees or mm and read, for example, as follows,

The inlet valve opens 10° before the dead-centre

The inlet valve closes 50° after bottom dead-centre

The exhaust valve closes 10° after top dead centre

The exhaust valve opens 50° before bottom-dead centre

The following diagram shows the approximate time for opening and closing valves and the period they remains open as shown in Fig. 15.23

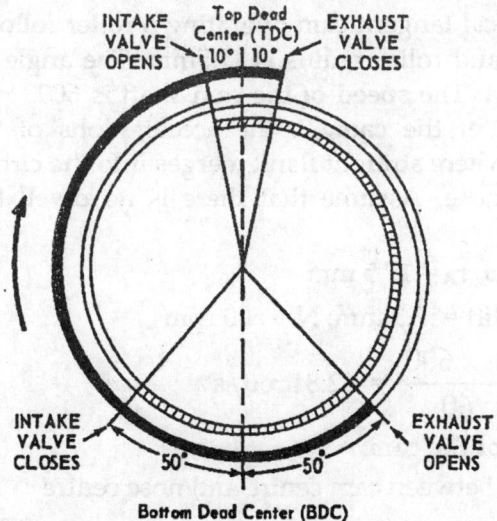

Fig. 5.23. Valve Timing Diagrams of A 4-stroke engine

Prob. 5.1 The equation of the turning moment curve of a three crank engine is (5000 + 15000 sin3θ) Nm, where q is the crank angle in radians. The moment of inertia of the flywheel is 1000 kg m² and mean speed is 300 rpm power compute of the engine.

Soln: Given T = (5000 + 1500 sin 3θ) Nm, I = 1000 kg m²

$\qquad$ N = 300 rpm or ω = 2π × 300/60 = 31.42 rod/s

$\qquad$ 1. Power of the engine

we know that word done per revolution

$$= \int_0^{2\pi} (5000 + 1500 \cos 3\theta) \, d\theta$$

$$= \left[5000 - \frac{1500 \cos 3\theta}{3} \right]_0^{2\pi} = 10,000 \, \pi \text{ Nm}$$

∴ Mean resisting torque,

$$T_{mean} = \frac{\text{Work done per revolution}}{2\pi}$$

$$= \frac{10,000 \, \pi}{2\pi}$$

$$= 5000 \text{ Nm}$$

we know that power of the engine

$$P = T_{mean} \, \omega = 5000 \times 31{:}42 = 157100 \text{ W}$$

$$= 157.1 \text{ kW Ans.}$$

Prob. 5.2 In a symetrical tangent cam operating a roller follower the least radius of the cam is 30 mm and roller radius is 17.5mm. The angle of ascent is 75⁰ and the total lift is 17.5mm. The speed of the cam shaft is 6000 rpm. Calculate 1. the principal dimensions of the cam; 2. the accelerations of the follower at the beginning of the lift, where straight flank merges into the circular nose and at the apex of the circular nose. Assume that there is no dwell between ascent and descent.

Solⁿ. Given $r_B = 30$ mm, $r_R = 17.5$ mm

$\alpha = 75°$, Total lift =17.5 mm; N = 600 rpm

$$\omega = \frac{2\pi N}{60} = \frac{2\pi \times 600}{60} = 62.84 \text{ rod/s}$$

Principle dimension of the cam:

Let r = OK = Distance between cam centre and nose centre

r_N = Nose radius, and

ϕ = Angle of contact of cam with straight flanks

From the geometry of Fig. 15.18.

$$r + r_N = r_B + \text{total lift}$$

$$= 30 + 17.5 = 47.5 \text{mm}$$

$$\therefore r = 47.5 - r_N$$

Also OE = OP + PE

or $r_B = OP + r_N$

$$OP = r_B - r_N = 30 - r_N \qquad (11)$$

Now from right angled triangle OKP

$$OP = OK \times \cos \alpha$$

or $30 - r_N = (47.5 - r_N) \cos 75°$

$$(47.5 - r_N) \times 0.2588$$

$$= 12.3 - 0.2588\, r_N$$

$$\therefore r_N = 23.88 \text{ mm Ans.}$$

and $r = OK = 47.5 - r_N - 47.5 - 23.88$

$$= 23.62 \text{ mm Ans.}$$

Again from right angled triangle ODB,

$$\tan \phi = \frac{DB}{OB} = \frac{KP}{OB} = \frac{OK \sin \alpha}{r_B + r_R}$$

$$= \frac{23.62 \sin 75°}{30 + 17.5}$$

$$= 0.4803$$

$$\phi = 25.6° \text{ Ans.}$$

2. Acceleration of the follower at the beginning of the lift

We know that acceleration of the follower at the beginning of the lift. i.e., when the roller has contact at E on the straight flank,

$a_{min} = \omega^2 (r_B + r_R) = (62.84)^2 (30+17.5)^2$

$$= 187600 \text{ mm /s}^2$$

$$= 187.6 \text{ m/s}^2 \text{ Ans.}$$

Acceleration of the follwer where straight flank merges into a circular nose

We know that acceleration of the follower where straight flank merges into a circular nose i.e.; when the roller just leaves contact at G,

$$a_{max} = \omega^2 (r_B + r_R) \left[\frac{2 - \cos^2 \phi}{\cos^3 \phi} \right]$$

$$= (62.84)^2 (30+17.5) \left[\frac{2 - \cos^2 25.6}{\cos^3 25.6} \right] = 187600 \left[\frac{2 - 0.813}{0.733} \right]$$

$$= 303800 \text{ mm/s}^2 = 303.8 \text{ m/s}^2 \text{ Ans.}$$

Acceleration of the follower at the open of the circular nose

We know that acceleration of the follower for contact with the circular nose,

$$a = \omega^2.r \left[\cos\theta + \frac{L^2.r\cos2\theta_1 + r^3 \sin^4\theta_1}{[L^2 - r^2 \sin^2\theta_1]^{3/2}} \right]$$

since θ, is measured form the top position of the follower, therefore for the follower, to have contact at the open of the circular nose (i.e., at point H), $\theta_1 = 0$

∴ Acceleration of the follower at the apex of the circular nose,

$$\alpha = \omega^2.r \left[1 + \frac{L^2.r}{L^2} \right] = \omega^2.r \left(1 + \frac{r}{L} \right) = \omega^2.r \left(1 + \frac{r}{r_R + r_N} \right)$$

$$= (62.84)^2 \times 23.62 \left(1 + \frac{23.62}{17.5 + 23.88} \right)$$

$$= 146\,530 \text{ mm/s}^2$$

$$= 146.53 \text{ m/s}^2 \text{ Ans.}$$

Prob. 5.3. The torque output T_α of an engine is given by $T_\alpha = 18000 + 8400 \sin 2a - 4600 \cos 2\alpha$ Nm, where α is the angle moved by the crank from inner dead centre. If the resisting torque is constant. Find the horse power developed by the engine at 200 rpm and the excess energy for designing the flywheel at $\alpha = 2/4$
        [GATE - 1998]

Soln. Given. N = 200 rpm,

$T_\alpha = 18000 + 8400 \sin 2\alpha - 4600 \cos 2\alpha$ Nm

We know that,

Work done per revolution $= \displaystyle\int_0^{2\pi} T\, d\alpha$

$$= \int_0^{\pi^2} (18000 + 8400 \sin2\alpha - 4600 \cos 2a)\, d\alpha$$

$$= \left[18000\,\alpha - \frac{8400.\cos 2\alpha}{2} - \frac{4600 \sin 2\alpha}{2} \right]_0^{2\pi}$$

$$= 180000 \times 2\pi \text{ Nm}$$

$$T_{mean} = \frac{\text{Work done per revolution}}{2\pi}$$

$$= \frac{18000 \times 2\pi}{2\pi}$$

$$= 18000 \text{ Nm}$$

Prob 5.4. The turning moment diagram of an engine is represented by the following equation

T = 25000 + 7650 sin 2α - 6400 cos 2α

Where, T = Torque, Nm

α = angle moved by the crank from inner dead centre. Assuming the resisting torque to be constant, compute

(a) the power developed by the engine at a mean speed of 200 rpm. (b) The engine in torque at any given instant (c) the angular acceleration of flywheel at α

$= \dfrac{\pi}{4}$ and at the moment of inertia of 4500 Nm² of the flywheel.   [GATE-2002]

Soln. Given N = 200 rpm

T = 25000 + 7650 sin 2α - 6400 cos 2α

$$T_{mean} = \dfrac{\displaystyle\int_0^{2\pi}(25000 + 7650 \sin 2\alpha - 6400 \cos 2\alpha)\, d\phi}{\displaystyle\int_0^{2\pi} d\alpha}$$

$$= \dfrac{[25000\,\alpha + 3825 \cos 2\alpha - 3200 \sin 2\,\alpha]_0^{2\pi}}{2\pi}$$

$$= \dfrac{25000 \times 2\pi}{2\pi} - \dfrac{3825}{2\pi}[\cos 2 \times 2\pi - \cos 0] - 0$$

$$= 25000 - \dfrac{3825}{2\pi}[1-1]$$

= 25000 Nm Ans.

Power (P) = T$_w$ = T.$\dfrac{2\pi N}{60}$ 25000 × 2 π × $\dfrac{200}{60}$

    = 523.598 kW Ans.

(b) Change in Torque

$\dfrac{dT}{d\alpha}$ = 15300 cos 2α + 12800 sin 2α

(c) T_{excess} = T- T$_{mean}$

      = 7650 sin 2α - 6400 cos 2α

$\left(T_{excess}\right)_{\alpha = \frac{\pi}{4}}$ = 7650 Nm

Angular Acc $(a_\alpha) = \dfrac{7650}{\dfrac{(45000)}{9.8}}$ 1.66 rad/s² Ans.

Prob. 5.5 The mass of flywheel is 3.25 tonnes and radius of gyration is 0.90 m. It is found from the turning moment diagram that the fluctuation of energy is 56 kNm. If the mean speed of the engine is 80 rpm. Find the maximum and minimum speed.

Soln. Given. $\Delta E = 56$ kJ $= 56 \times 10^3$ J

$\qquad m = 3.25 \times 10^3$ kg $= 3250$ kg

$\qquad K = 0.90$ m

We know that

$$\Delta E = \frac{\pi^2}{900} mk^2 N (N_1-N_2)$$

or $56 \times 10^3 = \dfrac{\pi^2}{900} \times 3250 \times (0.9)^2 \times 80 (N_1-N_2)$

$\qquad N_1 - N_2 = \qquad$ (i)

Again $N = \dfrac{N_1+N_2}{2}$

$\qquad \therefore N_1 + N_2 = 160 \qquad$ (ii)

From equation (i) and (ii), we have,

Prob 5.6 Determine the time exhaust and inlet valve of a 4-stroke cycle engine remain closed together. If the inlet valve opens 10° before. TDC and closes 40° after BDC, exhaust valve opens 30° before BDC and closes 5° after TDC.

N = 2000 rpm. [GATE -99]

Sol. Fig. 5.26 shows the valve timing.

Inlet valve remains open = 180 + 10 + 40 = 230°

Similarly :-

Exhaust valve remains open.

$\qquad = 180 + 30 + 5$

$\qquad = 215°$

Therefore, Inlet and Exhaust valve remains closed together = 720 - 230 - 215

$\theta = 285°$

Again, therefore, time of closing

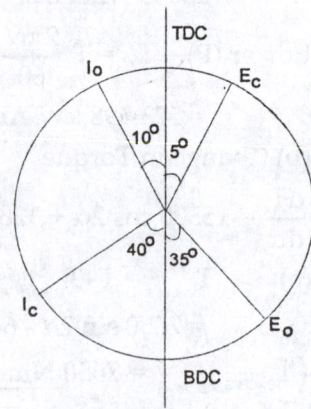

Fig. 5.24

$$= \frac{\theta}{360} \times \frac{1}{2000}\,\text{min}$$

$$= \frac{285}{360} \times \frac{60}{2000}\,\text{sec}$$

$$= 0.02375\,\text{sec.}$$

PROBLEMS:

1. Fig. 5.25 shows the valve timing to tractor. Engine has three cylinders with stroke length 90 mm and bend 75 mm. If the piston reciprocates 2000 times per minutes and length of connecting rod is 30cm. Calculate

    (a)   Location of vlave (mm)

    (b)   at what percentage of displacement, the exhaust valve remains, open,

    (c)   What is the time in second, the intake

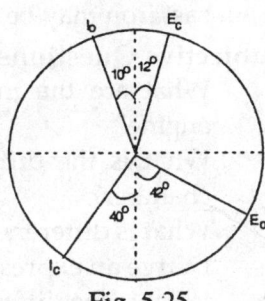

Fig. 5.25

and exhaust valves

    will remain open.

    (d)   If the cam gear has 48 teeth, find the number of gear teeth of carnk shaft, will be shifted from intake open to intake close and exhaust open to exhaust close.

(Ans. (a) 0.683 mm, (b) 10.52 mm 11.52 mm and 0.98 mm (c) 32.2% (c) 31.94% (d) 7.65

2. An engine flywheel has a mass of 6.5×10^3 kg and radius of gyration is 2000 mm. If maximum and minimum speeds are 120 rpm and 118 rpm respectively, find maximum fluctuations of energy.   (Ans. 67.875 Nm)

3. The flywheel of a steam engine has a radius of gyration of 1 m and mass 2500 kg. The starting torque of the steam engine is 1500 Nm and may be assumed constant.

    Determine 1. The angular acceleration of the flywheel and 2. The kinetic energy of the flywheel after 10 seconds from the start. [Ans. 0.6 rod/s², 45 kNm]

4. The equation of the turning moment diagram for the three crank engine is given by: T = 2500 - 7500 sin 30 Nm

    Where θ radius is the crank angle from inner dead centre. The moment of inertia of the fly-vheel is 400 kg wt, the mean engine speed is 300 rpm. Calculate the power of the engine and the total percentage fluctuation of speed of the flywheel, if the resisting torque is constant, and 2. The resisting torque is (25000 + 36000 sin θ) Nm. [Ans. 785 kW, 1.27%, 2.28%]

5.   A cast iron flywheel used for a four stroke I.C. engine is developing 187.5 kW at 250 rpm. The hoop stress developed in the flywheel is 5.2 MPa. The total fluctuation of speed is to be limited 3% of the mean speed. If the work done during the power stroke is 1/3 times more than the average workdone during whole cycle, find:

1. Mean diameter of flywheel 2. Mass of the flywheel and 3. cross-sectional dimensions of the rim when the width is twice the thickness. The density of cast iron may be than as 7220 kg/m³.   [Ans. 2.05m, 4561 kg, 44cm, 22cm]

Subjective Questions

1.   What are the main components or parts and their functions of an I.C. engine?
2.   What is the difference between direct and indirect injection combustion chamber?
3.   What is difference between oil wetted mesh air cleaner and dry air cleaner.
4.   Derive an expression for velocity and acceleration of the piston.
5.   What is the difference between compression and oil control ring?
6.   What is the purpose of flywheel in an engine?
7.   Derive an expression for energy stored in a flywheel.
8.   State the function of a cam in an I.C. engine.
9.   Describe the valve operating mechanism of a spark ignition engine.
10.   Write short notes on:
      (i) Combustion chamber (ii) Muffler (iii) Intake manifold
      (iv) Piston (v) Piston rings (vi) camb shaft (vii) Pressure angle (viii) Base circle (xi) Prime circle (x) Valve Timing (xi) Connecting rod.

Multiple Choice Questions

1.   Engine cylinders are made of
      (a)   high carbon steel   (b)   Nickel
      (c)   high grade cast iron   (d)   steel
2.   Piston are made of:
      (a)   cast iron   (b)   aluminium and its alloy
      (c)   steel   (d)   both (a) & (b)
3.   Piston ring is made of
      (a)   cast iron   (b)   copper
      (c)   pressed steel   (d)   both (a) & (c)
4.   Compression rings are placed in
      (a)   piston groves near the piston head
      (b)   sleeve
      (c)   skirt

    (d)   none of the above

5.   Oil rings are provided in

    (a)   power grove above the piston pin

    (b)   sleeve

    (c)   the grove above piston skirt

    (d)   both (a) & (c)

6.   Ring clearance merely per 200 mm diameter is

    (a)   1mm   (b)   5 mm

    (c)   2.5 mm   (d)   3.0 mm

7.   Piston pins are usually made of

    (a)   case hardened alloy steel (b)   cast iron

    (c)   nickel   (d)   copper

8.   Cylinder heads are usually made of

    (a)   cast iron   (b)   cap aluminium

    (c)   nickel   (d)   both (a) & (b)

9.   Connecting rod is made of

    (a)   forged steel & aluminium alloy (b)   nickel

    (c)   cast iron   (d)   copper

10.   Crank shaft is made of

    (a)   forged steel and cast steel

    (b)   Forged steel & nickel

    (c)   both (a) and (b)

    (d)   none of the above

11.   Main bearings are made of:

    (a)   white metal   (b)   forged steel

    (c)   nickel   (d)   copper

12.   Cam shaft is made of

    (a)   forged steel   (b)   cast iron

    (c)   cast steel   (d)   all of the above

13.   Flywheel is made of

    (a)   cast iron   (b)   forged steel

    (c)   cast steel   (d)   none of the above

14.   Timing gear controls

    (a)   fuel injection

    (b)   timing of ignition

     (c)   timing of opening & closing of valve

     (d)   all of the above

15.   Gaskets are made of

     (a)   copper   (b)   asbestos

     (c)   both   (d)   none of the above

16.   In cylinder, the side thrust of piston, is absorbed by

     (a)   sleeve   (b)   skrit

     (c)   liner   (d)   crown

17.   Top of the piston is called

     (a)   crown   (b)   skrit

     (c)   sleeve   (d)   none of the above

18.   Cam shaft is driven by

     (a)   drive wheel   (b)   piston rod

     (c)   crank shaft   (d)   none of the above

19.   In four-stroke engines, the ignition timing is controlled by

     (a)   timing gear   (b)   camshaft

     (c)   both   (d)   none of the above

20.   Manifolds are fitted to

     (a)   the side of cylinder head

     (b)   the exhaust valve

     (c)   the intake valve

     (d)   the lower part of the cylinder

21.   In I.C. engines, the tappet is made of

     (a)   hardended steel (b)   cast iron

     (c)   mild steel   (d)   chromium

22.   In I.C. engines, theoretically, the intake valve should be closed at

     (a)   T.D.C.   (b)   B.D.C.

     (c)   both   (d)   none of the above

23.   In I.C. engine, theoretically, the exhaust valve should be closed at

     (a)   T.D.C.   (b)   B.D.C.

     (c)   both   (d)   none of the above

24.   Generally, in 4- stroke diesel engines, the inlet valves gets opened at

     (a) 5^0 before T.D.C.

     (b) 5° after B.D.C.

     (c) 10° after B.D.C.

(d)   5º after T.D.C.
25.   The size of cam depends upon
       (a)   base circle   (b)   pitch circle
       (c)   prime circle   (d)   none of the above
26.   The angle between the direction of the follower motion and a normal to the pitch curve is called
       (a)   pressure angle   (b)   pitch angle
       (c)   base angle   (d) prime angle
27.   A circle drawn with centre as the cam centre and radius equal to the distance between the cam centre and the point on the pitch curve at which the pressure angle is maximum, is called
       (a)   prime circle   (b)   base circle
       (c)   pitch circle   (d)   none of the above
28.   In a radial cam, the follower moves
       (a)   In a direction of perpendicular to the cam axis
       (b)   in a direction of parallel to the cam axis
       (c)   along the cam axis
       (d)   none of the above
29.   For high speed engine, the follower should move with
       (a)   uniform velocity
       (b)   simple harmonic motion
       (c)   uniform acceleration and retardation
       (d)   cylindrical motion

FILL UP THE BLANKS

1.   Piston is made of .... and ....
2.   Cast iron cylinder blocks better .... properties than aluminium cylinder block.
3.   Cylinder head is made of .... and ....
4.   The muffler reduces the noise of the exhaust gases by .... the pressure.
5.   Piston pin clearance varies from .... to ....mm.
6.   Piston is made of .... and ....
7.   The follower oscillates .... to the cam axis in radial cams.
8.   Turning moment diagram is also known as .... diagram.
9.   Sodium is filled up to about .... % volume of the hollow stem of the valve.
10.   The range of valve face angle is from .... to ....

Ans. 1. Cast iron, cast aluminium. 2. Sound damping 3. Cast iron and aluminium alloy. 4. Reducing 5. 0.0127, 0.0178 6. Cast iron, aluminium, alloy 7. Perpendicular 8. Crank effort 9. 40 10. 30 to 40°.

ANSWER OF MULTIPLE CHOICE QUESTIONS

1(a) 2(d) 3 (d) 4 (a) 5 (d) 6 (a) 7 (a) 8 (a) 9 (a) 10 (a) 11 (a) 12 (a) 13 (d) 14 (c) 15 (b) 16 (a) 17 (d) 18 (a) 19 (a) 20 (a) 21 (b) 22 (a) 23 (a) 24 (a) 25 (a) 26 (c) 27 (a) 28 (d)

Chapter 6

Terminology and Power Measurment

6.1. Bore and Stroke: The diameter of the cylinder is called Bore and the displacement of the piston, i.e., it travels from top dead centre (TDC) to bottom dead centre (BDC) is called Stroke as shown in Fig. 6.1. In old engines, the stroke was always greater than the bore but the recent trend is towards a shorter piston stroke, the loss of friction is minimised. Also, the inertial and centrifugal load on the brings are reduced. In the square engine, which is the least in technology, the bore and strokes are equal.

6.2. Piston Displacement or Swept Volume (Vs):

This is the volume that the piston displaces during is movement from BDC to TDC as shown in Fig. It is given by following relationship,

$$V_s = \frac{\pi}{4} D^2 \cdot L \qquad (6.1)$$

Where,

D = Bore dia

L = Stroke length.

6.3. Displacement Volume of an Engine (Vs): It is the total swept volume of all piston during power strokes occurring in the minute. Mathematically, it is expressed as

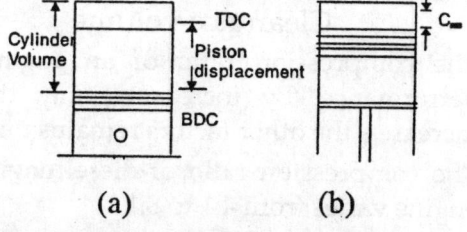

(a)   (b)

Fig. 6.1. Showing Piston Displacement and Clearance Volume

$V_d = A \times L \times N, \ x^{n/2}$ for four stroke engine, (6.2)

$= A \times L \times N \times n, =$ of two stroke engine (6.3)

6.4. Piston speed (Ps): It is the total length of travel of the piston in a cylinder in one minute. Mathematically, it is expressed as,

$P_s = 2 \times L \times N$ (6.4)

6.5 Brake Mean Effective Pressure (BMEP): It is the average pressure acting throughout the entire power strokes which are necessary to produce brake power of the engine.

155

$$BMEP = \frac{BP \times 60 \times 10^{12}}{L \times A \times N \times \frac{n}{2}} \text{, Pa, for four stroke engine} \quad (6.5)$$

$$BMEP = \frac{BP \times 60 \times 10^{12}}{L \times A \times N \times n} \text{, Pa , for two stroke engine} \quad (6.6)$$

Where,

BP = Brake Power, kW

L = Stroke length, mm

A = Area of piston, mm^2

N = Speed, rpm

6.6 Compression Ratio (CR): The compression ratio of an engine is a measure of how much the air/air-fuel mixture is compressed in the cylinder. It is obtained by ratio of the clearance volume of the charge at the beginning of the compression stroke to that at the end of compression stroke. It is given by following relationship,

$$CR = \frac{\text{Total cyclinder volume } (V_1)}{\text{Clearance volume } (V_2)} \quad (6.7)$$

$$= \frac{\text{Swept volume + clearance volume}}{\text{Clearance volume}} \quad (6.8)$$

The compression ratio of an engine is an important factor in the engine performance. By increasing only the compression ratio, the engine power increases, the other factors remains unchanged.

The compression ratio of diesel engine varies from 14:1 to 22:1 and for petrol engine varies from 4:1 to 8:1

6.7. Power: It is the rate of doing work. It is generally denoted by 'P' and mathematically, expressed as

$$P = \frac{W}{t} \text{, watt} \quad (6.9)$$

$$= T\omega \text{, watt} \quad (6.10)$$

Where,

W = work done, J

t = time, s

T = torque, Nm

ω = Angular velocity, rad/s

The various methods of defining power on described below

156

6.7.1 Indicated Power (IP): It is the power generated in the engine cylinder and received by the piston. It is the power developed in a cylinder without friction or auxiliary unit. It is given by following relationship,

$$IP = \frac{P_m \, L \, A \, N}{60 \times 10^{12}} \times \frac{n}{2}, \quad kW, \text{ for four stroke engine.} \quad (6.11)$$

$$= \frac{P_m \, L \, A \, N}{60 \times 10^{12}} \times n \; kW, \text{ for two stroke engine} \quad (6.12)$$

where,

P_m = Mean effective pressure, Pa

L = Length of the stroke, mm

A = Area of piston, mm²

$\dot{N}$ = Speed, rpm

$$I.P. = \frac{P_m \, L \, A \, N}{6,000} \; kW \quad (6.13)$$

Where,

L = Length of stroke, m

A = Area of piston, m²

N_p = Number of power strokes

6.7.2. Brake Power (BP): It is the power delivered by the engine and is available at the end of the crankshaft or flywheel and measured by a suitable brake dynamometer.

6.7.3 Belt Power: It is the power of the engine measured at the end of a suitable belt receiving drive from the PTO shaft of a the tractor.

6.7.4. Frictional Power (FP): It is power required to run the engine at a given speed without producing any useful work.

It represents the function and pumping losses of an engine.

It is given by following relationship,

F. P. = IP - BP   (6.14)

6.7.5. Take off Power: It is the power delivered by a tractor through its PTO shaft. In general the belt and PTO power of a tractor will approximately be the same and is measured by either a hydraulic or an electrical dynamometers.

6.7.6. Drawbar Power: It is the power of tractor measured at the end of the drawbar. It is that power which is available to pull loads.

6.7.7. Maximum Power and Net Power: The maximum power is measured at the engine flywheel without any of the power consuming accesories being attached. This is not a practical rating as it does not represent "usable" power.

Net power is measured at the engine flywheel in the same manner as the maximum power. The difference in the two is because the engine is equipped with acessories. Net power is the basis for rating the power of industrial and farm tractors.

6.7.8. Effect of Environment on Power: Power is affected by atmospheric pressure and atmospheric temperature. Therefore, what ever actual power is observed on the dynamometer is called the observed power, whereas the corrected power is the observed power corrected to standard atmospheric conditions as per IS: 1601-1960. The standard operating conditions are:

1. Mean barometric pressure of 736 mm of mercury corresponding to an altitude of 300 m above mean sea level.

2. Water vapour pressure of 27.4 mm of mercury corresponding to a relative humidity of 65 percent at 35°C.

3. Intake air temperature of 35°C.

For decreases in the atmospheric pressure, a deduction from the rated output of the engine shall be made at the rate of 1.4 percent per 100 m of altitude above 300 m. This de-rating is valid up to an altitude of 2500 m.

Also, for any increase of the intake air temperature above 35°C, a further deduction shall be made at the rate of 0.25 percent per °C.

6.9. Mean Effective Power (MEP): It is the average pressure during the power stroke minus the average pressure during other strokes. Mean Effective Pressure is the pressure that actually forces the piston down during the power stroke.

6.10. Volmetric Efficiency (Mv) : The amount of air entering to the cylinder due to the vacuum created by the downword movement of the piston is always less than the actual displacements f the piston because of construction of the air intake system. Therefore, the actual air taken into the cylinder divided by the swept volume is known as volumetric efficiency. Mathematically, it is expressed as

$$\eta_r = \frac{V_a}{V_s} \qquad (6.15)$$

$$= \frac{\text{Volume of air aspirated at intake condition per min}}{\text{stroke volume} \times N \times n}$$

Where,

V_a = Volume of actual air

V_s = Swept volume

N = Speed rpm

n = Number of cylinders

Note: Actual quantity of the air or charge admitted is less than the quantity corresponding to the displacement due to the fact that temperature in the cylinder and pressure is lower than the normal or standard values and also it depends on dynamics of air flow through suction valve.

6.11. Mechanical Efficiency (η_m): It is the ratio of brake power to indicated power. Mathematically, it is expressed as.

$$\eta_m = \frac{BP}{IP} \qquad (6.16)$$

Mechanical efficiency depends on the design of the engine, on the piston and rotary speeds, on cooling condition. On the method of quality and quantity of lubricating and on the accuracy used in manufacturing, fitting and aligning various engine parts, when assembling the engine.

The mechanical efficiency of an engine varies with load, falling off with a decrease in load.

As a first approximation, the looses, i.e, FP, may be taken as independent of load where engines runs at a particulars speed. Thus, for idle running with no shaft out put the indicating horse power is the same as friction horse power or it can be expressed as,

$$\eta_m = \frac{BP}{BP + IP} = \frac{BMEP}{IMEP} = \frac{\eta_s}{\eta_i} \quad (6.17)$$

The mechanical efficiency is indicative of mechanical losses in machine. It depends upon the operating conditions especially speed power out put and lubrication.

The losses in a machine can be put into four main groups as follows

(a) Friction losses in pistons, a bearings, gears, valves and valve mechanism. These losses vary from 7 to 10% of IP.

(b) Ventilating action of the flywheel. This loss varies from 1 to 3% of I.P.

(c) The work of charging absorbed during the suction and exhaust strokes in four stroke engine or by scavenge pumps in two strokes engines these losses vary from 2 to 6 percent of I.P.

(d) Power absorbed by different auxiliaries such as just pumps, lubricating pumps, wate circulating pumps, radiator fans, magnets and distributor drives and electric generators. These losses vary from 1 to 0 percent of IP.

Therefore, all these mechanical losses together vary from 11 to 28 percent of IP, causing the variation of mechanical efficiency from 72 to 79 percent.

6.12 Thermal Efficiency: It is classified as follows:

(a) Indicated Thermal Efficiency (η_i): The indicated thermal efficiency shows that fraction of the heat supplies is converted into indicated worked. Mathematically, it is expressed as,

$$\eta_i = \frac{\text{Indicated work in heat units}}{\text{evergy supplied}}$$

$$= \frac{60\ IP}{W_f C_v}$$

$$= \frac{3600}{S_f C_v} \tag{6.18}$$

Where,

W_f = Fuel supplied, kg/min.

Cv = Calorie valve, kJ kg.

S_f = Specific fule consumption $\tag{6.19}$

(b) Brake Thermal Efficiency (ηb): The brake thermal efficiency indicates the fraction of the heat supplied that is transformed into engine shaft work. Mathematically, it is expressed as

$$\eta_b = \frac{\text{Brake work done in heat units}}{\text{Energy supplied}}$$

$$= \frac{60\ BP}{W_f C_v} \tag{6.20}$$

$$\eta_b = \frac{3600}{S_f C_v} \tag{6.21}$$

Where,

S_f = sp. fuel consumption kg/kW.h

6.13. Scavenge Efficiency (ηs): For two-stroke engines, the concept of volumetric efficiency does not apply so, another term is called Scavenge Efficiency is employed. It is measure of the extent to which burnt gases our removed from the cylinder, and the cylinder is filled with fresh air of charge. Mathematically, it is expressed as,

$$\eta_s = \frac{m_a}{(V_d V_c)\,\rho a} \tag{6.22}$$

where,

m_a = Mass of charge or air retained in the cylinder, kg

V_d = Displacement volume, m^3

V_c = Combustion space volume, m^3

ρ_a = Density of air or charge, kg/m^3

6..14 Relative Efficiency (ηr): It is the ratio of the indicated thermal efficiency to the corresponding ideal air standard efficinecy. Thus for petrol engine the relative efficiency is given by

$$\eta_r = \frac{\eta_i}{1 - \left(\dfrac{1}{r}\right)^\gamma} \qquad (6.23)$$

The practice is also to refer the relative efficiency to brake power basis or to brake thermal efficiency.

6.15. Morse Test: The I.P. and mechanical efficiency of a multicylinder engine is found out in very short time by this test. During test the engine is run at a constant speed and at same throttle opening. First, the B.P. of the engine with all cylinders operative is measured by means of dynamometer. Next, the BP of the engine is measured with each cylinder rendered in operative one by one by shorting the spark plug in case of petrol engine or by cutting off the fuel supply in case of diesel engine.

When any cylinder is rendered inoperative, the speed abruptly goes down. Before, taking any reading, the initial speed must be restored by adjusting the load.

It is assumed that F.P. of the inoperative cylinder remains same as it were when the cylinder was operative.

Let B = B.P. of the engine with all cylinder operative

B_1 = B.P. of the engine with all cylinder No 1. inoperative

B_2 = B.P. of the engine with all cylinder No. 2 inoperative

B_3 = B.P. of the engine with all cylinder No. 3 inoperative

B_4 = B.P. of the engine with all cylinder No. 4 inoperative

I_1, I_2, I_3 and I_4 = I.P. of cylinder 1, 2, 3 and 4 respectively

F_1, F_2, F_3 and F_4 = F.P. of cylinders 1, 2, 3, 4 respectively.

$= (I_1 + I_2 + I_3 + I_4) - (F_1 + F_2 + F_3 + F_4) ....$ (6.24)

When cylinder No. 1 is rendered inoperative, it does not develop any power, on the contrary some power is lost due to movement of piston inside the cylinder. Then,

$B_1 = (I_2 + I_3 + I_4) - (F_1 + F_2 + F_3 + F_4) ......$ (6.25)

From the equations (6.23) and (6.24) we have

$B - B_1 = I_1$ (6.26)

Similarly we can have,

$B - B_2 = I_2$

$B - B_3 = I_3$

and $B - B_4 = I_4$

Therefore, total IP of the engine $= I_1 + I_2 + I_3 + I_4 = I$ say and mechanical efficiency

$$= \frac{B}{I}$$

When the Morse test is carried out

(i) The BP should be measured as soon as possible after making cylinder inoperative.

(ii) The dynamometer load should be adjusted soon to bring the speed to its constant value for the test, otherwise the engine may race. In order to plot IP, BP and 1 m a series of tests should be conducted at predetermined engine speed because BP varies with load & speed.

6.16. Torque:

Like power, torque is another important measures of engine performance. Any force applied on some point to cause a turning effect is called Torque (T). Mathematically, it is expressed as,

$T = F \times r$ (6.27)

Where,

F = Force

r = Distance of force from the centre of shaft

In an engine, the piston applies a torque to the crank shaft through the connecting rod and crank when it is moving down in the power stroke. The amount of torque depends on the pressure exerted by the piston and the length of crank arm. The greater the push on the piston, the greater the torque as shown in Fig.6.2. Torque should not confused with power. Torque is the twisting effort that the engine applies through the crank shaft, whereas power is the rate at which the engine works. The S.I. unit of torque is Nm.

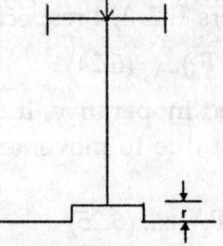

Fig. 6.2 Engine torque (T) = Force (F) x Crank arm (r)   (6.28)

6.17.1. BRAKE POWER MEASUREMENT: To measure the brake power, brake dynamameters are used.

6.17.2 Classification of Brake Dynamometer: They are classified as follows:

(i) Absorption Dynamometer: The total energy or power produced by the engine delivered by the engine is absorbed by the friction resistance of the brake and is transmitted into heat, during the process of measurement.

(ii) Transmision Dynamometers: Here, the energy is used to do work. The energy or power delivered by the engine is transmitted through the dymamometer to some other machines where the power develops is suitably measured.

6.17.3. Classification of Absorption Dynamometers: They are classified as follows:

(i) Prony brake dynamometer and (ii) Rope brake dynamometers

(i) Prony Brake Dynamometer: Prony brake dynamometer is a simple form of an absorption type dynamoeter as shown in Fig. 6.3. It consists of a friction band ring that may be placed around a pulley or flywheel and attached to a lever bearing upon a weighing scale. The friction between the surfaces in contact will tend to rotate the arm in the direction in which the shaft is revolving. This motion is resisted and measured. In setting up the prony brake, the distance between the centre of the shaft and the point of contact with the scale, must be accurately measured-the point being placed at the same elevation as the centre of shaft. By this arrangement the amount of friction between the brake band and the revolving pulley or wheel is weighed upon the scales.

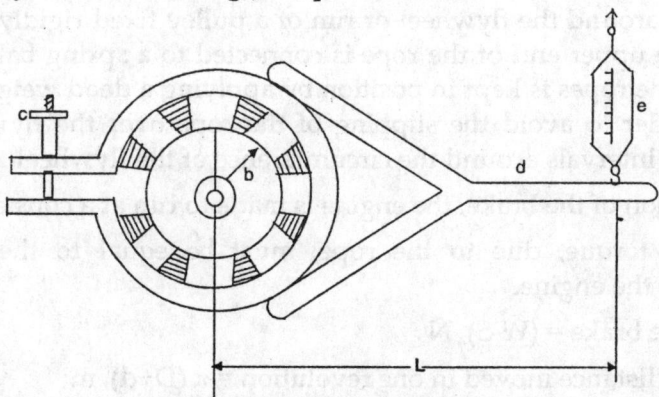

Fig. 6.3. Prony Brake Dynanometer

Since the brake fits tightly and could be carried around by the pulley, but for the arm bearing upon the scale, the amount of frictional power exerted by the revolving pulley in turning free within the brake band, may be measured just as would a load or a machine attached to the wheel or shaft.

The distance between the centre of the shaft and the point of contact with the scales, is called lever arm.

We know that the moment of the frictional resistance or torque on the shaft.

$$T = W.L, Nm \qquad\qquad (6.29)$$

work done in one revolution = Torque x Angle turned in radian

$$= T \times 2\pi, Nm$$

$\therefore$ work done per minute = 2π NT, Nm $\qquad\qquad (6.30)$

we know that brake power of engine

$$BP = \frac{\text{work done per minute}}{60}$$

$$= \frac{2\pi \, NT}{60}$$

$$= \frac{WL \, 2\pi \, N}{60}, W \qquad\qquad (6.31)$$

where, W = weight on scale, N

L = Length of lever arm from centre of shaft to point on scale, m

N = speed, rpm

(ii) Rope Brake Dynamometer: It is the also an absorption type dymamometer which is used to measure the brake power of the engine. It has one, two or more ropes wound, around the flywheel or rim of a pulley fixed rigidly to the shaft of an engine. The upper end of the rope is connected to a spring balance while the lower end of the ropes is kept in position by applying a dead weight as shown in Fig. 6.4. In order to avoid the slipping of the rope over the flywheel, wooden blocks fixed at intervals around the circumference of the flywheel.

During operation of the brake, the engine is made to run at a constant speed.

The frictional torque, due to the rope, must be equal to the torque being transmitted by the engine.

Net load on the brake = (W-S), N $\qquad\qquad (6.32)$

we know that distance moved in one revolution = π (D+d), m

Therefore, work done per revolution = (W-S) x π (D +d), Nm $\qquad\qquad (6.33)$

and workdone per minute = (W-S) π (D + d) N, Nm $\qquad\qquad (6.34)$

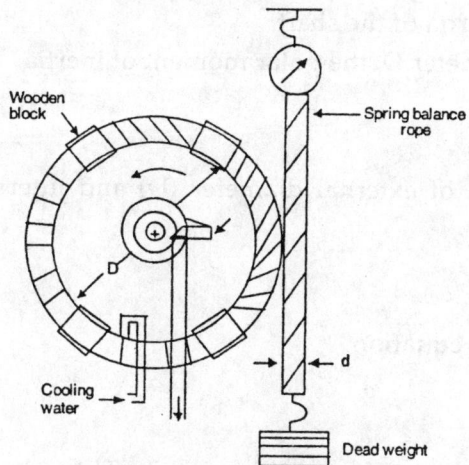

Fig. 6.4. Rope Brake Dynamometer

∴ Brake power of the engine, BP. = $\dfrac{\text{Work done per min}}{60}$

$$= \frac{(W - S)\,\pi\,(D + d)\,N}{60}\,, W \qquad\qquad (6.35)$$

If the diameter of the rope (d) is neglected, then brake power of the engine

$$\text{B.P.} = \frac{(W - S)\,\pi\,DN}{60}\,, W \qquad\qquad (6.36)$$

Where,

W = Dead load, N

S = Spring balance reading, N

D = Diameter of the wheel, m

d = diameter of rope, m

N = Speed of the engine shaft, rpm

6.17.4. Torsion Dynamometer: A torsion dynamometer is used to measuring large powers like the power transmitted along propeller shaft of a turbine. A little consideration will show that when the power is being transmitted, the driving end of the shaft twists through a small angle relative to the driven end of the shaft. The amount of twist depends upon many factors likewise torque acting on the shaft (T). length of the shaft (l), diameter of the shaft (D) and modules of rigidity (C) of the material of the shaft. We know that the torsion equation is

$$\frac{T}{J} = \frac{C.\theta}{l} \qquad\qquad (6.37)$$

Where, θ = Angle of twist, radian

J = Polar moment of inertia of the shaft.

For a solid shaft of diameter D, the polar moment of inertia,

$$J = \frac{\pi}{32} \times D^4 \qquad (6.38)$$

and for a hollow shaft of external diameter (D) and internal diameter (d), the polar moment of inertia,

$$J = \frac{\pi}{32}(D^4 - d^4) \qquad (6.39)$$

From the above torsion equation,

$$T = \frac{C \cdot J}{1} \times \theta = K. \theta \qquad (6.40)$$

Where k = C.J/1 is a constant for particular shaft. Thus, the torque acting on the shaft is proportional to the angle of twist. This means that if the angle of twist is measured by some means, then the torque and hence the power transmitted may be determined.

We know that

$$P = \frac{2\pi N \times T}{60}, W \qquad (6.41)$$

6.18. Drawbar Dynamometer: This is commonly used to measure the drawbar pull of power units or ascertain the draft of field implements. They can be classified as spring dynamometer, hydraulic dynamometer and strain gauge dynamometer.

(i) Spring Dynamometer: It makes use of spring, which elongates under tension and shorten under compression. The actuation of spring is directly linked with the needle provided on the dial. The spring is designed for different loading capacity are per requirement. This type of dynamo meters are suitable for rough measurement of draft because rapid fluctuation of needle on dial as shown in Fig. 6.5.

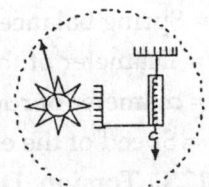

Fig. 6.5. Spring Dynamometer

(ii) Hydraulic Dynamometer: The hydraulic dynamoeter is an assembly of hydraulic cylinder, piston, pressure gauge and connecting linkage. The piston is fitted tightedly inside the cylinder with the help of rubber 'O' ring in such a manner that leakage can be prevented. Usually SAE-40 lubricating oil is used in the hydraulic cylinder. A pressure gause is connected to the hydraulic cylinder through a flexible pipe. The drawabar causes an increase in oil pressure which is calibrated in such a pressure gauge. The gauge is calibrated in such a way that it gives direct reading of the implement draft in Newton (N).

Momentary deflection in the pull are dampered out with the use of hydraulic oil, over loads do not seriously affect the unit. It is simple, sensity and accurate device for measuing drawbar pull.

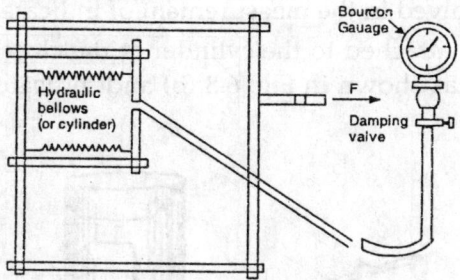

Fig. 6.6. Hydraulic Dynamometer

(ii) Strain Gauge Dynamometer: The electrical strain gauges dynamometer are very commonly used for the measurement of force. The actual working principle of strain gauge are the changing electrical resitance of a strain gauge is proportional to the mechanical strain to which it is subjected when it is physically mounted on a test surface and electrically corrected as an arm of a bridge and resulting output signal represents a voltage analog of the mechanical deformation of the surface. Fig. 6.7 shows one type of drawbar dynamometer using four strain gauge units. Units A and B are mounted such that as to react in tension, while C and D are in compression. It is made with three main components namely (i) Sensing unit (ii) Indicator or recorder of (iii) Connecting wire.

The measurement of force is done by connecting the strain gauge in a wheat stone bridge circuit such that the out-put from the circuit is proportional to the change in resistance of the gauge due to deformation. The rate of travel can be determined by observing the time to cover some distance. Then, power developed can be calculated as follows:

$P_D = F \times v$

Where,

F = Draft

v = Velocity

This is very precise and accurate but the recording instruments are very costly as shown in Fig. 6.7 (i), (ii) and (iii).

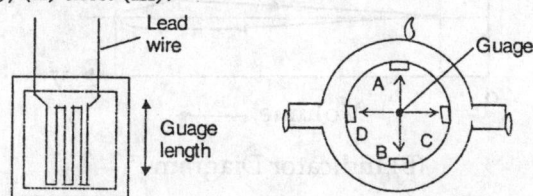

Fig. 6.7. Strain-gauge dynamometer

6.19. The power generated in the engine cylinder and received by the piston is said to be indicated power. Indicated power is measured by indicator. The following steps are involved in the measurement of indicated power.

Step I: The indicator is attached to the cylinder at the closed end and prepare or plot indicator diagram as shown in Fig. 6.8 (b) and indicator is shown in Fig. 6.8 (a).

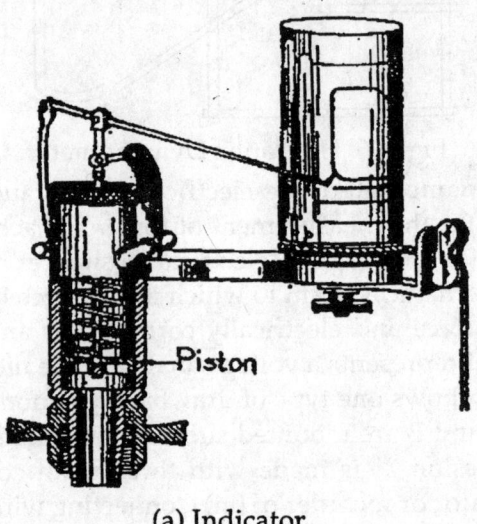

(a) Indicator

Step II: Determine the are of FCDE with the help of plannimeter.

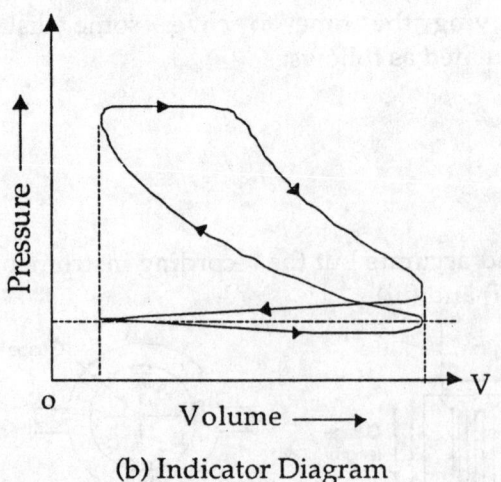

(b) Indicator Diagram

Step III: Dividing the are by its length horizontal distance px will give the average height. Then height is multiplied by the scale of the indicator spring will give the average mean effective pressure of cylinder corss-sectional area.

Step IV: Determine the operating engine speed (rpm), bore of cylinder and length of piston.

Step V: Then indicated power can be calculated as follows.

$$\text{I.P.} = \frac{P_m L A N_p N n}{60}, W$$

$$= \frac{P_m L A N_p N n}{6,000}, kW$$

Where,

P_m = Mean effective pressure, Pa

L = Stroke Length, m

A = Area of cylinder, m²

N_p = Number of power stroke

n = Number of cylinders

Prob. 6.1. A torsion dynamometer is fitted to a propeller shaft of a marine engine. It is found that the shaft twists 2' in a length of 20 meters at 120 rpm. If the shaft is hollow with 400 mm external diameter and 300 mm internal diameter find the power of the engine. Take modulus of rigidity for the shaft material as 80 GPa.

Soln. Given: $\theta = 2° = 2 \times \pi / 180 = 0.035$ rad; $l = 20$ m

N = 120 rpm ; D = 400 mm = 0.4 mm ; d = 300 mm = 0.3 m C = 80 GPa = 80 × 10³ PA

we know that polar moment of inertia of the shaft,

$$J = \frac{\pi}{32} (D^4 - d^4) = \frac{\pi}{32} [(0.4)^4 - (0.3)^4]$$

$$= 0.0017 \, m^4$$

and torque applied to the shaft,

$$T = \frac{C.J}{l} \times \theta = \frac{8 \times 10^9 \times 0.0017}{20} \times 0.035$$

$$= 238 \times 10^3 \, Nm$$

We know that power of the engine

$$P = \frac{2\pi NT}{60} = \frac{238 \times 10^3 \times 2\pi \times 120}{60}$$

$$= 2990 \times 10^3 \, W = 2990 \, kW \, Ans.$$

Prob. 6.2 An engine test revealed that the cylinder pressure (Pc) at the end of the compression stroke at normal cranking speeds is approximately related to the atmospheric pressure (Pa) and the compression ratio (r) at the engine in the following way.

$P_c = P_a - r^{1.28}$.

Compute the fuel cut off ratio for diesel in a diesel engine at an absolute cylinder pressure at 3377 KPa and at a gauge pressure of 100 KPa. Assume a thermal efficiency of 32% of the engine.[GATE-2002]

Sol. Given: h = 32% = 0.32, Pa = 100 KPa, Pc = 3377 KPa cut off ratio ρ = ?, γ =1.28.

$P_c = P_a . r^{1.28}$

or $r^{1.28} = \dfrac{P_c}{P_a}$

or $r = \left(\dfrac{P_c}{P_a}\right)^{\frac{1}{1.28}} = \left(\dfrac{3377}{100}\right)^{\frac{1}{1.28}}$.

$\therefore$ r = 15.63 : 1

we know that

$$\eta_d = 1 - \left(\dfrac{1}{r}\right)^{r-1}\left[\left(\dfrac{\rho^\gamma - 1}{\gamma\,(\rho-1)}\right)\right]$$

$$0.32 = 1 - \left(\dfrac{1}{15.63}\right)^{0.28}\left(\dfrac{(\rho^{1.28} - 1)}{1.28\,(\rho - 1)}\right)$$

or $0.68 = \left(\dfrac{1}{15.63}\right)^{0.28} \times \dfrac{1}{1.28}\dfrac{(\rho^{1.28}-1)}{(\rho-1)}$

or $0.68 \times (15.63)^{0.28} \times 1.28 = \dfrac{\rho^{1.28}-1}{\rho-1}$

or, $1.88\, P - 1.88 = \rho^{1.28} - 1$

or $1.88\, P - \rho^{1.28} = 0.88$

or $\rho^{1.28} - 1.88\,\rho + 0.88 = 0$

Prob 6.3. A MF-1035 tractor operates at 2000 rpm and uses 16.5 litre at fuel per hour. What is the average volume in cubic-millimeters of the individual injection? Assume a compression ratio of 16.7:1 and the engine displacement as 4520×10^{-3} L. What is the ratio of the clearance volume to the volume of an injection? [GATE-1998]

Soln. Given: N = 2000 rpm

Fuel consumption per hour = 16.5 L

$$r = \frac{V_t}{V_c} = \frac{16.7}{1}$$ Engine displacement = 4520 x 10⁻³ L

Fuel consumption per minute $= \frac{16.5}{60}$ L

$$= 0.275 \text{ L}$$

Number of power stroke per minute $= \frac{2000}{2} = 1000$

∴ 1000 power strokes consumes = 0.275 L of fuel.

Hence, 1 power stroke consumes $= \frac{0.275}{1000}$ L of fuel

$= 0.275 \times 10^{-3}$ L

$= 0.275 \times 10^{-3} \times 10^{-3}$ m³

$= 0.275 \times 10^{-6} \times 10^3$ mm³

$= 0.275 \times 10^3$ mm³.

Prob. 6.4. A two cylinder four stroke C.I. engine with volumetric efficiency 0.88 has stroke to bore ratio 1.12 : 1, stroke length = 100 mm, clearance volume of each cylinder is 100 cc and mean effective pressure is 6 x 10⁵ P$_a$. If the piston makes 3000 strokes per minute, calculate.

(a) B.H.P. of the engine.

(b) Air flow rate in m³/min

(c) Compression ratio   [GATE- 1997]

Soln. Given V$_c$ = 100 cm³, d $= \frac{100}{1.72}$ 89.3 mm,

$p = 6 \times 10^5$ Pa, $V_s = \frac{\pi}{4} d^2 L = \frac{\pi}{4} \times (8.93)^2 \times 10$

$= 626.31$ cm³

$= 626.31 \times 10^{-6}$ m₃

n = 2, N = 1500 rpm

(a) B.P. $= \frac{PLAN}{60,000} \times \frac{n}{2}$ kW

$$= \frac{6 \times 10^5 \times 626.31 \times 10^{-6} \times 1500 \times 2}{60,000 \times 2}$$

= 9.39 KW = 12.6 hp Ans.

(c) Volume of air taken = $626.31 \times 0.88 \times 2 \times 10^{-6}$ m^3/min $\frac{1500}{2}$

= 0.826 m^3 /min. Ans.

(c) C.R. = $\dfrac{V_s + V_c}{V_c} = \dfrac{626.31 + 100}{100}$

= 7.26 Ans.

Prob. 6.5. A four cylinder two-stroke cycle engine with a swept volume of 750 cm^3 cylinder gives a sp. fuel consumption of 0.25 kg/kW-h, when developing a break mean effective pressure 650 kPa at 1500 rpm. If the calorific valve of the fuel is 40 MJ/kg, the brakes thermal efficiency of the engine is.

(a) 9% (b) 18% (c) 32% (d) 36% [GATE- 2004]

Soln. Given. n = 4, ω_s = 0.25 kg/KW -h

V_s = AL = 750 cm^3 = 750 $\times$ 10^{-6} m^3

C_f = 40 MJ/ kg, p = 650 kPa, N = 1500

we know

$$BP = \frac{PLAN \times n}{60,000} \ KW$$

$$= \frac{650 \times 750 \times 10^{-6}, 1500 \times 4 \times 10^3}{60,000}$$

= 48.75 kW.

Brake thermal efficiency = $\dfrac{B.P. \times 60}{w_f \times C_f}$

$$= \frac{48.75 \times 60}{0.203 \times 40 \times 10^3}$$

= 0.3603

= 36% Ans.

Thus, answer is (d).

Prob. 6.6 The carburetor of 4 cylinder engine was adjusted evaporate 70% of fuel at the manifold at full throttle when engine speed was 1200 rpm. The rope brake dynamometer attached to this engine showed spring balance reading at 150 N at a dead load on the brake is 780 N. Th drum diameter was 70 cm. The dead weights at 578, 570, 563 and 561 N and spring tension as 121, 116, 120 and 113 N were recorded to maintain the same speed when the spark plug of each cylinder was short circulated intern respectively. Determine (a) Mechanical efficiency of engine (b) air fuel ratio for air vapour ratio of 17.14: 1.

Assume rope diameter is 2.0 cm.   [GATE-1997]

Sol. Given, D = 70 cm, d = 2 cm W = 780 N, S = 150 N

we know that

$$B.P. = \frac{W.S. \times (D + d) \times N}{60,000} , kW$$

$$= \frac{780.150 \times \pi \times (0.7 + 0.02) \times 1220}{60,000}$$

$$= 28.48608 \ kW$$

BHP of the engine, when Ist plug is short circuited

$$P1 = \frac{(578-121) \times \pi \times 0.72 \times 1200}{60,000} = 20.663 \ kW.$$

$$P_2 = \frac{(570-116) \times \pi \times 0.72 \times 1200}{60,000} = 20.53 \ kW$$

$$P_3 = \frac{(563-120) \times \pi \times 0.72 \times 1200}{60,000} = 19.516 \ kW'$$

$$P_4 = \frac{(561-113) \times \pi \times 0.72 \times 1200}{60,000} = 20.267 \ kW.$$

Again,

$I_1 = P-P_1 = 28.48608--20.663 = 7.82308 \ kW$

$I_2 = P-P_2 = 28.48608-20.53 = 7.95608 \ kW$

$I_3 = P-P_3 = 28.48608-19.51 = 8.97608 \ kW$

$I_4 = P-P_4 = 28.48608-20.267 = 8.21908 \ kW$

$$IP = 32.97432 \ kW$$

IP = 32.97432 kW

$$\eta m = \frac{BP}{IP} \times 100 = \frac{28.48608}{32.97432} \times 100$$

$$= 8.6.38\% \ Ans.$$

$$A/q. = \frac{Air}{Vapour} = \frac{17.14}{1}$$

Since 70% fuel evaporated

$$\frac{\text{Vapour}}{\text{Fuel}} = 0.7$$

$$\therefore \frac{\text{Air}}{\text{Fuel}} = \frac{\text{Air}}{\text{Vapour}} \times \frac{\text{Vapour}}{\text{Fuel}}$$

= 17.14 x 0.7 = 11.998 Ans.

Prob. 6.7. A four cylinder, four-cycle diesel tractor engine has cylinder bore of 90 mm and piston stroke of 100 mm. The engine develops 43.25 kW at 2300 rpm when coupled to a dynamometer. All the same speed and with the fuel shut off, the tractor engine required 7.5 kW to motor it. During the test when 43.5 kW was developed, the engine used 15.5 l/h of diesel fuel that contained heat energy of 45 MJ/kg with fuel density of 0.835 kg/l. Determine

(a) Indicated mean effective pressure

(b) Engine thermal efficiency.   [GATE-1999]

Sol. Given. N = 2300 rpm, ρ = 43.5 kW,

n = 4 , calorific valve (C_f) = 45 MJ/kg,

l = 0.835 kg/l, B.P. = 43.5 kw

D = 90 mm = 0.09 m, F.P. = 7.5 KW, L = 100 mm = 0.1 m

we know that

IP = B.P. + F.P.

= 43.5 + 7.5 = 51 KW

$$IP = P.L.A.N. \frac{n}{2}$$

$$51 \times 10^3 = p \times 0.1 \times \frac{\pi}{4} \times (0.09)^2 \times \frac{2300}{60} \times \frac{4}{2}$$

$$P = \frac{5 \times 10^3 \times 3 \times 4}{0.1 \times \pi \times (0.09)^2 \times 230}$$

= 1.0457 x 10⁶ N /m² = 1.0457 x 10⁶ Pa.

(b)   Engine thermal efficiency

$\therefore$ Total Heat Energy = Fuel Cnosumption x Calorific value

$$= 15.5 \left(\frac{1}{h}\right) \times 45 \left(\frac{MJ}{kg}\right) \times 0.835 \frac{kg}{l}$$

= 582.4125 MJ/h

$$= \frac{582.4125}{3600} = 01.6178 \text{ MW}$$

= 161.78 KW

$$\text{Engine Thermal Efficiency} = \frac{\text{Heat Energy}}{\text{Total Heat Energy}}$$

$$= \frac{43.5}{161.78} = 0.2689$$

= 26.89%

Prob. 6.8. The diesel engine of a tractor is required to start cold at -20°C. The fuel has an auto ignition temperature of 350°C. What minimum compression ratio must be engine consumes 0.25 kg of diesel fuel per kWh. What thermal efficiency; r = 1.3, calorific value 42000 kJ/kg.   [GATE-1991]

Soln. Given T_1 = 273 + (-20) = 253 K

T_2 = 273 + 350 = 623 K

we know that, in diesel cycle, state 1-2 adiabatic

$$T_1 V_1{}^{\gamma-1} = T_2 V_2{}^{\gamma-1}$$

$$\therefore \frac{V_1}{V_2} = \left(\frac{T_2}{T_1}\right)^{\frac{1}{\gamma-1}} = \left(\frac{623}{253}\right)^{\frac{1}{1.3-1}}$$

$$= \frac{20.16}{1} \text{ Ans.}$$

$$\text{Thermal efficiency of the engine} = \frac{\text{Thermal power of engine}}{\text{fuel power}}$$

$$= \frac{3600 \times 10^3}{42000 \times 0.25 \times 10^3}$$

= 34.28%. Ans.

PROBLEMS.

1.   An eight-cylinder engine of 85.7 mm bore and 82.5 mm stroke with a compression ratio of 7 is tested at 4000 rpm on a dynamometer which has a 0.5335 m arm. During 10 minutes test at a dynamomter scale beam reading of 400 N, 4.55 kg of gasoline for which the heating valve is 46,000 kJ.kg are burnt and air at 2.94K and 10 x 10⁴ N/m² is supplied to the carburettor at the rate of 5.44 kg min. Calculate

(a) The B.P. developed (b) The b.m.e.p. (c) b.s.f.c. (d) The specific air consumption (e) the brake thermal efficiency (f) the volumetric efficiency (g) Air fuel ratio

Ans. (a) 89.34 KW (b) 704.36 KPa (c) 0.306 Kg p KWh (d) 3.65 kg p KW h (e) 25.6% (f) 60% (g) 11.96

2. In a test with a four-cylinder four-stroke petrol engine, the following results were obtained for a particular setting and speed.

    B.P. with the all cylinders working 23.55 kW

    B.P. with No. 1 cylinders cut out 15.89 kW

    B.P. with No. 2 cylinder cut out 16.41 kW

    B.P. with No. 3 cylinder cut out 16.56 kW

    B.P. with No. 4 cylinder cut out 16.92 kW

    Estimate the IP of the engine and its mechanical efficiency.   (Ans. 28.41 kW, 83%)

3. A four-stroke cycle, four cylinder petrol engine has cylinder of 63.5 mm di and 95.2 mm stroke.

    On test it develops a torque of 62.66 Nms. When running at 3000 rpm. If the clearance volume in each cylinder is 663.00 nl, the brake thermal efficinecy ratio based on the air standard cycle is 0.5 and H.V. of petrol is 44 520 kJ/kg, determine the fuel consumption in kg/h and the brake thermal mean effective pressure. Take $\gamma = 1.4$ for air   (Ans.   6.28   kg/h; 652.4 kPa)

4. A four cylinder petrol engine is coupled to a brake dynamometer having an effective radius of 50 cm and running 2000 rpm. The brake load was 12 kg, when spark plug of each cylinder was short circuited in turn. The brake load adjusted to the same volume of speed were 8.5 kg, 8.75 kg, 8.0 kg and 8.9 kg find, IHP, BHP and mechanical efficinecy of the engine.

    Also, if at the time of, when carburettor was adjusted to air fuel ratio of 12 to evaporate 60% of the fuel at the manifold of fuel throttle, find Pp of the fuel.   (Ans. [19.35 hp, 16 hp, 0.0634 kg cm²]

5. A six cylinder engine has 130 mm stroke and 109.4 mm bore what is the displacement of engine at a compression 17:1. (Ans. 7.32 litres)

6. A four cylinder four stroke compression ignition engine has a stroke bore ratio = 0.96. The total swept volume of engine = 4000 cm³ and clearance per cylinder = 62.5 cm³ piston speed 7.5 m/s, power = 40 kW calculate (a) Compression ratio (b) Brake mean effective pressure. [GATE-1995]

    (Ans. (a) 17:1 (b) 562.55 kPa)

7. A four cylinder tractor engine develop 50 kW of 2500 engine rpm, when tested on a proney brake dynamomter on brake arm length of 35 cm. Compute brake net scale reading and torque in Nm.   [GATE-1989]

    (Ans. 190.98 Nm)

8. A single cylinder four stroke diesel engine runs at 750 rpm. The diameter of the cylinder is 15 cm. The stroke bore ratio is 1.2. The clearance volume

is 600 cm3 and the mean effective pressure is 5 kgf/cm^2. The mechanical efficiency is 75% calculate

(i) IHP (ii) BHP (iii) IHP (iv) Compression ratio and (v) swept volume.
(Ans. (a) 3.24 hp, (ii) 3.93 hp (iii) 3.30 hp (iv) 6.3 (v) 3180.86 cm^3)

9.   A torsion dynamometer is fitted on a turbine shaft to measure the angle of twist. It is observed that the shaft twists 1.5° in a length of 5 m at 50 rpm. The shaft is oiled and has a diameter of 200 mm. If the modulus of rigidity for the shaft material is 85 GPa, find power transmitted by turbine. (Ans. 3662 kW).

10. In a laboratory experiment, the following data were recorded with rope brake.

Diameter of the flywheel 1.2 m; diameter of the rope 12.5 mm; speed of the engine 200 rpm; dead load on the brake 600 N; spring balance reading 150 N; calculate the brake power of engine. (Ans. 5.715 kW).

SUBJECTIVE QUESTIONS

1.   Define the terms: (i) Swept volume (ii) mean effective pressure (iii) volumetric efficiency (iv) piston speed (v) compression ratio (vi) power (vii) break mean effective pressure (viii) volumetric efficiency (ix) scavenge efficiency (x) relative efficiency (xi) torque (xii) stroke bore ratio

2.   Explain the terms: (i) BHP (ii) FHP (iii) IHP (iv) DBHP (v) sp. fuel consumption (vi) indicated thermal efficiency (vii) brake thermal efficiency (viii) mechanical efficiency (ix) power take of power (x) net power.

3.   Describe the construction and operation of a prony brake and rope brake adsorption dynamomter.

4.   Describe with sketches one form of torsion dynamometer and explain with detail the calculation involved in finding the power transmitted.

5.   What is the difference between brake dynamometer and drawbar dynamometer used on farms?

6.   Explain the working of spring type and hydraulic type drawbar dynamometer used on farms.

7.   How a strain gauge dynamometer is used for calculating pull on a member?

MULTIPLE CHOICE QUESTION

1.   The diameter of engine cylinder is known as
     (a)   bore   (b)   stroke
     (c)   sleeve   (d)   none of the above

2.   The linear distance between BDC to TDC is called.
       (a)   bore   (b)   stroke
       (c)   swept volume   (d)   none of the above

3.   The stroke bore ratio of the engines veries from
       (a)   2 to 8   (b)   1 to 1.145
       (c)   3 to 4   (d)   none of the above

4.   In tractor engines, the stroke bore ratio is about
       (a)   2.0   (b)   1.25
       (c)   3.0   (d)   4.0

5.   The volume displacement by an stroke of the piston is known as
       (a)   Piston displacement   (b)   piston speed
       (c)   both   (d)   none of the above

6.   The ratio of total cylinder volume to the clearance volume is known as
       (a)   compression ratio   (b)   clearance ratio
       (c)   stroke-bore ratio   (d)   none of the above

7.   The ratio of actual air taken into the cylinder to swept volume is called
       (a)   volumetric efficiency   (b)   mechanical efficiency
       (c)   thermal efficiency   (d)   none of the above

8.   The ratio of brake power to indicated power is called
       (a)   mechanical efficiency   (b)   volumetric efficiency
       (c)   thermal efficinecy   (d)   none of the above

9.   The power obtained cylinder is known as
       (a)   indicated power   (b)   brake power
       (c)   both   (d)   none of the above

10.   The power obtained at crank shaft is called
       (a)   brake power   (b)   indicated power
       (c)   thermal power   (d)   none of the above

11.   The ratio of the indicated thermal efficinecy to the corresponding standard efficiency is called
       (a)   volumetric efficiency   (b)   relative efficinecy
       (c)   mechanical efficinecy   (d)   none of the above

12.   The sum of brake power and frictional power is known as
       (a)   indicated power   (b)   thermal power
       (c)   both   (d)   none of the above

13.   Sleavenge efficiency (ηc) is related to
       (a)   4-stroke engine   (b)   2-stroke engine

(c)   both   (d)   none of the above

14.   The S.I. unit of torque is

      (a)   Nm   (b)   Pa

      (c)   J   (d)   none of the above

15.   Prony brake dynamometer is used to measure

      (a)   torque   (b)   force

      (c)   both   (d)   none of the above

16.   Drawbar dynamometer is used to measure

      (a)   Draft   (b)   torque

      (c)   pressure   (d)   all of the above

17.   The most sensitive dynamometer is

      (a)   spring dynamometer   (b) hydraulic dynamometer

      (c)   strain gauge dynamometer

18.   Which of the following is an adsorption type dymamometer

      (a)   prony brake dynamometer

      (b)   rope brake dynamometer

      (c)   both   (d) none of the above

19.   Which of the following is a drawbar dynamomter

      (a)   spring dynamomter

      (b)   hydraulic dynamomter

      (c)   strain.gauge dynmameter

      (d) all of the above

20.   The displacement volume of 4-stroke engine is given by

      (a) $ALN\dfrac{n}{2}$ (b) $ALNn$

      (c) $ALN\dfrac{n}{4}$ (d)   none of the above

21.   The indicated power of 4-stroke engine in KW is given by

      (a) $\dfrac{P_m \text{ LAN}}{60 \times 10^{12}} \times \dfrac{n}{2}$ (b) $\dfrac{P_m \text{ LAN}}{60 \times 10^{10}} \times \dfrac{n}{2}$

      (c) $\dfrac{P_m \text{ LANn}}{60 \times 10^{12}}$ (d)   none of the above

FILL IN THE BLANKS

1.   The diameter of the cylinder is called .... the displacement of piston of from top dead centre to bottom dead is called ....

2.   .... is the volume displaces by the one stroke of piston.

3.   The compression ratio of diesel engine varies from .... and for petrol engine varies from ....

4.   Power measured at the piston of the engine is called ....

5.   Power available at the end of the crank shaft on flywheel is called .... and measured by a suitable ....

6.   .... actually forces the piston down during the power stroke.

7.   .... is the ratio of brake power to .... indicated power.

8.   Mechanical efficinecy varies from .... to ....

9.   Prony brake dynamometer is an .... type dynamometer.

10.   Drawbar dynamometer is used to measure....................

ANSWER OF THE FILL UP THE BLANKS

1. Bore, stroke, 2 Piston displacement or swept volume 3. 14 : 1 to 22 : 1 4. Indicated power 5. Brake power dynamometer 6. Mean-effective pressure 7. Mechanical efficinecy. 8. 72 to 79. 9. Absorption 10. Drawbar pull.

ANSWER OF MULTIPLE CHOICE QUESTIONS

1 (a) 2 (b) 3 (b) 4 (b) 5 (a) 6 (a) 7 (a) 8 (a) 9 (a) 10 (a) 11 (b) 12 (a) 13 (b) 14 (a) 15 (a) 16 (a) 17 (c) 18 (c) 19 (d) 20 (a) 21 (a)

Chapter 7
Fuel, Combustion and Fuel System of I.C. Engine

7.1   Fuel: The materials which burn to produce controlled amount of heat energy are known as fuels. Examples of fuels are: wood cal, domestic gas (LPG), Kerosene, Diesel, C.N.G. and petrol etc.

But fuels commonly used in farm tractors are the products of crude petroleum. The fossils, fuels, especially petroleum oil, are depleting at a fast rate year after year and are bound to get exhausted in near future. Therefore, petroleum oil is always under threat of supply instabilities and cost escalations. This has led to use other fuels. There are many factors that must be considered in the selection of the alternate fuel. Some of these are cost per unit work done, engine performance, effect on engine components, availability, safety, storage managment and convenience.

There days, liquified petroleum gas (bottle gas), bio-diesels, plant oil esters, biogas, poweralcohal, methane gas are used as the substitute for petroleum oil is stationary as well as tractor engines.

7.2   Petroleum: Petroleum is a dark coloured, viscous and fuel smelling crude oil. The name petroleum means rock oil (petra=rock, oleum=oil). It is called petroleum because it is found the crust of earth trapped in rocks. The crude oil petroleum is a complex mixtures of severals solid, liquid and gaseous hydrocarbons mixed with water, salt and earth particles. Thus, the crude petroleum oil is not a single chemical compound but it is a mixture of compound. Petroleum is lighter than water and insoluble in it.

7.2.1. Chemical Composition of Petroleum: It is made up of 100's of different chemical fram methane to asphalt. It consists of hydrocarbon with very small amount of nitrogenous solution and sulphur compound. The hydrocarbons are paraffine (C_nH_{2n+2}), Olefin (C_nH_{2n}), diolefin (C_nH_{2n-2}) and aromatic hydrocarbon (C_nH_{2n-6}, n_6).

The percentage composition of petroleum is C (89-given in Tables)

Table 7.1

Name of elements	C	H	N	S	O
Percent of elements	83 - 87	11 - 15	0.5	0.6	3.5

The disaguable odour of petroleum is due to the sulphur compound present in it.

7.2.2 Origin of Petroleum: Petroleum oil was formed by the decomposition of the remains of extremely small plants and animals (micro-organisms) buried under the sea, millions of years ago. It is believed that millions of years ago, the microscopic plants and animals (or micro-organisms) which lied in seas died. Their bodies sank to the bottom of the sea and in course of time they mixed with mud and sand. The chemical effects of presence, of heat and bacterias, converted the remains of microscopic plants and animals into petroleum oil just as they converted forest trees into coal. This conversion took place in the absence of oxygen or air. The petroleum thus formed got trapped between two layers of irripervious rocks forming an oil trap.

7.2.3 Refining of Petroleum : The process of separating crude petroleum oil into more useful fractions is called refining. The refining of petroleum is done by the process of fractional distillation. The distillation kin is shown in Fig. Various fractions obtained by the fractional distillation of crude petroleum oil are: Petroleum gas, (C_1 to C_4) Gasoline or Petrol, (C_5 to C_{10}), Kerosene oil (C_{10} to C_{12}), Diesel oil (C_{13} to C_{16}), Fuel oil (C_{16} to C_{18}), Lubricating oil (C_{17} to C_{20}), paraffin wax (C_{20} to C_{30}) and Asphalt (C_{30} to C_{50}).

Since the most of the fractions obtained from petroleum like petroleum gas, gasoline (or petrol), Kerosene oil, diesel oil, fuel oil burn radily, so they are used as fuel.

7.2.4 Products of Fractional distillation of Petroleum: Fractions of petroleum are followings:

(1)   Petroleum Gas: The molecular composition of petroleum gas is from C_1 to C_4 hydrocarbon. Its boiling range is below 40°C Petroleum gas is used as fuel as such or in the form of liqufied petroleum gas (LPG). Petroleum gas is also used in the production of carbon black (needed in type industry) and of hydrogen (needed in fertilizer industry). It is also used in the manufacture of gasolene (petrol) by the proces of polymerization.

(2)   Gasoline or Petrol: The molecular composition of gasoline is from C_5 to C_{10} hydrocarbons and its boiling range is 40°C to 170°C. Gasoline or petrol is used as a fuel in motor cars, scooters, motor-cycles and other lighter vehicles. Petrol is also used as a solvent; for dry cleaning clothes, and for making petrol gas.

(3)   Kerosene oil: The molecular composition of kerosene oil is from C_{10} to C_{12} hydrocarbons, and its boiling range is from 170°C to 250°C. Kerosene oil is used as a household fuel. For examples kerosene is used in wich stoves or pressure stoves to cook food. It is also used as an illuminant (for lighting purposes) in himicane or petroleum lamps, It is also used for making oil gas. A special grade of kerosene oil is used as 'aviation fuel' in jet aeroplanes. It is less volatile than petrol.

(4) **Diesel Oil:** The molecular composition of diesel oil is form C_{13} to C_{16} hydrocarbon and its boiling range is 250°C to 350°C. Diesel oil is used as a fuel for heavier vehicles like buses, trucks, railways engines and ships. Diesel is also used to run water pumps required for irrigation in fields, and in diesel generators to produce electricity on small scale.

(5) **Fuel Oil:** The melecular composition of fuel is from C_{16} to C_{18} hudrocarbon and its boiling range is 350°C to 400°C. Fuel oil is used in industries to heat boilers and in furnaces. Fuel oil is a better fuel than coal because fuel oil bunrs completely and does not leave any residuce, on the other hand, when coal is burnt it leaves behind a lot of ashes which has to be removed regularly from the coal furnace.

(6) **Lubricants oil:** The molecular composition of lubricating oil is C_{17} to C_{20} hydrocarbon, and its boiling range is beyond 400°C. Lubricating oil is obtained during the further fraction of residual oils It is used for lubricating machinary.

(7) **Paraffin wax:** The molecular composition of paraffin wax is from C_{20} to C_{30} hydrocarbons, and its boiling range is above 400°C. Paraffin wax is also obtained during the further fraction of residual oils. It is used for making candles, vascline, ointments, wax paper, toilet goods and grease.

(8) **Asphalt:** Asphalt is black, sticky substances having molecular composition of C_{30} to C_{50} hydrocarbons. Asphalt is non-volatile substance. So it does not vaporise. It is left behind as a residue in the fractionation of residual oils. Asphalt is used for making road surface.

Note: After its separation the fuel must be chemically treated to remove impurities, chiefly sulphur and gum.

7.3 Quality of Gasoline:

Gasoline obtained from the petroleum refining is used as a fuel in the internal combustion engines of scooters, motor cars and aeroplanes. In these engines, the mixutre of petrol or gasoline vapours and air is compressed by a piston in the cylinder of the engine and this compressed mixutre in then ignited by the spark from the spark plug. The efficiency and power of the engine depends upon the extent to which the fuel-air mixture gets compressed at the time of ignition. The greater the compression, greater will be efficiency of the engine. However, compression cannot be increased beyond a certain limit because it will result into sudden and irregular burning of the fuel mixture causing jerks against the piston and give rise to violent sound. This is known as knocking. The knocking reduces the power of the engine and also causes damage to the piston and the cylinder.

The maximum compression that can be attained in a given engine without any knocking depends upon the nature of the fuel. This is also called antiknocking value of fuel. This is expressed in terms of octane number.

7.4   Octane Number: It is defined as the percentage by volume of iso-octone in the mixuture of the iso-octane and n-heptane which has the same anti-kenocking qualities as the fuel under test or examination.

Petrol is graded in terms of octane number. It is an arbitray scale based on n-heptane and iso-octane (2, 2, 4-trimethyl pentone).

CH_3-CH_2-CH_2-CH_2-CH_2-CH_3, Octane number = 0

$$CH_3 \quad CH_3$$
$$| \qquad |$$

CH_3-C-CH_2-CH-CH_2, Octane number = 100

$$|$$
$$CH_3$$

All gasolines with octane number 80 or more are regarded as good fuels. It is interesting to note that quite recently. Chemists have prepared some hydrocarbons with octane no. less than zero (e.g., n-nonane has octane no. (45), as well as hydrocarbons with octane number grater than 100 (e.g.; 2, 2, 3-trimethyl heptene has octane no. 124).

7.5   Influence of structure of the Hydrocarbons on the Octane Rating: The octane number of a hydrocarbon depends upon its structure.

In general,

(a)   Straight chain alkanes have very low octane numbers.

The value increases with the increase in the length of the chain.

(b)   The branching of the chain increases the octane number of fuel.

(c)   Cyclic alkanes have higher octane numbers than the corresponding straight chain alkanes.

(d)   The unsaturated hydrocarbons (alkenes and alkynes) have higher octane numbers than the corresponding straight chain hydrocarbons.as

(e)   Aromatic hydrocarbons have very high octane numbers .

7.6   Antiknocking compounds: Knocking in engines in harmful. It can be decreased by the addition of certain compounds called antiknocking compounds. These are the compounds which when mixed with gasoline or petrol, tend to improve the octone numbers and therefore, decrease the knocking in the cylinder of the internal combustion engines.

The commonly used antiknocking compound is tetraethyl lead [$(C_2H_4)_4$ Pb], which is mixed in very small amount (about 0.01%) with the gasoline. The mixture thus, formed is called leaded gasoline or Ethly gasoline.

7.6.1   Preparation of Tetrethyl lead (TEL) : It is prepared by following methods:

(I)   From Gringnard reagent: When ethylmagnesium bromide in treated with lead tetrachoride, tetraethyl lead is obtaind.

$$C_2 H_5 Br + Mg \xrightarrow{\text{dry ether}} C_2 H_5 Mg Br$$

$$PbCl_4 + 4 C_2H_5Br \rightarrow (C_2H_5)_4 Pb + 4 Mg BrCl$$

(II)   From sodium lead alloy: When sodium lead alloy is treated with ethyl iodine, tetraehtyl lead is obtained

$$4C_2H_5I + 4 Pb (Na) \rightarrow (C_2H_5)_4 Pb + 3Pb + 4Na$$

7.6.2. Function of TEL: In the cylinder of internal combution engine,TEL $[(C_2H_5)_4]$ Pb decomposes to form ethyl radical.

$$(C_2H_5)_4 Pb \rightarrow Pb + 4 CH_3 CH_2$$

The ethyl radicals combine with the radical produced due to irregular combustion. As a result, reaction chains are broken and burning of the fule takes place smoothly. This prevents knocking. As leaded gasoline buses, lead metal gets deposited in the engine. This is removed by adding ehtylene dibromide which reacts with lead to form lead bromide. The lead bromide is volatile and is carried off with the exhaust gases from the engine.

CH₂-CH₂ + Pb → CH₂ + PbBr₂

  | | ||

Br   Br   CH₂ Lead bromide

Ethylene dibrmide   Ethylene

7.7   Cetane numbers: The whole number nearest to the percentage by volume of nornal contane ($C_{16}H_{34}$) in a blend with a methyl nephathalens that matches the ignition quality of the fuel when compared under prescribed conditions of operation in a special engine (such as ASTM-CFR engine).

Cetane ignites rapidly and in arbitraily given the centane number 100 while a-methyl nephthalene ignites slowly and is assigned centane number zero.

$CH_3–(CH_2)_{14}–CH_3$

n-Hexadecane (Cetane)   Cetane number = 100

CH_3

Cetane number = 0

α-Methylnephthalene

Cetane number of a fuel is computed by using following relationship;

Cetane number = percent of n-cetane + 0.15 (percent of a-methylenephthane)

Note I: In general, high-cetane fuels permit an engine to get started at lower air temperature, provide faster engine warm-up without misfiring or producing white smokes reduce the formation of varnish and carbon deposites, and elminate diesel knock.

Note II: Generally, dieseal fuels marketed in India range from 30 to 60 Centane mumber.

Proterties of Fuel:

7.8.   Quality of   Fuel: The quality of the fuel mainly depends upon the following properties:

(a)   Calorific value of fuel

(b)   Volatility of the fuel

(c)   Ignition quality of fuel.

(d)   Residue

(e)   Ignition temperature.

(f)   Transportating and storage

(a)   Calorific Values of Fuels: The amount of heat produced by burning unit mass of the fuel completely is known as its calarific value. The unit of mass usually taken for measuring the calorific value of fuel is 'kilo gram', so, we can also say that "The amount of heat produced by burning 1 kilo gram of a fuel completely is called its calorific value. Thus, the common unit of measurin g calorific value is kilojoules per kilo gram (kJ/kg). The calorific values of some common fuels are given in Table 1.2.

Note: The more is the proportion of hydrogen in a fuel, the more is its calorific value.

Determination of Calorific Value of a Fuel: A rough estimates of the Calorific value of a fuel can be made as follows. We take a known mass, say gram of the fuel, which calorific value is to be determined, and burn it below a beaker containing a known mass, in grams, of water. The fuel, on burning, produces heat and this heat is absorbed by water taken in the beaker, so the temperature of water rises. The rise of temperature of water is t^{o}C. The amount of the fuel is burnt in formed out from the initial and final temperature readings of water. Knowing the mass of water(m) taken in the beaker, specific heat (s) of water and the rise in temperature (t) of water, the quantity of heat produced by burning x grams of fuel is calculated by using the formula.

Heat produced (Q) = m x s x t   (7.1)

where,

m = Mass of water, kg

s = Sp. heat of water, $Jkg^{-1o}C^{-1}$

t = Rise in temperature of water, ^{o}C

This heat (Q) has been produced by burning x grams of the fuel. We can find out the calorific value in Joules per gram by dividing heat Q by t he mass x of the fuel burnt.

Calorific value = $\dfrac{Q}{x}$; kJ kg^{-1} (7.2)

Table 1.2

S.N.	Name of fuel	Calorific value (kJ/kg)
1.	Dung cake (upla)	6000-8000
2.	Wood	17 000
3.	Coal	30 000
4.	Charcoal	33 000
5.	Alcohol (ethanol)	30 000
6.	Diesel (and fuel oil)	45 000
7.	Kerosene oil	48 000
8.	Petrol	50 000
9.	Biogas	35 000-40 000
10.	Natural gas	33 000-50 000
11.	Butane (L.P.G.)	50 000
12.	Methane	55 000
13.	Hydrogen gas	150 000

(b) Volatility: It measues the tendency of fuel to convert liquid form to vapour form. In I. C. engine, all the liquid fuel must be converted into vapour fuel before burning. It depends upon intermolecular force between the molecules of liquid fuel. The more is the inter molecular force the less will be volatility. If the liquid fuel is not well vaporised it results into crankase oil dilution. A fuel having more volatility has got more ignition chances, so there is chances to vapour lock in the fuel system. Quickness in vapourising the fuel helps in producing more power swiftly which accelerates the engine.

The oil that vapouries quickly can be distributed well in different cylinders of the engine hence distribution of fuel in different cyliners is better in petrol engine than that of diesel engine.

(c) Ignition quality of fuel. It refers to ease of burning the fuel in combustion chamber.

(d) Residue: Fuel does not leave any poisonous or residue by products on combustion. A fuel is said to better fuel which does not leave any residues after combusion.

(e) Ignition temperature: The fuel should have proper ignition temperature.

(f) Transportation and storage: There should be convenience in transporting the fuel and should be easily storable.

7.9 Terminology Related Fuel and Combustion

7.9.1 Brake Specific Fuel Consumption: It is the quantity of fuel consumed by an engine per hour per unit brake power generated. It's S.I. unit is kg/kWh.

7.9.2. Brake Thermal Efficiency : It is the ratio of the heat realized as brake power to the heat content of the fuel used. It is expressed in percent and is computed by following relationship.

$$\eta_{th} = \frac{\text{Indicated work in heat units}}{\text{Energy supplied}} \qquad (7.3)$$

$$= \frac{60 \times BP}{w_f. (Cv)} \quad \text{where, } w_f = \text{Fuels supplied, kg/min.}$$

C_v = Calorific value kJ/kg

7.9.3 Gross Heating Value : The gross heating valve of a fuel at constant volume is the number of heat units which could be liberated when a unit weight of the fuel is burnt at constant volume in oxygen saturated with water vapour, the original and final material being at 15°C, the residual products being carbondioxide, nitrogen and water other than that orginally present as vapour, being in the liquid state. Units are Mega-Joules per kilogram (MJ/kg).

7.9.4 Cloud Point : The temperature, at which a cloud or hazre of wax crystals appear at the botton of the test jar when the oil is cooled under prescribed condtion.

7.9.5 Flash Point : The temperature at which a material produces sufficient vapour on mixing with the ambient air, leads to an ignitable mixutures and gives a momentary flash on application of a small pilot flame.

7.9.6 Pour Point : The lowest temperature, at which fuel ceases to flow under prescribed condition.

7.9.7 Direct Injection Type : A direct injection or open chamber diesel engine has the entire compressive volume in one chamber formed between the piston and head.

7.9.8 Indirect Injection Type : An indirect injection or divided chamber diesel engine has the entire compression volume in two (or three) distinct chamber, each separated by a restricting (throttiling) passage way.

7.9.9 Kinematic Viscosity : It is a measurse of the resistance to gravity flow of a liquid, the pressure head being proportional to its density. It is denoted by V and is given by following relationship.

$$v = \frac{\eta}{e} \qquad (7.4)$$

7.9.10 Cetane number : The whole number nearest to the percentage by volume of normal cetone ($C_{16} H_{24}$) in a blend with a-methyl naphathlene that matches the ignition quality of the fuel when compared under prescribed conditions of operation in a special engine (such as ASTM-CFR engine).

7.9.11 Octane Number : It is defined as the percentage by volume of iso-octane is the mixture of iso-octane and n-heptane which has the same anti-knockig qualitites as the fuel under test.

7.9.12 Ignition Temperature : The lowest temperature at which a substances catches fire and starts burning is known as the Ignition temperature.

7.9.13 Pre-ignition : Pre-ignition is an unwanted process of igniting charge earlier than desired which results into great thrust an piston restricting it to move up, resulting in production of sound. Pre-ignition may result in blowing of piston crown, or breaking of piston or bending of connecting or any other part of engine. It occurs in petrol engine.

7.9.14 Detonation :

(A) Definition: It is spontaneous combustion of remaining portion of charge of fuel and air (i.e., auto ignition of remaining charge) causing knocking due to rapid high pressure rise on a petrol gasoline.

(B) Process of Detonation: When the air-fuel mixture in an engine is ignited by spark plug, it does not burnt all at once. On the other hand, a wave front is formed at the spark plug which travels further with a certain flame velocity, gradually compressing the unburnt charge till it may so happen that the whole of unburnt charge is burnt all at once in the form of an explosion. This sets up a pressure wave which travels inside the combustion chamber to and fro, striking the wall. The gas in the combustion chamber will be compressed and expanded alternately by the pressure wave till equilibrium is restored. This disturbance forces the walls of the combustion chamber to vibrate at the same frequency as the gas. A peculiar ringing sound is thus produced and the phenomenon is called detonation or knocking.

(C) Difference between Detonation and Inflammation: In inflammation, flame travels along at the rate of few metre per sec but in detonation process the flame travels at few thousand metre per second.

(D) Factor Affecting Detonation: The following are the main factors which affect detonation.

(i) The use of pure oxygen instead of air.

(ii) The use of acetylene and air as the explosive mixture: After burning creats excessive pressure and temperature causes detonation ultimately severely stressed results into fractured cylinders and pistons.

(iii) To high compression pressure for the fuel used: It causes excessive temperature causes detonation.

(iv) To much turbulance in the mixture: Since turbulance decides the rate of flame propagation, it is evident that given sufficient turbulence in a small combustion chamber, the flame may pass across the chamber before the preliminary reactions in the detonating zone have had time to be completed. In such circumstancs, although detonation is absent the engine may be very rough.

(v) Mixture Strength: Moisture strength affects the delay period and the rate of flame propagation, and since both these exercise a fundamental influence on detoriation, variation in mixture strength is bound to affect detonation. The tendecy to detonate is greater with a mixture 20% rich.

(vi) Incorrect design of combustion chamber: The design of the combustion chamber has a most important effet on the liability of an engine to detonate, since tis controls:

(a) The position of spark plug

(b) The position of exhaust valve

(c) the position of pockets in which unburnt gas may be trapped.

The position of the spark plug determines the distance that the flame has the travel before reaching the detonation zone, the greater the travel of the flame, then, the greater the liability to detonation.

In the best form of cylinder head the sparking plug is placed centrally, but this involved the use of either twin camshaft or sleeve valves.

The presence of the hot exhaust valve in the detonation zone will promote detonation.

(vii) Fuel: Detonation to a large extent depends upon the fuel employed; any fuel rich in paraffins is liable to it. On the other hand, coal tar products known as Aromatics (because of thier aroma) are anti-detonation like benzol & alcohol. Unfortuntely both benzol and alcohal have lower calofrific values than petrol; hence fuel consumption is increased by their use.

Further objections to alcohol are that it is difficult to bend with petrol, especially in the presence of water. It attacks metals, specially alluminium alloys and is difficult to store through being unstable.

7.9.15 Testing of Liquid Fuel: The following tested are carried out to test the liquid fuel.

(A) Gravity Test of Liquid Fuel: The gravity of a fuel may eb expressed as specific gravity or as API. the specific gravity of a liquid is the ratio of density of substance to the density of water API (American Petroleum Institute gravity is expressed as

$$API_{degree} = \frac{141.5}{\text{sp. gravity of oil at} 15.5°C} - 131.5$$

API gravity fuel commonly contians more calorific value per unit mass but because of its lightness, will have a lower calorific value per unit volume.

Note: API gravity of water is 10.

(B) Distillation Test of Liquid Fuel: A more reliable and widely used method of determining the value of liquid fuels is known as the ASTM distillation tes. In making such a test a given quantity of the fule is placed in flask, heated, and its so called intial boiling pint noted from the thermometer inserted in the top of the flask. Then, as the heating is continued a certain amount vaporizes, pass off and in condesned. The tempreature at which certain percentaged of the fuel pass off are noted, and finally the end point is observed. The following terms are sued for distillation test.

(a) 10 per cent point: The "10 per cent point", as it is commonly called, is of primary importnace as a specification related to engine starting. The lower this tempreature, the better will be starting characteristics of the gasoline.

(b) 50 per cent point: It refers the engine warm-up characteristics of gasoline; i.e., the lower the 50 percent point tempreature the faster will be warm up.

(c) 90 percent point: The 90 per cent temperature refers a good indication fot he fuel performance.

(d) End point: It has little significance and is not usually included in gasoline specifications.

7.10 Emperical and Molecular Formula

7.10.1 Emperical Formula: It is the formula of a compound which gives the simple whole ratio of atoms of various elements prsent in one molecule of compound, e.g., the empirical formula hydrogen peroxide HO and of benzene is CH.

7.10.2. Determination of Empirical Formula: Procedure for determining the empirical formula is sumrised in Table 1.3.

Table 1.3 Emirical Formula

S.No.	Name of elements	At. wt of elements	Percentage of elements	Simplest ratio	Simples whole No. ratio	Empirical formula
1.	C	12	84	84/12	7	C7H16
2.	H	1	16	46/1	16	

Notes:

1. The atomic ratio is divided by its least value to get the simplest ratio.

2. If the simplest ratio is not a whole number then it is made so either by changing the value to the nearest whole number of by multiplying with suitable inter thoughout.

Note: Two or more molecules or compounds having same empirical formula.

7.10.3 Empirical Formula Mass: The sum of the atomic mass of various atoms represented by the empirical formula of the compound is known as its empirical formula mass. For example, the empirical formula of glucose in CH_2O. Thus, the empirical formula mass of glucose is $12 + 2 + 16 = 30$

7.10.4 Molecular Formula: It is the formula of compound which gives the actual number of the atoms of various elements present in one molecule of the compound e.g., the molecular formula hydrogen peroxide is H_2O_2 and benzene is C_6H_6.

7.10.5 Relation between Empirical Formula and Molecular Formula: Molecular formula of a compound is a simple whole number of its empirical formula.

Moelclar formula = n x empirical formula

where, n = simple whole number i.e., 1, 2, 3,........

Mathematically, $n = \dfrac{\text{Molecular mass}}{\text{Empirical mass}}$ (7.5)

7.10.5 Percentage Composition: Percentage of an element in a chemical compound is the number of parts by weight of it present in 100 parts by wesight of the compound. Mathematically it is expressed as.

Percentage of the element $= \dfrac{\text{Number of parts by weight of the element}}{\text{Molecular mass of compound}} \times 100$ (7.6)

7.10.6 Percentage of Carbon: It is given by following relationship,

% of carbon $= \dfrac{\text{Weight of carbon}}{\text{Weight of the compound}} \times 100$ (7.7)

$= \dfrac{12 x}{44} \times \dfrac{100}{W}$ (7.8)

7.10.7 Percentage of Hydrogen: It is given by following relationship,

% of Hydrogen $= \dfrac{2y}{18} \times \dfrac{100}{W}$ (7.9)

where, x = weight of CO_2 obtaind by combustion of 'W' gram of compound.

y = weight of water (H_2O) obtained by a combustion of 'W' gram of compound.

7.11. Combustion: The burning of a substance in oxygen of air in which heat and light are produced is known as combustion. The substance being burned can be an element or a compound. Here some examples of combustion.

7.11.1 Combustion of Hydro carbons: The general equation of combustion of hydrocarbon is given below,

$$3.8\left(\dfrac{x+y}{4}\right)N_2 + C_x H_y + \left(x + \dfrac{y}{2}\right)O_2 \rightarrow xCO_2 + \dfrac{y}{2}H_2O + 3.8\left(\dfrac{x+y}{4}\right)N_2 \quad (7.10)$$

Since, Air by volume consists of 20.8 percent oxygen and 79.2 percent nitrogen.

(a) **Combustion of methane (CH$_4$):** When methane burnes in air, it combines with the oxygen of air to form carbondioxide and water vapour. A lot of heat is also released during the combustion of methane.

CH_4 (g) + $2O_2$ (g) + 7.6 N_2(g) CO_2 + $2H_2O$ (g) + 7.6 N2 (g) + Heat

12 + 1 x 4   2 x 32   7.6 x 28   12 + 32 2(1x 2 + 16) + 7.6 x 28

16   64   212.6   44   36   212.8

weight of rectant = 16 + 64 + 212.8 = 292.8

weight of product = 44 + 36 + 212.8 = 292.8

Hence, weight rectant = weight of product

$$\frac{Air}{Fuel} = \frac{Wt.\ of\ air}{Wt.\ of\ Fuel} = \frac{276.8}{16} = \frac{17.3}{1}$$

i.e., the theoritically correct air-fuel ratio is $\frac{17.3}{1}$

(b) **Combustion o benzene:**

2 C_6H_6 + $15O_2$ + 57 N_2+ $\rightarrow$ 12 CO_2 + $6H_2O$ + 57 N_2 + Heat

7.11.2 Combustion of Charcoal: When charcoal burns in air, then carbon combines with the air is form carbondioxide.

A lot of heat is also released during this reaction.

C   + O_2 ──────→ CO_2 +   Heat

Carbon   Oxygen   Carbondioxide

(From charcol) (From air)

7.11.3 Conditions Necessary for combustion: There are three conditions for combustion to take place. These are:

(a)   Presence of a combustible susbstance (A substance which can burn)

(b)   Presence of supporter of combustion (like air or oxygen)

(c)   Heating the combustible substance to its ignition temperature (w ignition point).

7.11.4 Classification of Combustion:

There are two types of combustion

(a)   Spontaneous combustion   (b)   Rapid combustion

(a) **Spontaneous Combustion:** A combustion in which no internal heat is given to start, it is knwon as spontaneous combustion. The burning of white phosphorous on its own, when exposed to air for some time is an example of spontaneous combustion. The heat required to start this spontaneous combustion is produced internally by the slow oxidation of white phosphorus in air.

(b) **Rapid Combustion:** A combustion in which a large amount of heat and light are evolved in a short time, is known as rapid combustion. The immediate burning of domestic cooking gas in a gas bunner to given heat and light is an example of rapid combustion.

7.11.5. Fuel combustion in Petrol Engine:

(A) A mixture of fuel and air is compressed and ignited by a spark. Since, ignition is not spontaneous process, therefore the spark occurs just before the end of the compression. The time interval between spark occurs and ignition is said to be spark advance. It has been found that the delay period of approximately 0.0015 second is affected by mixture strength $\left(\dfrac{\text{Wt. of air in charge}}{\text{Wt. of fuel in charge}}\right)$, tempreature or pressure or both at the time of ignition, the proportion of exhaust gas present and the fuel. It has been also found that the more is the speed the more will be spark advance. The spark advance is shown on an indicator diagram in Fig. 7.1

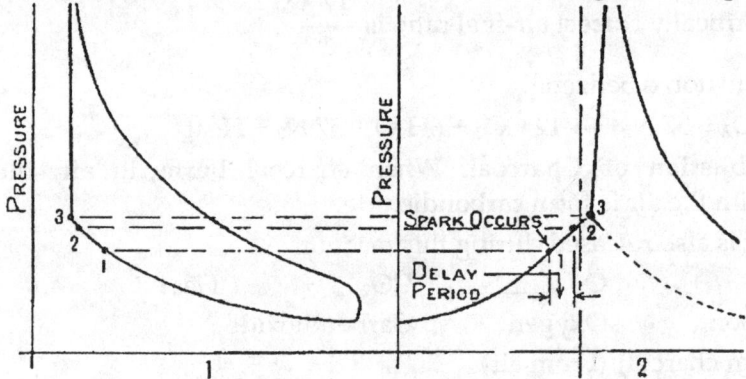

Fig. 7.1 Process of combustion in Petrol Engine

(B) Fuel combustion in Diesel Engine: Air alone is compressed and fuel is injected near the end of compression stroke resulting into burning of fuel due to heat of compression. Since, ignition is not a spontaneous process, therefore, fuel is added before the ignition starts. The time interval between fuel injection and ignition is called the Delay period. Immediately delay period, uncontrolled combustion starts resulting into very high cylinder pressure. The value of high pressure depends upon the accumulation of fuel charge in the cylinder. Even after the uncontrolled combustion, the fuel continues to be injected into the cylinder. During this period the rate of combustion depends upon the rate of fuel charge but pressure develop during this period is less than uncontrolled combustion because of that the piston goes downward in its power stroke.

Therefore, combustion of fuel is completed in three distinct steps namely delay period, period of uncontrolled combutsion and period of controlled combustion as shown in Fig. 7.2

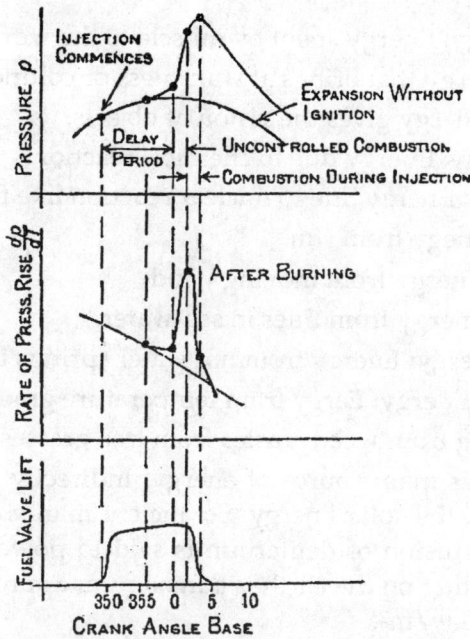

Fig 7.2. Process of Combustion in Diesel Engine

7.9 Energy: It is defined as the ablity to do work. Its unit (S.I.) is J.

7.9.1 Source of Energy: Any system from where energy can be trapped is called source of energy.

7.9.2 Charactertistics of Source of Energy:

(a)   Capable of providing adequate amount of energy.

(b)   Convenient to use and easy to store and transport.

(c)   Should be capable of giving desired quantity at required rate steadily over a long period.

(d)   should release energy in mostly all forms in which day's requirement exists.

7.9.3. Classfication of Source of Energy:

(i)   Conventional or Non-renewable Sources: Energy sources which are used traditionally far many years and are to deplete over a period of time are called conventional sources such as coal, petroleum, Natural gas etc.

7.9.4 Non-Conventional or Renewable Sources: Energy sources which do not deplete and are scavely used by the population are called non-conventional or renewable sources of enrgy e.g., solar energy, wind energy, vegetable refuse, wood, falling wake, geothermal power etc.

7.9.5 Forms of Energy:

(i)   **Muscular Energy:** Energy spent by muscle to the work.

(ii)   **Heat Energy:** Eergy that brings at warmness or coldness.

(iii) **Light Energy:** Energy gives the vision of objects.

(iv)   **Chemical Energy:** Energy due to chemical reaction.

(v)   **Nuclear Energy:** Energy due to nuclear reaction like fission & fusion

(vi)   **Solar Energy:** Enegy from sun.

(vii) **Wind Energy:** Energy from moving wind.

(viii) **Tidal Energy:** Energy from tides in sea-water.

(ix)   **Geothermal Energy:** Energy from hot water springs found under the earth.

(x)   **Ocean thermal Energy:** Eergy from temperature gradient in ocean water.

(xi)   **Biomass:** Eneryg from weed wastes from tree grasses crop.

7.10 Solar Energy: It is main source of energy. Indirectly or directly all form of energy originate from the solar energy. So ancient man workshipped sun as the source/God. Nuclear fusion of deuterium is said to power of the sun. A rough measure of energy falling on the earth is a maximum approximately of 940 w/m^2 and the average of 630 w/m^2.

The amount of solar energy received per square meter per second on the surface of earth is called solar constant. It is approximately 1.4 kJ/m^2. Only 0.47% of the solar energy reaching of the atmosphere, reaches the surface of earth. Although this energy source will likely become very useful for space heating and for agricultural operations such as crop drying. At present it is doubtful that it will be useful for operating tractors because of the low concentration of energy and a lack of suitable means of collecting and concentrating it. Another problem is the large differences in the amount of available solar energy at different times of year or day an at different locations.

7.11 Nuclear Energy: Energy produced by fission or fusion of the nucleus of atoms (of uranium) is called nuclear energy. Nuclear energy will ease the load on fossil fuels, as it is well adopted to large power plant operations where radiation shielding can be employed. It is a concentrated, clean and easily, controlled energy source, the energy in 4 ml of U235 is equivalent to the energy stored in 140 m^3 of coal ("Nuclar Energy" 1961).

Controlled fusion, the process of combining the lighter elements rather than breaking up the heavy atom as in done in the fusion process, may offer some hope from fusion power plants, even those as small as a farm tractor fusion fatomic energy does not require heavy shielding because it is not redioactive.

7.12. Biomass: Biomass has been traditional source of energy such as wood, crop residue, biogas are burnt to produce heat for domestic as well as industrial purposes.

Biogas is prepared from biomass. Biogas is a mixture of methane (55-70%) and carbondioxide (30-40%) and rest being impurition like ammonia, hydrogen. Its calorific value varies from 4500 to 5000 kcal/m³. Biogas could provide not only energy for cooking and lighting but also for diverse agricultural operation by running stationary engine. These days, biogas satisfactorily being used in SI as well as CI engine. Thus biogas is acceptable alternate fuels at present.

Some of the biomass-based fuels which have been used in IC engines, either as a partial or complete substitute to the gasoline/diesel fuel are as listed below:

(i)   Alcohals derived from grain and starchy/sugar crops, plants and trees.

(ii)   Biogas produced by anairobic fermentation of biomass, dung and refuge available from animal sources..

(iii)   Producer gas prepared by the partial burning (i.e., with less quantity of oxygen) of carbon rich biomass in a gasifier.

(iv)   Straight or modified plants oils derived from oil-rich seeds/nuts of farm crops and and fruit trees.

7.13 Fuel Injection System:

7.13.1 Purposes of Fuel Injection System:

The following are the main functions of fuel injections system is shown in Fig.

(i)   To provide correct fuel charge to each cylinder according to the load and speed.

(ii)   To inject fuel at the appropriate time in the cylinder.

(iii)   To facilitate efficient fuel utilization by atomizing the charge at the time of injection.

7.13.2 Classification of Fuel Injection System: There are two types of fuel injection system are used namely (i) Air injection system and (ii) Airless or solid injection system.

(2)   Air injection system: Air injection system makes use of streams of air under high pressure at about 5500 to 8000 kPa to force the fuel from the injector into the combustion chamber. This system is only adopted in very large stationary four-stroke-cycle engine and becoming obsolete becasue of necesscity of air storage tanks and other parts.

(ii)   Solid Injection System: In this system high pressure is applied directly by a pump to force the liquid fuel into the nozzles and then to combustion chamber.

It is further sub divided into system (i) Common rail injection system (ii) Individual pump injection system.

(a)   Common Rail Injection System: Layout of Fig. 7.3 Shows lay out of the common rail fuel injection system. In this type a single injection pump with injector called as unit injector is employed on each cylinder. The unit injector by rocker arm and spring similar to the engine's valve. A linkage connect the control rock of all the unit injectors, so that the fuel injection in all the cylinder may be equal and also controlled. The fuel is taken from the fuel tank by the fuel pump and is supplied to all the unit injection through a filter. Any fuel from the relief value is returned to the fuel tank.

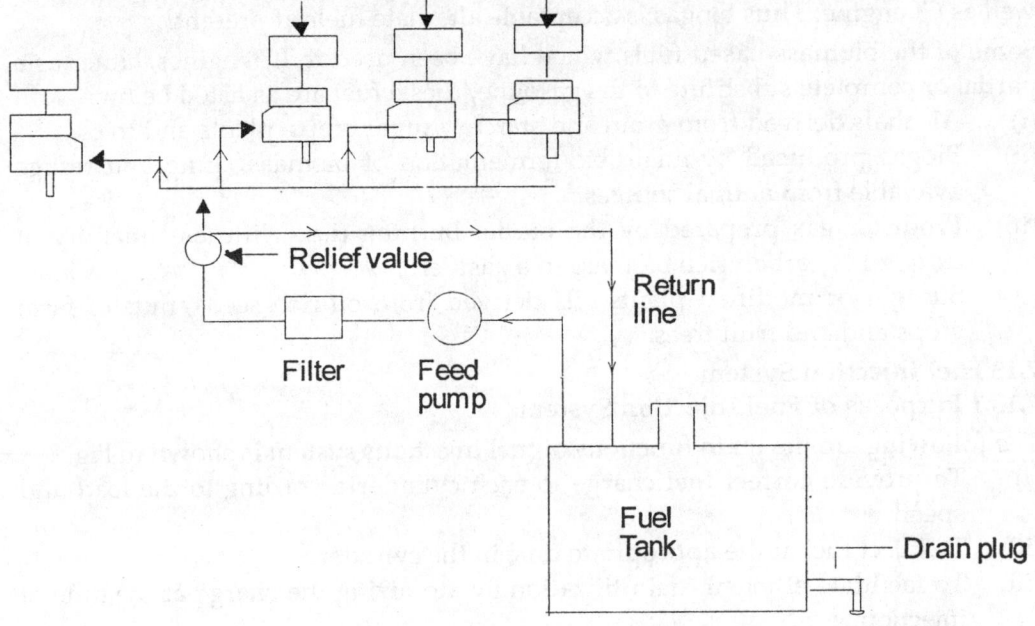

Fig. 7.3. Common Rail Injection System

(b)   Individual Pump Injection System: Fig. 7.4 shows the layout of common individual pump injectioin system. Fuel is drawn from the fuel tank by means of a fuel feed pump which is operated from the injection pump camshaft. The pump is provided with hand priming lever, so that the diesel oil can be forced into the system and air bleed out without turning the engine. The fuel is then passed through a filter and then to the fuel injection pump without the filter or with a poor quality, filter, abrasive material would reach the fuel injection pump and injectors resulting in poor starting irregular idling and deterioration in performance due to decreased fuel delivery from the injection pump. The abrosive material could also cause faulty spraying and leakage in the injectors results in the increased fuel consumption and heavy exhaust smoke.

Distributory system : This system consists of distributory unit along with the pump. The pump supplies fuel to the distributory unit from where the fuel is distributed to every cylinder separately.

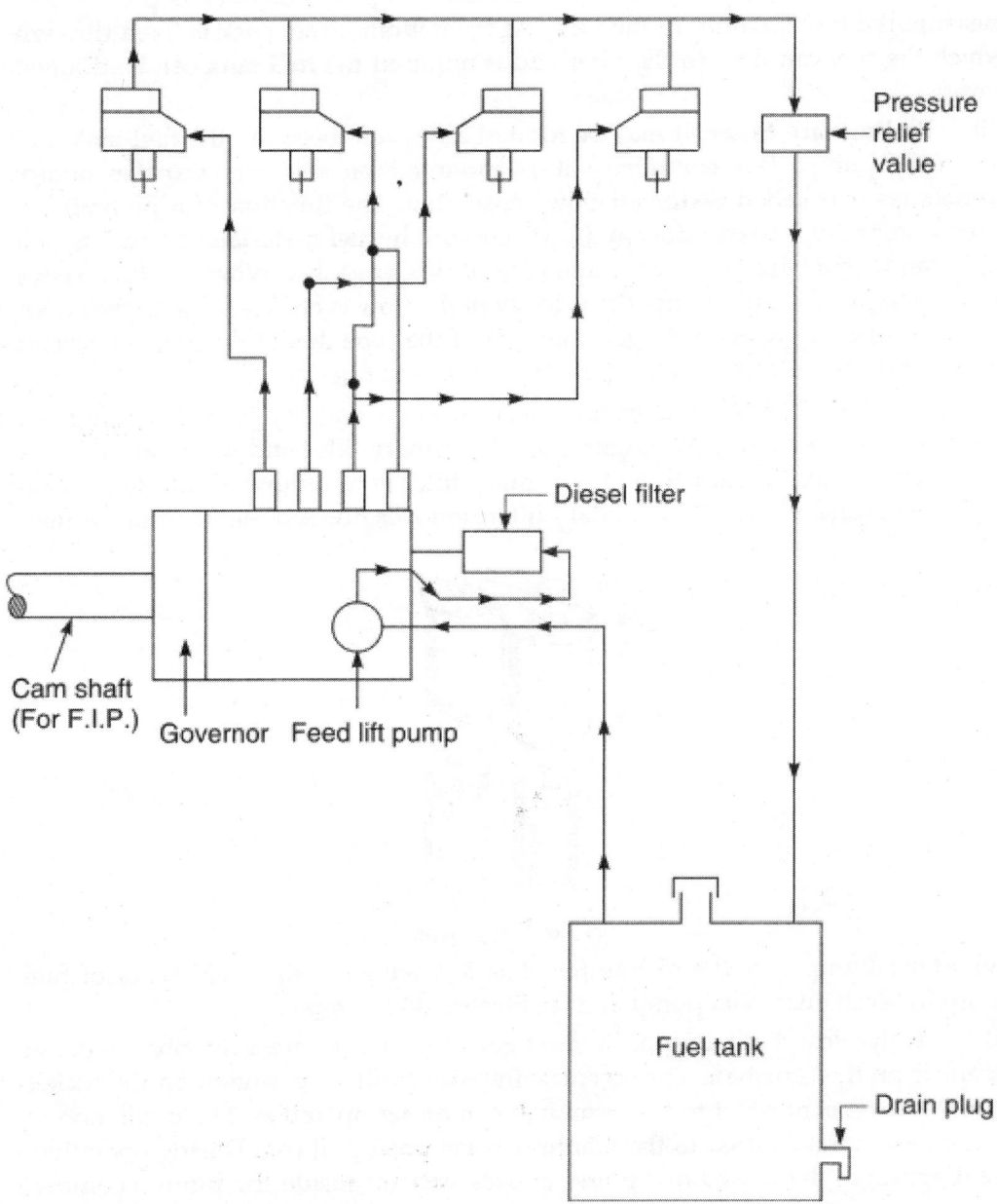

Fig. 7.4. Individual Pump injection system in diesel engine.

A pin hole is provided in the cap to maintain atmospheric pressure in the tank. When the pin gets checked, the fuel can not flow from the tank to the filter.

Generally fuel filter consists of a wire gauge strainer to filter the fuel, so that dust particles may not enter into the tank. In some engine, a dipstick is provided to measure the fuel quantity in the tank. At the bottom, drain cock is fixed through which the fuel can flow to the filter and if required the fuel tank can be drained empty.

(ii)   Preliminary Filter: It may be located anywhere between the fuel tank and fuel feed pump. But commonly it is mounted on the fuel transfer pump. Sometimes it is called Sediment Bowl Assembly. The function of a preliminary filter is to prevent coarse dust and dirt pressure in fuel materials. It consists of a glass cap with a wire gauge filter and cork or rubber gasket. When the fuel passes from the tank to the glass cup, the velocity of the flow is reduced due to the cross-section of the cup which is larger than that of the pipe due to the heavy particles of dirt settle at the bottom while clean fuel passes to filter.

(iii)   Fuel Filter: Most diese engines work on two stage system of filtering i.e., there are two filters in diesel engine namely primary filter and secondary filter as shown in Fig.7.6. The function of a primary filter is to remove water and coarse particles of dust while. The secondary filter removes fine sediments from the fuel.

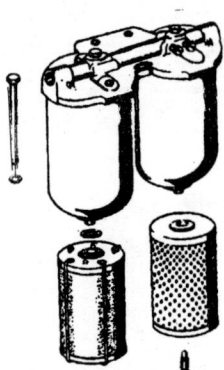

Fig. 7.6. Fuel Filter

(iv)   Fuel Pump (For Petrol Engine): The following are the main types of fuel pump (i) Mechanical fuel pump and (b) Electric fuel pump

(a)   Mechanical Fuel Pump: A mechanical pump receives motion from an eccentric on the camshaft. The eccentric imparts oscillatory motion on the rocker arm. A spring connected to this arm, helps in quiter operation. The oscillation of rocker arm is transmitted to the diaphragm via push-pull rod. During operation, the diaphragm depressed down and creates vaccum inside the pump chamber. The atmospheric air present causing so, the air makes flow of fuel into the pump from the tank. The lower motion of the diaphragm from sunction stroke and causes the inlet valve to open.

At the end of sunction stroke the inlet valve clooes and outlet valve now opens when the diaphragm executes delivery stroke. The delivery is performed under the influence of diaphragm returning to the spring the loading of which thus determines the delivey pressure of fuel. A mechanical fuel pump is shown in Fig. 7.7.

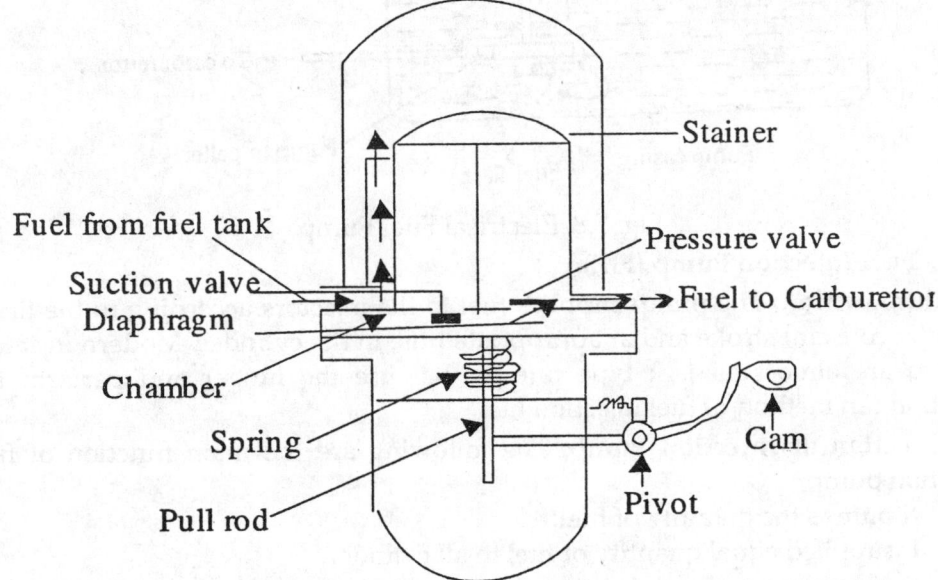

Fig. 7.7. Mechanical Fuel Pump

(b)   Electric Fuel Pump:

It consists of a diaphragm but it is operated electrically. When is turned on solenoid winding generates, magnetic flux, which pulls the armature and diaphragm above upward fuel and is drawn into fuel chamber through the inlet valve. But as soon as the armture moves up it disconnected the electricity supply. The magnetic flux collapse and the armature fall down, causing the diaphragm to move from creating the pressure in the pump chambers. This course the outlet valve to open and inlet valve to close. The fuel goes out to the carburettor. The downward movement of the armature again sets electric supply to the solenoid and the same process is repeated, the pump continues to operate untill the ignition switch is turned off.

Electric fuel pump is shown in Fig. 7.8.

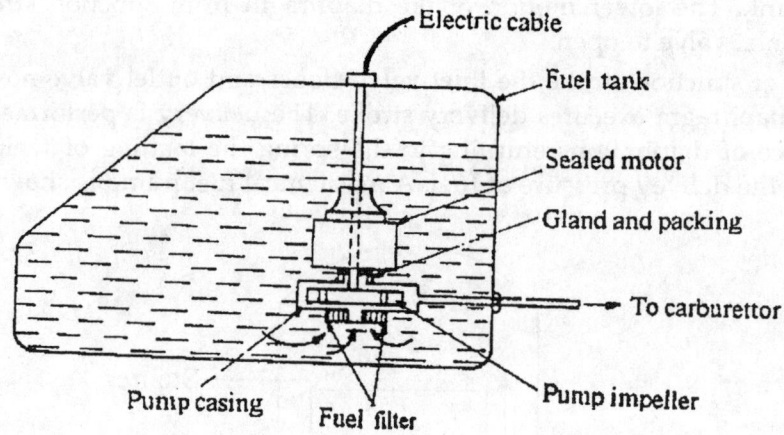

Fig. 7.8. Electrical Fuel Pump

(v) Fuel Injection Pump (FIP):

(A) Introduction: The pump supplies fuel to the injectors according to the firing order at constant stroke and at appropriate time in the cylinder. Modern injection pumps are almost all jerk type pumps that use the lunger and perform the function can method of fuel injection fuel.

(B) Function of Injection Pump: The following are the main function of fuel injection pump

(i)   It pumps the quantity of fuel.

(ii)   It supplied equal quantity of fuel to all cylinder.

(iii) It commences supplying the metered quantity of fuel at same degrees before TDC, to all cylinder.

(iv)   It builds up sufficient pressure so that diesel can be injected in the form of atomised spray.

(v)   The injection of diesel should be such that combustion process is kept under control.

(C) Classification of Jerk Type Fuel Injection Pump: They are classified as follows:

(a)   Multi element pump

(b)   Distribution (Rotary) type pump

(a) Multi Element Pump: The main components of pump is shown in Fig. 7.9. The plunger having helical upper part reciprocates in close fitting barrel. The helix makes it possible to vary the amount of the fuel delivered. An annular groove in the central part of the plunger facilitates the distribution of fuel over the barrel. The pluger reciprocates in the barrel through tappet and spring. As the pluger moves down, the fuel enters the barrel from inlet side and it goes up it closes the inlet part of the barrel, pressurises the fuel in barrel causing delivery

202

valve to lift off its seal and allows the fuel to enter into the injection line, leading the fuel injector. As soon as the edge of helix uncovers the split part of the barrel, the fuel pressure quickly drops.

Fuel injection pump is a high pressure pump used in diesel engine and creates very high pressure in the fuel pipe from injectig fuel into cylinder. It is based to creates pressure varying from 12,000 kPa to 20,000 kPa in the fuel pipe for injection of the diesel fuel in the cylinder.

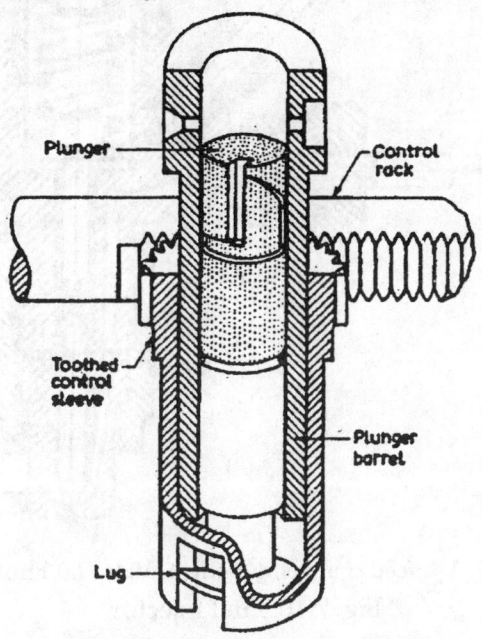

Fig. 7.9. Fuel Injection pump

(vi) Fuel Injector: It is a device which delivers smoothly atomised fuel under high pressure to the combustion chamber of the engine. Modern tractor engines have multiple holes injector. Main components of injector are (i) nozzle body and (ii) needle valve. Both of them are made of alloy steel. The needle valve is pressed against a conical seat in the nozzle body by a spring as shown in Fig. 7.8. The pressure of injection pump is adjusted by adjusting the screw. In working condition, fuel from fuel injection pump enters in the nozzle body through high presure pump. When the fuel pressure becomes so high that it exceeds the set spring pressure, the needle valve lifts off its seat. The fuel is forced out of the nozzle spray holes into the combustion chamber. The nozzle is fitted in a brass tube or sleave which is installed in the cylinder and is held in position by a special clamp.

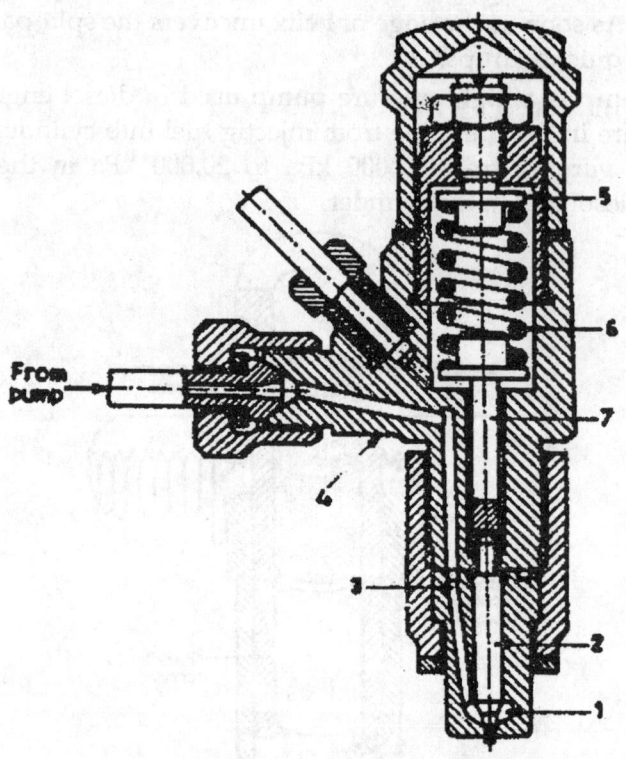

1. Atomizer, 2. Valve, 3. Infeed channel, 4. Body, 5. Valve lift limiter, 6. Spring, 7 Rod

Fig. 7.10. Fuel Injector

The nozzle of injector are of the following types:

(i)   Pintle Type: It consists of a nozzle tip of projection, which is slightly thinner than the nozzle tip. This prevents the nozzle tip from being clogged with carbon.

(ii)   Throttle Type: It is a nozzle with specially shaped nozzle tip projection which results into economy of fuel.

(iii)   Hole Type: It does not have nozzle tip. The valve seat is directly connected to a conically shaped outlet.

7.13.4 Fuel Injection System in Petrol Engine:

Introduction: Petrol from the fuel tank is fed to carburettor so that it can be mixed with air for onward feeding the cylinder as shown in Fig. 7.10.

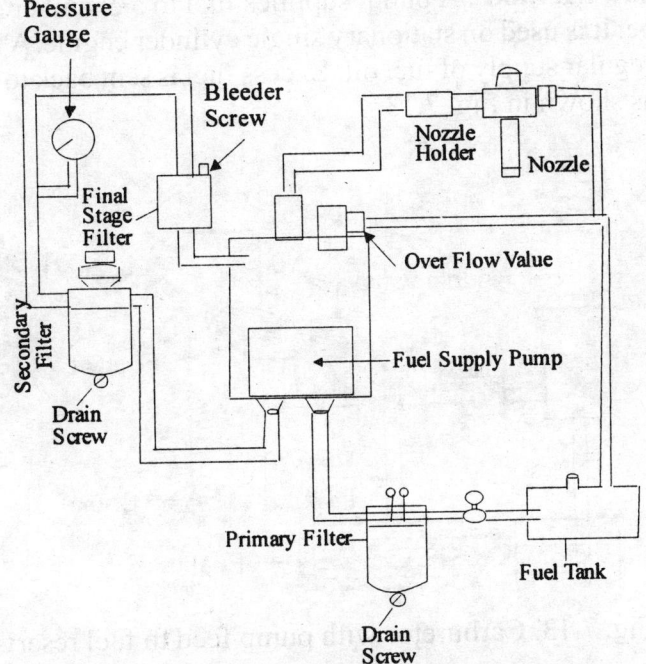

Fig. 7.11 Fuel Supply System in Petrol Engine

Fuel is fed to carburettor by the following two methods:

(i)   Gravity Feed Method (ii) Force Feed Method

(i)   Gravity Feed Method: In this method, fuel tank is placed above the level of carburettor and is connected with the help of pipe, fuel flows to the carburettor due to its own gravity. Such system is not popular in motor vehicles as there is no place to keep the tank at a higher level, however this method is used in almost all the motor cycles and scoorters, being very cheap.

(ii)   Force Feed Method: In this method tank is placed at a distance and also under the level of carburettor. To pump the fuel from the level and feed it to carburettor fuel, pump is used as shown in Fig. In almost all the vehicles this method is used and

(a)   Suction method (b) over flow method (c) Float valve method.

(a)   Suction method: In this methed, there is a chcck valve, provided in the fuel tank. The check valve is connected to the needle valve through a pipe. It is mainly used on single cylinder engine

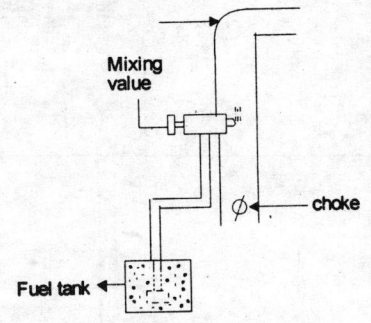

Fig. 7.12. Carburetor with Suction Feed and Check Valve.

(b) Overflow Method : A pump supplies fuel to a chamber equipped with an overflow pipe. It is used on stationary single cylinder engine. A fuel pump is used to maintain regular supply of fuel oil. Excess fuel is sent back to the fuel tank by a return pipe as shown in Fig. 7.13.

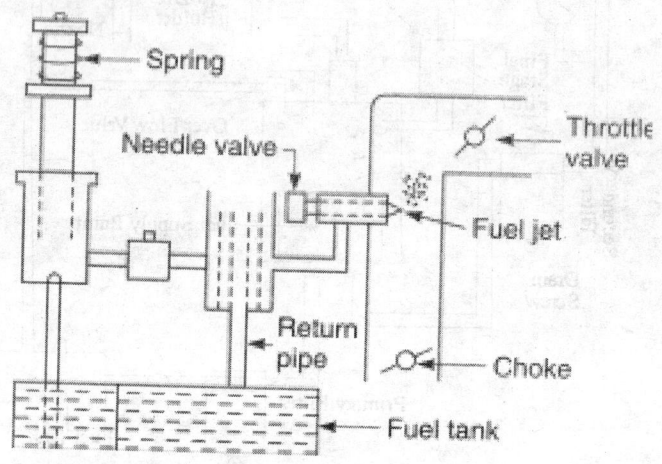

Fig. 7.13. Carburetor with pump feed to fuel reservoir.

(c) Float valve Method : A diaphragm pump is used to lift the fuel from the tank to the floating chamber. This method is common on multicylinder engines. The amount of fuel is controlled by a float operated needle valve in the pressure line as shown in Fig. 7.14.

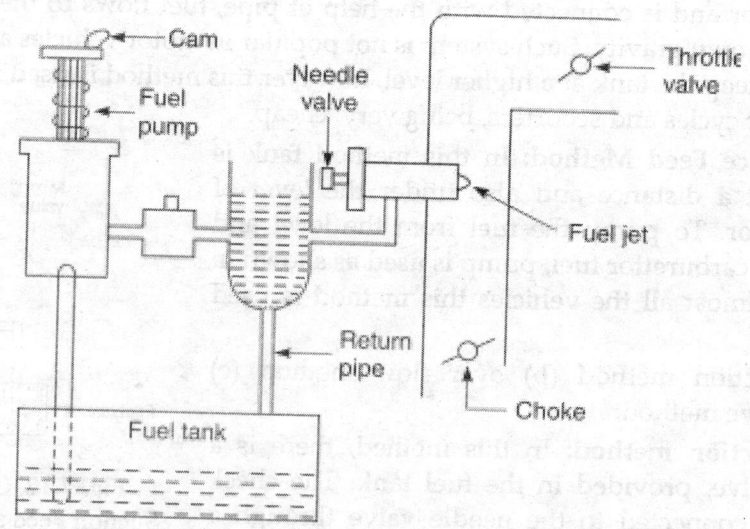

Fig. 7.14. Carburetor with pump feed to fuel reservoir.

7.13. 5 Carburetion System:

Presence of oxygen inside the cylinder is necessary for rapid combustion of the fuel. The fuel in vapour form is most suitable for combustion. If air is only in contact with the fuel, it will not help much. The best result is obtained when air is throughly mixed with the fuel. These conditions can be illustrated very well by the kerosene pumping stoves generaly used by students. If we have simply kerosene in a pot and we try to brun it, it will take time and even if it burns there will be no pressure in the flame. But as we pump the stove and oil starts coming out, just a flame touch, gives a powerful burning. The difference between the two is that in first the fuel was in liquid state and air was only in touch with it while in second case the air is throughly mixed with the fuel and at the same time the fuel breaks into small particles by allowing it to pass through the slove injector at very high pressure and velocity. The intensity of flows is controlled by air pressure inside the tank. Besides these, since engine runs at varying speeds and loads, we need some available devices having different mixtures automatically available at different speeds and loads. All these function together known as Carburetion and the device in which these function take place is known as Carburetor as shown in Fig. 7.15. These function of caburetor can be summerised as below.

(i)   To mix the air and fuel throughly.

(ii)   To atomise the fuel.

(iii) To regulate the air-fuel ratio of different speeds and loads.

(iv)   To supply correct amount of mixture of varying speeds and loads.

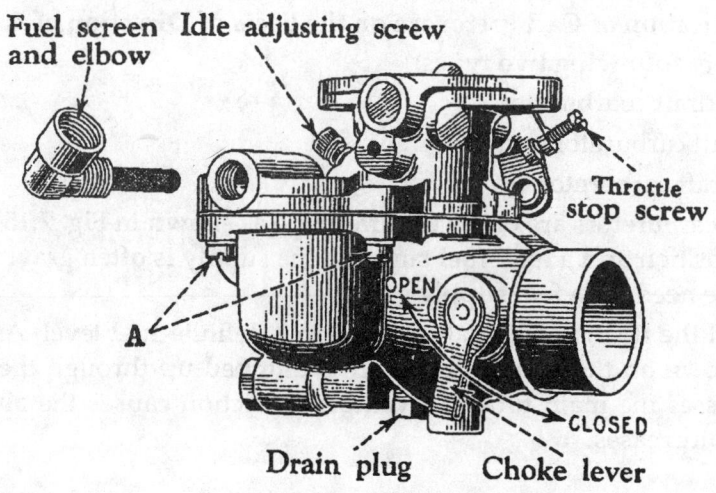

Fig. 7.15 Carburetor

7.13.6.Mixture Strength Required or Air-Fuel Ratio Requirement: While the air-fuel ratio (A-F) theoretically correct for gasoline, actually the carburetor should deliver different air-fuel ratio for different engine speeds as shown in Fig. 7.16.

When the engine is at slow speed, the air-fuel mixture should be richer since the valve timing valves are unsuited to slow speeds. The other speed ranges are economy and power, the former requires as lean an

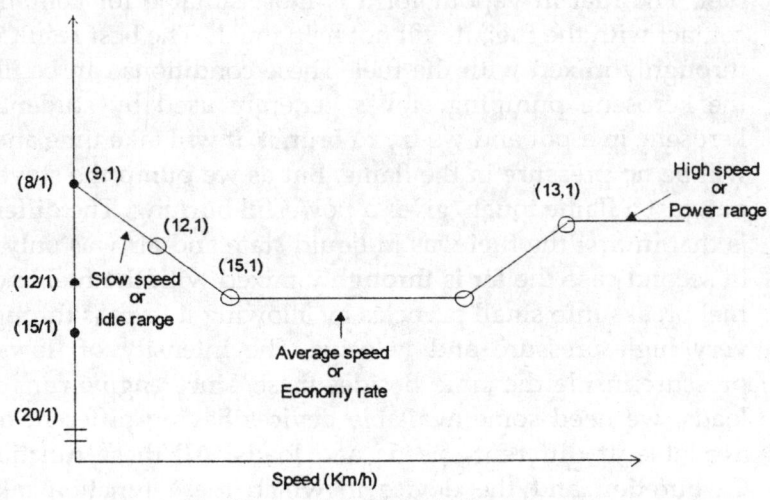

Fig. 7.16. Air Fuel Ratio Requirement

air-fuel Fig. 7.14. Air-fuel ratio requirements ratio as permissible, while the latter sacrifies economy for maxmium power performance.

Farm tractors engines do not perform as wide a speed range as other automotive engines consequently, their carburetors are simpler in construction and opearation.

7.13.7 Classification of Carburetor are on the basis of Direction of Air flow:

Caburetors are following two types:

(i)   Down-draft coarburetor

(ii)   UP-draft carburetor and

(iii)   Side-draft carburetor

Most tractor carburetors are of the up-draft type as shown in Fig. 7.15. With a low carburetor position and a high fuel tank, the fue supply is often gravity fed which eliminates the need for a fuel supply pump.

The float and the float, needle valve maintain a definite fuel level. As the engine pistons go down on the intake stroke, air is pumped up through the carburetor. When air passes the main tube, the venturi restriction causes the air velocity to momentarily increases.

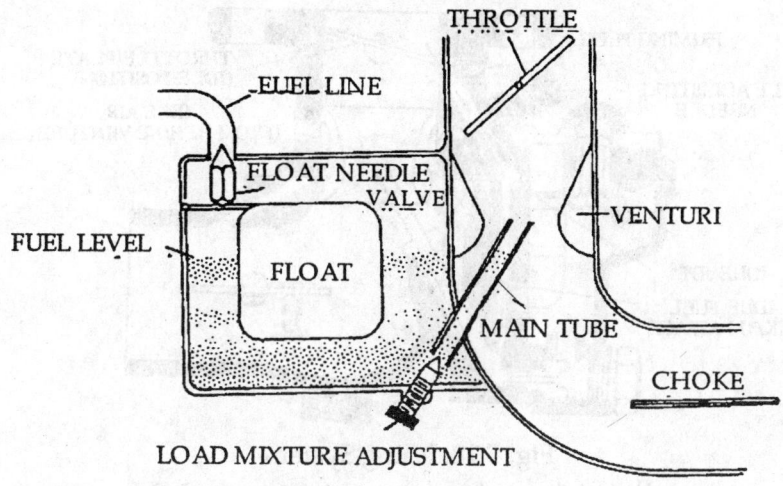

Fig. 7.17. Simple Up-draft Carburetor

As the velocity increases, its static pressure decreases and difference between the pressure and the float chamber pressure forces fuel out of the tube and into the air streams.

The throttle controls the amount of air and fuel entering the engine. As the choke is closed a greater pressure drop exits between the venturi section and the float chamber (of the throttle is open), thus on extr-reach mixture is pulled into the engine to aid in starting.

The load mixture needle valve is an adjustment to vary the air-fuel ratio by controlling the amount of the fuel entering the tube.

This simple carburetor works well for a constant speed engine but a completely inadequate for idling performance for a variable-speed engine. With the simple carburetor there is a tendency to produce increasingly rich air-fuel mixtures with increasing engine speed.

A complete tractor engine carburetor has an idling system and same type of compensating system in addition to the elements of the simple carburetor.

Idling jet supplies fuel at ideling or low speed only. It discharges fuel near the throttle as shown in Fig. 7.18. When the throttle plate is in a nearly closed position (engine idling), the air velocity part the main discharge tube in too low to pull out the fuel. But fuel is sucked up through the ideal (idle) passage channel. Its level being higher than the mainjet, in normal condition, fuel is supplied by the mainjet.

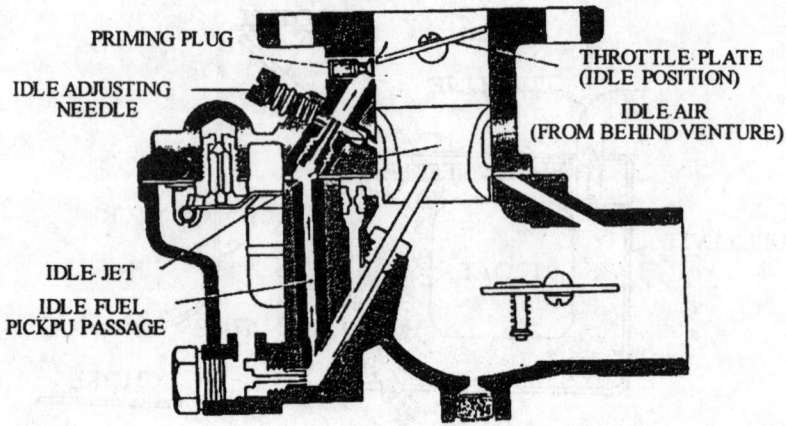

PRIMING PLUG

IDLE ADJUSTING
NEEDLE

THROTTLE PLATE
(IDLE POSITION)

IDLE AIR
(FROM BEHIND VENTURE)

IDLE JET

IDLE FUEL
PICKPU PASSAGE

Fig. 7.18. Idling System.

When main jet supplies richer mixture at higher speed the compensating jet supplies leaver mixture at that speed due to which a nearly constant air-fuel ratio occurs that results over a speed range and loads. These is well accelerating through which the jet g ets the fuel as shown in Fig.

Farm tractor carburetors are usually equipped with a balance line extending from the air intake form horn to the top of of the fleat chamber as shown in in Fig. 7.19. This device assures a constant pressure relation between the venturi and the fleat chamber regardless of external air resistances. The air-fuel ratio will not get richer due to clagged air cleaner.

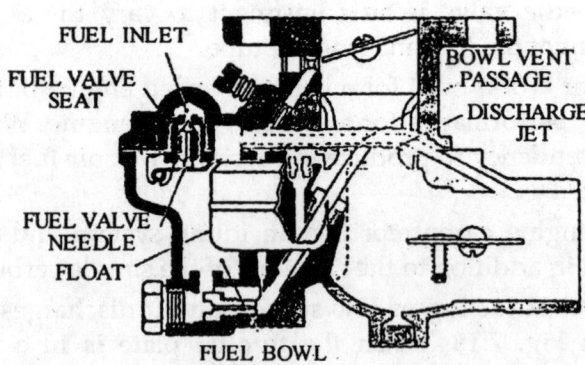

FUEL INLET

FUEL VALVE
SEAT

BOWL VENT
PASSAGE

DISCHARGE
JET

FUEL VALVE
NEEDLE

FLOAT

FUEL BOWL

Fig. 7.19. Fuel supply system

A back-suction economizer may be used to lean the air-fuel ratio or mixtures at part loads. The difference of air pressures at the air intake and above the throttle, effects the movement of piston.

7.13.8 Air Flow:

(i) Air is incompressible

(ii) Flow is frictionless

(iii) Process is adiabatic

The law of flow can be expressed by Bernouli's energy equation,

$$\frac{v^2}{2} + \frac{p}{\rho} + z = \text{constant}$$

where,

v = Velocity, m/s

r = Pressure, Pa

ρ = Density, kg/m³

z = Datum head, m

Hence neglecting the difference in height, we can write down for sution 1-1 and 2-2 as shown in Fig.

$$\frac{v_1^2}{2} + \frac{p_1}{\rho_a} = \frac{v_2^2}{2} + \frac{p_2}{\rho_a}$$

Where, ρa = Density of air, kg/m³

Since, v_1 is neglicgible in compression to v_2, the ideal velocity of the air at the throat is given by

$$v_2 = \sqrt{\frac{2(p_1 - p_2)}{\rho_a}}$$

$$= \sqrt{\frac{2\Delta p_a}{\rho_a}}$$

Due to contraction of stream and friction, the actual velocity of air throat is expressed as

$$V_a = C_a V_2 = C_a \sqrt{\frac{2\Delta p_a}{\rho_a}}$$

$$= C_a \sqrt{2gh}$$

Where,

Ca = Co-efficien tof discharge for air

$h = \dfrac{\Delta p_a}{\rho_a}$ = Head casuing flow, m

The weight of air flowing per second

211

$W_a = P_a A_a V_a$

$= \rho_a A_a C_a \sqrt{\dfrac{2\Delta p_a}{\rho_a}}$

$= C_a A_a \sqrt{2\rho_a \, \Delta p_a}$

Note: The value of Ca is genrally taken to be 0.84.

7.13.9 Appropriate Expression for the Air Flow:

The accurate or ideal velocity of air can be computed by applying the energy equation for steady flow assuming adiabatic expansion.

Taking one kg of air into consideration.

Let Q = Heat Energy, J/kg

W = work, J/kg

V = Specific volume, m³/kg

$$Q - W = U_2 - U_1 + p_2 v_2 - p_1 v_1 + \frac{v_2^2}{2} - \frac{v_1^2}{2}$$

Here,

$\theta = 0$, W = o and v_1 is negligible because v_1 is very-very small, in comparison to v_2.

Therefore,

$$\frac{v_2^2}{2} = (U + p_1 v_1) - (U_2 + p_2 v_2)$$

$$= H_1 - H_2$$

$$\therefore v_2 = \sqrt{2 (H_1 - H_2)}$$

Where, $(H_1 - H_2)$ = Adiabatic heat drop, J/kg

Now as the expansion follows adiabatic law

$pV^\gamma = k$

Here, Heat drop = $H_1 - H_2$

$$\frac{\gamma}{\gamma - 1} (p_1 v_1 - p_2 v_2)$$

= Shaded part on p-v diagram

Now, $v_2 = \sqrt{2(H_1 - H_2)}$

$$= \sqrt{2 . \frac{\gamma}{\gamma - 1} p_1 v_1 \left(1 - \frac{p_2 v_2}{p_1 v_1}\right)}$$

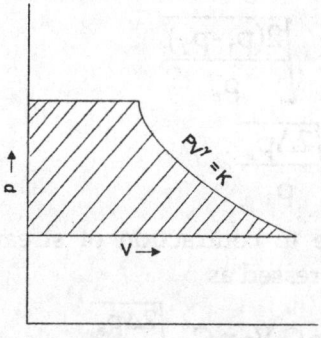

Fig. 7.20 PV diagram

Since $p_1 v_1^\gamma = p_2 v_2^\gamma$

or $\dfrac{v_2}{v_1} \left(\dfrac{p_1}{p_2}\right)^{\frac{1}{\gamma}} = \left(\dfrac{p_2}{p_1}\right)^{-\frac{1}{\gamma}}$

or $v_2 = \sqrt{\dfrac{2\gamma}{\gamma-1} RT_1 \left[1 - \left(\dfrac{p_2}{p_1}\right)^{\frac{\gamma-1}{\gamma}}\right]}$

Therefore, actual velocity of air at throat is given by

$v_a = c_a v_2 = ca \sqrt{\dfrac{2\gamma}{\gamma-1} RT_1 \left[1 - \left(\dfrac{p_2}{p_1}\right)^{\frac{\gamma-1}{\gamma}}\right]}$

since, $w_a = \dfrac{V_a A_a}{v_a}$

$v_2 = v_1 \left(\dfrac{V_1}{V_2}\right)^{\frac{1}{\gamma}}$

Therefore,

$W_a = A_a Ca \sqrt{\dfrac{2\gamma}{\gamma-1} \left(\dfrac{p_1}{v_1}\right)\left[\left(\dfrac{p_2}{p_1}\right)^{\frac{2}{\gamma}} - \left(\dfrac{p_2}{p_1}\right)^{\frac{\gamma-1}{\gamma}}\right]}$

Hence, Heat drop

$H_1 - H_2 = \displaystyle\int_2^1 v dp$

$= \dfrac{\gamma}{\gamma-1}(p_1 v_1 - P_2 v_2)$

7.13.10 Fuel-Flow: In carburetors the top of the fuel jet is always higher than the float-chamber fuel level so that the fuel maynot run out of the jet when the engine isnot in operation as shown in fig. 7.9.

Let x = Height of the jet above the fuel-level in the float chamber, m

g = Acceleratin due to gravity, m/s²

ρ_f = Fuel density, kg/m³

Δp_f = Drop in pressure causing the fuel flow, Pa

Δ_f = Cross sectional area of jet, m²

213

C_f = Co-efficient of discharge of fuel.

Now, Δ_f = Pressure of fuel surface in float chamber - Pressure at the top of the fuel

= $p_1 - (p_2 + g \times \rho f) = (p_1 - p_2) - g \times \rho_f$

$\Delta p_f - x \rho_f g$

Therefore, velocity of fuel,

$$V_f = C_f \sqrt{\frac{2(\Delta P_f - x \rho_f y)}{\rho_f}}$$

Weight of the fuel flow per second = $A_f . V_f . \rho_f$

$$= A_f C_f r_f \frac{\sqrt{2 \rho_f (\Delta P_f - x \rho_f g)}}{\rho_f}$$

$$= A_f C_f \sqrt{2 \rho_f (\Delta P_f - x \rho f g)}$$

Note: The value of C_f is genrally taken 0.7.

7.13.13 Expression for Air-Fuel Ratio :

Air Fuel ratio = $\dfrac{W_a}{w_f}$

or $\dfrac{W_a}{w_f} = \dfrac{A_a C_a}{A_f C_f} \sqrt{\dfrac{\rho_a \Delta p_a}{\rho_f (\Delta p_f - x \rho_f g)}}$

or Substituting the value of x = 0, i.e; neglect the effect of jet tip, we have

$$\frac{W_a}{w_f} = \frac{A_a C_a}{A_f C_f} \sqrt{\frac{\rho_a}{\rho_f}}$$

7.14. Super Charger:

Introduction: Its friction is obtained a comparatively greater power out put from a given size of engine simply inproving volumetric efficiency of the engine with the help of super charger.

Super Charging: Super charging is the process of supplying charge at pressure above the atmostphoric pressure to the engine.

In an ordinary engine without a superchargers, the downward pistion movement during the intake, stroke creats a vacuum in the inlet mainfold, which is used to drop the charge through carburettor into the cylinders. With supercharging, the density of charge increases due to high pressure. Therefore, weight of charge is increased for the same swept volume. It is seen that the power output of an engine is almost directily proporitional to the weight of charge per minutes. Therefore, the super chaged engine gives more output as shown in Fig.

Further at higher altitude, the air gets thin that results into low density. Therefore, supercharging is the most effective for operating at high altitudes.

Supercharging can be done with the help of a supercharger which may be a centrifugal, roots blower and vane type. Usually a supercharger is driven by the engine itself. Despite this supercharging in considerably raises the power of the engine. The work spent on compression or obtained during expansion of gas is proportional to its initial temperature. In the compressor the air is compressed at relatively low tempreature and expands in the engine cylinder at a high temperature thus delivery work tha that spent on compression. When , the supercharges is driven by an exhaust gas turbine, the engine is called turbo charges engines as shown in Fig. 7.21.

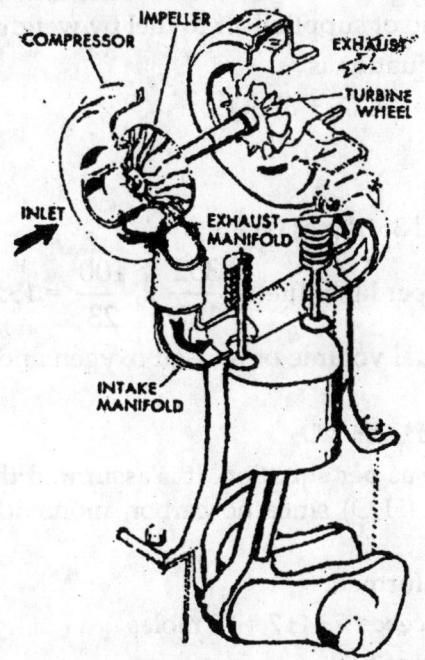

Fig. 7.21. Turbocharging Action

Notes: The increase in engine power is apprised by the degree of supercharging which is defined as the ratio of b.m.e.p of a supercharged engine to the b.m.e.p. of a the same engine without supercharging.

7.14.2 Additional Advantages of Supercharged Engine:

(i)   In cars of Petrol Engine.

(a)   Engine torque is inproved over whole speed range.

(b)   Faster acceleration.

(c)   Improved mixing of the fuel and air.

7.14.3 Additional Advantages of Supercharged Diesel Engine:
(a) Reduction in diesel knock
(b) Batter torque specially at a low rmp.
(c) Running in smoother and faster
(d) Improved cold starting
(e) Elimination of exhaust smoke expecially during low speed acceleration.

PROBLEMS

Prob. 17.1 A Petrol engine is supplied with fuel having the formula C_7H_6. Calculate the theoretical weight of air required per kg of fuel for complete combustion. In an actual experiment, the analysis of exhaust gases should equal volume of unused oxygen and carbondioxide and there was no carbon monooxide. Fing the ratio of supplied air to fuel by weight.

Soln. The combustion equation is

$C_7H_6 + \qquad 11O_2 \quad \rightarrow 7CO_2 + 8H_2O$

$7 \times 12 + 1 \times 16 \quad 11 \times 32$

$= 100 \qquad\qquad = 352$

i.e; 100 k g of fuel reqired 352 kg of O_2.

Therefore, weight of air per kg of fuel $= \dfrac{352}{100} \times \dfrac{100}{23} = 15.3$ kg

In actual experiment equal volume of unused oxygen and carbondixide is found. The equation becomes

$C_7H_{16} + xO_2 \rightarrow yCO_2 + 8H_2O + yO_2$

This equation is in valve as per equation. It is assumred that all the hydrogen has bee converted to water (H_2O) since no carbon monoxide is present all carbon have been burned.

Hence 7 moles of CO_2 is formed.

Therefore, y = 7 and hence x = 7+4+7 = 18 moles

Threfore, kg of air per kg of fuel

$= \dfrac{18 \times 32}{100} \times \dfrac{100}{23} = 25$ kg Ans.

Prob. 7.2 A fuel contains 84% carbon 16% hydrogen by mass. The necessary air-fuel ratio for chemically correct combustion is (a) 10.42:1 (b) 15.28:1 (c) 20.36:1 (d) 30.04:1 [GATE-2001]

Soln. Let CxHy be the fuel

Molecular wt of CxHy =12x + y

A/q, $\dfrac{12x}{12x + y} \times 100 = 84$ (i)

$\dfrac{y}{12x + y} \times 100 = 16$ (ii)

Solving equation (1) and (ii) we have

x = 7 and y = 16

Thus formula of fuel is C_7H_{16}

C_7H_{16} + $11O_2$ → $7CO_2 + 8H2O$

$12 \times 7 + 1 \times 16$ 11×32

= 100   = 352

$\dfrac{Air}{Fuel} = \dfrac{352}{100 \times 23} = \dfrac{15.3}{1}$

Hence, Answer is (b)

Prob. 7.3 A petrol containing 86% carbon and 14% hydrogen by weight is injected is to a engine cylinder for combustion. During combusion 25% of the required air is supplied to the cylinder. Analyse the dry exhaust gas by volume, assuming that all hydrogen have been burnt and carbon burnt to form CO and CO_2 and no free carbon is left here.

Soln. Let CxHy be the fuel, as it has only corbon and hydrogen moleuclar mass of CxHy =

= 12x + y

Given, 86%, Carbon

i.e., $\dfrac{12x}{12x + y} \times 100 = 86$ (i)

Similarly $\dfrac{y}{12 x + y} \times 100 = 14$ (ii)

Solving equation (i) and (ii), we have

$\dfrac{x}{y} = \dfrac{86}{14 \times 12} = \dfrac{43}{84}$

Therefore, the formula of petrol is $C_{43}H_{84}$

The combustion equation for $C_{43}H_{84}$ is

$$C_{43}H_{84} + 0.95 \left(43 + \dfrac{84}{4}\right) O_2 + 0.95 \times 3.8 \times \left(\left(43 + \dfrac{84}{4}\right) N_2 \rightarrow H_2O + NCO + (4.3n)\right.$$

$$CO_2 + 0.95 \times 3.8 \left(43 + \dfrac{84}{4}\right) N_2.$$

O_2 required for hydrogen = $\dfrac{42}{2}$ = 21

Amount of O_2 supplied = 0.95 (43 + 21)

$\qquad = 60.8$

Amount of O_2 utilized for burning the carbon = (60.8-21) = 39.8

i.e; (43-n) $\dfrac{n}{2}$ = 39.8

$\qquad => n = 6.4$

Therefore, final combustion equation is

$C_{43}H_{84} + 60.8O_2 = 231.04N_2 \rightarrow 42H_2O + 231.4N_2 + 6.4\ CO + 36.6CO_2$

Total number of moles of product = 42 + 231.4 + 6.4 + 3 6.6

$\qquad\qquad = 316.4$

Therefore,

% of H_2O = $\dfrac{42 \times 100}{316.4}$ = 13.27

% of N_2 = $\dfrac{231.4 \times 100}{316.4}$ = 73.13

% of CO = $\dfrac{6.4 \times 100}{316.4}$ = 2.2

% of CO_2 = $\dfrac{36.6 \times 100}{316.4}$ = 11.56

Ans.

Prob. 7.4: Find air fuel ratio for the complete combustion of C_8H_{18} (Assume air containing

23% of CO_2 by weight)

Soln. C_8H_{18} burns as

$C_8H_{18}\ \dfrac{25}{2} O_2 \rightarrow 8CO_2 + 9H_2O$

8 x 12 + 1x 18   12.5 x 32

114   400

∴ Air fuel ratio = $\dfrac{400}{114 \times 0.23}$ = $\dfrac{15.25}{1}$ Ans.

Prob. 7.5 A sample of gaseous hydrocarbon occupying 2.24% at STP is completely burnt in the air and released about 4.4 g CO_2 and 3.6 g water (H_2O). Calculate the weight of compound taken and volume of O_2 required at NTP for burning. Also, find out the molecular formula of hydrogen.

Soln. Given:

Volume of hydrocarbon (V_{hy}) = 2.24 L

i.e; mole of hydrocarbon $= \dfrac{2.24}{22.4} = 0.10$

Moles of CO2 $(nCO2) = \dfrac{4.4}{4.4} = 0.1$

Moles of water $(n\ H2O) = \dfrac{3.6}{18} = 0.2$

Let C_xH_y be the hydrocarbon

$$C_xH_y + \left(x + \frac{y}{4}\right)O_2 \to CO_2 + \frac{y}{2}\ H_2O$$

1 mole of C_xH_y gives x mole of CO_2

$\because$ 0.10 C_xH_y will give = 0.10 x mole of CO_2

0.1 x = 0.10

$\therefore$ x = 1

Again, $\therefore$ 1 mole of C_xH_y gives $\dfrac{y}{2}$ mole of H_2O

$\because$ 0.10 mole of C_xH_y gives 0.10 $\dfrac{y}{2}$ H_2O

i.e.; $0.10 \times \dfrac{y}{2} = 0.2$

Therefore, hydrocarbon is CH_4 Ans.

Combustion equation becomes

$CH_4 + 2O_2 + CO_2 + 2H_2O$

$\therefore$ 1 mole CH4 requires 64 g O2

$\therefore$ 0.10 mole CH4 requires 64 x 0.x = 6.4 O2 = 4.48 L of O_2 Ans.

Prob. 7.6. Determine the wt. and volume of fuel per cylinder in a 4 cylinder 4-storke engine developing 200 bhp at 1200 rpm. 32° API oil is used as a fuel at the rate of 0.2 kg/bp/h. The injection pressure is 120 bar. Determine the diameter of the fuel orifice for this engine if injection duration is 30° of crank travel calculate.

(a)   For a single hole nozzle

(b) For a five hole nozzle sp.gravity of 32° API oil is 0.866 and co-efficient of discharge of injection orifice in 0.6 for both cases.

(c) Power has injecting the fuel.

Soln. Given : $\Delta P = 120$ bar $= 120 \times 10^3$ g/cm²

Sp. fuel consumption = 0.2 kg/bhp /h

$\rho_f = 0.866$ g/cm³, $h = \dfrac{\Delta p}{\rho_f}$

(a) Fuel consumption for cylinder $= \dfrac{bhp \times sp.\ fuel\ consumption}{No.\ of\ cylinder}$

$= \dfrac{200 \times 0.2}{4} = 10$ kg

Fuel Consumption per cylinder per cycle $= \dfrac{10}{60 \times 600}$ kg

$= \dfrac{10}{60 \times 600}$

$= 0.277$ g

$= \dfrac{0.277}{0.66} = 0.412$ ml

Injection time of fuel $= \dfrac{\theta}{360} \times \dfrac{1}{N}$, min

$= \dfrac{30}{360} \times \dfrac{1}{1200} \times 60$, s

$= 4.166 \times 10^{-4}$ s

Volume $= A_f\, C_{df} \sqrt{2g\dfrac{\Delta p}{\rho_f}} \times t$

$= A_f \times 0.6 \sqrt{\dfrac{2 \times 981 \times 120 \times 10^3}{0.866}} \times 4.166 \times 10^{-4}$

$A_f = \dfrac{0.412}{6.869}$ cm²

$\dfrac{\pi}{4} d^2 = \dfrac{4.12}{6.869}$ cm²

$\therefore d = \sqrt{0.07626}$

= 0.276 cm

= 2.76 mm Ans.

(b) For fine hole $Af = 5 \cdot \dfrac{\pi}{4} \cdot d^2$

$\therefore d_o^2 = \dfrac{0.05994 \times 4}{5 \times 3.14}$

$\therefore d_0 = 0.1235$ cm

= 1.235 mm Ans.

(c) Power lost in injection = $\theta.\Delta p$

$= \dfrac{40}{60 \times 60} \times 120 \times 10^3$

$= \dfrac{40}{60 \times 60} \times \dfrac{120 \times 10^3 \times 10^{-2}}{0.866 \times 75}$ kgm/s

0.205 hp

$\therefore$ Power lost $= \dfrac{0.285}{200} \times 100$

= 0. 1026 Ans.

Prob. 7.8: A diesel fuel contain 85% carbon, 15% hydrogen and API gravity as 40. If it is consumed at the rate of 6.52L per 90 minute, calculate

(i)   air-fuel ration   (ii) air admitted ainto cylinder per minute

(iii)   fuel-water ratio by weight

(Assume that, the complete combustion takes place at 288.5 K termperature and 1.02×10^5 Pa pressure of mixture.

Soln. Let C_xH_y be the fuel, as it has only carbon & hydrogen

Molecular wt. of fuel is $12x + y$

A/q; $\dfrac{12x}{12x + y} \times 100 = 85$ (i)

$\dfrac{y}{12x + y} \times 100 = 15$ (ii)

From equation (i) and (ii),we have

$\dfrac{x}{y} = \dfrac{17}{36}$

Thus, the molecular formula of fuel is $C_{17}H_{36}$ combustion equation for $C_{17}H_{16}$ is

$$C_{17}H_{36} + \left(17 + \frac{36}{4}\right)O_2 + 3.8\left(17 + \frac{36}{4}\right)N_2 \rightarrow 18\,H_2O + 98.8\,N_2 + 17\,O_2$$

$$C_{17}H_{36} + 26\,O_2 + 98.8\,N_2 \rightarrow 18\,H_2O + 98.8\,N_2 + 17\,CO_2$$

$12 \times 17 + 1 \times 36$	26×32	98.8×28	$18\,(1 \times 2 + 16)$	2766.617×44
240	832	2766.6	324	748

$$A/F = \frac{824 + 2766.4}{240} = \frac{14.99}{1} = 15:1 \text{ Ans.}$$

(ii) $API = 40 = \dfrac{141.5}{\text{sp. gravity of 288.5 K}} - 131.5$

sp. gravity of fuel at 288.5 K $= \dfrac{141.5}{171.5} = 0.825$

Density of fuel at 288.5 K = density of water x sp. gravity of fuel

$= 1000 \times 0.825$

$= 825 \text{ kg/m}^3$

$= 0.825 \text{ kg/L}$

Air admitted at S.T.P. in the cylinder

$PV = nRT$

$$n = \frac{W}{M_m \text{ of air}} = \frac{832 + 2766.4}{29} = 124.48$$

$$V_{air} = \frac{nRT}{P}$$

$$= \frac{124.08 \times 8.314 \times 273}{1.03 \times 10^5} = 2.75 \text{ m3}$$

Therefore volume of air for 1 kg of fuel $= \dfrac{1000}{240} \times 2.75$

$= 11.,42 \text{ m3}$

Given that,

$P_1 = 1.02 \times 10^5 \text{ Pa}$

$P_2 = 1.03 \times 10^5 \text{ Pa}$

$T_2 = 288.5 \text{ K}$

$T_2 = 273$

$\rho_1 = 0.825 \text{ kg/L}$

$\rho_2 = ?$

we know that

$$\frac{P_1}{\rho_1 T_1} = \frac{P_2}{P_2 T_2}$$

$$P_2 = \frac{P_2 \times p_1 \; T_1}{PT_2}$$

$$= \frac{1.03 \times 10^5 \times 0.825 \times 288.5}{1.02 \times 10^5 \times 273}$$

= 0.801 kg/L Ans.

(iii) Mass of fuel consumed in 90 minutes = 6.5 × 0.801

$$= 5.2 \text{ kg}$$

Therefore mass of fuel consumed per minute = $\dfrac{5.2}{90}$ = 0.0577 kg

∵ 1 kg of fuel requires 11.42 m³ air

∴ 0.0577 kg of fuel requries 11.42 × 0.0577

= 0.697 m³ Ans.

PROBLEMS

1. A diesel fuel contains 85% carbon, 15% hudrogen and API gravity as 40. If it is consumed at the rate of 6.5x 10⁻³ m³ per 80 minutes, calculate.
   (i) Air-fuel ratio
   (ii) air admitted into cylinder per minute
   iii) fuel-water ratio by weight
   Assume that, the complete combustioin takes place at 288.5 K temperature, 102 k Pa pressure of mixture and Mm of air = 29]
   Ans. 15 [0.7423 m³, 0.74]

2. Gasoline can be represented by the hydrogcarbon on (C_8H_{18}) assume that when grasoline is used in an engine, the air supply is 95% of that theoretically required for complete combustion (a rich miture). Assume that all the hydrocabon is burned and that the carbon burns to carbon monoxide and carbon dioxide. So that these is no free carbon left. Calculate the percentage analysis of the dry exhaut gases by volume. Air contain 23% oxygen by weight.
   % of H2O=27.06%, % of N_2 = 48.87%]
   % of CO = 3.72, % of CO_2 = 20.33%]

3. The calorific value of a fule is 66,796.4 kJ/kg. It contains 87% carbon and 4% hydrogen by weight and rest is ash. Calculate, the amount of air required for complets combustion of 1kg of this fuel.
   Ans. 11.852 kg]

4. Assume that fuel can be represented by the hydrocarbon cetane ($C_{16}H_{34}$). When used in an engine the air supply is 5% greater than that theoretically required for complete combustion (a lean mixture). Assuming that that the hydrocarbon is burned and that no free carbon is left in the exhaust. Calculate the percentage analysis of the dry exhaust gases by volume. Also how much water is produced per kg of fuel.
   Ans. of H_2O = 13%, N_2 = 74.76% of CO_2 = 12.24% and 1.35 kg H_2O]

5. Determine the molecular formula of the compound. If the molecular mass of fuel in 78 and in percentage composition is 92.3% C and 7.6% H.
   Ans. C_6H_6]

6. A diesel oil fuel has the fol lowing gravimetric analysis: carbon 84%, hydrogen 12%, Sulphur 1.5%. The remainder being incombustible, estimate the minimim weight of air required for complete combustion of one kg of the fuel. If 20 kg of air is supplied per kg of fuel, estimate the percentage composition by vulme, supplied per kg of fuel, estimate the percentage composition by volume of the dry fuel gases. Which would be detected by an orsat apparatus.
   If for the same air supply, 4% carbon in the fuel is burnt to form carbonmonoxide, calculate the percentage of volume of CO_2 now present in dry exhuast gas.

Ans.

Constituent	CO_2	CO	SO_2	O_2	N_2
by volume	10.11	0.44	0.08	6.77	82.6

7. The diamter of the jet of a sim ple carburettor is 1mm. The venturi detression is 102 cm wateer and the co-efficient of discharge of jet is 0.60. The specific gravity of petrol is 0.77 with one m³ of water weighing 1000 kg. Calculate the wt. of petrol discharge per second. [Ans. 1.848 g/s]

8. A petrol engine consume 6.8 kg of petrol per hour. The specific gravity of the fuel 0.7 and its temperature 30.5 K. The air-fuel ratio is 15. The choke tube has a diameter of 20mm. Calculate the diameter of the single jet of carburettor of the top of the jet is 5mm above the petrol level is the float chamber. Take R = 287.14 J/kg K for air. [Ans. 1.14 mm]

SUBJCTIVE QUESTIONS

1. Define the terms: (i) fuel (ii) petroleum (iii) octane number (iv) centone number (v) calorific value (vi) antiknocking compounds (vii) pour point (viii) combustion.

2. What are functions of petroleum and their uses?
3. What do you understand by the quality of fuel oil? What are the different factors affecting the quality of fuel?
4. How does the volality of the fuel affects the engine performance?
5. How does detonation differ from preignition?
6. What is the chemical composition of petroleum?
7. What are necessary conditions for combustions?
8. With a neat diagram describe the fuel system fo a diesel and petrol engine.
9. What is the differences between idling jet, main jet compensating jet and economiser?
10. What is difference btween downdraft and updraft carburetor?
11. What do you understand by fuel injection system? What are the different methods of fuel injection injection in a diesel engine.
12. What are the effects of supercharing of I.C. engine?
13. What are advantages and disadvantages of supercharge?

MULTIPLE CHOUCE QUESTIONS

1. Normal heptane content in fuel spark ignition engines
   (a) accelrates auto-ignition
   (b) retards auto-ignition
   (c) does not affect auto-ignition
   (d) none of the above
2. Iso-octane content in a fuel for spark ignition engines
   (a) accelerates auto-ignition
   (b) retards auto-ignition
   (c) does not affect auto-ignition
   (d) none of the above
3. The auto-ignition reaction time for spark ignition fuels
   (a) increase with richer mixtures
   (b) increase with weaker mixture
   (c) is minimum for chemically corroct mixture
   (d) none of the above
4. The kcnocking in spark ignition engine increses with
   (a) increase in compression ratio
   (b) increase in inlet air temperature
   (c) increase in colling water temperature
   (d) all of the above
5. Advancing the spark timing in spark ignition engines.

    (a)   increase the tendency for knocking

    (b)   decrese the tendency for knocking

    (c)   does not affect knocking

    (d)   none of the above

6.   Decreasing the temperature of cooling water in spark ignition engines

    (a)   increases the tendenny by knocking

    (b)   decreases the tendency for knocking

    (c)   does not affect knocking in any way

    (d)   none of the above

7.   Increases the speed in spark ignition engines

    (a)   increases the tendency for knocking

    (d)   decreases the tendency for knocking

    (c)   does not affect knocking

    (d)   none of the abvoe

8.   Petrol commercially available in India for Indian has actane number

    (a)   40 to 45   (b)   30-60

    (c)   60-80   (d)   80-90

9.   Detonation in spark ignition occurs due to

    (a)   pre-ignition of change before spark is struck

    (b)   Auto-ignition of the charge after spark is struck

    (c)   both   (d)   none of the above

10.   The knocking tendency in C.I. engines incrase with

    (a)   increase of compression ratio

    (b)   decreases of compression ratio

    (c)   increasing the temperature of inlet air

    (d)   none of the above

11.   The tendency to knock in compression ignition engines increases with

    (a)   lowering the compression ratio

    (b)   lowering the air inlet temperature

    (c)   lowering the cooling water temperature

    (d)   all of the above

13.   In actual practice the maximum temperature attained taking dissociation into account, after combustion is

    (a)   with chemically correct mixture of fuel and air

    (b)   with weak mixture of fuel and air

    (c)   with rich mixture of fuel and air

(d)   none of the above

14. Fig. 17.22 Shows the temperature after combustion with mixture strength variation of fuel, ignoring dissociation.

(a)   A (b)   B
(c)   C (d)   D

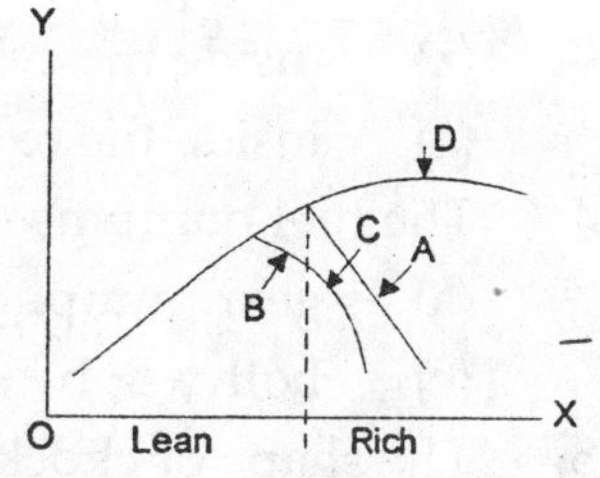

15. Fig. 17.22 Shows the temperature after combustion with mixture strength variation of fuel air considering dissociation.

(a)   A (b)   B
(c)   C (d)   D

Fig. 17.22

16. Calorific value of fuel determined of constant volme

(a)   is equal to calorific value of fuel at constant pressur

(b)   is more than the calorific value of fuel at constant pressure

(c)   is less than the calorific value of fuel at constant pressure

(d)   may be more or may be less depending upon molecular contraction or expansion of the products or combustion

17. Calorific value of each gaseous fuel can be found by

(a)   Bomb calorimeter   (b)   Junker calorimeter
(c)   Flash poinapparatus   (d)   none of the abvoe

18. vulmetric analysis of sample of the dry products of combustion are CO_2 = 10%, CO = 1%, O_2 = 8% N_2 = 81%. The proportions by weight are given as

(a)   44 : 28 : 256 : 2268   (b)   10 : 1 : 8 : 81
(c)   22 : 14 : 256 : 2268   (d)   22 : 14 : 128 : 2268

19. The common fuels for the engines are

(a)   petrol and kerosene   (b)   petrol and diesel
(c)   kerosene and diesel   (d)   none of the above

20. Quality of the fuel is judged by its (a) volatility (b) ignition quality (c) consuption alue (d) both (a) & (b) contain number is associated with

(a)   fuel consumption   (b)   calorific value
(c)   ignition quality of fuel

21. Detonatin occurs, after

(a)   exhaust stroke   (b)   ignition
(c)   intake of fuel   (d)   none of the above

22. In I.C. engine throttle is equipped

(a)   near radiator   (b)   between mixing chamber and inlet

(c)   in engine cylinder   (d)   none of the above

23.   In diesel engine,s the fule is automized

    (a)   inside the cylinder   (b)   inside combustion chamber

    (c)   inside the carburetor   (d)   none of the above

24.   The fuel pump used in carburetor type engine is

    (a)   gear pump   (b)   centrifugal pump

    (c)   both a & b   (d)   none of thea bove

25.   The shape of chock is

    (a)   T   (b)   L

    (c)   butterfly   (d)   none of the above

26.   API gravity of pure water is

    (a)   10   (b)   5

    (c)   20   (d)   30

27.   For getting maximum power from petrol engine, the air-fuel ratio should be about

    (a)   15 : 1   (b)   1 : 10

    (c)   1 : 15   (d)   1 : 12

FLL UP THE BLANKS

1.   Petroleum contains is about .... % of carbon.

2.   Cyclic alkanes have higher octane number than the corresponding.............. alkanes.

3.   Tetra-ethyl-lead is well known as .... compound.

4.   Diesel fuels in India haiving cetane number from .... to ....

5.   Calorific value of upla varies from .... to .... kJ/kg.

6.   Preignition occurs in the .... engine.

7.   The pressure range from .... to .... kPa in air injection system.

8.   The pressure is created by fuel injection pump is varies from .... to kPa.

9.   Fuel tank is placed .... the level of carburettor in gravity feed method.

10.   Super charging is the process of suppying charge at pressure .... the atmopheric pressure to the engine.

    1. 86% 2. Straight chain 3. antiknocking 4. 30 to 60 5. 6000 to 8000 6. petrol 7. 5,500 to 8,000 8. 12,000 to 20,000 9. above 10. above

ANSWER FOR MULTIPLE CHOICE QUESTONS

1 (a) 2 (b) 3 () 4 (d) 5 (a) 6 (b) 7 (b) 8 (b) 9 (b) 10 (b) 11 (d) 12 (e) 13 (a) 14 (c) 15 (d) 16 (b) 17 (a) 18 (b) 19 (d) 20 (c) 21 (b) 22 (b) 23 (c) 24 (a) 25 (c) 26 (a) 27 (b)

Chapter 8
Ignition System of I.C. Engine

8.10   Introduction

Ignition system is an arrangement of different components to ignite fuel inside the cylinder. The ignition has to be performed at a pre-set timing. If it is not done a appropriate time, engine may not produce sufficient power or may run of erretically or may run at all.

8.2.   Requirement of an Efficient Ignition System: The following are the main requirements of efficient ignition system:

(i)   Spark must occur continuously at appropriate time.

(ii)   These should not be any misfire.

(iii)   The spark should be strong enough to ignite the charge.

(iv)   The ignition should be simple cheap and contained as a compact unit.

(v)   The system should be operated at all engine speeds.

(vi)   The maintenance, repair and servicing of the ignition system should be easy and   convenient.

8.3   Classification of Ignition System: The following system are used for igniting the fuel in various internal combustion engine:

(i)   Open flame system

(ii)   Hot surface system or ignition by hot tube or hot bulb.

(iii)   Compression ignition system or ignition by heat of combustion.

(iv)   Electric spark system.

Only the last two are important methods for modern engines.

8.4   Compression Ignition System: Compression ignition is the chief characteristics of diesel engines, due to which they are often termed as compression ignition (C.I.) engines. It utilizes the heat developed due compressing the charge to a very high compression ratio. A pressure of nearly 3000 to 3500 kPa is developed by a compression ratio of 15:1 to 17:1 producing a temperature of 450 to 550°c, which is high enough to explode the fuel.

8.5   Electric Spark Ignition System:

The duty of spark ignition system is to provide a hot spark in highly compressed gases at proper time and proper sequences. A systematic diagram of tractor spark ignition system is shown in Fig. 8.1.

8.6   Classification of S.I. System on the Basis of Source of Electric Power

The following are the S.I. systems on the basis of source of electric power:

(a)   Battery Ignition system (b) Magneto ignition systems.

8.6.1 Battery Ignition System:

(i)   Introduction: Battery ignition system is used in all the petrol vehicles except in small engine such as engines are used in motor cycles, scooters, motor boats etc.

(ii)   Working Principle: Battery ignition system consists of two circuits.

(i)   Primary circuit or Low voltage circuit

(ii)   Secondary circuit or High voltage circuit

The components of the low voltage circuit and high voltage circuit has shown in Fig. 8.1

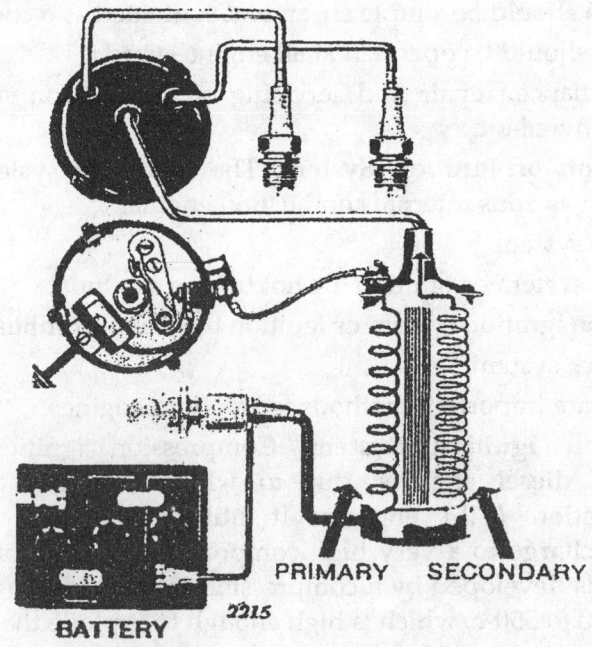

Low voltage side   High Voltage side

Fig. 8.1 Battery Ignition System

(A) Components of L.V. Side
1. Dynmo
2. Rectifier
3. Relay
4. Switch
5. Ammeter
6. Battery
7. Breaker
8. Condenser
8. Primary coil

(B) Components of H.V. side
1. Secodary coil
2. Distributor
3. High voltage cable
4. Spark plugs

Note: Primary winding and secondary winding collectively called ignition coil.

In battery ignition system, the current is taken from battery to the ignition switch, from ignition switch to the ignition coil, from ignition coil to primary circuit to distributor to the contact breaker condenser and is earthed.

For secondary circuit, a high tension lead is taken from the ignition coil to the distributor cap central terminal. From this terminal current is taken to the rotor and distributed to various segments depending upon the number of cylinders. From these segments of distributors to the terminals and from these terminals to various spark plugs. The complete ignition system is shows in Fig. 8.1.

8.8 Descriptions of Components of Battery Ignition.

8.7.1 Ignition coil. In ignition coil, 6 or 12 v current is supplied in the primary winding and from the secondary winding a very high voltage, as 10000 V to 20,000 V is trapped.

The primary winding having approximately 200 turns of thick wire (dia =- 0.8 mm) is wound on a soft of iron core on top of primary winding, a secondary winding of thin wire (dia = 0.1 mm) is wound which has 20000 terms. When contact paint joins, the 6 or 12 or current flows in the primary winding. Due to flowing this current magnetic fields is generated around it. Now when we break the current supply through contact point, the magnetic lines of force collapse causing high voltage electric current in secondary winding of the coil.

This high tension current is then fed to the spark plug through distributor. In a simple diagram the construction of an ignition coil with primary and secondary winding in shown in Fig. 8.2

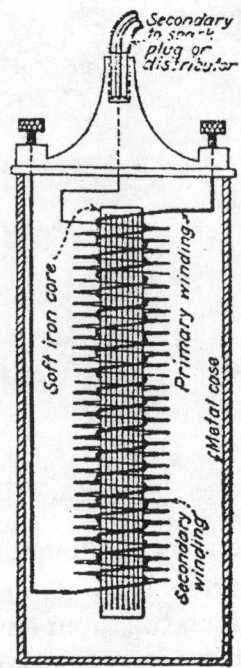

Fig. 8.2 Ignition Coil with Primary and Secondary Winding

Transformer coil is filled by vacuumized processes in the ignition coil. This not only help in proper insulation but also does not allow moisture to get into the winding.

Note: The high tension coils are not repairable.

8.7.2 Condenser: Condensers is a device which stores electric charge for a short time. As it is connected across the contact point. When these points open, condenser momentarily provides a place for current to flow in and get fully charged and send back the current when points close again. It also helps avoid anching in the contact point thus increasing their life. If the condenser were not there in the circuit, the current would continue to flow across the points after they begin to open thus providing producing on arch. This arch would not only burn the points but also reduce the voltage. As such the condesser acts as storage of electricity and stops the flowing current quickly.

A condesser consists of a pair of flat metal plates, separated by air. The most common type of condenser is of metal foil strips, separated by wax paper. It is used for quick reduction of magnetic field in the coil to obtained on extremely high voltage current. Its capacity is measured in terms **Fard.**

Note: In internal combustion engines, generally, the range of condenser varies from 0.15 to 0.45 μF.

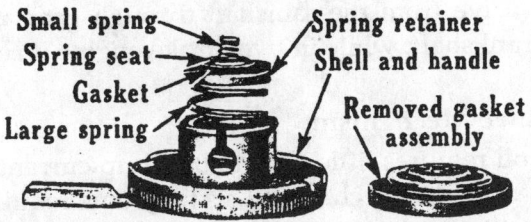

Fig. 8.3 Shows the components of a distributior and its Cross-Section

8.7.3. Distributor: The function of distributor is to make and break the primary circuit and distribute high tension current to various plugs. The lowest portion of distributor assembly does not the work of low tension current making and breaking while the upper portion i.e., cap and rotor distributes the high tension current.

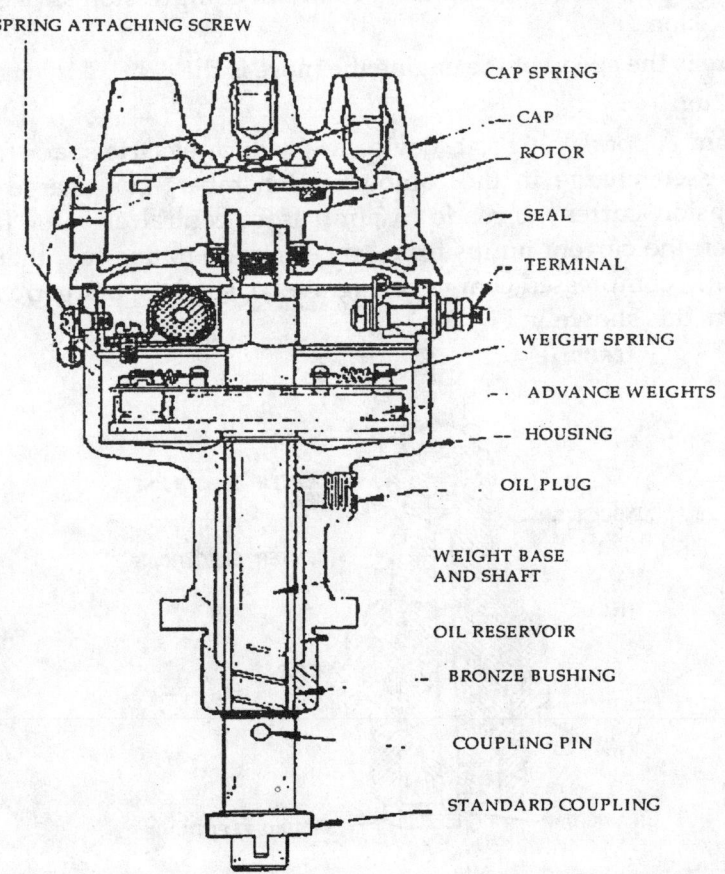

Fig. 8.3. Cross-section and Compenents of a Distributor

Distributor get its drive from the camshaft through gear and shaft and runs at half the speed of crankshaft; while in two-stroke engine it runs at the same speed of engine.

8.7.4 Spark Advance Mechanism:

The high tension coil requires little time to build up current and spark plug also require a short time to burn the change. This total time required is called time lag. Let us assume that the time required for high tension coil to build current and also for the spark plug to start burning the charge i.e., time lag is 2×10^{-3} sec. If the engine is running at 1500 rpm, the time required the completely burn the charge in degree of flywheel rotation will be $\dfrac{1500 \times 360}{60 \times 500} = 18^\circ$ and is engine is running at 3,000 rpm, we will have to initiate ignition 36° before the dead centre so that when piston reaches the top dead centre in compression stroke, charge is ready for expansion.

Note: The more is the speed of the engine the more is the spark advance needed.

7.5 Spark Plug:

(i) Introduction: A spark plug is a device to produce electric spark for igniting highly compressed charge in the combustion chamber. The charge is ignited when high tension current is made to jump from central elevator to the side electrode. When the current jumps from one electrode to another, there is spark due to this spark, compressed charge gets ignited. Usually spark gap varies from 0.50 to 0.85 mm. It is shown in Fig. 8.4.

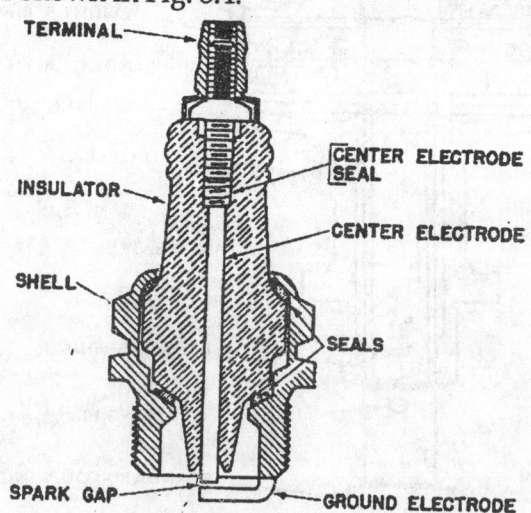

TYPICAL PRESENT-DAY SPARK PLUG CONSTRUCTION

Fig. 8.4 Spark Plug

(ii)   Requirements of spark plug: The following are the main requirements of good spark plug:

(i)   A good spark plug must be able to function under all working condition of temperature and pressure. It is designed to operate under 20,000 to 30,000V.

(ii)   It must maintain the proper gap between two electrodes under all condition.

(iii)   The spark plug must offer very high resistance current leakage.

(iv)   It must be corrosion resistant.

(v)   It must be perfectly insulated, so that high current can not leak.

(vi)   It should have reduced interference to radio and television from ignition system.

(vii)   It should also reduce the electrode corrosion caused by excessively long sparking.

(iii)   Classification of Spark Plug:

(A)   Types of spark Plug According to Threads size (dia)

They are classified as

(i)   14 mm   (ii)   18 mm and (iii) 22 m

(B)   Types of Spark Plug according to Reach Length

(i)   Short reach = 9.5 mm

(ii)   Medium reach = 12.7 mm

(iii)   Long reach = 19 mm

(C)   Types of Spark Plug According to Electrode

(i)   Side electrode (used for slow speed engine)

(ii)   Twin electrode and (used in two-stroke engine)

(iii)   Front electrode (used in automobiles)

(D)   Types of Spark Plug According to heat Range

They are classified as (i) Hot plug and (ii) cold plug.

(i)   Hot Plugs: The plugs which have comparatively long insulator extending into the cylinder is known as hot plugs. Due to longer insulator, the heat has to pass through a longer path to Reach cooling water which results into slow cooling of the plug. These are used on slow speed low compression engine. It is shown in Fig. 8.5 (a)

(ii)   Cold Plug: The plugs which have short insulator, extending into the cylinder is known as cold plug. The heat has to pass through a short path to cooling water resulting in fast cooling of the plug. These are used on high speed high compression engines, which is shown in Fig. 8.5 (b).

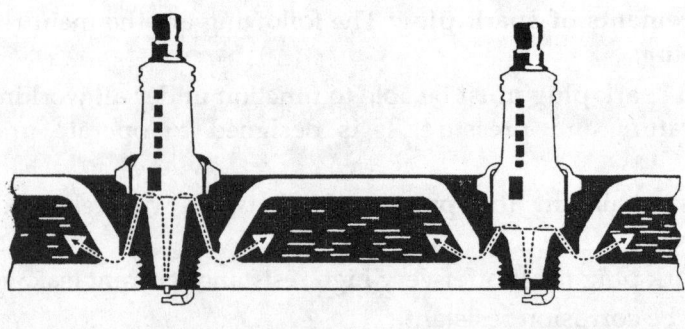

Hot plug   Cold plug

Fig. 8.5 Spark Plug

(iv) **Spark Plug Failure:** The following are the main reasons of spark plug failure:

(i)   Plug fowled by engine oil entering combustion chamber.

(ii)   Plug badly covered with carbon.

(iii)   Plug gap incorrect.

(iv)   Burned elecrtrodes or broken lower insulator caused by over heating.

(v)   Red, brown or yellow oxide, deposition on plug interior that short the insulator.

Ignition Timing: It is the time at which spark jumps across the spark gaps to ignite the charge.

If the ignition timing of an engine is not corrent i.e., either before or after of ignition timing results into poor performance increasd fuel consumption and slow idling in the case of before ignition whereas in the case of after ignition results into slow and jerky cranking with the warm engine. Detonation may also be experienced while accelerating.

(v) **Spark Plug Identification Marks:** In a micro spark plug word W 175 Z1 is punched in which word W denotes thread size 18 mm thread, 175 stands for heat range, Z is for type of electrode and 1 for reach of plug.

8.7.6. Ignition Switch: A switch provided in the primary circuit for starting and stopping the engine is called ignition switch.

8.7.7. Dynamo: It is a device which converts mechanical energy into electrical energy. The dynamo supplies direct current to the battery and keeps it fully charged.

8.7.8. Battery:

(i) **Introduction:** Batteries or storage cells are essential part of modern tractor and engine starting system. There are several types of battery, but lead storage battery is most popular for I.C. engine.

(ii) Lead Storage cell: This is the most commonly used battery in automobiles. Each battery consists of a number of voltaic cells connected in series. Each voltaic cell contains three to six such cells and combined to get 6 to 12 v battery. In each cell, the anode is a grid of lead packed with finely divided spongy lead and the cathode is grid of lead packed with PbO_2. The electrolyte is aqueous solution of sulphuric acid (38% by mass) having a density 1 g cm^{-3} sulphuric acid. When the lead plates are kept for sometimes, a deposit of lead sulphate is formed on them. Lead storage cell is shown in Fig. 8.6. Each cell one more negative plate than positive plate.

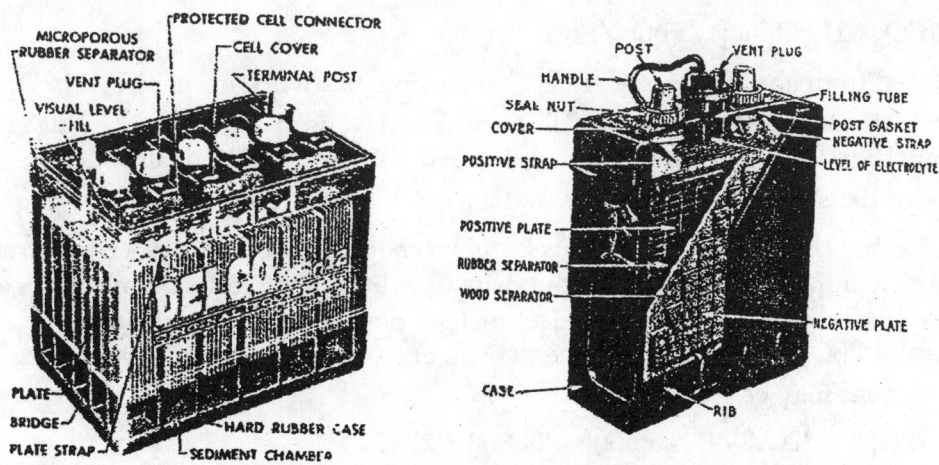

Fig. 8.6. Lead Storage battery.

At the anode, lead is oxidised to Pb^{2+} ions and insoluble $PbSO_4$ is formed. At the cathode PbO_2 is reduced to Pb^{2+} ions and $PbSO_4$ is formed.

The following reactions take place in the lead storage cells.

At anode, the lead loses two electrons and is oxidised to Pb^{2+} ions.

$$Pb\,(s) \rightarrow Pb^{2+}\,(aq) + 2e^-$$

$$Pb^{2+}\,(aq) + SO_4^{-2}\,(aq) \rightarrow PbSO_4\,(s)$$

i.e., overall anode reaction is

$$Pb\,(s) + SO_4^{2-}\,(aq) \rightarrow PbSO_4\,(s) + 2e^-$$

At cathode, The PbO_2 reduced to Pb^{2+} as

$$PbO_2\,(s) + 4\,H^+ + 2e^- \rightarrow Pb^{2+}\,(aq) + 2H_2O$$

Pb^{2+} (aq) + SO_4^{2-} (aq) → $PbSO_4$ (s)

i.e; overall cathode reaction is

PbO_2 (s) + 4 H^+ + SO_4^{2-} + 2e$^-$ → $PbSO_4$ + $2H_2O$

Thus, the complete electrode reactions and overall cell reactions are:

Pb (s) + SO_4^{2-} (aq) → $PbSO_4$ (s) + 2e$^-$, at anode

PbO_2 + $4H^+$ + SO_4^{2-} + 2e$^-$ → $PbSO_4$ (s) + $2H_2O$, at cathode

Pb (s) + PbO_2 (s) + $2H_2SO_4$ (aq) ® 2 $PbSO_4$ (s) + $2H_2O$ over all

The cell may be represented as

$Pb/PbSO_4$ + H_2SO_4 (aq) /PbO_2 /Pb

It is clear from the above reactions that during the working of cell, $PbSO_4$ is formed at each electrode and sulphuric acid is used up. As a result, the concentration of H_2SO_4 decreases and the density of solution also decreases. When the density of H_2SO_4 falls below 1.2 g cm-3, the battery needs recharging.

(iii)   Recharging the Battery: The cell can be charged by passing electric current (D.C.) of a suitable voltage in the opposite direction. The electrode reaction gets reversed. As a results, the flow of electrons get reversed and lead is deposited on anode and PbO_2 on the cathode. The density of sulphuric acid and also increases. The reactions may be written as

2PbSO4 (s) + 2H2O $\xrightarrow{\text{charge}}$ Pb(s) + PbO2(s) + 2H2SO4

Note: It acts as voltaic cell as well as electrolytic cell.

8.8 Magneto Ignition System:

Fig. 8.7 shows magnetic ignition system for a four cylinder engine. It consists of a magnets, instead of a battery which produces and supplies current in the primary winding. The remaining arrangement in this system is the same as battery ignition system. The magneto consists of a fired armature having primary winding and secondary winding and rotating magnetic assembly which is driven by engine. When the magnet rotates, current flows in the primary winding. The sundry winding gives high voltage current o the distributor, which distributes it to the respective spark plugs.

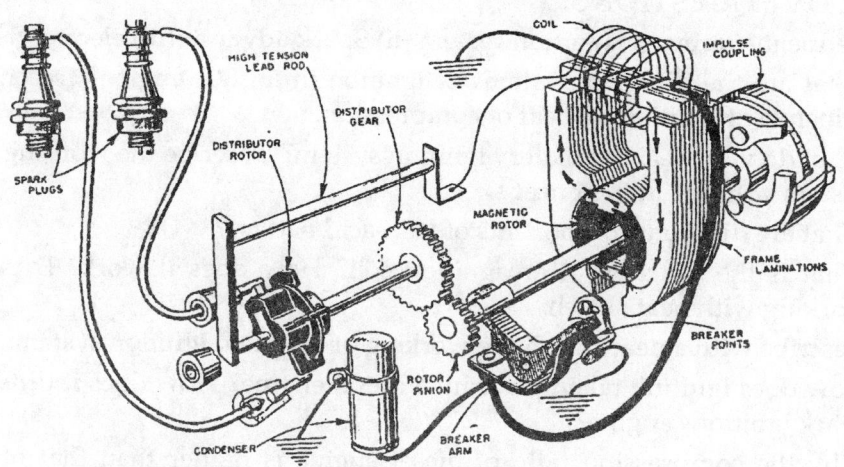

Fig. 8.7. Magneto Ignition system for a 4-cylinder engine

8.9 Classification of Magneto Ignition System:

They are classified as

(i)   Moving or Rotating magnet and

(ii)   Moving coil or Rotating armature type

The rotating magnet is more commonly used due to being simple in constructions. It consists of a powerful permanent magnet and laminated iron core with primary and secondary windings. The winding set up the voltage as explained earlier. Whereas in the rotating armature type magnet the armature carrying primary and secondary winding and rotating around the poles of a stationary horse shoe magnet.

8.10. Comparison between Battery Ignition and Magneto Ignition System.

Battery Ignition System	Magneto Ignition System
1. Current is obtained from battery	Current is generated by magneto
2. Sparking is good even at low speed.	Poor sparking at low speed
3. Starting of the engine is easier	Difficulty in starting
4. Occupy more space	Occupies less space
5. Complicated wiring	Simple wiring
6. Less cost	More cost
7. Spark intensity falls as the engine speed rises.	Spark intensity improves as the engine speed increases.
8. If the battery is discharged and resulting into engine is not started.	Such difficulty is not present
9. Used in car, bus, tractor, truck	Used in motor cycles, scooter, racing cars etc.

SUBJECTIVE QUESTIONS:

1. Define the terms: (i) Ignition system (ii) Spark advance (iii) electrolytes

2. What are the different systems of ignition in an I.C. engine? Describe the principle of ignition by heat of compression.

3. What do you mean by battery ignition system? Describe the working of this system with the help of neat sketch.

4. What are different components of lead-acid battery?

5. What is the function of an ignition coil? How does it work? Explain its working with neat sketch.

6. Describe with a neat sketch the working of magneto ignition system.

7. How does ignition taken place in a diesel engine? How does it differ from spark ignitions engine?

8. Why the compression ratio of diesel engine is higher than that of petrol engine?

9. What is the difference between hot and cold plug?

10. What are the functions of the spark plug?

MULTIPLE QUESTIONS

1. In. I.C. engine, the spark plug electrode gap setting varies from
   (a) 1.0 to 1.2 mm   (b) 0.5 to 0.85 mm
   (c) 0.1 to 0.2 mm   (d) 1.5 to 1.8 mm

2. A cold spark plug disappears the heat through
   (a) short path   (b) big path
   (c) both   (d) none of the above

3. The main function of distributor of ignition of system of engine is, to
   (a) open the primary circuit   (b) close the primary electrical circuit
   (c) both   (d) none of the above

4. The primary winding of ignition coil is made of mm dia of copper wire
   (a) 1.0 mm   (b) 1.5 mm
   (c) 0.8 mm   (d) none of the above

5. The function of condenser in battery igntion system is, to
   (a) produce a quick collapse of magnetic field in the coil
   (b) produce a high voltage
   (c) both
   (d) none of the above

6. The common type of battery used in tractor i
   (a) lead-acid battery   (b) dry battery
   (c) both   (d) none of the above

7. In lead-acid battery, the negative plates are made of
   (a) Copper lead   (b) Spongy lead
   (c) both   (d) none of the above

8. In lead-acid battery, the positive plates are made of
   (a) spongy lead   (b) lead
   (c) copper lead   (d) none of the above

9. Which one of the following is used as electrolyte in lead-acid battery
   (a) 38% by mass H_2SO_4 (b) 50% by mass H_2SO_4
   (c) 60% by mass H_2SO_4 (d) 70% by mass H_2SO_4

10. A fully charge battery should indicates the sp. gravity about
    (a) 1.25   (b) 1.28
    (c) 1.30   (d) 1.5

11. Capacity of battery is measured in terms of
    (a) A   (b) A-h
    (c) N   (d) J

FILL IN THE BLANKS

1. Temperature varies from.................. to............... in compression ignition system.

2. Pressure varies from..................... to.................. KPa in compression ignitions system.

3. Condenser stores............................... for a short time.

4. In internal combustion engine, the range of condense varies from.................. to............. HF.

5. Spark plug gap varies from ....to .... mm.

6. Dynamo converts mechanical energy to .... energy.

7. ....% by mass H_2SO_4 is used as electrolyte in lead storage battery.

8. The thickness of primary winding is about ....mm.

Ans. (1) 450 to 550°C. (2) 3000 to 3500 (3) electric charge (4) 0.15 to 0.45 (5) 0.50 to 0.85 (6) electrical (7) 38 (8) 0.8

ANSWERS OF MULTIPLE CHOICE QUESTIONS

1 (b) 2 (a) 3 (c) 4 (c) 5 (c) 6 (a) 7 (b) 8 (b) 9 (a) 10 (b) 11 (b)

Chapter 9

Cooling System of I.C. Engine

9.1 Introduction: Cooling helps proper carburation, provides satisfactory oil viscosity and gives correct part clearance within the engine. Peak combustion temperature in the engine cycle ranges from 2500 K to 3600 K and that of exhaust gases from 875 K to 1076 K. Thus the average temperature is quite high throughout the operating cycle. But the minimum normal temperature controlled by a thermostat is around 350 K to 360 K i.e., by Cooling system. A cut way of a cooling system is shown in Fig. 9.1. The temperature at which an engine operates affects both fuel economy and wear.

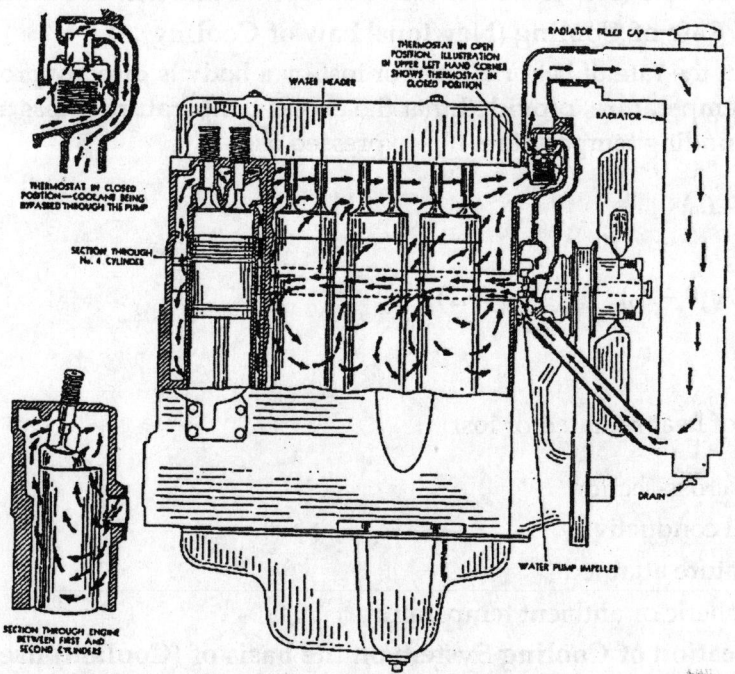

Fig. 9.1 A cut way of a cooling system

In practice, it has been observed that only 35% of the total heat produced is utilized for useful work. About 26% is washed as exhaust gas, 28% in the Cooling System, 2% in overcoming friction during transmission and about 5% in over coming friction and remainder is lost by radiation.

9.2 Necessity of Cooling System.

(i)   Melting point of different metals is lower than heat generated in the engine.

(ii)   Burning of the lubrication oil, deposition of carbon of the sliding and moving parts-resulting in engine seizure.

(iii)   Thermal stress may distort different components.

(iv)   Thermal efficiency is decreased, when engine is operated at over cooling and under cooling.

(v)   The vaporization of the fuel is less which results in fall of combustion efficiency, when engine is operated at over cooling.

9.3 Factors Affecting Rate of Cooling:

The following are main factors;

(i)   thermal conductivity

(ii)   Surface area

(iii)   Viscosity

(iv)   Temperature differences between atmosphere and heated surface.

9.4. Law of Rate of Cooling (Newtons' Law of Cooling).

It states that, the rate of heat radiated or lost by a body is directly proportional to the excess temperature, provided that the excess temperature is less as compared to the surrounding temperature. It is expressed as,

$$\frac{d\theta}{dt} \propto A\,(\theta - \theta_0)$$

$$\text{or } \frac{d\theta}{dt} = K\,A\,(\theta - \theta_0) \qquad (9.1)$$

Where,

$\dfrac{d\theta}{dt}$ = Rate of heat radiated or lost

A = Area of cross-section

K = Thermal conductivity

θ = Temperature attained

θ_0 = Atmospheric or ambient temperature

9.5 Classification of Cooling System on the basis of (Coolant) used:

They are classified as follows:

(i)   Air cooling system and

(ii)   Water cooling system

9.5.1 Air Cooling System: In air Cooling System, air is used as Coolant.

Methods of Air Cooling: The following are the main methods of air cooling:

(i)   By Cooling Fins: The surface are over the cylinder is increased by means of fins as shown in fig. 9.1. These fines either cast or as integral part of the cylinder or separate finned barrels are inserted over the cylinder barrel.

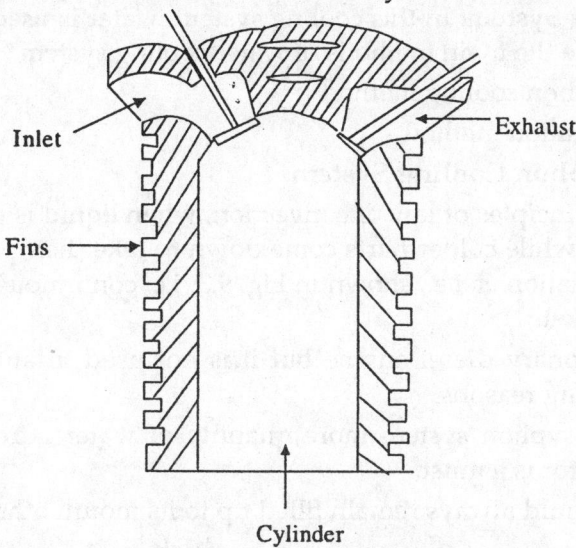

Fig. 9.2. Showing Cooling Fins

(ii)   By Fan Cooling: Fan cooling is used in larger air cooled engines. A fan having two or four or more blades, is driven either at engine's speed or twice engine's speed and the air flow is directed on the cycle.

Uses of the Air Cooling System: Air cooling system is mostly used in motor cycle, garden tractors, aeroplanes, scooters but now a days air cooling system is begin used for heavy diesel engines as used in Eicher tractor, Escort tractor etc.

Advantages of Air Cooling: The following are the main advantages of air cooled engine:

(i)   Lighter in weigh due to absence of radiator, coolant, water pump, cooling fan etc.

(ii)   No topping up the cooling system.

(iii)   No risk of leakage

(iv)   Anti-freeze is not required

(v)   Engine warms up faster than water cooled engine.

(vi)   It can be operated in cold climates where water may freeze.

(vii)   It can be used in areas where there is scarcity of cooling water.

The following are the main disadvantages of air cooled engine;

(i)   Less efficient cooling because the co-efficient of heat transfer of air is less than water.

(ii)   Not easy to maintain even cooling all around the cylinder.

(iii)   More noisy operation.

(iv)   Limited use in two wheelers generally.

9.6 Water Cooling System: In this cooling system, water is used to take away the heat. Following are the main methods of water cooling system.

(i)   Thermo syphon cooling method

(ii)   Pump circulation method

9.6.1 Thermo Syphon Cooling System:

It works on the principles of law of convection, when liquid is heated, it becomes light and rise up, while colder parts come down to take their place which results into starting circulation as i.e., shown in Fig. 9.3. i.e. continuous circulation of the water through jacket.

It is used in stationary diesel engine but it is not used in automobiles engines because of following reasons.

(i)   for thermo syphon system more quantity of water is required for which heavy radiator is a must.

(ii)   Radiator should always remain filled up to its mouth otherwise system will not work.

(iii)   In case of damage or choked base pipe the complete system will stop working.

(iv)   For carrying more water and bigger radiator, dead weight of vehicle increases.

9.6.2. Pump Circulation System: This system is similar to the thermo syphon except that in thermo syphon system water circulates by the law of connection, while in pump circulation system a pump is provided in the bottom as shown in Fig. 9.3., which forces the water to circulate through the cylinder jackets. This is one of the most commonly used systems for cooling the engine, especially in trucks.

Note:

1.   In tractors, the required flow rate of water is 0.16 litre per second per kW to drop the radiator temperature 8.5°C to 5.5°C.

2.   At 2000 rpm the diesel engine and petrol engine rejects 0.58 and 0.75 kW for each kilo watt and put respectively.

246

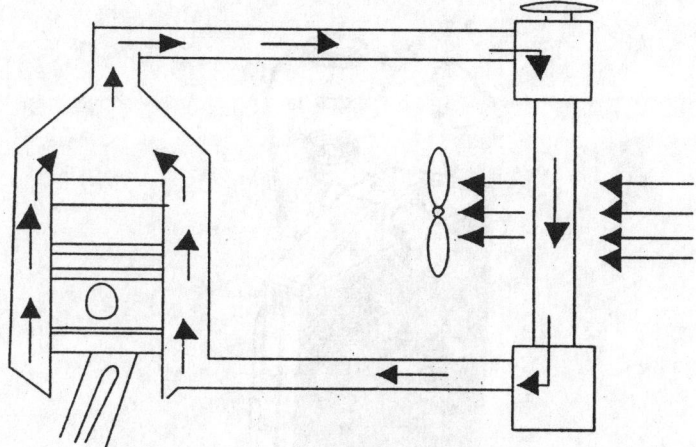

Fig. 9.3. Impeller therms syphon system

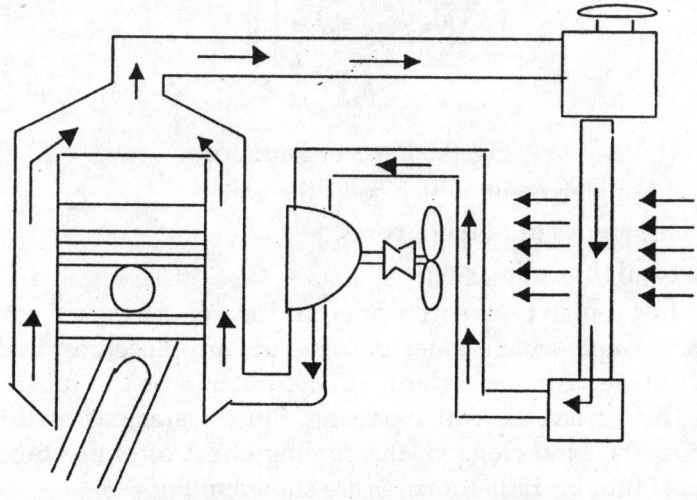

Fig. 9.4. Pump circulating system

9.7. Components of water cooling system

(i) Radiator (ii) Pressure cap (ii) Fan and fan belt (iv) Water jackets in cylinder block and head (v) thermostat (vi) Hoes (vii) Water and (viii) Water pump

9.7.1. Radiator

Radiator is a device which has a large amount of cooling surface, to large quantity of air, so that water circulate through it is cooled efficiently. It consists of an upper tank and lower tank & between them a core as shown in Fig. 9.5. Upper tank is connected to the water outlet from the engine jacket by a hose pipe and lower tank is connected to the jacket inlet through the water pump as shown in the Figure.

Fig. 9.5 Parts of Radiator

The core is a radiating element, which cools the water.

There are two basic types of radiator cores:

(i) Tubular type and (ii) Cellular type

Tubular type: In tubular type core upper and lower panes are connected by a series of tubes through which water passes. Fins are placed around the tube to improve heat transfer Air power around the outside of the tubes between the fins, absorbing heat from the water passing. Since water passes through all the tubes, if one tube become clogged, the cooling effect of entire tube is lost. The different forms of tubular radiator cores are shown in Fig. 9.6.

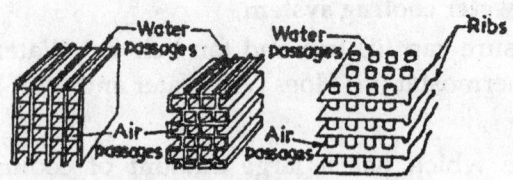

Tubular radiator sections

Fig. 9.6. Tubular Radiator

Cellular Type core: In cellular type core upper and lower panes are connected by a series of tubes through which air passes. Fins are placed around the tubes to improve heat transfer. Water circulates around the outer sides of the tubes between this fin. The core is composed of a large number of individual air cells which are surrounded by water. Because of its appearance the cellular type is usually known as honey comb radiator, especially when the cells in front are hexagonal shape. The different forms of cellular cores are shown in Fig. 9.7.

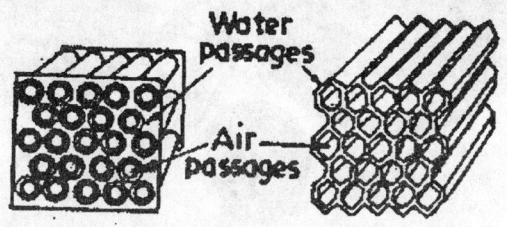

Cellular radiator sections

Fig. 9.7. Cellular Type Core

Radiators are usually made of copper and brass because of their heat conductivity.

9.7.2. Water Pump:

A coolant pump is necessary for forced circulation type engine cooling system. The pump is mounted at the front end of the engine and is driven from the crank shaft by means of a V' belt. Centrifugal type pump is the one which is used for this purpose. Fig. 9.8 shows the centrifugal type coolant pump. The coolant from the radiator enters the pumps at the centres where inlet is located. The flow of the coolant depends upon the pump speed which is proportional to engine speed. The scroll is connected in front of the engine to direct the conduct to the block. For 'V' engine the coolant pump has two outlet one for each bank of cylinder.

The main parts of the pump are a casing and shaft mounted impeller having a number of vanes. The impeller shaft is mounted on bearing while the real serve to prevent the leakage of the coolant around the shaft.

When the impellar rotates, the coolant between the vanes is thrown due to the centrifugal force, thus forcing the cooled coolant at the periphery with a force depending upon the speed of rotation of the pump spindle which itself is proportional to the engine speed. This water leaving the periphery of the impeller tangentially and having maximum Kinetic energy, then outers the involute, which is smoothly curved passage cast in the casing, whose cross-section gradually increases towards the outlet port. Thus, the scroll converts the kinetic energy of the coolant to pressure energy.

In this way a coolant pressure created at the pump outlet that forces he coolant through the cooling system.

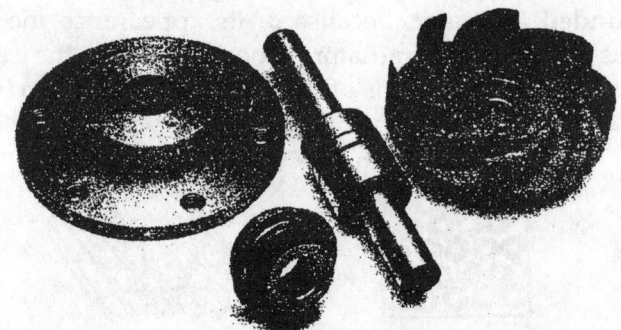

Fig. 9.8. Components of Water Pump

9.7.3. Radiator Cap: The radiator caps are specially designed for controlling the temperature of water. It consists of two spring loaded valves fitted in one cap as shown in Fig. 9.9. Small valve is vacuum valve and bigger one is pressure value. The pressure valve opens while pressure inside the radiator increases 50 KPa and allows the pressure to drop to safe limit while the tractor stops and left to cool down. As temperature of inside goes down, the water contracts and create a vaccum in it. At this stage vacuum valve opens and allows air to come which results into rapid decrease of temperature.

Note:

1. By use of radiator cap, boiling temperature of water increases and boil at 110°C which results in preventing the condensation in oil sump.

2. The boiling point will decrease approximately 1.4°C. for each 500 m above sea level.

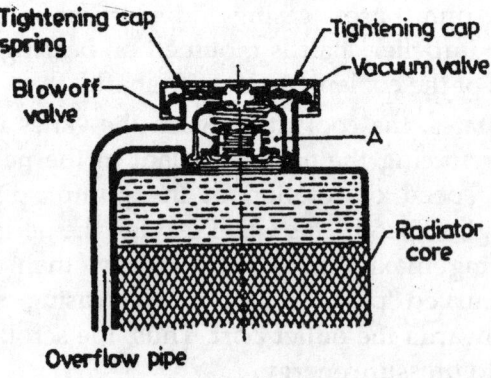

Fig. 9.9. Radiator Cap

9.7.4 Thermostat:

A thermostat valve is used in the water cooling system to regulate the circulation of water in system to maintain the normal working temperature of engine parts during different operating conditions. The thermostat valve automatically works in cooling system. When the engine is started from low temperature the thermostat valve prevents the flow of water from engine to radiator so that the engine readily reaches its working temperature, after which it is automatically comes into action. Generally, the thermostat valve does not permit to pass the water below 70°C. The arrangement of thermostat is shown in Fig. 9.10

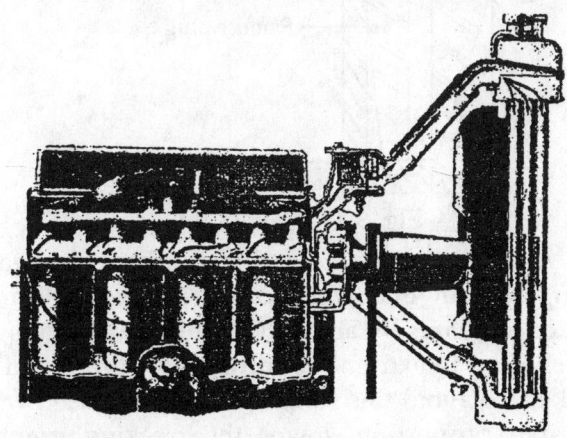

Fig. 9.10 A cutaway drawing of a cooling system, showing the thermostat and presure cap (Courtesy Massey-Ferguson, Inc.)

Note: Thermo states are designed to start opening at 70°C to 75°C and then fully open at 82°C for petrol engine and 88-90°C for diesel engine.

Classification of Thermostat: They are classified as follows:

(i)   Bellows type and (ii) Wax pallet type

Bellow's Type:

The heat unit consists of a closed bellow's with a volatile liquid (such as acetone, alcohol ether). Under reduced pressure, when the bellow is heated, the liquid vapourizes and creates enough pressure to expand the bellow. The movement of bellow operates a linkage which opens the valve to pass the water through it. When the bellow in cooled the gas condenses the pressure reduces and the bellow clones the valve, thus stops the water circulation.

Wax Pallet Type:

Fig. 9.10 shows the wax pallet type thermostat. As the coolant is heated, it transmits its heat to the copper leaded wax having high co-efficient of volumetric thermal expansion, which expands so that the rubber plug contracts against the pluger and exerts a force on it upwardly. So that it moves vertically. This movement of the plunger opens a valve in the thermostat to allow coolant to flow through radiator.

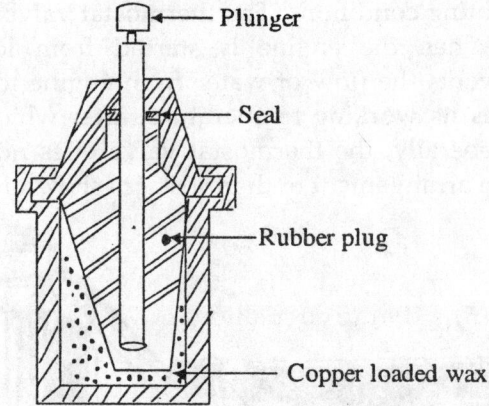

Fig. 9.11 Wax Pallet

9.8 Introduction of Anti-Freezer -In cold climate, there is always a danger that water in the cooling system may get frozen. As the volume of water after converting into the ice increases by about 10%, this may results in the damage of the entire-system including in extreme condition the bursting of the radiator core and the cylinder jacket. To avoid this some additives are used which when mixed with water in suitable proportion, lower the freezing point of water, such additives are called anti freezer. The anti freezer solution also increases the boiling point of water due to which it is also used in hot climates.

9.8.2 Properties of a Good Anti freezer:

The following are the main properties of a good anti freezes:

(i)   It should be throughly miscible with coolant and should prevent the freezing of the coolent.

(ii)   It should not have any corrosive action on system components

(iii) Its boiling point should be high so that there is minimum loss due to evaporation and the coolent can operate at higher temperatures.

(iv)   It should not deposit any foreign matter in the jackets, hose pipes and radiator core.

(v)   It should not be inflammable and its flash point should be higher than the maximum possible operating temperature.

(vi)   Its viscosity should not be very large.

9.8.5. Common Anti-Freezer:

The common anti-freezers are wood alcohol (methyl alcohol) denatured alcohol (ethyl alcohol), glycerine, ethylene glycol etc.

Each of these has its own advantages and disadvantages.

(A)   Alcohol: It is quite effective, but it is very much volatile and due to this reason evaporation losses are high.

(B)   Ethylene glycol: Ethylene glycol corrodes copper, aluminium and tin-lead solder alloys.

(C)   Glycerine: The glycerine is less volatile. (basic) but it is comparatively costly and also it attacks rubber horse pipe.

(D)   Calcium chloride: This is a good anti freezer, corrosion of metals are reduced by adding sodium chromate with calcium chloride.

SUBJECTIVE QUESTIONS

1.   What is the purposes of cooling system in an I.C. engine?
2.   What are the different methods of cooling of an I.C. engine?
3.   What is the difference between air and water cooled engines?
4.   Describe the working of thermo syphon system of cooling.
5.   What are functions of water pump and radiator. What are different types of radiators used in an I.C.. engines?
6.   Describe the different components of forced circulation system.
7.   What are the functions of thermostat valve? What are different types of thermostat used in tractor engine?
8.   What are the advantages and disadvantages of air cooled engines?
9.   Write short notes on:
(a)   Radiator cap   (b)   Water cooling system

MULTIPLE CHOICE QUESTIONS

1.   In I.C. engines, the temperature attained during power stroke in about
(a) 1600°C   (b) 1000°C
(c) 500°C   (d) 100°C
2.   In I.C. engines percent of heat dissipates by cooling is:
(a) 10%   (b) 20%
(c) 30%   (d) 40%
3.   Best operating temperature of I.C. engines lie between
(a) 82 to 90°C   (b) 100 to 150°C
(c) 200 to 250°C   (d) 150-200°C
4.   In air-cooled engines, fins are the component of
(a) cooling system   (b) ignition system
(c) fuel system   (d) none of the above
5.   Water-cooled engines are cooled by
(a) Open jacket method   (b) air firm
(c) thermostat method   (d) (a) & (c)

6. In an I.C. engines, the thermostat valve is opened at the temperature from
    (a) 50 to 60°C   (b) 70 to 75°C
    (c) 80 to 90°C   (d) 90 to 100°C
    In petrol engines, the thermo stat valve open fully at the temperature
    (a) 50°C   (b) 60°C
    (c) 75°C   (d) 82°C

7. Scale formation inside the water passage of cooling system can be presented by using
    (a) Lime free water   (b) Lime water
    (c) H_2SO_4 solution   (d) HNO_3 solution

8. Normally, air cooled engine runs
    (a) Faster than the water cooled engines
    (b) better than water cooled engine
    (c) both
    (d) none of the above

9. In bellows type thermostat valve, the liquid contains
    (a) alcohol   (b) ether
    (c) benzene   (d) carbon tetrochloride

10. An Air cooled engine, requires
    (a) heavier lubricating oil   (b) lighter lubricating oil
    (c) high compression pressure   (d) none of the above

11. Melting point of aluminium is about
    (a) 1100°C   (b) 1000°C
    (c) 900°C   (d) 800°C

12. Melting point of steel is about
    (a) 1450°C   (b) 1600°C
    (c) 1700°C   (d) 1800°C

FILL UP THE BLANKS

1. The temperature at which an engine operate affects both ....and ....

2. Thermal efficiency .... under cooling.

3. Rate of cooling is .... proportional to area.

4. Radiator cap consists of .... and .... valve.

5. The boiling point will decreases approximately 1.4°C of each............ on above sea level.

6. Thermostat valve doesn't permit to pass water below .... °C.

7. Thermostat completely opens at............ °C for diesel engine.

8.   Volumes of water after converting into ice increases by about .... %.

9.   About .... % is washed as exhaust gas.

10. About .... % in the cooling system.

Ans. 1. Fuel economy, wear 2. Decreases 3. Directly 4. Pressure, vacuum 5. 500 6. 70 7. 88-90 8. 10 9. 26 10.

ANSWERS OF MULTIPLE CHOICE QUESTIONS

1 (a) 2 (c) 3 (a) 4 (a) 5 (d) 6 (b) 7 (d) 8 (a) 9 (c) 10 (a) 11 (a) 12 (a) 13 (a)

Chapter 10
Lubricants and Lubrication System of I.C. engine

10.1. Introduction; Lubrication is the property of lubricant for reducing friction between moving or sliding parts of internal combustion engine by maintaining a film of lubricant in between two surfaces and thus completely separating them. These films, then slip one over the other as the parts move which results into reducing the amount of friction. The path of the lubricating oil through a diesel engine is shown in Fig. 10.1.

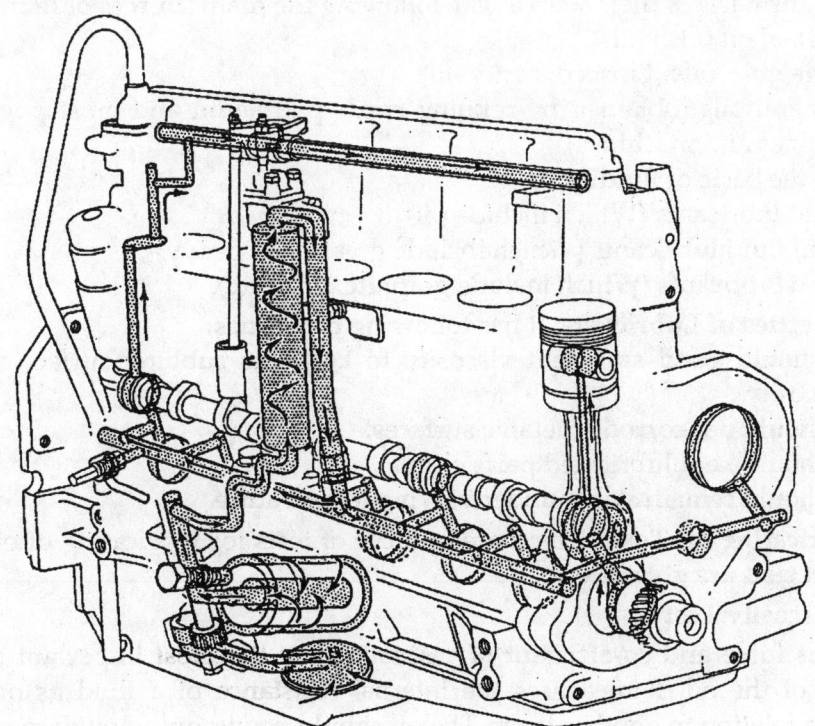

Fig. 10.1 Lubricating System

The following are the main objectives of lubrication.

(i)   To reduce friction between moving parts and supporting members which results into reducing loss of power and wear.

(ii)   To act as a cooling medium for removing heat.

(iii)   To keep the engine parts clean like piston rings, ring grooves, oil passage etc.

(iv)   To absorb the shocks between the two parts.

(v)   To absorb the engine noises and increases part's life.

(vi)   To real the piston ring with cylinder wall.

(vii)   To resist oxidation of metal.

10.2 Factors Affecting the Amount of Friction: The following are the main factors affecting the amount of friction:

(i)   Nature of the surface.

(ii)   Pressure which forces the surface together.

(iii)   Kinds of material.

10.3 Classification of Lubricants: They are classified as follows:

(a)   On the Basis of their source: The following the main sources of lubricants:

(i)   Animal oil (Fish oils)

(ii)   Vegetable oils (Linseed, carter oil)

(iii)   Mineral oils (obtained by refining crude patroleum and most popular for engines and machines)

(b)   On the basic of fluidity:

(i)   Fluid lubricants (Which include oil)

(ii)   Semi fluid lubricants (Which include grease and heavy)

(iii)   Solid lubricants (Which include graphite, mica etc).

10.4 Properties of Lubricants: It has following properties,

(i)   It should good sufficient viscosity to keep the rubbing surface apart (i) viscosity

(ii)   It should not corrode metallic surfaces.

(iii)   It should kept lubricated parts clean.

(iv)   It should remain stable under varying temperature.

10.5 Lubricating oil Tests: There are number of tests for lubricating of oil. Some important tests are given as

10.5.1 Viscosity Test

(i) viscous force and co-efficient of viscosity: It is the most important physical property of the oil. It measures the internal resistance of a fluid as one layer moved, in relation to another layer. The oil should be viscous enough to maintain a fluid film between the moving parts or sliding surface or bearing and its journal?

Sir Isaac Newton deducted the following relationship for a fluid being stressed-sternad between two plates.

$$F = \eta \, A. \frac{dv}{dx} \qquad (10.1)$$

where,

F = Fiscus Force, N

η = Co-efficient of viscosity, Pa. s (Ns/m^2)

A = cross-sectional area, m^2

$\dfrac{d_v}{d_\alpha}$ = velocity gradient, s^{-1}

Note: A fluid is said to be Newtonion if the viscosity is constant at content temperature changes.

i.e.; $\eta = \dfrac{F/A}{d_v/d_x}$ = constant

(ii) Flow through capillary tube: It is related to Poisevill's Law

It is given by following relationship

$$\eta = \frac{\pi p r^4 t}{8vl} \qquad (10.2)$$

Where,

p = pressure difference, dynes/cm^2

r = Radius of the tube, cm

t = Time , s

v = Volume of liquid, cm^3

l = Length of tube, cm

η = Absolute viscosity, poises.

Note: Equation is valid only for lamin or flow because viscosity measurement by capillary tube is fast or rapid.

Viscosity of an oil is measured by Saybolt universal viscometer and is reported in Saybolt universal seconds (SUS or SSU).

(ii) Kinematic viscosity (v): It is defined as the ratio of absolute viscosity (η) to density (ρ) and is given by following relationship.

$$v = \frac{\eta}{\rho} \qquad (10.3)$$

Oil used for lubrication purposes are graded as per viscosity in SAE numbers, SAE means society of Automobile Engineer, they have graded the oil as SAE 20, SAE 30, SAE 40 and so on; as the number increases viscosity increases i.e., oil becomes thick.

10.5.2 Carbon Residue Test: Method of finding the amount of carbon residue obtained when a given sample of oil is heated and evaporated under predetermined conditions is called carbon residue test.

10.6 Lubrication System: Generally following systems of lubrication are found in internal combustion engines:

(i).   Splash system (ii) Force feed or Pressure type

(iii)   Combination system (force feed and splash)

10.6.1 Splash System: Splash means spattering liquid over different parts. On splash lubrication system splash is produced due to the crank rotation in the oil pan as shown in (Fig. 10.2) and thus the different parts are lubricated. It has following characteristics features.

(a)   There is no uniformity or uneven lubrication.

(b)   It is generally used on single-cylinder engines with closed crankcases.

(c)   Maintenance of proper level is necessary for effective lubrication.

(d)   If the rings are worn out, lubricating oil reaches the combustion chamber which results in blue smoke, carbon deposition and plug fouling.

(e)   The oil may carry dust with it and worn metal to the rubbing surfaces causing wear.

(f)   Effectiveness depends upon the size of the holes, clearance etc.

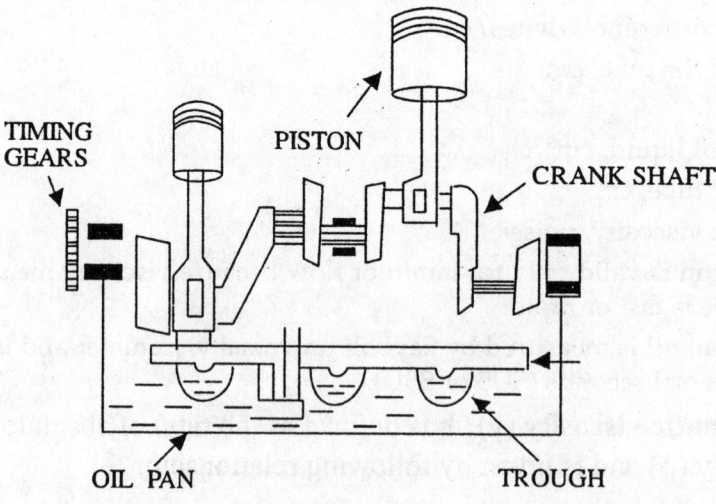

Fig. 10.2. Splash Lubrication system

10.6.2. Pressure Type Lubrication:

This system is most commonly used in four stroke and high speed multi cylinder engine as shown in Fig. 10.3. In this system, and oil pump takes the oil from the oil sump through a strainer and delivers it through a filter to the main oil galleries at a predefined pressure. The oil pressure is controlled by means of a pressure relief valve, situated in the filter unit or the pump housing.

There is one main gallary in the case of in lined engines, where the two main oil gallaries may be present in the case of V-shape engines, from the main gallary, the oil goes through drilled passages to the main bearings from where some of the air after lubricating falls back to the sump, some is splashed to lubricate cylinder walls, while the rest goes in the connecting leads through a hole to the piston pin. After lubricating the piston pin bearings, the oil falls back. In some of the engines most commonly used method of cylinder and piston lubrication is by big and splash for the cam shaft end timing gears, lubricating oil is lead through separate oil lines from the oil gallary to each camshaft bearing. To lubricate the timing gears and the sprocket chain, some times a directed oil jet is employed. The valve tappes are lubricated by connecting the main oil gallary to the tapped guide surface through drilled holes. In case of overhead valve mechanism, the rocker arms are sometimes mounted on hollow shafts. Which carry oil under pressure from the oil gallary. These hollow shafts feed oil for the lubrication of rocker arms.

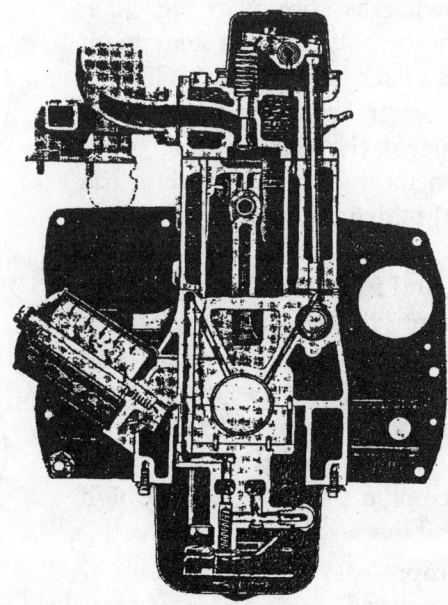

Fig. 10.3. Pressure Lubricating System

In some other designs, the push rods are made hollow and the oil under pressure is made to flow up to provide lubrication of various parts of the valve train. The oil seeps from the valve train as above is returned to the oil pan through drain holes, which are some times so placed that the oil drains on the camshaft and the timing gears the lubricate them. At the end of the main oil gallery oil pressure with is provided which operates the warming light on the dash board. During the circulation, the oil gains heat from various engine parts, which is given out to the sump walls. In some heavy engines, separate oil cooler may also be employed.

10.6.3 Components of Lubricating System: The main components of Lubricating system are as follows:

(i) oil pump (ii) oil filter (iii) Pressure regulating valves (iv) By pass valves (v) Breather system (vi) oil coolers.

(i) Pumps: Lubricating pump is generally a positive displacement pump. Some common pump:

(a)   Gear pump

(b)   Rotor type pump

(c)   Plunger or Piston type Pump

(d)   Vone type pump

(a) Gear Type Oil Pump

Gear type oil pump consists of two meshed spur gears included in a showing as shown in Fig. 10.4. There is very little clearance between the gear teeth and housing. One gear is attached to a shaft which is driven through suitable gear from the cam shaft (generally) or crank shaft of the engine. The outer gear is free to revolve on its own bearing when the pump is in action, the oil is driven between the gear teeth from the inlet side, carried around between the gears and pump housing and force out the outlet side. The pressure and the quantity of the oil supplied by the pump depend upon the speed of the gears. This type of pump is widely used in the automotive engines due to its simplicity in construction. A pressure relief valve is also provided in many oil pumps to relieve the excessive pressure due to high engine speed or clogged oil lives.

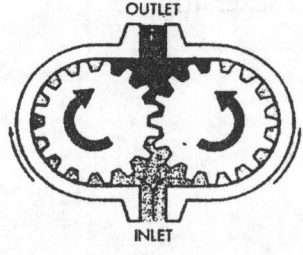

Fig. 10.4 Gear Pump

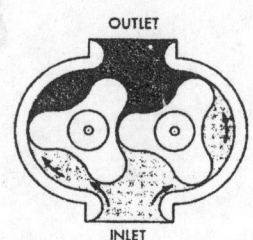

Fig. 10.5 Rotory pump

(b)   Rotor Type Oil Pump:

Rotor pump consists of an inner and outer rotor within the pump body inplace of gears, i.e., two gears meshed internally as shown in Fig. 10.5. The external gear has the number teeth one more than on the internal gear. The oil is displaced from the inlet to the outlet side in the same way as in the case of gear type oil pump.

(c)   Plunger Type Pump: Plunger type pump consists of pluge which reciprocates in the pump body, while moving up, the plunger sucks oil from the inlet the while moving down it forces out the oil to the outlet as shown in Fig. 10.6

(d)   Vane Type Pump: It consists of cylindrical casing with outlet and inlet and drum as shown in Fig. 10.6. The drum is mounted centrically in the casing and contains two valves for more vens in even number with springs, when the drum rotates, the vans sweep the oil from inlet to the out let side, because the drum in mounted eccentrically, the volume

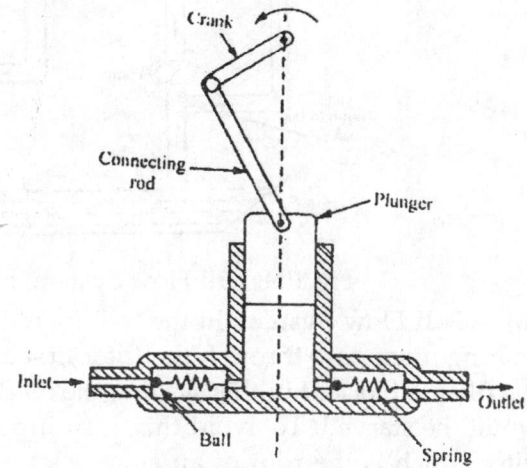

Fig. 10.6. Plunger Pump

between the drum and the casing constantly decreases and oil pressure increases at the outlet.

(e)   Oil Filtering System: Some of the most commonly used oil filter system are given below

(a)   By pass system (b) Full flow system.

(a)   By pass system: In by pass system the whole of the oil does not pass through the filter at the same time. as shown in Fig. 10.7. Most of the oil without being filtered goes to bearings whereas the rest (about 10%) passing through the filter cleaned out, the rate of oil flow through the filter is slow so that very fine filtering element can also be used. However, this system is now absolute.

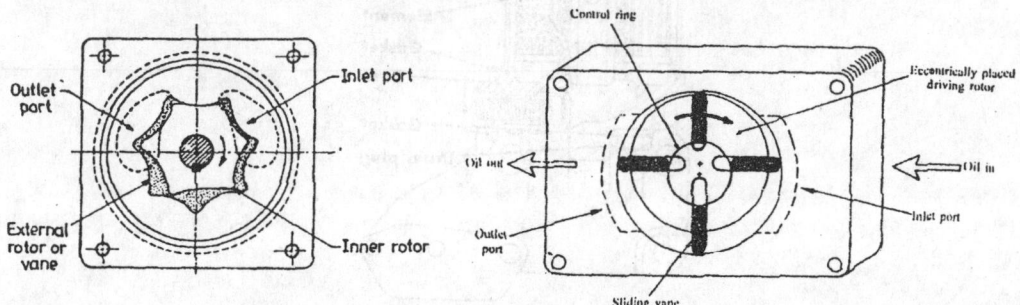

Fig. 10.7 Vane Pump

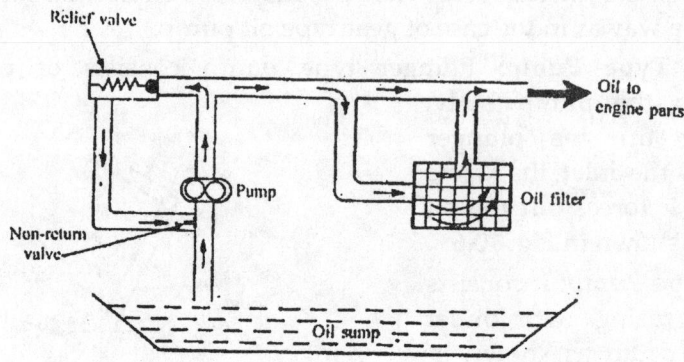

Fig 10.8 Full Flow System; Fig. 10.9. By Pass System

(b)   Full Flow System: In the full flow filtering system, all the oil which goes to bearing must pass through the filter first as shown in Fig. 10.9. Thus, if any time the filter is blocked in this system, the oil flow would be stopped and the bearing would be starved. To avoid this, a spring loaded relief valve incorporated in the filter which is the rout of an emergency supply of unfiltered oil to the bearing. Thus saving them from oil starvation. This relief valve is designed to open at a pre-determined pressure, the actual valve depending upon the engine model and the normal pressure drop across the filter.

(ii) Oil Filter: Fig. 10.10 shows a cut view of the oil filter. The following are the types of the oil filter:

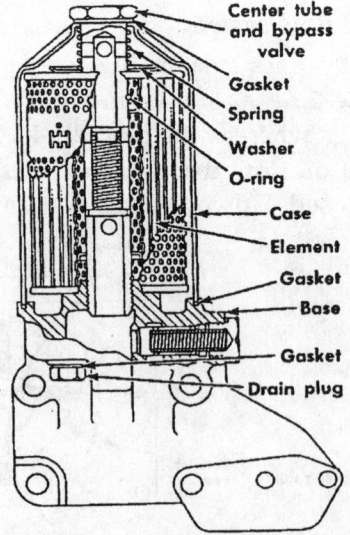

Fig. 10.10 A cut view of a Oil Filter

(i)   Cartidge type

(ii)   Edge type

(ii)   Centrifugal type

(i)   Cartidge Type: It consists of a filtering element placed in metallic casing as shown in Fig. 10.10. The impure lubricating oil is made to pass through the filtering element which takes up all the impurities. The filter element is given a pleated form to maximise the surface area of the filter for a given size of element in cartidge type, the oil enters the filter at the top and passes through the filtering elements (Fig. 11).

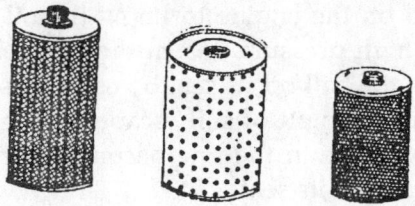

Fig. 10.11 Cartidge Type Oil Filter

The pure oil then goes to the perforated metallic tube from where, it goes to the outlet for circulation. A drain plug is also provided.

The filtering elements of two types are available, (i) cleauable (ii) replaceable type

(ii)   Centrifugal Type:

In the centrifugal type oil filter, the impure or dirty oil from engine enters the hollow centred spindle (tube) having holes around its periphery as shown in fig. 10.12. The dirty oil comes at from these holes and fills the rotor after which it passes through the tubes at the ends of which jets are attached. The oil under pressure passes these jets, the reaction of which gives the motion of the rotor casing in opposite direction results into rotating motion. The oil impinges on the outer stationary casing under high pressure, where the impurities are retained and clean oil falls out from where it is taken out.

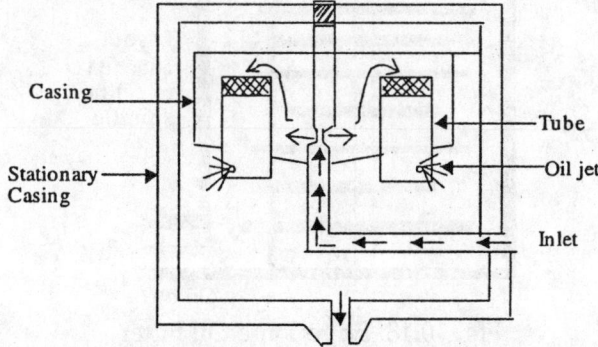

Fig. 10.12 Centrifugal Type Oil Filter

Edge Type oil Filter:

Edge type of oil filter is also called stack type filter. In this type, the oil is made to pass through a number of closely space discs. The alternate discs are mounted over a central spindle, while the dises in between these are attached to a separate sequence rod (fixed) as shown in Fig. 10.13. The space between two successive discs are kept very small. The oil is made to flow through the spaces between these discs and because of the very smalls paces in volved left on discs periphery from where these and periodically removed.

(iii) Pressure regulating value: It is a spring loaded valve mostly fixed in the oil gallary. This is provided on the engine to know the oil pressure which gives a warning against low or high pressure. When the oil pressure increases than the specified valve, it bushes the ball off its seat by compressing the spring when the ball is listed off its certain amount of soil escape through this and goes back to sump. As soon as the pressure in the line becomes normal the spring.Pressure makes the ball to come back on its seat.

(iv) By pass valve: It is also a spring loaded valve and is usually fitted in cover housing of filter. In absence of this valve, in case the filter gets chock, it will not allow the oil to pass to oil gallary resulting in the loss of lubrication and seizing of engine. For safety, a bypass valve is fitted in the system in such a way that it opens when the filters gets chocked and pressure builts up in the line thereby allowing oil to go directly to oil gallary without going to filter housing.

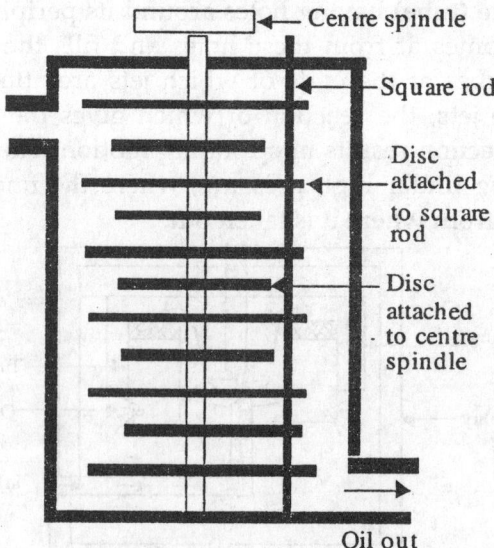

Fig. 10.13. Edge Type Oil Filter

10.7 Crank Case Dilution and Crank Case Ventilation:

The product of combustion contains mainly nitrogen, water and carbondioxide. Moreover sulphuric acid may also present due to sulphur content in the fuel. It is quite possible that the product of combustion may leak through the piston rings into the crank case. This leakage is called "blow by". The fuel may also mix into the crank case oil. The lubricating oil in the crank case becomes dilute. When mixed with water and gasoline (fuel) which leak past the piston ring. This mixing with engine oil is called crank case dilution. The acid causes corrosion of the crankcase metal as does water.

The crank case ventilation remove all the unwanted particles from the crank which leak passed through the piston rings. It prevents the lubricating oils from being dilute and corrosion of crankcase metals, due to acid formation. The crank ventilation is used in all engines. A constant stream of air is passed through crankcase ventilation which pickup and caries away most of the fuel vapour and water vapour before they can condense out and dilute the lubricating oil. Air is drawn into crankcase ventilation through the breather cap and is discharged through an outlet at the side of the engine as shown in Fig. 10.14.

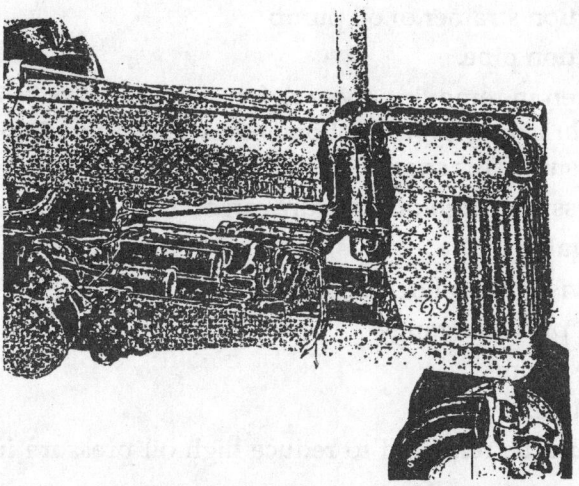

Fig. 10.14 Showing Crank Case Ventilation

10.8 Oil Coolers: Oil does not thin out as thin oil can no lubricate the parts efficiently. For this, different systems are used namely oil sump cooling, oil radiator or oil cooler and heat exchanger.

(a)   Oil sump cooling: Fins are made on oil sumps. Thus more cool air can come in contact with the sump and keep the oil cool.

(b)   Oil cooler: In some of the engines, a separate tubular type heat exchanger is fitted in front of main radiator so fresh cool air before getting into main radiator first touches this heat exchanger and cools the oil in it and then goes into the main radiator. Heat exchanger is connected to the engine oil main gallery through flexible pipes.

10.9. Trouble in Lubrication System: There are a few common troubles in lubricating system such as (i) Low oil pressure (ii) High oil pressure and (iii) Excessive oil consumption

10.9 Low oil pressure: Low oil pressure can take place due to the following reasons:

(i)   Less oil in crankcase

(ii)   Weak relief valve spring

(iii)   Worm oil pump

(iv)   Use of low viscosity oil

(v)   By pass valve spring defective

(vi)   Damaged regulating ball seat

(vii)   Defective oil pressure gauge

(viii) Too much play in oil pump

(ix)   Chocked suction strainer of oil pump

(x)   Chocked suction pipe.

Care should be taken in removing these defects as soon as possible to increase oil pressure in the lubricating systems. Sometimes defective oil pressure indicator shows low oil pressure. This should be checked.

10.9.2 High oil Pressure: High oil pressure can occur due to following reasons:

(i)   Stuck relief valve

(ii)   Use of high viscosity oil in crankcase

(iii)   Defective oil pressure gauge

(iv)   Strong valve spring

(v)   Clogged oil line.

These defects should be removed to reduce high oil pressure in the lurbricating system.

10.9.3 Excessive Oil Consumption: Excessive oil consumption can occur due to following reasons:

(i)   External leakage

(ii)   Internal leakage

(iii)   Operating deficiency

(iv)   Loss of oil in form of vapour through ventilations system.

Oil can enter the combustion chamber through rings and cylinder walls, piston rings and worm bearings.

SUBJECTIVE QUESTIONS

1. What is the purpose of lubrication in an I.C. engine?
2. What are the lubrication theories?
3. What are the different types of lubricants, which are more common for an I.C. engine?
4. What are the different types of lubricating oil tests?
5. What is the principles of splash system of lubrication? Explain with the help of a neat diagram?
6. How forced feed system of lubrication works in an I.C. engine? What are the different components of the system?
7. Explain the term viscosity and kinematic viscosity.
8. Why is breathing system used in engines?
9. What can be the reason for low oil pressure in engines?
10. What can be the reason for the high oil pressure in an engine?

MULTIPLE CHOICE QUESTIONS

1. Lubrication creates
   (a) cooling effect on engine parts
   (b) wear between to parts
   (c) Sharpness in moving parts
   (d) all of the above

2. Lubrication causes the effects.
   (a) cooling effect
   (b) cleaning effect
   (c) reduced friction effect
   (d) sealing effect
   (e) all of the above

3. Lubricants are prepared from
   (a) animal fat
   (b) vegetables
   (c) mineral
   (d) all of the above

4. Vegetable lubricant is
   (a) cotton seed oil
   (b) olive oil
   (c) caster oil
   (d) all of the above

5. Source of mineral lubricant is
   (a) petrol
   (b) crude petroleum
   (c) both
   (d) none of the above

6. For 4-stroke engines, the suitable lubricant is
   (a) animal fat
   (b) vegetable lubricant
   (c) mineral lubricant
   (d) all of the above

7. Viscosity of lubricant is measured by
   (a) saybilt viscosimeter
   (b) venturi meter
   (c) hydrometer
   (d) none of the above

269

8. The temperature, at which an oil just flows under prescribed condition is called
   - (a) flash point
   - (b) cloud point
   - (c) pour point
   - (d) none of the above

9. The splash system of lubrication is generally used for
   - (a) single cylinder engines with closed crank case
   - (b) multicyler engines
   - (c) both
   - (d) none of the above

10. The pump is used in forced feed systems of lubrication
    - (a) reciprocating type
    - (b) positive displacement pump
    - (c) both
    - (d) none of the above

11. The lubrication system is used in high speed multi-cylinder engines
    - (a) splash system
    - (b) force feed system
    - (c) both
    - (d) none of the above

12. The lubrication system is used in tractor
    - (a) forced feed system
    - (b) splash system
    - (c) both
    - (d) none of the above

13. The pressure of lubricating system in tractor is about
    - (a) 1000 kPa
    - (b) 300 kPa
    - (c) 1500 kPa
    - (d) 200 kPa

14. Which of the following reason causes low oil pressure in lubricating system
    - (a) a weak relief valve spring
    - (b) use of very thin lubricating oil
    - (c) use of heavy lubricating oil
    - (d) both (a) & (b)

15. Semi-soild lubricants are
    - (a) Greace
    - (b) SAE-30
    - (c) Graphite
    - (d) None of the above

16. solid lubricant is
    - (a) grease
    - (b) SAE-90
    - (c) graphite
    - (d) none of the above

17. viscosity of a heavy oil is
    - (a) high
    - (b) low
    - (c) medium
    - (d) none of the above

18. Oil is used for lubricating the gear.
    - (a) high
    - (b) low
    - (c) medium
    - (d) None of the above

19. The function of additives used in gear oil is
    (a) improve the oil performance   (b) protect the gears
    (c) protect the bearing   (d) all of the above

20. The pump is used in force feed of lubrication system
    (a) gear pump   (b) jet pump
    (c) both   (d) none of the above

21. The force feed system of lubrication, the pump is driven by
    (a) electric motor   (b) camshaft
    (c) crank shaft   (d) none of the above

22. When engine is operated under average working condition the crank case oil should be changed, after about
    (a) 120 h   (b) 150 h
    (c) 200 h   (d) 250 h

23. As per API, the number of classes of oil for spark ignition engines are
    (a) 3   (b) 2
    (c) 4   (d) 5

24. As per APE, the number of classes of oil for C.I. engines are
    (a) 2   (b) 3
    (c) 4   (d) 5

FILL UP THE BLANKS

1. Graphite and mica are .... lubricants.
2. .... is the most important physical property of the oil.
3. Newtonian fluid has .... at constant temperature.
4. Flow through capillary tube is related to ....
5. Viscosity of an oil is measured by...................
6. Ratio of absolute viscosity to density is known as ....
7. Lubricating pump is a .... displacement pump.
8. Cear pump is a ....
9. ....lubricating system used in multicylinder engine
10. In splash lubricating system splash is produced due to the .... in the oil pan.

Ans. 1. solid 2. viscosity 3. constant viscosity 4. Poisevill's law 5. saybolt universal viscometer 6. kinematic viscosity 7. positive 8. positive displacement pump 9. pressure 10. crank rotation.

ANSWER OF THE MULTIPLE CHOICE QUESTIONS

1 (a) 2 (e) 3 (d) 4 (d) 5 (b) 6 (c) 7 (a) 8 (c) 9 (a) 10 (b) 11 (b) 12 (a) 13 (b) 14 (d) 15 (a) 16 (d) 17 (a) 18 (a) 19 (d) 20 (a) 21 (b) 22 (a) 23 (a) 24 (b)

Chapter 11
Governing System of I.C. Engine

11.1 Introduction: Tractors and other stationary engines run at varying ends consequently the speed will change with change in loads, if it is not provided with a suitable controlling device. It means there will be a changing speed at every moment. It is desirable to maintain a steady speed at varying loads and to protect the engine parts from high speeds. To achieve this objectives they are equipped with a suitable device called Governor.

Note: In car, the supply of fuel is controlled by accelerator padel.

11.2. Governor: Governor is a mechanical device. Its function is to regulate the speed of an engine, when there are variations in the load on engine. To achieve the steady speed of engine to decrease or increase the supply of fuel depending on change in load through governor.

11.3 Diesel Engine Governor:

The governor may be connected directly to one end of the injection pump housing so that it can operation the control rod of the injecting pump which rotates the pledger thus regulating the amount of fuel injected into the engine.

11.4 Classification of Diesel Engine Governor

According to the principle of operation, governor may be classified into two categories, which are as follows:

1. Pneumatic Governor: It is operated by the depression created by the air flow in the inlet manifold.

2. Mechanical Governor: These are controlled by the engine speed and can be further divided into two categories:

(i) Constant Speed Governor: It is mounted on engine so that it can rotate at constant speed, like a stationary engine used for electricity generation plant.

(ii) Variable Speed Governor: It is a type of governor which keeps the speed of the engine constant with vary lead at any given value within generating range.

Tractor engines are equipped with variable speed governor in view of the following advantages.

(i) Easy and convenient operation of the tractor and implements which leads to easy and rapid variation of the engine speed and out put.

(ii) Less time required to change from gear to gear while operation the tractor with implements which into increase in rate of covering working area.

(iii) it decreases fuel consumption at partial load.

(iv) Operating at slow speed while concurrently clearing an obstacle backing the tractor which resulted longer service life of both tractor and implements.

11.5 Classification of Governing System: Governing system is classified as follows:

(i) Hit and miss system and (ii) Throttle system.

11.5 Hit and Miss System: In this frequency of explosion or power strokes of engine are regulated in this, the number of explosions per unit time depends upon the power requirement because intensity of explosion is same. A latch is provided on the exhaust valve push rod which prevents the valve from closing when the speed in too high. The inlet valve remains closed as long as the exhaust valve is held open. As a result neither charge is drawn into the cylinder on the suction strike or power is developed in the engine cylinder due to complete absence of fuel which results into the fall of speed. Thus, it is observed that explosions are missed intermittently but every change has same intensity. This method is commonly used on gas engines.

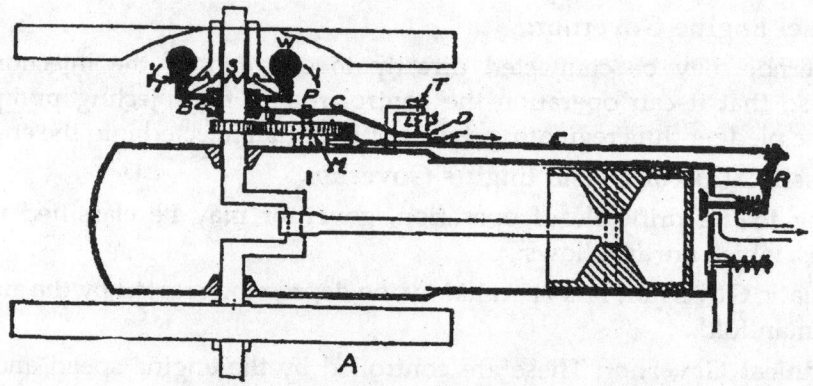

Fig.11.1 Hit and miss governing system

11.5.2 Throttle System: This system is applied for controlling the amount of fuel mixture or fuel during suction stroke and there by changing the explosion intensity in the cylinder. In this system the number of explosion are same, only intensity of explosion is changed. Uniform fixing takes place inside the cylinder throughout period of operation. A suitable butterfyl valve is provided in the air passage between the inlet manifold and the carburetor as shown in Fig. 11.2

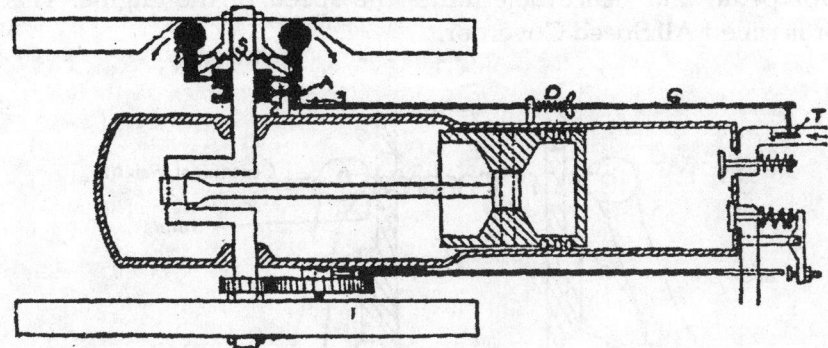

Fig. 11.2. Throttle Governing System

As the speed decreases, the throttel remains wide opena dn more charge enters he engine cylinder. When the speed enhances, the throttle comes to nearly closed position and less charge outers inside the engine cylinder.

11.6 Classification of Throttle System of Governor: They are classified as follows:

(a)   Centrifugal governor (b) Pneumatic governor and (c) Hydraulic governor.

11.6.1 Centrifugal Governor: The basic principle of a centrifugal Governor is that when a weight rotates about a point, it tends to fly away in tangential direction from the centre of rotation. Two spring loaded weighted are mounted on the governor shaft which gets drive from the engine as shown in Fig. 11.3. One end, the bell crank levers carried balls. Where as their other ends touches the lower surface of the flings of a sleep on the governor shaft. As the engine speed increases, the centrifugal forces due to the weights acts against he spring tension that in turn increases.

Once the engine speed exceeds the spring tension, the weight fly apart, causing the other ends of the bell crank leaves to raise the sleeve and hence operating the control lever in the downward direction, which further actuates the control rack on the fuel injection pump in a direction which reduces the amount of field levered and hence decreases the engine speed tends to decreases.

Thus, the spring tension can be so adjusted as to actuate the control rack for decreases in fuel delivery at same maximum speed, the control rock on fuel injection pump may be directly operated by the operator through accelerators pedal and linkages, with a provision to override the driver control of maximum speed which is limited by the amount of spring tension, such a governor is called maximum speed governor.

In another type of governor, however, there is no direct connection between the accelerator pedal and the pump control rack. The two are linked only through the governor. The operation can then change spring tension with the help of the accelerator pedal and hence determines the speed of the engine. This type of governor is called All Speed Governor.

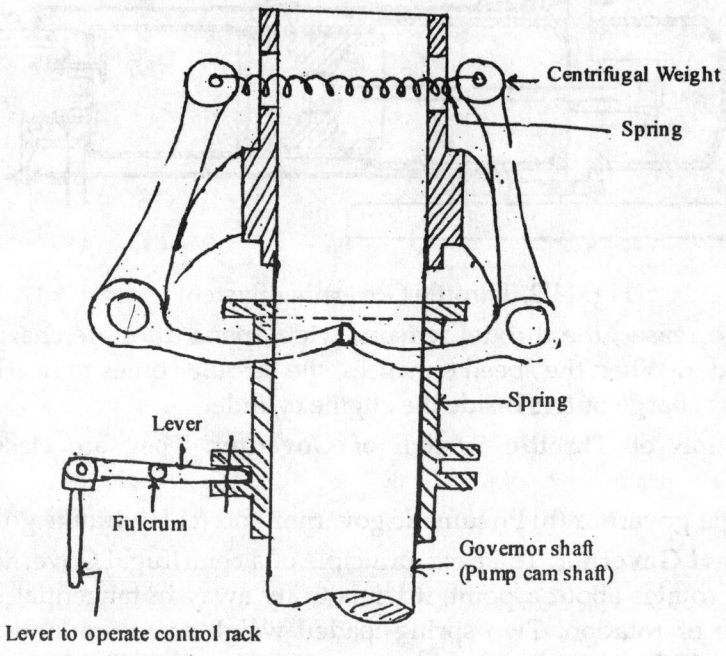

Fig. 11.3. Centrifugal Governer

11.6.2. Pneumatic Governor: The Fig. 11.4 shows a simple pneumatic governor. This type of governor consists of two main parts (i) the venturi unit and (ii) diaphragm unit. The venturi unit is connected to the engine inlet manifold and the diaphragms unit is mounted on the fuel injection pump. The two units are connected by a vacuum pipe.

Accelerator pedal controls the position of the butterfly in the venturi unit and hence controls the amount of vaccum from in let manifold, which is equipped to the diaphragm via the vaccum pipe. As the control rock is pumped, the rock is operated left or right depending upon amount of vaccum applied. Thus the position of the pump controls control rack and hence the amount of fuel injection. Idling string adjustment is also provided by means of a separate spring and lever and spring tension can be adjusted with and adjusting not provided as shown in Fig. 11.4 This is an all speed type of governor.

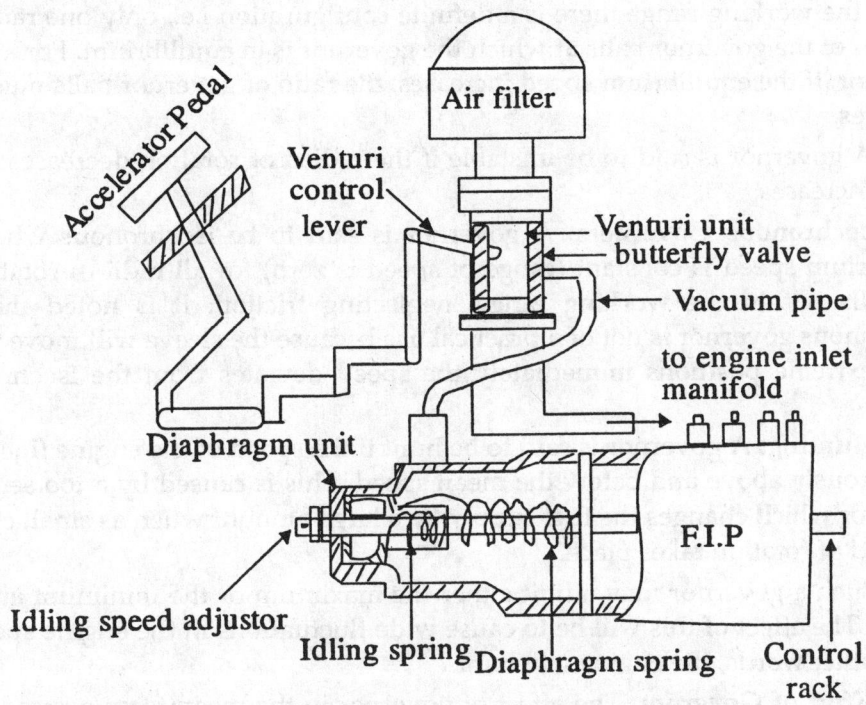

Fig. 11.4. Pneumatic Governer

11.7. Sensitiveness of Governors: It is defined as the ratio of the difference the maximum and minimum equilibrium speeds to the mean equilibrium speed. It is given by following relationship

$$\text{Sensitiveness of the governor} = \left(\frac{\tan\phi}{m}\right)^{\frac{1}{2}} \frac{N_2 - N_1}{N} = \frac{\Delta N}{N} \qquad (11.1)$$

$$= \frac{2(N_1 - N_2)}{N_1 + N_2} = \frac{2(\omega_1 - \omega_2)}{N} \qquad (11.2)$$

Where,

N_1 = Minimum equilibrium speed, rpm

N_2 = Maximum equilibrium speed, rpm

N = Mean equilibrium speed, rpm, $\dfrac{N_1 + N_2}{2}$

ω_1 = Minimum equilibrium angular speed, rod/s

ω_2 = Maximum equilibrium angular speed, rod/s

ω = Mean equilibrium, angular speed, rod/s, $\dfrac{\omega_1 + \omega_2}{2}$

11.8 Stability of Governor: A governor is said to be stable when for every speed within the working range there is a definite configuration i.e., only one radius of rotation of the governor balls at which the governor is in equilibrium. For a stable governor, if the equilibrium speed increases, the ratio of governor balls must also increases.

Note: A governor is said to be unstable if the radius of rotation decreases as the speed increases.

11.9. Isochronous Governors: A governor is said to be isochronous when the equilibrium speed is constant (range of speed is zero) for all radii of rotation of the balls within the working range, neglecting friction. It is noted that the Isochronous governor is not of a practical use because the sleeve will move to one of its extreme positions immediately the speed deviates from the isochronous speed.

11.10. Hunting: A governor is said to be hunt if the speed of the engine fluctuates continuously above and below the mean speed. This is caused by a too sensitive governor which changes the fuel supply by a large amount when as small change in speed of rotation takes place.

Note: Such a governor may admit either the maximum or the minimum amount of fuel. The effect of this will be to cause wide fluctuations in the engine speed or in the other words, the engine will hunt.

11.11 Effort of Governor: The effect of governor in the mean force exerted by at the sleeve for a given percentage change of speed (or lift of sleeve). It may be noted that when the governor is running steadily, there is no force no sleeve. But, when the speed changes, there is a resistance at the sleeve which opposes its motion.

11.12. Power of Governor: The power of a governor is the work done at the sleeve for a given percentage change of speed. It is the product of the mean value of the effort and the distance through which the sleeve moves. Mathematically, it is given by following relationship,

Power = Mean effort x lift of sleeve   (11.3)

11.13. Controlling Force: We have seen that when a body rotates in a circular path, there is an inward force or centripetal force acting on it. In case of a governor running at a steady speed, the inward force acting on the rotating balls is known are controlling force. It is equal to opposite the centrifugal reaction.

$\therefore$ Controlling force (F_c) = $m\omega^2 r$ (11.4)

The controlling force is provided by the weight of the sleeve and balls as in Porter governor and by spring and weight as in Hart nell governor (r spring controlled governor).

When the graph between the controlling force (F_c) as ordinate and radius of rotation (r) as abscissa is drawn, then the graph obtained is known as controlling force diagram as shown in Fig 11.5 This diagram enables the stability and senstivences of the governor to the examined and also shows the effect of friction.

11.14 Controlling Force Diagram for Spring: Controlled Governors:

The controlling force diagram for the spring controlled governor is a straight line, as shown in Fig. 11.5

We know that controlling force,

$$F_c = m. \omega^2.r \qquad (11.5)$$

or, $\dfrac{F_c}{r} = m. w^2$ (11.6)

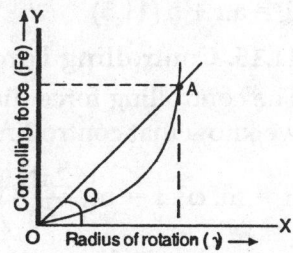

Fig. 11.5. Controlling Force Diagram

The following points, for the stability of spring controlled governors, may be noted

1. For the governor to be stable, the controlling force (Fc) must increase as the radius of rotation (r) increases, i.e., F3/r must increase as r increase. Hence the controlling, force line AB when produced must intersect the controlling force axis below the origin, as shown in Fig. 11.6

The relation between the controlling force (Fc) and the radius of rotation (r) for the stability of spring controlled governor is given by the following equation.

$$F_c = ar - b \qquad (11.7)$$

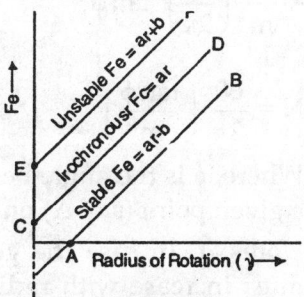

Fig. 11.6 Controlling Force for spring-controlled Governor

Where,

a and b are constants.

2. The value of ab in equation (11.7) may be made either zero or positive by increasing the initial tension of the spring. If b is zero, the controlling force line CD passes through the origin and governor becomes isochronous because Fc/r will remain constant for all radii of rotation.

The relation between the controlling force and the radius of rotation, for isochronous governor, is therefore,

$$F_c = a. r. \qquad (11.8)$$

3. If b is greater than zero i.e. positive, then F_c/r decreases as r increases, so that the equilibrium speed of governor decreases with an increase of the radius of rotation of balls, which is impracticable.

Such a governor is said to be unstable and relation between the controlling force and raise of rotation is, therefore,

F_c = a.r.+ b (11.5)

11.15. Controlling Force Diagram for Porter Governor.

The controlling force diagram for a porter governor is curve as shown in Fig. 11.5 we know that controlling force,

$$F_c = m. \omega^2. r = m\left(\frac{2\pi N}{60}\right)^2 r \qquad (11.9)$$

$$N_2 = \frac{1}{m} \left(\frac{60}{2\pi}\right)^2 \left(\frac{F_c}{r}\right)$$

$$= \frac{1}{m} \left(\frac{60}{2\pi}\right)^2 \tan\phi$$

$$N = \frac{60}{2\pi} \left(\frac{\tan\phi}{m}\right)^{\frac{1}{2}} \qquad (11.10)$$

Where, ϕ is the angle between the axis of radius of the rotation and a line joining a given point (say A) on the curve to the origin 'o'.

Notes: 1. In case the governor satisfies the condition for stability, the range ϕ must increase with radius of rotation of the governor balls. In other words, the equilibrium speed must increase with the increase of radius of rotation of the governor balls.

2. For the governor to be more sensitive, the change in the value of over the change of radius of rotation should be as small as possible.

3. For isochronous governor, the controlling force curve is a straight line passing through the origin. The angle f will be constant for all values of the radius of rotation of the governor.

From equations

$$\tan\phi = \frac{F_c}{r}$$

$$= \frac{m.\omega^2 r}{r} = m\omega^2$$

$$= m\left(\frac{2\pi r}{60}\right)^2$$

$$= CN^2 \qquad (11.11)$$

Where,

$$C = m\left(\frac{2\pi r}{60}\right)^2 = \text{constant}$$

Using the above relation, the angle f may be determined for different values of N and the lines are drawn from the origin. These lines enable the equilibrium speed corresponding to the given radius of rotation to be determined.

Prob: 11.1 A Governor is said to be stable when for each speed with working range, there is only one radius of rotation of the governor balls at which the governor is in equilibrium. What would be the nature of the controlling curve if the balls in such a spring controlled. governor are 350 mm apart at a controlling force at 1200 N and 200 mm apart when the balls are 250 mm apart if each of them has a mass of 6 kg.   [GATE-1998]

Soln. Let 'r' be the radius of rotation and Fc is the controlling force.

Given:

$$r_1 = \frac{200}{2} = 100 \text{ mm} = 0.1 \text{ m}$$

$$r_2 = \frac{350}{2} = 175 \text{ mm} = 0.17 \text{ m}$$

$F_{cp} = 600$ N   , $Fc_2 = 1200$ N

$m = 6$ kg, $r = 0.125$ m

For a stable governor, we know that

$$F_c = ar - b \qquad\qquad (1)$$

Accordingly,

$$600 = a \times 0.1 - b \qquad\qquad (2)$$
$$1200 = a \times 0.175 - b \qquad\qquad (3)$$

Solving equation (2) and (3) we get

a = 8000 b = 200

Substituting the value of a and b in equation (1)

$$F_c = 8000 \, r - 200$$

Controlling force at 250 mm apart of balls

$$F_c = 8000 \times 0.125 - 200$$

$$= 800 \text{ N}$$

We know that,

$$F_c = m\omega^2 r$$

or $F_c = m \left(\dfrac{2\pi N}{60} \right)^2 \times r$

or $800 = 6 \times \left(\dfrac{2\pi N}{60} \right)^2 \times 0.125$

N = 312 rpm

Prob. 11.2 : In a spring controlled governor, the curve the controlling force is a straight line when balls are 400 mm apart, the controlling force is 1200 N and when 200 mm apart, the controlling force is 450 N. At what speed will the governor run when the balls an 250 mm apart. What initial tension on the spring would be required for isochronism and what would then be the speed. The mass of each ball is 9 kg.

Sol. Given. When balls are 400 mm apart i.e., when radius of rotation (r_2) is 200 mm the controlling force, F_{c2} = 1200 N

Similarly r_1 = 100 mm and F_{c1} = 450 N

Mass of each ball (m) = 9 kg

Speed of governor when the ball are 250 mm apart i.e., when radius of rotation (r) is 125 mm.

Let N be the required speed

We know that for the stability of the spring controlled governor the controlling force (Fc) is expressed as

$F_c = ar-b$ (x)

$\therefore F_{c1} = 450 = a \times 0.1 - b$ (i)

$F_{c2} = 1200 = a \times 0.2 - b$ (ii)

Solving equation (i) and (ii), we have

a = 7500 and b = 300

Now; from equation (x) we have

F_c = 7500 r-300 (iii)

Substituting r = 0.125 m in equation (iii), we have

F_c = 7500 x 0.125 - 300 = 637.5 N

$F_c = m\omega^2 r = m \left(\dfrac{2\pi N}{60} \right)^2 r$

N = 227.3 rpm

For an isochronous governor the controlling force line passed through origin (i.e.; b = 0)

Let N' and Fc' be the isochronous speed and controlling force at the isochronous speed.

$F'_c = ar$

or $m\left(\dfrac{2\pi N^1}{60}\right)^2 r = ar$

$\therefore a = m\left(\dfrac{2\pi N^1}{60}\right)^2$

$\therefore N^{12} = a \times \left(\dfrac{60}{2\pi}\right)^2 \times \dfrac{1}{m}$

$= 7500 \times \left(\dfrac{60}{2\pi}\right)^2 \times \dfrac{1}{9}$

or $N^1 = 275$ rpm Ans.

PROBLEMS

1. The controlling force (F_c) in newtons and the radius (r) in metres for a spring controlled governor is given by the expression.
    $F_c = 2800r - 76$
    The mass of ball is 5 kg and the extreme radii of rotation of the balls are 100 m and 175 mm. Find the maximum and minimum speeds of equilibrium. If the friction of the governor mechanism is equivalent to a force of 5 N at each ball. Find the co-efficient of in sensitiveness of the governor at the extreme radii.
    [Ans. 192.6 rpm, 207.6 rpm, 9.4%]

2. Calculate percent regulation of governor, if speed at no load and load is 1500 and 1400 rpm, respectively.
    [Ans. 6.896%]

3. Calculate speed of governor at the condition of load, if percent regulation is 6.4 and speed at no load is 1600 rpm. [1500 rpm]

4. In a spring controlled governor, the radial force acting on the balls was 4500 N when the centre of balls was 200 mm the axis and 7500 N when at 300 mm. Assuming that the force varies directly as the radius, find the radius of the ball path when the governor runsat 270 rpm. Also find what alteration in spring load is required in order to make the governor isochronous and the speed at which it would then run. The mass of each balls is 30 kg.
    [Ans. 250 mm, 1500N, 301.5 rpm]

SUBJECTIVE QUESTIONS

1. Why has a tractor a governor? How a tractor engine differs from a car engine with respect to governor.

2. Explain the working principle of hit and miss system of governing with the help of a neat diagram.

3. Explain the working of throttle governing system with the help of a neat diagram.

4. What is the basic difference between hit and miss system of governing and throttle system of governing.

5. What is the principal of centrifugal governor? Explain with a neat sketch.

6. What are different components of pneumatic governor? Explain its working with the help of a diagram.

7. How a hydraulic governor work?

8. Write short notes on: (i) Governor regulation (ii) governor hunting (iii) effort of governor (iv) power of governor (v) stable governor.

MULTIPLE CHOICE QUESTIONS

1. The device used to control engine speed within a specified limit is called
   (a) Governor (b) turbo-charger
   (c) both (d) none of the above

2. The height of a watt's governor (in meters) is equal to
   (a) $8.95/N^2$ (b) $89.5/N^2$
   (c) $895/N^2$ (d) $8950/N^2$
   where, N= speed of the arm and ball about the spindle axis.

3. When the sleeve of a porter governor moves upwards, the governor speed
   (a) increases (b) decreases
   (c) remains constant (d) none of the above

4. Which of the following in a spring control governor
   (a) Wall governor (b) porter governor
   (c) both (d) none of the above

5. Which of the following is a spring controlled governor
   (a) hartnell (b) hartung
   (c) pictering (d) all of the above

6. The sensitiveness of governors is given by
   (a) $\dfrac{\omega_{mean}}{\omega_2 - \omega_1}$ (b) $\dfrac{\omega_2 - \omega_1}{\omega_{mean}}$

(c) $\dfrac{\omega_2 - \omega_i}{2\omega_{mean}}$ (d)   none of the above

7.   A governor is said to be hunting, if the speed of the engine
     (a)   fluctuates continuously above and below the mean speed
     (b)   remains constant at the mean speed
     (c)   is above the mean speed
     (d)   is below the mean speed

8.   A hunting governor is
     (a)   more stable   (b)   more sensitive
     (c)   less sensitive   (d)   none of the above

9.   Isochronism in a governor is desirable when
     (a)   the engine operates at low speeds
     (b)   the engine operates at high speed
     (c)   the engine operates at variable speed
     (d)   one speed is desired under one load.

10. When the relation between the controlling force (Fc) and radius (r) for a spring controlled governor is $F_c = ar + b$, then the governor will be
     (a)   stable   (b)   unstable
     (c)   isochronous   (d)   none of the above

FILL UP THE BLANKS

1.   Governor .... the speed of engine at varying load.
2.   .... is generally used in tractor.
3.   .... is the ratio of the differences the maximum and minimum equilibrium speeds to the mean equilibirium speed.
4.   A Hunting governor is................ sensitive.
5.   Hit and miss system and throttle system are ....

Ans. controls 2. centrifugal governor 3. sensitiveness of govenor 4. more 5. governing system

Chapter **12**

Front Axle, Steering Mechanism and Differential

12.1 Introduction: The front axles are generally referred as dead axles. It supports idler wheels of both ends and engine at the centre. The following are the main functions of front axle.

(i) It carries king pin, steering arm through which the tractor can be steered properly.

(ii) It supports the weight of the front end of vehicle (tractor)

(iii) It keeps the tractor in levelled position by its swinging action.

(iv) It provides pivotal connection between front axle and axle pivot.

(v) In case of four wheel drive it also transmits the power to gouted wheel.

12.2. Classification of the Front Axle: They are classified as follows:

(i) Rigid front axle and (ii) Swinging type front axle

(i) Rigid Front Axle: In earlier, tractors were equipped with rigid front axle, where the and axle beam was rigidly tied up with the chasis front member. As the tractor body used to get tilted on slope, this system has now been replaced by swinging type of axles.

(ii) Swing Front Axle: In modern tractor swinging front axle is employed by all manufactures as shown in Fig. 12.1. In this case centre of axle is pivoted to the front cross member of the tractor chasis with the help of centre pin which runs in bushes. With this right or left wheel can go up or down or swing to certain degree on either side. This allows the tractor as whole in maintain level to some extent.

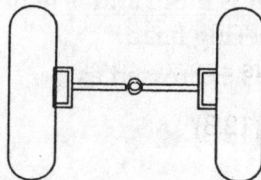

Fig. 12.1 Swinging type front axle

12.3 Kinematics of Front Axle: Front axles experience two types of stress (a) Bending and (b) Shearning stress. In the static condition, the axle may be treated as a beam supported vertically upward at the ends. The vertical bending moment, is zero at the point of support and rises linearly to a maximum at the point of loading and the remain constant

Therefore,

The maximum bending moment = WZ, Nm   (12.1)

Where,

W = Load on the wheel

Z = Distance between the centre of wheel and the spring pad, m

Under vehicle in motion, the vertical bending moment is increased due to uneven road. But its absolute measurement is not possible and hence accounted for a factor of safety. A horizontal bending moment also acts on the front axle because of resistance to motion this is as like as the vertical one but its magnitude is very small and hence can be neglected, except these situations, when it is comparatively large.

The resistance to motion also include, a torque in the case of drop type front axle. Thus, the part after the spring are experienced to combined effect of bending and torsion. The magnitude of torque (τ) is expressed as

τ = R. x; Nm   (12.2)

Where,

R = Resistance to motion, N

x = Drop from the spindle axis to the centre of the section, m

The shear stress in the axle is due to breaking toque where magnitude i given as

= μWr......   (12.3)

Where, r = Road wheel radium, m

μ = Co-efficient of ardhesion between road & tyre

= 0.6 for dry, hard road surface.

The breaking torque is minimum for the section laying in between the spring pads and is expressed as μW (r-x). The bending moment is more at this section whereas, torsion is more at steering head due to which I-section is used for portion where bending moment is more and is generally changed to circular, oval or rectangular section at the steering head.

For I-section, the relation used is expressed as

$$\frac{M}{I} = \frac{f_b}{y}$$ (12.3)

Where,

M = Maximum bending moment, Nm

f_b = Allowable bending stress for the material, N/m^2 or Pa y = Maximum distance of the fibres from neutral axis,

$\frac{d}{2}$, m

I = Moment of inertia of the I-section about natural axis.

$$I = \frac{bd^3 - ch^3}{12}, m^4 \qquad (12.4)$$

Where, d = overall depth of I-section, m

b = Flange width, m

t = Flange thickness, m

w = Web thickness, m

C = b - t

a = d-2W

In general

d = 6t

b = 4.25 t

w = 2.5 t

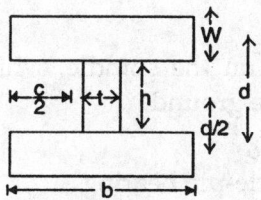

Fig. 12.2 I-Section

For the section where torsion predominates, the relation is express as

$$\frac{\eta}{Ip} = \frac{f_a}{y} \qquad (12.5)$$

Where, η = Maximum torque in the plane section, Nm

f_s = Allowable shear stress in the material, Pa

y = Distance from the neutral axis to the outermost fibre of the axle

$\frac{d}{2}$, m

d = Diameter for the circular section, m

= Major axis for the oval section, m

I_p = Polar moment of inertia of the section

$\frac{\pi}{32} d^4$ for circular section, m⁴

$\dfrac{\pi}{32}d^3b$ for oval section with minor axis, b

Bearing Loads on Front axle

Fig. 12.3 shows the forces and the reaction on steering knuckle when the vehicle is at rest. The thrust load and the knuckle-pin-bearing load can be expressed in terms of the reaction of wheel on wheel spindle.

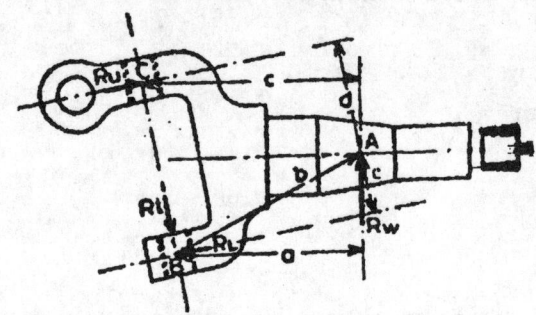

Fig. 12.3 Forces and Reaction on Steering Knuckle

Let

$R\omega$ = Reaction of the wheel on the spindle, which acts vertically through the centre of contact of type on the ground.

R_t = Load on the thrust bearing

R_u = Load on the upper knuckle-pin bearing

R_l = Load on the lower knuckle-pin

B and C epresent the centre of lower and upper knuckle-pin bearing respectively.

Now, $\Sigma Mc = 0$ gives

$R\omega C - R_t (d+e) = 0$

$$\therefore R_l = \left(\dfrac{C}{d+e}\right) R_\omega \qquad (12.7)$$

Similarly, $\Sigma MB = 0$ gives

$R_w.a - R_u (d+e) = 0$

$$\text{or } R_u = \left(\dfrac{a}{d+e}\right) R_\omega \qquad (12.8)$$

Again, $\Sigma MA = 0$ [Where A is a point on the spindle axis in the centre place of the wheel] gives,

$R_t b - R_{te} - R_u d = 0$

or $R_t b = R_l e + R_u d$

Substituting the value of R$_t$ and Ru,

$$Rt = \frac{Ce + \alpha d}{b\,(d+e)} \cdot R\omega \qquad (12.9)$$

The other lods on knuckle-pin bearing those due to the rolling resistance and road shows loads are proportional to the static load and hence can accounted for.

12.5. Wheel Alignment:

12.5.1 Introduction: The Wheel alignment refers to the positioning of the front wheel and steering mechanism that provides the vehicle directional stability, promotes ease of steering and minimum tyre wear. A vehicle is said to be have directional stability or directional central if it can run straight down on a road centre and leave a turn easily and resist road shocks. The following are the factors of the wheel alignment:

1. Factors pertaining to wheel

(a)   Balance of wheel

(b)   Inflation pressure of tyre

(c)   Brake adjustments

2. Stearing Geometry: It includes following as given below:

(a)   Camber angle (b) Caster angle (c) King pin inclination

(d)   True-in and (e) Toe-out

3. Steering linkages

4. Suspension system

12.6 Stearing Geometry

12.6.1. Camber Angle or Wheel Rake.

(i)   Definition: It is the angle between the centre lines of the tyre and the vertical line, viewed from front as shown in Fig. 12.4 (b). It may be positive (front wheel are titled 'out' at top) and negative camber (front wheels are titled 'in' at top).

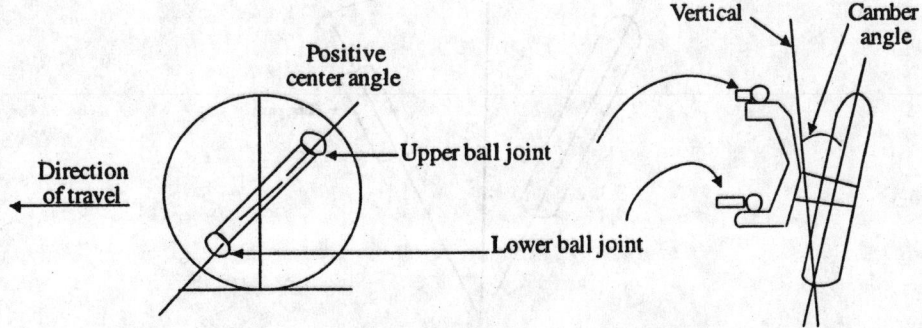

Fig. 12.4 Camber Angle and Cater Angle

Note: Mostly vehicles are provided with positive camber than negative camber.

Purpose: Camber is provided to prevent inward tilting of top of the wheel caused due to

(i)   excessive load (ii) play in the king-pins and

(iii)   play in the wheel bearings.

The camber on both the wheel must be identical in amount otherwise the vehicle will roll-on in the direction of the wheel having a more camber. It not only endangers the directional stability rather scuffs the treads also of the opposite tyre.

Range: 0.25 to 4°, in tractor

12.6.2. Caster:

(A) Definition: It is the angle between the centre line of the kingpin of the tractor and vertical i.e., the tilt of the king pin or ball joint centre line from the vertical towards within the front (negative caster) or rear (positive caster) of the vehicle as shown in Fig. 12.4.

(B) Purpose: The following are the main purposes of providing caster

(i)   To produce directional stability

(ii)   To avoid or minimize the tendency of wheel wander and (iii) to avoid shimmy

        (i.e., oscillation of the front wheel)

(c)   Range: 0 to 4° in tractor

12.6.3. King pin Inclination:

(A) Definition: It is the angle between centre line of a cambered wheel and the centre line of kingpin join at tyre, touching the ground as shown in Fig. 12.5.

(B) Purpose: The following are the main purposes of providing king-pin inclination.

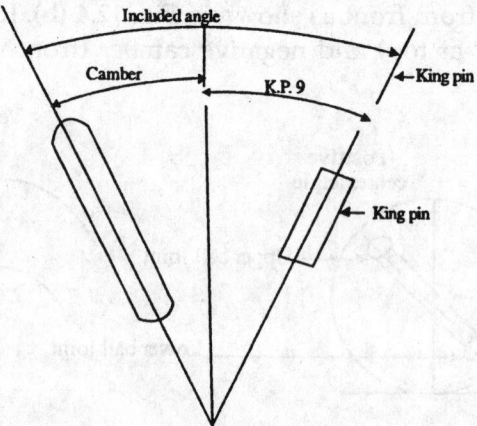

Fig. 12.5 King pin Inclination

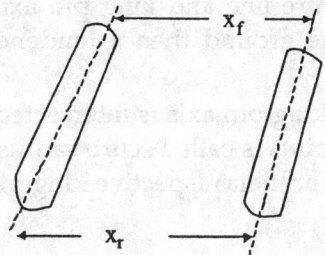

Fig. 12.6. Toe In

(i) It provides directional stability in a vehicle by tending to return the wheels to straight ahead position after any turn.

(ii) It reduces steering effort particularly when the vehicle is stationary.

(iii) It reduces tyre wear.

(C) Range: 6 to 8° in tractor

12.6.4 Toe in:

Definition: It is the difference in distance between back of wheel and front of wheels, measured at huts as shown in Fig. 12.5 and is given as

Toe in = X_r - X_f (12.10)

Purpose: The purpose of providing toe-in is to offset the tendency of wheel rolling.

(i) On the curves due to the limitation of correct steering.

(ii) due to the possible play in the steering linkages.

(iii) due to the camber effect.

Range. 0 to 12 mm

12.6.5. Toe Out:

(A) Definition: It is the difference in distance of front wheel and back of the wheel.

(B) Purpose: The toe-out is provided to counter the tendency of inward rolling of the wheels

(i) due to the soil condition on agricultural land.

(ii) on account of side thrusts and cross-wind effects.

(C) Range: 0 to 6 mm

12.6.6 Included Angle or Combined Angle and Scurb Radius:

Definition: It is an angle between wheel centre line and king pin axis, viewed from front of the vehicle as shown in Fig. 12.7.

Note: Its numerical value is equal to the sum of camber angle and king pin inclination.

(B) Facts: (i) When wheel centre line and king pin axis is intersected with each other at a point (1) above the ground then a tendency of toe-in is induced in vehicle.

Where wheel centre line and king pin axis is intersected on the ground, there is a distance between these two points is called scurb radius (Rs). In Fig. 12.7. M, -M2, a and M1-M3 in scrub radius for their respective king pin inclination.

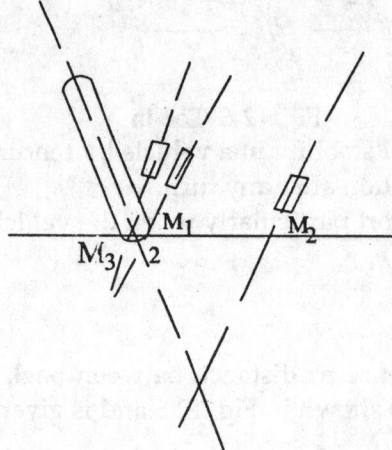

Fig. 12.7 Included Angle and Scrub Radius

(ii)   When the intersection at point-2, means on the ground. So, a tendency of centre-point steering is produced, toe-in in vehicle.

(iii)   When the intersection of at point-3 then a tendency of the toe-out is induced in vehicle.

12.7 Steering System

12.7.1 Introduction: Steering System is provided in the vehicle (tractor) is used to steer (to turn) the vehicle when desired by the driver throughout its range of speed irrespective of load and road or field condition.

The function of the steering system is to concert the rotary motion of the steering wheel into the angular turn of the front road wheels.

12.7.2 Qualities of Steering System: The following are the qualities of good steering system:

(i)   it should have provision for front wheel spacing.

(ii)   It should be self-adjusting and self-aligning.

(iii)   It should be easy in operation.

(iv)   It should be fool proof.

(v)   It should not transmit field shocks to steering wheel.

(vi)   It should not disturb steering geometry on bad field conditions or on over loading.

12.7.3. Layout of Steering System: Simple layout of steering system is shown in Fig. 12.8. It consists of following main component.

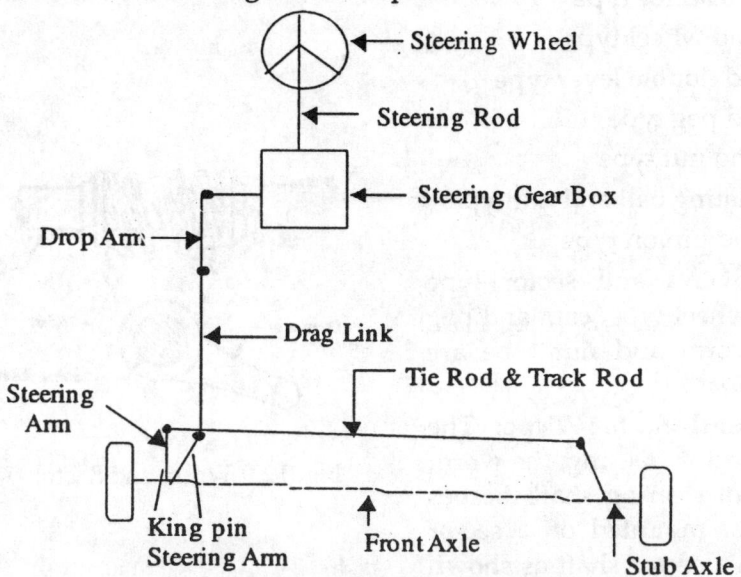

Fig. 12.8. Layout of Steering System

(i) Steering wheel (ii) Steering column (iii) Steering gear (iv) Drop arm or pitman arm (v) Drag link or link rod (vi) Tie rod (vii) Steering arm (vii) Track and adjustment (ix) Front wheels (x) Tie rod and joints (xi) King-pin.

The steering wheel is made circular so that driver may apply the effort conveniently when the operator turns the steering wheel, the motion is transmitted through the steering shaft to the angular motion of the pitman arm through a set of gears. The angular movement of the pitman arm is further transmitte to the stearing arm through the drag link and tie rods steering arms are keyed to the respective king pins which are integral part of the stub axle on which wheels are mounted. The movement of steering arm affects the angular movement of the fromt wheel.

Note : Steering ratio lies between 15 to 35.1 on different categories of vehicle.

12.7.4 Functions of Steering System: The following are the main functions of steering system.

(i) to convert the rotary motion of the steering wheel into the angular turn of the front road wheel.

(ii) to provide directional stability fo the vehicle (tractor)

(iii) to facilitates straicgh ahead recoverying after completing a turn.

(iv) to minimise tyre wear.

(v) the effort required to steer should be minimum

12.7.5 Classification of Steering Gear Box System: They are classified as follows

(i) Worm and sector type

(ii) Worm and wheel type

(iii) Cam and double lever type

(iv) Cam and peg type

(v) Worm and nut type

(vi) Recirculating ball and nut type

(vii) Rack and pinion type

Generally, worm and sector type worm and wheel type, cam and peg type and worm and nut type are used in tractor.

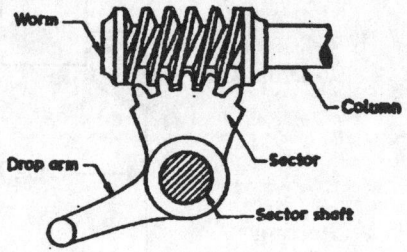

Fig. 12.9 Worm and Sector Type

(i) Worm and Sector Type: The worm and sector steering, the worm on the end of steering shaft meshes with a sector mounted on a sector mounted on a sector shaft as shown in Fig. 12.9. When the worm is rotated by a rotation of the steering wheel, the sector also turns rotating the sector shaft. Its motion is transmitted to the road wheel through the linkage.

(ii) Worm and Wheel Type: fig. 12.10 shows a simplified diagram of a worm and wheel type steering gear. The movement of the steering wheel turns the worm, which in turn drives the worm wheel.

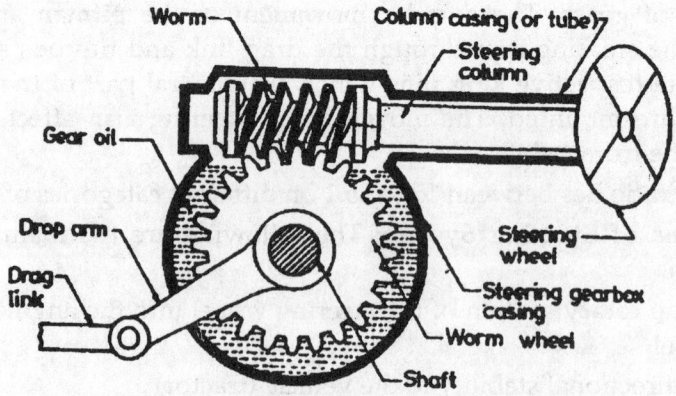

Fig. 12.10 Worm and Wheel Type Steering Gear

Attached to the wheel spindle rigidity is drop arm, so that a rotation of the steering wheel, corresponds to a linear motion of the drop arm end, which is connected to link rod or drag link.

There is an advantage of this type over the worm and sector type. In this case blacklash due to wearing out of the teeth of the worm and worm wheel can be easily adjusted for this purpose, the worm wheel is mounted over and eccentic both. When the teeth have worm out the problem is how to bring the worm and the wheel together to take cup the wear. This is done by rotating the bush through a certain angle.

(iii) Worm and Nut type Steering Gear : Fig. 12.11 shows the construction of a worm and nut type steering gear. The steering wheel rotation rotates the worm which inturn moves the nut along its length.

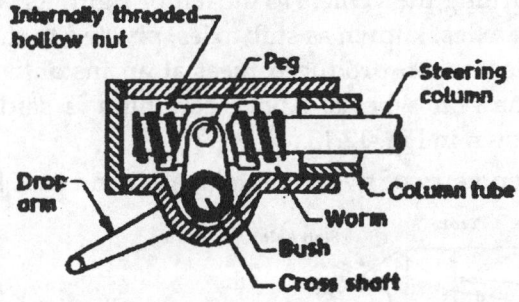

Fig. 12.11 Worm and Nut Type Steering Gear

This causes, the drop arm end to move linearly, further moving the link rod and thus steering the wheels.

(iv) Cam and Peg Type Steering Gear: Fig. 12.12 shows the cam and peg type and steering gear.

A taper peg is attached to the rocker arm. This taper peg engages in the cam. When the cam rotates, the peg moves along the cam groove causing the rocker shaft to rotate. The movement of the rocker shaft is transmitted to drop-arm drag link etc.

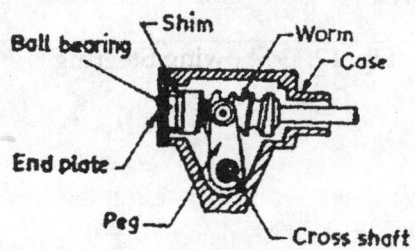

Fig. 12.12 Cam and Peg Type Steering Gear

12.8. Steering System

12.8.1 Introduction: Steering system is used to steer (to turn) the vehicle (tractor) when desired by the operator or driver. The function of the steering is the convert the rotary motion of the steering wheel into the angular turn of the front road wheel.

12.8.2. Fundamental Condition for Correct Principle of Steering of Correct Steering.

When the vehicle (tractor) takes a turn the outer wheel move faster than the inner wheels. The four wheels must roll on the road, so that there is line contact between the road surface and tyres. This is essential to prevent tyre wear. The rooling motion of the wheels on he road surface is possible only if there describe concentric circles on the road at instant aneoius centre, when the tractor is taking a turn. In order for turning the vehicle to the left or right, its two front wheels are mounted on the short axles, known as stub axles, pivoted to the chesis of vehicles. The axis of these axles, when produced meet at an instantaneous centre which lies on the axis of the rear wheels. Above condition is said to be principle of correct steering as shown in Fig. 12.13.

On considering the geometry of two triangles ΔAOB and ΔCOD, we have

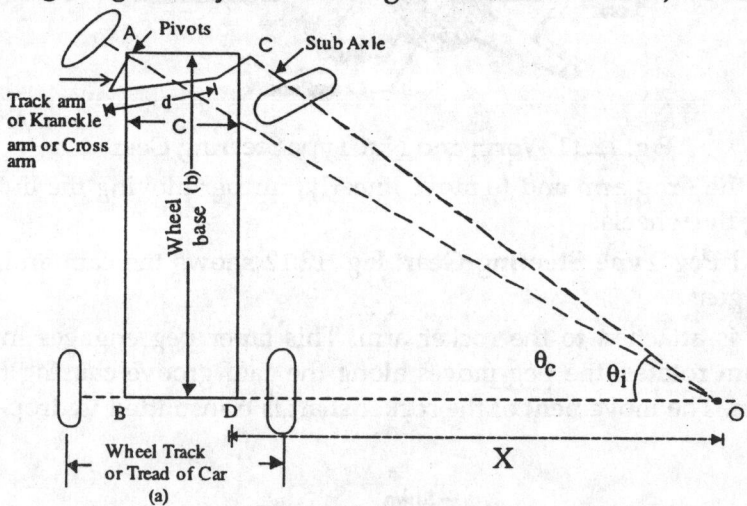

Fig. 12.13 Showing Steering

Where,

O = Instantaneous centre

θ_i = Angle of inside lock

θ_0 =Angle of outside lock

C = Distance between the pivot centres.

b = Wheel base of the vehicle

a = Wheel track

$$\tan \theta_i = \frac{OD}{b} \text{ and } \tan \theta_o = \frac{b}{OB}$$

$$\cot \theta_i = \frac{OD}{b} \text{ and } \cos \theta_Q = \frac{OB}{b}$$

$$\therefore \cot \theta_0 - \cot \theta_i = \frac{OB-OD}{b} = \frac{c}{b} \qquad (12.8)$$

The equation represent correct steering of the vehicle and equation is called fundamental equation for correct steering. If this equation is satisfied, there will not any lateralslip by the wheels, when the vehicle is taking a turn.

From above condition, A vehicle can have only three correct steering position as per followings;

(i) while is running straight

(ii) while it is turning in extreme right

(iii) while it is turning to extreme right

12.8.3. Steering Mechanism: The mechanism used for automatically adjusting the values of qi and q0 for correct steering are known as steering gear mechanism.

Steering mechanism are two types (i) Davis steering mechanism and (ii) Ackermann steering mechanism.

The main difference between two steering mechanism is that the Devis steering mechanism has sliding pairs, whereas the Ackermorm steering gear has only turning pairs, therefore, the Devis steering gear will wear out earlier and become inaccurate after certain time. Although, their Ackermann steering gear is not mathematically accurate except above stated three positions, contrary to the Devis steering mechanism which is mathematically correct in all positions.

However, Ackermann steering mechanism is preferred to the Devis steering mechanism.

12.7 Terms Related to Steering Mechanism

12.7.1. Wheel Lock Angle (θ_{WL}) : Mathematically it is expressed as

$\theta_{WL} = \theta i + \theta_0$ (12.9)

12.7.2. Steering Lock Angle (qSL); Mathematically, it is expresses as

$\theta_{SL} = 2\theta i$ (12.10)

12.8. Wheel Wobble: Excessive vibration of type as seen from the front when vehicle is slow motion is called wobble. This is generally due to dynamic imbalance of the wheel assembly which way develop due following reasons:

(i) Tyres may worn unevenly, which should be replaced

(ii)   Incorrect balanced weights fitted, which can be refitted correctly.

(iii) The type pressure may be uneven.

(iv)   Steering, gear or wheel bearing may be loose which can be adjusted or replaced as required.

(v)   The ball joints may have worm act which should be replaced.

(vi)   The stiffiness of spring may be less. In such a case either add additional leaf to both the springs or replaced them both with shifter springs.

(vii) The camber may be incorrector uneven which may be suitably adjusted.

(viii) The caster may have become excessive due to wear of bushes or damage to front suspension. The damaged parts in such as case have to be placed.

12.9 Turning Circle Radius: When a vehicle (tractor) takes turn without experiencing any lateral step, all the wheels rotate about a common centre along different circles as shown in Fig. 12.13. The front out wheel transverse a circle of maximum radius (Rmax) and the areas inner wheel moves in the smallest turning circle. It radius Rmin in the least of all the four wheels.

The turning circle radii for different wheels can be determined from the geometry of Fig. 12.13. There are given below in the decreasing order of their value.

Turning circle radius of the outer front wheel (R & f)

$$R_{of} = \frac{b}{\sin \theta_0} + \left(\frac{a-c}{2}\right) \qquad (12.11)$$

Turning circle radius of the outer rear wheel (R_{ro})

$$Ror = b \cot q0 + \left(\frac{a-c}{2}\right) \qquad (12.12)$$

Turning circle radius of the inner front wheel (Fif)

$$R_{if} = \frac{b}{\sin \theta} - \left(\frac{a-c}{2}\right) \qquad (12.13)$$

Turning circle radius of the inner rear wheel (Rir)

$$R_{if} = b \cot \theta_2 - \frac{a-c}{2} \qquad (12.14)$$

Note: Turning circle radius for tractor varies from 11 to 13 m.

12.10 Power Steeeing

12.10.1 Introduction

Large amount of torque is required for steering of medium, and heavy vehicles i.e., large amount of effort is applied by drives to steer the medium and heavy vehicle. The power steering provides automatic assistance to the turning effort apply to the manual steering system. The system is always so designed that in the event of the failure of the power system, the operator or drives is able to steer the vehicles manually although with increased effort.

The power steering system are operated by fluid under pressure. The principle of working of all the power steering system is same.

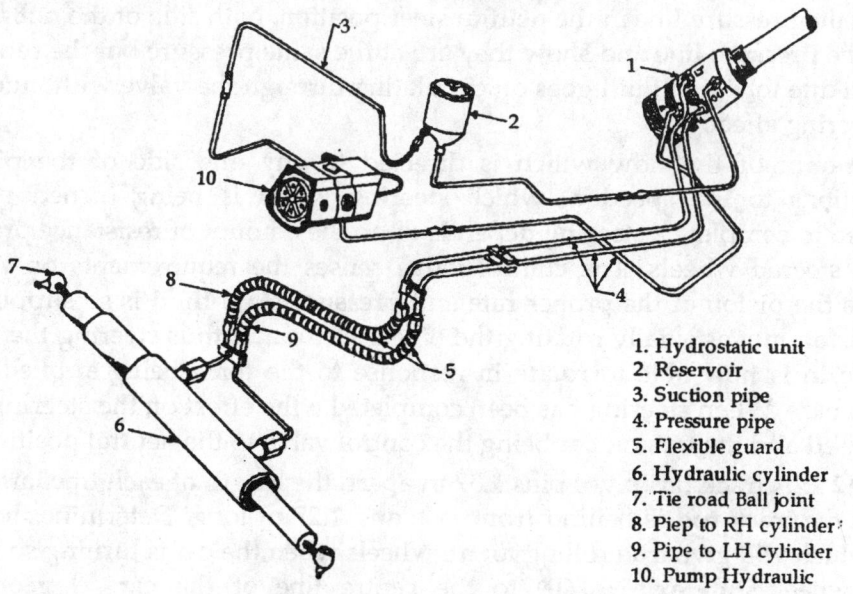

1. Hydrostatic unit
2. Reservoir
3. Suction pipe
4. Pressure pipe
5. Flexible guard
6. Hydraulic cylinder
7. Tie road Ball joint
8. Piep to RH cylinder
9. Pipe to LH cylinder
10. Pump Hydraulic

Fig. 12.14 Power Stearing

12.10.2 Steering Gear Box for Power Steering System:

The slide movement of the steering wheels actuates a valve so that the liquid enters on the appropriate side of cylinder, thereby applying pressure on one side of a piston to operate the steering linkage which steers the wheel in appropriate direction.

The power steering are two types (i) The integral type and (ii) The Linkage type.

In the integral type the power steering gear where as in the linkage type it is a part of linkage.

The main component of an steering power system consists of a hydraulic pump type assembly and a steering gear assembly connected by means of a hoses. A rotary valve power steering gear for the integral system using recirculating ball type worm and wheel steering gear is shown in Fig. 12.14 The steering wheel is connected to the right end of the torsion box through steering shaft the other end of the torsion bar is connected to the worm and also to the spool about which the rotatary valve is positioned. When the driver applies a force Wheel to steer, the other end of the torsion bar, being connected to the spool of the rotary value and the worm offers resistance, when the force at the wheel exceeds as per determined valve, the spool turn through a small angle, when the returned pipe in closed and the fluid under pressure goes to one side of the rack, piston and move sit to effort steering in desired direction. The torsion bar is meant to give a fuel of the steering wheel in opposite direction connects the other side of steering gear to the pressure line in the neutral steer position, both side of the nut are shut off to the pressure line and show they are at the same pressure but the return line in open due to which fluid goes on circulating through the valve without causing any steering effect.

The amount of the flow which is directed to any one side of the piston is proportions to the speed at which steering wheel is being turned pressure required to complete a steering depends upon the amount of resistance presented by the steered wheels. The control valve senses the requirements on supplies fluid to the piston at the proper rate and pressure. And fluid is so supplied, the rack piston moves axially rotating the wheel sector and thus steering the wheels. The worm is now able to rotate in response to the force being applied by the torsion bars. When steering has been completed a the effort on the steering wheel is released and the torsion bar being the control valve to the neutral position.

Prob. 12 1: A track has pivot pins 1.37 m apart, the length of each tract arm is 0.18 m and the track rod is behind front axle and 1.27 m long. Determine the wheel base which will give true rolling for all wheels when the car is turning so that the inner wheel stub axle is 60° to the centre line of the car. A geometrical construction may be used.

Sol. Given:

C = 1.37 m, d = 1.27 m, r = 0.18 m, θ = 30°

Referring Fig.

$$\text{Sin } \alpha = \frac{c-d}{2r} = \frac{1.37-1.27}{2 \times 0.18} = 0.278$$

or $\alpha = \sin^{-1}(0.278) = 16.2°$

Again,

Sin $(\alpha + \theta)$ + Sin $(\alpha - \phi)$ = 2 Sin α

or Sin (16.2+30°) + Sin (16.12 - ϕ) = 2 x Sin 16.2

or Sin (16.12 - ϕ) = 0.556 - Sin (46-12)

= 0.556-0.720

= -0.164

or 16.12 -ϕ = Sin^{-1} (-0.164)

or 16.12 -ϕ = -9.44

$\therefore$ ϕ = 25.56°

We know that, for correct steering

$$\cot \theta_o - \cot \theta_i = \frac{c}{b}$$

or $\cot 25.56 - \cot 30 = \dfrac{1.37}{b}$

or $2.081 - 1.732 = \dfrac{1.37}{b}$

$\therefore b = \dfrac{1.37}{0.349} = 3.92$ m Ans.

Prob. 12.2 While turning a 4-wheel tractor equipped with the Ackermann steering mechanism the axis of the inner-front wheel makes an angles 45°, whereas the angle made by the axis of the outer front wheel is 30° with horizontal line parallel to the front axle. The kingpins of the axle are 1300 mm part. The spindle genths are essentially zero. What should be wheel base if their is no slippage of any of the wheel?

Sol. Given:

$\theta_i = 45°$, $\theta_0 = 30°$, $C = 1300$ mm

We know that $\cot \theta_0 - \cot \theta_0 = \dfrac{c}{b}$

or $\cot 30 - \cot 45 = \dfrac{c}{b}$

$\therefore b = \dfrac{1300}{\cot 30 - \cot 45}$

$= 1775.83$ mm Ans.

Prob. 12.3 If the inner and outer steering angles in a tractor are 9° and 9.8° respectively then for correct steering condition the value of the ratio of pivot axis spacing to tract length is equal to

(a) 0.256 (b) 0.525 (c) 0.756 (d) 0.990

Sol. Given, $\theta_i = 9.8°$, $\theta_0 = 9.0°$

We know that $\cot \theta_0 - \cot \theta_i = \dfrac{c}{b}$

or $6.314 - 5.789 = \dfrac{c}{b}$

or $\dfrac{c}{b} = 0.525$

Therefore, Answer is (b).

Prob. 12.4 A tractor has a wheel base of 2100 mm and pivot centre of 1665 mm. The front and rear wheel track is 1850 mm. Calculate the correct angle of outside lack and turning circle radius of the outer front and inner rear wheels when the angle of inside lack is 40°.

Soln:

Given: $\theta_0 = 40°$, C = 1665 mm = 1.665 m and b = 2100 mm = 2.100 m

a = 1850 mm = 1.850 m

We know that for correct steering.

$$\cot \theta_0 - \cot \theta_i = \frac{c}{b}$$

$$\therefore \cot \theta_0 = \frac{c}{b} + \cot \theta_i$$

$$= \frac{1.665}{2.100} + \cot 40°$$

$$\therefore \theta_0 = \cot^{-1} ( )$$

Turning circle radius of the front wheel

$$R_{of} = \frac{b}{\sin \phi} + \left(\frac{a - c}{2} \right)$$

$$= \frac{2.1}{\sin ( )} + \left(\frac{1.850 + 1.665}{2} \right)$$

Turning circle radius of the inner rear wheel,

$$R_{ir} = b \cot \theta_0 - \left(\frac{a - c}{2} \right)$$

$$= 2.1 \cot 40 - \left(\frac{1.85 - 1.665}{2} \right)$$

PROBLEMS

1. A tractor has wheel base 1775 83 mm and pivot centre of 1300 mm. The front and rear wheel track is 1505 mm. Calculate the correct angle of lack and turning circle radius of the outer and inner rear wheel when the angle of inside lack 45°.

2. A tractor with a wheel base of 1950 mm has a trend with (both front and rear wheel) of 1650 mm. If the tractor is negotiating a 5 m (measured from centre of turning along rear side. Centre line to point midway between rear wheels) turn at 6 km/h and rolling radius of the wheel is 600 mm.
   (a) Calculate the speed (in rpm) of the inside and the outside wheels.
   (b) During the turn, what percentage of engine power and torque is transmitted through each of the two rear wheels.

MULTIPLE CHOICE QUESTIONS

1. Front axle is generally
   - (a) dead axle
   - (b) line axle
   - (c) both
   - (d) none of the above

2. The tilt of the king pin from the vertical towards front is called
   - (a) negative caster
   - (b) positive caster
   - (c) caster
   - (d) none of the above

3. The angle between the centre line of the king pin of the tractor and vertical is called
   - (a) caster
   - (b) camber
   - (c) king pin inclination
   - (d) none of the above

4. Caster angle varies from
   - (a) $4^o - 8^o$
   - (b) $0^o - 4^o$
   - (c) $10^o - 12^o$
   - (d) $12^o - 16^o$

5. Which type of caster is generally given in motor vehicle and agriculture machines
   - (a) negative caster
   - (b) positive caster
   - (c) both
   - (d) none of the above

6. The angle between the centre line of the tyre and vertical line is known as
   - (a) caster
   - (b) camber
   - (c) kingpin inclination
   - (d) none of the above

7. Camber angle varies from
   - (a) 0.25 to 4°
   - (b) $10^o - 12^o$
   - (c) $12^o - 15^o$
   - (d) $15^o - 20^o$

8. The angle between centre line of cambered wheel and the centre line of king-pin join at tyre is touching the ground is
   - (a) camber
   - (b) caster
   - (c) kingpin inclination
   - (d) none of the above

9. King pin inclination varies from
   - (a) 6 to 8°
   - (b) $10 - 12^o$
   - (c) $12 - 15^o$
   - (d) $15 - 20^o$

10. Toe in varies from
    - (a) 0 to 12 mm
    - (b) 12 - 20 mm
    - (c) 20 - 30 mm
    - (d) 30 - 35 mm

11. Toe out varies from
    - (a) 0 - 1 mm
    - (b) 0 - 4 mm
    - (c) 4 - 8 mm
    - (d) 8 - 12 mm

12. Excessive vibration of type as seen from the front when vehicle is moving is called
    (a) wobble
    (b) camber
    (c) caster
    (d) king pin inclination

13. Fundamental condition for rolling is given by
    (a) $\cot\phi - \cot\theta = \dfrac{c}{b}$
    (b) $\cot\theta - \cot\phi = \dfrac{c}{b}$
    (c) $\cot\phi - \cot\theta = \dfrac{b}{c}$
    (d) none of the above

    Where θ and ϕ are the angles of inside and out side lack respectively
    b = wheel base and c = distance between the pivot centres

14. Steering geometry includes:
    (a) caster angle
    (b) camber angle
    (c) king pin inclination
    (d) toe-in
    (e) toe-out
    (f) all of the above

15. Causes of wobble are faulty in
    (a) camber angle
    (b) caster angle
    (c) toe in
    (d) all of the above

16. Polar moment of inertia of circular section is given by
    (a) $\dfrac{\pi}{32}d^4$
    (b) $\dfrac{\pi}{16}d^4$
    (c) $\dfrac{\pi}{8}d^4$
    (d) $\dfrac{\pi}{4}d^4$

17. Polar moment of inertia of oval section is given by
    (a) $\dfrac{\pi}{8}d^4b$
    (b) $\dfrac{\pi}{16}d^4b$
    (c) $\dfrac{\pi}{32}d^4b$
    (d) $\dfrac{\pi}{48}d^4b$

18. Which type is front axle is generally used these days
    (a) Rigid front axle
    (b) swinging type front axle
    (c) both
    (d) none of the above

FILL IN THE BLANKS

1. Front axle experience .... and .... stresses.
2. Mostly vehicles are provided with .... camber.
3. Caster varies from .... to .... in a tractor.

4. King pin inclination varies from .... to .... in a tractor.
5. Steering ratio varies from .... to .... for different vehicles.
6. Excessive vibration of type is seen from front is ....
7. Power steering works on the principle of ....
8. Front axle is also known as .... axle.

Ans. 1. pending, shearing, 2. positive 3.0 to 4 4. 6 to 8 5. 15 : 1 to 35 : 1 6. wobble 7. Pascal's law 8. dead

ANSWER OF MULTIPLE CHOICE QUESTIONS

1 (a) 2 (a) 3 (a) 4 (b) 5 (b) 6 (b) 7 (a) 8 (c) 9 (a) 10 (b) 11 (a) 12 (a) 13 (f) 14 (e) 15 (a) 16 (b) 17 (b)

Chapter 13
Wheels and Tyres

13.1 Brief History: In the beginning of tractors era, they were provided with iron wheel with small spokes to grip the ground. These tractors were very heavy in weight very slow in speed made let of noise. But modern tractors are equipped with a wheel-type assembly.

A wheel-tyre assembly consists of the following main parts (i) wheel body with rim (ii) tyre and tube

(iii) brake drum and (iv) air valve

A wheel-tyre assembly serves the following purposes

(i)   To make the vehicle mobile

(ii)   the bear the total load of the vehicle

(iii) to provide cushioning effect to vehicle

(iv) to help in smooth steering and directional stability.

13.2. Wheels: A wheel is an assembly of hub, disc, rim, and spokes (spokes are not essential in many types). The following are the desirable properties of a good wheel:

(i)   Strong enough to withstand the weight of the vehicle.

(ii)   Flexible to absorb the road shocks

(iii) Able to grip the ground

(iv) Perfectly balanced

(v)   Light in weight and easily removable..

13.2.1 Types of Wheels: They are classified as follows:

(i)   Wire-spoked wheel   (ii) Pressed steel disc wheel

(iii) Light alloy cost wheel   (iv) Composite wheel

Modern tractors are equipped with pressed steel disc wheel. A typical construction of disc wheel is shown in Fig. A disc wheel consists of two parts (i) rim and (ii) disc. Both are made of pressed steel, and can be either made integrally or permanently attached by welding. The rim generally accomodates a tyre while the disc provides strength of wheel.

The disc has a whole in its centre to accomodate the axle. Provision of hole is made on the periphery for bolting the axle flage with disc. Some cooling vents are also provided on them to allow the air to flow inside. This helps in cooling of the brake drum which gets during braking.

13.2.2. Wheel Specification: The wheels are available in different sizes. Their dimensions differ from vehicle to vehicle as well as model to model. An automobile wheel is specified in the following sequential manner.

W	RT	D
Rim width	Type of rim	Rim diameter
(in inches)		(in inches)

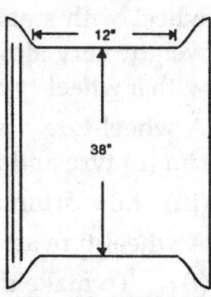

For examples 12.6-38 wheel size represent a wheel with 12.6" nominal cross-sectional with rim diameter of 38" as shown in Fig. 13.1.

13.3. Tyres: Pneumatic wheels are usually known as tyre.

The tyre is an especially rubber product that remains mounted on the wheel periphery. There are two types of tyres (i) solid tyres and (ii) pneumatic tyre.

Pneumatic tyres are usually known as pneumatic wheel. They were first introduced in 1920 and since then are being used as standard fitting on all the tractors. They mainly consists of an outer part (the main type) and a tube inside. The tyre-tube

Fig. 13.1 Wheel specification

combination is fitted or mounted on the wheel rim. Tube is fitted inside the type filled with compressed air. Infact this compressed air in the tube carries the vehicle and also imparts cushing of the vehicle.

13.3.1 Function of Tyre: They perform the following functions.

(i) They support the load of the vehicle (tractor)

(ii) They provide traction for driving and braking

(ii) They allow steering control and the directional stability

(iv) They offer cushion to the vehicle over the ground surface irregularities and against the road shocks.

(v) They transmit driving and braking forces to the road.

13..2 Requirements of a Good Tyre: The following are the main requirements of a good tyre:

(i) Non skidding (ii) Uniform wear (iii) Load carrying (iv) Cushioning (v) power consumption (vi) Tyre noise (vii) Balancing

(i) Non-Skidding: This is one of the most important tyre property. The trend pattern on the tyre must be suitably designed to permit least amount of skidding, even on wet road.

(ii) Uniform wear: To maintain the non-skidding properties it is very essential that the wear on the tyre tread must be uniform.

(iii) Load carrying: The tyre should be strong enough to carry the gross wt. of the vehicle. The strength in the tyre is imparted by the number of plies involved in construction. The load sustaining ability of a tyre having higher ply-rating (PR) will be more.

(iv) Cushioning: The tyre should be able to absorb small high vibration set up by the road surface and this provided cushioning effect.

(v) Power consumption: The vehicle tyre does absorb some power which is due to friction between the tread rubber and road surface. This power comes from the engine fuel and should be least possible. It is seen that the synthetic tyres consume more power which rolling than the tyre made out of natural rubber.

(vi) Tyre noise: The tyre noise may be in the form of different patter sing in a particular style. It is desirable that the noise should be minimum.

(vii) Balancing: Balancing is very important consideration. The type being rotating that part of the vehicle. It must be balance properly. The absence of balancing gives rise to peculiar oscillations called wheel wobbling.

13.3.3. Tyre Skeleton: The body of a tyre is mainly composed of carcass or skeleton of cards arranged in definite pattern. The skeleton is the main structural constituent that takes the load transferred on the tyre during its operation.

Bias -ply, or Cross ply skeleton, Redial-ply skeleton and Belted-bias ply skeleton are the skeleton of the tyre.

Which are shown in Fig. But a radial tyre is mostly used on vehicle due to following characteristics.

(i) Side Wall: The side walls of radial ply tyres can bend easily which results into ride comfortable.

(ii) Shock absorption: Their shock absorbing capacity is about 25% more than the cross ply tyres. Thus they can absorb more bounce of rough road and are thus more comfortable at high speed.

(iii) Possibility of puncture: Due to steel belt construction possibility of puncture is minimum or less.

(iv) Construction: It offers better road grip since the tread is also supported by the breaker strips in addition to side wall.

(v) Surface area of road tyre contact: There is a continuous and almost flat contact path area with the road surface, improving acceleration and breaking.

(vi) Rolling Resistance: Lower rolling resistance which ultimately reduced fuel consumption.

(vii) Configuration of the tyre print on the road: Balance straight on shown in Fig. 13.2 adds extra life to the tyre.

(vii) Tread life: Longer tread life. the extra life may be up to 100% in some cases due to the less heat built up.

(ix) Braking efficiency and acceleration performance: It has better braking efficiency as well as acceleration performance.

(x) Steering characteristics: It has better steering characteristice due to higher covering force and self-righting couple.

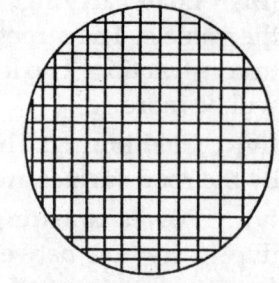

Fig. 13.2 Balance straight

(xi) Curve negotiating behaviour: It has stable curve negotiating behaviour, since tendency to distort and life-off the road is less.

13.4. Aspect Ratio (Ar): It is the geometrical parameter of a tyre and mathematically expressed as,

$$A_R = \frac{\text{Height of the tyre section (H)}}{\text{Width of the tyre section}} \quad (13.1)$$

It is expressed in percentage.

If a tyre has 100% aspect ratio is called high profile tyre. But now-a-days, tyre having aspect ratio (AR) around to are more popular due to following advantages.

(i)   Better road holding (ii) More tread contact

(iii)   High Load carrying capacity (iv) Improved high speed performance (v) Less wear (vi) High cornering power (vii) Longer life.

13.5. Tyre Specification and Designation can be given in either English system or metric system:

13.5. Specifications for Non-Radial Tyres: A non-radial tyre is specified by two different manners (i) speed rating (SR) basis and (ii) Ply rating (PR) basis when specified by speed rating basis, it is expressed sequentially as

W   SR   D

Width (in inches)   Speed rating   Diameter (in inches)·

Here, W is the width measured between the widest sections of a tyre when the tyre is correctly inflated and D is the diameter measured between points of the tyre and the connecting rim.

The speed ratings bear different codes for different operating speeds which are given below:

VW for speeds upto 150 km/h

SR for speeds upto 170 km/h

HR for speeds upto 210 km/h

VR for speeds above 210 km/h

Ply Rating Designation: In this style of tyre designation the number of plies in its construction is also indicated alongwith the width and diameter such as

Tractor front tyres, 6.0-16-6 PR

i.e., W =65.0 inch and D =16 inch and number of plies = 06

13.5.2. Specifications for Radial Tyres: A radial tyre is designated in sequential order as follows:

145/70 SR 12

Where,

145 indicates X-sectional width of the tyre in mm

70 indicates aspect ratio of the tyre

S indicates maximum speed limit which is 180 kmph

R indicates radial construction and 12 indicates rim diameter in inches

13.6. Inflation Pressure and its Effect: The use of proper pressure is the most important for proper working and longer life of tyre as in shown in Fig. 13.4 (iii). Both under-inflation (less than recommended) and over-inflation (more than recommended) are undesired and are harmful. The inflation pressure in the rear wheels of the tractor varies between 80 to 150 kPa. The inflation pressure of the front wheel variesfrom 150 to 250 kPa.

Note: The correct tyre inflation depends upon load distribution on the tyre and climatic condition.

13.6.1. Effects of Under-inflation: The following are the harmful effects of under inflation tyre.

(i) They cause excessive flexing, unreparable damage to the tyre skeleton and cracking of the tyre side walls Fig. 13.4 (i) The trends were more on the sides than in the centre

(iii) They result in separation of plies and loosening of the corals.

(iv) An under-inflated tyre gets damaged due to 'rim bruises' which is caused due to the an impact between the rim and the side wall, and due to misalignment of.

13.6.2. Effects of the Over-inflation: The following are the harmful effects of the over-inflation.

(i) They wear rapidly in their centres as shown in Fig. 13.4. (iii)

(ii) The already stressed tyres exhibit concussion breaks due to over-inflation which causes fabric tear owing to any impact with the tyre.

(iii) They are experienced to separation of plies, cracking and separation of the tread due to localised stresses and strains and heat in the tread region.

(iv) They are unable to provide cushioning effect to itself which results into inharsh, uncomfortable and skidding behaviour.

(v) The contact area between the tread and the rod diminishes, which causes decreased resistance with the road surface.

13.7. Factors Affecting the Tyre Performance and Life:

The performance and life of a tyre are influenced by several factors, which are given below.

13.7.1. Improper inflation: Both under-inflation and over-inflation are harmful is discussed previous. We have observed that the tyre mileage lowers-down if the tyre is either under-inflation or over inflation as shown in Fig 13.3.

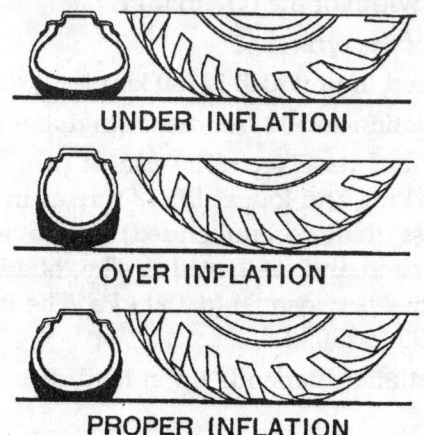

Fig. 13. 3. Effect of Inflation on Tyre Cross-section

13.7.2 Overloading: In art we have discussed the vehicles weight, gross vehicle and pay load on it, overloading results into the rim and the tyre carcass will get over-stained. Thus the effect of overloading will be not only to reduce the tyre life but will also result in the decrease of tyre performance.

13.7.3. Vehicle Speed: The tread of a tyre wears fast, beyond a certain speed which is generally varies between 50 to 65 kmph. Hence, speeding of the vehicle above this speed range reduces the tyre life as well as into mileage.

13.7.4. Wheel Alignment: Misalignment of wheel results into rapid wear of tyre tread. Therefore, misalignment of wheel reduces the tyre life as well as its mileage.

13.8. Tyre Economy: Mathematically, it is expressed as

$$\text{Tyre economy} = \frac{\text{Its total cost}}{\text{Total mileage covered by it}}$$

$$= \frac{C_I + C_{R_1} + C_{R_2}}{M_1 + M_{R_1} + M_{R_2}}, \text{Rs/km} \qquad (13.2)$$

Where,

C_I = Initial cost, Rs

C_R = Retreading prices, Rs

M_I = Mileage obtained from the new tyre

M_R = Mileage obtained from the retreading tyre.

1, 2 are for a first and second retreadings.

13.9. Tube: It is rubber bag in which air is filled through valve. It is placed over the rim in the tyre. The pressure in the tube must be maintained at prescribed a specified level.

13.10. Tube Vulcanization: Generally a tube is made of natural rubber whose monomer is isoprene. When natural rubber is heated with 3.5% sulpher, vulcanized rubber is obtained and process is called vulcanization. Vulcanized rubber has greater strength than natural rubber.

13.11. BALLASTING

To improve the traction of drive wheels, additional weight is added to the reas tyres. This is known as Ballasting and can be achieved by any of the following methods.

1.   Bolting cast iron weights to the wheels, and

2.   Use of liquid in the inner tube

Beside improved traction, ballast helps in (i) reducing the slippage (ii) increasing the drawbar, pull, (ii) slower tread wear and (iv) less fuel consumption. For road operations and light work, such as cultivating, harrowing, planting etc. ballasting is not required.

13.11.1. Method of Ballasting: There are followings methods of ballasting.

(a)   Bolting cast iron weights: Cost iron weights are secured to the rim by, extension bolts. This method of ballasting has an advantage over water ballasting in that these can be easily removed when not required. The maximum amount of weight a tyre can carry depends upon the tyre size, ply rating and maximum pressure. Hence, it is always recommended to follow the operational manual to decide the weight.

Front wheels are also sometimes counter balanced with weights to increase the stability when heavy loads are superimposed on the drawbar or heavy equipment is to be mounted on the drawbar or heavy equipment is to be mounted on the rear end of the tractor.

(b)   Use of Liquid in Inner Tube: This method is used only in those areas where temperature does not fall to the freezing point of the water. In this method clean water is used for this purpose. In areas where water freezing can take place Calcium Chloride ($CaCl_2$) is added to make anti freeze solution.

13.11.2 Reason for Adding wt. to Rear Wheel: There are following reasons, which are given as

(i)   it gives added traction for ploughing.

(ii)   To maintain traction with heavy load on the front

13.11.3 Reason for Adding wt. to Front Wheel: There are following reasons

(i)   To balance the lifting action of front wheel due to rear mounted implement.

(ii)   To help in keeping the front wheels on road while driving up a slope i.e., steering stability.

SUBJECTIVE QUESTIONS

1.   What are the important functions of the tyre?

2.   Explain the size of tyre.

3.   Write short notes on:

        (i)   Ballasting (ii) Pneumatic wheel (iii) Ply rating.

MULTIPLE CHOICE QUESTIONS

1.   Tyres were first intruduced in

        (a)   1920   (b)   1870   (c)   1820   (d)   1720

2.   Functions of tyres are

        (a)   absorbs the small shocks

        (b)   carries the lead of vehicles

        (c)   damps down the vibration to some extent

        (d)   all of the above

3.   If plying is more, that tyre is

        (a)   capable of tacking more load

        (b)   capable to absorb small shocks

        (c)   both

        (d)   none of the above

4.   12.6-38 tyre size represents

        (a)   12.6" nominal cross-sectional with having rim diameter of 38".

        (b)   38" nominal cross-sectional with having a rim diameter of 12.6"

        (c)   both

        (d)   none of the above

5.   Under-inflation causes

        (a)   a series of diagonal breaks in cord fabric in the side wall area.

        (b)   loss of friction

      (c)   both

      (d)   none of the above

6.   The inflation pressure in the rear wheels of tractor varies from

      (a)   80 to 150 KPa

      (b)   150 to 250 KPa

      (c)   250 to 300 KPa

      (d)   none of the above

7.   The inflation pressure in the front wheels of tractor varies from

      (a)   80 to 150 KPa

      (b)   150 to 250 KPa

      (c)   250 to 300 Kpa

      (d)   none of the above

8.   Ballasting helps in

      (a)   reducing the slippage

      (b)   increasing drawbar pull

      (c)   slow tread wear

      (d)   all of the above

9.   Ballasting of rear wheels of tractor improves

      (a)   traction   (b)   directional stability

      (c)   both   (d)   none of the above

10.   Ballasting of front wheels of tractor improves

      (a)   traction   (b)   directional stability

      (c)   both   (d)   none of the above

11.   Which one is generally used to make an anti freeze solution

      (a) $CaCl_2$ (b) $Ca(OH)_2$

      (c) $CaCO_3$ (d)   none of the above

12.   The comparative strength of tyre is indicated by

      (a)   size and try width   (b)   ply rating

      (c)   both   (d)   none of the above

13.   The ply ratings of the tyres used in tractor is

      (a)   4, 6 or 8   (b)   6, 8 or 12

      (c)   2, 4 or 6   (d)   10, 12 or 14

14.   In tyre size of 12-38, the number 12, represents the

      (a)   sectional diameter of tyre   (b)   tyre ply

      (c)   rim diameter   (d)   none of the above

15. The strength of tyre increases with
    (a) increase in ply rating
    (b) decrease in ply rating
    (c) no-effect of ply rating

FILL UP THE BLANKS

1. Tyre was first introduced in ....
2. Tyre .... the power from the engine and transmission of the ground with which the tractor moves.
3. 12-36 tyre size represents a tyre with .... nominal cross-section with having a rim diameter of ....
4. The inflation pressure in the rear wheels of the tractor varies between .... MPa.
5. Ballasting improves the traction of .... wheels.

Answers : 1. 1920 2. transmits 3. 12" and 36" 4. 0.08 to 0.15 5. drive

Chapter 14
Traction

Introduction: Transmission of engine power to the drawbar, and 3-point links if agricultural, implements is achieved through traction devices, namely wheels and tracks. Among power take off, hydraulic, drawbar and 3-point link the later is the most commonly used power outlet of agricultural vehicles. The ability to provide draft for pulling various types of implements is primary measure of efficiency of tractor or power tiller.

14.2. Terminology Related to Traction.

14.2.1 Traction: Traction is obtained by intraction between traction devices (wheel, track) and traction medium (road, soil) interface. In other works "Traction is the term applied to the driving force developed by a wheel, track or other traction devices."

14.2.2 Net Co-efficient of Traction: it is the ratio of net force obtained from the traction device to the dynamic weight. It is generally denoted by 'μ' and is given by following relationship,

$$\mu = \frac{\text{Net pull (P or H)}}{\text{Dynamic Weight (W)}} \qquad (14.1)$$

14.2.3. Traction Device: It is a device which propell, a vehicle using traction force obtained from supporting surface.

14.2.4. Tractive Efficiency: It is the ratio of output power to the input power expressed in percent. It is given by following relationship,

$$\eta_{trac} = \frac{\text{Traction obtained from ground contact}}{\text{Rim pull}} \times 100 \qquad (14.2)$$

Actually, it is a measures of the efficiency with which the traction device transforms the torque acting on its axle into linear drawbar pull. i.e.,

$$\eta_{trac} = \frac{\text{Drawbar Power}}{\text{Axle Power}} \qquad (14.3)$$

i.e., It is the ratio of output power to the input power for a traction device.

12.2.5. Rimpull: It is the tractive force available from engine power at tyre an ground contact (supporting surface). It is given by following relationship,

319

$$\text{Rim pull} = \frac{3600 \times BP \times \eta_e}{s} \qquad\qquad (14.4)$$

Where, BP = Brake power, kW

s = speed, km/h

η_e = Engine efficiency

14.2.6. Rolling Resistance (R). It is the amount of resistive force offered to a moving object in the process of it soil being compacted by the object opposite to the direction of motion as shown in Fig. 14.1. It is given by following relationship,

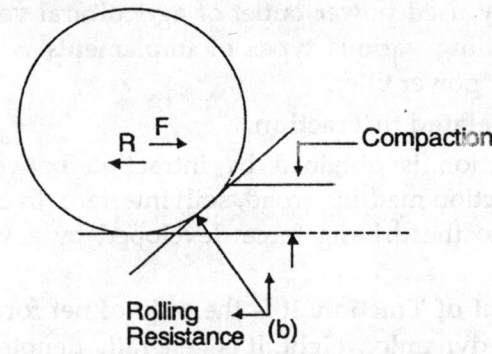

Fig. 14.1. Showing Compaction

$$R = \frac{2}{(n+1)(K_c + BK_\varphi)^{\frac{1}{n}}} \left(\frac{W}{2L}\right)^{\frac{n+1}{n}} \qquad\qquad (14.5)$$

where,

n = co-efficient of wheel sinkage

K_c = Cohesive modulus of soil deformation

K_ϕ = Friction modulus of soil deformation

B = Width of each track

W = Vertical load on shearing area

L = Length of the track in contact

Note: This equation is derived by assuming a flat plate as in a crawler tractor. But this equation is approximately correct for rubber tyre tractors.

14.2.7. Motion Resistance Ratio (ρ): It is defined as the ratio of the rolling resistance (R) to the normal load (W) on traction device. It is given by following relationship,

$$\rho = \frac{R}{W} \qquad (14.6)$$

14.2.8. Wheel slip (S): Wheel ship is the relative movement of the wheel in the direction of travel for a given distance under load and no load conditions and as shown in Fig. 14.2. Mathematically, it is expressed as,

$$S = \frac{N_1 - N_0}{N_1} \times 100, \% \qquad (14.7)$$

where, N_1 = Number of revolutions of the driving wheel for a given distance under load.

N_0 = Number of revolution of driving wheel for given distance under no load condition.

Slip (s) is also defined as

$$S = 1 - \frac{v_a}{v_t} \qquad (14.8)$$

Where, v_a = Actual travel speed

v_t = Theoretical wheel speed, rw

r = Rolling radius

ω = Angular velocity

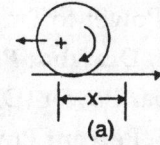

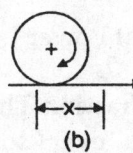

Fig. 14.2. Measurement of Wheel Slip

14.2.9 Towed Wheel condition: The transition, point between the braked and driven force states is the towed wheel condition. A towed wheel is unpowered; axle torque is zero.

14.2.10. Rolling Radius: Rolling Radius is defined as the distance travelled per revolution of the traction device divided by 2π (pi) when operating at the specified condition.

14.2.11. Gross Traction Co-efficient (μ_g): It is the ratio of soil thrust in the direction or Tractive force (F) to normal load (W). It is given by following relationship,

$$\mu_g = \frac{F}{W} \qquad (14.9)$$

The variation of the gress tractive force with soil strength and slip have been incorporated into a relationship including the effect of wheel load on tire size.

$$\mu_g = \frac{F}{W} = \frac{T}{rW} = 0.75 \, (1 - e^{-0.3Cns}) \qquad (14.10)$$

Where, C_n = Wheel numetic = $\dfrac{CIbd}{W} \qquad (14.11)$

321

14.2.12. Cone Index : It is defined as the average force per unit base area required to force a cone-shaped probe into soil at steady rate.

14.2.13. Input Power to Traction device: It is given by following relationship,

Input Power to Traction device = Input Power to tractor - Transmission loss

14.2.14. Drawbar Power: It is calculated as,

Drawbar Power (DP) = Drawbar Pull x Linear speed of tractor

14.2.15. Percent Power Loss in traction: It is calculates as,

$$\text{Percent Power Loss in traction} = \frac{\text{Input power - Drawbar Power}}{\text{Input power}} \times 100 \qquad (14.14)$$

14.3 Traction Theory: Pneumatic tyres are used for common when such a tractor moves over soil, it has to overcome the rolling resistance R as shown in Fig. 14.3.

Maximum tractive force that can be obtained from ground reaction (soil shear) is given by following relationship,

$F_p = AC + W \tan \phi, N$ (14.15)

Where,

A = Area under tyre = 0.78 BL, m²

C = Cohesion of soi, Pa

W = Load that soil can support under the rear wheel.

$W = \dfrac{W_t}{2}$, for track type tractor

= AP vertical load of shear area, N

r = Radius of rear tyre bearing

p = Soil being pressure, Pa

ϕ = Angle of internal friction of soil, Pa

or F = AC + Ap tanϕ

or F= A(C + P tanϕ) = BL (C+P tanϕ); for track

or F= 0.78 BL (C + P tan ϕ); for neumatic tyre on seeing over leaf, we obtained

Area under tyre is shown in Fig. 14.4

$r = \left(\dfrac{L}{2}\right)^2 \times \dfrac{1}{2h}$

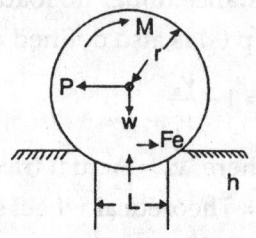

Fig. 14.3 Showing Compaction

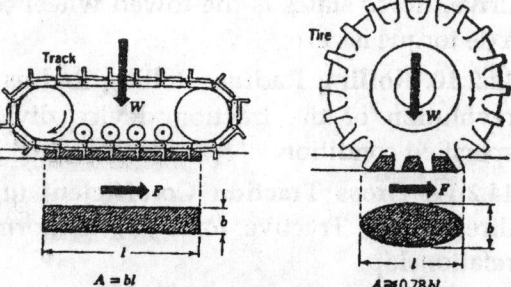

Fig. 14.4 Comparison of Contract Area between Tyre and Track

$$\therefore L = \sqrt{8rh} \qquad (14.17)$$

Where,

h = Depression, m

L = Chord length of tyre which coems in conta‹

14.4. Tractive Force (rim pull) Made Availa

Contact: It is shown in Fig. 14.5

$$F_a = \frac{3600 \times BP \times E}{S}, \, kw \quad (14.18)$$

Where,

F_a = Rim pull, N

BP = Brake power of the engine, kW

E = Efficiency of the gear train between engine

S = Speed of tractor, km/h

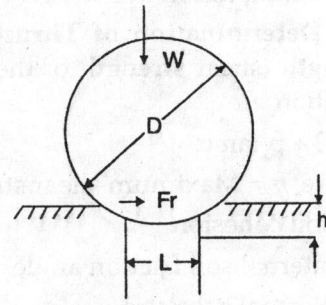

Fig. 14.5 Rim Pull

Tractive force required (Fr) to pulled the load

$$F_r = P + R, \, N \qquad (14.19)$$

Where,

P = Pull, N

R = Rolling resistance, N

$$L = 2\sqrt{Dh} \qquad (14.20)$$

Where,

D = Diameter of wheel, m

h = Compaction, m

Condition for motion of the tractor

$$F_r \le F_P \le F_a$$

Radius of Rear tyre (r) : It is shown in Fig. 14.6

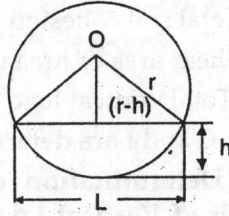

Fig. 14.6 Radius of Tyre

From Fig. 14.6, $r^2 = \left(\dfrac{L}{2}\right)^2 + (r-h)^2$

$$r \approx \left(\frac{L}{2}\right)^2 \times \frac{1}{h} \qquad (14.21)$$

Where, L = chord length of tyre which combus is contact with soil, m

h = Depression

14.5. Pulling Force Developed by Tractor: Becker developed the pulling force developed by the tractor by following mathematically model:

$$P = F - R \qquad (14.22)$$

Where,

F = Thrust force or Tractive force

P = Pull

R = Rolling resistance

14.6 Determination of Thrust Force (F): Assuming force is developed by soils strength (shear strength of the soil). Shear strength of soil is given by coulomb's equation

$$\sigma = C + p \tan \alpha \qquad (14.23)$$

Where, y = Maximum shear stress

C = soil cohesion

ϕ = Internal soil friction angle

p = Normal pressure

Multiplying the equation (14.23) by 'A', we have

$$\sigma A = CA + p \tan \phi$$

$$or \ F = C + W \tan\phi \qquad (14.24)$$

where,

F = Maximum shear force

C = Total soil cohesion force

A = Shear area or area under tyre

W = Total vertical load

Note: C and f are determined in the laboratory for different soil.

14.7 Determination of Maximum Value of Shearing Force for Various Levels of Vertical Loading:

(a) Force-displacement curve at different normal wt or vertical loading: Application of the Mohr-Coulomb criteria to a soil plate situation insights into the nature of the plate loading

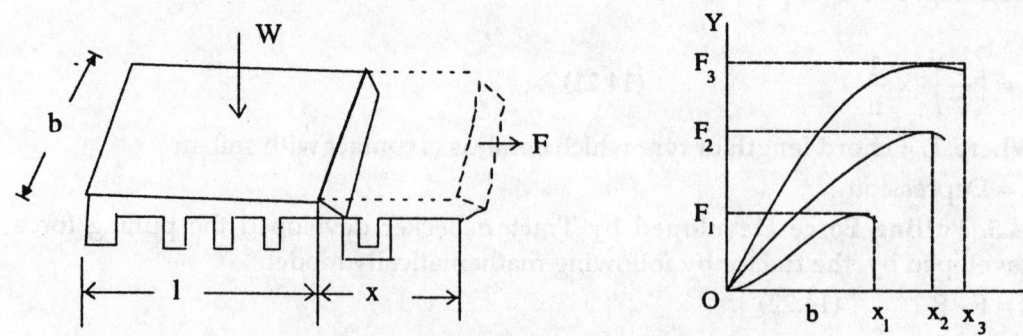

Fig. 14.7 Shearing Force to Soil Plate

and soil shear we find that the force required is usually depend upon both the normal force and area.

Fig. 14.7 Method of Determining Maximum Value of shearing Force for Various Levels of Vertical loads.

(b) Determination of the soil parameters C and ϕ from a plate of maximum valve of the shearing force (F) verses the normal force W.

From Fig. 14.8. We observed for soils having some cohesion that F does not approach zero as W approaches zero. If the maximum valves are plotted for a soil that has both cohesion (c) and internal friction (ϕ), the result will be similar to Fig. 14.8 The equation for such a curve is given by Coulomb's equation.

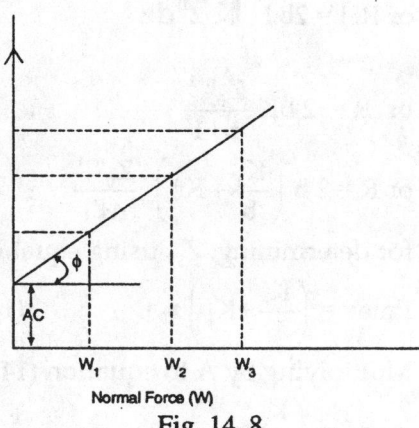

Fig. 14. 8.

$$F = AC = W \tan \phi \qquad (14.25)$$

14.8. Determination of Rolling Resistance (R): Assuming that since wheel is rigid and moving on soft soil, then

Energy of soil deformation = Energy of rolling resistance

Pressure shinkage Relationship is given by followisng relationship,

$$p = Kz^n \qquad (14.29)$$

Where,

K = Constant

z = Shinkage

n = Exponent

After modification by Becker, it given by

$$p = \left(\frac{K_e}{b} + K\phi \right) Z^n \qquad (14.30)$$

Where, K_c and K_ϕ = Shinkage constant or modulus

b = characteistics width of the plate

n = shinkage constant

Work of rolling resistance = Work of compaction

$$R.\,l. = A \int_0^{z_0} pdz$$

For track

$$A = 2\,bl$$

Where,

b = Width of one track

l = Length of the track

or $R.\,l = 2b.l \int_0^{z_0} K\, z^n dz$

or $R = 2\,bK \dfrac{Z_0^{n+1}}{n+1}$

or $R = 2\,b \left(\dfrac{K_c}{b} + K\phi\right) \dfrac{Z_0^{n+1}}{n+1}$ (14.31)

for determining, Z_0, using equation (14.30)

$Pmax = \left(\dfrac{K_c}{b} + K_\phi\right) z_\rho^n$ (14.32)

Multiplying by A to equation (14.32), we have

$W = 2bl \left(\dfrac{K_c}{b} + k_\phi\right) z_0^n$

$W = 2l\,(K_c + bK_\phi)\,Z_0^n$

or $Z_0 = \left(\dfrac{W}{2l\,(k_c + bk_\phi)}\right)^{\frac{1}{n}}$ (14.32)

Substituting the valve of z_0 in equation (13.31), we have

$R = \dfrac{2}{(n+1)\,(K_c + bK_\phi)^{\frac{1}{n}}} \left(\dfrac{W}{2l}\right)^{\frac{n+1}{n}}$ (14.33)

For track type tractor

$W = R_r$ = Nromal reaction on rear wheel

Predication Equations:

$P = F - R$ (14.34)

$F = AC + W \tan \phi$ (14.35)

$R = \dfrac{2}{(n+1)\,(K_c + bK_\phi)^{\frac{1}{n}}} \left(\dfrac{W}{2l}\right)^{\frac{n+1}{n}}$, for track

$R = \dfrac{\left(\dfrac{3W}{D^{0.5}}\right)^{\frac{2n+1}{2n+1}}}{(3-n)^{2n+2/2n+1}\,(n+1)\,(K_c + k_\phi)^{\frac{1}{2n+1}}}$, (for wheel) (14.34)

Where,

D = Diameter of wheel

Notes:

1. For sand,

C = o, ϕ = _____

F = 0 + W tan ϕ

i.e., if we add more weight then thrust force in crases. It is independent of contact area (A).

For clay,

C = _____, ϕ = 0

F = AC + 0

By increasing contact area thrust force increases but independent from weight.

14.19. Cone Index: It is defined as the average force per unit base area, required to force a cone-shaped probe into soil at steady rate. It is given by the following relationship,

$$C.I. = \frac{F}{A} \qquad (14.35)$$

Where,

A = Base are of cone

F = Force

14.10. Wisner's method to predict pull and Efficiency (for single wheel)

Parameters: Dimensionless number

$$\frac{TF}{W}, \frac{P}{W}, \frac{Q}{r.w} = f\left(\frac{CIbd}{W}, \frac{b}{d}, \frac{r}{d}, s\right)$$

TF = Towing force, rolling resistance force

W = Weight on the wheel (normal)

Q = Torque applied on the wheel

r = Rolling radius

CI = Cone index

b = Width of the tyre

S = Wheel stip

C_n = Wheel numeric

14.11.1 Relationship between Towing Force Number $\left(\frac{TF}{W}\right)$ and Wheel Numeric (C_n): It is represented in Fig. 14.9. From Fig. 14.9 we observed that as the valve of wheel numeric increases, towing force number decreases.

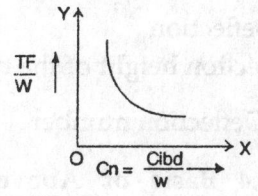

Fig. 14.9. Showing Towing Force No. and Wheel Numeric

14.11.2 Relationship between Pull Number $\left(\dfrac{P}{W}\right)$ and Cone Index: It is represented in Fig. 14.10 From Fig. 14.10, we observed that as the wheel numeric increases, the pull number increases steadily.

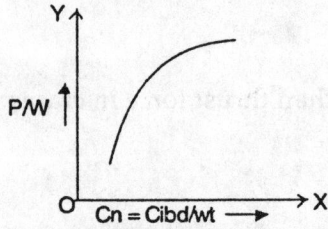

Fig. 14.10 Showing Pull No. and Cone Index

14.10.3 Relationship between Torque Number (q/rw) and Cone-Index: It is represented in Fig. 14.11. From Fig. 14.11 intially torque number increases with increasing cone index. But after obtaining maximum value it becomes constant.

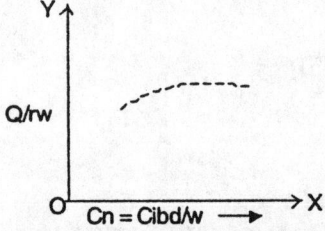

Fig. 14.11 Showing Torque No. and Cone Index

Above Figures (14.10 and 14.11) are drawn on the following assumptions:

$$\frac{b}{d} \square \; 0.30$$

$$\frac{\delta}{h} = 0.20$$

$$\frac{r}{d} \square \; 0.475$$

Where,

δ = Deflection

h = Section height of the tyre

$\dfrac{\delta}{h}$ = Deflection number

14.10.4 Basis of Above Figures and Assumption, Some Equations were Developed:

$$\left(\frac{TF}{W_\theta}\right)^F = \frac{1.2}{C_n} + 0.04 \qquad\qquad (14.36)$$

328

$$\frac{\theta}{rW} = 0.75(1-e^{-0.3CnS}) \qquad (14.37)$$

$$\frac{P}{W} = 0.75(1 - e^{-0.3\,CnS}) - \left(\frac{1.2}{C_n} + 0.4\right) \qquad (14.38)$$

Pull number = Torque number - Towing force number

14.11. Tyre Tractive Efficiency for Single Tyre: It is given by following relationship,

$$TE = \frac{P/W}{Q/rw}(1-S) \qquad (14.40)$$

$$TE = \left[1 - \left(\frac{1.2/C_n + 0.04}{0.75(1 - e^{0.3\,CnS})}\right)\right](1-S) \qquad (14.41)$$

14.12. Forces Acting on the Towed Wheel: It is shown in Fig. 14.12.

Where,

G = Soil Reaction, soil reaction (G) is resolved in two components towed force (TF) and R.

For towed wheel, axle torque is zero.

i.e., (TF).r - Re = 0

$$\therefore e = \left[\frac{TF}{R}\right].r \qquad (14.41)$$

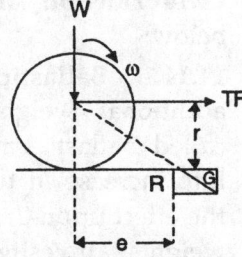

Fig. 14.12 Forces Acting on the Towed Wheel

$$Now, \frac{TF}{R} = \frac{TF}{W} = \rho\left[\because R = W\right]$$

Where

e = Distance between normal load and vertical component of soil reaction

ρ = Motion resistance ratio

$$\therefore e = \rho.r. \qquad (14.42)$$

14.13 Forces Acting on Driving Wheel: It is shown in Fig. 14.13

and horizontal component is given by

H = F - TF

Where,

F = Gross-traction force

TF = Motion resistance force

Dividing numerator and denominator by 'W', we have

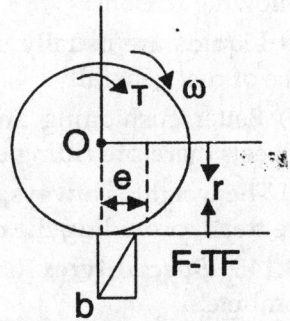

Fig. 14.13 Forces Acting on Driving Wheel

$$\frac{H}{W} = \frac{F}{W} - \frac{TF}{W}$$ (14.43)

$$\mu = \mu_g - \rho$$ (14.44)

where,

μ_g = Gross traction co-efficient

Summing the moments acting on wheel,

T - (F - TF) r - Re = 0

or T = Fr

∵ (TF) r = R. e (14.45)

14.14 Traction Aids: Aids by which traction is increased. The aids are given below:

14.14.1. Ballasting of tractor: Putting additional weight on tractor wheel is called 'ballast'. Ballasting of tractor results into increase in traction. Fig. 14.14 shows the effect upon drawbar pull adding wheel weights. Investigations show that the increased drawbar pull will be approximately 50 percent of the weight added the wheel. Weighting rubber-tired tractor wheels by partly filling the inner tube with water or some other suitable liquid is now in practice and seems to be preferable to using external weight for the following reasons:

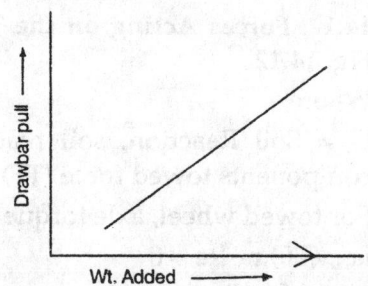

Fig. 14.14 Effect upon Drawbar pull of Adding Weight to Rear Wheels

(a) Liquids are usually easy to obtain and free of cost generally.

(b) Better cushioning and shock-absorbing effects are obtained weight to Rear Wheels therefore riding qualities.

(c) The weight is always located in the lower portion of the type and directly over the tread, providing the most effective traction possible.

14.14.2. Special tyre: Rice tyre is special tyre which is used in rice field in rice combine.

14.14.3. Wheel extension: the followings are wheel extensions, which are given below:

(a) Cage wheel extension: Use of cage wheel extension which results into width increases. Increases in width which results into increase shearing area. Since pull is equal to product of shearing area and cohesion, therefore, ultimatially traction increased. It is generally used for puddling purpose in paddy field before transplanting.

(b) Wheel strake: It is shown in Fig. 14.15 and are used to increases traction.

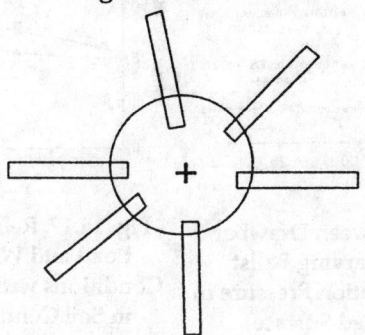

Fig. 14.15 Wheel Strake

(c) Dual tyre: We have observed that when dual tyre is used then we increases width of tyre. Increase in width which results into increase in shearing area. Since pull is equal to product of shearing and cohesion, thus increase in traction takes place.

14.15. Effect of Inflation Pressure and Ballasting on the Tractive Performance of a Tractor:

S. Kumar Lohan and and. S. Agarwal (2001) conducted test to determine tractive performance as function of inflation pressure and ballasting condition. The experiment was conducted on a Ford-3600 with average mass of 1850 kg and tyre size of 13.6-28". Three levels of ballasting conditions were achieved by adding cast iron weight to rear tyres, i.e., 0 kg, 75 kg and 100 kg per tyres. Four levels of drawbar load on tractor were chosen, i.e., 0 kN, 7.5 kN, 17.5 kN and 27.5 kN. Two condition, of soil were selected for the test, namely ploughed and unplough conditions with moisture content level at 6.6% and 5.85% respectively. The bulk density and cone index for ploughed soil were 1.2 g/cc and 886 kPa respectively whereas for unploughed soil type it was 1.02 g/cc and 1016 kPa respectively.

14.16 Relationship between Drawbar Load and Wheel Slip: Experiment conducted at the research area of college of Agricultural Engineering and Technology, CCSHAU, Hisar states that as the drawbar load is increased the value of wheel slip increased, at all inflation pressure and ballasting conditions.

Experiment reveales that maximum slip of 11.64% and occurred at 27.5 kN drawbar load on tractor with 110 kg ballast per tyre. At the same inflation pressure and same ballasting conditions, slip got increased with an increase in drawbar load on tractor, as shown in Fig. 14.16

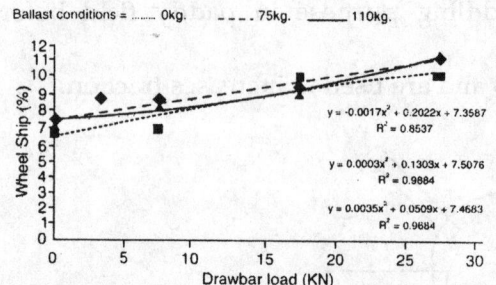

Fig. 14.16. Relationship between Drawbar Load and Wheel Slip at Varying Ballst Conditions with 78.5kPa Inflation Pressure in Soil Condition-I (Ploughed Surface).

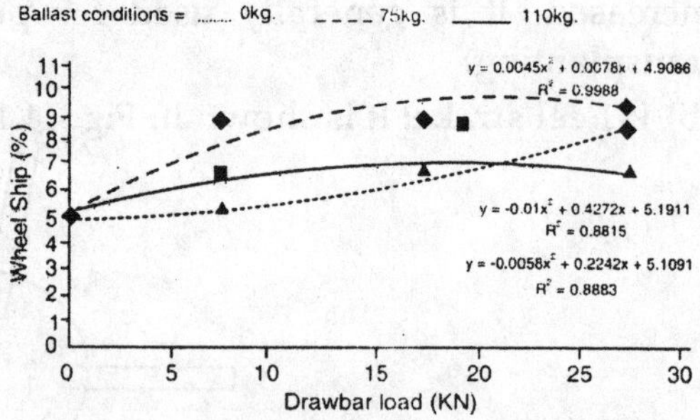

Fig. 14.17. Relationship between Drawbar Load and Wheel Slip at Varying Ballst Conditions with 112.8kPa Inflation Pressure in Soil Condition-I (Ploughed Surface)

Drawbar load (kN) Wheel slip increase with an increase in the ballast condition from 0 kg to 75 kg. But the slip was decreased when ballast was increased from 75 kg to 110 kg as shown in Fig. 14.17.

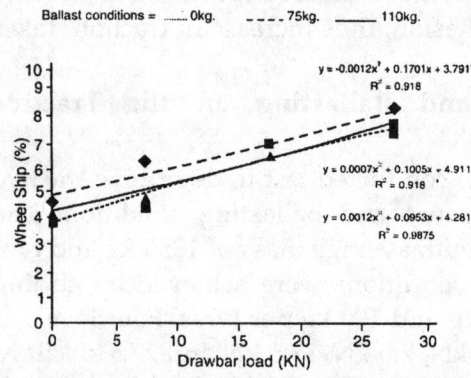

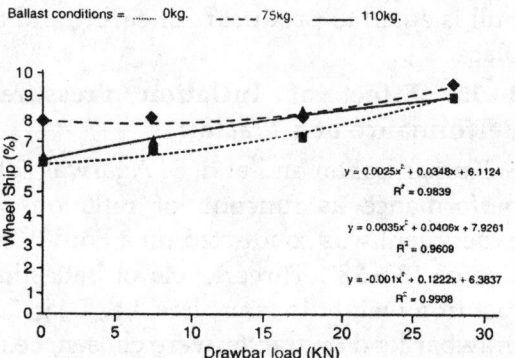

Fig. 14.18. Relationship between Drawbar Load and Wheel Slip Varying Ballast Conditions with 147.1 kPa Inflation Pressure in Soil Condition-I (ploughed Surface)

Fig. 14.19. Relationship between Drawbar Load and Wheels Lip at Varying Ballast Conditions with 78.5 kPa Inflation Pressure in Soil Condition-I (Unploughed Surface).

Similarly, Fig. 14.18, Fig. 14.19, Fig. 14.20 and Fig. 14.21. Show the relationship between drawbar load and wheel slip at varying ballast conditions at different inflation pressure in ploughed and unploughed soil condition.

Finally, we can conclude that at all inflation pressures and ballasting conditions the wheel slip increased with an increase in drawbar load for both ploughed and unploughed soil.

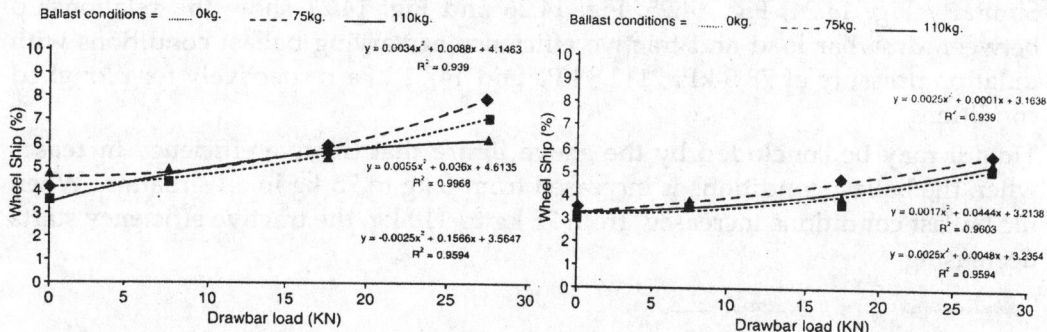

Fig. 14.20. Relationship between Drawbar Load and Wheel Slip at Varying Ballast Conditions with 112.8 kPa Inflation Pressure in Soil Condition-II (Unploughed Surface).

Fig. 14.21. Relationship between Drawbar Load and Wheel slip at Varying Ballast Conditions with 147.1 kPa Inflation Pressure in Soil Condition-II (Unploughed Surface).

14.17. Relationship between Drawbar Load and Tractive Efficiency: Experiments show that in the ploughed and unploughed soils and net value of tractive efficiency goes on decreasing as the inflation pressure increased from 78.5 kPa to 147.1 kPa.

Fig. 14.22. Shows that tractive efficiency increased with an increase in the ballast conditions from 0 to 75 kg. When the ballast condition is increased from 75 kg to 110 kg the tractive efficiency decreased as shown in Fig. 14.23.

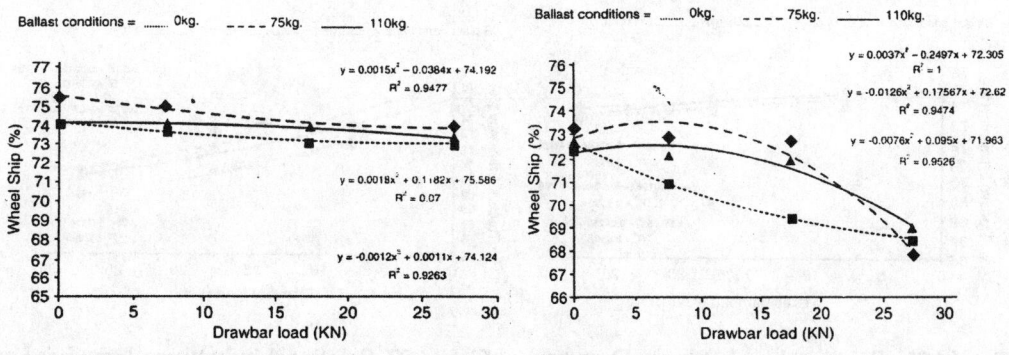

Fig. 14.22. Relationship Drawbar Load and Tractive Efficiency at Varying Ballast Conditions with 78.5 kPa Inflation Pressure in Soil Conditions-I (Ploughed Surface).

Fig. 14.23 Relationship between Drawbar Load and Tractive Efficiency at Varying Ballast Conditions with 112.8 kpa Inflation Pressure in Soil Condition-I (Ploughed Surface).

Similarly Fig. 14.24, Fig. 14.25, Fig. 14.26 and Fig. 14.27 show the relationship between drawbar load and tractive efficiency at varying ballast conditions with inflation pressure at 78.5 kPa, 112.8 kPa and 147.1 kPa respectively for ploughed conditions.

Thus it may be concluded by the above figure that tractive efficiency increases when the ballast conditions is increased from 0 kg to 75 kg in all situation. When the ballast conditions increased, from 75 kg to 110 kg, the tractive efficiency starts decreasing.

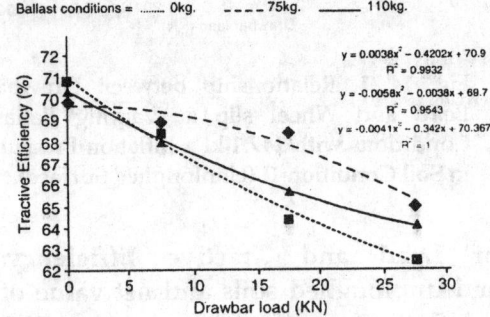

Fig.14.23. Relationship between Drawbar Load and Tractive Efficiency at Varying Ballast Conditions with 147.1 kPa Inflation Pressure in Soil Condition-I (Ploughed Surface).

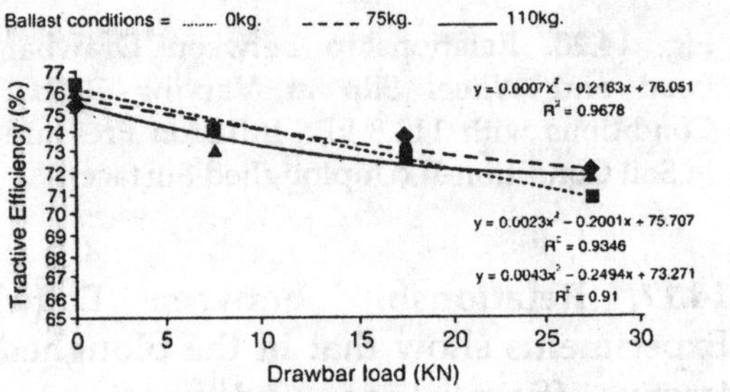

Fig. 14.24. Relationship between Drawbar Load and Tractive Efficiency at Varying Ballast Conditions with 78.5 kPa Inflation Pressure in Soil Condition-II (Unploughed Surface).

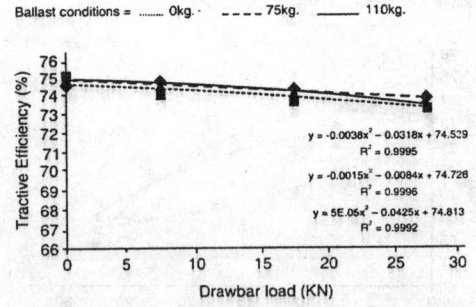

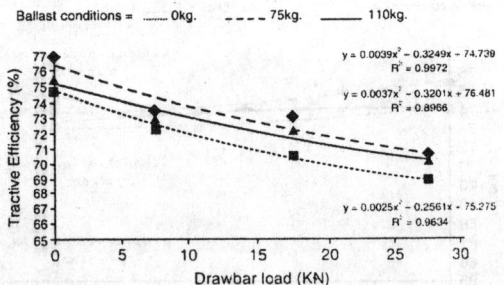

Fig. 14.26. Relationship between Drawbar Load and Tractive Efficiency at Varying Ballast Conditions with 112.8 kPa Inflation Pressure in Soil Condition-II (Unploughed Surface).

Fig. 14.27. Relationship between Drawbar Load and Tractive Efficiency at Varying Ballast Conditions with 147.1 kPa Inflation Pressure in Soil Condition-II (Unploughed Surface).

Source : AMA Vol. 32 No. 3, Summer 2001.

Note 1. Investigations show that the larger diameter of tyre performed better than the small tyres in improving the soil tractive efficiency.

Note 2. Investigations show the effect of tyre width in increasing the tractive efficiency is relatively less as compared to tyre diameter.

Note 3. Investigations show that the power loss in traction decreased with an increase in drawbar pull and linear speed.

Note 4. Investigation show that the effect of lug angle and lug spacing are negligible on traction performance.

Prob. 14.1. A towed wheel with rolling radius of 0.35 m and normal load of 500 N requires a horizontal force of 5N to move it forward. The vertical soil reaction against the wheel can be considered to act ahead of vertical line passing through the wheel axis at a distance of (a) 3.18×10^{-1} m (b) 3.5×10^{-1} m (c) 3.18×10^{-2} m (d) 3.5×10^{-2} m [GATE-2004]

Sol. Given : TF = 50 N, R = 500 N, r = 0.35 m e = ?

Referring Fig. 8

(T.F.). r = R. e

$$\therefore e = \frac{(T.F.). \, r}{R} = \frac{50 \times 0.35}{500} = 3.5 \times 10^{-2} \text{ m}$$

Therefore, Answer is (d)

Prob 14.2 A four wheel drive tractor with a total weight to 135 kN is pulling a level drawbar load of 55 kN on a concrete track. The actual travel speed is 10 km/h owing to unequal tyre pressures and uneven wear of tyres, the theoretical speed of front tyres is maintained 6 percent higher than that of the rear tyres. The axle power to the front tyres is 110 kW and to the rear tyres is 90 kW.

A. If travel reduction of the front tyres is 15 percent, the travel reduction of the rear tyres is

(a) 9.90% (b) 15.00% (c) 20.00% (d) 30.00%

B. The tractive efficiency of the tractor for this, operation is

(a)　40.74% (c) 61.11% (c) 76.39% (d) 84.87% [GATE-2004]

Sol. $S_1 = 0.15$, F = 55 KN, v = 10 km/h

　　　Front　　Rear

$(1 - S_1) \, 1.06 \, v_t = (1 - S_2) \, v_t$

or $(1 - 0.15) \times 1.06 = 1 - S_2$

or $1.06 - 0.159 = 1 - S_2$

or $S_2 = 1 - 0.901$

$S_2 = 0.099$

= 9.9%

Therefore, answer of A is (a)

$$\text{Drawbar power} = \text{F.V.} = 55 \times 10^3 \times \frac{10000}{3600}$$

$= 152.77 \text{ kW}$

$$\text{Tractive efficiency} = \frac{\text{Drawbar Power}}{\text{axle power}} = \frac{152.77}{200} \times 100$$

$= 76.39\%$

Therefore, answer of B is (c)

Prob. 14.3. A rear wheel drive tractor weight 18 kN has the static weight divided in such a way that 12 kN is on the rear wheels and 6 kN on the front. The tractor is pulling a plough at a forward speed of 5 km/h. The plough exerts an inclined drawbar pull of 10 kN with the line of pull making an angle $\alpha = 15°$ with the horizontal in the vertical plane (see the figure 14.28). The axle power required is 20 kW. The wheel base of the tractor L is 2100 mm and distance y is 500 mm.

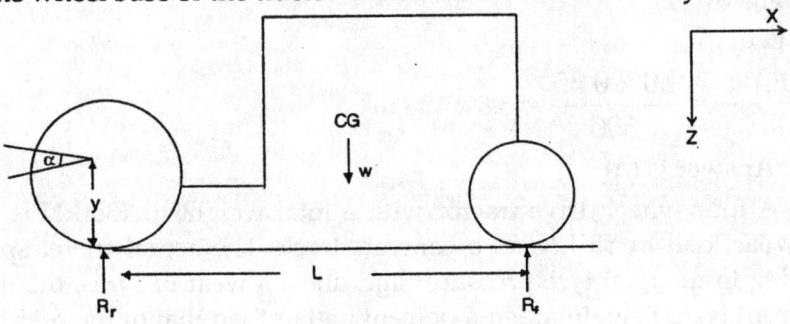

Fig. 14.28

R_r - Soil reaction against rear wheel

R_f - Soil reaction against front wheel

W -Static wt. of tractor

(A)   The dynamic weight on the rear axle is (a) 12.00 kN (b) 12.62 kN (c) 11.30 kN (d) 16.89 kN

(B)   The tractive efficiency of the tractor for this operation is

(a)   17.97% (b) 40.25% (c) 67.08% (d) 69.11% [GATE-2003]

Sol. Given, y = 500 mm L = 2100 mm

W = 18 kN $\alpha = 15°$

v = 5 km/h   Rr = 12 kN

R_f = 6 kN   P = 10 kN

$$\text{Wt. Transfer} = \frac{10 \times \cos 15° \times 500}{2100} = 2.29 \text{ kN}$$

Therefore dynamic wt. on the rear axle = 12 + 2.29 + P sin α

= 12 + 2.29 + 10 sin 15°

= 12 + 2.29 + 2.60 = 16 .89 kN

Hence answer of (A) is (d)

$$\text{Tractive efficiency} = \frac{\text{Drawbar power}}{\text{Axle power}} \times 100\%$$

$$= \frac{P \cos \alpha . v}{\text{axle power}} \times 100\%$$

$$= \frac{10 \times \cos 15° \times 5000}{3600 \times 20} \times 100\%$$

= 67.08% ans.

Therefore answer of (B) is (c)

Prob. 14.4. A traction wheel having 600 mm diameter was tested in soil bin and the following data were recorded angular speed of wheel = 10 rev/min, input torque to wheel axle = 60 Nm, drawbar pull= 150 N, normal load on wheel axle = 500 N, wheel forward speed = 0.25 m./s. Calculate

(a)   Co-efficient of traction

(b)   Wheel slippage

(c)   Tractive efficiency [GATE- 1991]

Sol^n. Given: D = 600 mm = 0.6 m; N = 10 rev/s

Input torque to wheel axle (T) = 60 Nm

Forward speed (V_a) = 0.25 m/s

Normal load (W) = 500 N

Drawbar pull = 150 N

$$(a) \text{ Co-efficient of tractor} = \frac{\text{Drawbar pull}}{\text{Normal load}}$$

$$= \frac{150}{500} = 0.3 \text{ Ans.}$$

$$(b) \text{ Wheel slippage} = \left(1 - \frac{V_a}{V_t}\right) \times 100,\%$$

$$= \left(1 - \frac{0.25}{2\pi \, ND/2}\right) \times 100$$

$$= \left(1 - \frac{0.25 \times 2 \times 60}{2\pi \, 10 \times 0.6}\right) \times 100$$

337

$$= \left(1 - \frac{30}{2\pi \times 10 \times 0.6}\right) \times 100$$

$= 20.32\%$

(c) Tractive efficiency $= \dfrac{H}{F} (1 - S)$

$\dfrac{150 \times 0.3}{60} (1 - 0.2032)$

$= 0.5976$

59.76% Ans.

Prob 14.5. The rear wheel diameter of a tractor is 130 cm and its wheel base is 185 cm. If a horizontal pull of 6 kN is applied at a distance of 25 cm below the rear axle, the weight transfer will be

(a) 0.811 kN (b) 1.30 kN (c) 3.75 kN (d) 4.70 kN   [GATE -2000]

Soln.

Given, $r_R = 65$ cm

$L = 185$ cm $= 1.85$ m

$P = 6$ w, $\theta = 0$

$y_1 = (65-25)$ cm $= 40$ cm $= 0.4$ m

weight transfer = ?

We know that

Weight transfer $= \dfrac{P(y_1 \cos \theta)}{L}$

$= \dfrac{6 \times 0.4 \times \cos \theta}{1.85}$

$= 1.30$ kN Ans.

Hence, answer is (b)

PROBLEMS.

1. Predict the maximum traction thrust of a track type tractor with two track each 360 mm wide by 1680 mm long. The wt. of tractor is 31.75 kN. Assume that the lugs on the track are such that the soil is sheared off in a plane area at the ends of the lugs.

    Soil. parameters are C = 14 kPa and $\phi = 30°$ [GATE - 1994]

    (Ans. 35.264 kN)

2. If the tractor of the above problem is extering a drawbar pull of 7.8 Kn and if $y_f = 700$ mm $= y_r$ and from the Fig. 14.28 and $L_1 = 2160$ mm, calculate

    (a) the true tyre load

    (b) the required co-efficient of traction for the rear wheels.

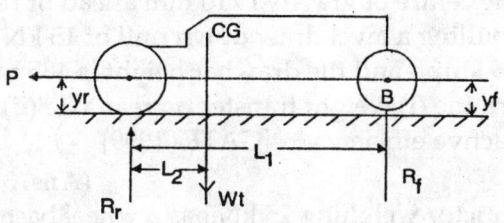

Fig. 14.29

3. A 2-wheel drive 35 hp tractor has 1.5 m rear wheel diameter. The engine runs at 1200 rpm/min. The total reduction of speed is 30:1. Find the travelling speed of tractor is km/h and the tractive force at each driving wheel.   [GATE -1972]
(Ans. 8.315 kN)

4. Determine theoretical maximum drawbar pull of track type tractor 28000 kN with 360 mm width and 1.70 m long track. Soil parameters are as follows:
(i) Soil cohesion, C = 12 kPa.
(ii) Angle of repose ϕ = 28°
(iii) Cohesive modulus of deformation K_c = 3
(iv) friction modulus of deformation K_ϕ = 0.5
(v) Co-efficient of sinkage of wheel = 0.2
Assume that, the lugs of tractor to be such that, the soil is sheared off in a plane area, at the ends of lugs.

(Ans. 33.58 kN)

5. Determine maximum drawbar pull of a track type tractor with 350 mm wide and 16 m long track. The weight of a tractor is 35,000 kN. The lugs on the tractors are such that the soil is sheared off in a plane are at the ends of lug. The soil parameters are as
C = 14 KPa ; K_ϕ = 0.5
ϕ = 30°; n = 2
K_c = 3
(Ans. 35,88 kN)

6. valuate the maximum traction thrust of a track type tractor with two track each 36 cm wide and 168 cm long. The weight of tractor is 31750 N.
Assume that the lugs on the track are such that the soil is sheared off in a plane area at the ends of the lugs-soils parametur are as follows.
(i) C = 14 kPa   (ii) ϕ = 30°

(Ans. 35.26 kN)

7. A rear wheel drive tractor with a total weight of 23 kN has a wheel base of 200 mm and the centre of gravity i 710 mm ahead of rear axle centre line. The tractor is puliing a level draw down pull of 15 kN on a concrete surface at as speed of 6 kmph and the drawbar height is 485 mm. The axle power is 33.3 kW. Determine (i) weight transfer on rear axle (ii) co-efficient of traction (iii) tractive efficiency   [GATE- 1999]

(Ans. 3.462 kN, 0.802, 74.7%)

8. A four wheel tractor weighing 25 kN has a wheel base 1.2 m. The C.G. is located on a vertical plane 0.4 m ahead of rear axle. Detemine the maximum drawbar pull that a tractor can exert on a level road where co-efficient of rolling resistance is 0.04 and co-efficient of traction between the road surface and tyres is 0.5 The hitch height may be taken as 0.4 m. Also calculate the rimpull if there is no slip.   [GATE -1995]

(Ans. 9.48 kN).

9. A rear wheel drive tractor is operating on a level ground. The static weight of the tractor is 25 kN and wheel base is 2100 mm. The centre of gravity is located 800 mm ahead of the rear axle centre. The rolling radius of each drive wheel is 600 mm. Assume the rear and front wheel reactions pass through their respective axle centre. Compute

(a) the steady-state horizontal pull required to maintain just 20% of tractor static weight on front axle and

(b) the corresponding co-efficient of traction. [GATE -2001]

(Ans. 14.55 kN, 0.59)

SUBJECTIVE QUESTION

1. What do you mean by traction? What are different factors affecting traction?

2. Prove that $R = \dfrac{2}{(n+1)\,(Kc + bK\phi)^{\frac{1}{n}}} \left(\dfrac{W}{2L}\right)^{\frac{n+1}{n}}$

Where,

R = Rolling resistance

n = co-efficient of wheel sinkage

K_c = cohesive modulus of soil deformation

K_ϕ = Friction modulus of soil deformation

B = Width of the each track

W = Vertical load on shearing area.

L = Length track in contact.

3. Write short notes on:
(a) Traction (b) Traction efficiency
(c) Rolling resistance (d) slip
(e) Rimpull (f) Weight transfer
(g) Cane index (h) Towing force number
(i) Motion resistance ratio

MULTIPLE QUESTIONS

1. The term applied to the driving force developed by a wheel track or other traction devices is known as
   (a) Traction (b) traction co-efficient
   (c) rim pull (d) tractive efficinecy

2. The ratio of total force obtained from the traction device to the dynamic weight is known as
   (a) traction (b) net co-efficient of traction
   (c) rim pull (d) tractive efficiency

3. The ratio of drawbar power to axle power is known as
   (a) traction (b) tractive efficiency
   (c) co-efficient of friction (d) none of the above

4. Tractive force available from engine power at tyre on ground contact is known as
   (a) rim·pull (b) tractive efficinecy
   (c) both (d) none of the above

5. The efficiecny of the most of tractors and trucks varies between
   (a) 50 to 60% (b) 60 to 70%
   (c) 80-85 % (d) none of the above

6. The ratio of the rolling resistance to the normal load (W) on traction device is known as
   (a) rim pull (b) tractive efficiency
   (c) motion resistance ratio (d) traction

7. Wheel (s) sleep is given by
   (a) $1 - \dfrac{V_a}{V_t}$ (b) $1 + \dfrac{V_a}{V_t}$
   (c) $1 - \dfrac{V_t}{V_a}$ (d) $1 + \dfrac{V_t}{V_a}$

8. The distance travelled per revolution of the traction device divided by 2π when operating at the specified condition
   - (a) traction
   - (b) rolling radius
   - (c) traction-efficiency
   - (d) none of the above

9. The torque of towed wheel is
   - (a) infinity
   - (b) zero
   - (c) both
   - (d) none of the above

10. The average force per unit base area required to force a cone shaped probe into soil at steady rate is known as
   - (a) cone index
   - (b) traction
   - (c) rolling radius
   - (d) none of the above

11. The ratio of soil thrust in the direction to normal land is known as
   - (a) traction co-efficient
   - (b) gross traction co-efficient
   - (c) traction efficiency
   - (d) none of the above

12. Drawbar power (DP) is given by
   - (a) drawbar pull & linear speed of tractor
   - (b) drawbar pull & linear acceleration of tractor
   - (c) both
   - (d) none

13. The drawbar load is increased the value of slip
   - (a) increases
   - (b) decreases
   - (c) remains constant
   - (d) none of the above

14. The power loss in traction decreases with
   - (a) increases in drawbar pull & linear speed
   - (b) decrease in drawbar pull & linear speed
   - (c) both
   - (d) none of the above

15. The power loss in traction increased with
   - (a) increase in moisture content
   - (b) decrease in moisture content
   - (c) In both condition
   - (d) none of the above

16. The weight transfer in traction is given by
   - (a) $\dfrac{\text{Pull x hitch height}}{\text{Wheel base}}$
   - (b) $\dfrac{\text{Wheel base}}{\text{hitch height}}$

342

(c) $\dfrac{\text{Pull}}{\text{Wheel base}}$

(d)   none of the above

17. The weight transfer in tractor increases with

     (a)   increases in pull   (b)   decrease in pull

     (c)   both   (d)   none of the above

18. In tractors, the rear part is heavier than the front to

     (a)   balance the body load

     (b)   get higher tractive efficiency

     (c)   both   (d)   none of the above

FILL UP THE BLANKS

1. The ability to provide draft to .... various types of implement is primary measure .... of a tractor.

2. .... is the term applied t the driving force developed by a wheel, tract or other traction devices.

3. .... is the ratio of total force obtained from the traction device to the dynamic weight.

4. .... propells a vehicle using traction force obtained from supporting force.

5. Ratio of drawbar power to axel power is known as ....

6. .... is the tractive force available from engine power at tyre an ground contact.

7. .... is the rolling resistance to the normal load.

8. Tractor trolley is .... a wheel.

9. Axle torque of towed wheel is ....

10. The average force per unit base area required to force a cone-shaped probe into soil at steady rate in known as ....

11. The efficiency of the most of tractors and trucks varies from .... %.

12. The S.I. unit of cane-index is ....

Ans. 1. pull, effectiveness 2. traction 3. net co-efficient of traction 4. traction device 5. tractive efficiency 6. rimpull 7. motion resistance ratio 8. towed or unpowered 9. zero 10. cone index 11. 80-85 12. N/m² or Pa.

ANSWER OF MULTIPLE CHOICE QUESTIONS

1 (a) 2 (b) 3 (b) 4 (a) 5 (c) 6 (c) 7 (a) 8 (b) 9 (b) 10 (a) 11 (b) 12 (a) 13 (a) 14 (a) 15 (a) 16 (a) 17 (a) 18 (a) 19 (b)

that

(d) None of the above

1. The required pull in traction increases with

(a) increase in pull   (b) decrease in pull
(c)   (d) none of the above

2. In tractors, the rear part is so made that the front to

(a) decrease the brief load
(c) high brake tractive efficiency
(e) both   (c) none of the above

FILL UP THE BLANKS

1. The ability to provide draft to the various types of implement is primary measure of a tractor.

2. .... is the term implied the driving force developed by a wheel, track or other traction device.

3. .... is the ratio of total force obtained from the traction device to the dynamic weight.

4. .... propels a vehicle using traction force obtained in transporting force.

5. Ratio of drawbar power to axle power is known as ....

6. .... is the tractive force available from engine power at tyre an ground contact.

7. .... is the rolling resistance to the normal load.

8. Tractor trolley load .... axle load.

9. Axle torque of towed wheel is ....

10. The average force per unit base area required to force a cone shaped probe into soil at steady rate is known as ....

11. The efficiency is the most of traction and much tractive force ....

12. The static of total cone index is ....

Ans. 1 pull efficiency 2 traction 3 net to efficient of traction 4 traction device 5 tractive efficiency 6 input 7 motion resistance ratio allowed or unpowered 9 zero 10 cone index 11 68 35 12 N, he or Ft.

ANSWER OF MULTIPLE CHOICE QUESTIONS

1 (a) 2 (b) 3 (b) 4 (c) 5 (c) 6 (c) 7 (c) 8 (b) 9 (b) 10 (a) 11 (b) 12 (b) 13 (b) 14 (a) 15 (a) 16 (a) 17 (a) 18 (a) 19 (b)

Chapter 15

Mechanics of Tractor

15.1 Machines of Rear Wheel Driven Tractor:

Assumption: The following asumptions are made regarding tractor are given below

(i) The ground surface is planer and nondeformable

(ii) The motion of the tractor can be analysed as two dimensional

(iii) Rotational motion of the front wheels is neglected.

(iv) Aerodynamic forces neglected.

Fig. 15.1 shows the forces and the reaction on tractor.

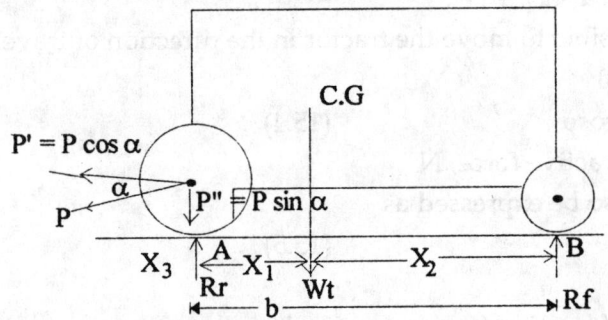

Fig. 15.1 Showing Forces and Reactions on Tractor

Let

P = Load behind the tractor

W_t = Wt. of tractor

R_r = Load on tyre of rear axle

R_f = Load on tyre of front axle

b = wheel base

Condition for stability

1. $\Sigma H = 0$

2. $\Sigma V = 0$

3. $\Sigma M = 0$

Where,

H = Horizontal forces

V = Vertical forces

M = Momentum

Case I: Tractor resting on ground (force P due to load is ineffective)

$\Sigma H = 0$, as tractor is not moving.

$$\Sigma V = 0 = R_r + R_f \qquad (15.1)$$

Taking moment about point A.

$\Sigma M_A = 0$

$w_t x_1 - R_f b = 0$

or $R_f = \dfrac{w_t x_1}{b} \qquad (15.2)$

Taking moment about point B.

$$\Sigma M_B = w_f x_2 - R_r b = 0 \qquad (15.3)$$

$R_r = \dfrac{w_t x_2}{b}$

Case (II): The tractor moving with a constant load P.

Assumption $F = F_a = F_p = F_r$

F = Force responsible to move the tractor in the direction of travel.

1. $\Sigma H = F - R - P' = 0$

or $P' = F - R = P \cos\alpha \qquad (15.4)$

$F - R = P' = $ Net tractive force, N

Equation may also be expressed as

$$P' = \mu N = \mu R_r \qquad (15.5)$$

Where,

μ = co-efficient of traction (property of soil)

i.e.; $R_r = \dfrac{w_t x_2}{b} + P'' + w_t \cdot b$

considering vertical force

$\Sigma V = R_r + R_f - W_t - P'' = 0$

or $R_r + R_f = w_t + P \cdot \sin\alpha \qquad (15.6)$

Considering moment about A

$\Sigma M_A = 0 = w_t x_1 - R_f b - P'' x_3 - P' y_1 = 0$

$R_f b = w_t x_1 - (x_3 P \sin\alpha + y_1 P \cos\alpha)$

or $R_f = \dfrac{w_t x_1}{b} - \dfrac{y_1 P \cos\alpha + x_3 P \sin\alpha}{b} \qquad (15.7)$

The term $\dfrac{y_1 P \cos\alpha + x_3 P \sin\alpha}{b}$ is called as weight transfer.

For stability in vertical plane

$$\frac{w_t x_1}{b} - \left(\frac{y_1 P\cos\alpha + x_3 P\sin\alpha}{b}\right) \geq 0$$

or $w_t x_1 \geq P (y_1 \cos \alpha + x_3 . \sin \alpha)$

$$\therefore P \leq \frac{w_t x_1}{y_1 \cos\alpha + x_3 . \sin\alpha} \qquad (15.8)$$

This gives limiting value of P considering weight transfer.

Considering moment about B,

$\Sigma M_B = R_r b - w_t x_2 - P' y_1 - P'' (b + x_3) = 0$

or $R_r b = w_t x_2 + y_1 P \cos\alpha + (b + x_3) P \sin\alpha$

or $R_r = \dfrac{w_t x_2}{b} + P \sin \alpha + \dfrac{P(y_1\cos\alpha + x_3\sin\alpha)}{b}$ $\qquad (15.9)$

$\dfrac{w_t x_2}{b}$ = Portion of the tractor weight coming over rear wheel

$P \sin \alpha$ = Vertical component of pull

$\dfrac{P(y_1\cos\alpha + x_3\sin\alpha)}{b}$ = Load transferred to the rear wheel

R_r is known as dynamic weight used to compute tractive capacity

$P' = \mu N = \mu R_r$

$$P' = \mu \left[\frac{w_t x_2}{b} + P\sin\alpha + \frac{P(y_1\cos\alpha + x_3\sin\alpha)}{b}\right]$$

or, $P\cos \alpha = \mu \; \dfrac{w_t x_2}{b} + \mu P \sin \alpha + \dfrac{P\mu(y_1\cos\alpha + x_3\sin\alpha)}{b}$

or $P \cos \alpha - \mu p \sin \alpha - \dfrac{P\mu(y\cos\alpha + x_3\sin\alpha)}{b} = \mu \, \dfrac{w_t x_2}{b}$

$$P = \frac{\mu w_t x_2}{(b - \mu y_1)\cos\alpha - (b + x_3)\mu\sin\alpha} \qquad (15.10)$$

This gives the limiting vale of P considering co-efficient of friction of soil under rear wheel. The lowest value of P computes from equation (15.10) and has to be used.

15.2 Mechanics of Grade and Non-Parallel Pull Drive Tractor: Fig. 15.2 shows the forces and the reaction on tractor.

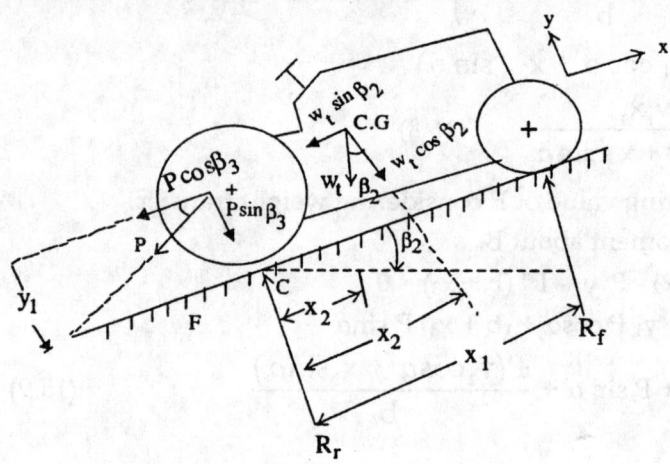

Fig. 15.2 Shwoing Forces and Reactions on Tractor

1. Force Equillibrium

(a) Force in x - direction

$\Sigma Fx = 0$

$F - W_t \sin \beta_2 - P \cos \beta_3 = 0$ (15.11)

(b) Forces in y-direction

$\Sigma Fy = 0$

$R_r + R_f - W_t \cos \beta_2 - P \sin \beta_3 = 0$ (15.12)

2. Moment Equillibrium:

Taking moment about point C, we have

$\Sigma M_c = 0$

$w_t x_2' - Py_1' - R_f . x_1 = 0$

or $R_f = \dfrac{w_t x'_2 - Py'_1}{x_1}$ (15.13)

Substituting the value in equation ( ), we have

$R = P \sin \beta_3 + \dfrac{P_{yi}}{x_1} + w_t \cos \beta_2 - \dfrac{w_t x_2}{x_1}$ (15.14)

Here, the weight transfer is because of pull (P),

Weight transfer $= \dfrac{Py'_1}{x_1} P \sin \beta$ (15.15)

Effect of angle β_2 and β_3 on tipping condition:

(a) Effect of β_2: The more is value of B₃, the more is value of drawbar pull or pulling force.

(b) Effect to β_3:

Since ; $F - w_t \sin \beta_2 - P \cos \beta_3 = 0$

$$\therefore P = \frac{F - w_t \sin \beta_2}{\cos \beta_3}$$

From above relation, we see that increase in valve β_2 which results into decrease in pulling force.

It has been also find that increase in value of B₂ which results into decrease in soil reaction force (R_r).

15.3 Turning of Tractor at High Speed:

(a) Tricyclic tractor:

Fig. 15.3 (a) and Fig. 15.3 (b) show the forces on three wheel tractor

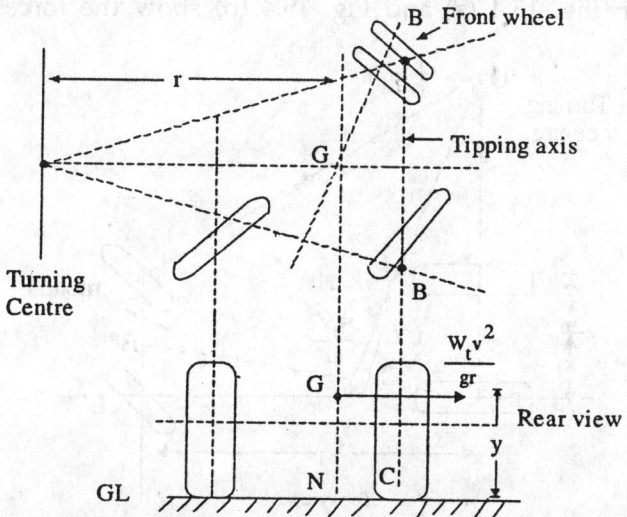

Fig. 15.3 Showing Forces and Reactions on Tricyclic Tractor

Two types of moment acting about C' which are commonly known as overturning moment and stabilizing moment. To avoid over-turning of tractor in sideways, the following condition must be satisfy,

Over turning moment ≥ stabilizing moment.

$$\frac{w_t v_2}{gr} \times y \geq w_t . x$$

or $\dfrac{v^2}{gr} \times y \geq x$

$$\therefore v \geq \sqrt{\frac{grx}{y}} \qquad (15.17)$$

Where, r = Radius of turning

g = Acceleration due to gravity

x = Tread width/2

y = vertical distance of C.G. of the tractor

v = velocity of the tractor

Condition to avoid over turning of tractor at high speed: The following are the main conditions to avoid over-turning of a tractor at high speed.

(a) C.G. should be as low as possible to the ground.

(b) Truck width should be larger.

(c) Turning radius should be large.

4. Wheel tractor: Fig. 15.4 (a) and Fig. 15.4 (b) show the forces in four wheel tractor.

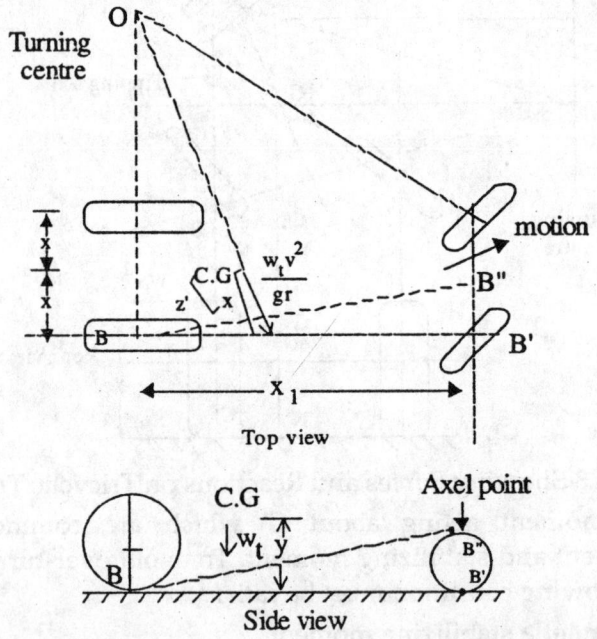

Fig. 15.4 Showing Forces and Reactions on Tractor

15.5. Centre of Gravity (C.G):

Centre of gravity of a tractor refers to that point on body at which its weight is acting. In a tractor, the centre of gravity (C.G.) should be located rod of the wheel base ahead of the rear wheel. In most of the tractors the centre of gravity located towards the rear wheel. Exact location of the centre of gravity can be determined by the following methods.

1. Suspension method 2. Balancing method 3. Weighing method.

15.5.1. Suspension Method: The tractor is suspended from any convenient point (part), strong enough to carry its as shown in Fig.. 15.5 (a). The centre of gravity will be the vertical plane through the point of suspension. By repeating this operation with another point of suspension another plane may be located and its intersection with the previous line well determine the centre of gravity as shown in Fig.15.5. (b)

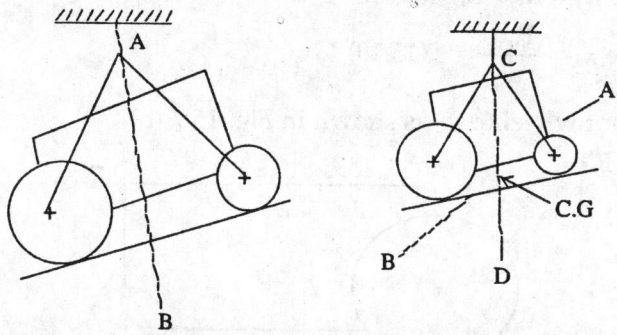

Fig. 15.5. Showing measurement of centre of Gravity by Suspension Method

15.5.2. Balancing Method: This method is used in track type of tractor. A plumb bob and a large timber block equal in length to overall width of tractor and about six inches or more thick are required.

Drive the block upto balance (tipping point) as shown in Fig. 15.6 (a). Making the line AB with the help of plumb bob. Then something is done in reverse direction as shown in Fig. 15.6 (b). Draw the line CD. Intersection of AB and CD be C.G.

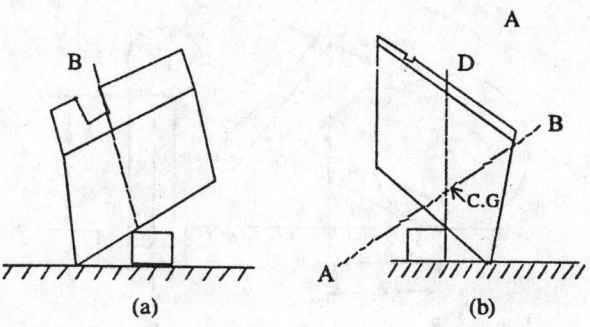

(a)   (b)

Fig. 15.6. Measurement of centre of Gravity by Balancing Method

15.3.3. Weighing Method: This method is used in wheel type of tractor.

Procedure to locate C.G. of a tractor through weighing method:

Assumptions:

1. C.G. lies at coordinates (x_1, y_1) as shown in the figure.

2. Operator, oil and fuel does not offset locating C.G.

Objective: To compute or locate x_1 and y_1, the coordinates of the C.G.

Procedure:

Step 1: Measure wheel base 'b'.

Step 2: Measure R_r and R_f using a plate form balance/weight bridge as shown in Fig. 15.7 (a)

Step 3: Calculate $w_t = R_r + R_f$ (15.18)

Step 4 : Calculate $x_1 = \dfrac{R_f.b}{w_t}$ (15.19)

Step 5 : Raise front wheel to y_2 as shown in Fig. 15.7 (b)

Step 6: Measure R'_f

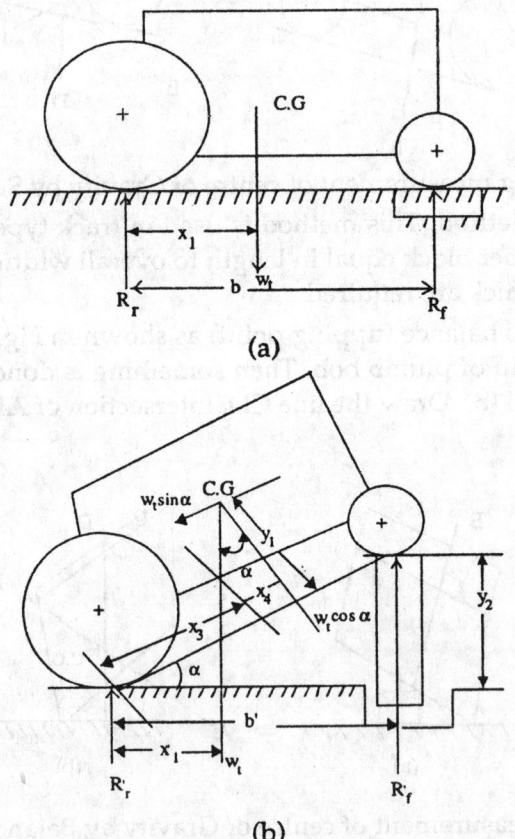

(a)

(b)

Fig. 15.7 Showing Forces and Reactions on Tractor

Step 7: Compute, $\alpha = \left(\sin^{-1}\left(\dfrac{y_2}{b}\right)\right)$ (15.20)

Step 8: Compute $b' = y_2 \cdot \cot \alpha$ (15.21)

Step 9 : Compute $x_1' = \dfrac{R_f' b'}{w_t}$ (15.22)

Step 10: Compute $x_3 = x_1' \sec \alpha$ (15.23)

Step 11: Compute $x_4 = x_1 - x_3$ (15.24)

Step 12: compute $y_1 = x_4 \cdot \cot \alpha$ (15.25)

$\therefore$ Coordinate of C.G. (x_1, y_1) from step-4 and step-12

Another Method (Weighting Method):

Referring Fig. 15.8 (a) and Fig. 15.8 (b), C.G. of tractor can be determined as follows

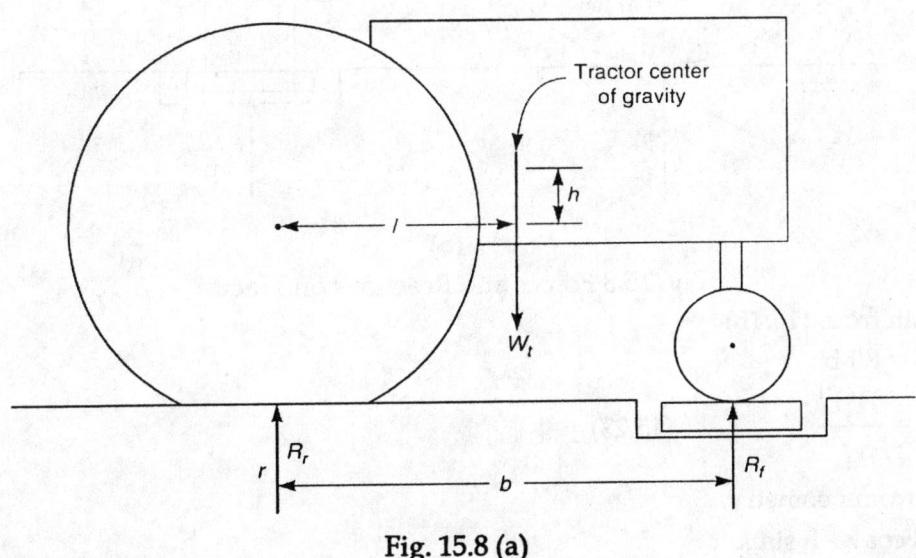

Fig. 15.8 (a)

Taking moment about A.

$\Sigma M_A = 0$

$w_t \cdot l = R_f b$

$\therefore l = \dfrac{R_f b}{w_t}$ (15.26)

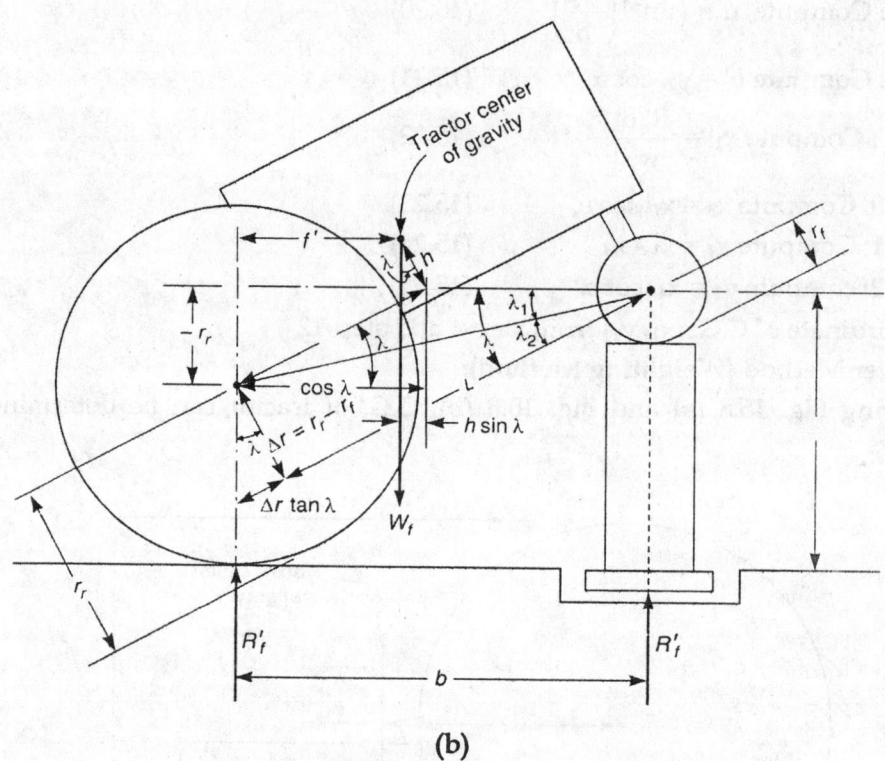

(b)

Fig. 15.8 Forces and Reactions on Tractor

Again from Fig. (b)

$w_t \, l' = R'f \, b'$

or $l' = \dfrac{R'_f b'}{w_t}$ (15.27)

But from geometry,

$l' = l \cos \lambda - h \sin \lambda$

Thus equatin (15.27) can be written as

$\dfrac{R'_f b'}{w_t} = l \cos \lambda - h \sin \lambda$ (15.28)

$\therefore b' = (l \cos \lambda - h \sin \lambda) \dfrac{w_t}{R'_f}$

$\therefore b' = (b + \Delta r \tan \lambda) \cos \lambda$ (15.29)

Substituting Equating equations

354

$$(l \cos \lambda - h \sin \lambda) \frac{w_t}{R_f} = (b + \Delta r \tan \lambda) \cos \lambda$$

or $h = \dfrac{w_t . l - R'_f b}{w_t . \tan \lambda} - \dfrac{R'_f . \Delta r}{w_t}$ (15.30)

Again, $\lambda = \lambda_1 + \lambda_2$ (15.31)

$\text{Tan } \lambda_1 = \dfrac{(n-r_r)}{b'}$ (15.32)

$\text{Tan } \lambda_2 - \dfrac{\Delta r}{b}$ (15.33)

An approximate value of b' for determining the value of b' is also given as

$b' = \sqrt{b^2 - (n-r_r)^2 + (\Delta r)^2}$ (15.34)

Weight Transfer: The process of weight transfer works simply on law of mechanics as discussed below.

Take a rod of 1.5 m. put a wedge at a distance of 0.5 m as shown in Fig. 15.9 Now add a weight of 10 N an smaller end. This wt can be balanced by

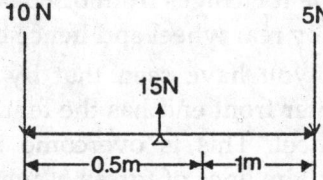

Fig. 15.9 Showing Forces on a Rod

adding a wt. of 5N on bigger side of the rod and the pivot point has taken up a load of 15 N. Thus we have seen by arranging a fulcrum in such a way we have been able to balance the rod by putting a wt. of 15 N so that the total wt. of 15 N is affected by at fulcrum.

The same principle can be applied to a tractor with implements, by designing the same in such a way that the wheel base of the tractor acts as long and the distance from the centre of the rear wheel to the implement centre of gravity as a short end which is kept as a half length of wheel base. Thus the centre of the wheel becomes 1.5 times heavier than the rear wt. of tractor, which inturn improves grip on field as shown in Fig. 15.10.

In actual practice it is not on the implement. wt., but there the other wts. also like soil wt., resistance etc. which is tabulated as under with 2-bottom Mold Board plough.

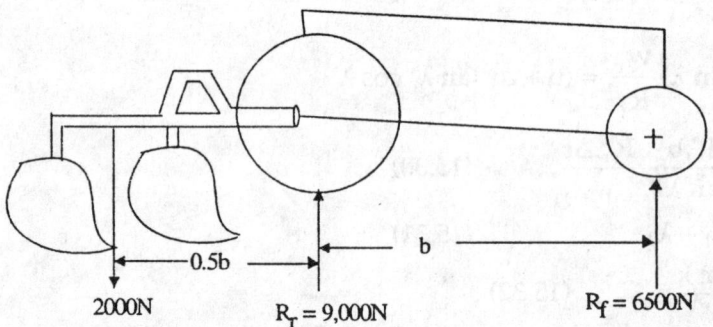

0.5b

b

2000N R_r = 9,000N R_f = 6500N

Fig. 15.10 Forces and Reactions on Tractor and Implements

Table 15.1

1 term	Rear axle (R_r)	Front axle (R_f)
Tractor wt (15,500 N)	9,000 N	6,500 N
Implement wt. (2000 N)	+ 3,000 N	- 1,000 N
Resistance (1000 N)	+ 1,500 N	- 500 N
Soil wt. (500 N)	+ 750 N	-250 N
	14,250 N	4,750 N

From the Table 15.1 it will be seen that load on rear axle changes from 9,000 N to 14,250 N and on the front axle it changes from 6,500 N to 4,750 N as implement is put to work, which big gain by rear wheel and hence better traction.

From the above paragraph you have seen that by wt. transfer the front end becomes lighter, but the lighter front end has the tendency to lift the front and or twist back around rear wheel. This is overcome by the compression forces developed by in the top link, the lines of forces of which acts on the centre of the front axle also over comes the draft force tending to take plough pivot above the cross-shaft as such implements are known as semi mounted.

Note: The drawbar pull of the tractor tyre is usually equal to half the weight carried on the rear wheel.

Prob. 15.1 A tractor weighing 14.5 kN and wheel base as 140 cm is moving up the slope 1 in 20 (vertical : horizontal) without load at a speed of 30 km/h. The C.G. is located 20 cm ahead of rear axle and 75 cm above the ground level. if the co-efficient of friction between the ground and the tyres is 04. Find the distance travelled after the application of brake in rear wheel.   [GATE-1997]

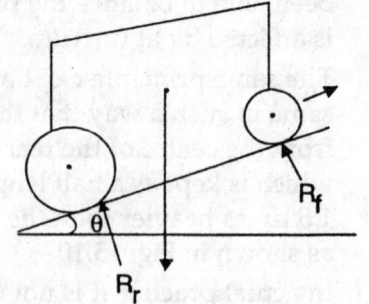

Fig. 15.11

Soln. Given u = 30 km/h = 8.33 m/s

v = 0, h = 0.75 m

L_1 = 140 cm = 1.4 m

$L_2 = 20$ cm $= 0.2$ m

$\tan \theta = \dfrac{1}{20}$, $\mu = 0.4$

$\cos \theta = 0.998$

we know that

$v^2 = u^2 - 2as$

or $S = \dfrac{u^2 - v^2}{2a} = \dfrac{(8.33)^2 - 0}{2a}$

$S = \dfrac{34.72}{a}$ \hspace{1cm} (1)

When the brakes applied on Rear wheel then

$a = \dfrac{\mu g \cos \theta \, (L_1 - L_2)}{L_1 + \mu h} + g \sin \theta$

$\dfrac{0.4 \times 9.8 \times 0.998 \times (1.4 - 0.2)}{(1.4 + 0.4 \times 0.75)} + 9.8 \times 0.05$

$= 3.25$ m/s^2

Substituting these valves of a in equation (i) we get,

$S = \dfrac{34.72}{3.25}$ m

$= 10.69$ m Ans.

Prob. 15.2. A tractor with a mass of 1600 kg develops a maximum tractive effort of 3000 N in top gear on a concrete surface. The total rolling resistance is 160 N. If the gradient angle is defined as the angle that the inclined plane makes with the horizontal, the maximum gradient can be negotiated by the tractor is (a) 10.44° (b) 11.63° (c) 29.4° (d) 34.29°　　　[GATE-2004]

Soln. Given, F = 3000 N

$m_t = 1600$ kg

TF or R = 160 N

Refering Fig. 15.12

In the limiting case

$3000 = m_t g \sin \theta + 160$

or $mg \sin \theta = 2840$

or $\sin \theta = \dfrac{2840}{m_t g} = \dfrac{2840}{1600 \times 9.8}$

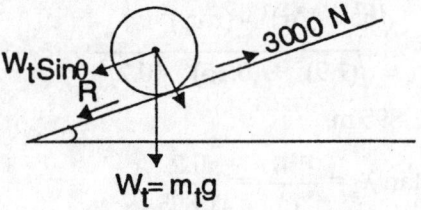

Fig. 15.12

357

= 0.18112

$\therefore \theta = \sin^{-1}(0.18112)$

= 10.44°

Therefore answer is (a)

Prob. 15.3. Static front and rear end reactions of a tractor on level ground are 3.92 kN and 11.77 kN respectively. The corresponding wheel diameters are 0.9 m and 1.2 m and the wheel base is 1.9 m. When front wheels were raised by 0.8 m. The rear end reaction was increased to 12.75 kN. Calculate the position of centre of gravity of the tractor. [GATE-2000]

Sol. Given: R_f = 3.92 kN. R_r = 11.77 kN

D_f = 0.9 m, D_r = 1.2 m

R_f = 0.45 m, r_r = 0.6 m

b = 1.90 m, n = 0.8 m

R_r' = 12.75 kN

Refering fig. 9.3 and 9.4

$W_t = R_r + R_f$

= (3.92 + 11.77)

= 15.162 kN

$\Delta_r = r_r - r_f = 0.60 - 0.45$

= 0.15 m

$n - r_r = 0.8 - 0.6 = 0.2$

we know that

$$l = \frac{R_f \times b}{W_t} = \frac{3.92 \times 1.9}{15.162} = 0.496 \text{ m}$$

$R'f$ = 15.162 - 12.75

= 2.42 kN

Again,

$$b' = \frac{\sqrt{b^2 + (\Delta r)^2 - (n - r_r)^2}}{}$$

$$= \sqrt{(1.9)^2 + (0.15)^2 - (0.2)^2}$$

= 1.895 m

or $\tan \lambda_1 = \dfrac{n - r_r}{L'} = \dfrac{0.2}{1.895}$

or $\tan \lambda_1 = 0.1055$

or $\lambda_1 = \tan^{-1}(0.1055)$

$\therefore \lambda_1 = 6.0235$

$$\tan \lambda_2 = \frac{\Delta r}{b} = \frac{0.15}{0.19} = 0.079$$

or $\lambda_2 = \tan^{-1}(0.079)$

$\therefore \lambda_2 = 4.5$

Again $\lambda = \lambda_1 + \lambda_2 = 6.0235 + 4.5$

$\lambda = 10.54$

$b' = (b + \Delta r \tan\lambda)\cos\lambda$

$= (1.9 + 0.15 \tan 10.54)\cos 10.54$

$= 1.8953$ m Ans.

$$l' = \frac{R'b'}{w_t} = \frac{2.42 \times 10^3 \times 1.8953}{15.169 \times 10^3} = 1.17 \text{ m}$$

$$h = \frac{w_t . l - R'_f b}{w_t \tan \lambda} - \frac{R'_f \Delta r}{w_t}$$

$$\frac{15.169 \times 0.496 - 2.42 \times 1.9}{15.169} - \frac{2.42 \times 0.2}{15.169}$$

$= 100.4$ cm

Therefore, C.G. $= 60 + 100.4 = 160.4$ cm Ans.

Prob. 15.4 A four wheel tractor weighing 25 kN has a wheel base =1.2 m. The C.G. is located on a vertical plane 0.4 m ahead of rear axle. Determine the maximum drawbar pull that a tractor can exert on a level road where co-efficient of rolling resistance is 0.04 and co-efficient of traction between the road surface and tyres is 0.5. The hitch height may be between 0.4 m Also calculate the rimpull if time is no slip.   [GATE-1995]

Soln. Given. $b = 1.2$ m, $x_1 = 0.4$ m, $x_1 = 0.4$ m

$W_t = 25$ kN

Referring fig. 15.1

Taking moment about A.

$W_t x_1 - R_f b - Py_1 = 0$

or $25 \times 0.4 - R_f \times 1.2 - P \times 0.4 = 0$

or $1.2 R_f + 0.4 p = 10$ (i)

and, $R_r + R_f = 25$.   (ii)

Again, $\dfrac{P}{R_r} = (0.5 - 0.04)$

Therefore, equation (i) becomes

$1.2 R_f + 0.4 \times 0.46 R_r = 10$ (iii)

Solving equation (ii) and (iii) we have

R_r = 19.68 KN

∴ Maximum drawbar pull = 0.46 x R_r = 0.46 x 19.68 = 9.05 KN Ans.

Rimpull = N.R_r

= 0.5 x 19.68 = 9.84 kN Ans.

Prob. 15.5 Tractor may over turn during high centre of gravity. The critical speed (Sc) of a tractor weighing W kg taking a turn at high speed is a function of the radius of the turn (r), the location of the C.G. (Xeg, Zcy) and the distance from tractor C.G. to tipping axis (Y). Calculate the critical turning speed at which side tipping would begin with minimum wheel spacing, given that r = 5200 mm, Xeg = 658 mm, Z cy = 988 m, rear thread with = 1253 mm, wheel base = 3450 mm and W = 25.6 kN   [GATE-2001]

Refering figure 9.2 (b)

Soln. Given : W = 25.6 kN, Zcy = 988 mm,

$r = 5200$ mm = 5.2 m, $\dfrac{y}{2} = \dfrac{1253}{2} = 0.6265$ m

we know

$$\frac{w}{g} \cdot \frac{v^2}{r} \cdot Zcy = W \cdot \frac{y}{2}$$

$$v = \sqrt{\frac{g.r.y}{2.Zcy}}$$

$$= \sqrt{\frac{9.8 \times 5.2 \times 0.6265}{0.988}}$$

= 5.683 m/s Ans.

Prob. 15.6 Frequency of oscillation of 1700 kg tractor when suspended from a point 0.35 Hz. If the distance between the centre of gravity (C.G.) and the pivot is 1.3 m, Calculate the moment of inertia of the tractor about on axis passing through its C.G.   [GATE-2000]

Soln. Given: m = 1700 kg, v (frequency = 0.35 Hz), R_0 = 1.3 m, l_0 = ?

we know

$$T = 2\pi \sqrt{\frac{I_o}{mgL}}$$

$$\text{or } \frac{1}{v} = 2\pi \sqrt{\frac{I_o}{mgL}}$$

or $I_o = \dfrac{1}{v^2} \dfrac{mgL}{4\pi^2}$

$= \dfrac{1}{(0.35)^2} \cdot \dfrac{1700 \times 9.8 \times 1.3}{4 \times (3.14)^2} = 4482.94 \text{ kgm}^2$

$I_t = I_o - mR_o^2$

$= 4483.9 - 1700 \times (1.3)^2$

$= 1609.97 \text{ kgm}^2$ Ans.

Prob. 15.7 A tractor having 130 cm tread, travels along a 30 m diameters path. The C.G. of the tractor is at a height of the 0.85 m from the ground. Calculate the speed of travel at which the tractor will experience a sideways overturning.
[GATE-2000]

Soln. Given : Refering Fig. 9.2 (b)

$y = 130 \text{ cm} = 1.3 \text{ m}, D = 30 \text{ m} Zcy = 0.85 \text{ m}$

$r = 15 \text{ m}, \dfrac{y}{2} = \dfrac{1.3}{2} = 0.65 \text{ m}$

we know

$\dfrac{w_t}{g} \cdot \dfrac{v_2}{r} = w_t \cdot \dfrac{y}{2}$

or, $v = \sqrt{\dfrac{y}{2} \cdot \dfrac{gr}{Zcy}}$

$= \sqrt{\dfrac{0.65 \times 9.8 \times 15}{0.85}}$

$v = 10.6 \text{ m/s}.$

PROBLEMS

1.   A four wheel tractor weigh in 30 kN has a drawbar power of 22.4 kW. It pulls a trail implement at a speed of 5 kmph on a level ground. The centre of gravity of tractor is 800 mm ahead of rear axle and 1000 mm above the ground and wheel base is 2500 mm. The total contact area of the rear wheel is 0.1 m² while point of hitch is located 400 mm above the ground surface and behind the rear axle. Assuming angle of internal friction as 20o and cohesion co-efficient as 10 kPa. Compute.

     (i) The angle of inclination of the line of pull.

     (ii) Soil reaction at rear and front wheel.

     (iii)Weight transfer if angle of inclination remains unchanged what is the maximum pull. (49.47o, 9.78 kN, 7.86 kN)

2. A four wheel rubber tyre tractor is moving with a speed of 18 kmph up a slope of 12°. The tractor is pulling 3 bottom 40 cm MB plough makes as angle of 20° with ground and is a distance of 37.50 cm from rear wheel contact point. Calculate the drawbar pull and drawbar power at the limiting case i.e., the tractor is about to topple on rear wheel. Assume weight is 700 mm and radius of front wheel is 350 mm. Weight carried by front wheel on level ground is 6.30 kN. Weight carried by front when lifted 46 cm is 5.4 kN. Taking average soil pressure 70 K_B. Calculate depth of penetration. (40.63 cm)

   Calculate the C.G. of a tractor of following dimensions.
   (i) Wheel base -2500 mm
   (ii) Radius m of rear wheel = 720 mm
   (iii)Width of rear wheel = 260 mm
   (iv)Total weight of tractor = 18 kN
   (v) Weight carried by front wheel = 6.5 kN
   (vii) Weight carried by front wheels when lifted 460 mm from ground is 5.40 kN.   (0.903 m, 1.09 m)

3. A four-wheel tractor weigh in 3000 kN is climbing up a slope of 20%. The tractor is having wheel base of 2000 cm a dn drawbar height of 40 cm. The centre of gravity is located 100 cm infront of the rear axle and 80 cm gravity of ground. The area of contact of each rear wheel with soil is 1.0 m². The soil parameters are cohesion, C = 13.37 kPa, angle of internal friction, ϕ = 27°. Find the maximum drawbar pull of the pull is assumed to be parallel to the soil surface and the engine power is not limiting. The rolling resistance can be neglected. Also calculate the maximum grace, which the tractor can negotiate without dangering the side and longitudinal stability. (Ans. 971.62 kN)

4. A rear wheel drive tractor with a total weight of 23 kN has a wheel base of 2100 mm and centre of gravity of a 710 mm ahead of rear axle centre live. The tractor is pulling a level drawbar pull of 15 kN an a concrete surface at a forward speed of 6 km/h and the drawbar height is 485 mm. The axle power is 33.3 kW. Determine
   (a) Weight transfer on rear axle.
   (b) Co-efficient of traction
   (c) Tractive efficiency. (Ans. 3.47 KN, 80.2%, 74.7%)

MULTIPLE CHOICE QUESTIONS

1. Weight transfer of tractor depends upon
   (a) dead wt. of tractor supported by rear wheel (b) vertical component of pull (c) weight transfer from front wheel (d) all of the above

2. $P \dfrac{(y_1 \cos + x_3 \sin)}{b}$ refers.

    (a) Load transfered to the rear wheel (b) weight transfer (c) both (d) none of the above

3. The drawbar pull of the tractor tyre is usually equal to
    (a) half the wt. carried on rear wheel (b) three fourth the wt. carried on real wheel (c) equal the wt. carried on rear wheel on rear wheel (d) none of the above

4. Overturning moment is generally
    (a) less than stablizing moment (b) greater than stablizing moment (c) equal (d) (b) & (c)

5. Centre of gravity of a tractor refer to a point on body at which
    (a) Its wt. acting (b) its mass acting
    (c) both   (d) none of the above

6. Centre of gravity of tractor is located by
    (a) Suspension method (b) balancing method (c) weighing method (d) all of the above

7. Kinetic energy of tractor is given by

    (a) $\dfrac{1}{2}m_t v^2$ (b) $\dfrac{1.1}{2}m_t v^2$

    (c) $\dfrac{1}{3}m_t v^2$ (d) $\dfrac{1}{4}m_t v^2$

8. Dead weight of tractor is given by
    (a) dynamic weight   (b) weight transfer
    (c) both   (d) None of the above

9. The more is the wt. transfer results into
    (a) better tractive power   (b) poor tractive power
    (c) constant tractive power   (d) none of the above

ANSWER OF MULTIPLE CHOICE QUESTIONS
1 (d) 2 (a) 3 (a) 4 (d) 5 (c) 6 (d) 7 (b) 8 (a) 9 (a)

Chapter 16
Hydraulic System & Control

16.1. Introduction: Hydraulic system is a circuit in which force and power are transmitted through a fluid, generally an oil. This system has great importance in tractor. Hydraulic system is a mechanism provided in tractors to raise, hold or lower the mounted or semi-mounted implements. The hydraulic system of a modern tractor enables the operator to operate mounted or pull-type implements quickly and easily with a weight transfer attachment , the hydraulic system aids in improving traction by transfering weight brom trailing implements and the front of the tractor to the drive wheels as shown in Fig. 16.1 and Fig. 16.2. It helps in working of three point hitch of the tractor safety.

The hydraulic system, as in the case of electrical circuit, is complicated to under stand it. Therefore, specific symbols are used to describe them. The symbols known as graphical symbol for fluid power diagram must necessarily be understand to learn hydraulic system.

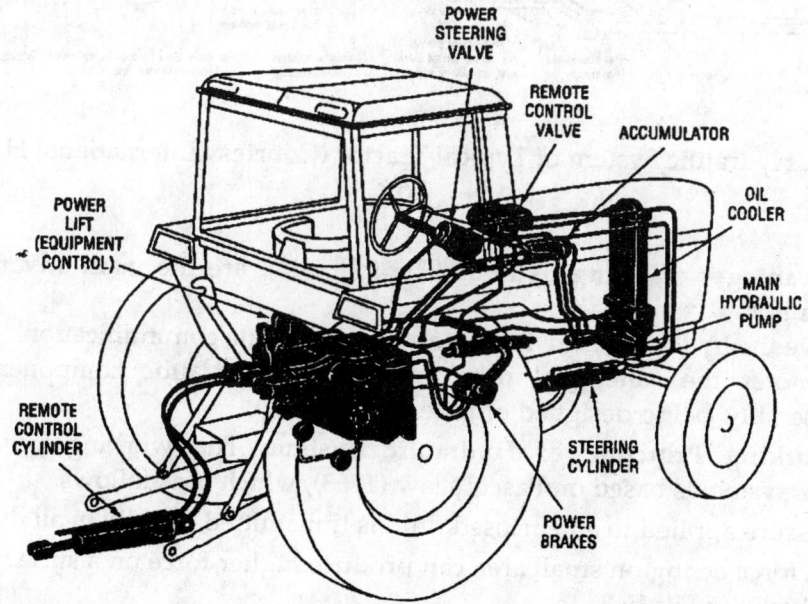

Fig. 16.1 Tractor with Full Hydrauls (Courtesy John Deere Moline ill)

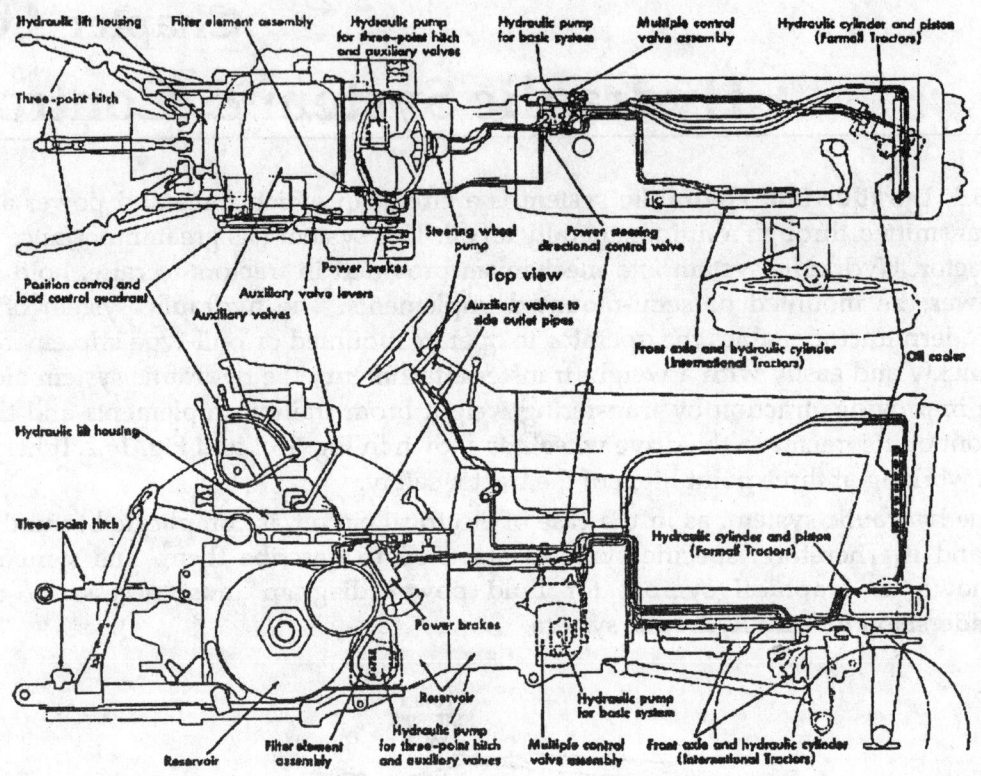

Fig. 16.2. Hydraulic System of Typical Tractor (Courtesy International Harvester Co.)

16.2. Advantages of Using Symbol: The following are the main advantages of using symbol:

(i)   Save the hydraulic drawing time and simplify its communication.

(ii)   Denotes the functional requirement of a hydraulic component or its assembly being designed or redesigned.

16.3. Working Principle of Hydraulic System: The working principal of hydraulic system is based on Pascal's law (1963), which is as follows:

"The pressure applied to an enclosed fluid is transmitted equally in all direction".

i.e.; shall force acting on small area can produce higher force on a surface of large area as shown in Fig 16.3.

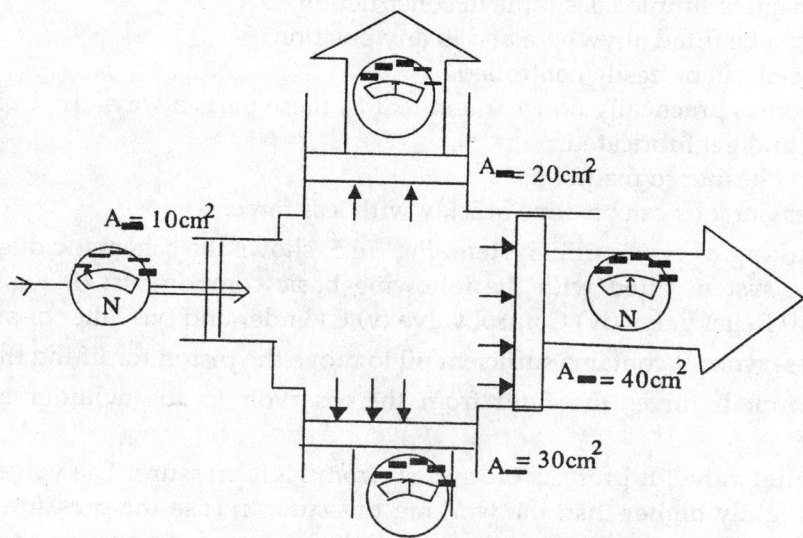

Fig. 16.3 Showing Forces Acting on Area

Examples: If we take two cylinder one having cross-sectional area 0.10 m² and the other having cross-sectional area 1.0 m² contact both the cylinder with a suitable pipe as shown in Fig. 16.4. Fill these cylinders with water or any other fluid and place to matching piston in both the cylinder. Then press the smaller cylinder with 10 N weight by 100 mm (0.1 m). The bigger cylinder being interconnected with raise its piston by 10 mm (0.01 m) and carry a load 100 N.

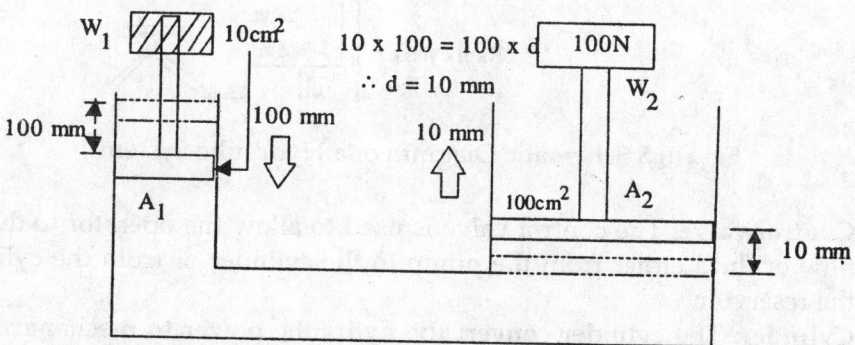

Fig. 16.4 Forces Acting on Different Dimension Area

Volume of fluid displaced by piston A = volume displace by piston B.

16.4 Advantages of Hydraulic System: It has following advantages:

(i)   It is easy in operation.

(ii) Design is simple i.e. simple in construction.

(iii) It can be fitted anywhere and in any position.

(iv) Speed can be easily controlled.

(v) There is practically no wear and tear as these parts always run in hydraulic oil and get lubricated.

(vi) It is cheaper to maintain.

(vii) Heavier jobs can be done quickly with less force.

16.5. Working of Hydraulic System: Fig. 16.5. shows the schematic diagram of a hydraulic system fitted with the following basic components: (i) Reservoir (ii) Pump (iii) Relief valve (iv) Control valve (v) Cylinder and (vi) Filter or strainer.

(i) **Reservoir:** It contains sufficient oil to move the piston for lifting the load.

(ii) **Pump:** It forces the fluid from the reservoir to the cylinder at specific pressure.

(iii) **Relief valve:** It protects the system from high pressure. The valve is set for slightly higher than the working pressure. In case the pressure increases beyond the working pressure the relief valve opens allowing the fluid to pass into the reservoir. Also, when the piston reaches its extreme position, the relief valve opens to bypass the oil.

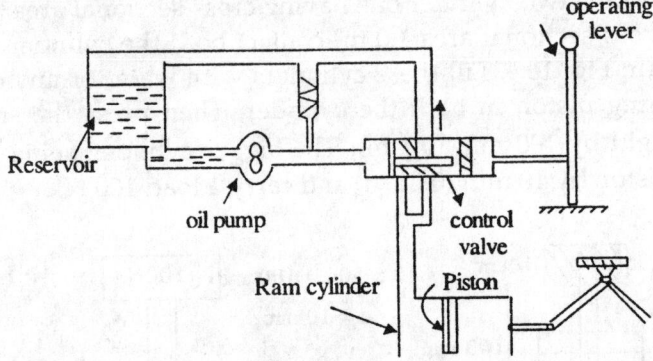

Fig. 16.5 Schematic Diagram of a Hydraulic System

(iv) **Control valve:** The control valve is used to allow the operator to direct the flow of fluid either from the pump to the cylinder or from the cylinder to the reservoir.

(v) **Cylinder:** The cylinder convert the hydraulic power to mechanical power for doing various jobs.

16.5 Components of Hydraulic Circuit: Following are the main components of hydraulic circuit.

16.6.1 Pump: The pump is basically a mechanical device which increases pressure energy of a liquid. Hydraulic pump is the heart of the hydraulic system.

Hydraulic pump pumps the hydraulic oil to the various components of hydraulic system.

(A) Types of Pump: Basically following two types of pumps are used in agricultural machine.

(i)   Variable displacement pump

(ii) Positive displacement pump

But in hydraulic system, positive displacement pumps are used. Positive displacement may be categories into two types namely: (a) reciprocating pump and (b) rotary pump

But rotary pumps are used in hydraulic system because of space limitation. The rotary pump may be constant flow pump (gear pump, screw pump, vane pump, etc.) and variable flow pump (axial and radial piston pump).

In a constant flow pump volume of oil for a given speed remains the same. The rate of flow will change with change in speed. In hydraulic system fitted with a constant flow pump, when the piston of the cylinder reaches its dead end or when the spool valve is brought to the neutral position, the oil delivered by the pump is diverted to the reservoir either through relief valve or spool valve. In the case of the variable-flow pump the volume of oil can be changed even-at the same speed. When the pistion of the cylinder reaches dead end or the valve is put to neutral, the pump stops delivering further oil. The rate of flow is governed by the presure-sensing devices of the pumps. A spur gear pump is normally used on tractor hydraulic systems of lower pressure as shown in Fig. 16.6.

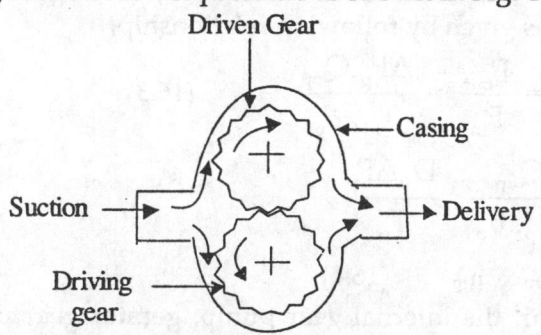

Fig. 16.6 Gear pump

(B) Matheology of Pump:

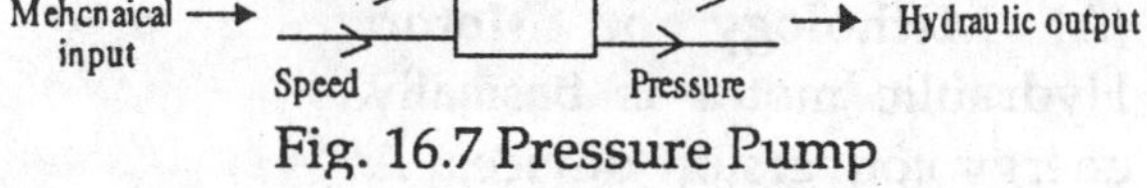

Hydraulic pump is basically energy conversion devices. A pump converts mechanical energy into hydraulic energy. Its inputs are mechanical torque speed and output are discharge and pressure as shown in Fig. 16.7.

Fig. 16.7 Pressure Pump

(C) Pump Performance:

(i)   Volumetric Efficiency (η_{VP}): It is defined as the ratio of flow that results in pump speed (the ideal flow) to the flow supplied to pump. It is given by following relationship,

$$\eta_{Vp} = \left(\frac{\theta_{op}}{\theta_{ip}}\right) = \frac{Q_{op}}{D_p.\theta p} \times 100 \text{ , \%} \qquad (16.1)$$

where,

Q_{ip} = Discharge input to pump, m³/s

Q_{op} = Discharge rate of pump, m³/min

D_p = Pump displacement per revolution, m³/rev

θ_p = Pump speed, rpm

(ii) Torque or Mechanical Efficiency (η_{tp}): It is defined as the ratio of actual to ideal torque delivered by the pump. It is given by following relationship,

$$\eta_{tp} = \frac{D_p.\Delta P_p}{2\pi T_{pi}} \times 100 \text{ , \%} \qquad (16.2)$$

Where,

T_{Pi} = Input torque of the motor, Nm

ΔP_p = Pressure drop across pump, N/m²

Overall Efficiency: It is defined as the ratio of actual power to the hydraulic power supplied. It is given by following relationship,

$$\eta_{op} = \frac{P_{out}}{P_{in}} = \frac{\Delta P_p.Q_{op}}{T_{Pi}.\theta_p} \qquad (16.3)$$

$$= \frac{Q_{op}}{D_p.\theta_p} \cdot \frac{D_p\Delta P_p}{T_{pi}}$$

$$= \eta_{vp} \times \eta_{tp} \qquad (16.4)$$

Note: The spur-gear, the internal gear pump, gerator gear pump and the vane-type pump are all used on tractor hydraulic system where lower pressure are used.

16.6.2 Motor:

(A) Methology of Motor: Hydraulic motor is basically energy conversion devices. A

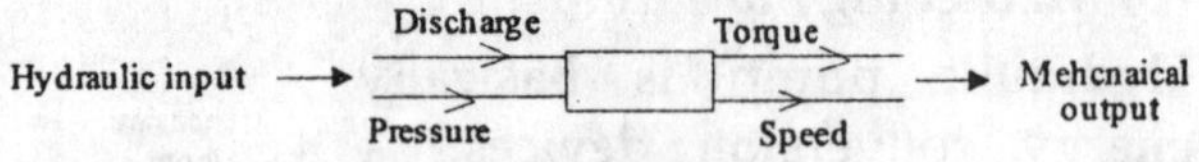

Fig. 16.8 Motor

motor converts hydraulic energy into mechanical energy. Its inputs are discharge and pressure and outputs are torque and speed as shown in Fig. 16.8.

(B) Motor Performance:

(i) Volcemetric Efficiency (η_{vm}): It is defined as the ratio of flow that results into motor speed (the ideal flow) to the flow supplied to the motor. It is given by following relationship,

$$\eta_{vm} = \frac{D_m . \theta_m}{Q_{op}} \times 100, \% \qquad (16.5)$$

D_m = Motor displacement per revolution, m^3/rev

θm = Motor speed, rpm

(ii) Torque or Mechanical Efficiency: It is defined as the ratio of actual to ideal torque delivered by the motor. It is given by following relationship,

$$\eta_{tm} = \frac{2\pi T_{om}}{D_m . \Delta P_m} \times 100, \% \qquad (16.6)$$

Where, T_{om} = Output torque of motor, Nm

Δp_m = Total pressure drop across the motor, N/m^2

Dm = Motor displacement, m^3/rev

(iii) Overall efficiency (η_{om}): It is defined as the ratio of actual power output to the hydraulic power supplied. It is given by following relationship,

$$\eta_{om} = \frac{P_{out}}{P_{in}} = \frac{T_{om} . \theta_m}{Q_{op} \Delta P_m} \qquad (16.7)$$

$$= \frac{T_{om}}{Dm\Delta P_m} \times \frac{D_m \theta_M}{Q_{op}}$$

$$= \eta_{vm} \times \eta_{tm} \qquad (16.8)$$

If the efficiencies (volumetric, torque and overall) are plotted as function of the dimensionless term ($\mu\theta m/p$), where μ is the absolute viscosity, a typical set of curves, as shown in Fig. 16.9. will be obtained.

From Fig. 16.7, it is clear that a motor has an optimum combination of pressure and speed. Fluid viscosity the shaft speed decreases, the motor approaches a stall condition at which efficiency approaches zero. As pressure becomes very small and/or the shaft velocity becomes very high, the motor approaches a condition just overcoming friction, and again motor becomes inefficient.

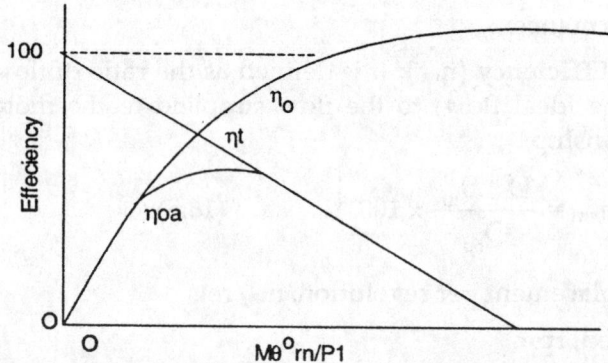

Fig. 16.9 Showing Relationship between Motor speed and Pressure

16.6.3. Accumulator: It is the only convenient device for storing energy in a hydraulic system. It is used to supply energy when the demand of the motors and cylinders is greater than the capacity of the pump. It is also intended for stand by or emergency used in case of pump or engine failure for braking and steering off highway vehicles. It also serves as shock absorber to reduce maximum stresses if the system is subjected to unequal dynamic loads. The hydraulic accumulator consists of a cylinder and a plunger generally known as a ram as shown in Fig. 16.10. One side of the to the cylinder connected to the hydraulic machine and other press pump. Either the cylinder or the ram may be fixed. Generally the cylinder is fixed and the ram moves up and down to accomodate a variable quantity of liquid inside by the cylinder.

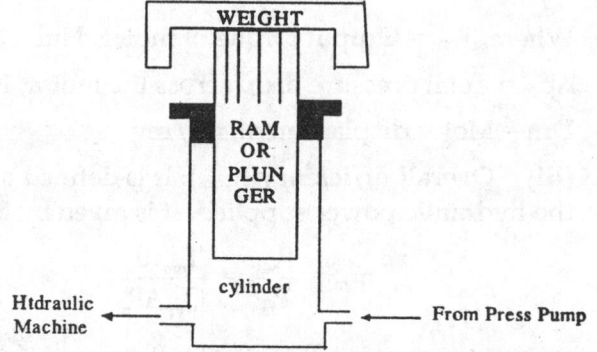

Fig. 16.10. Hydraulic Accumulators

Accumulators may be dead load type or variable load. In the former, dead weights. To hydraulic press pump while are employed to press the ram in, while the latter employs steam pressure.

16.6.3.1 Capacity of Accumulator: It is maximum amount of energy which is stored by it. The storage capacity is equal to the potential energy of the lifted ram together with weight.

Let d = Diameter of ram

s = Stroke or lift of ram

p = Intensity of pressure of fluid supplied.

Total moving weight or weights of ram (W) = $\frac{\pi}{4}d^2p$

Work done in lifting ram or capacity of accumulator

$$W.s. = \frac{\pi}{4} . d^2.p.s \qquad (16.9)$$

Volume of accumulator = $\frac{\pi}{4} d^2. s$

∴ Capacity of ram = p x volume   (16.10)

Therefore, capacity of accumulator and that ram are same.

16.6.4. Hydraulic Cylinder: The hydraulic energy is converted to mechanical energy with the help of cylinders. There are two types of hydraulic cylinder used in hydraulic system. (i) Single acting cylinder (ii) Double acting cylinder.

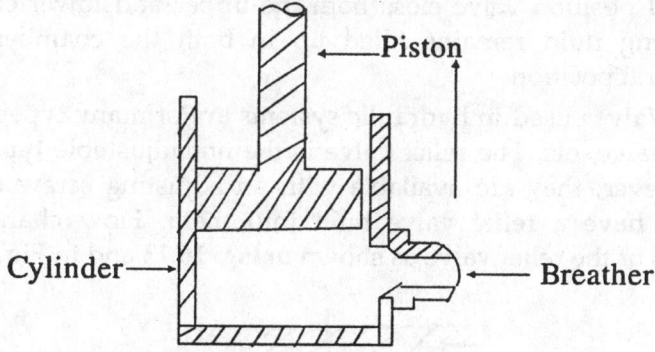

Fig. 16.11. Single Acting Hydraulic Cylinder

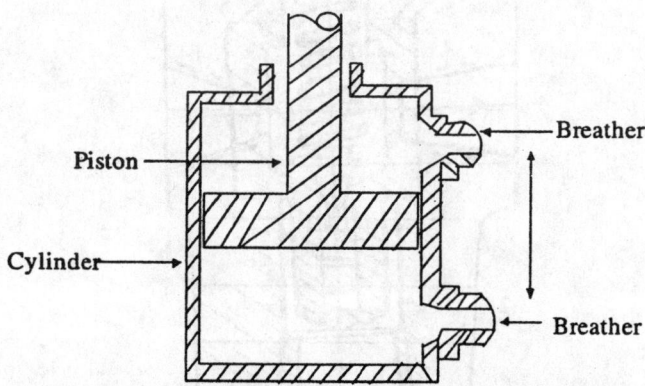

Fig. 16.12. Double Acting Hydraulic Cylinder

1. Single Acting Cylinder: In a single acting cylinder the piston fitted in the cylinder is lifted up due to pressure of fluid. When the pressure is released the piston comes back due to the weight of implements or its own weight as shown in Fig. 16.11.

In single acting cylinder where pressure is only applied from the bottom a breather is fitted on the uppermost part of the upper chamber. The purpose of fitting this breather is to allow clean air to get out when the piston moves up. Breather is fitted with a wire gauge filter so that clean air can get in.

2. Double Acting Cylinder: In this type of cylinder piston is lifted up o lower down with hydraulic pressure as shown in Fig. 16.12. When we have to lift the piston in the cylinder, the hydraulic oil under pressure is sent to the lower part of the cylinder which makes the piston lifted up. At the same time position is made in the valve to drain back the fluid from the upper part of the cylinder to tank. Similarly when the piston has to be lowered down the upper chamber is connected to pressure line while lower chamber to the tank. For keeping the cylinder neutral position valve close both the upper and lower chamber of the cylinder resulting fluid remains filled up in both the chambers and piston remains in neutral position.

16.6.5 Valves: Valves used in hydraulic systems are of many types such as relief valve, control valve, etc. The relief valve is the nonadjustable type as shown in Fig.16.11. However, they are available with an adjusting screw on the spring. Pumps mostly have a relief valve built into them. Flow characteristics and operating limits of the relief valve as shown in Fig. 16.13 and in Fig. 16.14.

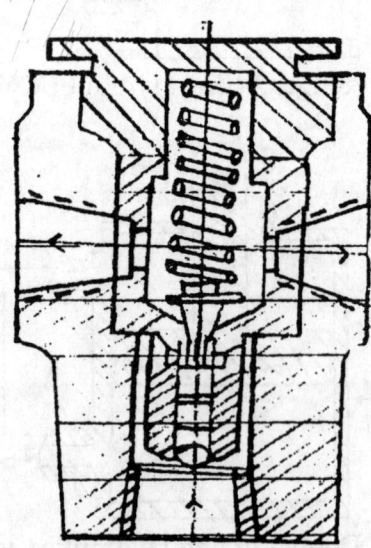

Fig. 16.13. Relief Valve

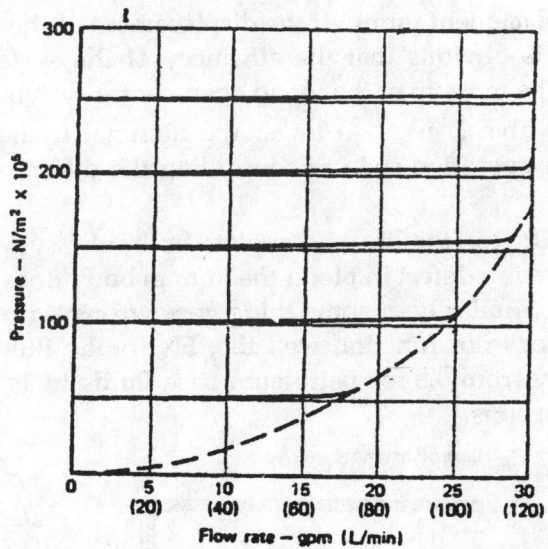

Fig. 16.14. Control Characteristics and Operating Limits of the Pilot-Operated
Relief Valve Shown in figure (Courtesy Robert Bosch CmbH.)

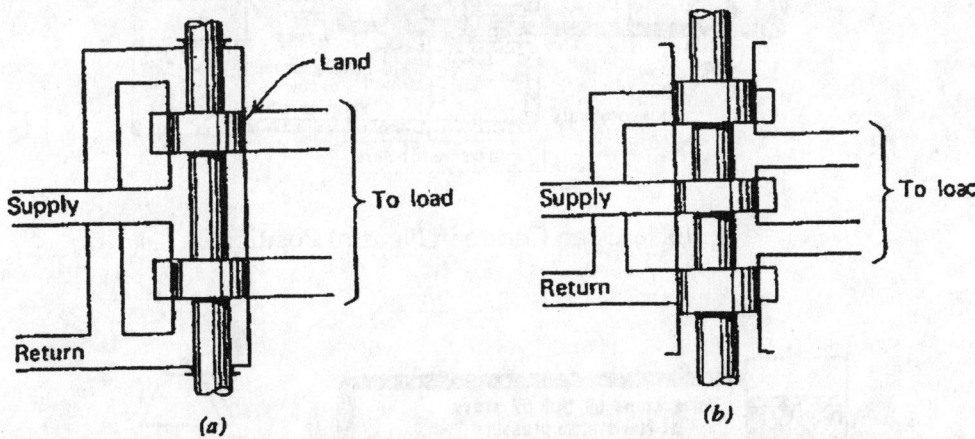

Fig. 16.15. Typical hydraulic spool valves. (a) Four-way, two way and
(b) four-way, three land.

Spool valveis a type of control valve used in pumps shown in Fig. 16.15. At has at
least three ports and two lands the width of the port in the valve sleeve, the
valves is said to be open centre valve and system is said to be open system, as
shown in Fig. 16.16. A closed centre valve has land widths greater than the pot
width spool is neutral and system is a said to be closed system, as shown in Fig.
16.17. The major advantage of the closed-centre valveis realized when it is used

with a variable displacement pump. If the displacement of the pump is controlled by the pressure, it is obvious that the efficinecy of the system using a closed-centre valve would be more than that of an open-centre system.

Pressure reducing valve is used to lower the nominal hydraulic pressure to a desired level for on operation such as controlling the differential lock, the PTO clutch and brake.

16.6.6. Hydraulic oil: It is the life of complete hydraulic system as blood in the human body. If there is a defect in blood the human body does not work well and the man become ill. Similarily of some thing goes wrong with hydraulic oil then hydraulic system does not function well too. Hydraulic fluids used in tractors have specific gravity from 0.8 for petroleum base fluids to as high as 1.5 for the chlorinated hydrocarbons.

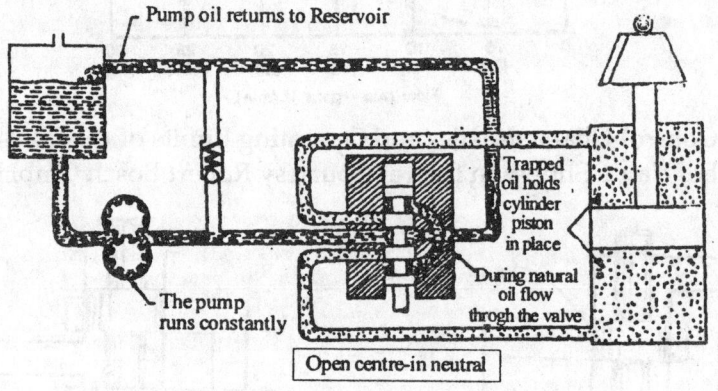

Fig. 16.16 Open Centre in Neutral Position

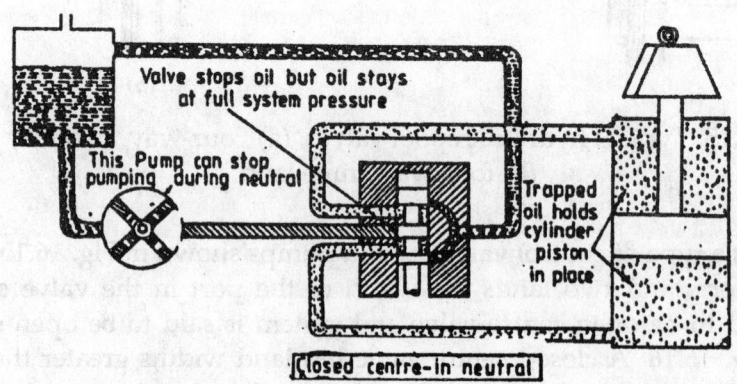

Fig. 16.17 Closed Centre in Neutral

(i) Specific gravity: It is the ratio of the mass density of a substance to the mass density of water at constant temperature.

(ii) Kinematic viscosity (υ): It is the ratio of absolute viscosity to mass density of a substance at constant temperature. Mathematically, it is expressed as,

$$\upsilon = \frac{\mu}{\rho} \qquad\qquad (16.11)$$

Where, μ = Absolute density of the substance

ρ = Mass density of the substance.

Kinematics viscosity is measured by Saybolt universal viscometer.

Where, SVS = Soybolt universal seconds.

$$u = 0.216\,SVS - \frac{166}{SVS} \qquad\qquad (16.12)$$

16.7. Implement Control: The following methods are used to control implements, (i) Nudging system (ii) Position control system (iii) Draft control and (iv) Mixed control system

16.7.1 Nudging System: It is used to raise, lower or position an implement, either mounted or trailed by moving a hand lever either forward or backward from its neutral position. If the control lever is moved (nudged), the hydraulic cylinder will move a complete stroke. If the lever is returned manually its neutral position before the end of the complete stroke, the cylinder will stop and remain in that position, provided leaks do not exists in the system. In the nudging system there is no relationship between the position of the hand control lever and the cylinder piston. Actually it is an open loop system. It is normally associated with a three point hitch system.

16.7.2 Automatic position control System: The system provides automatic control of attached implement and allows the driver or operator to preselect and to position the implement by the hand control lever as shown in Fig. 16.18. It is normally associated with a three point hitch system. It is generally used in plane field as well as travelling on road with implements.

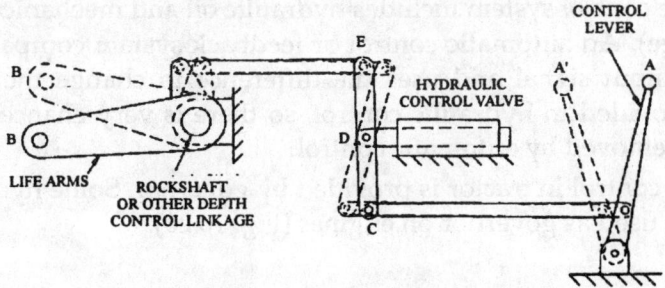

Fig. 16.18 Basic Principle of Position Control System

16.7.3 Automatic Draft Control: This system will automatic raise or lower an implement as the draft or resistance of the attached implement increases or decreases as shown in Fig. 16.17. The sensing device, which tells the hydraulic system to lower or raise the hitch system is located on either the lower links or the upper link, depending upon the size of the tractor.

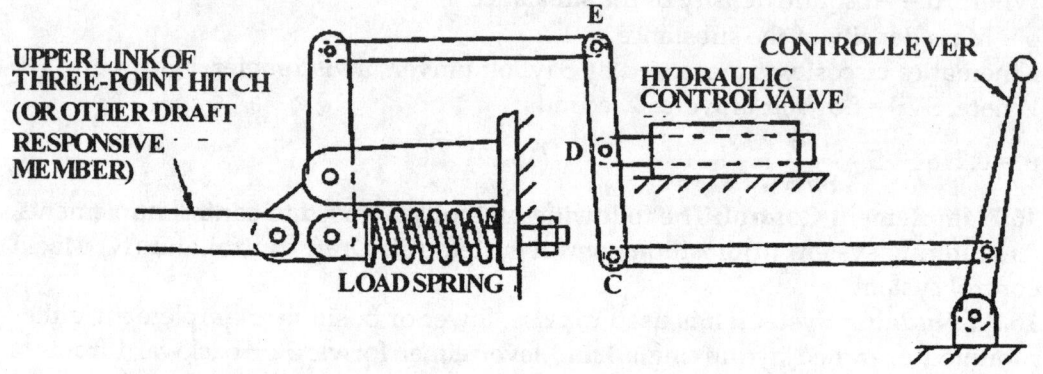

Fig. 16.19. Draft Control System

16.7. Draft Sensing: For a draft control system, draft sensing device was located on the upper link and responded to a comprehensive force. For a close coupled implement, i.e., a two bottom plough, the upper links will normally be in compression and as the draft increases the comprehensive force will increase. The comprehensive force in the upper link decreases as the size of the mounted plough increases.

16.8. Automatic Control: The objective of an automatic control system is to control the system without the aid of a human operator. Automatic control in most hydraulic control system includes hydraulic oil and mechanical devices (i.e., springs, linkage). An automatic control or feedback system compares the output signal to the input signal and uses the difference to change the output. Since feedback is provided in hydraulic control, so there is very chance of unstability which can be removed by automatic control.

The automatic control in tractor is provided by governor. Some hydraulic devices have also been used as governor on engines (Fig. 16.20).

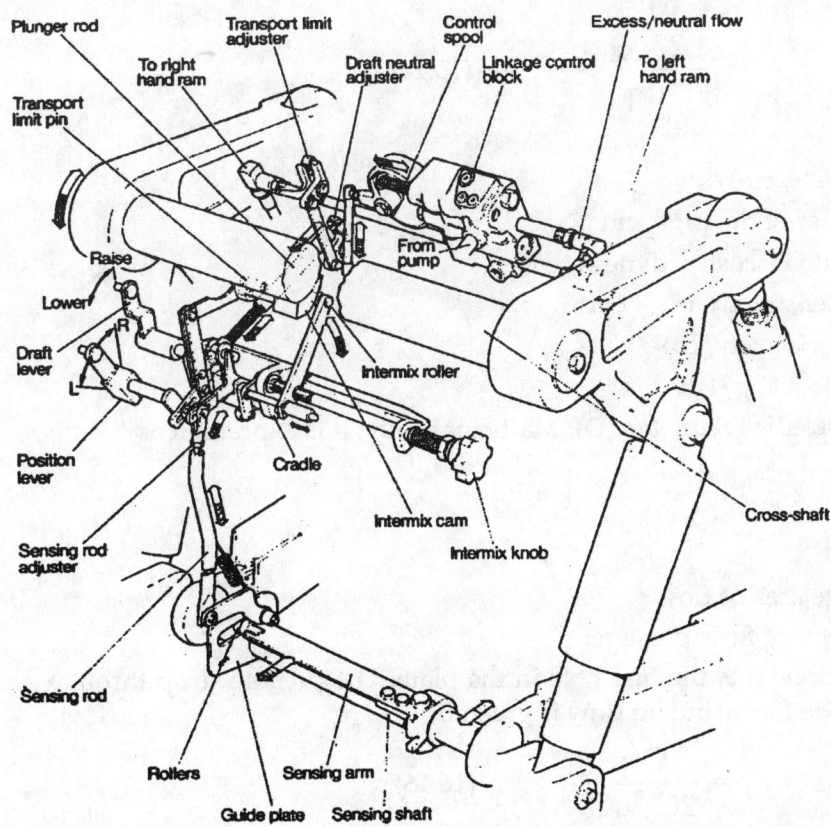

Tractors: Constructional Features

Fig. 16.20. Automatic Draft Control System

16.9. Lines, Hoses and Internal Passages

(i) The flow rate in farm tractors varies from 1.5 m/s for suction lines to 9.1 m/s for pressure lines.

(ii) operating temperature is from 65 to 95°C.

(iii) oil viscosity is from 70-100 SUS at 65°C and 45-60 SUS at 93°C.

(iv) The transmission form laminor to turbulance flow or vice-versa is determined on Reynold's number basin. Mathematically, Reynold's number (R) is expressed as

$$R = \frac{\rho.v.d}{\eta} \qquad (16.13)$$

$$= \frac{1.27 \cdot Q}{d\nu}$$

$$= \frac{1.27 \cdot Q \cdot p}{d\eta} \qquad (16.14)$$

Where,

Q = Flow rate, cm³/s

d = Diameter of the pipe, cm

η = Absolute viscosity, dyne. s/cm²

ρ = mass density, dyne s²/cm⁴

υ = kinetic viscosity, cm²/s

ω = specific wt., g/cm³

16.10. Hydraulic Diameter (D): Mathematically, it is expressed as

$$= \frac{4A}{S} \qquad (16.15)$$

Where,

A = Passage area of flow

S = Perimeter of flow passage.

16.11. Orifices: It is the fine hole in the plate. The presure drop through a sharp-edged orifice for turbulent flow is given by

$$\Delta p = \frac{Q^2 p}{2C_d^{\,2} \cdot A^2} \qquad (16.16)$$

Where,

A = Orifice area

ρ = Mass density

C_d = Orifice discharge

16.12 Power of Steering Pumps: Power (P) of pump is determined by the following formula.

$$P = \frac{V \cdot \Delta p \cdot N}{E}, \ W \qquad (16.17)$$

Where,

Δp = Pressure rise through pump, Pa

E = Over all pump efficiency

N = Speed, rps

16.14. HITCHING OF IMPLEMENTS

For efficient and safe operation of tractors, the implements need to be hitched properly. Because if it is improperly hitched, it will results into:

(i) wastage of power (ii) Excessive load on steering (iii) Uneven ploughing (iv) uneven transfer of load on tractor resulting in fast wearing of parts.

(v) Before we study further let us study the type of draw bar available for hitching purposes.

16.15. Terminology Related to Hitching

16.15.1 Trailed Type Implement: It is one that is pulled and guided from single hitch point but its weight is not supported by the tractor such trolley, trailed mould board plough etc.

16.15.2 Semi-mounted type implement: This type of implement is one which is attached to the tractor along a hinge axis and not at a single hitch point. It is controlled directly not at a single hitch point. It is controlled directly by tractor steering unit but its weight is partly supported by the tractor such as semi mounted mould board plough etc.

16.15.3 Mounted Type Implement: A mounted implement is one which is attached to the tractor, such that it can be controlled directly by the tractor steering unit. The implement is carried fully by the tractor when out of work.

16.15.4 Centre of Power: It is the true point of hitch of a tractor as shown in Fig. 16.21.

16.15. 5 Centre of Resistance: It is the point at which the resultant of all the horizontal and vertical forces act as shown in Fig. 16.21.

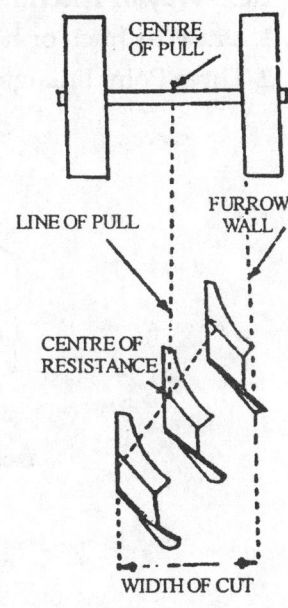

Fig. 16.21. Centre of resistensce

The centre lies at a distance equal to 3/4 the size f the plough from the share wing.

16.15.6. Line of Pull: It is an imaginary straight line passing from the centre of resistance through the clevis to the centre of pull (power) as shown in Fig. 16.21.

16.15.7 Pull: It is the total force required to pull an implement.

16.15.8. Draft: It is the horizontal component of pull. Parallel to the line of motion.

Draft (D) = P cos θ, N $\qquad$ (16.18)

Where,

P = Pull, N

θ = Angle between line of pull and horizontal.

16.15.9 Side Draft: It is the horizontal component of the pull perpendicular to the direction of motion.

Note: This is developed if the centre of resistance is not directly behind the centre of pull.

15.15.10 Unit Draft: It is the draft per unit cross sectional area of the furrow.

16.15 Way of Hitching: Implements can be hitched in two ways.

1. Drawbar hitch or horizontal hitch

2. Three Point linkage as shown in Fig. 16.22

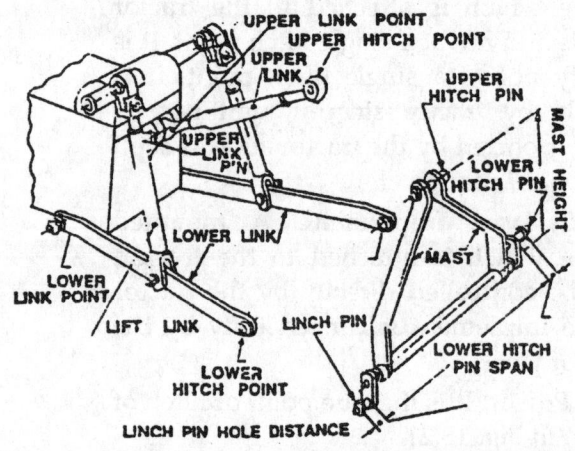

Fig. 16.22. Three point hitch with hydraulic lift

16.15. Drawbar Hitch: Drawbar is a device through the pulling power of the tractor is provided to the trailing equipment. It consists of crossbar with suitable holes, attached to the lower hitch link. It is fitted tot he rear end of the tractor.

16.15.2. Three Point Linkage: It is a combination of three links. One top link and other two lower links as shown in Fig. 16.22

Advantages of Three Point Linkage: There are following advantages of three point linkage.

(i)   Easy control of working implements.

(ii)   Quick attachment of implements.

(iii)   Automatic control through hydraulic system.

(iv)   Good balancing of attached implements.

Note: For drawbar hitching the hitching point should be within the limit of 0.325 to 0.425 m.

16.17. Weight Transfer: When a tractor is pulling some load either at drawbar or connected to three point linkage, the weight of implement along with a part of the weight of the front axle is transferred to the rear axle. The shifting of weight of the rear axle is known as weight transfer which improves the tractive efficinecy of the tractor.

Mathematically, it is expressed as

$$\text{weight transfer} = \frac{\text{Pull} \times \text{Hitch height}}{\text{Wheel base}} \quad (16.17)$$

where, the line of pull is assumed parallel to the ground.

From above relation, we observed that following observations:

(i) Longitudinal stability of tractor depends on hitch height.

(ii) The higher the hitch height more is the weight transfer.

Notes: 1. The more is the weight transfer the more is the tractive power.

2. The more is the weight transfer the more is the change of lifting and toppling of tractor front wheel.

3. Normally, the weight transfer from the front axle to rear axle is allowed 30-40% without affecting the steering ability.

16.18. Three Point Hitch: When an implement is mounted on a three point hitch the lines projected from the lower and upper links intersect at a pull point known as "vertical point" or "Centre of pull" and the implement appear to be pulled from that point as shown in Fig. 16.23. The point lines in between rear and front axle.

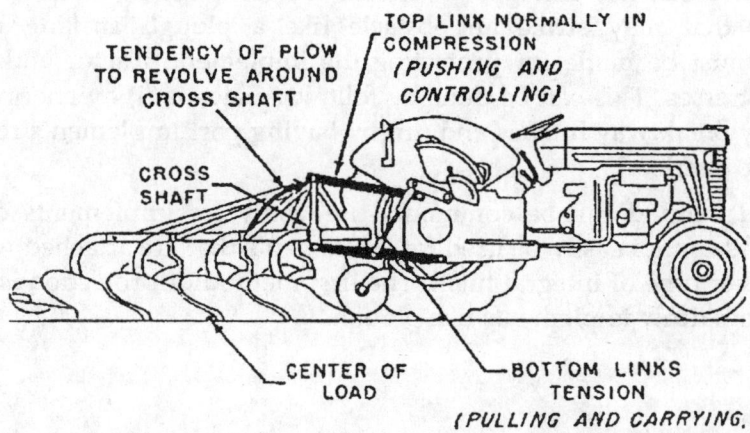

Fig. 16.23 Principle of weight transfer implement lowered

When the implement is raised position the virtual point is rear to ground is shown and when the implement is lowered the virtual point is lifted up, as shown in Fig. 16.21. The rise of virtual point causes weight transfers rear wheells which results in increase of tractive efficiency.

Free Link Operation of Three Point Hitche: With free link operation the depth is controleld by gauge-wheels or other supporing surfaces on the implements. Though depth control is also obtained by rear furrrow wheell and heel of rear land slide but guage wheels are most popular.

Restrained Link Operation of Three Point Hitch: In retrained link operation the implement gets all or the most of the its vertical support from the tractor, the hitch links being free only when the tool is entering the ground. As soon as the mold board plough for example reaches the working depth, it is held by hydraulic system of tractor. Automatic draft control is a type of restrained link operation.

Hitching of Semi-Mounted Implements: Semi-mounted implements are pulled through lower links only. The weight of implement is supported by rear furro where. The line of pull passes through horizontal hinge axis from centre of lower links is shown in Fig. 16.24.

Hitching of Trailed Implements: The trailed implements are hitched by following ways:

(i) Connection to the regular swinging drawbar provided on the tractor.

(ii) Connection to the lower links of three-point hitch-through a supplemntary-drawbar.

(iii) Connection to (additional) trailer hitch point.

16.23. Tractor Kinetic Energy: When the tractor is being used to propel an implement that may strike an obstacle like a plough striking rock. Some provision must be made for protecting the implement, tractor and hitch from excessive stresses. This can be done by following means (i) by energy-absorbing hitch (ii) by break way hitches and (iii) by having part implements release when subjected to overload.

The second method can be commonly used only for implements drawn by a drawbar and cannot easily be used for implements that are attached with a three-point or other type of integral hitch. The first method of protection is of valve of an the hitches draw implements like plough.

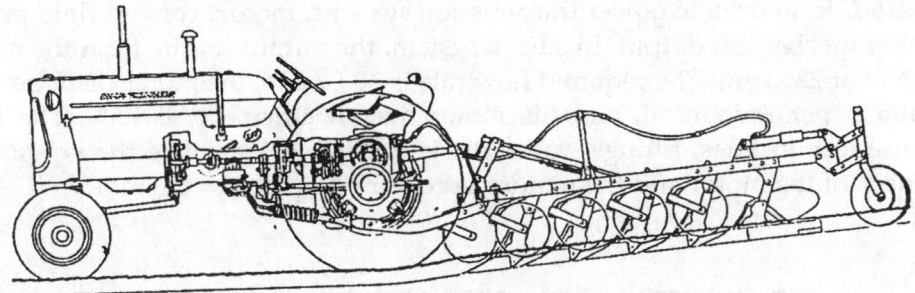

Fig. 16.24. Hitching of semi mounted implement

A moving tractor has kinetic energy, which must be absorbed in slowing down or stopping. In addition to the kinetic energy resulting from the mass of the tractor, the engine, wheels and transmission have additional kinetic energy as a result of their rotation. For rubber-tired tractors the kinetic energy of revolving parts is approximately equal to ten percent of the total K.E. resulting from the linear motion of the tractor (Clyde 1949). Therefore, K.E. of wheeled tractor is given as

$$\text{K.E.} = \frac{1}{2}\, m_t\, v^2 \qquad (16.19)$$

Where m_t = Mass of the tractor

v = velocity of the tractor

of the tractor is equipped with a linear spring type of energy-absorbing hitch and of the tractor clutch remains engaged after the implement is stopped, they by the conservation of energy equation it is apparent that the kinetic energy in the tractor plus the work being done by the drive wheel while the tractor is stopping must be equal the increase in potential energy stored in the spring.

$$T_1\,(x_2-x_1) + \frac{1.1}{2}\, m_t v^2 = (x_2-x_1)\left[\frac{(P_{max} + T_2)}{2}\right] \qquad (16.20)$$

Where,

T_1 = Tractive force before implement stops

$(x_2 - x_1)$ = Deformation of spring after the implement strikes an obstacle

P_{max} = Maximum force on the hitch

T_2 = Tractive force after implement stops

Note: It has been observed that the energy to be absorbed by the spring will be less if the clutch can be released at the instant of impact, in which case the tractive force, T_2 will be zero.

Prob. 16.1. In hydraulic power transmission systems, motors convert fluid power to rotary mechanical output. In such a system, the output torque from the motor is 90 Nm at 225 rpm. The required flow rate is 30 L/min, the motor displacement is 0.105 L per revolution, and the motor overall efficinecy, is 75%. The total pressure loss in lines, fittings, valve etc. is negligible. Calculate the volumetric efficinecy of the motor and the required pressure drop across the motor. [GATE-1998]

Soln.

Given η_{om} = 75% Q_{op} = 30 lpm = 30 x 10^{-3} m^3/min.

Revolution of motor (θ m) = 225 rpm.

Δm = 0.105 L/rev.

T_m =90 Nm

we know that

$$\eta om = \frac{T_m \times \theta m}{Dp} = \frac{90\ (Nm) \times 225\ (rev/min)}{30 \times 10^{-3} m^3/min \times \Delta p_m}$$

$$0.75 = \frac{3 \times 225 \times 10^3}{\Delta P_m}$$

$\therefore$ Pm = 900 kPa Ans.

Again volumetric efficiency

$$\eta vm = \frac{Dm.\theta m}{Q_{op}} \times 100 = \frac{0.105\ L/rev \times 225\ rev/min}{30\ L/min}$$

$$= 78.75\%$$

Prob. 16.2. A Tractor with rubber tyre is pulling a plough at 5 kmph speed on level ground, when the plough hooks a large builders, causing the until to stop suddenly. The co-efficient of traction is 0.5, the maximum possible drawbar power is 18 kW, the rear wheel wt. is 14700 N and front wheel is 7350 N. Compute.

(a)   K.E. to be observed in stopping the tractor

(b)   In tractor is stopped (not declutched) in 15 cm by a drawbar spring.

What is the increase in the drawbar pull above the maximum tractive ability.

Soln. Given., v = 6.0 kmh = 1.666 m/s,. P_D = 18 kW, μ = 0.5, x_2-x_1 = 0.15 cm = 15 m, Rr = 14,700 N, Rf = 7,250 N W_t = Rr + Rf = 14700 + 7350 = 22050 N

i.e., m_t = 2205 kg

we know that,

$$K.E. = \frac{1.1}{2} \times m_t\ v^2 = \frac{1.1}{2} \times 2205 \times (1.660)^2$$

$$= 3,341.85$$

(b) Since clutch is being engaged after the implement is stopped, therefore increase in potential energy of drawbar spring will be equal to the sum of K.E. and work done by the drive wheel while tractor is stopped.

According to law of conservation of energy

$$(x_2 - x_1)\left(\frac{P_{max} + T_2}{2}\right) = \frac{1.1}{2} m_t v^2 + T_1(x_2 - x_1) \qquad \text{(i)}$$

$$\text{Drawbar pull} = \frac{\text{Drawbar power}}{\text{Speed}} = \frac{18.10^3}{1.666} \quad 10.80 \times 10^3 \text{ N}$$

Tractive force before the tractor is stopped $(T_1) = 10800$ N

Tractive force after the tractor is stopped $(T_2) = \mu R_r = 0.5 \times 14700 = 7350$ N

Substituting the valve of T_1 and T_2 in equation (i) we have

$$0.15\left(\frac{P_{max} + 7350}{2}\right) = 3341.85 + 10800 \times 0 \times 0.15$$

$$P_{max} = \frac{9,923.70 - 0.15 \times 7.350}{0.15}$$

$$= 58,808 \text{ N}$$

Therefore, increase in drawbar pull = 58,808 - 10,800 = 48,008 N

∴ Increase in pull with respect to maximum pull of the tractor

$$\frac{48,008}{58.808} \times 100 = 81.635\% \text{ Ans.}$$

Prob. 16.3 A hydraulic motor is required to develop torque of 125 Nm at a max speed of 600 rpm. The maximum pressure drop across the motor is to be 150 bar. The torque and volumetric efficiencies are both 0.9. Determine

(a) the suitable motor displacement.

(b) the flow required in the motor is L/minute   [GATE-2001]

Soln. Given $T_m = 125$ Nm $\theta°m = 600$ rpm

$\Delta P_m = 150$ bar $= 150 \times 10^5$ N/m^2.

$\eta_{vm} = \eta_{tm} = 0.9$

$D_m = ?$ and $Q_{op} = ?$

(a) We know that

$$\eta_{tm} = \frac{2\pi \, T_m}{D_m \cdot DP_m} = \frac{2\pi \times 125}{0.9 \times 150 \times 10^5} \quad \frac{Nm}{N/m_2}$$

$$= 5.8148 \times 10^{-5} \text{ m}^3/\text{revolution.}$$

(b) Again, we know

$$\eta_{vm} = \frac{Dm.\,\theta m}{Q_{op}}$$

$$Qop = \frac{Dm.\,\theta m}{\eta_{vm}} = \frac{5.814 \times 10^{-5} \times 600}{9}$$

$$= 387.6 \times 10^{-5} \text{ m}^3/\text{min.}$$

$$= 3.87 \text{ L/min}$$

Prob. 16.4 An accumulator has a ram 300 mm in diameter an effective stroke of 6 m and is loaded with a total weight of 5×10^5 N. If the friction of ram amounts 3% of the total load, find the total power delivered to the hydraulic machine if the ram falls steadily through its full stroke in 2 minute, while at the same time the pump delivers 7.5×10^{-3} m³/s

Soln. Given. d = 300 mm = 0.3 m, s = 6 m.

Load W = 5×10^5 N, Friction loss = 3%

∴ Net Load = $5 \times 10^5 \times 0.97 = 485000$ N

Time of ram fall = 2 min = $2 \times 60 = 120$ S

Qp = 7.5×10^{-3} m³/s

(i) Work supplied by accumulator ram per second

$$= 485000 \times \frac{6}{120}$$

$$= 24250 \text{ J/s}$$

(ii) Intensity of pressure in accumulator

$$p = \frac{w}{a}$$

$$= \frac{485000}{\frac{\pi}{4} \times 0.3^2} = 6870000 \text{ Pa}$$

Head h due to this pressure = $\dfrac{p}{\gamma.g}$

$$= \frac{6870000}{1000 \times 10} = 687\text{m}$$

$$h = 687 \text{ m}$$

work supplied by the pump per second = $(\gamma.\,\theta p)\,h$

$$= 1000 \times 0.0075 \times 687 = 5.5250 \text{ J/s}$$

∴ Total work supplied to hydraulic machine per second

  = work supplied by ram + work supplied by pump

  = 24250 + 515250 = 539500 J/s

Power (P) = 559500 W

  = 0.5395 MW Ans.

Prob. 16.5. An hydraulic pump having 37.5 cm³ displacement per revolution, develops 15 MPa at 887. Volumetric efficiency. At 3000 rpm the pump supplies oil to a torque converter, whose shaft rotates at 60 rpm and has 85% overall efficinecy. Calculate, the torque available at the shaft of the Governor.

  [GATE-2000]

Soln. Given D_p = 37.5 cm³/rev = 37.5 x 10⁻³ L/rev

hvp = 88%, ΔP_c = 15 x 106 Pa ηac = 85%

θ_c = 60 rpm = 1rev/s θ_p = 3000 rpm

we know that,

$$Q_{op} = \theta_{op} = \eta_{vp} \times D_p \times \theta_p = 0.88 \times 37.5 \times 10^{-6} \times 3000$$

$$= 99 \times 10^{-3} \text{ m}^3/\text{min}$$

Output power of pump = $\theta_{op} \times \Delta p$

$$= \frac{99 \times 10^{-3} \times 15 \times 10^6}{60}$$

$$= 24.75 \text{ kW}$$

$$\eta_{oa} = \frac{P_{om}}{P_{im}}$$

$$P_{om} = 24.75 \times 0.85$$

$$= 21.037 \text{ kW}$$

$$T = \frac{P_{om} \times 60000}{2\pi \times \theta_m} = \frac{21.037 \times 60,000}{2\pi \times 60}$$

Ans = 3.348 kNm

Prob. 16.6. Find the length of stroke required for an accumulator having a displacement of 110 litres. The diameter of the pluger is 350 mm.

Soln. Given. d = 350 mm = 0.350 m

Volume or Displacement (vf) 110 L = 110 x 10⁻³ m³

$$a = \frac{\pi}{4} d^2$$

$$= \frac{\pi}{4} \times (0.35)^2 = 0.096 \text{ m}^2$$

$$\therefore \text{ Length of stroke} = \frac{v}{a} = \frac{0.11}{0.096}$$

= 1.145 m Ans.

Prob. 16.7. In a open loop hydrostatic transmission a pump running at 1440 rev/min is used to supply fluid to drive a motor. The motor displacement 0.5 x 10⁻³ m³/rev and it is to run 65 rev/min. The pressure drop across the motor is 132 bar and the pressure drop between the motor and the pump is 5 bar. The torque and the volumetric efficiencies of both the pump and motor are 95 percent and 90 percent, respectively. **[GATE-2004]**

(A)   The torque required at the motor is

(a)   898 Nm   (b) 945 Nm

(c)   998 Nm   (d) 1228 Nm

(B)   The input power to operate the pump is

(a)   7.81 kW   (b) 8.68 kW

(c)   9.29 kW   (d) 9.64. kW

Soln. Given. θp = 1440 rpm, D_m = 0.5 x 10⁻³ m³/rev

θm = 65 rev/min, ΔP_m = 132 bar = 132 x 10⁵ N/m²

ΔP_{mp} = 5 bar = 5 x 10⁵ N/m².

ΔP_m = 132 x 10⁵ N/m², Δp_p = ΔP_{mp} + ΔP_m = 137x 105 Pa

η_{tm} = η_{tp} = 0.95 and η_{vm} = η_{tp} = 0.95

we know

$$\eta_{tm} = \frac{2\pi T_m}{D_m . \Delta p_m} = T_m = \frac{\eta_{tm} \times \Delta P_m \times D_m}{2\pi}$$

$$= \frac{0.95 \times 132 \times 10^5 \times 0.5 \times 10^{-3}}{2\pi}$$

T_m = 997.9 Nm

Therefore, answer of A is (c)

$$\eta_{vm} = \frac{D_m \, \theta m}{Q_{in}}$$

or $Q_{in} = \dfrac{D_m \, \theta_m}{\eta_{vm}} = \dfrac{0.5 \times 10^{-3} \times 65}{0.9 \times 60} = 6.0185 \times 10^{-4} \text{m}^3/\text{s}$

P_{op} = $\theta . \Delta P_p$ = 6.0185 x 10⁻⁵ x 137 x 10⁵ = 8.24 kW.

$$\eta_{op} = \frac{P_{out}}{P_{in}} = \frac{8.245}{0.95 \times 0.9} = 9.64 \text{ kW}$$

Therefore, answer of B is (d)

Prob 16.8. The weight of a 350 mm plunger of an accumulator is 45000 N. What additional weight is to be placed upon it to develop a hydraulic pressure of 4200 kPa.

Soln. Given. d = 350 mm, p = 4200 kPa = 42 x 10^5 kPa w$_1$ = 45,000 N

Cross-sectional area of plunger = $\dfrac{\pi}{4}$ (0.35)^2

$$= 0.096 \text{ m}^2$$

Total weight to balance the hydraulic poressure

w = w$_1$ + w$_2$

Now w = p.a.

42 x 0.986 x 105

= 403500

w$_2$ = w- w$_1$

= 403500-45000

= 358500 N Ans.

Prob. 16.8 A tractor is equipped with a hydrostatic drive which includes a variable displacement pump and a fixed displacement motor. The input to the drive include torque of 250 Nm and speed of 2500 rpm. The pump displacement can vary from 42 cm3/rev to zero to 42 cm³/rev in opposite direction while motor has fixed displacement of 42 cm³/revolution, the volumetric efficiencies of pump and motor are 96% and torque efficiencies are each 90%. The maximum per missible pressure drop across the motor is 35 MPa.

[GATE-2005]

(A) The maximum out put power of the motor will be

(a) 50.80 kW (b) 55 13 kW

(c) 59.82 kW (d) 62.72 kW

(B) The transmission efficiencies of the drive will be

(a) 77.62% (b) 84.23%

(c) 91.40% (d) 95.83% [GATE 2005]

Soln. Given. Tip = 250 Nm. N = θp = 2500 rpm = θm

D$_p$ = 42 to zero cm³/rev.

D$_m$ = 42 cm³/rev.

$\eta_{tp} = \eta_{tm} = 0.9$

$\eta_{vp} = \eta_{vm} = 0.96$

$\Delta P_m = 35\ \text{MPa} = 35 \times 10^6\ \text{Pa}$

$Q_{out} = \eta_{vp} \times D_p \times \theta^{\circ}_{p}$

$0.96 \times 42 \times 10^{-6} \times \dfrac{2500}{60}$

$= 168 \times 10^{-5}\ \text{m}^3/\text{s}$

$P_h = \theta_{op} \times \Delta P$

$168 \times 10^{-5} \times 35 \times 10^6$

$= 58.80\ \text{kW}.$

$P_s = \eta_{op} \times P_h = \eta_{vp} \times \eta_{tp} \times P_w$

$= 0.96 \times 0.9 \times 58.80$

$= 50.80\ \text{kW}$

Therefore, answer of A is (a)

$$\eta_{tp} = 2\pi \times T_p \times \theta_P$$

$$= \frac{2\pi \times 250 \times 2500}{60}$$

$$= 65.45\ \text{kW}.$$

$$\eta_{transmission} = \frac{50.80}{65.45}$$

$$= 72.2$$

Therefore, answer of B is (a).

Prob. 16.9. A tractor trailed sub sailer weighs 4.0 kN with centre of gravity located 8 cm in front of the shavel point. The soil resistance on the cutting edge is estimated to be 65.0 kN working horizontally parallel to he direction of motion. The resultant reaction on the supporting wheels is found to be 10.5 kN which can be assumed to be working vertically at distance 34 cm in front of the shovel point.

(a) Calculate the magnitude, direction and location of the pulling force.

(b) For perfect balance what should be the height of vertical hitch point located 35 cm ahead of the shovel point?

(c) What power is exerted or developed by the tractor moving at a speed of 3 kph?

Soln. Given.

(a) Let P_v is the vertical component can P_h be the horizontal component of the pulling force P. Then from summation of forces separately invertical and horizontal planes in Fig. 16.25

392

$P_v + 10.5 - 4.0 = 0$

or $P_v = 2.95$ kN

and $P_h - 6.50 = 0$

∴ $P_h = 6.50$ kN

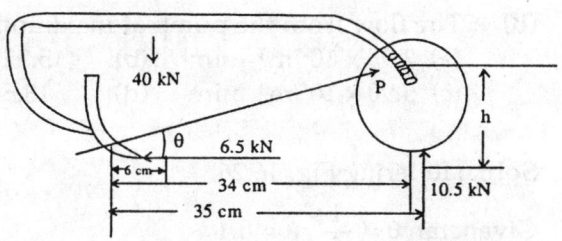

Therefore, $P = \sqrt{P_v^2 + P_h^2}$

$$= \sqrt{(2.95)^2 + (6.5)^2}$$

$$= 7.13 \text{ kN}$$

Fig. 16.25 Forces acting on a sub soiler

Angle of inclination

$$\theta = \tan^{-1}\left(\frac{P_v}{P_h}\right)$$

$$= \tan^{-1}\left(\frac{2.95}{6.5}\right) = 24.5°$$

Taking moments about the shovel point

$$p \times y + 4.0 \times 0.08 - 1.05 \times 0.54 = 0 \qquad \text{(i)}$$

Where, y is the perpendicular distance of P from the shovel point.

Substituting $P = 7.13$ kN is equation (i), we have

$$y = 0.52 \times 10\text{-}2 \text{ m Ans.}$$

(b)   The vertical distance of the time of pull above shovel point,

$$h = \frac{0.52 \times 10^{-2}}{\cos\theta} = \frac{0.52 \times 10^{-2}}{\cos 24.5}$$

$$= 0.572 \times 10\text{-}2 \text{ mans.}$$

(c) $P = P_h \times$ speed

$$= 6.50 \times \frac{3000}{3600}$$

$$= 5.42 \text{ kW Ans.}$$

Prob. 16.10 A Tractor weighing 20 kN is to be driven up a slope of 1 in 10 (1 vertical in 10 measured along the slope) at a speed of 20 Kmh^{-1}. The co-efficient of rolling resistance may be taken as 0.1. The tractor is driven hydraulically by two fixed displacement motor fitted in the rear wheels having an effective diameter of 1.2 m. The Volumetric and torque efficiency of the motors are both 0.95. The maximum pressure drop across the motors is 250 bar.

(A)   The required motor displacement per revolution is

   (a) 1.00×10^{-4}m³ (b) 3.01×10^{-4}m³

   (c) 3.17×10^{-4}m³ (d) 6.34×10^{-4}m³

(B) The flow from the pump at maximum speed is
    (a) $2.95 \times 10^{-2} m^3$ min^{-1} (b) $5.32 \times 10^{-2} m^3$ min^{-1}
    (c) $5.90 \times 10^{-2} m^3$ min^{-1} (d) $18.54 \times 10^{-2} m^3$ min^{-1} [GATE 2006]

Soln. : Refering Fig. 16.26

Given, $\tan \theta = \dfrac{1}{10}$, $\mu = 0.1$

$\therefore \sin \theta = 0.1$ and $\cos\theta = 0.99$

$m_t g = 20$ kN

$v = 20$ km/h

$= \dfrac{20 \times 1000}{3600} m/s$

$\eta_{vm} = \eta_{tm} = 0.9$

$\Delta_{pm} = 250$ bar $= 250 \times 10^5$ Pa

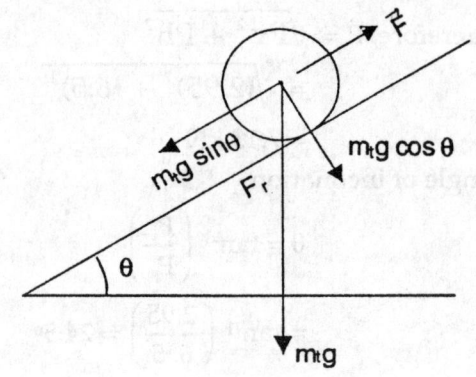

Fig. 16.26

(A) Driving force (F) acting on the wheel

$F = m_t g \sin \theta + Fr$

$= mtg \sin\theta + \mu m_t g \cos\square$

$= 20 \times 0.1 + 0.1 \times 20 \times 0.99$

$= 3.94$ kN

Therefore torque acting on the wheel $= Fr$

$\therefore$ Tm = Fr

or Tm $= 0.398 \times 0.6$

$\qquad = 2.388$ kNm

We know that for motor,

$$\eta tm = \dfrac{2\pi \, Tm}{Dn \, \Delta Pm}$$

or Dm $= \dfrac{2\pi \, T_m}{\eta_{tm} \Delta P} = \dfrac{2\pi \times 2.88 \times 10^3}{0.95 \times 250 \times 10^5} = 6.34 \times 10^{-4}$ m³ Ans

Therefore, answer of A is (d)

(B) We know that

$\qquad v = \omega.r$

$\qquad$ or $v = 2\pi \, \theta r$

$$\therefore \theta = \frac{v}{2\pi r} = \frac{20 \times 1000}{3600 \times 2\pi \times 0.6}$$

$$= 1.47 \text{ rad/s}$$

Again for the pump

$$\eta_{vp} = \frac{Q_p}{\theta_p \, D_p}$$

$$Q_p = \eta_{vp} \, \theta_p . \, D_p$$

$$= 0.95 \times 1.47 \times 6.34 \times 10^{-4} \times 60 \text{ m}^3 \text{ min}^{-1}$$
$$= 5.32 \times 10^{-2} \text{ m}^3 \text{ min}^{-1}$$

Therefore, the answer of B is (b)

PROBLEMS
1. A pump delivers 40L/min to 100 mm diameter cylinder that is required to produce 2200N force. What pressure is required to extend the cylinder? what hydraulic power is required.   (280 kPa, 186.6 W)
2. A hydraulic pump having 37.5 cm² displacement per revolution develop 15 MPa at 88% volumetric efficinecy at 3000 rpm the pump supplies oil to a torque convertor, whose shaft rotates at 60 rpm and has 85% overall efficiency. Calculate the torque available the shaft of the convertor. (3.348 kNm)
3. A hydraulic circuit uses 25 litres of fluid per minute. The fluid is supplied by a pump having a fixed displacement of 12.5 cm³ per revolution drive at 3000 rpm. The pump has volumetric efficiency of a 0.85 and torque efficiency of 0.88. If the system pressure is et at 18 MPa by the relief valve. Calculate.
   (a) The power required to drive the pump
   (b) Heat generated owing the excess flow passing over the relief valve.

   Ans. [12.78 kW, 40.69 Nm]
4. The ram of a hydraulic accumulator is 450 mm in diameter. The stroke is 7m and the water pressure is 8000 KPa. If the useful work given by the accumulator during one full downward stroke utilized in raising W tonnes to a height of 15 m by means of hydraulic crane, whose efficiency is 60%, find the valve of W if this work is done in 3 minutes. What is gross power of the crane.   (35,7000 N, 49.236 kN)

5.   While a disc plough was being pulled by a tractor through a three point converging link hitch, the stresses produced in each of three links were measured with the use of strain gauges. The compressive load in the top line inclined at an angle of 8° with the horizontal was 2.50 kN. The lower links were in tension and the horizontal and upward vertical components of the reactions at the implement end of each of the lhps were 7.50 kN and 1.25 kN respectively. If the distance between upper and lower hitch points is 450 mm. Find the magnitudes, direction and location of line of pull with reference to lphs.

(Ans. 12.8°, 1.3 kN)

SUBJECTIVE QUESTIONS

1.   What is the principle to hydraulic system? Explain its principle with the help o a diagram.

2.   What are the functions of hydraulic system.

3.   What are the components of hydraulic system.

4.   Explain the terms centre of power, centre of resistance, draft and side draft.

5.   Write short note on
    (a) Draft control
    (b) Open centre system
    (c) Closed centre system
    (d) Position Control
    (e) Trailed implement
    (f) Semi mounted implement
    (g) Mounted implement
    (h) Three point linkage
    (i) Weight transfer
    (i) Double acting cylinder

MULTIPLE CHOICE QUESTIONS

1.   The working principle of hydraulic system is based on
    (a) Newton's laws
    (b) Pascal's law
    (c) Raoult's law
    (d) None of them

2.   Pascal's law is given in
    (a) 1753
    (b) 1653
    (c) 1553
    (d) 1453

3.   The pum is mechanical device which increases in the hydraulic system.
    (a) Pressure energy of liquid
    (b) gas
    (c) both
    (d) none of the above

4.   Heavier jobs can be done quickly with less force by
    (a) transmission system
    (b) hydraulic system
    (c) differential
    (d) clutch

5.   Which of the following convert the hydraulic power to mechanical power
    (a) Control valve
    (b) cylinder
    (c) pump
    (d) none of the above

6. Which of the following pump is most efficient in hydraulic system
   (a) centrifugal pump   (b) gear pump
   (c) both   (d)s none of the above

7. Motor efficiency is the ratio of
   (a) shaft power to the hydraulic power
   (b) hydraulic power to the shaft power
   (c) both
   (d) none of the above

8. Accumulator serves as a
   (a) storage of energy   (b) shock absorbers
   (c) both   (d) none of the above

9. Horizontal component of pull, parallel to the line of motion is
   (a) side draft   (b) draft
   (c) both   (d) none of the above

10. The draft per unit cross sectional area of furrow is
    (a) side draft   (b) unit draft
    (c) draft   (d) none of the above

11. Which of the following is trailed type implement
    (a) trolley   (b) cultivator
    (c) both   (d) none of the above

12. Depth controlled in free link operation of the three-point hitch is
    (a) gauge wheel   (b) rear furrow wheel
    (c) heel of the rear land side   (d) all of the above

13. Which is the following is a type restrained link operation:
    (a) draft control   (b) position control
    (c) both   (d) all of the above

14. Which of the following is a control valve
    (a) spool   (b) priority valve
    (c) both   (d) none of the above

15. Kinetic viscosity is the ratio of
    (a) absolute viscosity to mass density
    (b) mass density to absolute viscosity
    (c) absolute viscosity to mass
    (d) none of these

FILL UP THE BLANKS

1. The pressure applied to an enclose fluid is transmitted .... in all directions.

2. The cylinder convert the hydraulic power to .... power for doing various jobs.

3.	Positive displacement pump can be categorized into reciprocating pump and ....

4.	The rotary pump is a .... pump.

5.	A .... gear pump is normally used on tractor hydraulic systems of lower pressure.

6.	Pump efficiency is the ratio of .... and shaft power.

7.	Overall efficiency is the product of volumetric and .... efficiency.

8.	Motor has an optimum combination of pressure and ....

9.	An accumulators also serves as a .... absorber.

10.	A closed-centre valve has land width greater than ....

11.	.... is one which is pulled and guided from single hitch point.

12.	Centre of power is .... point of hitch of a tractor.

13.	.... draft is the horizontal component of the pull perpendicular to the direction of motion.

14.	.... is the total force required to pull an impliment.

15.	Centre of resistance lies at a distance .... of the plough from the share wing.

16.	The hitch point within the limit of 32.5 to .... cm.

ANSWERS OF FILL UP THE BLANKS
1. equally 2. mechanical 3. rotary pump 4. constant flow 5. spur 6. hydraulic 7. torque 8. speed 9. shock 10. port width 11. trailed implement 12. true 13. side 14. pull 15. 3/4 15. 50

ANSWER OF MULTIPLE CHOICE QUESTIONS
1 (b) 2 (b) 3 (a) 4 (b) 5 (b) 6 (b) 7 (a) 8 (c) 9 (b) 10 (b) 11 (a) 12 (d) 13 (a) 14 (d) 15 (a)

Chapter 17
Transmission and Drive Trains

17.1 Intruduction: Engine power is transmitted to the rear wheels through power train, which perform four basic jobs. They are:

(i)   To connect an disconnect engine power to transmission system.

(ii)   To select speed-ratio to suit road and different load conditions.

(iii)   To provide means of reversing.

(iv)   To equalize power to the drive wheels for turning.

To perform the above said functions, three basic units are connected namely clutch transmission and differential as shown in Fig. 17.1. and tractor gear box in Fig. 17.2

1.   **Clutch:** It is used to connect and disconnect the power from engine to the transmission system.

2.   **Transmission:** It is used to select speed ratio at suit road, load and operating conditions.

3.   **Differential:** It is used to eqalize power at turning vehicle.

7.2.   Clutch: The clutch is mounted at the gear box as shown in Fig. 17.1. It has coupling used for connecting or disconnecting the engine power from transmission system. The main functions of a clutch are as follows.

1.   To disconnect the engine power from tranmission system as required under following circumstances:

(a)   In order to start the engine it warms up the engine and runs it at high.

Clutch: Speed is order to develop sufficient power to move the tractor from rest.

(b)   It disconnects power from transmission

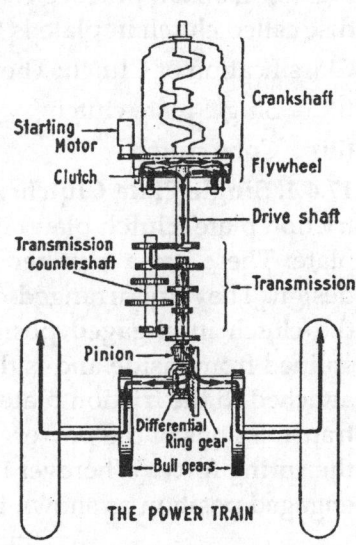

Fig. 17.1 Power Transmission Syste

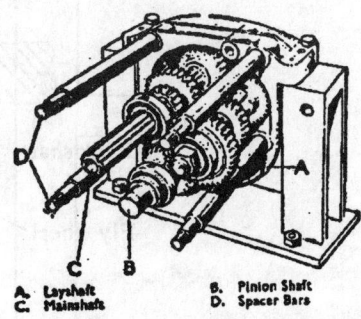

A. Layshaft   B. Pinion Shaft
C. Mainshaft   D. Spacer Bars

Fig. 17.2 Tractor Gear Box

399

system for easy shifting of gear.

(c)   It disconnects drive from the engine to step the tractor after application of brakes.

2.   It permits the engine to take up load gradually without jerk.

17.3 Principle of clutch: It works on the principle of friction in which when one stationary surface is brought in contact with rotating surface, the stationary surface also starts rotating. Take two flywheels with centre shaft fixed in it. Keep these a part as shown in Fig. (a) if you rotate one flywheel, the other will not rotate as they are kept apart. Now, bring the 2nd wheel close to first wheel and press them together. If you turn one wheel, the other will also rotate as shown in Fig. (b) in actual practice two metal wheels are not pressed together but a friction disc called clutch in plate is fixed in between.

Classification of Clutch: They are classified as follows:

(i)   Single plate clutch   (ii)   Multiple clutch

(iii)   Cone clutch

17.4.1. Single Plate Clutch: A simple single plate clutch is as shown in Fig. 17.3 A friction plate (clutch plate) is mounted in between the fly wheel and the pressure plate. These are a number of corl spring (helical spring) which depends upon design. They are arranged circumferentially, which provides axial force to keep the clutch in engaged position. The friction plate is mounted on a bus which splined from inside and is thus free to slide over the clutch side. Friction facing is attached to the friction plate on both sides to provide two friction surface. For the transmissions of the power. A pedal is provided to pull the pressure plate against the spring force. Wherever it is required to be disengaged, generally it remains in engaged position as shown in Fig. 17.3.

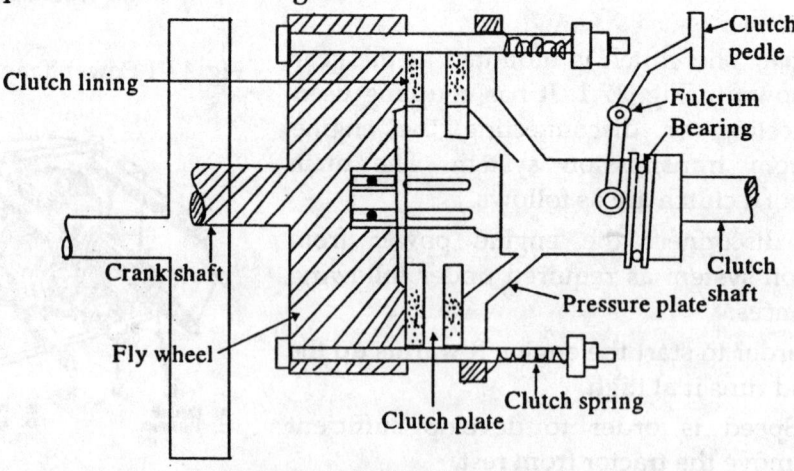

Fig. 17.3. Single Plate Clutch

When the clutch pedal is given pressure, the pressure plate is moved to right against the spring force. This is achieved by means of a suitable linkage and thrust bearing with this movement of the pressure plate, the friction plate is released and the clutch is disengaged.

(A) Advantages of Single Plate Clutch: The following are the main advantages of single plate clutch:

(i)   Gear changing in easier than with the coni clutch, because the pedal movement is less in this case.

(ii)   It doesn't suffer from disadvantages of cone clutch like bending of cones and hence, it is more reliable.

(iii)   It is more sigger than the multiplied type clutch.

(B)   Disadvantages of Single Plate Clutch:

Size of the clutch plate is more bigger than the clutch plate is used in the multiplate type. Hence, more space is required.

17.4.2. Multiplate Type Clutch: (i) Introduction:- A simple multiplate clutch is shown in Fig. 17.4 Multiplate clutch consists of a number of clutch plate, instead of only one clutch plate as in the case of single plate clutch. As the number of clutch plates are increased the friction surface increases the capacity of clutch to transmit torque. The plates are alternately fitted to the engine shaft and gear box shaft. They are firmly pressed by strong coil springs and assembled in a drum shaped flywheel. Each of the plates alternate slides groves on the flywheel and other slides on splines on the pressure plate. Thus, each alternate plate has inner and outer supplies.

The multiplate clutch works in the same way as the single plate clutch operating the clutch pedal.

When the clutch pedal is pressed, the pressure is moved to the right side against the force of the spring. This is achieved by means of suitable linkage and thrust bearing this movement of the pressure plate. (The clutch plate having external splime and internal splines). The clutch plates are released from the pressure. In disengaged position the externally slined plate clutch plate will continue to rotate with the flywheel. But the internally splined clutch plate will be stopped.

Multiplate clutch is if two types namely (i) Dry type and (ii) wet types

Note: West type clutch plates are mostly used in 2. Wheelers. In this case their is a oil bath in which the clutch plates an submerged.

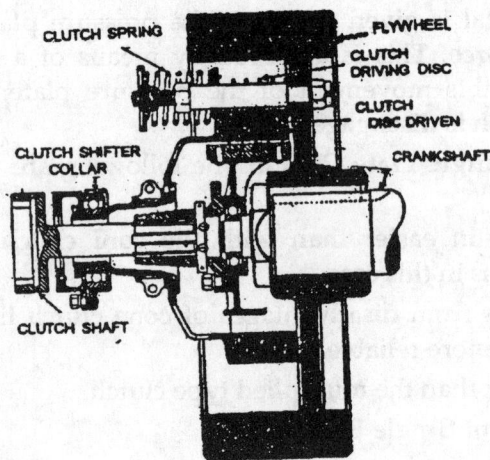

Fig. 17.4. Multiple Clutch

(A) Advantages of Multiplate Clutch: The following are the main advantages of multiplate clutch:

(i) It's capacity to transmit torque is greater than single plate clutch.

(ii) For the same torque transmission, the diameter of clutch plate is less than single plate clutch.

(B) Kinematics of the Plate Clutch: Refering Fig. 17.5 Let r_i and r_o = Internal and External radii of contact surface respectively, (m)

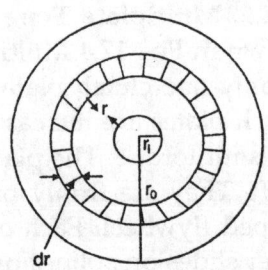

Fig. 17.5 Cross section of contact Surface

W = Axial load extered by actuating spring, N

μ = Co-efficient of frction between the contact surface

Elemental area of ring of radius r with radial width dr,

dA = 2πrdr

if p = Normal pressure

Then total axial load

$$w = \int_{r_i}^{r_o} p.2\pi r.dr \qquad (17.1)$$

and total frictional torque

$$T = \int_{r_i}^{r_o} 2\mu \pi r^2 dr.p \qquad (17.2)$$

$$\begin{bmatrix} \therefore T = F.\, r \\ F = \mu w \end{bmatrix}$$

Case 1. Intensity of pressure of uniform

$$\text{i.e., } P = \frac{w}{\pi(r_0^2 - r_i^2)}$$

Putting the value p in equation, we have

$$T = \int_{r_i}^{r_o} \frac{w}{\pi(r_0^2 - r_i^2)}\, 2\,\mu\, p\, r\,^2 dr$$

$$= \frac{2\mu w}{(r_0^2 - r_i^2)} \int_{r_i}^{r_o} r^2\, dr$$

$$= \frac{2\mu w}{r_o^2 - r_i^2} \left[\frac{r^3}{3} \right]_{r^i}^{r^o}$$

$$= \frac{2}{3}\,\mu w \left[\frac{r_o^3 - r_i^3}{r_o^2 - r_i^2} \right]_{ }^{ri}$$

$$= \mu w r_m$$

$$\left[r_m = \frac{2}{3}\left(\frac{r_o^3 - r_i^3}{r_o^2 - r_i^2} \right) \right]$$

$$T = \mu W r_m\ \text{Nm}\quad (17.3)$$

In general, total frictional torque acting on the friction surface is given by

$$T = n\mu W r_m,\ \text{Nm}\qquad (15.4)$$

Where,

$$n = n_1 + n_2 - 1$$

n_1 = Number of discs of the driving shaft

n_2 = Number of discs on the driven shaft

Case II: Uniform rate of wear;

i.e., pr = C

$$W = 2\pi\, C \int_{r_i}^{r_o} dr$$

$$= 2\,\pi C\,(r_0 - r_i)$$

$$\therefore C = \frac{w}{2\pi(r_o - r_i)} \qquad (17.5)$$

Total frictional torque becomes

$$T = 2\pi\, C\mu \int_{r_i}^{r_0} r\,dr$$

$$= 2\mu\pi\, C \left[\frac{r_o^2 - r_i}{2} \right]$$

$$= \mu\pi\, C\, (r_o^2 - r_i^2) \quad (17.6)$$

Substituting he value of C in equation (17.6), we have

$$= \mu\pi\, \frac{w}{2\pi(r_o - r_i)}\, (r_o + r_i)\,(r_o - r_i)$$

$$= \mu w \left(\frac{r_o - r_i}{2} \right)$$

$$= \mu w r_m \text{ Nm} \qquad (17.7)$$

In general, total frictional torque acting on the friction surface is given by

$$T = n\mu w \left(\frac{r_o + r_i}{2} \right)$$

$$= n\mu w\, r_m \left[r_m = \frac{r_o + r_i}{2} \right] (17.8)$$

Note: The uniform pressure theory gives a higher frictional torque than uniform wear. Therefore, in case of friction, clutches uniform wear should be considered unless otherwise stated.

(C) Energy Lost by Plate Clutch During Engagement: Consider, I_1 and I_2 are the mass moment of inertia of the rotor attached to driving and driven shafts of the clutch respectively,

ω_1 and ω_2 are the angular speeds of driving and drives shafts respectively before engagement of clutch. w is the common speed of both the shaft after engagement of clutch.

Apply law of conservation of momentum, we have

$$I_1\omega_1 + I_2\omega_2 = (I_1 + I_2)\omega$$

$$\therefore \omega = \frac{I_1\omega_1 + I_2\omega_2}{((I_1 + I_2)} \qquad (17.9)$$

Total kinetic energy of the system before engagement,

$$E_1 = \frac{1}{2g} I_1 w_1^2 + \frac{1}{2g} I_2 w_2^2$$

$$= \frac{1}{2g} [I_1 w_1^2 + I_2 W_2^2] \quad (17.10)$$

Total kinetic energy of the system after engagement

$$E_2 = \frac{1}{2g} (I_1 + I_2) w^2$$

$$= \frac{1}{2g} \frac{(I_1 + I_2)(I_1 \omega_1 + I_2 \omega_2)^2}{(I_1 + I_2)^2} \quad (17.11)$$

Hence, loss of kinetic energy during engagement

$$\Delta E = E_1 - E_2$$

$$= \frac{(I_1 \omega_1^2 + I_2 \omega_2^2)}{2g} - \frac{(I_1 \omega_1 + I_2 \omega_2)^2}{2(I_1 + I_2)g}$$

$$= \frac{I_1 I_2 (\omega_1 - \omega_2)^2}{2g (I_1 + I_2)} \quad (17.12)$$

Case-I if driven shaft is at rest, than $\omega_2 = 0$

$$\text{Therefore, } w = \frac{I_1 \omega_2}{(I_1 + I_2)} \quad (17.13)$$

$$\text{and } \Delta E = \frac{I_1 I_2 \omega_1^2}{2 (I_1 + I_2)g}$$

case-II of I_2 is very small compared to I_1 and $w_2 = 0$

$$\omega = \frac{I_1 \omega_1}{(I_1 + I_2)} = \omega_1$$

$$\text{and } \Delta E = \frac{1}{2g} I_2 \omega \omega_1 = \frac{1}{2g} I2 \omega^2 \quad (17.14)$$

$$= \text{Energy given to driven shaft}$$

17.4.3. Cone Clutch:

(i)   Introduction: A simple cone clutch is as shown in Fig. 17.6. Cone clutch consists of friction in the form of cones. The engine shaft consists of a female cone. The male cone is mounted on the splined clutch shaft. It has frictional

. surface on the conical portion. The male cone can slide on the clutch shaft. When the clutch in disengaged, the friction surfaces of the male cone are in contact with that of the female cone, due to the force of spring when the clutch pedal is pressed, the male cone slides, against the spring force and the clutch is disengaged.

The only advantage of the cone clutch is that the normal force acting on the friction surface is greater than the axial force as compared to the single plate clutch. In this case, the normal force acting on the frictional surface is equal to the axial force.

(A) Kinematics of cone clutch: Ref. Fig. 17.6 consider a thin ring at a 'r' running around the cone, the radial width of which is 'dr' and width parallel to conical surface dw.

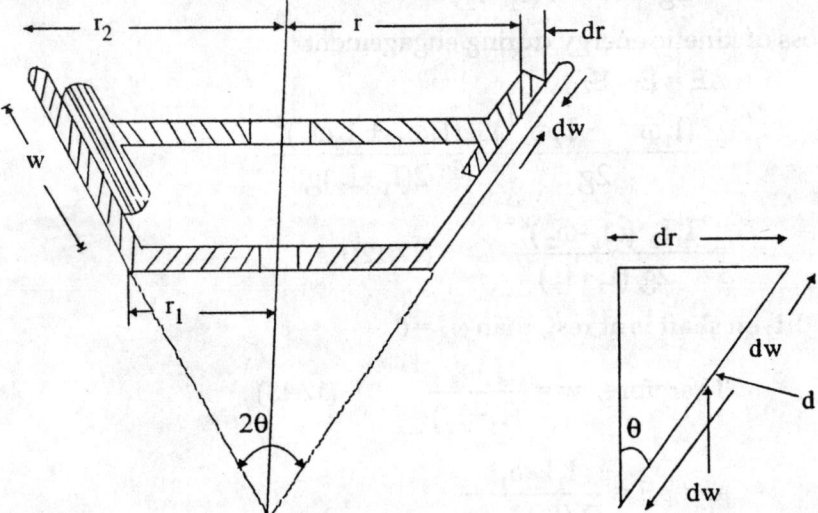

Fig. 17.6 Cone Clutch

Therefore, Area of ring (A) = $2\theta\pi d\omega$

$$= 2\pi r . \frac{dr}{\sin\theta}$$

Normal load on ring,

$$dp = p . 2\pi r \frac{dr}{d\theta}$$

Axial load on ring,

$$dW = dP\sin\theta$$
$$= p\ 2\pi r dr$$

Therefore, total axial load,

$$w = \int_{r_1}^{r_2} p.2\pi r.dr$$

Total torque about the axis,

$$T = \int_{r_1}^{r_2} \mu dpr$$

$$= \int_{r_1}^{r_2} \mu.p.2\pi r.\frac{dr}{\sin\theta}.r$$

$$= \frac{2\mu r}{\sin\theta} \int_{r_1}^{r_2} .p.r^2 dr \qquad (17.15)$$

Case-I. Unifrom pressure rate

$$W = \int_{r_1}^{r_2} .2\pi \ p.r.dr$$

$$= 2\pi p \left(\frac{r^2}{2}\right)_{r_1}^{r_2}$$

$$= \pi p \ [r_2^2 - r_1^2], \text{N} \qquad (17.16)$$

$$p = \frac{w}{\pi\left(r_2^2 - r_1^2\right)}, \text{N/m}^2 \quad (17.17)$$

$$\text{and } T = \frac{2\pi\mu}{\sin\theta} \int_{r_1}^{r_2} pr^2 dr$$

$$= \frac{2\pi\mu p}{\sin\theta} \left(\frac{r^3}{3}\right)_{r_1}^{r_2}$$

$$= \frac{2\pi\mu p}{\sin\theta} \left(\frac{r_2^3 - r_1^3}{3}\right)$$

$$= \frac{2}{3} \frac{\mu w}{\sin\theta} \left[\frac{r_2^3 - r_1^3}{r_2^2 - r_1^2}\right], \text{Nm}$$

$$= \frac{\mu wrm}{\sin\theta}, \text{Nm} \qquad (17.18)$$

$$r_m = \frac{2}{3}\left[\frac{r_2^{\ 3}-r_1^{\ 3}}{r_2^{\ 2}-r_1^{\ 2}}\right]$$

Case-II, Uniform rate of wear, pr = C

$$W = \int_{r_1}^{r_2} 2\pi c\,dr$$

$$= 2\pi\,C\,(r_2 - r_1),\,N \qquad (17.19)$$

$$T = \frac{2\mu\pi C}{\sin\theta}(r_2^{\ 2}-r_1^{\ 2})$$

$$= \frac{\mu\,(r_2+r_1)\,w}{2\sin\theta}$$

$$= \frac{\mu w r_m}{\sin\theta}\quad r_m = \frac{r_1+r_2}{2}$$

$$= 2\pi\mu p w r_m \qquad (17.20)$$

The power capacity of the clutch $= \dfrac{2\pi NT}{60,000}$, kW $\qquad (17.20)$

where, N = speed, rpm

T = Torque of the shaft, Nm

(B) Energy Dissipated due to Clutch Slip and the Time Required to Reach Full Speed from Rest During the Acceleration Period

let,

T = Frictional torque, Nm

I= Moment of inertia of flywheel due to rotation of flywheel, Nm^2

N= speed, rpm

ω = angular velocity, rad/s

θ = Time, s

Then,

$$T = \frac{I}{g}\alpha$$

$$= \frac{I}{g}\cdot\frac{w}{t}\left[\therefore \alpha = \frac{w}{t}\right]$$

$$= \frac{I}{g}\cdot\frac{2\pi N}{60}\cdot\frac{I}{t}$$

$$\text{or } t = \frac{I}{gt} \frac{2\pi N}{60}, \pi \qquad (17.21)$$

Energy supplied during period of clutch slip = Twt, Nm

Kinetic energy developed in the shaft or the flywheel

$$\frac{I\omega^2}{2g} \text{ Nm or J} \qquad (17.22)$$

Energy dissipated due to clutch slip

$$= T\omega t - \frac{I\omega^2}{2g}, \text{ Nm or J} \qquad (17.23)$$

17.5 Clutch Facings: The following are the main characteristics of good clutch facings:

(a)   Good wearing properties

(b)   Presence of good binder on it.

(c)   Cheap and easy to manufacture

(d)   High co-efficient of friction

(e)   High resistance to heat.

17.5.1 Classification of the Clutch facings on the Basis of their Manufacturing Methods: They are classified as follows:

(i)   Mill board type or sheet type (ii) Moulded type and

(iii)   Woven type

(i)   **Mill Board Tyre of Sheet Type:** The word board comes from the fact that a board type construction is prepared in a mill in the form of a sheet. The facing is then cut into different sizes from this sheet. The sheet is manufactured from asbestos imprignated with certain chemicals. This is the cheapest form of the facing.

(ii)   **Moulded Type:** This type of clutch facings are prepared from the mixture of asbestos fibres and suitable binding materials. This mixture is heated to a certain temperature and then moulded under pressure. The moulding is done in a done whose shape and size are similar to that of the facing sometimes, metallic wire are also inserted to enhance were resisting ability of the facing.

(iii)   **Woven Type:** It is further classified into two categories namely (a) Solid type and (b) Laminated type woven clutch type facings are made from cloth impregnated with certain binders. The cloth can be ordinary woven in the warp and weft direction or may be fibres bound in circumferentially direction.

In solid woven facing, there is a weaving in just one-layer required to form the suitable thickness, but there are layers of laminated consists of many lamina.

409

Each of these layers are bounded to each other. These layers are also stitched together in addition to binding.

17.5 2 Clutch Facing Materials: The following materials are used to make facing:
(a)   Asbestos (b) Reybestos and ferodo
(c)   Fabric (d) Leather (e) cork (f) organic fibre composites (g) sinerted metal (h) metal ceramic

Co-efficient of friction in these material varies between 0.3 to 0.75. Fabric leather rand cork are not suitable for high temperature application. The asbestos and reybesto posses high anti-heat property besides high co-efficient of friction and hence are very suitable materials. They are universally accepted material for use as clutch facing.

Fibrous composites are light weight and strong materials. Its use is increasing now-a-days. Facing made of sintered metal can sustain a very high temperature without showing any appreciable negative effect. They are therefore, sustained for use in severe condition. A metal ceramic composite is yet another suitable facing material for high temperature and extreme condition.

17.5.3. Clutch Linkage: The clutch linkage is used for mechanical operation. On pressing the clutch pedal the shaft 'A' turns which moves the effort level and then through the shaft 'B' actuates the forks to the press thrust bearing. This movement is further conveyed to release fingers to disengeage the clutch. Generally, mechanical leverage from 10:1 to 12:1 is employed, when the clutch pedal is pressed, the thrust bearing is not pressed immediately. Rather a part of the pedal movement is purposely kept idle. This is done to avoid a rapid wear of the thrust bearing and the clutch plaster an is called clutch free pedal plate.

17.5.4. Clutch Plate: A clutch plate basically consists of a central steel plate with a susplined hub friction facing and the rivets are made for attaching friction facing on both sides of the steel plate.

17.5.5. Classification of Clutch Plate: They are classified as follows:
(i)   Solid clutch plate (having no spring)
(ii)   Axially cushioned clutch plate (having cushioning spring only)
(iii)   Axially and torsionaly cushioned clutch plate (having cushioning and tersional spring)

A clutch plate consists of 2-sets of clutch facing or friction material mounted on steel cushion springs. The facings and cushions springs are riverted to a centre plate. Sub-assembly and spring retainer plate, which are slotted for the insertion of the tersional spring. These springs contact the hub flages that fit between the spring retainer plates and the center plate sub-assembly. This construction helps to transmit the twisting force which is applied to the facings to the splined hub. The spring action serves to reduce torsional vibration and shocks between the engine and the tranmission during clutch operation. The facings and the plates rotate with respect to the hub to the limit of the springs or to the limit of the spring stops. When the clutch is engaged, the pressure on the facings compresses the cushion the spring sufficiently to course the unit to decrease in thickness. This construction helps to make clutch engagement smooth.

17.5.6. Important Parts of a Clutch Housing-Pressure Plate Assembly: The following are the main parts of the clutch assembly: (i) cover (ii) Release finger (iii) Anti-rottel spring (iv) Pressure plate (v) Thrust spring (vi) Eye bolt (vii) Eye bolt nut (viii) Release lever pin (ix) Strupt (x) Ferrule for strap (xi) Bolt for strap.

17.6. Gear Box: The gear box is fitted just after the clutch and transmits power from clutch to final drive. The transmission box (gear box) consists of train of gears of different sizes contained in case.

The functions of the transmission are the following:

(i)   The gear in neutral position, disconnects the clutch shaft from the driving shaft. Hence, it does the same function of the diengaged clutch.

(ii)   It changes the direction of rotation of driving wheels, when gear are meshed in reverse position, giving back-work movement of tractor (vehicle).

(iii)   In low or second gear the engines crankshaft revolves at a higher speed while the wheels turn at lower speed. Thus tranmission delivers sufficient torque at the driving wheels that is required to the vehicles, carrying heavy loads, climbing a hill or transversing rough road.

(iv)   At top gear the transmission enables the vehicle to turn at the highest speed.

17.7. Resistance to A Tractor (vehicle) in Motion:

The moving vehicle has to force the following resistance on track.

(i)   **Air resistance (R_a).** The faster the tractor runs the more resistance it has to face. To reduce the resistance the front portion of the tractor (bonnet) is given slope so that air can be easily turn apart.

Note: $R_a \alpha v^2$

where, v = velocity

(ii)   **Grade Resistance:** A Tractor (vehicle) has to exert more GR while climbing steep hills. It depends upon gradient, type of road and load on tractor.

(ii)   **Roling Resistance:** We know that more force is required to more the stationary tractor and once the tractor starts rolling, less force is required. This is known as rolling resistance and this depends upon ground, tyres and weight.

17.8. Tractive Effort: It is a force available at the points of contact between the rear wheel type and ground & road, kachcha road etc.

19.9. Terminology Related to Transmission:

19.9.1 Engine Torque (Te):
Mathematically it is expressed as

$$T_e = \frac{60 \times P_e}{2\pi N_e}, Nm \quad (17.24)$$

where,

P_e = Power of the Engine, W

T_e = Engine torque, Nm

N_e = Engine speed, rpm

19.9.2 Road Wheel Torque (Tw) =
Mathematically, it is expressed as

$$T_w = \frac{g_r \times a_r \times \eta_t \times T_e}{N_e}, Nm \quad (17.25)$$

$$= \frac{g_r \times \eta_t \times T_e}{N_e}, Nm \quad (17.26)$$

Where,

g_r = Gear box ratio

a_r = Rear axle ratio

G_r = overall gear ratio ($g_r \times a_r$)

η_t = overall transmission efficiency

19.9.3 Tractive Effort (Tef):
Mathematically, it is expressed as,

$$Tef = \frac{T_w}{r}. \quad (17.27)$$

19.9.4 Gear Ratio (Ge):
Mathematically, it is expressed as

$$Gs = \frac{N_2}{N_1} = \frac{1}{V.R.} \quad (17.28)$$

$$\frac{D_1}{D_2} = \frac{T_1}{T_2}$$

Where, N_1 = Speed of drive, rpm

N_2 = Speed of driven, rpm

D_1 = Diameter of driver shaft

D_2 = Diameter of driven shaft

T_1 = Teeth on driver

T_2 = Teeth on driven

19.9.5 Compound Gear Ratio (G_c): Mathematically, it is expressed as,

$$G_c = \frac{\text{Velocity of last driven}}{\text{Velocity of Ist driven}} \quad (17.29)$$

$$= \frac{\text{Product of teeth of driver}}{\text{Product of teeth of driven}} \quad (17.30)$$

19.9.6 Circular Pitch (P_c): Mathematically, it is expressed as,

$$Pc = \pi D/T \quad (17.31)$$

Where,

D = Diameter of the pitch circle

T = Number of the teeth on wheel

Note: Meshing gears have same circular pitch.

19.9.7 Diametral Pitch (P_d): It is the ratio of number of teeth on the pitch circle diameter in mm and mathematically expressed as

$$P_d = \frac{T}{D} = \frac{\pi}{P_c} \quad (17.32)$$

$$P_d = \frac{2Cd}{1+R}, \text{ for pinion} \quad (17.33)$$

$$2C_d - P_d = \frac{2C_d}{\left(1+\dfrac{1}{R}\right)} \quad (17.34)$$

Where,

T = Number of Teeth

D = Pitch circle diameter

R = Gear Ratio

19.9.8 Module (m): It is the ratio of the pitch circle diameter millimeters to the number of teeth. Mathematically it is expressed.

$$m = \frac{D}{T} \quad (17.35)$$

Root Circular Diameters: Mathematically, it is expressed as,

Root Circle diameter = Pitch circular diameter x $\cos\phi$ - $\quad$ (17.36)

Where, ϕ = pressure angle

17.10 Classification of Gear:

17.15.1 On the Basis of Arrangement of Teeth Along the Width of the Gears: They are classified as follows:

(i) Straight (spur gear) (ii) Spiral (helical)

and (iii) Double spiral (herring bone gear)

(i)   Spur Gear: The arrangement of teeth in spur gear is straight across the face of gear as shown in Fig. The fig 17.7 also illustrates the plane type of spur gear with the two-shafts parallel. Spur gears have advantages of strength and simplicity. Spur gear can be mounted easily for sliding mesh. Since, it is difficult to mesh fully more than one pair at a time, spur gear teeth must be strong enough to with stand the bending stresses produced by transferring the load from one pair of teeth to the next. They are noiser in operation than helical or spiral gear.

Fig.17.7. Spur Gear

(ii)   Helical Gear: On the helical gear the gears teeth are extended helically across the face as the gears shown in Fig. 17.8. The fig also shows a plane helical gear with this design. It is easier to distribute the load to two or more teeth at the same time. For this reason, helical gear can be made lighter and can run at high speed without creating trouble. These gear provide silent operation and smooth operation.

Fig. 17.8. Helical Gear

(iii)   Hearing Bone gera or Double Spiral Gear: The hearing bone gears are shown on Fig. 17.9. In this the gear the teeth are cut across the face of gears in hearing bone pattern. This pattern can not be used in sliding mesh type gears

17.10.2 On the Basis of Relative Position of the two Shafts: The following are main types of gears on the basis of relative position of the two shafts:

(i)   Bevel Gear: Bevel gears are generally employed, so that power can be transmitted from one shaft to another shaft at an angle to it but in the same plane. This angle is usually right angle (90°) as shown in Fig. 17.10. Bevel gear can be of the helical or spur type. The out lines of beval gear teeth are generated in the form of a pair of cones. Whose vertices coincide at the point of intersection of their axis. The small gear is called Bevel pinion or gear and the gear is the Ring gear. There is of course a gear reduction from the small to the large gear. When its teeth are straight than it is called Spur Bevel Gear but

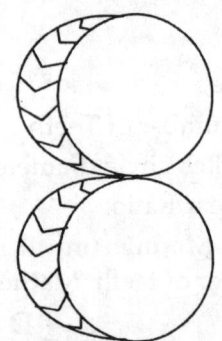

Fig. 17.9 Herring
Bone Gear

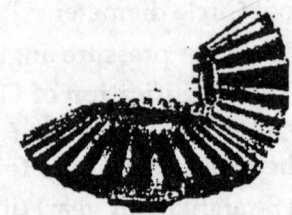

Fig. 17.10 Bevel Gear

when their teeth are helical or spiral then it is called Helical Bevel Gear. Helical bevel gears are quieter and smoother in operation than the Spur Bevel gear.

(ii)   Hypod Gear or Spiral Gear

Fig. 17.11. shows a set of hypoid gears. These gears are used in the final drive also. As shown in the Fig their shaft, is at 90 angle but are not in the same plane. It is special type of helical bevel gear in which the axis of the pinion is perpendicular to the axis of the ring gear but doesn't intersect with it. This difference in level between the axis of two gear permits the floors of cam to be lower with the same axle clearance than when spiral bevel gear are used.

Fig. 17.11. Spiral Gear

17.11 Components of Drive Trains: The following are the main or major components of a complete drive train of a tractor.

(i)   Traction and PTO friction clutch: It is used to connect and disconnect torque transmitting elements rotating at different speeds.

(ii)   Transmission: The driver-controlled speed change portion of the drive train.

(iii)   PTO drive: It is used to transmit power from the engine to the PTO out-shaft.

(iv)   Mechanical front wheel drive: It is used to transmit power to the front axle drive lines on tractor equipped with front-wheel drive.

(v)   Transmission and hydraulic pump drive: It is used to transmit power to pumps for the transmission and hydraulic systems on tractor.

(vi)   Spiral bevel gear set: A special gear set that provides a right angle drive a speed reduction.

(vii)   Differential: A set of bevel gears which is used to create difference in the speed of outer wheel and inner wheel at curve path.

(viii) Final drive: It is used to provide the accurate axle speeds and to reduce torque loads on and size of the differential and spiral bevel set.

(ix)   Individual axle brakes: It is used to restrict or smooth the rotation of one or both the axle shafts by driver.

(x)   Rear axle: It is used to transmit power to the tractor rear wheels and transmit the wheel loads to the tractor structure.

17.17. Classification of Transmission: The following main types transmission are used in Tractor:

(i)   Crash mesh or sliding mesh (ii) Constant mesh (iii) synchro mesh and (iv) Planetary

17.12 Sliding Mesh Gear Box: It is the simplest type gear box. These type of gears were used in earlier days in which one moving gear was pulled out and pushed to mesh another gear. Fig. 17.12 to 17.17 show three forward speeds and one reverse speed of a 3-speed gear box of sliding mesh type. The arrangement of gears shown in the Fig. 17.12 are in neutral position. The clutch gear is rigidly fixed to the clutch shaft (A). It is always connected to the drive gear to the counter shaft (B). Gears-1, 2 and reverse are mounted on the splined mainshaft, and they can be slided by corresponding gears of the counter shaft. A reverse idler gear is mounted on the another shaft and always connected to the reverse gear of the counter shaft.

(i)   Gear in Neutral position: Gears are in neutral position shown in Fig. 17.2 when the engine is running and clutch is engaged, the clutch shaft gear drives the counter shaft gear. The counter shaft rotates in opposite direction of clutch shaft. In neutral position only the clutch shaft gear are used. Other gears are free and hence the tranmission of main shaft is not turning. In this condition, the vehicle is stationary.

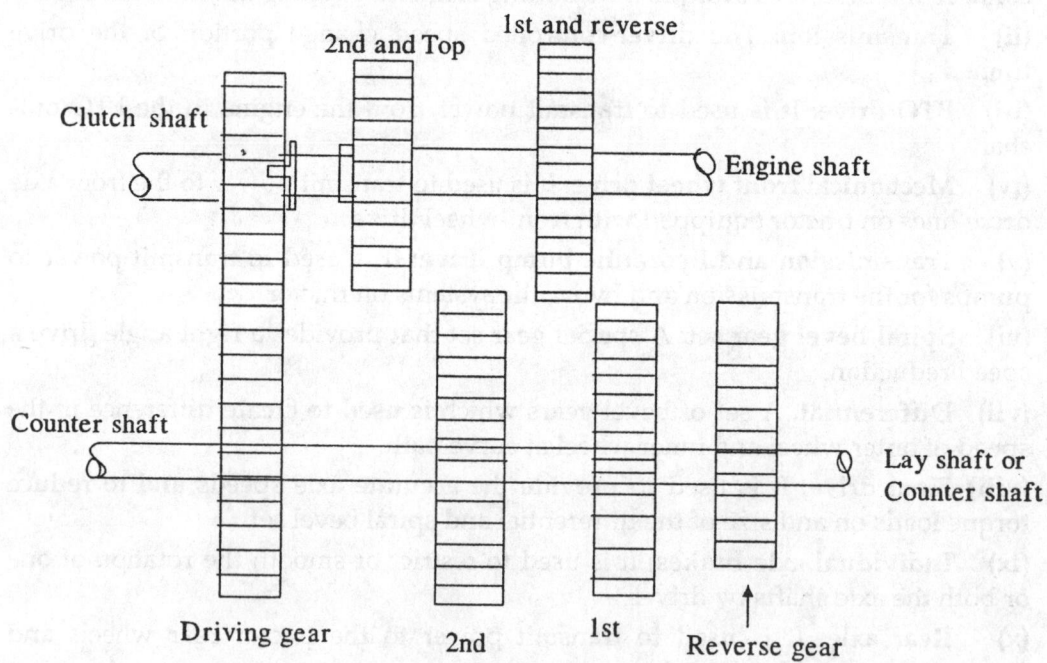

Fig. 17.12. Gear In Neutral Position

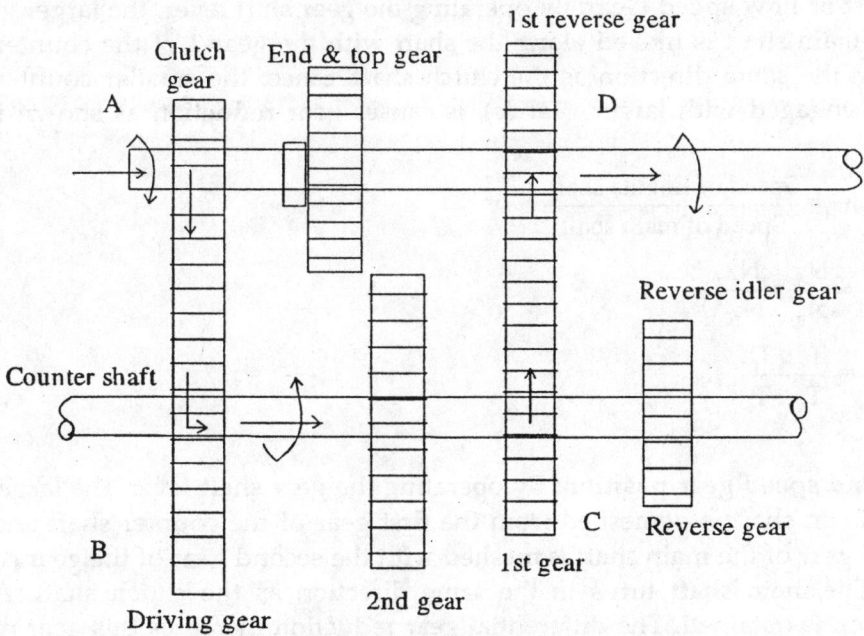

Fig. 17.13. 1st Gear Engagement

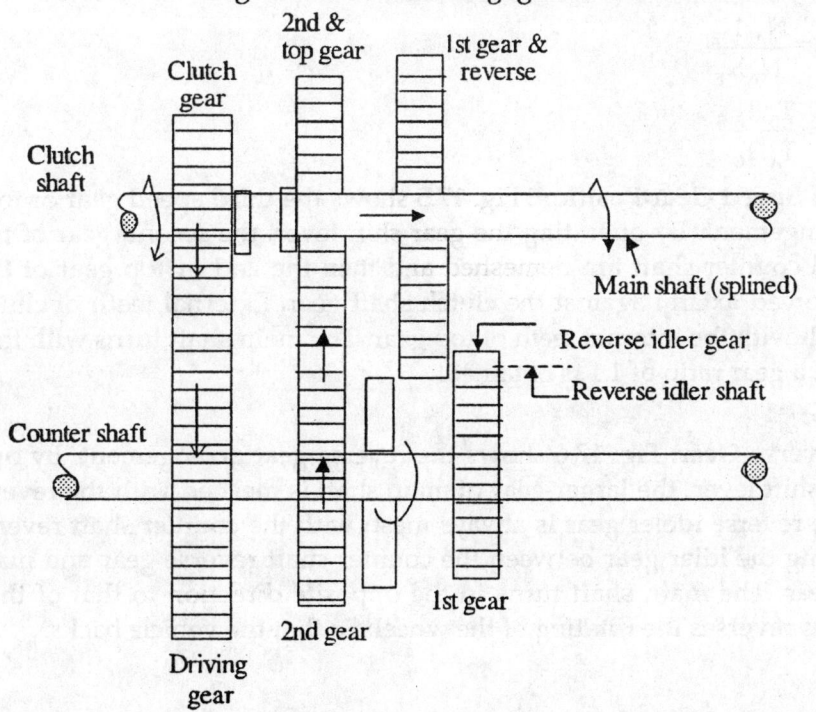

Fig. 17.14. Second Gear Engagement Position

(ii)   Ist or Low speed Gear: By operating the gear shift lever, the larger gear (c) on the main shaft is moved along the shaft with the gear-1 of the counter shaft turns in the same direction as the clutch shaft. Since, the smaller counter shaft gear is engaged with larger gear (c), is causes gear reduction as shown in Fig. 17.3.

$$G_1 = \frac{\text{Speed of Engine shaft}}{\text{Speed of main shaft}}$$

$$= \frac{N_A}{N_B} \times \frac{N_c}{N_D}$$

$$= \frac{T_B \cdot T_D}{T_A \cdot T_c}$$

(iii)   2nd speed gear position: By operating the gear shaft lever, the larger gear of the main shaft is demeshed from the first gear of the counter shaft and then smaller gear of the main shaft is meshed with the second gear of the gear counter shaft. The main shaft turns in the same direction as the clutch shaft. A gear reduction is obtained. The differential gear reduction increases this gear ratio as shown in Fig. 17.4.

$$G2 = \frac{N_A N_E}{N_B N_F}$$

$$= \frac{T_B \cdot T_F}{T_A \cdot T_E}$$

(iv)   3rd Speed Gear Position: Fig. 17.5 shows the third speed gear or top speed gear arrangement. By operating the gear shift lever, the second gear of the main shaft and counter shaft are demeshed and then the 2nd or top gear of the main shaft is forced axially against the clutch shaft gear. External teeth of clutch shaft gear mesh with the internal teeth of top gear. The main shaft turns with the clutch shaft and a gear ratio of 1:1 is obtained.

$$G_3 = 1$$

(v)   Reverse Gear: Fig. 17.6 shows the reverse gear arrangement. By operating the gear shift lever, the larger gear of main shaft is meshed with the reverse idler gear. The reverse ideler gear is always mesh with the counter shaft reverse gear. Interposing the idler gear between the counter shaft reverse gear and main shaft bigger gear. The main shaft turns in the opposite direction to that of the clutch shaft. This reverses the rotating of the wheel. So that the vehicle backs.

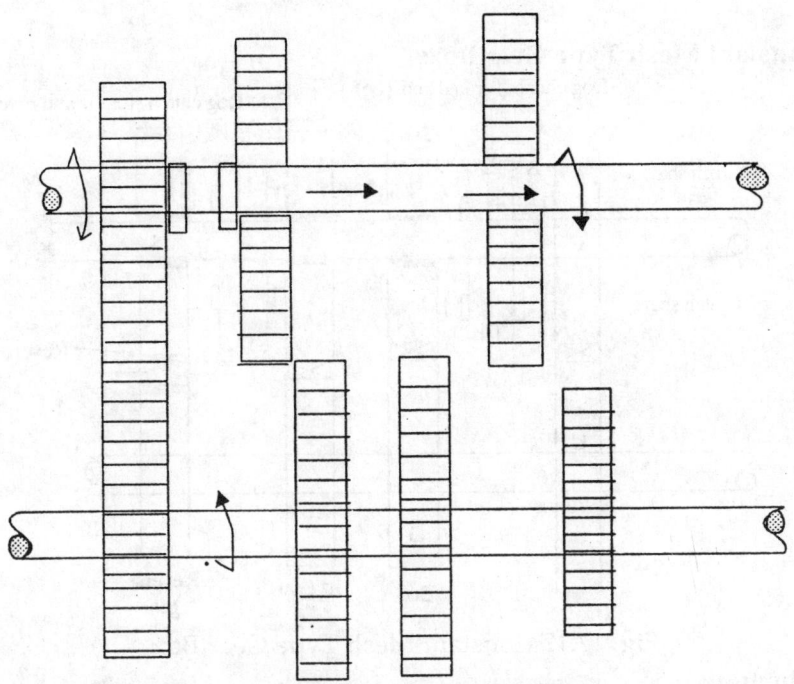

Fig. 17.15 Third Gear Arrangement

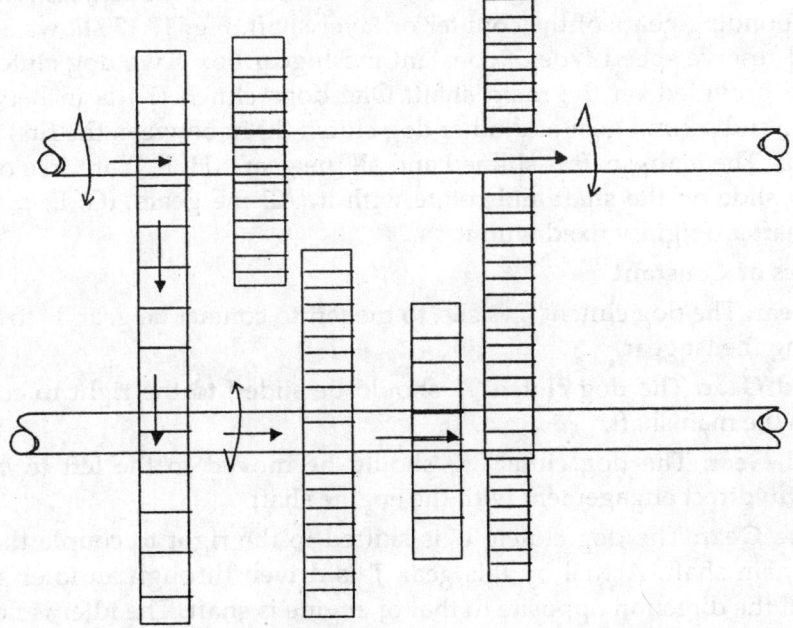

Fig. 17.16. Reverse Gear Engagement Position

17.12.2 Constant Mesh Type Gear Box:

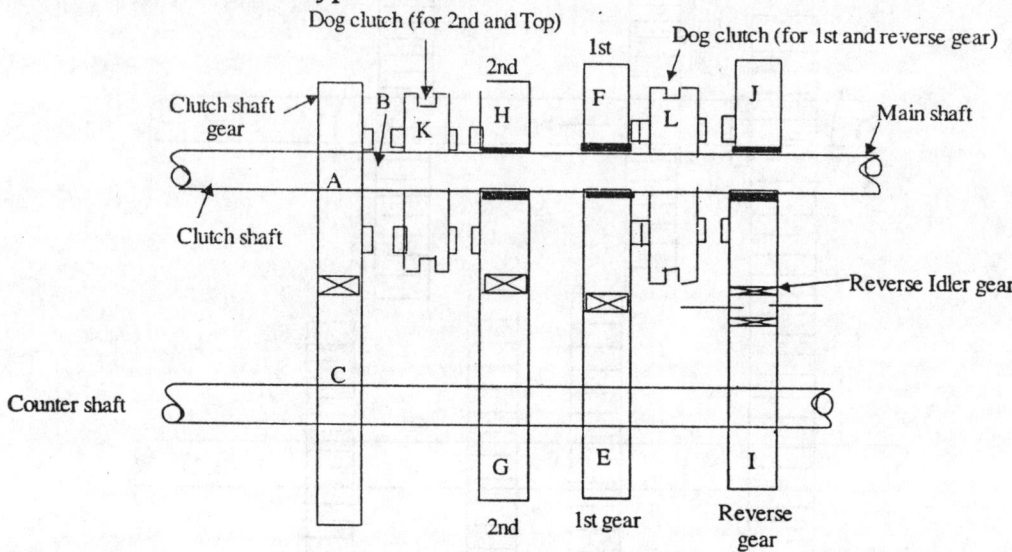

Fig. 17.17 Constant Mesh Type Gear Box

(A) Introduction:

In this type of gear box, all the gears of the main shaft are the constant mesh with the corresponding gears of the counter or layer shaft. Fig. 17.17 shows 3-forward speed and-reserve speed type of constant mesh gear box. Two dog clutches (L & K) are the provided on the main shaft. One dogs clutch (K) is in between the clutch gear and second gear and other dog clutch (L) in between the first gear and revese gear. The main shaft is splined and all the gears (H, F, J) are free on it. Dog clutch can slide on the shaft and rotate with it. All the gears, (G, E, & I) on the counter shaft are rigidly fixed with it.

Kinematics of Constant

(i) First Gear: The dog clutch 'L' is slid to the left to contact he gear 'F' to the main shaft giving the Ist gear.

(ii) Second Gear: The dog clutch 'K' should be slided to the right to couple the gear 'H' to the mainshaft.

(iii) Third Gear: The dog clutch 'K' should be moved to the left to bring the mainshaft in direct engagement with the engine shaft.

(iv) Revese Gear: The dog clutch 'L' is shifted to the right to couple the gear 'J' with the main shaft. Actual by this gear 'J' is driven through an idler so that it revolves in the direction opposite to that of engine is shaft. The idler is not visible in the figure.

For the gear box all the different gear ratios can be obtained in the similar way as in the sliding mesh type.

17.12.3. Epi Cyclic or Planetary Gear:

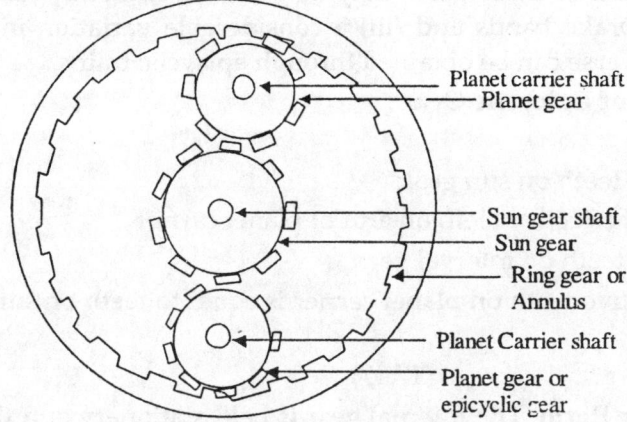

Fig. 17.18. Planetary Gear

(A) Introduction:

An epicyclic gear box consists of two, three or even four epicyclic or planetary gear sets. Fig. 17.18 and 17.19 show an epicylcic gear box in the simple form. In centre, there is a sun gear about which Planet gears turn round. These planets gears are carried by a carrier and a shaft and are also in mesh internally with a ring gear. The ring gear is also called Annular gear or Internal gear.

Different torque ratio i.e., speed ratio are obtained by making any one of the part (the sun gear, the ring gear or the planet gear) stationary Epicyclic gear are widely used in automatic transmission because,

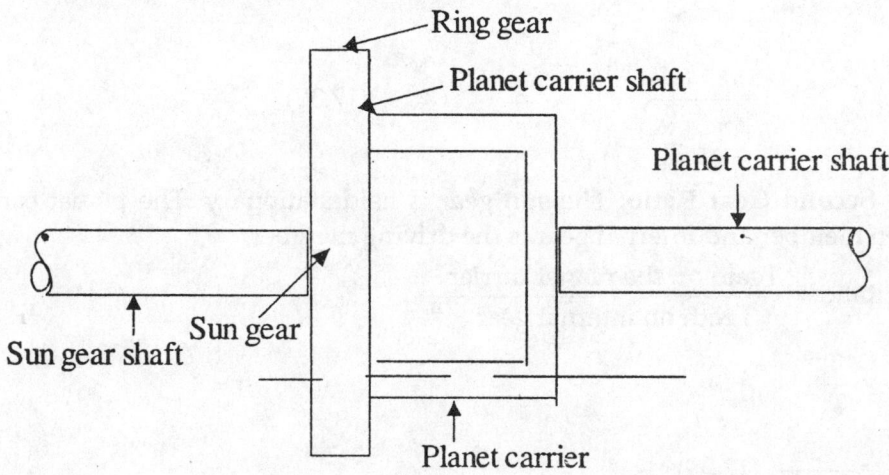

Fig. 17.19. Sectional View of Planetary Gear.

(i)   They are always in contact mesh

(ii) Engagement of these gears may be obtained smoothly and quickly by the application of brake bands and **(iii)** a considerable variation in gear ratio both forward and reverse can be obtained through epicyclic trains.

(B) Kinematics of Epicyclic Gear

Let

T_S = Number of teeth on sun gear,

T_A = Number of effective teeth on arm of planet carrier

T_I = Number of teeth on interval gear

Therefore, effective teeth on planet carrier is equal to teeth on sun gear plus teeth on internal gear.

i.e., $T_A = T_S + T_I$ (17.37)

(i) **First Gear Ratio:** The internal gear is held stationary and the planet carrier is driven by the power supplied to the sun gear

$$\text{Gear Ratio} = \frac{\text{Speed of driven shaft}}{\text{Speed of driving shaft}}$$

$$= \frac{\text{Teeth on the driving shaft}}{\text{Teeth on the driven shaft}}$$

$$= \frac{\text{Teeth on sun gear}}{\text{Teeth on planet carrier}}$$

$$\text{or } \frac{T_S}{T_A} = \frac{1}{\dfrac{T_A}{T_S}}$$

$$= \frac{1}{1 + \dfrac{T_A}{T_S}} \qquad (17.38)$$

(ii) **Second Gear Ratio:** The sun gear is held stationary. The planet carries is driven member and internal gear is the driving member,

$$\text{Gear Ratio} = \frac{\text{Teeth on the planet carrier}}{\text{Teeth on internal gear}}$$

$$= \frac{T_i}{T_A}$$

$$= \frac{1}{1 + \dfrac{T_s}{T_i}} \qquad (17.39)$$

(iii) **Reverse Gear:** Here, the planet carrier is held stationary the internal gear is driven by the sun gear to which the power is applied,

$$\text{Gear Ratio} = \frac{\text{Teeth on the sun gear}}{\text{Teeth on the internal gear}}$$

$$= \frac{T_s}{T_i} \qquad (17.40)$$

(C)   Tabular Method: Assumption: Anticlockwise rotation is positive and vice versa

When the sun gear makes one revolution anticlockwise, the platnet carrier makes $\dfrac{T_S}{T_A}$ clockwise

i.e., The angular gear will make $= \dfrac{T_S}{T_I} \times \dfrac{T_A}{T_S}$

$$= - \frac{T_S}{T_I}$$

This statement is entered in the first column of table

If the sun gear makes x revolutions, then planet carrier makes $-x \dfrac{T_S}{T_A}$ revolution

and annular gear makes $-x \dfrac{T_S}{T_I}$ revolution. These statements are entered in 2nd row of the table.

Each element of the epicyclie gear is given y-revolutions and entered in the third row of column the table.

Finally the motion of each element of the train is added up and entered in the fourth row of table. The use of table for compound epicyclic gear will be clear through examples.

Step No	Condition of motion	Revolution of elements		
		Sun gear	Planet carrier	Angular gear
1.	Sun gear rotates + 1 revolution	+1	$-\dfrac{T_s}{T_A}$	$-\dfrac{T_s}{T_I}$
2.	Sun gear rotates through x-revolution	+x	$-x\dfrac{T_s}{T_A}$	$-x\dfrac{T_s}{T_I}$
3.	Add + by revolution to all elements	+ y	+y	+y
4.	Total motion	x+y	$y - x \dfrac{T_s}{T_A}$	y-x

Note: A epicylic gear box is a compound epicyclic gear trains which contains number of simple gear trains provides higher velocity ratios and to allow several rotation be obtained.

(c)   Torque and Tooth Loads in Epicyclic Gear Trains:

Let

t_i = input torque or driving torque having wheel speed w;

t_o = output or resisting torque having wheel speed, wo

t_w = holding torque or breaking torque which makes the corresponding wheel speed, w_n is zero.

i.e., $\Sigma t = 0$

or $t_i + t_o + t_h = 0$ (17.41)

If the friction loose of teeth during mesh and the friction losses at bearings are neglected, then total energy must be equal to zero.

$$ie., \Sigma t_o\omega = 0$$

$$or\ t_i\,\omega_i + t_o\omega_o + t_h\,\omega_h = 0$$

$$or\ ti\,\omega_i + t_o\omega_o = 0 \qquad (\because \omega_h = 0)$$

$$\therefore t_o = -\,t_i\frac{\omega_i}{\omega_o}$$

$$and\ t_n = -\,(t_i + t_o) = -\left(t_i - t_i\frac{\omega_i}{\omega_o}\right) \qquad (17.42)$$

$$\therefore t_h = t_i\left(\frac{\omega_i}{\omega_o} - 1\right) \qquad (17.39)s$$

Considering the simple gear trains as shown in Fig.

$$t_i = t_s,\ t_o = t_A$$

$$\frac{\omega_i}{\omega_o} = 1 + \frac{T_I}{T_S},\ for\ the\ first\ gear\ ratio, \quad (17.43)$$

$$t_o = t_A = -\,t_s\left(1 + \frac{T_I}{T_S}\right) \qquad (17.44)$$

Negative sign for the movement in opposite direction

$$and\ t_h = t_s\frac{T_I}{T_S} \qquad (17.45)$$

17.12.14 Synchromesh Type Gear: It is similar to the constant mesh with the corresponding gears on the counter shaft the gear on counter shaft or lay shaft fixed to it provide these on the main shaft are free to rotate on the same. It's working is also similar to the constant mesh type. But in the former there is a definite improvement over the latter. There is the provision of the synchromesh device which avoids the necessity of double de-clutching. The parts which ultimately are to be engaged are first brought into the frictional contact, which equalises their speed, after which this may be engaged smoothly.

Fig. 17.20 shows the construction and working of a synchromesh gear box. In most of the vehicles however. Synchromesh divice are not fitted to all the gears. They are fitted only on the high gears. On the low and reverse gears ordinary dog clutches are only provides for simplicity. This is done to reduce the cost.

In the Fig, 17.20 'A' is the engine shaft, 'B', 'C', 'D' and 'E' are free on the mainshaft and are always in mesh with corresponding gears on the lay shaft. Thus, the all gears on mainshaft as well as on lay shaft continue to rotating so as long as shaft 'A' is rotating there members 'F_1' and 'F'_2' are free to slide on supplies, on the mainshaft 'G' and 'G'_2' are ring shaped members having interval teeth fit on it to the external teeth members 'F_1' and 'F_2' respectively. 'K', and 'K_2' are dog teeth on 'B' and 'D' respectively and these also on to the teeth 'G_1' and 'G_2', 'S_1' and 'S_2' are fork, 'T_1' and 'T_2' are the balls supported by springs. These tend to prevent the sliding of members G_1 (G_2) F_1 (F_2). However, when the forks applied on G_1 (G_2) through fork S1 (S_2) exceeds a certain value, the balls are over come and members G_1 (G_2) slides over F_1 (F_2). There are usually six of three balls symmetrically placed circumferentially in one synchromesh device. M_1, M_2 N_1, N_2, P_1, P_2, R_1 and R_2 are frictional surface.

Fig. 17.20 Synchromesh Type Gear

425

17.18. Fluid Coupling: Fluid coupling posses a driving meber and a driven member. An impeller with radial vanes constitute the driving member and runner with radial varies. Constitutes the drives member as shown in Fig. 17.21 The impeller entire unit is housed in a proper casing. A coupler is mounted on the engine crankshaft and is $\frac{3}{4}$ th filled with suitable oil. A spring loaded sealing ring is provided to make the driven shaft oil tight. At the rotation of the crank shaft, the oil is thrown out by the action of centrifugal force from the centre to the outer edge of the impeller due to which the velocity and the energy of oil increases. After that it enters the runner values at the outer portion and flows towards the centre which causes rotation to the runner unit. The oil continues to circulate uniformly as long as impeller and runner rotate at different speeds but when the impeller and runner starts running at equal speed, the circulation of oil stops. There is no effect of coupling on applied torque but only transmits the torque in an uniform manner.

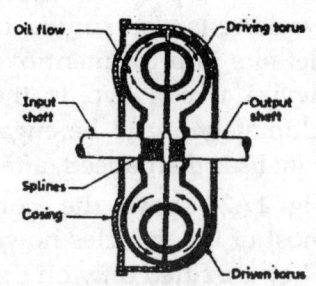

Fig. 17.21 Fluid Coupling

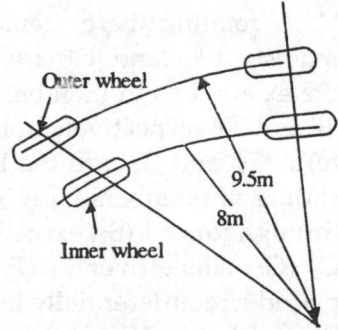

Fig. 17.22 Motion on Curved Path

Feature of Fluid coupling: The following are the main features of the fluid coupling.

(i) Absorption of shock and vibration.

(ii) Smooth starting

(iii) Easy operation

17.18. Diferential:

Introduction: It is a device which is used to create the difference in the speed of outer wheel and inner wheel at curve path.

When the tractor is taking a turn, the outer wheel have to travel greater distance as compared to the inner wheel in the same time as shown in Fig.17.23. If, therefore, the tractors has a solid rear axle only and no other device, there will be tendency for the outer wheel to skid. Hence if the wheel skidding is to be avoided some mechanism be used in the rear axle, which should reduced the speed of the outer wheel, when tracking turn and keeps speed of all wheel same on going straight. Such a device which serves the above function is called a Differential.

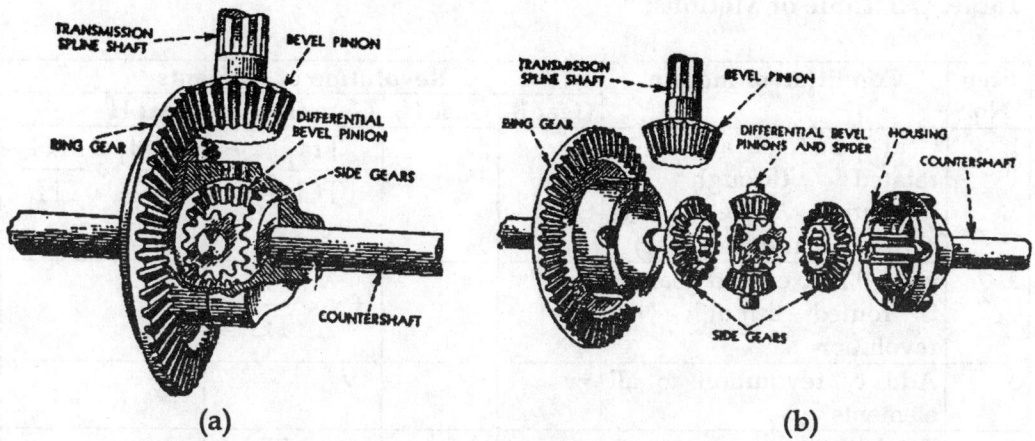

(a)   (b)

Fig. 17.23 Construction and Parts of a Differntial Gear Assembly

17.18. Function of Differential: The following are the main functions of differential:

(i)   To transmit the power from transmission shaft at right angle to the axle shaft to move the wheel.

(ii)   To differentiate the speed of two rear wheels while taking turn.

Fig. 17.24 shows the differential system

Commonly used on tractors: The engine drives the crown wheel or ring gear (R) through the bevel pinion (B). A metallic case known as differential case is mounted on the crown wheel. Two bevel differential pinions, P_1 and P_2 are mounted on the axle 'A' which is carried by the cage. The pinions are free to revolve on axle (A) Side Gears G_1 and G_2 are mounted on the splined end of the leaf axles, which are supported on roller bearing responsible for carrying both radial and thrust leads. The bearings give rigid support for the differential unit and are ready adjusted for end play.

On straight, paths, the cage moves along with crown wheel carrying the differential pinious and run gear without any relative motion among them, causing the half axles to rotate at the same speed.

As soon as any of the rear wheels of the tractor comes across a loose or wet soil, where resistance to both the wheels is not equal or when the tractor is on turn, the unequal resistance will came across both wheels hence speed of the wheel experienced to more resistance will be reduced and accordingly the other wheel acclearte in motion. This may be well understand by drawing the table of motions as follows:

Table: 17.1 Table of Motions:

Step No.	Condition of motion	Revolution of elements			
		Gear B	Gear H_1	Gera G	Gear H
1.	Gear-B in fixed and H_1 is rotated through t_1 revolution. (i.e., one revolution anticlockwise)	0	+1	$+\dfrac{TH_1}{TG_1}$	$-\dfrac{TH_1}{TG} x \dfrac{TG}{TH_1}$ $\Box\, TH_1 = TG_2$
2.	Gear-B is fixed and gear H_1 is routed through (+x) revolution	0	+x	$+ x \times \dfrac{TH_1}{TG_1}$	-x
3.	Add ty revolution to all elements	+y	+y	+y	+7
4.	Total motion	+y	x+y	$y = \dfrac{xTH_1}{TG_1}$	y-x

From the table, we see that when the gear-B, which derives motion from the engine shaft, rotates at y revolutions, then the speed of inner gear H_2 is less than y by x revolutions and the speed of the outer gear H_1 is greater than y by x revolutions. In otherwords, the two parts rear axle and thus the two wheel ro tate at different speed. We also see from the table that the speed of gear B is the mean speeds of the gear H_1 and H_2.

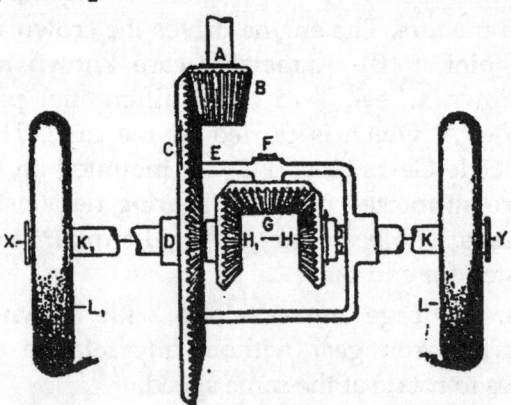

Fig. 17.24 Construction and Operation

Principle (i) When differention bevel pinions (P_1 & P_2) revolved on their own axes, permitting a relative movement between the reax-axle shafts, irrespective of the total drive (ii) one rear and wheel is turned formed the other one is turned via the differential gear through the same distances in opposite direction, at stationary condition i.e., one of the two rear road wheels is blocked, while the engine is running, the speed of the other wheel is doubled.

17.20. Differential Lock: The toruqe from the final drive is also divided between the half shafts. As per rule, equal toruqe is divided betweentwo wheel on the axle evenwhen their speed are different. If one wheel is on a slippery surface where it can simply skid and toruqe that it is transmitted to it will simply cause it to rotate idely, then no tractive force could be obtained from the wheell in this situation the slipping.,wheel will speed at twice crown wheell speed,while opposite wheel wil remain stationary due to differential action. To over come this problem, all tractors are provided with alacking system known as differential lack. It join both the hal faxle shafts. It helps tractor come out of mud where one wheells starts slipping as both wheels move with some speed and apply equal traction as shown in Fig. 17.25.

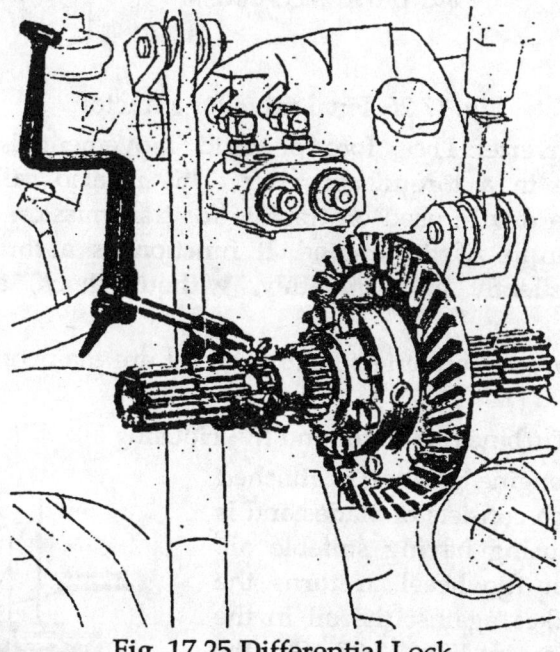

Fig. 17.25 Differential Lock

17.21. Final Drive: The final drive is mounted near the rear drive wheel of the tractor. It helps in minimizing the number of gears and shaft in the gear box to achieve higher torque with less speed on driving wheels. Final drive transmits the power finally to rear axle and the wheels. The tractors rear wheels are not directly attached to thehalf shafts but the drive is taken through a pair of spur gears. Each half shaft terminates in a small gear which meshes with a large gear called bull gear. The bull gear is mounted on the shaft, carrying the tractor rear wheel as shown in Fig. The divce for final speed reduction, suitable for tractor near wheels is known as final drive mechanism.

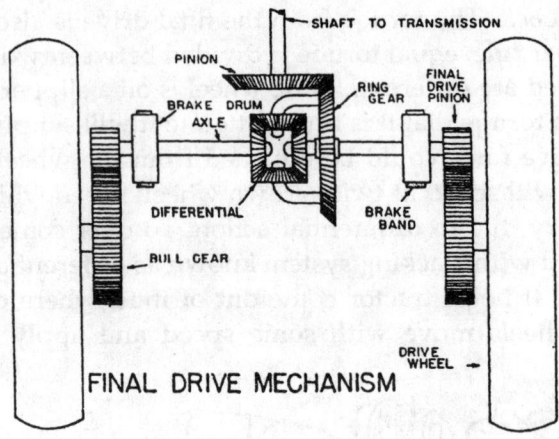

Fig. 17.26. Final drive for a tractor

17.22 Torque Converter: The forc of fluid movement is responsible for multiplying torque in a torque converter. This is also called hydro-kinetic transmission. It is a device used on tractors for transmission of power and for multiplying the torque of the engine. It function as a torque multiplier. It transmits power silently and smoothly, without shock, at various speed andtorque ratio.

Components of Torque converter: Following the are maincomponets of torque convert.

(i)   Impeller (ii) Turbine (iii) Stator and (iv) Housing

In this system, the engine flywheel is attached to an impeller which consists of blades and is contained in a housing having suitable oil. Due to rotation of flywheeel, it turns the impller, which strikes against the oil in the container as shown in Fig. 17.27. On the blades of the turbine driven oil strikes, forcing into spin, creating high input torque. The swirling oil rebounds the turbine blades against the stator. A back is created against the flow of oil. This is a reaction torque and it is added to the input torque. The swriling oil bounced off through the stator and is

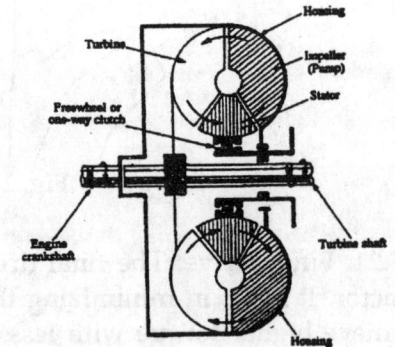

Fig. 17.27. Torque Convertor

redirected back into the spinning impeller blade. Thus the circulating oil is driven around and around.

430

Bouncing from impeller to tubnine, to tator to impeller, helping itselt to multiplying the torque. The turbine is connected to the output shaft to the toruqe converter. Its twisting power (torque) is geared to the rear wheels of the tractor. At high speed low torque is taken by torque converter and convert it to high torque at low speeds.

Prob. 17.1 A diesel tractor is raked at 24 kW and develops a maximum torque of 115 Nm. The largest diameter of a single plate clutch, with both sides effective,that may be fitted to the tractor is 0.25 m. The pressure being applies axially by means of spring is limited in 1.5 x 105 N/m². If the co-efficient of friction between the lining material and the contact surface is 0.26, the inner diameter of the clutch plate, assuming uniform pressure is

(a) 2.14 x 10⁻¹m (b) 1.57 x 10⁻¹ m (c) 2.33 x 10⁻¹ m (d) 2.42 x 10⁻¹ m   (GATE-2004)

Soln. Given P = 24 KW, T = 115 Nm

P_{av} = 1.5 x 10⁵ N/m², μ = 0.25 n = 2, r_o = 0.12 m, r_i = ?

We know that, for uniform pressure,

T = n $\mu W r_m$

$$= n\mu W \; \frac{2}{3} \cdot \left(\frac{r_o^3 - r_i^3}{r_o^2 - r_i^2} \right) \quad (i)$$

W = pav 2π² (r_o^2-r_i^2)   (ii)

Substituting the valve of 'W' in equation (1), we have

$$T = n\mu \; pav \; r_i \; 2\pi \; (r_o^2 - r_i^2) \times \frac{2}{3} \times \left(\frac{r_o^3 - r_i^2}{r_o^2 - r_i^2} \right)$$

or 115 = 2 x 0.25 x 1.5 x 10⁵ x 2π x $\dfrac{2}{3}$ x r_o^3-r_i^3

or, 7.32 x 10⁻⁴ = (0.125)³ -r_i^3

or r_i^3 = (0.125)³ – (7.32 x 10⁻⁴)

or r_i^3 = 1.22 x 10⁻³

$\therefore$ r_i = $\sqrt[3]{1.22 \times 10^{-3}}$

= 1.07 x 10⁻¹ m

Therefore, d_i = 2r_i = 2 x 1.07x 10⁻¹

= 2.14 x 10⁻¹ m

Thus, answer is (a)

Prob. 17.2. A single plate friction clutch with both sides effective is to transmit 15 KW at 2000 rpm. The axial pressure is limited to 0.1 N/mm². If outer diameter of the friction lining in 1.5 times the inner diameters. Find the required outer and inner diameter of the friction lining. Assume uniform wear conditions. The co-efficient of friction may be taken as 0.3. (ARS-2001)

Soln. Given n = 2, p = 15 KW, N = 2000 rpm

p_{max} = 0.1 N/mm^2, r_o = 1.5 r_i μ = 0.3

Since, uniform wear is considered,

$$r_m = \frac{r_o + r_i}{2}$$

$$p_{max} \, r_i = c$$

$$W = 2 \pi \, (r_o - r_i) \, c$$

we know that;

$$P = \frac{2\pi NT}{60,000} \, KW$$

$$\text{or } T = \frac{6000 \times P}{2\pi N}$$

$$= \frac{6000 \times 15}{2\pi \times 2000} = 71.66 \text{ Nm}$$

Again, we know that

$$T = n\mu \, W. \, r_m$$

$$= n\mu \, 2\pi \, (r_o - r_i) \, p_{max} \, r_i \left(\frac{r_o + r_i}{2} \right)$$

$$\text{or } 71.66 = 0.6 \times 2 \pi \, (0.5 \, r_i) \times 10^5 \times r_i \, (1.25 r_i)$$

$$r_i = .06725 \text{ m}$$

$$= 67.25 \text{ mm}$$

$$\therefore \, r_o = 1.5 \times r_i = 1.5 \times 67.25$$

$$= 100.875 \text{ mm Ans.}$$

Prob. 17.3. Two tractor are tested at central testing station. The aim is to determine the power train efficiency of each at a gear train efficiency fo 0.95. It is given that maximum p. t. 0 power of the tractor is euql tothe maximum flywheel power of an engine, and the efficiency of the drive train, including equal traction, is aproximately equal to the maximum available drawbar, power, obtained in a 2-hour maximum power test, divieded by the maximum p. t. o. power at rated speed. [GATE-1998]

Soln. Given,

$$\eta + g - 0.95$$

$$P_{p.t.o. \, max} = p_{max} \, \text{flywheel}$$

$$\eta_{drive} = \frac{P_{db}}{P_{pto}}$$

$$\eta_{power} = \frac{P_{db}}{P_{flywheel}}$$

$$= \frac{P_{db}}{P_{pto}} \times \frac{P_{pto}}{P_t}$$

0.95 x 0.95 = 0.9 Ans.

Prob. 17.4 A tractor engine develops brake power of 24 KW at 2000 rpm. When engaged in first gear drive provides a gear reduction ratio of 40:1 through main gear box and 4:1 through final differential unit. The overall tranmission efficiency in frirst gear is 90% on a right hand curve in first gear, the nearest wheel travels 40% of the crown wheel speed. Determine the torque speed and power at off side wheel. [GATE- 1999]

Soln. Given, P_e = 24 KW, N_e = 2000 rpm

$$N_i = 0.4\ N_e$$

$$\therefore N_i = N_c - x$$

$$N_o = N_c + x \quad (i)$$

Again, $0.4\ N_c = N_c - x$

$$\therefore x = 0.6\ N_c$$

Susstituting the value of x in equation (i) we have

$$N_o = N_c + 0.6\ N_c = 1.6\ N_c$$

Therefore,

$$N_o = 1.6 + N_c = 1.6 \times 12.5 = 20\ rpm$$

$$N_i = 0.4\ N_c = 0.4 \times 12.5 = 5\ rpm$$

We know that

$$Te = \frac{P_e \times 60000}{2\pi N_e} = \frac{24 \times 6000}{2\pi \times 2000}$$

= 114.65 Nm

Again

$$N_e T_e = \eta\ N_p.T_p,\ T_p = \eta\ \frac{N_e}{N_p} \times T_e$$

$$= 0.9 \times \frac{2000}{50} \times 114.5 = 4127.38\ Nm$$

Therefore, $T_c = 4127.38 \times 4$

$$= 16509.52 \text{ N}$$

$$= 16.509 \text{ kN}$$

$$T_{off} = \frac{16.5}{2} = 8.254 \text{ kN}$$

$$Poff = \frac{T_{off} \times 2\pi \times N_{off}}{60,000}$$

$$= \frac{8.254 \times 10^3 \times 2\pi \times 20}{60,000}$$

$$= 17.278 \text{ KW Ans.}$$

Prob. 17.5. MF-1035 tractor has planetary gear drive that has three planet gears each with 18 teeth carried on the carrier. The annular gear which has 54 teeth is held stationary. In the high speed arrangement the power comes into the driven on the sun gear, which also has 18 teeth and rotates clockwise at 1200 rpm giving a forward travel speed in this arrangement. What would be the direction of rotation of the planet carrier? [GATE-2002]

Soln. Given,

$$N_r = 54$$

$$N_s = 18$$

$$N = 1200 \text{ rpm}$$

We know that,

$$\frac{N_s}{N_c} = 1 + \frac{N_r}{N_s}$$

$$= 1 + \frac{54}{18}$$

$$= 4$$

Speed of travel = 300 rpm

Therefore, velocity of wheel = 7.5 Km/h Ans.

PROBLEMS

1. Detemine the maximum, minimum and average pressure in a plate clutch when the animal force is 4 kN. The inside radius of the contact surface is 50 mm and the outside radius is 100 mm.

[Ans. 2.5×10^5 N/m², 1.27×10^5 N/m², 1.7×10^5 N/m²]

2. Five spur wheels A, B, C, D, and E are in gear. A has 50 teeh and runs at 300 rpm, B has 80 teeth, C has 60 teeth, D has 40 teeth and E 120. What will be the speed of (i) B, (ii) C and (iii) E.

[B = 187.5 rpm, C = 250 rpm, E =83.34 rpm]

3. A 35 hp tractor has a four speed sliding, gear box. The speed ratios of the driving shaft to driven shaft are approximately 4:1, 25:1, 1.5 :1 and 1:1 in the first, second, third and top gears respectively.The pitch of gear in module is 7.32 mm and centre to centre distance between matching gears is 80 mm. Find suitable number of teeth on the gears resulting, in first, 2nd speed reduction. Assume the minimum number of teeth on the pinion to be 14.   [GATE-1998, ARB -2001]

[Ans. T_1 = 14, T_2 = 29, T_3 = 25, T_4 = 18, T_5 = 20 T_6 = 24, T_7 = 15 and T_8 =28]

4. The differential in the gear axle of a farm tractor has ring gear with 3.2 teeth driven by a bavel pinion with 8 teeth. Each side gear is connected to a rear axle through a final drive unit that provides a 5:1 speed-reduction. If the input torque to the bevel prinion is 1500 Nm and the input speed is 520 rpm. Calculate the torque and powe in each rear axle when the left wheel encounters poor traction and begins turning 50% faster that the right. Assume differential efficiency as 0.98.

[Ans. 14.7 kN, 31.378 kW]

5. A multiple disc clutch is composed of 5 steel and 4-bronze discs. The clutch is required to transmit 16 Nm of torque. If the inner diameter is restricted to 50 mm,determine the necessary outer diameter of the discs and the necessary axle force. The co-efficient of friction may be taken as 0.1 and the average pressure in not exceed 350 kN /m². Assume uniform presssure [Ans. 77 mm]

SUBJECTIVE QUESTIONS:

1. What do you mean by transmission system of a tractor? What are the functions of the tranmission system?

2. Why a tractor needs a clutch? What are the essential features of a good clutch?

3. What is the pricniple of friction clutch? Explain the working of single plate clutch with the help of diagram?

4. How a single plate clutch differs from a multiple plate clutch?

5. What is the function of a gear box in a tractor?

6. Explain the working of selective sliding type gear box with the help of a diagram.

7. How a constant mesh type gear box works?

8. Derive an expression for torque for single plate, multiple plate clutch.

9. What is the function of a differential in a tractor? Explain its working with the help of diagram.

10. What do you mean by final drive arrangement in a tractor?

11. Write short note on: (a) Fluid coupling (b) continously variable transmission (c) Epicylcic gear (d) sliding gear (e) constant mesh gear (f) Hydrochemical (g) Hydromechanical transmission (h) Toruqe converter (i) Wet clutch (j) Planetary efficiency (k) Differential lock

MULTIPLE CHOICE QUESTIONS

1. Engine power is transmitted to the rear wheel by the
   (a) Power train   (b) front axle
   (c) rear axle   (d) none of these

2. power train consists of
   (a) clutch   (b) transmission
   (c) differential   (d) all of the above

3. Differential is used to
   (a) equlize power   (b) suit different load
   (c) both   (d) none of these

4. Driven assembly contains only one clutch disc, the clutch is known as
   (a) single clutch   (b) multiple clutch
   (c) both   (d) none of the above

5. In cone clutch the contact surface between the driving and driven members froms a part of
   (a) square   (b) triangle
   (c) cone   (d) none of the above

6. Features of fluid coupling are
   (a) absorption of shock and vibration
   (b) smooth starting
   (c) easy operation
   (d) all of the above

7. Fluid coupling consits of a
   (a) driving member   (b) driven member
   (c) both   (d) none of the above

8. A synchrniozed has
   (a) small friction clutches   (b) big friction clutches
   (c) both   (d) none of the above

9. To transmit the power from transmission shaft at right angle to the axle shaft by
   (a) differential assebly   (b) gear
   (c) both   (d) none of the above

10. The gear train used in differential is
    (a) an epicylcli gear
    (b) constant-mesh gear
    (c) both
    (d) none of the these
11. Differential consists of
    (a) a set of bevel gears
    (b) helical gear
    (c) both
    (d) none of these
12. Differential lock provides both wheels
    (a) same speed and equal traction
    (b) different speed and equal traction
    (c) same speed and different traction
    (d) none of the above
13. For multiplying the torque of engine is used
    (a) fluid coupling
    (b) torque converter
    (c) both
    (d) none of these
14. Dog clutch is mostly used in
    (a) tractor
    (b) power tiller
    (c) both
    (d) none of the above
15. Dog clutch having
    (a) cone jaw
    (b) square jaw
    (c) triangle jaw
    (d) none of the above

FILL UP THE BLANKS

1. Differential is used to select speed to .... bad, road and operating conditon.
2. Engine is power is transmitted to the rear wheel by the.................
3. The clutch is fitted in between ....and the gear box.
4. ....is used to contact and disconnect the power from engine to tranmission.
5. In .... , driven assembly has only one clutch disc.
6. The coupling does not increases the applied.................
7. Transmission consists of a .... of different sizess contained in a case.
8. Automatic tranmission uses .... gear train.
9. .... is a special arrangment of gears permit one fo the rear wheels of the tractor to rotate slower or faster than the other constant mesh type consists of .... in shapde.
10. Constant mesh type consists of .... in shape.
11. .... oil is generally recommended for gear box.
12. Gear are usually made of.................
13. Final drive is a................ unit is the power trains between differential and the driven wheels.
14. Final derive transmits the power finally to the .... and the wheels.
15. .... is a speed reducing mechanism, equipped with gears.

ANSWERS

1. suit 2. power train 3. engine 4. clutch 5. single plate 6. clutch torque 7. train of gears 8. planetary 9. differential unit 10. helical 11. SAE -90 12. alloy steel 13. gear reduction 14. rear axle 15. transmission.

ANSWER OF MULTIPLE CHOICE QUESTIONS:

1 (a) 2 (d) 3 (a) 4 (a) 5 (c) 6 (d) 7 (c) 8 (a) 9 (a) 10 (a) 11 (a) 12 (c) 13 (b) 14 (b) 15 (b)

Chapter 18
Brakes

18.1 Introduction: Brakes are used to stop or slow-down the motion of a tractor (vehicel) depending upon the driver needs. Most of modern farm tractors have two brake pedals which are used for stopping (both pedals) or for low speed turning (left or right) brake pedal. When braked, each where of the vehicle (tractor) builds-up a certain braking force. For this reason, the more is the number of wheels braked, the more will be the braking effort, and sooner will the vehicle (tractor) come to rest.

The following are the basic requirements of a good braking system:

(i)   To stop the vehicle within a shortest possible distance.

(ii)   To act instantaneously in case of an urgent braking.

(iii)   To strong enough to sustain sudden braking force.

(iv)   To opearate with the least effort by the operator.

(v)   It must neither slip or nor should cause any skid to the vehicle.

18.2 principle of Braking: A brake is a device by means of which artificial friction is created which causes sped reduction or stop the motion of vehicle. In this process of performing this function, the brake absorbs their kinetic energy of moving member. However, this rate cannot high enough to stop the vehicle (tractor) instantaneously. Kinetic energy of vehicle (Tractor) is given as

$$\text{K.E.} = \frac{1}{2} m_t v^2 \qquad (18.1)$$

In order to bring the vehicle (tractor) to stop (K.E.=0),
some work has to done onthe wheel and is given by
Braking work done = $F_R \times d$ =K.E. $\qquad (18.2)$
Where F_R = Frictional resitance
d = Distance traveled by the vehicle before stop
= Stopping or braking distance
Based upon the similar concept, if a vehicle has to be slow down from velocity v_1 to v_2 in distance x, then, braking work done is euqal to the loss of kinetic energy.

$$F_R. = \frac{1}{2} m_t (v_1^2 - v_2^2) \qquad (18.3)$$

Again, we know that

$F_R = \mu R$

Where, μ = Co-efficient of friction

R = Normal reaction

$$\therefore \mu Rx = \frac{1}{2} m_t (v_1^2 - v_2^2) \qquad (18.4)$$

18.3 Braking Efficiency (η_{bra}) The rate at which the braking system brings a vehicle (tractor) to rest from a certain road speed is said to be braking efficiency. Mathmatically, it is expressed as

$$\eta_{bra} = \frac{a_{Br}}{g} \times 100 \ . \ \% \qquad (18.5)$$

Where,

a_{bra} = Braking retardation, m/s²

g = Gravity acceleration, m/s²

Its maximum value can be 100% when the braking force, on all the wheels is equal to the vehicle's wt and possible only if $\mu = 1$

18.4 Stopping distance:. Mathematically, it is expressed as

$$d = \frac{1}{2} \frac{v^2}{g\mu \ \eta_{bra}}, \text{ for wheel braking}$$

$$= \frac{1}{2} \frac{v^2}{ng\mu\eta_{bra}} \qquad (18.6)$$

where, n = Number of wheel braked,

18.5 Braking Effect: The effect of applying brakes on vehicle in motion is to cause transfer of its wieght partially, from the rear wheel to the front wheel. The fraction of the wt. transferrd incrases with increase in intensity of braking.

Mathematically, inertia force (I_f) is expressed as

$I_F = ma$ (18.7)

Where, m_t = Mass of the tractor

a = Acceleration of the vehicle tractor

when brakes are applied, the forces I_F and F_R form an anticlockwise couple 'C', whose tendency is cause overturning effect on vehicle. Mathematically, it is expressed as,

$$C = m.f \times h \qquad (18.8)$$

h = Height of C.G from ground

However, the vehicle (tractor) is not going to overturn due to a righting couple produced on the establishment of forces between the wheels and the ground as shown in Fig.

The directions of Fwg. on front and rear wheels are such so as to cause clockwise moment of righting couple and is express as

$$C_{right} = F_{wg}. b \qquad (18.9)$$

Where, b = wheel base

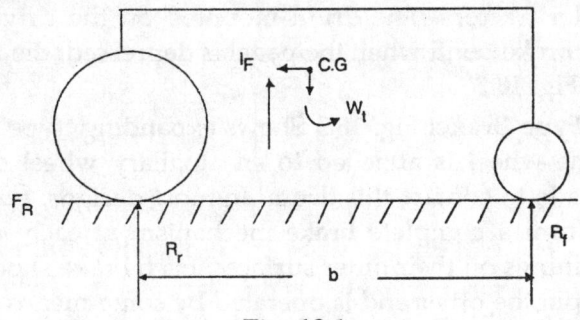

Fig. 18.1

Intially $W_t = 2 [R_r + R_f]$ (18.10)

After braking, $R_r = R_r - F_{wg}$ (18.11)

$R_f' = R_f - F_{wg}$ (18.12)

18.6 Fading· of Brake: Prolonged application of brakes, their effectiveness decreases. This is called fading of brakes. This happens on account of revesible changes, in friction properties of the brake linings on account of high temperature produce due to prolonged application. However, because such properties changes are reversible, usual effectiveness of the brake is restored when they cool off.

18.7 Classification of Brake: The brakes, according to the means used for transforming the energy by the braking element are classified as:

1. Mechanical brake 2. Hydraulic brake

18.7.1 Mechanical Brake: Most of the tractor manufactured in our country are equipped with mechanical brakes. This system is less costly and provide trouble-free service and easy to maintain.

The mechanical brakes, according to the direction of acting of force, may be classified into categories.

(a) Radial Brakes: In these brakes, the force acting on the brake drum is in radial direction. The radial brakes may be sub divided into external

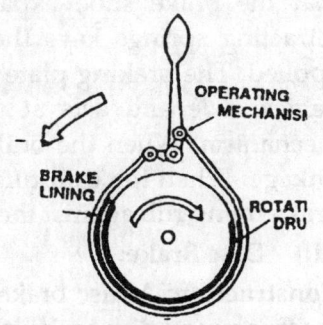

Fig. 18.2. External controlling she type brake

441

contracting brakes and internal expanding brakes. According to the shape of the friction elements,these brakes may be block or shoe brakes and band brakes.

(b)   Axial Brake: In these brakes, the force acting on the brake drum is in axial direction. The axial brakes may be disc brake and cone brakes. The analysis of these brakes is similar to clutches.

Radial Brakes: They can be classified into folowing types

(i) External Contracting Shoe-Type Brakes: This type of brake system is gnerally available on crawler tractors. The drum mounted on the drive axle is driectly sorrounded by the brake bond when the pedal is depressed, the band tightens the drum as shown in Fig. 18.2

(ii)   Expanding Type Brake: Fig. 18.3 Shows expanding type brake linkage. In a motor vehicle the wheel is attached to an auxillary wheel called drum. The brake shoes are made to contact this drum. In most designs, two shoes are used in each drum to form a complete brake mechanism at each wheel. The brake shoes have brake linings on their outer surfaces. Each brake shoe is hinged at one end by an anchor pin,the other end is operated by some means so that the brake shoes expands outward, the brake lining come into contact retraching springs, keep the brake shoe into position when the brakes are not applied. The braking plate complete the brake enclosure holds the assembly to the vehicle axle and acts at the base for fastening the brake shoes and operating mechanism. When the brake pedal is pressed the can turns by the means of brake linakge. When the can turns, the shoes expands out-ward against the drum. The brake lining rubs agains the drum and thus stop it is motions.

In a tractor (motor vehicle) the wheel is mounted to an auxially wheel called drum. The brake shoes are made to contact this drum. In most designs, two shoes are used which eachdrum to form a complete brake mechanism at each wheel. The brake shoes have brake linings on their outer surfaces. Each brake shoe is hinged at one end by an anchor pin, the other end is operated by some means so that the brake shoe expands outeward, the brake living come into contact retracting springs keys the brake shoes into positon when the brakes are not applied. The braking plate complete the brake enclose holds the assembly to the vehicle axle and acts at the base for fasting the brake shoes and operating mechanism. When the brake pedal is pressed the cam turns by means of brake linkage. When the cam turns,the shoes expands out ward against the drum. The brake lining rub against the drum and thus stop its motion.

(iii)   Disc Brake:

Construction: A disc brake resembles to a plate clutch fitted on each wheel. The most common disc brake is spol brake, which consists of following main parts.

(i)   caliper or cylinder casing-outer and inner.

442

(ii) Rotor disc (iii) Piston (iv) Friction pad

(v) Pad supporting plate (vi) Bleedler plug.

Besides above, the disc brake assembly also includes piston seals, dust boot, pad wear indicator etc as shown in Fig. 18.4

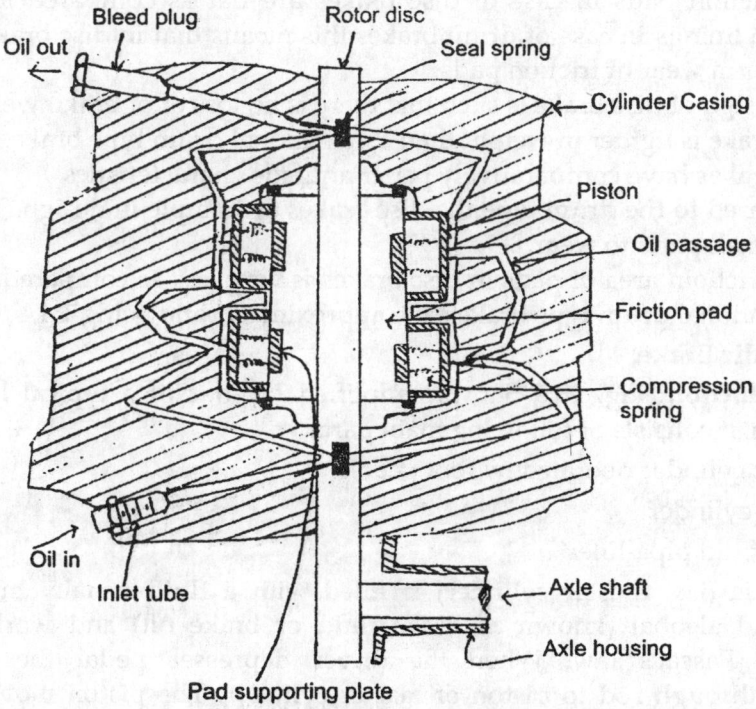

Fig. 18.3. Disc Brake

The cylinder casing is made in two halves named outer and inner cylinder and resembles a calipers. That is why disc brake is also known as caliper type. The caliper is attached to the axle housing in a rear wheel brake and to the steering knuckles in a front wheel brake. The rotor disc is connected to the road wheel through axle shafts. The assembly houses two friction pads, one on each side of disc. These pads are held in postion by steeel pad plats.

The disc brake is operated hdyraulically. When the vehicle is the be braked, the brake fluid pumped by the master cylinder brake pedal enters into the cylinder through inlet tube. It then flows through the passage provided there in and exerts pressure on the pistons. There are four pistons and each of them forces the friction pads against the rotating disc. The pressure of pads spots rotation of the disc and henc ethe axle stops.

When the brake are to be released, the compression springs force back the pistons to release pessure from the friction pads.

18.8 Comparison Betwen Disc. Brake and Drum Brake:

(i)   In case of disc brakes, friction surfaces are directly exposed to the cooling air where as in the drum type the friction occurs on the internal suface, from which heat canbe dissipated only by conduction through the drum.

(ii)   The friction pads in case of disc brakes are flat as compared to curved friction linings in case of drum brakes this means that in disc brakes, there is uniform wear of friction pads.

(iii) The design of disc brake is such that there is no loss of of braking efficiency.

(iv)   Disc brake is lighter in weight than conventional drum type brake.

(v)   Disc brakes have comparatively better antifade characteristics.

(vi)   Compared to the drum type the disc brakes are simple in design. There are very small parts to wear.

(vii) Total frictioin area of pads in disc brakes is very less as compared with the conventional drum type brakes, the approximate ratio being 1:4.

18.9. Hydraulic Brake:

18.9.1 Introduction: Fig. 18.5 Shows simplified lay out of a typical hydraulic brake system. it consists of following main parts:

(i)   Master cylinder operated by foot pedal.

(ii)   Wheel cylinder.

(iii) Brake fluid pipe-lines

The system is (i.e., master cylinder) is filled with a fluid usually mixture of glycerine and alcohal (known as brake fluid or brake oil) and work on the prinicple of Pascal's law. When the driver depresses pedal the effort is transmitted through rod to piston of master cylinder. The piston moves in the cylinder and compresses return spring, forcing out the fluid from the cylinder into brake line through a by-pass. Pistons of a brake cylinde are actuated by the fluid and press against shoe, bringing their linings tightly against the working surfaces of drums.

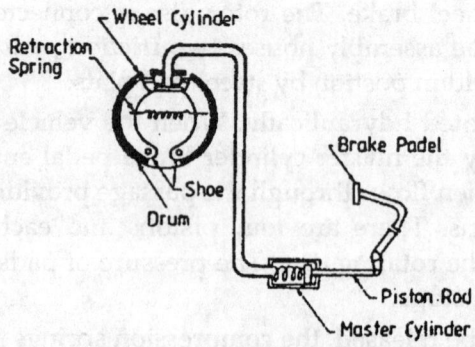

Fig. 18. 4 Hydraulic Brake

As soon as the pedal is released, the retracting spring pushes piston back. At the same time the compression springs of the barke shoe moves piston to their initial position and the fluid brings to flow in the reverse direction.

18.9.2 Advantages of Hydraulic Brake: The following are the main advantages of hydraulic brake.

Components of Hydraulic Brake system: The following are main components of hydralulic brake system.

(i)   Master cylinder (operated by foot pedal)

(ii)   Wheel cylinder and (iii) Brake fluid pipline

(i)   **Master cylinder:** It consists of following main parts

(i)   oil reservior (ii) primary piston (iii) secondary piston (iv)s Brake booster out put rod (v) spring and (vi) parts as shown in Fig. 18.5

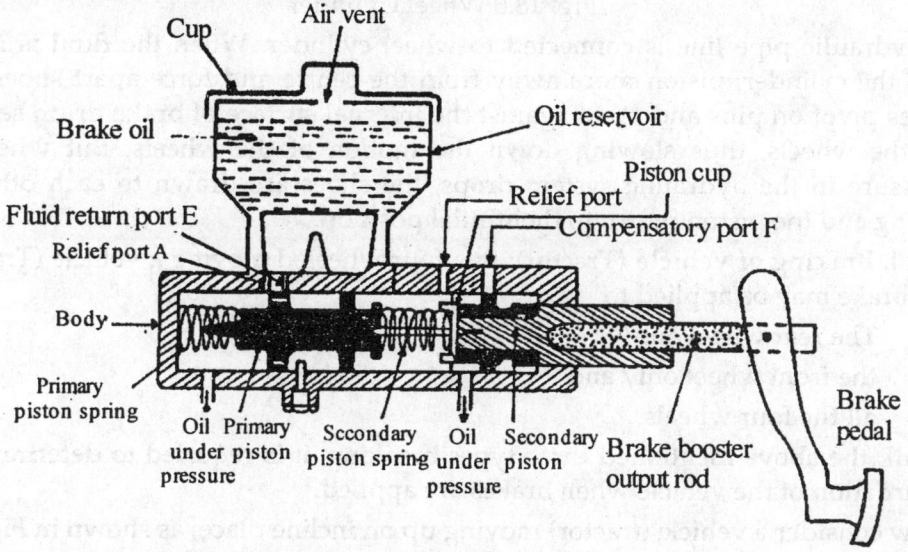

Fig. 18.5. Master Cylinder

When the brake pedal is depressed the brake booster output rod will push the secondary pistion and, at the same time, the primary piston will be pushed by tension force of the secondary piston be springs. As the result, relief parts A and B will be closed by thepiston cups and hydraulic pressure will arise on both the spring and seconary sides. Brake oil in the reservoir tank will flow into part E to compensate the piston stroke.

When the pedal is released both the secondary and primary piston will be return to their original positions by the hydraulic pressure in the pipes and returns force of the piston springs. Remaining fluid will return to the reservoir tank through E and F.

Wheel Cylinder: It consists of following main parts (i) Two pistons (ii) Piston return spring and (iii) Wheel cylinder body enclosing the piston and spring as shown in Fig. 18.6

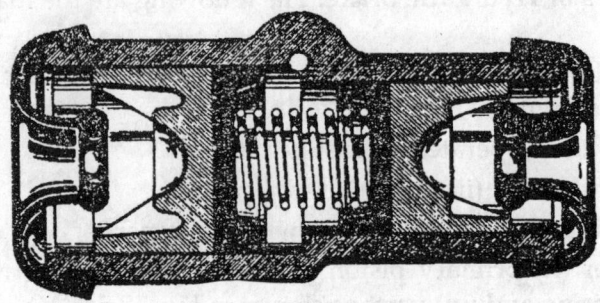

Fig. 18.6 Wheel Cylinder

A hydraulic pipe line is connected to wheel cylinder. When the fluid is forced into the cylinder, piston more away from the centre and force apart shoes. The shoes pivot on pins and press against the internal surface of brake drum secured on the wheels, thus slowing down the motion of the wheels. But when the pressure in the hydraulic system drops, the shoes are drawn to each other by spring and the piston return to their intial position.

18.10. Braking of vehicle (Tractor): In a four wheeled moving a vehicle (Tractor), the brake may be applied to

(i)   The rear wheel only

(ii)   the front wheel only and

(iii)   all the four wheels.

In alL the above mentioned three types breaking, it is requried to determine the retardation of the vehicle when brakes are applied.

Now consider a vehicle (tractor) moving up on incline place, as shown in Fig. 18.8 Various forces and reactions are shown in Fig.18.7

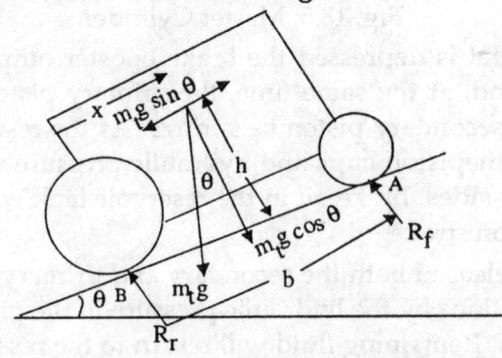

Fig. 18.7. Various forces and reaction acting on Tractor

Consider

θ = Angle of inclination of the plane to the horizontal, radian

m_t = Mass of the tractor, kg

h = Height of the C.G. of the tractor above the ground surface, m

x = perpendicular distance of C.G. from the rear axle, m

b = wheel base, m

R_f = Total normal reaction betweenthe ground and front wheels, N

R_r = Total normal reaction between the ground and the rear wheels, N

μ = Co-efficient of friction between the types and road surface.

a = Retardation of the vehicle (tractor), m/s²

18.10.1. When the brakes are applied to rear wheels only: It is a common way to braking the tractor, in which the breaking the force acts at the rear wheels only.,

Let

F_B = Toal braking force (N) acting at rear wheels due to the application of the brakes. Its maximum value is μR_r

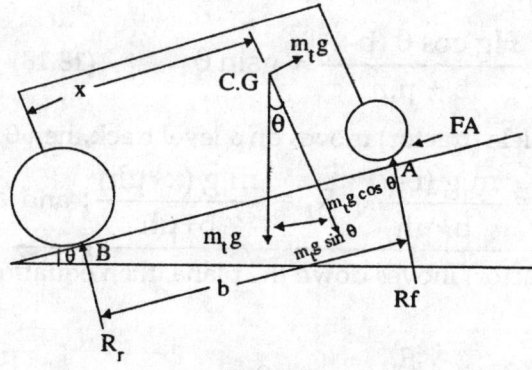

Fig. 18.8.

The various forces acting on a tractor are shown in Fig. 18.8. For equilibrium of the vehcile (tractor,) the force acting on the vehicle (tractor) must be in equilibrium.

Resolving the forces parallel to plane,

$$F_B + m_f.g \ Sin \ \theta = m_t a \qquad (18.14)$$

Resolving the forces perpendicular to the plane,

$$R_f + R_r = m_t \ g \ cos\theta \qquad (18.15)$$

Taking moment about G, the centre of gravity of the tractor,

$$F_B \ h + R_B \ x = R_f \ (b-x) \qquad (18.16)$$

Substituting the value of $F_B = \mu.R_r$ and $R_f = m.g. \ cos-R_r$

in equation of (18.16), we have

$$\mu R_r\, h + R_r\, x = (m_t.\, g \cos \theta - R_r)\,(b-x)$$

$$\text{or } R_r\,(b + \mu.h) = m_t\, g.\, \cos \theta\,(b-x)$$

$$\text{and } R_f = \frac{m_t g \cos (b-x)}{b + \mu h} \qquad (18.17)$$

$$\text{and } R_f = m_f\, g \cos \theta - R_r = m_t\, g \cos \theta\; \frac{m_f g \cos \theta\,(b-x)}{b + \mu h}$$

$$R_f = \frac{m_t.\, g \cos \theta\,(x + \mu h)}{(b + \mu h)} \qquad (18.18)$$

We know from equation (18.14)

$$a = \frac{F_B + m_t g \sin \theta}{m_t} = \frac{F_B}{m_t} + g \sin \theta \quad \text{[substituting the value of}$$

R_B]

$$= \frac{\mu R_r}{m} + g \sin \theta$$

$$a = \frac{Hg \cos \theta\,(b-x)}{b + \mu.h} + g \sin \theta \qquad (18.18)$$

Notes: 1. When vehicle (tractor) moves on a level track, then $\theta = 0$

$$R_r = \frac{m_t g\,(b-x)}{b + \mu h};\; R_f = \frac{m_t g\,(x + \mu h)}{b + \mu h};\; \text{and } a = \frac{Hg\,(L-x)}{b + \mu h};$$

2. If the vehicles (tractor) moves down the plane, then equation (i) becomes

$F_B - m_t g \sin \theta = m_t a$

$$\therefore \qquad a = \frac{F_B}{m_t} - g \sin \theta \qquad = \qquad \frac{\mu Rr}{m_t} - g \sin \theta \qquad =$$

$$\frac{\mu g \cos \theta\,(b-x)}{b + \mu h} - g \sin \theta$$

18.2. When the brakes are applied to front wheels only

It is very rare way of braking the vehicle (tractor). in which the braking force acts at the front wheels only

Let

F_A = Total braking force (N) acting at the front wheels, due to application of brakes. Its maximum value is μR_f

The various forces acting on the vehicle, as shown in Fig.18.9

Resolving the forces parallel to the plane
$$F_A + m_t g \sin\theta = m_t a \qquad (18.20)$$
Resolving the forces perpendicular to the plane,
$$R_f + R_r = m_t g \cos\theta \qquad (18.21)$$
Taking moments about G the centre of gravity of the vehicle,
$$F_A\, h + R_B x = R_f\,(b - x) \qquad (18.22)$$
Substituting the value of $F_A = \mu R_f$ and $R_r = m_t g \cos\theta - R_f$

in equation (18.22), we have
$$\mu R_f h + (m_t g \cos\theta - R_f)x = R_f\,(b - x)$$
or $\mu R_f h + m_t g \cos\theta\, x = R_f b$

$$\therefore\ R_f = \frac{m_t g \cos\theta\, x}{b - \mu h} \qquad (18.23)$$

and
$$R_r = m_t g \cos\theta - R_f = m_t g \cos\theta - \frac{m_t g \cos\theta \cdot x}{(b - \mu h)}$$

$$= m_t\, g \cos\theta\left(1 - \frac{x}{b - \mu h}\right) = m_t\, g \cos\theta\left(\frac{b - \mu h - x}{L - \mu h}\right) \qquad (18.24)$$

We know from equation (18.20).
$$a = \frac{F_A + m_t g \sin\theta}{m_t} = \frac{\mu R_f + m_t g \sin\theta}{m_t}$$

$$= \frac{\mu\, m_t g \cos\theta \times x}{(b - \mu h)\, m} + \frac{m_t g \sin\theta}{m_t} \quad \text{[Substituting value of Rf]}$$

$$= \frac{\mu g \cos\theta \times x}{b - \mu h} + g \sin\theta \qquad (18.25)$$

Notes: 1. When the vehicle moves on a level track, then $\theta = 0$

$$\therefore\ R_f = \frac{m_t g x}{b - \mu h}\,;\ R_B = \frac{m_t\, g\,(L - \mu h - x)}{b - \mu h} \ \text{and}\ a = \frac{\mu g \cdot x}{b - \mu h}$$

2. When the vehicle (tractor) moves down the plane, then equation ( ) becomes
$$F_A = m_t g \sin\theta = m_t a$$

$$\therefore\ a = \frac{F_A}{m_t} - g \sin\theta = \frac{\mu R_f}{m_t} - g \sin\theta = \frac{\mu g \cos\theta\, x}{b - \mu h} - g \sin\theta$$

18.10.3. When the brakes are applied to all the four wheels

This is the most common way of braking the tractor in which the braking force acts on both the rear and front wheels.

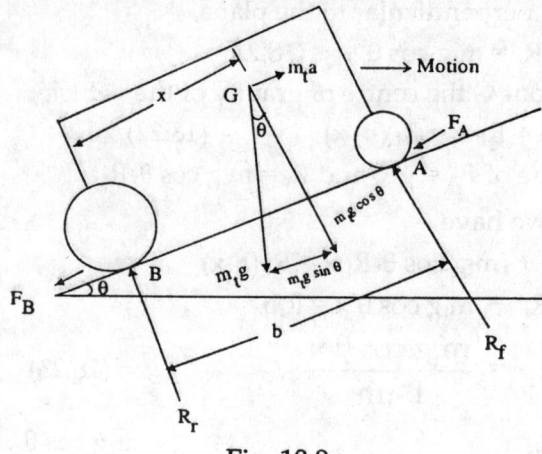

Fig. 18.9

Let

F_A = Braking force provided by the front wheels = μR_r

and

F_B = braking force provided by the rear wheels = μR_r

A little consideration will show that when the brakes are applied to all the four wheels, the braking will be least.

It is due to this reason that the brakes are applied to all the four wheels.

The various forces acting on the vehicle (tractor) are shown in Fig. 18.10

Resolving the forces parallel to the plane,

$$F_A + F_B + m_t g \sin \theta = m_t a \qquad (18.26)$$

Resolving the forces perpendicular to the plane,

$$R_f + R_r = m_t g \cos \theta \qquad (18.27)$$

Taking moment about, G_1 the centre of gravity of the vehicle

$$(F_A + F_B) h + R_r x = R_f (b-x) \qquad (18.28)$$

Substituting the value of $F_A = \mu R_f$; $F_B = \mu R_r$ and

$R_r = m_t g \cos\theta - R_f$ in the equation

we have

$$\mu (R_f + R_r) h + (m_t g \cos\theta - R_A) x = R_A (b-x)$$

$$\mu (R_f + m_t g \cos \theta - R_f) h + (m_t g \cos\theta - R_f) x = R_f (b-x)$$

$$\text{or } \mu m_t g \cos \theta \times h + m_t g \cos \theta \times x = R_f b$$

$$\therefore R_f = \frac{m_t g \cos\theta \,(\mu h + x)}{b} \qquad (18.29)$$

$$\text{and } R_r = m_t g \cos\theta - R_f - m_t g \cos\theta = \frac{m_t g \cos\theta(\mu h + x)}{b}$$

$$= m_t g \cos\theta \left(1 - \frac{\mu h + x}{b}\right) = m_t g \cos\theta \left(\frac{b - \mu h - x}{b}\right)$$

Now from equation (18.26)

$$\mu R_f + \mu R_r + \mu_t g \sin\theta = m_t a$$

$$\mu(R_f + R_r) + m_t g \sin\theta = m_t a$$

$$\mu m_t\, g \cos\theta + m_t\, g \sin\theta = m_t\, a \ (18.31) \text{ from equation} \qquad (18.30)$$

$$a = g\,(\mu \cos\theta + \sin\theta) \qquad (18.31)$$

Notes: 1. When the vehicle (tractor) moves on level tractor, then $\theta = 0$

$$R_f = mg\frac{(\mu h + x)}{b}; \ Rr = mg\frac{(b - \mu h - x)}{b} \text{ and } a = \mu g$$

2. if the vehicle moves down the plane, then equation (18.32) may be written as

$F_A + F_B - m_t g \sin\theta = m_t a$

or $\mu(R_f + R_r) - mg \sin\theta = m_t a$

or $\mu m_t g \cos\theta - m_t g \sin\theta = m_t a$

$\therefore g = (\mu \cos\theta - \sin\theta) \quad (18.27)$

SUBJECTIVE QUESTIONS

1. Discuss the various types of brakes?
2. Describe with the help of neat sketch the principles of operation of an internal expanding shoe.
3. What are the functions fo brake?
4. Describe with the help of neat sketch the principles of operation of the hydraulic brake.
5. Write short notes on:
   (a) Radial brakes   (b) Axial brakes
   (c) Expanding type brake with servo action

MULTIPLE CHOICE QUESTIONS

1. Which of the following requires least pedalforce
   (a) expanding typre brake with servo action
   (b) external contracting shoe type
   (c) disc brake

2. Which of the following is mechanical brake
   (a) radial brakes   (b) axial brakes
   (c) both   (d) none of the above

3. The working principle of hyraulic brake based upon
   (a) Newton's law   (b) Pascal law
   (c) Ohm's law   (d) None of the aboe

4. In crawler type tractor, which type of brake is used
   (a) hydraulic brake   (b) band brake
   (c) contracting shoe type   (d) none of the above

5. In hydraulic brakes, the brake fluid is the mixture of
   (a) H_2SO_4 and HNO_3 (b) glycerine and alcohal
   (c) water and glycerine   (d) none of the above

6. The external contracing shoe type brake is normally used
   (a) four wheel tractors   (b) powe tillers
   (c) scooters   (d) crawler tractor

7. The brake of tractor is mounted on
   (a) drive axel   (b) front wheel
   (c) pedals   (d)   none of the above

FILL UP THE BLANKS

1. Braking effort incrases with .... the number of wheels braked.

2. Arfiticial friction is created which causes speed reduction or stop the motion of vehicle is known as.................

3. The rate at which the braking system brings a vehicle to rest from a certain speed is known as .... efficiency.

4. Prolonged application of brakes, their effectiveness decreases is known as .... of brakes.

5. The brake lining rub against the .... and thus stop its motion.

6. In hyraulic brake, the brake fluid is the mixture of .... and.

7. The brake of tractor is mounted on.................

8. Total friction area of pads in disc brakes is .... than drum type brakes.

9. Disc brakes have .... anti fade characteristics than drum type brake.

10. The force acting on the brake drum is in radial direction is known as ....

Answers : 1. increase 2. brake 3. braking 4. fading 5. drum 6. glycerine, alcohal 7. drive axle 8. less 9. better 10. radial brake.

Chapter 19
Cost Estimation and Selection of Tractor

19.1 Intruduction: Tractor costs are divided into two categories, fixed costs and variable cost or operating cost.

19.2 Fixed costs: The cost, which is independent from

The following are the subcosts of fixed cost.

(i)   Debredication   (ii)   Interst on the capital

(c)   Insurance and (d) Taxes

19.2.1 Depreciation: Depreciation measures the amount by which the value of a machine deceases with passing of time whether used or not. The value declines due to following reasons.

(a)   Wear and Tear of Parts: The parts of the tractor (machine) became worn with uses and cannot perform proper function as effectively as previous. These parts are the conomically irreparable mechanism in a machine; for example, the basic frame may be worn or disterted.

(b)   Enhance Operating and Maintenance cost: The expense of operating the machine at its original performance increases as more power, labour, and repair and costs for the same unit of output may be rquired. Repair and adjustment can maintain the machine but at increasing rate of cost.

(c)   Obsolete Technology: A new, more efficient machine or practice becomes available when this situation develops, the existing machine is said to be obsolete. The existing may be functionally adequate but because of new technology it is uneconomic to continue to operate it.

(iv)   Size of Interprise: The size of the enterprize is changed and the existing machine's capacity is not appropriate for the new stituation.

19.2.2 Estimation of Depreciation

There are three specific methods of calculating depreciation as suggested by the Internal Revenue Service:

1. Straight-Line Method. The annual depreciation charge is given by following relationship, xxx Alternate Method. Depreciated value afte n-years may be expressed as

$$D = \frac{D-S}{L}, \text{ Rr/year} \quad (19.1)$$

Where,

P = Purchase price, Rs.

S = solvage value, Rs.

L = Economic machine life, year

This method is the simplest, as it changes on easily calculated, constant amount each year.

2. Declining-Balance Method: An uniform rate is applied each year to the remaining value (includes solvage value) of the machine at the beginning of the year. The depreciation amount is different for each year of the machines life. It is given by following relationship,

$$D = V_n - V_{n+1} \quad (19.2)$$

$$V_n = P\left(1 - \frac{x}{L}\right)^n \text{ and } V_{n+1} = P\left(1 - \frac{x}{L}\right)^{n+1}$$

Where,

D = The amount of depreciation charged for year (n + 1).

n = The number representing the age of the machine in years at the beginning of the year in question.

v = The remaining value at any time.

x = The ratio of the depreciation rate used to that of the straight line method. The value of x may be any number between 1 and 2.

XXX Alternate Method: Depreciated value after n-years may be expressed as

$$V_n = (1-r)^n \times P$$

and solvage value may be expressed as

$$S = (1-r)^L \cdot P$$

4. Sinking-Fund-Method: This method is generally used by engineering economist. This method consides the problem of depreciation as one of establishing a fund which will draw compound interest uniform annual payments to this fund are of such a sinze that by the end of life of machine the funds a their interst have accumulated to an amount which will puchase another equivanlent machine.

Sinking-fund annual payment (SFP) and the value at the end of year n are,

$$SFD = (P-S) \frac{i}{(1+i)^2} - 1$$

$$Vn = (P - S) \left(\frac{(1+i)^2 - (1+i)^n}{(1+i)^2 - 1} \right) + S$$

If $x = 2$, the method is called a double-declining. balance method permitted by IRS. For used machines the maximum rate is $x = 1.5$.

3. Sum of the years-Digits Method. It is given by following relationship,

$$D = \frac{(L - n)}{YD} (P - S) \qquad (19.3)$$

Where,

YD = The sum of years digists, $(1+2+3+ \dots + L)$

n = The age of the machine is years at the beginning of the year.

(b)   Interest (I): Interst is calculated on the average investment of the machine taking into consideration the value of the machine in first and last year. it is given by following relationship,

$$I = \frac{C + S}{2} \times \frac{i}{H} , Rs/h \quad (19.4)$$

Where, i = % rate of interest

H = working hours per year, h

(c)   Housing: Housing cost is calculated on the basis of the prevailing rates of the locality but roughily speaking, the housing cost may be taken as 1-percent of the purchase price of the machine per year.

(d)   Insurance: Insurance charge is taken on the basis of the actual payment to the insurance company but soils, weather and crops.

Even in the same geographical area, repair cost data are highly variaible. Some of variation is due to differences in machine usage, to the size fo the machine surveyed, and to the individual differences in machines as they come off the assembly line. Some is due to the effects of inflation of a significant time span is involved in the survey. Much of variation is due to the natural rordumness of breaddowns.

Cost of repairs and maintenance varies between 5 to 10 percent of the the purchase price of machine per year.

(d)Wages: Wages are computed on the basis of actual wages of the workers.

19.4. Terms Related to Field Performance of Machine

19.4.1 Theoretical Field Capacity (Fc): The Theoritical field capacity of an implement is the rate coverage that would be obtained if the machine were performing its function 100% of the time at the rated forward speed and always covered 100% of its related with. It is expressed as,

$$F_c = \frac{s \times w}{10}, \text{ha/h}$$

Where,

S = speed, km/h

W = width of implement, on

19.4.2. Effective Field Capacity (Fce): The effective field capacity is the actual average rate of coverage by the machine, based on its total time consumed and its width. It is exprssed as,

$$F_{ce} = \frac{S \times W}{10} \times \frac{Ef}{100}$$

19.5. Factors Affecting Selection of a Tractor

The various factors affecting the right selection of a tractor. They are as follows:

1. Land holding   2. cropping pattern
3. Solid condition 4. Climatic conditions.
5. Repair facilities 6. Running cost
7. Initial cost and resaleable value 8. Test report
9. Design
10. Trade Mark & Trade Names

1. Land holding; Under single cropping system it is normally recommended to consider 1 kW for every 2.7 ha. of land. In other words , 26.8 kW to 33.5 kW is suitable for 40 ha farm.

2. Cropping pattern: Generally 2.0 ha/kw recommended where adequate facilities are available and more than one crop is taken. Therefore, a 40-47 kW tractor is suitable for 40 ha farm.

3. Soil condition: A tractor with less wheel base, higher ground clearance and low overall weight may work successfully in lighter soil but it will not be able to give sufficient depth in black cotton soil.

4. Climatic condition: For every hot zone and desert area, air cooled engines are prefered, over water cooled engines. Similarity for higher altitude, air cooled, engines are prefered because water, 6 . liable to be brozen at higher altitude.

5. Repairing facilities: Before purchasing any tractor, it is feasible to look into the source of repair. it should be ensured that the tractor to be purchased has a dealer at rear by place with all the technical skills for repair and maintainance of tractor.

6. Running cost: The running cost play a vital role in the selection of tractor. Tractors with less specific fuel consumption are prefered by progressive farmers due to less running cost.

7. Initial cost and resale value: The life of different tractors,varies between wide limits. A tractor may wear out earlier, whereas another may serve for decades without much trouble and acquire good market resale value. While keeping the resale value in mind the initial cost should not be very high because higher amount of interest will have to be paid.

8. Test report: Test report of tractors released from farm Machinery Testing Stations should be considered for guidance.

9. Design: Indian farmers are lacking in technical knowledge. The machine (Tractor) should be operated easily and there should be very few adjustments.

The control should be easaily unders tandiable. The wearing parts should be as few as possible.

10. Trade Marks and Trade Names: Standard firm always try to make the reputation of their products. The products bear a registered trade mark and trade name, which, to some extent, is a guarantee of the firm. Painted equipments could not be checked by just seeing them, it is the trade mark which is generally seen, along with the other things, for purchasing them. Machines with a number of mechanism, could not be checked at glance, but it bears trade mark of good firm it is supported that the machine is worth purchasing.

Prob. 19.1 A 40 hp tractor purchasing Rs. 4,00,000 is expected to have useful life of 10 years. Calculate the depreciated value after 5 years by different methods, assuming the solvage value as 10% of purchaing price.

Soln. Given P = Rs. 4,00,000, L = 10 years

(i) Estimation of dpereciated value by straight line method

$$\text{Depreciation (D)} = \frac{4,00,000 - 40,000}{10} = \text{Rs. } 36,000/\text{yr}$$

Therefore, depreciated value after 5 years = 4,00,000 - 36,000 x 5

= Rs. 2,20,000

(ii) By decline method

$$V_n = (1-r)^n \times P$$

$$\frac{10}{100} \times P = (1-r)^{10} \times P$$

or $(1-r)^{10} = 0.1$

$$\therefore r = (0.1)^{\frac{1}{10}} = 0.2$$

Therefore, depreciated value after 5 years $(D_5) = P(1-r)^5$

$$= 4,00,000 (1-0.2)^5$$

Rs. 1,31,072

(iii)   Sum of year digit method

$$D_5 = (P - S) \left[1 - \frac{\sum_{n=1}^{L}(L - n + 1)}{\sum_{n=1}^{L} L} \right]$$

$$= (4,00,000 - 40,000) \left[1 - \frac{10 + 9 + 8 + 7 + 6}{55} \right]$$

$$= 3,60,000 \times \frac{15}{55}$$

$$= \text{Rs. } 98,181.81$$

Prob. 19.2 A farmer purchased 35 hp diesel tractor for Rs. 3,50,000. Its total working life 12000 hours and annual use 1000 hours. The annual interest is 10%. The tractor is being used with an eleven time cultivator costing Rs 10,000. This shovel spacing is 22.5 cm. speed of cultivation is 3 km/h and field efficiency is 70%. Compute

(a)   Cost of tractor is Rs/h.

(b)   Cost of cultiavation is Rs/h.

Soln. Given

P = Rs. 3,50,000

$$L = \frac{L - H}{P - S} \frac{12,000}{1000} = 12 \text{ years}$$

H = 1,000 h

i = 10% = 0.1

Assumption

(i)   Solvage value - 10% of purchase price

(ii)   Repair and maintenance cost = 70% of purchase price

(iii)   Rate of fuel consumption = 3 lph

(iv)   Rate of fuel = Rs. 35.0

(v)   Lubricant charge = 30% of fuel cost

(vi)   Wage of labour for 8 hours = Rs. 80.00

(vii)   Insurance, taxes and shelter = 3.5% of purchase price.

$$\text{Depreciation (D)} = \frac{P - S}{L \times H} = \frac{3,50,000 - 35,000}{12 \times 1000}$$

$$= \text{Rs. } 26.25/h$$

$$\text{Interest (I)} = \left(\frac{P + S}{2 \times H} \right) \times i = \left(\frac{3,50,000 + 35,000}{2 \times 1000} \right) \times 0.1$$

= Rs. 19.25/h

$$\text{Insurance, taxes and shelter} = \frac{3.5}{100} = \frac{3,50,000}{1000}$$

= Rs. 12.25/h

Therefore, total fixed cost = Rs. 57.75/h

$$\text{Repair and maintentance charge} = \frac{7}{100} \times \frac{3,50,000}{1000}$$

= Rs. 24.5 /h

Fuel charge = 35x 3 = Rs. 105/h

Lubricant charge = 0.3 x 105 = Rs. 31.5/h

$$\text{Labour charge} = \frac{80}{8} = \text{Rs } 10/h$$

Thus, total variable cost per hour = 24.5 + 105 + 31.5 +10 = Rs. 171

Therefore, total cost of use of tractor per hour = 171 + 57.75 = Rs. 228.75

Cost of cultivator:

L = 12 years

H = 210 h

S_c = 10% P = Rs 1,000

Price of cultivator (P_c) = Rs. 10,000

$$\text{Depreciation (D)} = \left(\frac{P_c - S_c}{L \times H}\right) = \frac{10,000 - 1000}{12 \times 210}$$

= Rs. 3.57 /h

Interest (I)

$$= \left(\frac{P_c - S_c}{2 \times H}\right) \times i$$

$$= \left(\frac{10,000 + 1000}{2 \times 210}\right) \times 0.1$$

Rs. 2.61/h

$$\text{Taxes, housing and insurance} = \frac{3.5}{100} \times \frac{1000}{210}$$

Rs. 1.66/h

Total fixed cost for cultivator per hour = Rs.

$$\text{Repair and maintenance cost} = \frac{7}{100} \times \frac{10000}{210}$$

Rs. 3.33/h

Total cost for cultivivator per hour = 3.57 + 2.6 + 1.6 + 3.33

Rs. 11.17 h^{-1}

Therefore, total cost of tractor and cultivator per hour = Rs. 228.75 + 11.17 = Rs. 239.92

$$\text{Area covered} = \frac{S \times W \times E_F}{10}$$

$$= \frac{3 \times 2.47 \times 0.7}{10} = 3.48 \text{ h}^{-1}$$

Hence, cost of cultivation = Rs 835.56 ha^{-1}

PROBLEMS

1. A farmer purchased 35 hp diesel tractor for Rs.1,45,000.00. Its total working life 1200 hours and annual use 1000 hours. The annual interest is 16%. The tractor is being used with an eleven time cultivator costing Rs. 8,000.00. The shovel spacing is 22.5 cm. Speed of cultivation is 6 km/hr and field effeciency is 70% calculate.

    (i) Cost of tractor in Rs./h.

    (ii) Cost of cultivation in Rs/ha. [ARS - 1991]

    [101.57, 97.95]

2. A 30 hp tractor costing Rs. 300,000 is expects to have an useful life of 10 years. Calculate the depreciation value after 5 years by different methods, assuming the solvage value 10% of purchase price.

    [Rs. 1,65,000 (by straight line mthods) Rs. 98,304.00 (by decline method) Rs. 73,636.36 (by sum of year digit method)]

3. A farmer is considering the purchase of a combine. His own small-grain acreage does not provide enough use to make the ownership of a combine economical. Hoever, the farmer knows that he can get all the custom work he wants if he can lower his custom charge of Rs. 250/acre. How many acres of combining must tie contract for (include his own) to pay himself a labour charge or wage of Rs 75/h and still returns Rs. 50,000 profit the first year?

    Data: PTO combine purchase price-Rs. 2,00,000

    Effective field capacity-2 acre/h

    Assume a 7-hours working day.

    Tractor purchase price-Rs. 27,50,000

    Fuel consumption 5 litre/h

    Note: Assume necessary data required.

4. Use the proper equations for each depreciation method and find the depreciation during the fifth year of life for a machine that was purchased

new for Rs 400000 and has an estimated life of 10 years. The solvage value is expected to be Rs. 80,000.

SUBJECTIVE QUESTIONS

1. What do you mean by depreciation?
2. What are the reasons the value of machine decline?
3. What are the different methods for estimating depreciation?
4. What are the factors affecting selection of tractor.
5. Write short notes on:
(i) Theoretical Field Capacity.
(ii) Effective Field Capacity.

MULTIPLE CHOICE

1. Which of the following has fixed cost.
   (a) depreciation   (b) fuel cost
   (c) lubricant cost   (d) all of them

2. Which of the following has variable cost
   (a) depreciation   (b) interest
   (c) taxes   (d) wages

3. Which of the following method is mostly used to measure depreciation of Agriculture Machines.
   (a) decling balance method   (b) straight line method
   (c) sum of the year digits method   (d) none of the above

4. The depreciation (D) of machine /hour is computed by the formula
   (a) $\dfrac{D - S}{L.H}$ (b) $\dfrac{L - H}{P - S}$
   (c) $\dfrac{L + H}{P - S}$ (d) $\dfrac{P + S}{L - S}$

5. The decreases of value of machine with passing of time is known as
   (a) Depreciation   (b) Solvage value
   (c) Both   (d) None of the above

6. 'Depreciation' of implements depends on
   (a) purchases price   (b) solvage value
   (c) economic life   (d) all of the above

7. Which of the following is not consider in the selective of tractor
   (a) land holding   (b) cropping pattern
   (c) repairing facilitites   (d) none of the above

8. 26.8 kW to 33.5 kW tractor is suitable for ha of land under singe cropping system

      (a) 20   (b) 30

      (c) 40   (d) 50

9.   A tractor with less wheel base, higher ground clerance and low overall wt. is suitable for
      (a) lighter soil   (b) black cotton soil
      (c) both   (d) none of the above

10.   Which of the following factors are considered for proper selection of machine
      (a) land holding   (b) soil condition
      (c) cropping pattern   (d) all of the above.

FILL UP THE BLANKS

1.   The decrese of value of machine with passing of time is known as ....

2.   .... is the simplest method to measure depreciation.

3.   Depreciated amout is ....each year in...................method.

4.   A................rate is applied each year in................. method.

5.   Lubricants cast varies between..................of the fuel cost.

6.   Cost of reparis and maintentance varies from ....to ....percent of the   purchase price of machine per year.

7.   Fixed cost includes (i) depreciation (ii) interest (iii) housing (iv) insurance and (v) ....

8.   Generally.......................ha/kW is recommended for more than one crop is taken.

9.   ....to.................kW to 33.5 kW is suitable for ha farm for single cropping   pattern.

10.   A tractor with less wheel base,...............ground clearance and low overall weight   work successful in.................soil.

ANSWERS

1. depreciation, 2. straight line method, 3. Constant, Straight line 4. Uniform, Declining-balance 5. 25 to 32, 6. 5 to 10, 7. taxes, 8. 2.0, 9. 27 to 33.5, 10 high, lighter

ANSWER OF MULTIPLE CHOICE QUESTIONS

1. (a) 2. (d) 3. (b) 4. (a) 5. (d) 6. (a) 7. (d) 8. (c) 9 (a) 10. (d)

Chapter 20

Tractor Testing and Performance

20.1 Introduction: Tractor is one of the important source of power. The great demand of tractar has promoted many manufacturer to increase the production of tractors. Since production of tractors need heavy investment, therefore, it its necessary to judge the performance of machine being manufactured by a particular manufacturer.

Thus, there was a need to have an impartial agency for evaluating the performance of the tractor. These testing agencies also act as a bridge between the manufacturers and users of tractor.

20.2 Test Facility in India:

The idea of opening a test facility in India was conceived in 1951, a tractor testing station was intially opened in 1956 at Nagpur, which was later on amalgamated with the item Tractor Training Centre, Budni in October 1959 and renamed as Tractor Training and Testing Station. The first test report was released in 1961. In 1983, the station was upgraded to the status of an Institute and renamed as Central. Farm Machinery Training and Testing Institute, Budni. The Institute is a member of Organisation for Economic Co-operation and Development (OECD) for testing of tractor and equipped with most modern testing facilities with instrumental system.

20.3 Testing Stations

20.3.1 Public Testing Agencies in India

The country has the following public testing agencies for agricultural machiens and tractor:

(i)   Central Farm Machinery Training and Testing Station, Budni (MP),

(ii)   Northern Region Farm Machinery and Tractor Taining and testing Centre, Hissar (Haryana), 1972.

(iii)   Southern Region Farm Machinery Training and Testing Institute, Anantpur (A.P.)   1983.

20.3.2. International Testing Stations: There are following international Testing Stations:

(i)   Agricultural Machinery Testing Institude, Uppsla (Sweden)

(ii)   National Institute of Agricultural Engineering, Siloe (U.K.)

(iii)   Nebraska Testing Station (U.S.A.)

20.4 Nature of Test Report: The test report released by the station are confidential and commercial in nature.

(i) **Confidential Tests:**These test are done to provide confidential informations on performance of tractor for suitability of commercial production. These tests are done at the initial stage of tractor development.

(ii) **Commercial Tests:** These tests are done for the tractor which are in commercial production or sale to establish their performance characteristics.

20.5 Batch Testing (Step by Step Testing)

Sinch January 1977 batch testing of tractor has been introduced and its broad objective are:

(i) To check whether the defects pointed out during the earlier tests have been rectified and to improve performance and durability.

(ii) To check the variation in the performance of tractor is if there is any change in design, manufacturing technique, material of construction and some other factor.

(iii) To acces the durability of the tractor operating under wide range of field condition.

(iv) To facilitate the manufacturer to update the specification of the tractor based on tests on the latest model of tractors.

(v) To assist the buyers to have information on the quality of tractor after sale & service facilities provided by the dealer network.

20.6 Types of Test:

Normally, two types of testing are carried out for any tractor namely Lab test and Field test.

20.6.1. Lab Test:

The lab tests comprise of general specification checking. Power test, position of central gravity, performance of brake, ambient noise emitted by the tractor and noise level at drivers ear level, power lift and hydraulic pump performance, air cleaner, oil pullover test, visibility from driver seat, vibration at various assembles. Laboratory tests can be summeriesed as below:

(A) **Power Test:**

(i) PTO performance test

(ii) Belt pulley performance test

(iii) Drawbar performance test

(iv) Hudraulic power and lifting capacity test

(B) **Saftey Test:**

(i) Brake test

(ii) Centre of gravity position.

(iii)   Turning ability test

(C)   Erogomical Test:

(i)   Noise measurement

(ii)   Mechanical vibration test

(iii)   Visibility from driver's seat

(iv)   Smoke level

(D)   Miscellaneous test:

(i)   Air cleaner oil pull over test

(ii)   Component/Assembly insepction.

20.6.2 Field Test:

The field performance is a section for operating the machine (tractor) in field for determining the important parameter like:

(i)   Rate of work

(ii)   Quality of work

(iii)   Fuel consumption

(iv)   Labour requirment

(v)   Handling characteristics

(vi)   Soundness of construction

20.7 Power Test:

20.7.1 PTO Performance Test:

(A)   General Test:

(a)   The torque value obtained from the dynamometers and power should be reported without applying any correction for losses in power tranmission between PTO and dynamometers.

(b)   In all the tests, shaft connecting the PTO and dynamometer should have minimum angularity at the universal joint. The angularity should not exceed 2°.

(c)   Stable operating condition should be obtained for a minimum period of five minutes at each leading setting, before beginning the test measurement.

(d)   The test report should include the representation of the following curve made for the full range of engine speed tested:

(i)   Equivalent Crankshaft torque as a function of speed i.e., T vs speed: It is graphically shown in Fig. 20.1. It is clear that the maximum torque is available at a much lower speed which indicates that when the engine is momentary over loaded, the speed of the engine will drop and consequently the torque will increase to take care of the momentary over loading. The difference in the values of maximum torque and torque at

465

maximum power is known as Reserve torque or Lugging ability of the engine. Better the lugging ability the better is tractor. It has been observed that the maximum torque is 110% of the torque at maxmimum power.

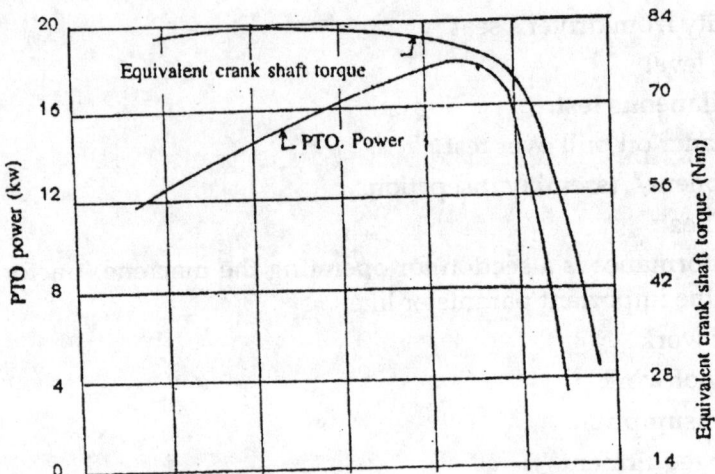

Fig. 20.1 PTO Power and Torque Vs Engine Speed

(ii) Specific fuel consumption as a function of PTO Power: Curve drawn between PTO power and specific fuel consumption is shown in Fig 20.2. It indicates that if it is flat in the zone of the high load, then it is a better curve. A 'too steep' rise in specific fuel consumption is not desired.

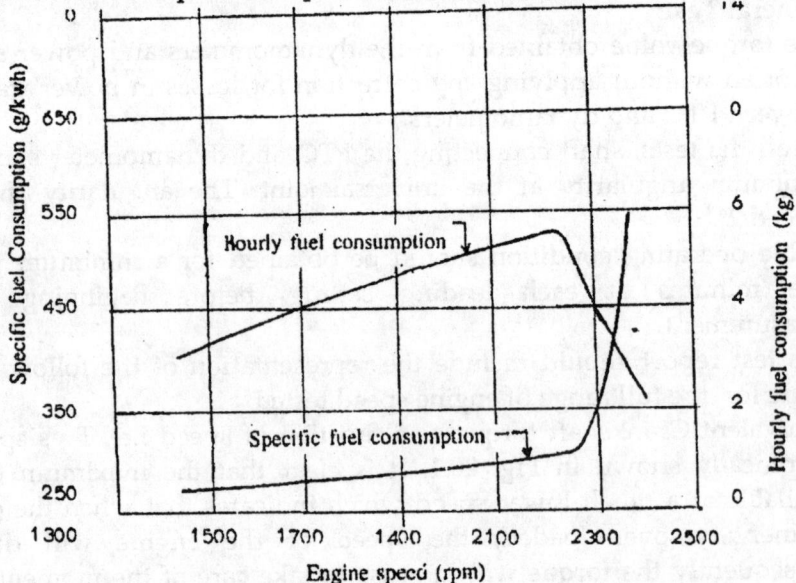

Fig. 20.2 Sp. Fuel Consumption Vs Engine Speed

Fig. 20.2 Sp. Fuel Consumption Vs Engine Speed

The value of specific fuel consumption corresponding to maximum PTO horse power indicate the specific fuel determination by the manufacture. The specific fuel comsumption limits have been fixed by the Govt. of India. These are:

Upto to 25 ph 205g /PTO hp/h

26 to 35 hp 200g/PTOhp/h

36 to 55 hp 195/PTOhp/h

Above 56 hp 185/PTOhp/h

Specific fuel consumption as a function of break means effective pressure:

Fig. 20.3 shows a relation bewteeenspecific fuel consumption and break mean effective pressure. At high loads, the sp. fuel consumption curve is almost flat. For economic operation, the load on the tractor should be such that engine may work on the flat portion of curve for longer duration of time. Care has should be taken that fuel consumption curve may not rise steeply as load is reduced.

(e)   During the test following should be recorded:

(i)   Temeperature of fuel

(ii)   Temperature of lubricating oil.

(iii)   Temperature of transmission oil.

(iv)   Temperature of exhaust gas

(v)   Atomospheric pressure

(vi)   Pressure of the engine lubricating oil

(vii)   Relative air humidity.

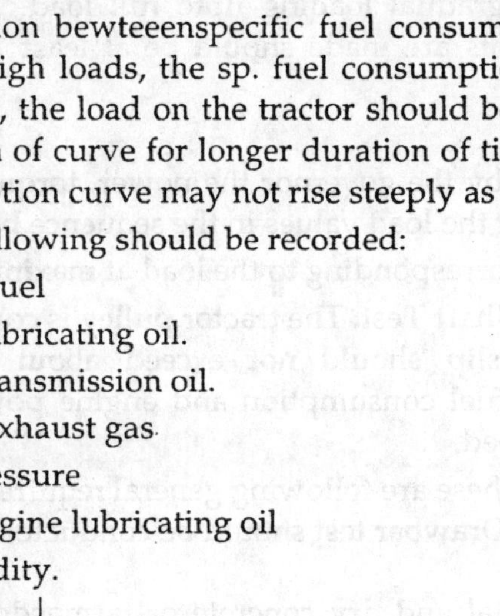

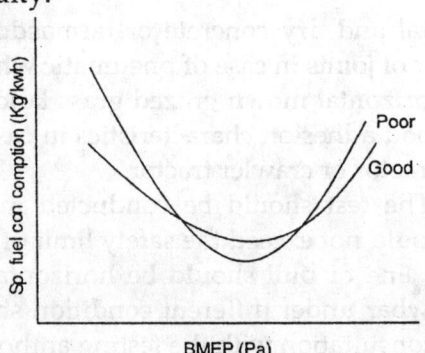

Fig. 20.3 Sp. Fuel Consumption Vs BMEP

(B)   Two Hour Test at Maximum Power:

The tractor should be operated at maximum power 2-h after the required warming up period for power to became stablised.

The governor control lever should be tractor manufactures for obtaining maximum power.

(b)   A minimum of air readings of equal interval of time should be taken during the 2-h test period. Recording of temperature, pressure and other observation should be made simultaneously.

(c)   The maximum power quoted in the report should be average of the reading taken during two hours period. If the power varies by more than ±2% fromthe average, the test should be repeated. If the variation continues to exceed ±2%, it should be reported in test report.

(C)   **Varying speed Test:** After the engine has reached the established working condition, the fuel consumption, torque and power should be measured as a function of speed by gradual loading upto full load. The minimum speed at which the measurements are made should be at least 15% below the speed at maximum torque.

Varying Load Test:

In the zone controlled by the governor the power, torque and fuel consumption should be measured for the load values in the sequence below:

(a)   85% of the load corresponding to the load at maximum power.

20.7 (2) Belt or Pulley Shaft Test: The tractor pulley is coupled to a dynamometer by a belt. The belt slip should not exceed about 2%. The hourlye fuel consumption, specific fuel consumption and engine power should be recorded according to engine speed.

20.7.3. Drawbar Test: These are following general requirements for drawar test:

(a)   Track condition: Drawbar test should be conducted on-one of the following tracks:

(i)   A clean, horizontal and dry concrete or tarmacdom surface containing a minimum number of joints in case of pneumatic wheeled tractor.

(ii)   A flat, dry and horizontal mown grazed grass land or a horizontal surface having equally good adhesion characteristics in case of trace line tractor or steeled wheeled tractor or crawler tractor.

(b)   Gear condition: The test should be conducted in the gear in which the forward speed should not exceed the safety limit of testing equipment.

(a)   Line of Pull: The line of pull should be horizontal ballast. The optimum height of the drawbar under different condition should be selected by the manufactures in consultation with the testing anthority.

It should be decided by the manufacturer for the following limitatioins:

(i)   The height of drawbar should be such that when the tractor developing maximum sustained pull, the load exerted on the front wheel is sufficient to control the direction of travel.

(c)   In the caseof wheelled tractor, the following formula is applied.

$$P = \epsilon = \frac{\text{Seat subpenions damping rate}}{\text{Critical damping rate}} = \frac{0.8 \times W \times Z}{H} , N$$

Where,

P = Maximum drawbar pull, N

W = Static load exerted by the front wheel on the ground, kg

Z = Wheel base, mm

H = Static height of the line of pull above the ground, mm

In the begining of the drawbar test theheight of the tyre lungs should not be less than 65% of the height of the lugs, when it is in new condition.

Test of Ballasted Tractor:

The tractor should be ballasted as approved by the tractor manufacturer with the load limits specified by the tyre manufacturer.

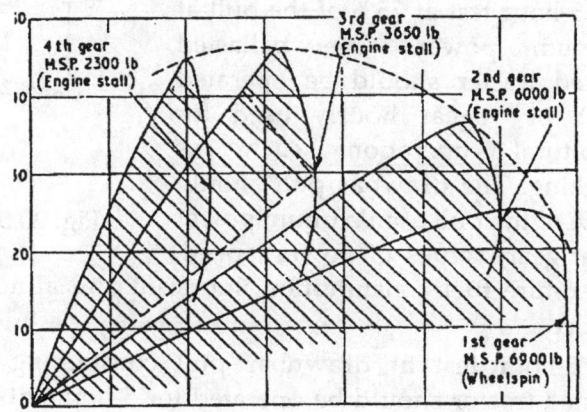

Fig. 20.4 Drawbar Performance Characteristics of Tractor

(b) The drawbar power at the rated engine speed of the ballasted tractor in each gear from the height of the gear in which maximum power is limited by wheel slop of 15% to the gear immediately that in which the height maximum power is developed.

(c) For each gear combination the test reports include combination of following curve:

1. Drawbar power and Forward Speed Vs Darwbar Pull:

Fig shows a relationship between drawbar pull and drawbar power. There is curve corresponding to each gear of the tractor.

The point of maximum-drawbar power of each gear can be joined by the envelop as shown in Fig. by a dotted line. Gera spacing is the distance between two points of drawbar pull as shown in the Fig. Hence greater the number of gears, closer the gear spacing and better is the working of the tractor. It is always desirable to have large number of equally speed gears on a tractor engine.

2. **Wheel slip as function of a drawbar pull**

Fig 20.5 shows a relation ship between wheel slip and drawbar pull. The relation shows that increase in drawbar pull which results into increase in slip.

10. HOUR TEST. This test is conducted in two parts as given below:-

(a) 5-hour test at 75% of the pull at maximum power: The ballasted wheeled tracter should be operated for 5h in agear hourly used for agricultural operation such as ploughing. The drawbar pull should be 75% of the pull at maximum power in that gear, values of power, speed,

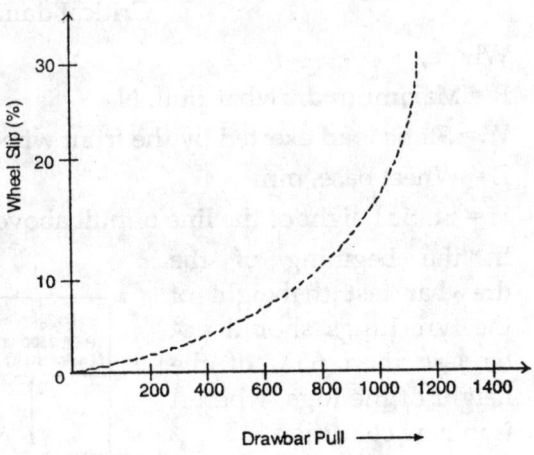

Fig. 20.5 Drawbar pull Vs Wheel Slip

temperature fuel consumption, lubricant and atmospheric condition should be recorded.

(b) 5-hour test at drawnbar pull considering with 15% wheel slip. The ballasted tractor should be operated for 5-hours at the drawbar pull giving 15% wheel slip. The gear used should be the fastest gear in which required pull can be achieved.

The purpose of the ten hour test is to detect any short coming in the transmission design, maneuverability, steering ability, etc.

Note: After completion of test the maximum power test should be repeated on unballasted tractor.

20.7.4. Hydraulic Power and Lifting Capacity Test: The test is aimed to find out the maximum static vertical force which can be exerted by the hydraulic lift at the lower hitch points and a point 610 mm to the rear of the pitch points on a frame attached to three point linkage through-out the full range of movement. The hydraulic pump and relief valve performance and the ability of the lifting system to maintain the load in the lifted position without hydraulic power.

20.8. Safety Tests: It includes the following tests:

20.8.1 Brake Test: The test is aimed to asses the performance of service brakes and parking brakes. The service brake performance is checked under cold brake and not in brake conditions at the maximum designed speed under ballasted and unballasted conditions. The performance of parking tractor is checked by parking the tractor on slopes. The stopping distance for cold and hot brake should not exceed 7.6 and 9.5 m respectively.

20.8.2 Location of Centre of Gravity: The stability of tractor depends upon the location of centre of gravity which is determined by a method of weight transfer by lifting it. Simple statics dictates that the centre of gravity falls outside the triangle formed by the point of contact of the two rear wheels and the centre pivot of the front axle. The distance of centre of speed of rear axle determine the weight distribution, height above the ground determines the stability an grades and during high speed terms. Also with reference to height of rear axle if centre of gravity is below the axle the tractor is better stablized.

20.8. (3) Turning Ability Test

Terminolgy rated to Turning Ability Test

Minimum Turning Diameter: It is the dia of a circle described by the outermost point of the tractor around the centre of rotation.

Minimum Clearance Diameter: It is a dia of the circle described by the centre of the tread of the outer most wheel around the centre of rotation. The turning radius is half of the minimum clearance diameter.

Procedure: the test is carried out at 1.5 to 2.0 km/h speed measured at the middle point of rear wheels. The test carried out withoutusing directional brake and above two parameter i.e.; minimum turning diameter and minimum clearnace diameter should be recoreded.

Turning Radius: Turning radius of awheel type tractor is the radius of circle described by the centre of tread of outermost wheel (front wheel) around centre of rotation.

20.8. Ergonomical/Environemntal Tests:

20.8.1 Noise Measurement: This aims at measurement of average amplitude of vibration on points mainly related to operator's comfort. The average amplitude of mechanical vibration should not exceed 100 microns. The average noise should not exceed 90 decibell for 8 working hours.

20.8. 2. Visibility from Driver's Seat:

Keeping the operator's eye level at 760 mm the area invisible is determined around the tractor. The furrow points of the tractor should be visible to the operator from his normal sitling position i.e., within 100 m of shifting of vision to either side.

20.8 (3). Smoke Level: The smoke level measured at 80% of maximum power should not exceed light absorption co-efficeint of 3.1/m (5.1 Bosch smoke units or 7.3 Hartridge smoke units.

20.9. Miscellaneous Test:

20.9.1. Air Cleaner Oil Pull Over:

The tractor should be parked on a levelled ground. The air cleaner should be cleaned and filled to the specified oil level with an oil of viscosity recommended by the manufacturer. The tractor should be operated at full governed speed for 15 minute. This should be followed by sudden acceleration and discelaration made after every 30 seconds for a period of 15 minutes the air cleaner assembly should be weighted before and after the test. The lose of mass of oil in gram and in percentage of mass should be reported.

If there is no oil pull over with the tractor in the level position the following additional test should be carried out.

(i)   In the case of wheeled type tractor, the test should be repeated with the tractor tilted 15° either side and then 15° forward and backward tilt should be 50°.

(ii)   Oil equal to 5% of the recommended quantity may be added to represent the over fill situation. Percentage loss of oil may be expresed as.

$$\% \text{ of Loss of oil} = \frac{\text{Loss of oil}}{\text{Mass of oil before test}} \times 100$$

20.9.2. Component/Assembly Inspection:
After the completion of all the laboratory track tests and field tests the tractor assemblies are dismantled for wear assessment of critical components. The discard limits are supplied by the manufactuerer applicant at the time of submission of the machine for test. Specific reference is also made to the literature supplied by the applicant/manufacturer. The premature failures and comparision of components wear in relation of discard limit are highlighted.

20.10 Favourable condition for operator:

(i)   Recirculation to fresh-air ratio will be 3:1.

(ii)   The metabolic rate of tractor drive wil be in the range of 70-174 W/m^2.

(iii)   Most individuals will be comfortable when effective temperature is between 24-27°C.

Sound Pressure Level (SPL):

Sound pressure can be expressed as a sound pressure level (SPL) relative to a reference sound pressure (P). Mathematically it is expressed as

$$SPL = 20 \log \frac{P}{P_0} \text{ dB}$$

Where,

P = Measured R.M.S. and sound pressure, P_a

P_o = Reference sound pressure level $2.0 \times 10^{-5} P_a$

Notes: 1. Sound pressure double with increase of 6 dB.

2. If unit of SPL in dBA then the value of $P_o = 1P_a$

Vibration Acceleration Level (VAL): Vibration is usually measured with an accelerometer. Vibration acceleration level (VAL) is expressed as

$$VAL = 20 \log \frac{V}{V_o}, dB$$

where,

V_o = Reference acceleraion, $1m/s^2$

V = Measured RMS acceleration, m/s^2

Note: Maximan human tolerance to vibration is 4-8 Hz.

Transmissibility (T): It is the ratio of out put vibration intensity to input vibration intensity and its value varies from 0.5 to 0.65.

Mathematically, it is expressed as

$$T = \left[\frac{1 + 4 \in^2 \left(\frac{\omega_t}{\omega_s} \right)^2}{\left[\left(1 - \frac{\omega_t}{\omega_s} \right)^2 \right] + 4 \in^2 \left(\frac{\omega_t}{\omega_s} \right)^2} \right]^{0.5}$$

Where,

$\in$ = Damping ratio

$$\in = \frac{\text{Seat suspension on damping rate}}{\text{Critical damping rate}}$$

ω_t = Frequency of tractor chasis

ω_s = undamped natural frquency of sheet seat

Note: Its value varies from 0.5 to 0.65

Prob. 20.1: Show through calculations that doubling the sound pressure results in 6-dB increase

Soln. Given = $P_2 = 2P_1$

We know that,

$$SPL = 20 \log \frac{P}{P_o}$$

$$\text{Therefore, } (SPL)_1 = 20 \log \frac{P_1}{P_o} \quad \text{(i)}$$

$$(SPL)_2 = 20 \log \frac{P_2}{P_o}$$

$$\text{or } (SPL)_2 = 20 \log \frac{2P}{P_o} \quad \text{(ii)}$$

Substrating equation (i) from (ii), we have

$$(SPL)_2 - (SPL)_1 = 20 \left[\log \frac{2P_1}{P_o} - \log \frac{P_1}{P_o} \right]$$

$$= 20 \log 2$$

$$= 20 \times 0.301$$

$$= 6.02 \text{ dB Proved}$$

Prob. 20.2 What is the maximum theoretical sound pressure in dB that can exits?

Given : P = atmospheric pressure

$$= 1 \times 10^5 \text{ N/m}^2$$

$$P_o = 2 \times 10^{-5} \text{ N/m}^2$$

We know that

$$SPL = 20 \log \frac{P}{P_o}$$

$$= 20 \log \frac{1 \times 10^5}{2 \times 10^{-5}}$$

$$= 20 \log 5 \times 10^9$$

$$= 20 (\log 5 + 9 \log 10)$$

$$= 20 (9.7)$$

$$= 19.4 \text{ dB Ans.}$$

Prob. 20.3 In a tractor, the noise was measured at the operator's ear level and at standard position, which come to be 84 and 76 dBA respectively. What should be corresponding R.M.S. values in N/m² at these positions. If sound pressure is increased four tims. Also determine the resulting sound pressure in decibles.

[GATE-1998]

Soln. Given: $SPL_1 = 84$ dBA, $SPL_2 = 76$dB

We know that, $P_1 = P$ and $P_2 = 4 P$, $P_o = 1P_a$

$$SPL = 20 \log \frac{P}{P_o}$$

$$\therefore P_1 = 10^{4.2}$$

We know that

$$(SPL)_1 = 20 \log \frac{P_1}{P_o} = 20 \log \frac{P}{P_o}$$

$$(SPL)_2 = 20 \log \frac{P_2}{P_o} = 20 \log \frac{4P}{P_o}$$

$$(SPL)_2 - (SPL)_1 = 20 \left[\log \frac{4P}{P_o} - \log \frac{P}{P_o} \right]$$

$$= 20 \log 4$$
$$= -12.04 \text{ dB}$$

SUBJECTIVE QUESTIONS

1. What are the broad objectives of testing? How it is beneficial to the manufacturer, users and extension worker?
2. What is the use of tractor testing? What are different tests of a tractor?
3. What are the important test conditions of a tractor? How belt performance tests differ from drawbar performance test?
4. What are the performance characteristics of tractor engines? Explain with help of various curves.
5. How can you find the most economical and efficient speed of a tractor engine? Explain with diagram.
6. What do you understand by gear spacing in a tractor? How it affects the performance of a tractor.
7. Write short notes on:
   (i) 10-hour test   (ii) safety tests
   (iii) Turning radius   (iv) Batch testing.
   (iv) Air cleaner oil pull over test (v)   Turning ability test
8. Enlist the various types of test conduct on agricultural tractors.
9. Describe P.T.O. performance test of an agricultural tractors.

MULTIPLE CHOICE QUESTIONS

1. Which of the following is an erogomical test
   (a) noise measurement   (b) turning ability test
   (c) brake test   (d) none of the above
2. Which of the following is a power test
   (a) PTO performance test   (b) brake test
   (c) smoke level   (d) noise measurement
3. Which of the following is a safety set
   (a) centre of gravity position (b) drawbar performance test
   (c) belt pulley performance test (d) none of the above

4. First tractor testing centre was open in India at
   - (a) Nagpur
   - (b) Budni
   - (c) Hissar
   - (d) Madras
5. First tractor testing centre was started in
   - (a) 1958
   - (b) 1959
   - (c) 1956
   - (d) none of the above
6. Batch testing of tractor have been introduced in
   - (a) Jan 1997
   - (b) Jan 1987
   - (c) Jan. 1977
   - (d) none of the above
7. The maximum torque is % of the torque at maximum power
   - (a) 88
   - (b) 110
   - (c) 150
   - (d) none of the above
8. Torque at maximum power is % of the maximum torque
   - (a) 88
   - (b) 110
   - (c) 120
   - (d) 150
9. The sp. fuel consumption for diesel tractor is about
   - (a) 0.2 kg/bhp-h
   - (b) 0.3 kg/bhp-h
   - (c) 0.4 kg/bhp-h
   - (d) none of the above
10. Most of the time, the engine is required to be operated between % of the fuel load.
   - (a) 90-100
   - (b) 80-90
   - (c) 50-70
   - (d) none of the above

FILL UP THE BLANKS

1. The difference in the values of maximum torque and torque at maximum power is known as ....
2. Nebraska testing is situated in...............
3. The speed requirement for different agricultural operation varies from ....kmph to .... kmph.
4. The diesel engine .... better than petrol engine.
5. In diesel engine, the torque is considerably high at .... than rated speed.
6. The difference is 100 rpm between no load and maximum BHP is said to be a ....
7. The sp. fuel consumption per bhp-h is a meausre of .... efficiency of the engine.
8. The diamete of the smallest circle, described by the outermost point of the tractor at a speed not exceeding 2 kmph is called ....
9. The slope of the land has got effects on .... and .... of the tractor.

ANSWER

Reserve torque or lugging ability 2. U.S.A.. 3. 0.5 to 25 4. slogs 5. lower 6. good governor. 7. overall 8. turning space. 9. tractive effort, stability.

ANSWER OF OBJECTIVE QUESTIONS

1 (a) 2 (a) 3 (a) 4 (a) 5 (c) 6 (c) 7 (b) 8 (a) 9 (a) 10 (c)

Chapter 21
Power Tiller

21.1. Introduction: Power tiller is versatile source of energy which is used to propel agricultural implements for different cropping, gardening, foresting etc. it is a small two wheel tractor in which the direction of travel and its control for field operation is controlled by the operator walking behind it. The concept of power tiller came in the world in the year 1920. Japan was the first country to use power tiller in large scale. In Japan, the first successful model power tiller was designed in year 1947. Production of power tiller rapidly increased during the year 1950 to 1965.

The power tiller was first introduced in India in 1963. Manufacturing of several makes of power tiller like Iake, Sata, Krishi, Kubota, Yanmar and Mistsubishi were started in India after 1962. But the power tiller has not became popular as shown in Table 1.1 and 1.2. The yearly production is about 10,000 units with a total population of 66,000 units only (Singh 1999), These are mainly used in the tastes of West Bengal, Tamil Nadu, Andhra Pradesh, Kerala, Karnataka and Assam, where rice is main crop.

Power tiller is a walking type tractor as shown in Fig. 21.1. The operator walks behind the power tiller, holding the two bandles sof power tiller in his own hands. Power tiller may be called a single axle walking type tractor, though a riding seat is provided in Certain designs.

Fig. 21.1. Power Tiller

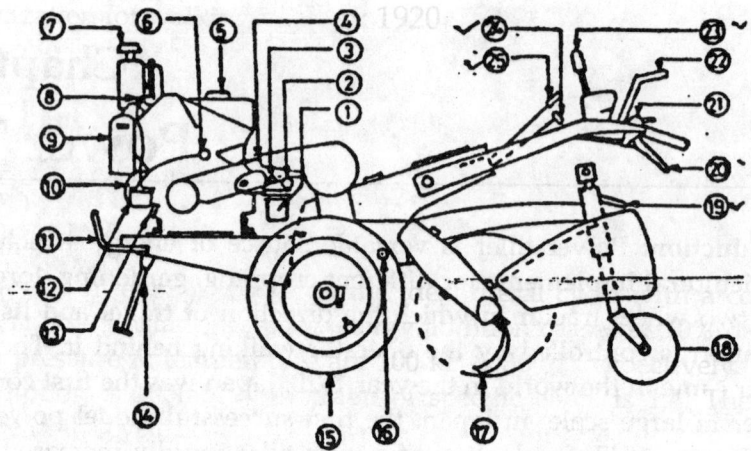

Fig. 21.2. Components of Power Tiller

1. Oil filter 2. Tension Pulley 3. Speed control lever 4. 'V' belt 5. Fuel Tank 6. Fuel cork. 7. Air cleaner 8. Nozzle or injector 9. M.suffler 10. Fuel injection pump 11. Bomper 12. Fuel filter 13. Deep Stick 14. Stand 15. Tyre 16. Oil drain plug 17. Tines 18. Tail wheel 19. Tail wheel adjust clamp 20. Steering clutch lever 21. Speed control lever 22. 23. Main clutch. 24. Rotary transmission lever 25. Main transmission lever.

21.2. Components of Power Tiller:

The following are the main components of power tiller.

(i) Engine (ii) Power transmission (iii) Brake (iv) Control lever (v) Rotary System units and (vi) Chasis

The components of power tiller is shown in Fig.

All the power tillers are mounted with single cylinder internal combustion engine. At present, most of the power tillers are mounted with diesel engine except Iseki (kerosine) Both air cooled as well as water cooled engine are used but water cooled engine is the most popular.

The power of I.C. engine, fited on power tiller goes to the wheel through main clutch with the help fo belt or chain. From main clutch, the power is divided into two routes, one goes to tranmission gears, steering clutch and then to wheel. The other part goes to the tilling clutch and then to the tilling attachment.

21.3. Power Transmission System: of Power Tiller:

Clutch and gear are the main components of the power tranmission system.

(A)   Clutch: The engine power goes to transmission unit through clutch. The clutch is in between engine and gear box.

The following are the main functions of clutch.

(i)   To transmit engine power to tranmission gear.

(ii)   To make power transmission gradual and smooth.

Normally, two discs and single disc friction clutch is used. The clutch is fitted inside the three groove. V-pulley of power tiller. There are two clutch with the help of six springs. In lower capacity power tiller, the friction roller attached with V-belt also works as clutch, which has not been successful. Dog clutch is used in smaller power tiller. The size of clutch, depends upon power of power tiller. Input and out shaft is connected with clutch. During power transmission jaws of input and outshaft is engaged in such a way that engine power goes to gear box conveniently. Both jaws of the clutch are separated during disengage.

(B)   Gear Box: Gear box is an important unit of power tranmission system and its functions are as per the following:

(i)   Transmission of torque and speed from the engine wheel or rotator as per the need.

(ii)   To direction and speed change as per the need.

(iii)   To prevent from powr transmission to wheel during stationary power tiller, while engine is running.

21.4 Transmision of Power Tiller: The engine power goes to the main clutch with the help of belt or chain. From main clutch, the power is divided in two routes, one goes to transmision gears, steering clutch, and then to the wheel. The other part goes to the tilling clutch and then to the tilling attachment.

The flow diagram for power transmissioin of powder tiller is given below:

Engine to Main Clutch Tranmission gear ® steering clutch ® wheel

Tilling clutch ® Tilling attachment.

21.5 Brake: All power tillers have some braking arrangment for stopping or slow down the speed of the power tiller depending upon the driver needs. Normaly brake is fitted after intermediate gears. Most of power tiller normal disc type or inner side exposion type brake. Brakes work on the principle of friction.

21.6 Steering System of Power Tiller: All power tillers have steering system for turning at working in the field or running at the road.

Steering clutch is in between intermediate gears and last gear set.

21.7. Traction units.

(i)   Rubber Tyre: Usually 2 to 4 ply pneumatic tyres are used in power tillers for all purposes except puddling. The pressure of tyre ranges from 110 K Pa to 140 KPa. The size of tyre is 6 x 19 for transporting.

There is facility to.

(ii)   Iron Tyre: Iron tyres are used during puddling as well as harvesting of paddy with reaper.

21.8. Rotary Unit: Power tiller has a rotary unit for field operation. It may be two types namely (A) centre drive type and (B) Side drive type

(A)   Centre Drive Type: Centre drive type has the following characteristics:

(a)   Tilling width can be widened.

(b)   Rotary unit is light in weight.

(c)   Fixing of attachement is easy.

(d)   The type of shaft can be detached easily.

(e)   Mounting and dismounting of rotary unit is very easy.

(f)   It may have some portion of the field untilled.

(g)   It has one point supported on the ground.

(B)   Side type drive: Side type drive has the following characteristics

(a)   deeper tilling is possible (b) the arrangement is useful for hard soil (c) It has two points support on the ground.

21.9. Rotary tines: Rotary tines are ussed in rotary unit for soil cutting and pulverisation purpose. Rotary tines are of three types. (A) Straight tines (B) Curved tines and (C) sliding tines

Korn (1957) studies were made of the performance of rotary cultivators with different sets of tines on various types of soil. Curved-spring tines were most suitable for deep of the soil and for forming a very fine tilth, board, flat, L-shaped tines for stubble working and shallow cultivation of weedly fields and wide,flat tines, the end of which are pointed for ward, for working soil after a root crop, or after ploughing.

Adamas and Furlong (1959) made a study on rotary tiller in soil preparation. Experiments were carried cut to comparethe performance characteristics of the hoe, slicer, and pick-type rotary cultivator times used in conjuction with 302.4-604.8 mm wide rotors operated at 2, 3.5 and 5 m/s and 50-151 mm deep, with cut increments of 66 m and tine-rake angles of 10-30° in dry to moist soil. The error is rearmounted on ahydraulic vehicle the rotary assembly is given 2° of freedom and is driven by fixed-displacement hydraulic motor in conjunction with a variable displacement pump. Records were made of rotary power requirement and reaction forces (vertical and horizontal components), the dispersion of surface organic matter, soil pulverization and subsoil condition. Hoe-type tines operated at the lower rotor tip speeds and intermediate increment of cut were the most satisfactory overall as regard power utilization, pulserization, etc. although they do not leave a loose uneven subsoil, necesary to promote water penetration.

(A)   Straight Tines: Straight tines have following characteristics:

(a)   Power consumption is less (b) tine pulverization of soil is possible (c) poor soil turning (d) grass entangles in the tines very easily and (e) it is suitable for hard soil.

(B)   Curved Tines: curved tines have following characteristics.

(a)   Good soil turning is possible (b) It is suitable for avoiding grasses (c) pulverization of soil is coarse and (d) power consumption is high.

(C)   Sliding Tines: Sliding tines have the characteristics of sliding on their positions according to the requirement

21.10 Arrangement of tynus: The tynes can be arranged in three ways.

(i)   inner heep "to break the ridges"

(ii)   outer heap "to make the ridges"

(iii)   even arrangment

21.11. Steering clutch lever: steering clutch is provided on the grip of the right and left handles. When the left side is gripped, power is cut-off on left side of the wheel and power tiller turns to the left. similarly when the right side is gripped, the power tiller turns to right.

21.12 Matching Commercially Available Equipment: They are classified as follows:

1. Equipment for land development and seed bed preparation: it includes terracer-cum-leveller, disc plough, rotary tiller, cultivator.

2. Sowing and fertilizer application equipment: It inludes see-cum-fertilizer drill, potato planter-cum-fertilizer applicator, Multi crop planter.

3. Interculture equipment: It includes seep cultivator

4. Irrigation equipment: It includes axial flow pump.

5. Harvesting and threshing equipment: It includes vertical conveyor reaper, potato digger, pady thresher,

6. Equipment suitable for social forestry and agro-forestry: It includes suger digger,

21.13 Constraints in Adoption of Power Tiller Technology:

There are various constraints which are given below:

(A)   Machine aspects:

(a)   Non-availability of machine

(b)   Lack of knowledge about the matching equipment of power tiller.

(c)   Non availability of original spare parts.

(d)   lake of knowledge about different makes.

(e)   Higher initial cost of power tiller.

(B)   Credit Aspects:

(i)   Difficulties in getting loan.

(ii)   Non availability of subsidy to all categories of farms.

(C)   Socio-economic Aspects::

(a)   Poor economic condition of farmer.

(b)   Non availability of road communication system.

(c)   Poor hiring demand.

(D)   General Awarenss:

(a)   Farmer are generally believes that such a small machine will not be able to do any tractive work.

(b)   Most of the farmers, are ignorant about such type of machine.

Velu (1976) made a study on review of the power tiller committee recommended the following points for adoption of power tiller:

(a)   Streamlining the bank credit to facilitate purchase of power tiller by small farmers.

(b)   Familianizatin of the power tiller to the small farmer through Government agencies.

(c)   Demonstration and publicity by all concerned.

(d)   Introduction of power tillers in Government farms, agriculture and agro-industries corporation.

a single axle walking type tractor, though a riding seat is provided in certain designs. Average size of holding in India is about.

21.14. Difference Between Tractor and Power Tiller: It is described in Table. 21.1

Table 21.1 Comparison Between Tractor & Power Tiller

S.N.	Power Tiller	Tractor
1.	It has a single axle	It has double axle.
2.	It may be walking or riding type tractor.	It is riding type tractor.
3.	Its power varies from 5 hp to 12 hp.	Its power generally varies from15-75 hp.
4.	Its sp. fuel cunsumption is greater than tractor.	Its sp. fuel consumption. is less than power tiller
5.	It has no differential	It has differential.
6.	It has steering clutch or lever	It has steering wheel.
7.	It has generally single cylinder engine.	It may have single or multicylinder engine.
8.	Low intial cost.	High initial cost
9.	It is suitable for small farm.	It is suitable for big farm.

21.15 Crawler Tractor:

21.15.1 Introduction: In this type fo tractors instead of wheels track is provided as shown in Fig. 21.3. It is two types (i) Full track type and (ii) Half track type.

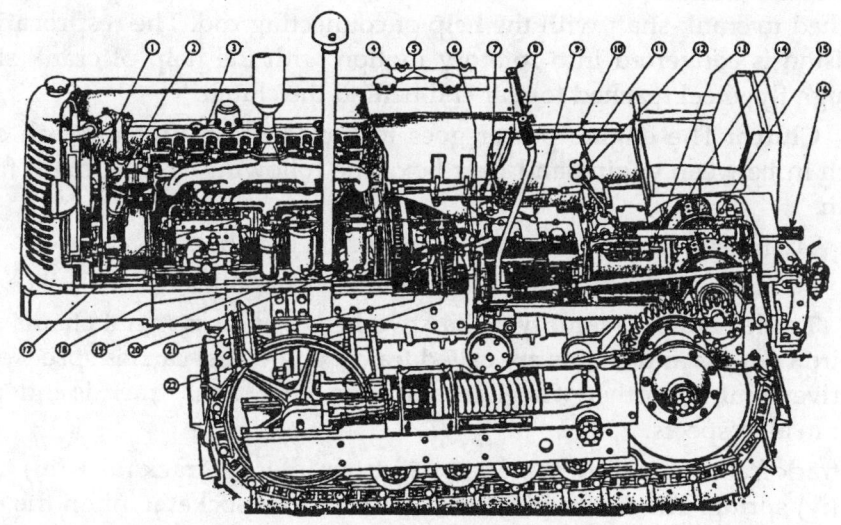

Fig. 21.3 Section of Crawler Tractor

KEY TO NUMBERS :

1. Dynamo, 2. Water pump, 3. 50 b.h.p 6cyl. Diesel engine, 4. Batteries, 5. Fuel fillers. 6. Parking brake ratchet pedal, 7. Clutch pedal, 8. Brake levers, 9. Engine speed control, 10. High/low ratio lever, 11. P.T.O. lever, 12. Gear change lever, 13.Twin range 3-speed and reverse gear-box 14. External contracting brake, 15. Spur type differential, 16. P.T.O. shaft, 17. Pneumatic governor, 18. Air cleaner, 19. Fuel fitler, 20. Lubricating oil filter. 21. Single plate clutch

The following are the main characteristics of crawler or chain type tractor:

(i)   It is designed to secure good adhesion and transmit high drawbar pull in difficult field condition, where the wheels unable to secure adequate grip on the soil.

(ii)   It provides large area of contact with the ground which results into traction power of the tractor increases considerably.

(iii)   It most suited for heavy work like earth moving work on dams and reclamation work of barren lands.

(iv)   It is used for all types of agricultural work with heavy implements.

21.15.2 Components of Crawler Tractor: The following are the main components of crawler tractor.

(i)   Engine (ii) Clutch

(iii)   Power transmission system (iv) Tract frame assembly

(v)   Track chain (vi) Steering system in Crawler Tractor

(i)   Engine: Infact engine is the only part which creats power. All the crawler tractor are mounted with 4-stroke-multi-cylinder engine. In this also piston is attached to crank-shaft with the help of connecting rod. The resprocating motion of piston is converted into rotatory motion with the help of crank shaft which through flywheel reached to rear end behind the clutch.

(ii)   Clutch: The engine power goes to transmission unit through clutch. The clutch in between engine and gear box. The following are the main functions of clutch.

(i)   To transmit engine power to tranmission gear box

(ii)   To make power tranmission gradual and smooth.

(iii)   Track Frame Assembly: It has two heavy endless metal chains moving on two iron wheels and chains are called traick. one wheel carries sprockets and acts as driver unit, the other wheel serves as an idler. Each track is independent of other in all respects.

The track frame assembly is made by (i) front idler (ii) track idler (iii) track rollers and (iv) spring. The tracks pivot from the ball and socket joint on the ends of the pivot shaft.A suitable spring which carries the front and weight of the tractor makes contact with the track frame. Suitable rollers are provided to maintain track spacing on the tractor. Heavy braces made of steel are fitted diagonally to make the track from erect and stable.

(iv)   Track Chain: Track chain consists of drop forged steel links, held together by pushings and pins to form continuous chain. The pins and pushings are pressed fit in the links with pins, pivoting inside the bushing. The left and right track chains are interchangeable. Track grousers are provided to track lines by cap screw and nuts.

(v) Tranmission System in Crawler Tractor: Like conventional tractor, crawler tractor also has the gear box and differential housed in common housing. Fig.. shows the layout of tranmission systemin crawler tractor where you can see that a pinion is mounted on gear box out put shaft which gives drive to the crown wheell or ring wheel of differential assembly. On the assembles on for right and the other for left tract. On the output shaft of steering clutches are fitted two pinions to reduce the speed and increases torque and drive gear of sprocket drive shaft.

(vi) Steering System in Crawler Tractor: The following are the main methods of steering in crawler Tractor.

(A)   Steering by Clutch.

(B)   Steering by Brake.

(C)   Steering by Differential.

(A)   Steering by Clutch: A clutch systemis fitted between both halves axles which goes from differential to sproket in chain type fo tractor. Which is linked with link and lever with right and left lever separately of the seat of the operator i.e., clutch is linked with right hand side axle is attached with right lever and vice versa. it is worth mentioning that to use the clutch for steering of chain type tractors, the power from differential are employed for both halves of axles. When operator draw clutch lever of left side then clutch of left axle is get disengaged i.e., power from left sproket is cut-off and vice-versa.

It is very obvious that if one wheel/sproket is made idle and power to other wheel/sprocket is continuing, the later wheel starts bending towards the idle farmer wheel. Therefore, in chain type tractor, the work of steering is done by the clutch.

(B)   Steering by Brake: In crawler tractor for small turnings, brakes axle used. For this in both sprockets are fitted with one brake drum and a brake shoe. The brakes shoes are connected in link and lever which is attached with right and left brake padels of the operator. When any padal is pressure the brake shoe spread in that direction and brake drum step rotation by friction. Therefore, to use brakes for steering the operator presses the brake of side to which it is intended to turn.

(C)   Steering by Differential: We know that function of differential is to reduce the speed of one wheel according to the nature of work and add to proportional speed to the other wheel.

For example, to turn a tractor to the left the left side sprocket has to revolve less and at the same time the right side sprocket hasto revolve more. Thus can be possible by a differential system. Therefore,differential is used as a steering in chain type tractor.

21.16 Comparison Between Crawler and Wheel Tractor: It is described in Table 21.2

Table 21.2 Comparison Between Crawler & Wheel Tractor

S.No	Crawler Tractor	Wheel Tractor
1.	It is suitable for undulated land because there is less chance to overturn	It is not suitable for undulated land.
2.	It is heavy	It is relatively light
3.	Instead of steering wheel, it has lever which is used to pull.	It has steering wheel.
4.	It moves with the help of chain-sprocket	It moves with the help of wheel and tyre

5.	It is not used for transportation	It is used for transportation.
6.	It is hard to repair because heavy parts has to be disconnectd.	Its repair is easy.
7.	It is costly.	It is relatively cheap.
8.	It travels in any condition without any difficulties.	It does not do so.
9.	Hydraulic system is used either front or back	Mainly implements are attached back side.
10.	Driving is difficult	Driving is easy.
11.	It is only suitable for large fields.	It is suitable for all types of field.
12.	Repair parts are not easily available.	Repair parts are easily available.
13.	It has high power.	It has relatively less power.

MULTIPLE CHOCIE QUESTIONS

1. Power tiller is also known as
   (a) small two wheel tractor
   (b) hand tractor
   (c) walking type tractor
   (d) all of the above

2. The power tiller was first introduced in India in
   (a) 1863
   (b) 1963
   (c) 1763
   (d) none of the above

3. Which of the following used kerosine engine.
   (a) Mitsubishi
   (b) Krishi
   (c) Kubta
   (d) Iseki

4. The pressure of power tiller tyres varies from
   (a) 80 to 100 KPa
   (b) 110 to 140 KPa
   (c) 150 to 200 KPa
   (d) none of the above

5. The power of power tiller varies from
   (a) 5-20 hp
   (b) 5 to 12 hp
   (c) 35 to 40 hp
   (d) none of the above

6. Which of the fllowing is not a component of power tiller
   (a) engine
   (b) brake
   (c) differential
   (d) lever

7. Power tiller has
   (a) one axle
   (b) two axle
   (c) both
   (d) none of the above

8. Speed of rotavatorof power-tiiller is
   (a) 200 rpm
   (b) 300 rpm
   (c) both
   (d) none of the above

9. Which of the following is not a component of power-tiller
   (a) Steering wheel
   (b) lever
   (c) engine
   (d) transmission gear

10. Tiner are available
    (a) straight tines
    (b) curved tines
    (c) sliding tines
    (d) all of them

11. Crawler is suitable for
    (a) reclamation work
    (b) transportation work
    (c) both
    (d) none

12. Which of the following is not a component of crawler tractor
    (a) Steering wheel
    (b) Wheel & tyre
    (c) both
    (d) none

13. Track frame assembly consists of
    (a) front idler
    (b) track idler
    (c) track roller
    (d) spring
    (e) all of them

14. The following are the main methods of steering in crawler tractor.
    (a) steering by clutch
    (b) steering by brake
    (c) both
    (d) none of the above

15. Hydraulic used in crawler tractor
    (a) only in front
    (b) only in back
    (c) either front or back
    (d) none of the above

FILL UP THE BLANKS

1. Injapn, the first successful model power tiller was designed in ....

2. The operator .... behindthe power tiller.

3. .... type multiple disc clutch is used for small power tiller.

4. Usually...............ply pneumatic tyre are used in power tiller.

5. Rotary tines are used in rotary unit for soil .... and .... purpose.

6. L.-shaped are used for .... working and .... cultivation of weedly fields.

7. Rotary tines are of three types (a) .... (b) .... and (c) ....

8. The power tiller was first indroduced in India in ....

9. Specific fuel consumption of power tiller is .... than tractor.

10. Power tillers has generally .... cylinder engine.

11. Power tiller has steering ....
12. Inner heat arrangment of tyres refers to .... the ridges.
13. Outer heap arrangement of tynes refers to .... the ridge.
14. .... is the first country to use power tiller on large scale.
15. .... is generally usedfor biger power tiller.

ANSWER

1. 1947 2. behind 3. dry 4. 2 to 4 5. cutting, pulverisation 6. stubble, shallow 7. straight, curved, sliding 8. 1963 9. greater 10. single. 11.clutch or lever 12. break 13. make 14. Japan 15. friction clutch.

ANSWER OF MULTIPLE CHOICE QUESTIONS

1 (d) 2 (b) 3 (d) 4 (b) 5 (b) 6 9c) 7 a) 8 (c) 9 (a) 10 (d) 11 (a) 12 (c) 13 (e) 14 (c) 15 (c)

Chapter 22
Ergonomics

22.1 Introduction: It is the scientific study of the relationship between worker and his working environment. It seeks to increase productivity, reduce drudgery & occupational health hazards in the following ways.

(i)   by use of equipments job ads for manual operations
(ii)   by ergonomic design of equipment and work method
(iii)   by improving the physical work environment and provision of personal protective wear to the workers.
(iv)   by adoption of proper safety measures and
(v)   by educating the workers and employers.

22.2. Ergonomic Design of equipment and work method

a)   Anthropometric Data : It is general technique to design the equipment in order to suit the needs of user population. Anthropometric data is useful in determining workplace layout. But it is mainly used to decide the dimensions of some components, e.g., handles, size of seat, height of feeding system.

b)   Bio-mechanical principles: To maintain that strength and ability muscles of the human body has got limitations, depending upon age and sex of worker. This is not negligible, rather it should be given due consideration. It is very important to understand muscular strength to be to suggest appropriate control and movement systems, to define the forces required in various manual tasks, to determine maximum & optimum control resistances and to ensure the adequate arrangements for safe and efficient manual material handling activities (Tichauer, 1978).

c)   Work physiology: As we grow older, our physical working capacity gradually decreases. It also depends upon certain factors, e.g. - weight, height, nutrition, etc of same age group.

The stamina of our body decreases due to muscular fatigue. Taking the same fact into account, the equipment should be designed so that the fatigue developed during work should get balanced by the rest pauses provided in the work schedule. If fatigue still occurs, then it should be overcome by proper rest. The working hours should be limited to a maximum of 8 hours per day, so that the labourers can also have a normal human life. It has been observed that capacity of an individual varies in the course of a day and does so in a rhythm i.e., independent of actual work. It increases in the moving form 6.30 am to 8.00 am

491

reaches its maximum about 10 am and declines towards 1 pm. In the middle of the day between noon and 1 pm, it is low and then it rises again. The afternoon maximum between 2 pm to 3 pm is a little lower than the morning maximum. After 4 pm working capacity falls rapidly. Therefore the working hours should be arranged keeping these points in consideration (ILO, 1979, Dewan, 1982).

d) **Job design as a basis for motivation of workers:** Intrinsic and extrinsic factors - these two effect the behaviour and output of a worker. Self esteem, use of skills and a feeling of making a notable contribution - constitute intrinsic factors while extrinsic factors include payment terms, recognition and organisational environment (Gite, 1988).

22.3 Physical Environment and Protective Wears:

Here the term Physical Environment is not a general word. Here it contains a vast meaning that includes thermal environment and other work conditions such as vibration, noise, dust, chemicals and exhaust emissions.

a) Thermal Environment: Agricultural operations are mostly carried out in the farms & fields and so the thermal environment plays a vital role on the work output. This can be overcome by taking suitable & preventive steps for different weathers and seasons. It is very important for tractor drivers that the tractors are provided with hoods to give protection from extreme weather conditions.

b) Vibration: Mechanical vibration is one of the dangerous factors for the operating worker of a machine. If affects work output and worker's health also. Those machines are more dangerous whose capacity of mechanical vibration for setting up synchronous vibrations in the body is more. The particular frequency of internal organs of man varies from 2 to 8 Hz and that of the body as a whole is less than 4 Hz. These specific frequencies are almost in the range of vibrations commonly caused by agril vehicles and machines (ILO, 1979; Oborne, 1982).

In case of tractor, the main reason for vibration is travel over uneven surfaces. Vertical oscillations of the vehicle on its tyres is the most important vibrations component. The dominant frequencies are generally in the range of 2.5 to 8 Hz, due to which tractor drivers face a lot of health problems. The international standard ISO-2631: Guide for the evaluation of human body exposure to whole body vibrations lays down limits of exposure to vibration. According to the Indian Standard IS 12343 - 1988, the maximum permissible amplitude of mechanical vibration as 100 μm. Vibration problem of tractors can be reduced by the proper design of seat.

If we take the case of power tiller, generally its frequency range is 20 to 250 Hz. The international standard ISO 5349 gives guidelines for vibration transmitted to the hand. To remove the drudgery in power tiller operation, handles should be properly designed so that vibrations should be isolated.

Vibrations, in the case of powered knapsack sprayer, generally arise from engine. When the speed of engine ranges 3000 to 8000 rpm, vibrations range at 50-130 Hz. It can also be lowered down by using proper techniques (Gite & Yadav, 1982).

c) **Noise:** Noise levels in 35-50 hp tractors are generally between 85 to 100 dBA. In power tiller operations, the noise level recorded are between 85-100 dBA. But according to ISO recommendation (ISO: 1999), the maximum permissible limit for 8 ha day exposure is 90 dBA. So many of our tractors and power tillers might be having detrimental effect on hearing of operators. Proper attention should be taken by the manufacturers on this problem. Operators should also take care of themselves and they should use proper preventive aids.

d) **Dust:** During various agricultural processes, such as tillage operations, threshing and chaff cutting, dust occurs naturally. It can be said that dust is unavoidable in agricultural work. Dust may cause irritation to the eyes, skin or lung. The threshold limit value for inert dust is taken as 8 mg/m^3, but the dust situation around agricultural machinery is observed to the about 500 mg/m^3 of air in soil cultivation and 300 mg/m^3 in combining operations. (Gustafsson & Noren 1982). Therefore, operator should take effective steps such as they should use cloth, face mask etc. to prevent dust.

e) **Exhaust Emission:** Almost all the combustion engines give of toxic gases. They are more dangerous than dust. Its main harmful effects are headache, nausea, weakness, dizziness and irritation of lungs. The best technique is to discharge the exhaust upwards and over operators head.

f) **Chemicals :** When plant protection equipments are used, the workers get in contact with pesticides powder/spray etc. which cause skin & eye irritations. These can be averted by using gloves, masks, aprons and goggle etc.

g) **Lighting:** It is an important factor that affects performance & worker's safety. So it should be cared. Minimum 300 lux light intensity should be available at the work place during operations.

22.4. Safety Measures

The machines and vehicles used during various agricultural process cause accidents that lead to loss of life or ability. Such accidents can be reduced by providing safe feeding systems, designing suitable work-place lay out, training the operators properly, following proper work-rest schedule etc. Also our tractor trailer system should be made safer.

22.5 Education

Work is of two types - Physical and Mental. Whichever type of work it would be, it should be given proper value. But in our society people doing physical work are looked down. This 'cheap mentality' should be changed and 'Dignity of Labour' should be established. (Dewan, 1982)

493

22.6 Summary

Ergonomics is a new concept in Indian Agriculture till this time. Its importance and contribution in improving the quality of life of workers should be given proper attention. It should be given due regard, especially by the equipments designers, work managers, employers and other that are related to this field.

SUBJECTIVE QUESTIONS

1. What is Ergonomics?
2. What is Work Physiology?
3. What are the objectives of Ergonomics?

MULTIPLE CHOICE QUESTIONS

1. Ergonomics is ....
    (a) Study physical condition
    (b) Scientific study of the relationship between worker and his working environment
    (c) Both
    (d) None

2. Work output of worker depends upon..................
    (a) Intrinsic   (b) Extrinsic
    (c) Both   (d) None

3. The dominant frequencies are generally in the range of
    (a) 2.5 - 8 Hz   (b) 8-12 Hz
    (c) 12-15 Hz   (d) None

4. The working hours is
    (a) 8   (b) 10
    (c) 12   (d) 14

5. The Noise varies between
    (a) 85 to 100 dB   (b) 120-150 dB
    (c) 150-200 dB   (d) None

Ans. 1 (b) 2 (c) 3 (a), 4 (a) 5 (a)

TECHNICAL DETAILS OF DIFFERENT TRACTORS

S. No.	Make	No. of Cylinder	Compression Ratio	Bores/ shrubs (mm)	Wheel base (mm)	Rated RPM	Draw-bar hp (PS)	P.T.O. hp (PS)	Sp. fuel consumption	Oil pump pressed hydraulic (KPa)	Type of cooling	Type of Engine
1.	Eicher 364 NC	2	17:1	100/125	1912	2130±30	29.2	31.7	196	17340	Air	Four strike Diesel Engine
2.	HMT 3511	3	17.9:1	95/110	2015	2000	24:5	28.5	221	15000	Water	Four stroke Diesel Engine
3.	Mahindra B-3-27SDI	3	18:1	88.9/101.6	-	2500±10	27.62	34.12	-	13220	Water	Four stroke Diesel Engine
4.	Farm Tractor 55	3	16.5	106.68/106.68	1935	2000	36.98	40.14	207	15300	Water	Four stroke Diesel Engine
5.	Swaraj 735 FE	3	17:1	100/110	2055	2000	26.8	34.1	184	15300	Water	Four stroke Diesel Engine
6.	New Halland 56330	4	17:1	100/115	2165	2500	49.11	58.19	185	16300	Water	Four stroke Diesel Engine
7.	Bajaj Tampo DX-45	4	18.5:1	90.19/100	1955	2500	30.67	38.86	175	15300	Water	Four stroke Diesel Engine
8.	MF 1035 DI	3	16.6:1	88.9/127	1820	2000	25.1	29.4	255	15300	Water	Four stroke Diesel Engine
9.	L & T John Deere 510	3	17.8:1	106/110	2050	2400	43.19	52.5	182.22	20000	Water	Four stroke Diesel Engine
10.	Same Greaves 583	3	17:1	105/115.5	2045	2055	35.70	42.51	188	14270	Water	Four stroke Diesel Engine
11.	Sanalica International	3	17.5:1	88.9/127	2060	2000	28.0	33.60	188	16300	Water	Four stroke Diesel Engine
12.	Harshat - 25	2	16:1	105/120	1633	1800	-	-	-	-	Air	Four Stroke Diesel Engine
13.	Kirloskar	3	17:1	100/120	1995	2150	-	-	-	-	Air	Four Stroke Diesel Engine

REPAIR, MAINTENANCE AND STORAGE OF TRACTOR

Problem No. (1) The Engine does not start

Causes	Correctionsâ
1. Battery terminals are not connected.	1. They should be connected.
2. Faulty injectors, switch or fuel pump	2. They should be checked and repaired to changed.
3. Battery is not fully charged	3. It should be charged fully.
4. Incorrect pump timing.	4. It should be checked.
5. Engine is very stiff.	5. Lubricating oil of low viscosity should be used.
6. Air lock in fuel system.	6. Fuel line should be bleeded.
7. Blocked fuel filter.	7. It should be cleaned.
8. Presence of water in fuel line.	8. Fuel oil should be changed.

Problem No. (2): Black smoke is given out by Engine

Causes	Corrections
1. Cooling is imperfect.	1. Cooling system should be checked.
2. More injection of fuel	2. Injection pump & injector should be checked in specialised shop.
3. Chocked air cleaner.	3. It should be cleaned well.
4. Fuel is unsuitable.	4. Correct fuel should be used.
5. Overload engine	5. Load should be reduced from the engine.

Problem (3): Blue Smoke is given by Engine.

Causes	Corrections
1. Very high level of lubricant oil.	1. Correct level should be maintained.
2. Use of low viscosity lubricating oil.	2. Correct viscosity oil should be used.
3. Wornout oil rings.	3. Oil rings should be replaced.

Problem No. (4): Sufficient load is not taken by Engine.

Causes	Corrections
1. Incorrect timing of injection.	1. It should be checked & correct.
2. Checked air cleaner or fuel filter.	2. They should be cleaned well.
3. Broken/damaged valve spring or head gasket.	3. They should be replaced.
4. Faulty injectors or governor.	4. They should be checked & repaired or changed.
5. Incorrect adjustment of decompression mechanism.	5. It should be adjusted correctly.
6. Worn out cylinder or rings.	4. They should be resleeved or changed.

Problem No. (5): Engine runs in idle. could, but stops in loaded could.

Causes	Corrections
1. Fuel filter or fuel tank, vent blocked.	1. The filter or rent should be cleaned.
2. Pressure of air in fuel system.	2. The fuel line should be bleeded.
3. Incorrect valve clearance.	3. It should be set.
4. Faulty fuel lift pump or injector.	4. It should be checked, repaired and replaced.
5. Worn out cylinder.	5. It should be rebored or resleened.
6. Worned or stucked rings.	6. They should be changed.

Problem No. (6): Engine burns on load but stops in idle could.

Causes	Corrections
1. Incorrect injection timing.	1. It should be checked & set properly.
2. Faulty injector or injection pump.	2. They should be checked & repaired in specialized shops.
3. Faulty governor adjustment or decompression mechanism.	3. They should be checked & repaired properly.
4. Incorrect valve clearance.	4. It should be adjusted nicely.
5. Worn cylinder or rings.	5. They should be replaced.

Problem No. (7): Engine gets overheated very soon.

Overheating may be caused due to:

(A) Faulty cooling systems, or

(B) Improper lubrication, or

(C) Inefficient combustion.

(A) Causes	Corrections
1. Improper openings of Thermostae valve.	1. It should be adjusted properly.
2. Defective water pump or radiator.	2. They should be cleaned & repaired.
3. Loose or broken Fan Belt.	4. It should be changed.
4. Dirt and scale on cooling surface.	4. It should be cleaned thoroughly.
5. Leakage in cooling system.	5. Leakage should be checked.

(B)	
1. Chocked exhaust pipe	1. It should be cleaned.
2. Overloaded engine	2. Load on the engine should be reduced.
3. Wrong injection timing	3. It should be checked.
4. Faulty injectors	4. They should be checked properly.

(C)

1. Dirty lubricating oil	1. It should be replaced.
2. Very high viscosity of oil.	2. Correct grade of oil should be used.
3. Defective lubricating pump.	3. It should be repaired in specialized shop.
4. Chocked oil filter.	4. Should be thoroughly cleaned.
5. Air cleaner out of order	5. It should be checked and repaired.

Problem (8): Poor braking:

1. Seized or worned brake lining.	1. The lining should be replaced.
2. Different acting strokes of right & the left pedal.	2. Stroke should be made same.
3. Oil leakage in brake chamber	3. Leakage should be checked.
4. Excess play of the brake pedal.	4. Play should be adjusted.

Problem (9): Not lifting of Hydraulic system.

1. Broken cylinder or control valve	1. They should be repaired or replaced.
2. Leakage of pipe	2. Leakage should be removed.
3. Defective hydraulic pump.	3. Should be repaired properly.
4. Lack of hydraluic oil.	4. Should be filled up to mark.
5. Air sucked by pipe.	5. Leakage should be removed.
6. Clogged filter.	6. Filter should be cleaned.

Problem No. (10): Clutch slips

1. The play should be adjusted.	1. Incorrected pedal adjustment.
2. Clutch lining burnt or worn.	2. It should be repaired or replaced.

STANDARD GRAPHICAL SYMBOLS

LINES AND LINE FUNCTION

LINE, WORKING,	
LINE PILOT (L>20W)	
LINE DRAIN (L<5W)	
CONNECTOR	
LINE FELXIBLE	
LINE JOINING	
LINE PASSING	
DIRECTION OF FLOW, HYDRAULIC	
LINE TO RESERVOIR ABOVE FLUID LEVEL BELOW FLUID LEVEL	
LINE TO VENTED MANIFOLD	
PLUG OR PLUGGED CONNECTION	
RESTRICTION, FIXED	
RESTRICTION, VARIABLE	

METHODS OF OPERATION

PRESSURE COMPENSATOR	
DETENT	
MANUAL	

MECHANICAL	
PEDAL OR TREADLE	
PUSH BUTTON	
PUMPS	
PUMP, SINGLE FIXED DISPLACEMENT	
PUMP SINGLE VARIABLE OIL PLACEMENT	
MOTOR AND CYLINDERS	
MOTOR, ROTARY FIXED DISPLACEMENT	
MOTOR, ROTARY VARIABLE DISPLACEMENT	
MOTOR, OSCILLATING	
CYLINDER, SINGLE ACTING	
CYLINDER, DOUBLE ACTING	
CYLINDER, DIFFERENTIAL, ROD	
CYLINDER, DOUBLE END ROD	
CYLINDER, CUSHIONS BOTH ENDS	
METHODS OF OPERATION	
LIVER	

PILOT PRESSURE	
SOLENOID	
SOLENOID CONTROLLED PILOT PRESSURE OPERATED	
SPRING	
SERVO	
MISCELLANEOUS UNITS	
DIRECTION OF ROTATION (CARROW IN FRONT IN SHAFT)	
COMPONENT ENCLOSURE	
RESERVOIR, PRESURIZED	
PRESSURE GAGE	
TEMPERATURE GAGE	
FLOW METER (FLOW RATE)	
ELECTRIC MOTOR	
ACCUMULATOR SPRING LOADED	
ACCUMULATOR, GAS CHARGED	
FILTER OR A STRAINGER	
HEATER	

COOLER

TEMPERATURE CONTROLLER

INTEREIFIER

PRESSURE SWITCH

RESERVOIR, VENTED

BASIC VALUE SYMBOLS

CHECK VALUE

MANUAL SHUT OFF VALUE

BASIC VALUE ENVELOR

VALVE, SINGLE FLOW PATH, NORMALLY CLOSED

BASIC VALUE SYMBOL'S (CONT.)

VALUE SINGE, FLOW PATH, NORMALLY OPEN

VALUE, MAXIMUM PRESSURE (RELIFE)

BASIC VALUE SYMBOL MULTIPLE FLOW PATHS

FLOW PATH BLOCKED IN CENTRE POSITION

MULTIPLE FLOW PATHS ARROW SHOW FLOW DIRECTION

VALUE EXAMPLES

UNLOADING VALVE INTERNAL DRAIN REMOVELY OPERATED	
DECELERATION VALVE NORMALLY OPEN	
SEQUENCE VALUE DIRECTLY OPERATED EXTENALLY DRAINED	
PRESSURE REDUCING VALVE	
COUNTER BALANCE VALVE WITH INTERNAL CHECK	
TEMPERATURE AND PRESSURE COMPENSATION FLOW - CONTROL WITH INTERNAL CHECK	
DIRECTION VALVE THREE POSITION, FOUR CONNECTION	
DIRECTION VALVE TWO POSITION, THREE CONNECTION	
VALVE INFINITE POSITIONING (INDICATED BY HORIZONTAL BARS)	

CONVERSION FACTORS

Unit	Abbreviation	Definition of Equivalent
Angstrom	A^o	10^{-10} m = 10^{-8} cm = 0.1 mm = 100 pm
Atmosphere	atm	1.0132×10^5 Pa = 760 torr = 760 mm of Hg.
Calorie	Cal	4.1840 J
Erg	erg	10^{-7} J
Joule	J	Nm = kg m^2 s^{-1} = 10^7 erg
Kelvin temperature scale	K	K = ^{o}C + 273.15
Fahrenheit	^{o}F	1.8^{o}C + 32
Pascal	Pa	Nm^{-2} = kgm^{-1} s^{-2}
Tarr	Torr	1.31579×10^{-3} atm or 1.33322×10^2 Pa
Inch	in	2.54 cm
Mile	-	1.61 cm = 5280 ft
Hectare	ha	10^4 m^2 = 2.5 acre = 42560 ft^2
Pound	lb	454.5 g
Ounce	-	28.3 g
Litre	lit	1000 ml = 10^{-3} m^3
Gallon	gal	3.185 lit.

S.I. SYSTEM : Standard Multiplication

Factor	Prefix	Factor	Prefix
10^{12}	tera, T	10^{-3}	milli, m
10^9	giga, G	10^{-6}	micro, m
10^6	mega, M	10^{-9}	nano, m
10^3	kilo, k	10^{-12}	pico, P

UNIT AND DIMENSIONS

System : Basic units

Quantity	Unit	Symbol
(i) Length (L)	meter	m
(ii) Mass (M)	kilogram	kg
(iii) Time (T)	second	s
(iv) Amount & Substance.	mole	mol
(v) Temperature (T)	kelvin	k
(vi) Electric current	Ampere	A
(vii) Luminous intencity	Candela	Cd
(viii) Plane angle	Radian	Rd
(ix) Solid angle	Steradian	Sr.

Dimensions of the other quantity are derived from these basic units.

Quantity	Unit	Alternative unit	Basic unit
Force (F)	Newton	(N)	$kg\,m/s^2$
Energy (E)	Jule	(J) Nm	$kg\,m^2/s^2$
Power	Wall	(W) J/s	$kg\,m^2/s^3$
Pressure	Pascal	(Pa) N/m^2	$kg\,/ms^2$
Frequency	Hertz	(Hz)	s^{-1}
Electric charge	Coulomb	(C)	As
Electric potential	Volt	(V) w/A = J/C	$kg\,m^2\,/\,s^3A$
Capacitance	Farad	(F) c/v	$s^4\,A^2\,/kgm^2$
Electric resistance	ohm	($\square$) v/A	$kg\,m^2\,s^3\,A^2$
Magnetic flux	weber	(Wb) Vs	$kg\,m^2/s^2A$
Magnetic flux density	Tesla	(T) wb/m^2	kg/s^2A
Inductance	Henry	(H) wb/A	$kg\,m^2/s^2A^2$

Bibliography

Ali, I Farm Power Machinery and Surveying Kitab Mahal

Arara, S.C; Damkundwar S. and Dom kundwar, Anand, V: Heat and Mass Transfer Dhanpat Rai and W (P) Ltd, Delhi.

Arlen D. Brown and R. Mack Strick land, The infested Printers and Publisher, Inc, Danrille Illinais.

Ballaney, P.L. Thermal Engineering, Khana Publishers, Delhi.

Bahadur, P: Numerical Chemistry, G.R. Bathla and Sona, Muzaffernagar.

Bill, Butter, Worth, Farm Tractors, E. and F.N. span II, New Fitter Lane London. EC4P4 EE 733, Third Avenue, New York Ny 10017.

Brown Arlen D and Strickland R. Mack, Tractor and small engine maintenance; The Interstate Printers and Publishers, Inc.

Culpin Claude, Farm Machinery, Collins professional and Technical Books, London.

Giri, N.K.; Automobile Mechanics, Khana Publisers, Delhi.

Gupta, K.M., Automobile Engineering; Umesh Publication, Delhi.

Jain. S.C. and Rai, C.R.: Farm Tractors, Standard Publisers, Distributors, Delhi.

Lal Radhey : Agricultural Engineering, Saroj Prakashan Allahabad.

Liljedahl, John, B. Turnquist, Paul K. and Smith David. W. : Tractor and their Power units, CBS Publishers and Distributors, New Delhi.

Michael, A. M. and Ojha, T.P. : Agricutural Engineering, Volume-J and II Jain Brothers, New Delhi.

Murty, V.V.N. : Land and Water Management Engineering, Kalyani Publishers, Cuttack.

Nakra, C.P. : Farm Machines and Equibments Dhanpat Rai Publishing, Company (P) Ltd, New Delhi.

Nag, P.K. : Engineering Thermal Dynamics, TMH Publishing Company, Ltd. New Delhi.

Shay, J : Elements of Agricultural Engineering Agro Book Agnecy, Patna

Kumar Sanjay : A Numerical Approach in Agril, Engineering with objectives, Kalyani Publisher, Ludhina

Suresh, R. and Kumar Sanjay Objectives and Solved Problems in Farm Power and Machinery Engineering, Standard Publishers Distributors, Delhi.

Index